VALUES
IN
HUMAN SOCIETY

VALUES IN
HUMAN SOCIETY

The Contributions of
Pitirim A. Sorokin
to Sociology

by
F. R. Cowell

An Extending Horizons Book

To the Memory of
Lillian, my wife
who saw and endured the
effort but not the result.

Acknowledgements

Grateful acknowledgement is made to all sources mentioned in the footnotes for quotations of copyrighted material, and particularly to the publishers of the works of the late Professor Pitirim A. Sorokin. Accordingly, thanks are here expressed to The American Book Company, New York, and to Messrs, George Allen & Unwin, London who published the first three volumes of *Social and Cultural Dynamics.* Acknowledgement is also made to Messrs. Harper & Brothers, publishers of Professor Sorokin's *Society, Culture and Personality,* 1947, in which many of his earlier views are restated and amplified. The figures and tables reproduced here previously appeared in *History, Civilizations, and Culture,* published by Beacon Press in 1962. In conclusion, I acknowledge with gratitude the invaluable aid given me by my publisher, to whose editorial staff, notably Miss Esther Doughty, Miss Pamela Johnson and Miss Sandi Mandeville, I am indebted for queries and suggestions, as well as for their patience in dealing with an unusually complicated typescript at a distance of some 3000 miles.

Contents

FIGURES   Page

Introduction

Whenever any subject of study gets a new foundation or new perspectives whereby knowledge is advanced, it is usually the result of pioneering work by one man. Bacon, Descartes, Leibniz, Newton, Kant, Darwin and others were outstanding for the ways in which they were able to assimilate the knowledge of their age in their own chosen fields and to order, arrange and develop it through the creative force of their own genius, so giving new form and direction to science and philosophy.

Sociology in our time badly needs a new synoptic vision able to light up all its heterogeneous elements with the glow of some new synthesis. Thus clarity, order, and intelligibility would suffuse the vast welter of miscellaneous ideas contributed in its name during the past century and more. In recent years sociologists have intensified their efforts without so far finding or creating any master-concepts by which such a fruitful consolidation might be realized. Certainly the name of a science cannot be claimed for sociology until it has been equipped, after a survey of its factual basis, with adequately defined concepts providing classifications which in turn yield some congruities and correlations able to provide explanatory principles over the whole vast area. A body of doctrine would then emerge to serve as a fruitful means of deepening and widening our understanding of the true nature of the antecedents, the structure, and the motive forces of all those complex facts which go to make up the life of men in societies.

No less an achievement than such a reformulation of sociology has rewarded the arduous study and research given to the subject throughout the long and remarkably energetic career of Pitirim A. Sorokin, an exile from Bolshevik Russia who became the first Professor of Sociology at Harvard University. If one or two short words often suffice, rightly or wrongly, to recall some of the grand discoveries made by great minds of the past — if the name of Socrates suggests "concepts"; Plato, "ideas"; Aristotle, "the mean"; Bacon, "experiment and induction"; Descartes, the "cogito"; Leibniz, "monadic energy"; Newton, "gravitation"; Dalton, "chemical atoms"; Darwin, "natural selection" — then for Sorokin, that word might be "values." Naturally scores of thinkers debated value before Sorokin, just as atoms were a commonplace in ancient philosophy, but none presented value as the password to open so many of the closed doors in sociology.

Sorokin, as this book will show, had written much on other topics before, in mid-career, he completed the massive labor upon which rests his demonstration of the primacy of value-theory in sociology. Already in his earlier work he had given proof of exceptional knowledge, unusually wide perspectives, and a firm grip upon the problems with which he grappled. Much of that work still stands, so that it would be as wrong to leave any impression that Sorokin is a man of one book or of one idea as it would be to lose Bacon, the legal mind, in Bacon the philosopher; or Leibniz, the mathematician and theologian, in Leibniz the metaphysician.

The very bulk of Sorokin's output makes any single formula inadequate as an assessment of it all. At the same time, it deserves more detailed summary description and appraisal than Sorokin, with the modesty of the true scholar, would ever himself provide. This book has therefore been written in the hope that it may serve as an introductory general survey of Sorokin's massive contribution. It is not the first time that I have attempted such a task, for in *History, Civilization and Culture* (1952) I tried to indicate the main outlines of the exceptionally detailed and precise historical findings presented by Sorokin in his *Social and Cultural Dynamics.* I now seek to give a general account of Sorokin's main achievements on a more generous scale than that of my earlier work, the bulk of which however is revised and included here as Chapter V. More attention is given therefore to Sorokin's deduction of sociological principles from history than to his other writings, a disproportion warranted by the outstanding quality of that work and by the consequences for sociology which derive from it. Of them all, that on which special emphasis will here be placed is the theory of value which it establishes as a grand interpretative principle in sociology and in all humanist studies. The full implications of Sorokin's achievements are not exhausted by that major discovery, the consequences of which have still to be worked out and applied, as they easily may be, in many directions in which Sorokin himself did not travel.

It is unlikely that anyone encountering Sorokin's ideas for the first time, particularly when presented as here by an unknown sponsor, will be otherwise than skeptical. "What," it may be asked, "has Sorokin to say that has not already been better said by some of the great sociologists of the past, such as Durkheim or Max Weber?" Greatly as such names are honored by sociologists everywhere, they did not full develop a viable, philosophically established theory of value.

Unless it is denied that fundamental explanations of life in human societies, or sociological theory, must include or presuppose some theory of value, it cannot be claimed that Max Weber said the last word on sociology. Like Dilthey's, his labors were immense, but their interpretative principles were not adequately developed. Sorokin does not deny that Weber made an immense contribution but he shows how it may be given a more adequate, because more comprehensive and general perspective.

Crucial examples are Max Weber's celebrated theories in economic history of the increasing rationality of life in modern times (in his *General Economic History*) and of the links between Protestantism and Capitalism (in his *Protestant Ethic*). Sorokin does not question the factual, descriptive relevance of Weber's remarks, but he holds that they do not fully explain the transition from the age of traditional Catholicism to the adventurous modern materialist age. His own discovery, by fact-finding, "empirical," investigations on an unprecedentedly vast scale and the theories he established upon them culminating in his discovery of culture complexes, "ideational, idealistic and sensate," incorporate all Max Weber's ideas which they are able to explain in a more comprehensive and conclusive manner. They explain, for example, the rise of rationality and "capitalist" enterprise in the Ancient World when there was no Protestantism.

This book has been written in the belief that Sorokin's findings make it possible for sociology to rise to a higher generality, a more all-inclusive scope, and that such a development is at present very badly needed. In the light of Sorokin's work a value theory is available which relates together philosophy, history, and sociology more directly and more vitally than has ever yet been possible. With an industry and an attention to detail which is unprecedented in humanistic studies, he has proposed a new map of the sociological universe. His cartography of social and cultural life may no doubt need revision, just as far greater precision has been given to the earlier maps of North America by those who came after Columbus. Sorokin himself would have welcomed such improvements. This effort to honor his memory, to give a general account of his career and his achievements, and to draw attention to some of the consequences which may follow from them could have no better sequel than that further development of sociology to which his lifework was devoted.

It was never my good fortune to meet Professor Sorokin, with whom I had never corresponded until the publication of a somewhat lengthy article on his work contributed by me to *The Times Literary Supplement.* His very kindly reception of my other writings in which I referred to him, including my books *History, Civilization and Culture* (1952 an account of his *Social and Cultural Dynamics)* and *Culture in Public and Private Life* (1959), as well as my contribution to *Pitirim A. Sorokin in Review* (1963), led me to believe that I had not misrepresented his ideas. This was particularly encouraging because I had submitted nothing to him before publication. At no time did he suggest that I should write. When, at the invitation of the Editor of *New Society,* I contributed on January 12, 1967, a summary account of Sorokin's contribution in a series *"The Founding Fathers of Sociology"* (since reprinted in a book of that title by the Penguin Press), the time seemed to have come to give a more extended account of his life and work. It became a more urgent task when he wrote to say that he was stricken by the malady which was to prove fatal. I was able to send him a typescript of the first draft of this book before his lamented death in February 1968. I would not, however, seek to claim his agreement to everything I have written, particularly because I have subsequently revised the text.

F. R. Cowell
February 1970

Apprenticeship in Sociology

Early Years in Russia 1889-1922

The career of Pitirim Alexandrovich Sorokin has been strange and extraordinary even for an age of violent upheaval and change. He was born on January 21, 1889 in an obscure village among the Komi folk who dwelt in that vast but little known area of Russia in latitudes stretching from Leningrad (then St. Petersburg) to the White Sea and Arctic Circle.

Sorokin says of himself: "Starting my life as a son of a poor itinerant artisan and a peasant mother, I have subsequently been a farmhand, itinerant artisan, factory worker, clerk, teacher, conductor of a choir, revolutionary, political prisoner, journalist, student, editor of a metropolitan paper, member of Kerensky's cabinet, an exile, professor at Russian, Czech and American universities."

"Born and reared among peasants," he had, he said, sprung from "the lowest peasant stratum." He hardly remembers his mother who died when he was three years old. She was, he learned later, beautiful and intelligent, but like the majority of Russian mothers at the time, illiterate. At the age of ten, he and a brother only four years older resolved to leave their father because his affection for them, of which Sorokin speaks warmly, was increasingly overclouded by dangerous spells of alcoholism, from which he died soon after they had left. A younger brother remained in the care of an illiterate aunt and uncle of whose kindness and affection Sorokin has the most grateful memories. The two young boys made their own way, plying the craft their father had taught them of painting ikons, gilding and silvering holy objects and the high domes of the village churches. They wandered from village to village among their own Komi folk, sometimes cold and hungry, sometimes risking their lives as at Yarensk, the only "town" they knew, of some 1000 inhabitants, where they were nearly blown off the high spire of the cathedral they were gilding in a sudden squall.

Somehow Pitirim picked up the rudiments of education from talks with friendly clergy, teachers, doctors, with the wise but often illiterate peasants, and from a few hours in the schools of the villages through which he and his brother passed in their search for work. One day he heard that an entrance examination was to be held at the school of one of the villages where he happened to be working. He entered on the whim of the moment, passed easily, and won a tiny scholarship which saw him through the nine months of the school year. During school holidays he continued to pay his way by his old craft of decorating churches, painting ikons and molding their copper or silver covers, a very practical foundation for the development of an aesthetic taste in painting, sculpture, and architecture.

He shared the plain fare and relatively primitve life of the peasantry, absorbing from them a traditional simple Christian morality, their folk songs, folk tales and heroic poetry, which he supplemented by reading the works of Tolstoi, Pushkin, Gogol and other Russian literary classics. Although sometimes short of food, clothing, and adequate shelter, he survived, thanks to the strong community spirit and mutual aid of the "mir," or the Russian village community. There was then no sharp economic, political, or social stratification.

Sorokin paints an idyllic picture of his calm and peaceful schooldays, for which his far from peaceful early manhood may well have given him a nostalgia. He lived amid the unspoiled beauty of the lakes, rivers, boundless forests, and sharp, clear air, sun and snow of the Komi country.

At school he succeeded well enough to be admitted at the age of 14 to a teacher-training school maintained by the Orthodox Church at Khrenovc where he first became aware of the new currents of political opinion sweeping over Russia at the time of the Russo-Japanese War. The Social Democratic Party had then very recently been formed (in 1898), but already a more radical wing under the leadership of Nikolai Lenin challenged the moderate leaders, with the result that the Bolsheviks, the extremists, parted company with the moderate Mensheviks in 1903. A Social Revolutionary Party had been formed in 1901 to begin its campaign of terrorism and assassination. The saner, more intellectual Union of Liberation, formed in 1903, attracted rather greater support than these extremist groups. The Tsarist Government was thus being sharply challenged at a time when its own incompetence was revealed by the disasters on land and sea during the Russo-Japanese War of 1904-5. Indignation and unrest seethed; these were manifest in violent outbursts —

strikes, mutinies and murders — culminating in 1905 in a General Strike, an insurrection of Moscow workers and, on the Government side, in the creation of the Imperial Duma and the proclamation of a constitution by the Tsar's October Manifesto.

Sorokin as a Revolutionary 1906 - 1917

An ardent young mind could not be indifferent while volcanic political explosions rocked the country. Within three years Sorokin had read and witnessed enough to become "modern," "progressive," and far from orthodox. Not content merely to think that way, he became a missionary for the new republican-democratic, socialist ideas and a leader in the violent Socialist Revolutionary party in the school and neighborhood. He must have made some impact, for on Christmas Eve 1906, shortly before his eighteenth birthday, he was arrested along with many other political offenders in whose company he spent five months in a Tsarist jail. Why he should have become so involved puzzled him all his life. Most of his fellow-students, his two brothers, their aunt and uncle whose house was the only "home" Sorokin knew, did not share his opinions, still less his activities. "Social position," "group structure," or the "class affiliation" categories of some sociologists cannot account for the change and the contrast. Sorokin describes his independence colloquially as "bull-headedness" and sociologically, as the outcome of "cultural-mental factors," not to be accounted for by "structural" concepts of groups or social classes. He was never a Marxian and he cannot explain the dynamic process of his mental life by economic interests. He was well-treated at the school and had no grudges or enmities to avenge. No evident psychological drive or instinct, still less any psychoanalytic, Freudian notion, explains his active spirit of revolt. These reflections later in life upon a vivid personal experience prompted and confirmed Sorokin's views about the phenomenon of creativity, the reality of "values, meanings and norms" as a guiding force in human conduct. How eventually this "integral" theory of human personality as the operative factor in sociology emerged from his stormy life-history will be more fully described in later pages of this book.

Sorokin and his fellow political prisoners seem to have turned their prison into a vigorous seminar for revolutionary ideas with the connivance and actual assistance of the sympathetic governor and prison staff. Having spent almost the first half of 1907 in this stimulating company, where he formed some friendships among other revolutionaries that were to stand him in great stead in more perilous times ahead, Sorokin was confirmed in his revolutionary zeal. He soon became more deeply involved. Expelled from the teacher training college, remaining under police surveillance, he carried on a desperate underground life as an unpaid and often starving missionary of revolution among villages and factories with the armed police again on his trail. Such was the strain of this life that he had to retreat to spend a few months in obscurity in the Komi country, where he worked as a farm-hand for his aunt.

In 1907 the urge for wider horizons was again so strong that he was off again. He went to St. Petersburg and there his life's work began – at a night-school. During the day he had to take any odd job he could get and he seems to have roughed it as the poor in a big city at that time had to do, often on a low standard of bare existence the like of which far fewer of the poor now experience in the so-called "affluent societies" of the West today, despite their still present need to redeem great numbers from poverty often falling below subsistence levels. Such was his resolute devotion to learning that in spite of this life of poverty and toil, in which many succumbed, he won entry by sheer merit in 1909 to the Psycho-Neurological Institute and in the following year to the University of St. Petersburg. There also he did brilliantly, but he did not succeed in keeping out of political trouble. In 1911 and 1913 he was again arrested for his revolutionary activities. He was now able to profit more from such experiences. He met his fellow political prisoners on their own ground, and also encountered at close quarters "the thieves, robbers, rapists and social deviants" among his fellow-prisoners. His academic interests stimulated him to write his first book in the light of his experiences, *Crime and Punishment, Service and Reward* (1913). Together with contributions to specialized and learned journals, this work earned him the reputation of a rising young scholar. The fact that he was known to be a violent opponent of the Tsarist Government does not seem to have embarrassed his academic career.

City life in St. Petersburg brought enriching cultural opportunities from music, the theater, the museums, painting, literature, which young Sorokin was eager to seize. He graduated with the highest honors at the university and was at once given an academic post. In 1916 he gained a Master's degree in criminal and administrative law. Sociology was not taught at St. Petersburg until 1918 when Sorokin was one of the first to pursue it. At that time it was predominantly of the empirical, neo-positivist school of critical realism based upon an amalgam of the ideas of Comte and Herbert Spencer and mixed with the popular ideas of evolution and progress. Sorokin read widely, not merely Russian authors, among whom were Kovalevsky, Petrajitzsky, de Roberty, Pavlov, Dostoievsky, and Tolstoi, but also Durkheim, Simmel, Weber, Stammler, Pareto, and Marx.

As Sorokin was giving his lectures at the university, the First World War, which had broken out in 1914, again revealed the incompetent direction of the mighty Russian army upon which the Allies had confidently relied as the "steam roller" that would crush the German forces. Instead, it experienced a succession of shattering defeats which culminated in the virtual collapse of the entire Russian front in 1917. Failure in the field and failure at home touched off a tremendous explosion of public indignation against the Government which the revolutionaries and anarchists of Russia had been fomenting and prophesying for years. The resulting crash of the Tsarist regime led to the creation of a Provisional Government on March 12, 1917 amid scenes of violence and horror. At first this event was hailed with the rapture with which "progressive" spirits greet the destruction of an old order.

Sorokin and the Russian Revolution 1917 - 1922

Sorokin was one of them, but when the storm burst, he saw sights and read news which made him exceedingly uneasy. He had sufficient knowledge of political history to feel the need for caution and restraint. He had heard enough speeches in the Duma and more than enough wild talk outside it during January and February 1917 to recall visions of the French ruling classes before the eighteenth century revolution. Well-to-do Russian businessmen and members of the aristocracy "applauded the scathing criticisms of the Government and acclaimed the approaching Revolution." With prophetic insight he warned a student who had asked him about the prospects of a guillotine that after killing the well fed, the Revolution would soon begin to find victims among the poor. At St. Petersburg, fire, looting, mutiny, the murder of officers by their men, and mounting chaos and starvation presaged the shape of things to come.

The fierce and bloody events of those early revolutionary days of horror are retold with graphic realism in Sorokin's *Leaves from a Russian Diary* (1924). His ardent work for thoroughgoing political, administrative, and economic renewal marked him out for prominence as an early revolutionary leader, and he threw himself with fierce energy into the task of supporting the Provisional Government established in March 1917, of which his friend Kerensky, at first Minister of Justice, became President on July 20, 1917. Sorokin had already become his Secretary or chief personal assistant. He worked day and night for the cause, writing, editing, and speaking. In the middle of it all he married in March 1917. Kerensky's reign was short. On November 6, 1917, Nikolai Lenin, whom the Germans had sent into Russia from Switzerland in April virtually as their secret agent in the well-founded belief that he would succeed in undermining the Russian will to fight, launched the armed attack he had been preparing with vigor and venom. Kerensky's government was overthrown at gun-point. Sorokin records some of the speeches he heard Lenin make, appealing to the crudest instincts of greed, lust, and destruction "rousing the lowest beast-instincts in the unthinking masses."

Sorokin noted at the time that Lenin's face "reminds me of those of congenital criminals in the albums of Lombroso and at the same time it has something in it which recalls religious fanatics of the old Orthodox Church . . . . Although a poor speaker and a repellent personality, it seems to me that this man may go far because he is ready and determined to encourage all the violence, the criminality and obscenity which the mob, under these demoralized conditions, is straining to let loose." Zinovieff, whom Sorokin also heard, he describes as "a disgusting creature. In his high womanish voice, his face, his fat figure, there is something hideous and obscene, an extraordinary moral and mental degenerate. A perfect pupil has Lenin found in this man" *(Leaves from a Russian Diary,* pp. 47-49).

It is not surprising that Sorokin, who had campaigned against the Bolshevik threat to the Rule of Law, to sanity, and to moderation, was in danger. On January 2, 1918 he was flung into prison by the Bolsheviks on the trumped-up charge of conspiring to murder Lenin, who had been frightened out of his life by a burst tire in a car in which he was riding. Fifty-seven days later Sorokin was released, thanks to the efforts of an old revolutionary, who knew Sorokin merely by repute. It was a short reprieve. Because Sorokin was fundamentally opposed to the Bolshevik tyranny, he merited their suspicion. He soon became a hunted man again. For two months he lived in the forests, wandering from village to village, befriended by peasants, eating berries and fungi, constantly evading the Red soldiers on his track. After two months and many narrow escapes, he realized that there was little hope for him, so, to spare his friends further danger, he walked resolutely to the nearest headquarters of the local

Bolshevik police, the Chekha, and gave himself up. He was told that he would soon be shot but that his eminence and activities in Petrograd and Moscow required a decision from the Central Chekha, which would postpone his execution for a few days. It was a fate he expected, for he knew that there was not more than one chance in a thousand of escape. His prison life, the brutal warders, the lice, the dirt, the stink, the horror of the daily selection of prisoners to be roused and told to march out and leave their few possessions behind as they would not need them again, the agony, despair and stoic bravery of the victims, the numb horror of those waiting their turn for a like fate unless typhus removed them first, the silence broken by a sudden burst of firing are a few among the many horrors of that ghastly epoch vividly depicted in Sorokin's *Leaves from a Russian Diary.*

After nearly three months spent in such a hell, Sorokin was suddenly summoned on December 12, 1918 to the prison commandant's office, and shown an article in the Communist newspaper *Pravda* by Lenin himself, in which he was praised as an intellectual who might be a useful teacher in Communist Russia. He was sent under guard to Moscow, and there set free. He owed his escape, the one chance in a thousand, of which he had despaired, to a few of his students and early revolutionary friends who had intervened on his behalf with Lenin. He went back to Petrograd, where his apartment and his property had been "nationalized," only to find that no one ever expected to see him again, so that nothing remained except a few books and papers piled in a corner, waiting to follow the rest of his library to the stove, where the new occupant, lacking fuel, had burned nearly everything.

Sorokin found that it was almost as difficult to survive free as in prison. There was a general lack of food, clothing, fuel, lighting and many of the elementary decencies of life. All around him were starvation, disease and despair, terrorism, arrest and summary execution. Such was the quality of life in what became known as a "police state" because of the absolute power of life and death of its autocratic rulers. Such totalitarian countries are better described as "prison states" because everybody in them must give unquestioning obedience, all are at the mercy of arbitrary arrest, punishment, torture and death, and they dare not and cannot try to escape across the frontiers.

Sorokin struggled to resume his lectures and, despite the appalling conditions, to begin to write his *System of Sociology.* Lacking many books and learned periodicals, undernourished, often without light or heat in the long arctic Russian winter, he nevertheless managed to produce it in 1920. It was read eagerly and soon sold out. It has never been translated and Sorokin described it later as inadequate. The wonder is that it was ever written under such crippling difficulties. Sorokin was made head of the university's Department of Sociology and given other appointments, although his book was vigorously denounced by the Communist press. It is not surprising, therefore, that he was very soon in grave peril once more. Again he had to combine as best he could a fugitive existence with his university work, from which he was periodically and prudently absent on account of a feigned illness. During 1920 such brave show of relative academic independence as the few remaining distinguished professors endeavored to maintain was no longer tolerated. Yet all resistance was not crushed. Pavlov, given special favors in 1921 to impress his admirers abroad, refused to accept them with a nobility and bravery which contrasted sharply with the actions of many others, such as Maxim Gorky.

A sudden respite had occurred in February 1921 when, after the great famine, even ardent Communists broke into revolt. The mutiny of the communist Kronstadt sailors, was, with difficulty, brutally suppressed. It led at once to the New Economic Policy, NEP, a reversion to something nearer free enterprise. Sorokin revived and resumed his teaching. At the university anniversary on February 3, 1922 he made an eloquent oration in favor of freedom, individual initiative, and private enterprise, which incensed the Communist press but won him great renown. In May 1922 his book *The Influence of Hunger on Human Behavior, on Social Life and Social Organization* appeared, but not before it had been severely mutilated by the censors. Even the restricted 'free' enterprise allowed by the Bolsheviks rapidly brought economic life to something approaching normal conditions. Food, clothes and other necessities reappeared in the shops of Petrograd. People began to make profits and the 'bourgeois' element of enterprising citizens began to revive. This was more than the Bolsheviks could endure. University life became impossible. Semi-literate students became undergraduates and teaching appointments were given to incompetents, whose only qualification was party loyalty or favoritism. The Rector was dismissed along with most of the remaining older professors. Many were imprisoned and executed, many committed suicide. University life virtually ceased in August 1922. Sorokin went to Moscow where he was not so clearly marked out as an enemy to the Bolsheviks as he was known to be by the Chekha of Petrograd. While there, the repression broke out anew; many of Sorokin's remaining academic friends were arrested both in Petrograd and Moscow, so he anticipated a similar fate. Then in a sudden fit of clemency, Trotzky published an announcement in Pravda that all such intellectuals as could not conform were to be released and banished. Sorokin at once went north, collected his wife, and returned quickly to Moscow where once more he gave himself up to the Chekha as a candidate for exile.

Sorokin In Exile 1922

Through the fortunate circumstance that the Acting Minister of Foreign Affairs had been a friend of his student days, he was able, after harrowing delays, to get passports and visas for himself and his wife. With her, allowed to take only $50 from the American Relief Administration, a watch, two wedding rings and a few books, pamphlets and the herbarium and botanical equipment of his wife, an eminent cytologist, he boarded the train which was to take him into exile and left Moscow on September 23, 1922. When the Soviet frontier was at last at a safe distance behind them, they were able to sleep at night for the first time for five years without the recurrent and chilling fear, "Will they come tonight?" They got away at the twelfth hour, for there was rage when their escape became known to the Bolshevik Commissaries in Moscow. The Acting Minister of Foreign Affairs and the head of the Chekha were both censured for having allowed them to go.

After a short stay in Berlin, Sorokin and his wife were welcomed in Prague by President Masaryk, whom they first met on their wedding day when he was on a visit to Russia. There he was able to resume work, helping to establish two magazines, so continuing the periodical journalism he had directed under Kerensky, *The Farm* and *The Peasants' Russia*; and lecturing in the Agricultural Institute and the agricultural and cooperative schools in Czechoslovakia. There he trained young Russians whom he hoped might later become peasant leaders in the Russia of his dreams. With a characteristic energy he produced five books in Russian there, including *Situation of Russia,* and *Popular Essays in Social Pedagogics and Politics* (1923). There also he began, with scientific objectivity and detachment, to write *The Sociology of Revolution.*

The Sociology of Revolution

In November 1923 an invitation to lecture in American universities took him from Europe, which he saw only rarely afterwards as a visitor to conferences of learned societies. So ended the first phase of Sorokin's career. No other eminent sociologist had a similar experience except Saint-Simon, and to a much lesser extent and for a shorter time, Karl Marx. No other academic sociologist has been so immersed in the daily work, at a high level, of government and administration, so often imprisoned, so long in peril of summary execution, so wracked by searing grief and hopeless tragedy. The story is far more than one of mere biographical interest, gripping as it is when told by Sorokin himself in his *Leaves from a Russian Diary* and *A Long Journey*. It also has a deep sociological interest as a special instance of a general principle.

Immersion in the practical business of life at any level is a valuable corrective of that learned detachment, amounting sometimes to obscurantism, which is liable to afflict those whose world is bounded by a college quadrangle, a university campus, academic committees, college and local politics. The academic world is often rightly critical of the blinkered politicians, bureaucrats and administrators who never consider, let alone question, the validity of the standards to which they unquestioningly adhere, those "concealed major premises" of all human activity which few except philosophers ever discover or discuss. Yet the day-to-day work of such practical men gives them advantages which the theorist lacks. All subjects can benefit when their practitioners must rub shoulders daily with their fellow men in the practical business of life, but in no subjects can academic aloofness be more dangerous than in sociology, government, and political theory. Having touched life on so many levels, having often very nearly perished, and surviving by a near miracle, Sorokin had savored to the full that pungent sense of reality of which William James wrote so eloquently. His students, and the far greater number who read his books, were to profit in later years from experiences so dearly bought, and so well transmuted by his personal abilities and character into a ripe sociological wisdom.

Vivid and bitter as Sorokin's experience of the revolution in Russia had been, even he could hardly have foreseen the full rigor of the iron control by which the revolutionaries perpetuated their power, subsequently extending and enforcing their rule over Poland, Hungary, East Germany, and Czechoslovakia. How that power has been exercised over all significant aspects of the lives of every one of these millions of subject peoples, how reactions against it or criticisms of it have been met by the Soviet authorities in any of these countries and within the Soviet Union itself is, in part at least, a matter of record needing no more than a reference here. Despite the anguish of mind with which Sorokin followed such events in his unshaken loyalty to the liberal philosophical and political faith for which he had more than once risked his life, he became more impressed by Russian material progress and more hopeful that the Soviet despotism would gradually become more tolerant. He did not live to see the manner in which Russian troops and tanks were used to crush what seemed to be incipient stirring of the desire for self-determination in Czechoslovakia in 1968-69, just as the Hungarians had been crushed in his own lifetime in 1956. At the same time, he remained always ready to denounce, according to his sociological principles, any shortcomings in the political, economic, and cultural life of the freer Western democracies.

Early Years in the United States

Minnesota 1924 - 1930

The invitation to lecture in the U.S.A. soon resulted in Sorokin's appointment as Professor of Sociology at the University of Minnesota. There, among the lakes, the forests, the winter snows, and summer heat he found a home which must have recalled the Komi land of North Russia from which he had so recently been banished. Many Minnesotans or their parents had also come from Northern Europe so in that respect also his New World was not a complete and utter contrast to the Old World that he had been forced to leave. The contrast, and it was merciful, was from the precarious and dangerous life of a suspect in a Prison State. He had lost his two brothers, his aunt and his uncle, victims with unnumbered hosts of other Russians, of the Bolshevik fury.

The iron will and resolution which had carried him through so many perils, now drove him to sink himself in work, in lecturing, writing, and home-making. He and his wife were slowly able to think less about the problems of exile as the nightmare of the past receded amid the stimulus of city life in Minneapolis, the bustle and business around the university campus and the peace and calm of the continental vastness beyond.

The first-fruit of Sorokin's life soon appeared there: his graphic *Leaves from a Russian Diary* (1924), put together from his notes and memories from January 1917 to September 1922. It is a gripping tale of horror, told not only for his own account, the reader feels, but also as a memorial tribute of bitter regret to honor scores of named and nameless fellow countrymen, women and children who perished in the Bolshevik terror. A gnawing anxiety and sympathy also haunted him for the many millions more who somehow survived to face an almost hopeless future of hunger, want, cold, misery and fear, but whom he had been forced to leave. In memorable words of deeply felt sincerity he concluded by proclaiming three convictions of heart and mind that would never leave him. "Life, even the hardest life, is the most beautiful, wonderful and miraculous treasure in the world. Fulfilment of duty is another beautiful thing, making life happy and giving the soul an unconquerable force to sustain ideals and third, that cruelty, hatred and injustice never can and never will be able to create a mental, moral or material millenium."

So fervid a profession of faith, although most unusual in a treatise on sociology, is a very suitable prelude to Sorokin's work. Not merely because it was a piece of wisdom that he had paid for by often risking his life, but because it strikes a note of rich humanity which rings in various tones throughout all the work he was in future to accomplish. His Russian Diary may be regarded as a *pièce justicative* if not as "volume one" of his next book, already finished at the beginning of December 1924, *The Sociology of Revolution* (1925). Begun during his first year of exile in Prague, it was published in the Lippincott Sociological Series under the editorship of Professor E. C. Hayes, Professor of Sociology at the neighboring University of Illinois, whom Sorokin thanked not only for adding the volume to his series, but for sympathy, advice, and encouragement, and not least for aid over English which Sorokin had begun to learn in prison, but had still to master. His first contribution in English to an aspect of sociological theory, the book already gave proof of qualities that were to be developed and improved during the succeeding forty years and more of Sorokin's active life as a teacher and writer in America. The book was inevitably colored throughout by his own direct experiences of the Russian Revolution but it makes manifest at the same time a strong historical interest and a scientific desire to present the subject objectively as a sociologist should. Not content, as many might well have been, to derive all his empirical findings from the crowded scenes and dramatic events during which he had somehow survived in Russia, he made some rapid surveys of the great revolutions of the past, from Ancient Egypt, Greece, Rome, the Peasants' Revolt in England of 1381, the Jacqueries of Hussite Europe in the early fifteenth century, the English Civil War, and above all, the French Revolution and its sequels in the nineteenth century. A graduate of the Psycho-Neurological Institute of St. Petersburg would not fail to concentrate on the nature and mechanism of human behavior and the transformations it undergoes in times of revolutionary stress and change. Seeking correlations between revolutionary manifestations at various times, Sorokin examined in turn the attitudes of the revolutionaries during several revolutions, to human life and human rights, to property, sexual relations, labor relations, government, law, order and authority, as well as changes in acquired forms of aesthetic and moral activity. He noted for instance changes in speech-reactions and the invention of a new cant vocabulary with words such as *citoyen* during the French Revolution, *tovarish* in the Bolshevik upheaval, and others. Part I of his book is devoted to this psychological survey and it is illustrated by a great many examples drawn from history. In Part II Sorokin presented some telling statistics, including some from Bolshevik sources, exposing the sinister effects which revolutions can have upon the composition of the population, its death, birth, and marriage rates. Part III deals with the effects of revolution upon social classes and the social aggregate in general, as a prelude to the study in Part IV of the shattering effect revolutions have, and are designed to have upon governmental activity and upon the economic life of communities in which they occur, with their concomitant disastrous impact upon educational, scientific, and cultural life. "From whatever angle we approach the subject," he concluded, "the result is always identical: destruction, destruction, destruction. In this respect as in so many others, the revolution has thrown back Russia for fifty or sixty years."

Such were the facts, historical and contemporary, such was the legacy of revolution. So many revolutions had happened so often in the past that there seemed little mystery about it all. "History is like an author who without interruption is writing ever new dramas, tragedies and comedies with new characters and heroes, with new scenery and environment but . . . with the old subjects which many times . . . have been repeated" (p. 5). It is not difficult to answer the question "What is Revolution ?" The serious question is what causes revolution.

Sorokin lists among the principal causes the repressions of deep-seated reflexes among which the desire for food, for self-preservation, is immensely powerful. So is the lack of housing, shelter, clothing. Sexual frustration and repression and condemnation to a life of poverty among the wealth of others also incite revolt. Up to this point Sorokin was giving priority to all the emphasis which a sociologist in the empirical, positivist tradition would be likely to put upon psycho-neurological, economic or material causes of revolution. He went on however to include recognition of the fact that to thwart individual urges for creative effort, for variety of experience and adventure, for freedom to communicate by speech and action, all contributes powerfully to provoke social explosions. It was as though he foresaw the malaise of the affluent society and the "revolt of youth" that were to come forty years later. In recognizing also that the collective self-preservation of cultural and religious groups will be fought for with the utmost tenacity, he was, at the same long distance in time, providing an explanation of the spirit and resolution of the ruling minorities in the Union of South Africa and Southern Rhodesia to sustain at all costs the culture of the West within the lands they ruled. He did not however single out all these various frustrations as distinctive 'cultural' forces.

Having succeeded, as it were, in getting much of the poison of revolution out of his system by writing these two books, Sorokin was able to return to the calmer kind of professional, academic sociology. Within five years he produced three more books, any one of which might have sustained a lesser man as his main contribution to the advancement of learning. The first, *Social Mobility* (1927) picked up the well-worn theme of social stratification and movements up and down the social scale. Sorokin tried in it to throw light not only upon the sort of individuals who go up and down the economic, occupational, and political ladders, but the frequency of such movements in comparison with the greater numbers who remain more or less fixed in their strata and who move only if it does. More interestingly, Sorokin raises and endeavors to answer questions on such subjects as the nature of the differences between these strata over historical times. The deeper he tried to get into these problems, the more difficult they seemed to be, for he was unable in 1927 to visualize the nature of the trends which his study revealed. "It was," he said, as though men had been "circling in various directions without any definite goal or point of arrival". Does social stratification serve a useful purpose in the life of societies, and if so how rigid can it be if social progress and individual well-being are not to be thwarted — perhaps to the extent of provoking a revolution? What, in short, should be said about the ethical aspect of class relations — if any? Progress in such investigations could not be very great in the 1920's partly because of the lack of adequate statistics. Even now, when many more are available and when the social and economic life of advanced Western industrial societies has made great strides forward, radically changing the class structure of many old traditional societies, it is not easy to penetrate more deeply into the merely factual aspect of the problem. Nor is this surprising because the social phenomena involved must first be defined. To define them involves making certain value judgments about what constitutes a "class" and about the conceptual framework into which the classes are supposed to fit. In the traditional societies of the past, the matter could be resolved quite simply, as a brief illustration from an English context may show. The prevailing idea in

England was that everyone had their "station in life." St. Paul had laid down the Christian doctrine in his First Epistle to the Corinthians, which was read in every English church in the magnificent language of the Authorized Version of the Bible, preached from as a text for many a sermon, and pondered by the faithful at home as they weighed every word of Holy Writ: "as God hath distributed to every man, as the Lord hath called every one, so let him walk . . . Let every man abide in the same calling wherein he was called. Art thou called being a servant? Care not for it but if thou mayest be free, use it rather." In the age of faith when the values governing social life were generally accepted with little or no questioning, such an attitude became part of a millennial tradition. It gave rise to an "order of society" which was not the product of thought about "social stratification." It was not until the validity of traditional morality, that is to say, the value judgments implicit in it, were called into question by a sensate age, that "stratification" became a problem. Little help was to be had from the philosophers in the discussion when the most eminent of them in England, F.H. Bradley, in an essay on "My Station and its Duties" in his *Ethical Studies* (1876) could write that "there is nothing better than my station and its duties, nor anything higher or more truly beautiful." Despite the skill and sophistication with which he elaborates his theme, he did not consider its application to the caste system of India, for example, nor even to the probable sentiments of the servants and waiters who labored to make his life comfortable at Merton College, Oxford, or in the various hotels to which he occasionally resorted for a holiday.

These digressions are intended to illustrate the dead end at which sociology was to be found as long as it was confined, or supposed to be confined, to the elaboration of facts and statistics. A science purporting to deal with men in action whose traditional behavior was changing; could obviously make no progress without standards or criteria of judgment of that action. Otherwise it is reduced to the banal conclusion that "some do, others don't." Economists and historians usually surmounted this formidable barrier by smuggling in unobstrusively the unavoidable minimum amount of value judgments in the hope, largely successful, that because their readers would possibly share them, as "ordinary common sense," they would not be singled out for criticism. The argument will be picked up again, because Sorokin was later to provide a theory able to explain both the firm basis of the traditional morality about class distinctions illustrated above from British experience, and at the same time to indicate how and when a dogma of equality, which many may consider just as arbitrary as the old idea of divine ordinance, came to supplant it.

Meanwhile, with the unresolved problems of social mobility still in his mind, Sorokin had switched his energies to another yet more demanding task in order to meet a constant need under which he and all who taught sociology had to labor. There was no succinct, comprehensive guide to the already vast and growing literature of the subject. With amazing speed, accuracy, and conciseness he filled the gap in knowledge with the 760-odd pages of his *Contemporary Sociological Theories* (1928). The book gave proof of interest, knowledge, and critical insight over so wide a field that it was probably the envy and despair of many contemporary sociologists. For the first time, the kaleidoscopic offerings of a multitude of writers were shaken down into a convenient and comprehensible pattern. It was well described at the time as "unique among works of social theory because of the enormous amount of factual and quantitative data assembled." Already in 1928 Sorokin exposed the merits and the defects of such sociological theories as those of the mechanistic, geographical, biological, racial, demographic, economic, Marxian, and crude evolutionary schools. He had sound and shrewd comments about the views of the pioneers of sociology such as those of Le Play and his followers, the work of Emile Durkheim, Max Weber, and others. His commentary was especially valuable in the U.S.A. at that time for the first-hand study it provided of the work of the great sociologists in German, Russian, French, Italian, as well as of those who wrote in English.* He divided the subject by groups of theories or "schools" rather than by discussing each author in chronological order, and he provided thoughtful, critical assessments of the ideas they had advanced. Sociology, he concluded, could be described as the study, firstly, of the relations and correlations between various classes of social phenomena (e.g. economic and religious, family and moral, juridical and economic, mobility and political phenomena); secondly, of the correlations between the social and the non-social phenomena (geographic, biological, etc.); and thirdly of the general characteristics common to all classes of social phenomena. If sociology from a scientific point of view was to be described, as many did describe it, as a wilderness, it was, he said, in no worse shape than psychology, political science, or economics. To detect and attack the "sterile flowers" in the wilderness was a part of the sociologists' task and one, it may be added, from which Sorokin has never been deterred.

---

*E. E. Eubank, *The Concepts of Sociology* (New York, D. C. Heath, 1932) is symptomatic of the scanty interest shown by American sociologists in non-American work at that time.

That *Contemporary Sociological Theories* successfully filled an obvious gap in the literature of sociology was soon shown by the number of translations in which it circulated round the world — German, French, Czech, Serbian, Chinese, Turkish, Spanish, Hindi, and Japanese.

While *Contemporary Sociological Theories* was in the press, and despite his daily teaching duties, Sorokin began with eager enthusiasm a systematic sociological survey of the nature and problems of rural life. It was work for the Department of Agriculture of the U.S. Federal Government upon the subject which he had come to America to pursue, one for which he was thoroughly well equipped. He and Professor Carle C. Zimmerman cooperated to produce the three-volume *Source Book in Rural Sociology* (1930-1932). Before a work of this magnitude could be published, they jointly produced, in the light of their reflections upon the mass of materials they had gathered, "an abbreviated manual" (of 636 pages), *Principles of Rural — Urban Sociology* (1929), rather more than half the chapters being written by Sorokin.

The Federal Government was at that time putting forth a lot of effort to improve rural life in America. The Department of Agriculture had a vigorous Extension Service in which all the available means of publicity were being used to raise standards and to make rural life more attractive. It produced a series of guides and leaflets, for example, on the design and equipment of the rural home, even down to the choice of window curtains, hints on cookery and the making of children's clothes. These were the days before the invention of television, when even the radio coverage of the American broadcasting agencies, nearly all of them privately owned and mostly operated for profit, was by no means complete. A serious plan of action of this type needed a firm foundation in fact and for this the department had wisely turned to Professors Sorokin and Zimmerman. There was no lack of studies of one sort and another of rural life, or of monographs dealing with some of its aspects in considerable detail. What was now forthcoming was the first effort to provide, on a major scale, a *Sociological* view of the problem as a whole by two actively involved social scientists, each of whom had grown up in remote rural areas. Sorokin, as has been seen, was himself of peasant stock. It was a scientific effort to attain precision which disclaimed any pretension to preach or to indulge in rash generalizations, many of such being mentioned only to be demolished. Problems were raised which remained "dark" and unresolved for the lack either of adequate facts or of their proper interpretation, or of both. After preliminary definitions, there was a joint chapter on the economic and class status of farmer-peasants, then the two authors each contributed roughly equal amounts to the fact-finding chapters on physique, health, disease, suicide, mortality, birth-rates and vitality, marriage, intelligence, mental disease, and psychological processes. Part IV attempted a cross-sectional comparison of rural and urban behavior, institutions and culture, while the whole of Part V was given up to the growing problem of migration.

The book was, for its time, a remarkable contribution, distinguished as was all Sorokin's work by its hunger for facts, its hesitancy in their absence, and its power of organizing available facts with the rest of his available material. Again his wide-ranging quest led him to draw upon Russian, German, French, Italian, and English sources as well as to refer to the situation in the classical world of Greece and Rome. The study was of course made before the technical developments of our own time had swiftly accelerated the process of change of which Sorokin and Zimmerman were very well aware. Roads, automobiles, radio, television, air travel, education and general economic developments have all transformed much of the world which Sorokin and Zimmerman described. Nevertheless their book was a classic statement so that, together with the *Source Book* on which it was based, it will remain a permanent contribution to the literature on rural life.

Harvard 1930-1959

Planning
SOCIAL AND CULTURAL DYNAMICS

When, in 1930, Harvard University created a Department of Sociology, no more than six years had elapsed since Sorokin had arrived as a refugee, knowing very little English and with no experience of the American environment. With a faith and foresight that does great credit to those who controlled the university's affairs, the appointment as head of the new department was offered to him. He could not have been given a greater compliment or a more distinguished and gratifying academic recognition. From then until his retirement in 1959, he not only continued to train many of the present generation of eminent American sociologists, but he added new and yet more weighty publications to the considerable corpus of sociological work already standing to his credit. During the years immediately following his appointment, with a new department to organize, he produced no new book. In a number of contributions to learned journals however, he began to show the direction in which his thoughts were tending. The readers of *Isis* in 1935 were presented with a paper of his upon "The Course of Arabian Intellectual Development A.D. 700 - 1300." Another on "Fluctuations of Materialism and Idealism from 600 B.C. to A.D. 1920" appeared in the *Festschrift* honoring the veteran Tonnies in 1936.

Background and Inspiration of
SOCIAL AND CULTURAL DYNAMICS

The years of preparation devoted to *Social and Cultural Dynamics* mark a turning point in the development of Sorokin's thought and also in the history of sociology. All his previous work had revealed the need for far more facts. Revolutions, the class structure of society, social mobility, rural and urban life and affairs, all had, as he called them, their "dark problems"; and they were not alone.

In *Contemporary Sociological Theories* Sorokin had passed in review a succession of pronouncements paraded as sociological wisdom, but nobody could feel at all secure about the factual foundations upon which they rested. Not enough was known to enable answers to be provided with any confidence to such questions as "What kinds of society have there been in the past?"; "In what did men then believe?"; "What did they know?"; "Why did they act as history says they acted?"; "When and why did they begin to change and to act otherwise?"; "How are their works and their records to be interpreted from a sociological point of view?"; "Are the facts upon which sociological doctrine presently rests fully sufficient?"; "Are they capable of sociological interpretations and correlations other than those which are now widely accepted?" There was no dearth of theories accompanied by historical evidence purporting to answer such questions. Sorokin, with the instincts of a true scholar and teacher, had done his best to profit from them all.

To begin with, there is the problem of the true nature of man, the unit from which societies are formed. The former student and Professor of the Psycho-Neurological Institute and student and colleague of Pavlov had long since ransacked the available literature on the mechanisms of human behavior from which sociological phenomena arise. He made what sense he could out of the notions thrown up in the past about the forces by which these original springs of human conduct were thought to be conditioned, controlled, or formed. Upon the earlier theories of Spencer and Darwin about the molding power of the environment and a resulting "natural selection," other sociologists had subsequently grafted various ideas about unconditioned and conditioned and hereditary reflexes or instincts. Beyond crude "behaviorism," others had stressed acquired religious, aesthetic, moral, and conventional actions. There had been the ideas such as the "suggestion" and "imitation" of Tarde and others, and more recently the speculations of Freud and Pareto about the compelling causative force of subconscious and unconscious impulses. As we have seen, it was upon an amalgam of such ideas that sociologists, including Sorokin, had formerly set to work. In his *Sociology of Revolution* in 1923/4 for instance, he summed up the result of his review of this medley of theories by saying that "human conduct is an extraordinary complex phenomenon, determined in an immense majority of cases by inborn reflexes and their stimuli. . . . . . the balance of conduct is achieved by way

of self-restriction and a complex struggle of various stimuli and reactions"
(p.31).

At this point it would assist the argument of this book if the reader
would reflect upon such a statement and decide whether it can be regarded
as an accurate summary of the state of knowledge about human
motivation and human actions in the 1920's. Would it not still, moreover,
be widely accepted as a fair if telegraphic summary of the mainsprings of
human conduct? The more Sorokin thought and wrestled with the
problem of building sociology upon such foundations, the more skeptical
he became. By the time he had written his long survey of *Contemporary
Sociological Theories*, four years later, he was able to discount all such
formulas. They were so loosely framed, so heterogeneous, so general and
so vague that, as he reported, they explained very little. They were not
even used by their authors to provide a factual account of actual human
achievements in society. No meanings could be got out of them with
which to construct an adequate, well-rounded sociology.

The poor harvest of operational concepts which a constructive sociology
could glean from physiological and neurological psychology deflected the
enquiry to a review of environmental, racial, biological, and economic
theories. In *Contemporary Sociological Theories* Sorokin had also already
weighed and found wanting many efforts to locate the agency of change in
human affairs elsewhere than in psychological causation and motivation.
Sociologists and historians had successively tried to find clues in such
matters as geographical, climatic, racial, political and economic forces, in
population levels and pressures, and in the evolutionary struggle for
survival — all mechanisms external to the character, personality, and
creative powers of individuals. Such were the factors upon which many
historians had relied, according to their personal predilections, in the
effort forced upon them to make the transitions which were necessary to
accommodate their record to the new directions taken in human affairs.
Although they could be employed sometimes with good effect, they
ultimately failed to measure up to the requirements of scientific validity.
For it was impossible to derive from them those satisfactory correlations
which, by an economy of causal concepts, would yield a scientific
explanation. The few matters they seemed to explain were swamped by
the many which they were powerless to explain. Neither is this surprising,
for no such explanatory concepts can transcend the narrow area over
which their subject matter extends. A geographical, anthropological,
economic or other such interpretation of social life has nothing but
geographical, anthropological or economic standards upon which to rely.

Other manifold human activities in art, philosophy, science, government, law, war and peace, must therefore be left imperfectly explained.

On two counts, therefore, sociology as traditionally presented was defective as a science. Nothing could be done to build a science of society out of the fragmentary findings of biology or of the psychology of instincts, reflexes, sub-conscious influences, habits and so forth. Nothing could be done to establish effective correlations in the development, the forms, the structure and the organization of societies, their aims and achievements, with the aid either of the psychological school or of the environmental sciences — climatology, geography, biology, anthropology, population pressures and so forth. If by combining them, an adequate account of zoological evolution could put together, no such combination was able to measure up to the needs of sociology as a science with all its myriad manifestations in art, in thought, in human behavior, in social groupings and their varied forms, in government, law, war, and revolution.

At this point it is useful to pause once more and ask if Sorokin was correct in regarding these two deficiencies in the traditional presentation of sociology as fatal to all hopes of making a science out of it — a science, that is to say, which would answer to a simple definition such as "knowledge based on the observation and testing of facts and worked into an ordered system acting as a base for new knowledge and a guide to ways of getting it"; an "ordered system" being "one controlled in agreement with tested facts and rules of reasoning."*

If the facts of sociology and history can be explained by relying solely upon the biological-anthropological-psychological nature of man and the power and influence of environmental forces to create, instead of merely to condition the life of man in society and civilization, then Sorokin's sociology might be unnecessary. He found it impossible to rest content with such explanations, and the positive, constructive advance which he has made in sociology consists in the manner in which he has gone beyond these traditional preliminaries to sociology in order to develop new concepts derived from other areas of human achievement.

It was indeed already obvious that sociologists could not remain upon levels of explanation which made it impossible to account sociologically for all that men had labored to produce, all that they had created in the way of artistic, literary, philosophical achievements; their laws, societies, and governments. Sorokin had given in *Contemporary Sociological Theories* (Chapter XII) a summary survey of the attempts made by such

---

* *The Science Dictionary in Basic English,* E. C. Graham, ed. (London, Evans, 1965).

predecessors as Fustel de Coulanges, Durkheim, Hobhouse, Lester Ward, Small, Max Weber and others to interpret social phenomena as a function of various cultural forces. While he acknowledged the force and brilliance with which they had put their points of view, he remained somewhat critically aloof. He considered that although "it is safe to say that in their trans-subjective form they (i.e. cultural forces) play some part in social control...... just how great it is, the existing theories do not answer." The conclusion at which he arrived would probably have been generally shared at the time he wrote, in 1927. It was that all that could be said about theories of cultural causation was that "they are vague and have not given us any valid correlations." So also in that work, when he came to survey various cyclical theories of history, he did not include his own name along with that of Weber as a theorist of the rhythm of spiritual and materialist civilizations with those of Danilevsky or Spengler as theorists of cycles in the life of a nation or culture, or with that of Nietzsche as one who thought that world history shows an eternal repetition of the same cycles.

Stress upon the great power of human values as well as human desires was however already "in the air", as Sorokin's survey made clear. As an aspect of the history of ideas it may be said to be almost as old as history itself. But special stress on the desirability of making history as a whole turn upon specifically cultural concepts was new. Sorokin points to the Russian, Nikolai Danilevsky (1822-1885) as a pioneer along such lines, but his books had not been translated and it is probable that, outside Russian-speaking lands, the learned world had never heard of him until Sorokin celebrated his work. Danilevsky does not seem to have founded a cultural-historical school of thought whose influence penetrated at all widely. Nowhere had concern about a "cultural" interpretation in history received a more powerful impetus and development than in Germany. The pregnant but little-known philosophical speculations of Dilthey, the more theologically involved attitudes of Eucken and Troeltsch had followed upon the pioneering thought of earlier writers, notably Schleiermacher and Hegel. In economics, Marx created a ferment, not because he denied the force of ideas as a power to change the world, but because he affirmed that they were a function of the economic means of production. Controversy on such lines powerfully concentrated thought upon the nature of such ideological influence and stimulated the study of cultural changes. In aesthetics, Wölfflin's contribution to the interpretation of the history of art had been striking. After Lamprecht's efforts to provide a positivistic and psychological interpretation of history, no writers had done more to stress the significance of cultural values than the philosophers Wilhelm Dilthey and Heinrich Rickert, and the historian Friedrich Meinecke, with all of whose work Sorokin was familiar. There is however, no evidence that he had seen Meinecke's striking essay "Kausalitäten und Werte in der Geschichte," which had appeared in the *Historische Zeitschrift* in 1928 and had once been republished in *Staat und Personlichkeit* (1933), a collection of Meinecke's essays. But it was above all Max Weber, of whom Sorokin always wrote with admiration, who had made a value-theory a central point of discussion in his sociology. Nobody had more vigorously urged that, as a science, sociology must avoid value judgments. Yet nobody was to do more to illustrate from history how value judgments changed men's lives. Earlier, Paul Barth had attempted to merge history and sociology in *Die Philosphie der Geschichte als Soziologie* (1897), a Russian translation of which had been published in St. Petersburg in 1900. Sorokin refers to it appreciatively, but it was far from anticipating his own approach to the problem of the nature of the agencies of sociological change. To this powerful new current of thought in Germany many writers contributed in addition to those mentioned here, among whom, however, Max Weber's brother, Alfred Weber, deserves special recognition. Novel and intriguing as this new development was, no consistent, well-rounded interpretation of sociology or of history had emerged from it. Very few echoes from it were heard in the Anglo-Saxon world. None of the major works of the thinkers mentioned above was available in English. Their writings were so little known that when Professor R. H. Tawney published his *Religion and the Rise of Capitalism* in 1926 the ideas he expressed in his own compellingly attractive style had all the appeal of novelty. English readers were largely ignorant of the pioneer thoughts of Troeltsch and Max Weber — which Tawney was inspired to apply in an English context. It has already been noted that Sorokin was the first to bring German and continental European sociological thought prominently to the notice of Americans, which stimulated a demand for the works of Max Weber in translation. Professor Talcott Parsons' version of *Protestant Ethics and the Spirit of Capitalism* with an introduction by R. H. Tawney had appeared in 1930, following a translation of Weber's lectures on general economic history. Many names could be added from Germany and from other countries, such as Jacob Burckhardt (1818-1897), Benedetto Croce (1866-1952), Ortega y Gasset (1883-1955), R. G. Collingwood (1889-1943) and others, by way of additional evidence of the growing interest in the formative power of general ideas and cultural influences in historical interpretation. The first man to create enthusiastic public interest in the new trend had undoubtedly been Oswald Spengler (1880-1936) whose *Der Untergang des Abendlandes* took the serious German reading public by storm as soon as it was published in 1918. Translated as *The Decline of the West* (1926), it also aroused immense interest in the English-speaking world. Condemned by every academic historian with a violence that varied with their personal tempers and force of personality, the book changed men's ways of looking at the past. It prepared the way for those sweeping reviews of world history written to satisfy the rising public interest, which the great German maestro of the *Götterdammerung,* with his fire and fury, had done so much to stimulate. Despite academic aversion, Spengler has never ceased to find readers or to create discussion. Yet, as Sorokin was to point out, from a sociological point of view the framework or philosophical basis of that great work was simple to the point of naivety, with the analogy of the childhood, youth, manhood and old age of cultures as its central concept of development.

Every reader must supplement from his own wider knowledge this sketchy outline of some of the main influences upon the development of thought about social evolution, as it stood before Sorokin wrote. He himself, as already seen above, has recorded the names of other writers by whom he was influenced, some of whom, such as Kovalevsky and Petrajitzsky, remain virtually unknown in the West. Readers must form their own judgment as to whether the composite picture of human social development which they are able to form from all such varied contributions amounts to the outlines of a valid sociology. Sorokin, who knew them all well, did not consider it possible to put together a satisfactory picture, either from them or from the various other philosophies of historical change to which reference will be made later, in discussing cyclical movements or rhythms in history. It was not possible to extract from them answers to the questions posed at the beginning of this chapter which could clearly be warranted by the facts, and which would, above all, yield hypotheses or generalizations showing correlations between each other sufficiently close and evident to warrant clearance as "scientific." Such hypotheses must qualify by meeting a definition such as that in *The Science Dictionary in Basic English* "theories put forward to give reasons for connection between certain facts, or suggestions to be tested, on which further work may be based." Every reader can again at this stage decide which, if any, of the many hypotheses proposed by previous writers to explain the course of sociological development have, in fact, demonstrated such connections, and if so, how wide a field it is that they are able to cover. It is equally important to know whether they have also led to fruitful lines of research upon which further work has been based. Far from achieving these happy results, most of the theories, however ingenious, seem to have died with their authors. They created no enduring doctrine, they founded no flourishing school after the manner of Plato, Aristotle, St. Thomas Aquinas, Leibniz, Kant or Hegel. They failed notably to advance the arguments to which they had been addressed. Their value, and it was great, lies in the interest and stimulus they evoked. They brought thousands to take a vivid interest in the past, at a time when the influence of most academic historians who were striving to extend the bounds of historical knowledge did not reach far beyond a few hundred students, their colleagues, and their students at other centres. So sociology as the *Science Dictionary* defines it, "the science of society among men, covering its history, development, forms, structure, the organization and relations to which it has given birth", lacked that embodiment in a network of congruous hypotheses which it needs.

The truth was that the facts between which connections could reasonably be demonstrated had not been collected. Many of course were available, but the historians and sociologists who had got them together could be charged, as indeed many were, of picking up only those facts which happened to suit their preconceived notions. Some preconceptions of course there had to be, otherwise there would be no hypotheses to test. No science has ever emerged from a collection of raw facts. When R. G. Collingwood at Oxford repeated vigorously that all advances in knowledge depend upon the ability to ask the right questions, he may seem to have been stating the obvious, but he was at least uttering a much needed caution as well as a piece of practical advice. What are the right questions in sociology? They must arise from and illuminate its subject matter — "the history, development, forms, structure and the organizations and relations to which human society has given birth." Sociology had already collected sufficient problems for it to be possible to ask some penetrating questions. Difficulties arose because they could not be answered for lack of sufficient information. Many more facts were needed about the life of men in societies and their achievements.

Undaunted, Sorokin took up no lesser task than to look for these facts — all of them, over as wide an area of sociological phenomena as possible. Before proceeding to give some account of this vast and novel enterprise, it is essential to get clear both the nature and purpose of his enquiry. It was to derive from the historical record all those facts which would throw light upon the creations, the achievements, and the social behavior of mankind from the earliest times to the present day. His was a piece of sociological research, although on a grand scale. He was not writing a history of mankind. He was not intending to propound a new philosophy of history. Unless this fact is clear at the outset there will be grave danger that he will continue to be bracketed with writers such as Spengler and Toynbee, as he has been and all too often still is. Those who have attacked him have usually made this mistake. Others who have referred to him in passing in this way betray a merely superficial or hearsay acquaintance with his achievement. A bad journalist might do so, but a good journalist at least tries to present the facts correctly. As a sociologist, therefore, Sorokin had a philosophical interest in trying to state and to understand the full sociological significance of the achievements of mankind in the formation and development of societies, in their ethical systems, laws, governments, wars and revolutions. He sought to discover the origin, nature, and development of all those activities by which the human race is distinguished: its art, science, music, literature and philosophy. "Significance" for him stood, in addition to its ordinary meaning of giving a sense or being a sign, for its more scientific meaning of being great enough to be important, thus indicating the degree to which the facts collected corresponded with the hypotheses he was testing. Such significant facts and the hypotheses based upon them must next show significant correlations with each other. That is to say they must not merely show the connection between one branch of human achievement and another, they also have to make clear the degree to which one changing value among the various human achievements could be shown to depend upon another. If the results of Sorokin's investigations succeeded in establishing such connections, they would naturally be likely to influence the interpretation of history, as well as of sociology, because both of these branches of learning depend upon facts, their interpretation and presentation.

What then were the significant facts for a scientific sociology?

The Empirical Basis of Social and Cultural Dynamics.

Of all the works of man which remain from remote times, their buildings, statuary, and other works of art are most conspicuous. They have all been intently studied in modern times. A large share of Sorokin's fact-finding enquiry was accordingly devoted to them. To study practically all the known pictures and sculptures of any period is a gigantic task, but

Sorokin attempted no less than that. He tried to include "all the pictures and all the sculptural works known in the history of art regardless of whether they belong to great or small or anonymous artists." "We are sure," he wrote, "that our samples embrace for most of the countries — the bulk of the works of each period."

The main work was done by collaborators in Prague and Cambridge, Massachusetts. Paintings and sculptures were examined from the following countries or cultures: Italy, France, England, Central Europe (Germany, Austria, Czechoslovakia), the Netherlands, Spain, Russia, Islam, and the ancient and medieval Christian period including that of Byzantium. Encyclopedias and other reference works, histories of art, monographs, museum catalogs, and art journals were consulted. Sorokin indicates that somewhat greater attention was given to the art of Italy, Central Europe, France and Russia than to that of Spain or England. He makes no claim to have exhausted the subject. He is candid about the extent to which he considers his work meets ideal tests of validity and reliability, saying about his results that "they may be unreliable, but they are more reliable than any data presented up to the present time so far as the general course of art fluctuation in the countries studied is concerned."

The enquiry was a sociological investigation, not an aesthetic one of the kind usually made to appraise the skill of artists in drawing, composition, color and design. It was directed instead to throw light on the state of mind, the aims, beliefs, and social climate of the time in which the art was produced. Consequently, the answers which Sorokin sought were of the following order: whether the paintings and sculptures were predominantly religious or secular; whether landscapes, everyday scenes, or portraits; whether the subject was royalty, the aristocracy, clergy, middle class, or laboring class. Such qualities were readily recognizable. More care was needed in deciding the next point, which was the number of paintings and sculptures of the nude human form. Here the investigators were asked to distinguish between ascetic, neutral, sensuous, and erotic styles. The degree of subjective bias arising from the interpretation of this classification is however unlikely to be serious, and Sorokin was able up to a point to check and allow for it by the fact that while one team of investigators was at work in Prague, another was busy independently in Cambridge, Massachusetts.

Regarding music, Sorokin had its history searched to compute from A.D. 1500-1900 the number of religious and the number of secular composers, rather than of actual compositions, owing to the manifest absurdity of equating a short madrigal with a Mass. The number of great religious works from A.D. 1600-1920 was however compared with the number of great secular works in that period. Other computations were made to show the proportion between major theatrical compositions and non-theatrical works in the seventeenth, eighteenth and nineteenth centuries. An interesting study was that which revealed the dominant tonalities of representative composers of the eighteenth and nineteenth centuries showing that the minor key increasingly gained ground on the major key of earlier times. The topics to which music could be said to have been devoted were also analyzed, showing how, between A.D. 1600 and 1920, mythological and pseudo-historical subjects diminished in number as *genre* and comedy pieces increased, as did also the compositions inspired by revolution, war, folklore, historicism, exoticism, and urbanism.

Sorokin's study of literary forms was similarly extensive. Just as his investigations of the history of art and music were sociological and not aesthetic in purpose, so in literature he was not concerned primarily with literary standards of judgment. Again computations were made of aspects of the literary product such as their religious, secular or critical character, the treatment of love and lust, the place of economic motives and behavior, the reflection of social classes, the topic of duty versus comfort and easy living. In the light of these investigations into the nature of man's aesthetic productions, Sorokin was able to draw provisional conclusions about the prevalent mentality and its sociological values, meanings and norms at various periods in the past. In addition to these enumerations and estimates the enquiry had revealed other useful sociological guides and pointers of a qualitative kind which could not be adequately represented by quantitative formulae.

From art, Sorokin turned to philosophy, science and law. An exhaustive study was indertaken to provide indicators to the fluctuations observable in the criteria by which knowledge was deemed to be true or false from 580 B.C. to A.D. 1900. Thinkers were listed according to their predominant tendencies in the following classes: — empiricism, rationalism, mysticism, criticism, skepticism and fideism. An immense amount of work was devoted to the detailed study of each of these branches of philosophy resulting in many striking statistical tables and graphs. Moreover the names of hundreds of philosphers classified under their various schools of thought, together with an indication of the weight allowed to each (indicating their influence) were presented in an appendix. A parallel effort was made to list the number of scientific discoveries and inventions in Greece and Rome from the eighth century B.C. to the sixth century A.D. and in Western Christian Europe from the seventh century to the nineteenth century. This was elaborated by separate listings of discoveries and inventions in the natural sciences, technology, and geography from 3500 B.C. to A.D. 1908, divided into mathematics, astronomy, biology, medical science, chemistry, physics, geology, technology and geographical discoveries. The thought that this tally of inventions would fortify the study of philosophical trends was justified. Between A.D. 1401 and 1900 the number of such important discoveries was shown in ten-year periods. A less successful table gave the relative amount of space devoted in the *Encyclopaedia Britannica* to the achievements of England, Germany, France, the U.S.A., Austria-Hungary and Bohemia, Russia and Poland, Belgium and Holland, China and India, in religion, literature, scholarship, science, philosophy, fine art and music. As the ninth edition of this great encyclopedia, published in 1875, was used, it naturally gave much more space to British achievements than to those of other countries. It was a bias largely rectified by another more comprehensive table of statistics taken from Darmstädter's *Handbuch zur Geschichte der Naturwissenschaften und der Technik* (1908) and from the statistics of patents issued in the U.S.A. (from 1840-1934) and Great Britain (from 1761 to 1931). Other sources were also used to indicate the output of scientific literature in modern times.

From philosophy and science, Sorokin turned to the more cosmological aspects of thought about human nature and destiny. Another immense labor was undertaken to assess the fluctuating emphasis given by thinkers of the past during twenty-year periods from 560 B.C. to A.D. 1900 to the grand questions of Being and Becoming, Permanence, and Change. Under the headings eternalism, temporalism, eternalism-temporalism, temporalism-eternalism, equilibrium of both, were listed the numbers of thinkers supporting each predominant tendency together with weights assigned to them indicating their influences in the stream of thought.

Various views about the nature of knowledge entertained by thinkers of the past from 540 B.C. to A.D. 1920 were then analyzed under the three heads of nominalism, conceptualism and realism, first in twenty-year periods and then in 100-year periods, giving as well the numbers and weights of all the thinkers included, whose names were also all listed in an appendix.

Ideas about singularism, universalism and mystic unity were next analyzed in the same way from 580 B.C. to A.D. 1920, also in twenty-year periods. A brief but illuminating table set out the currents observable in the ideas of singularism, universalism, and integralism between 600 B.C.

an; A.D. 1920, a table especially relevant to the study of society and group sociology.

One of the perennial divisions running through the history of philosophical thought has been the cleavage between the opposite ideas of determinism and indeterminism. Particularly useful therefore are Sorokin's tables listing between 540 B.C. and A.D. 1920, in twenty-year periods, the numbers supporting each of these opposed schools of thought as well as the number of mixed, undifferentiated opinions on the matter evident in very early times.

The next group of statistics was collected in the effort to trace the nature and development of ethical systems. For every twenty-year period from 580 B.C. to A.D. 1920, Sorokin listed indicators based upon the theories and the estimated influence of hundreds of writers whose opinions or some record of them had survived. He grouped them into the four broad categories: the ethics of happiness (eudaemonism, hedonism, utilitarianism); the ethics of principles; deontological ethical systems; the ethics of love. The result was then condensed to show the fluctuations of such influences by century periods between 600 B.C. and A.D. 1900. Again he printed in an appendix the names of all these thinkers, the class in which he grouped them, and the weight assigned to each. Again therefore, the questions he asked and the manner in which they were answered together with the sources on which the answers were based were fully disclosed. Such details occupy considerable space, and Sorokin could not reproduce them all. Thus for the allied ethico-philosophical question of the alternation of relativism and absolutism, criticism and belief, doubt and faith, the summary results alone are presented. The fluctuations of the vogue of pessimism and optimism are also summarized in statistical tables and a graph. When not printed in full, the work-sheets and data upon which all such conclusions were based were deposited in Harvard University Library.

Law represents another important branch of Sorokin's great sociological investigation for the obvious reason of its great value as an indicator of social conditions at various periods of history. Taking the main codes and laws of France, Germany, Austria and Italy as his sources, he subjected them to scrutiny in order to determine the nature of the acts regarded as criminal and the intensity of punishment inflicted upon offenders as successive changes in the law were made, from the earliest times for which records are available.

Volumes 1 and 2 of *Social and Cultural Dynamics* thus deal broadly with cultural values, aesthetic, scientific, philosophical, religious, moral, and juridical, using as a foundation the laborious fact-finding explorations of which those briefly referred to above were the chief. In Volume 3 Sorokin turned to specifically social problems, to the social groups through which cultural values are manifested.

Taking first the familistic, contractual, and compulsory relations in the main social groups evident in Europe since Carolingian times, Sorokin sought to discover whether the proportion of the relationship of each type, within each social group, as well as the totality of such groups, has been fluctuating, and, if so, when. Then he tried to see whether any correlations were to be detected between those fluctuations and the various main cultural changes already examined and reported in his first two volumes. Where any positive correlation appeared, he sought to explain the reasons for it. In this enquiry he was fortunate in securing the cooperation of his well-known countryman and specialist on the sociology of law, Professor N. S. Timasheff, just as he was assisted by other men who are now renowned, such as Professor Robert K. Merton, who helped with the laborious investigations into the scientific history of mankind reported in Sorokin's second volume. As the subject matter of this section on social groups was predominantly qualitative, no numerical data were presented. The succeeding socio-political phenomena, forms of government and socio-political leadership, were similarly treated. The quantitative aspects of such studies were next researched by means of an investigation into the social relationships created by the existence, within any social framework, of a network of organized groups. It was a problem which led directly to the study of totalitarian government on the one hand and of *laissez-faire* and liberal state practices on the other.

Topics such as the increase of governmental control in periods of social emergency were investigated also from the earliest times. The changing nature of the network of social relationships, the shifts or "mobility" observable within such relationships under the pressure of catastrophe, revolution, and so on, were all examined. Particular attention was given to the collection of information on economic conditions from the earliest times of Greece and Rome, a task of great difficulty which, as Sorokin points out, must leave large areas of uncertainty because of the lack of information. Such data as Sorokin could assemble were presented graphically, with all due reservations, for the Ancient World 600 B.C. to A.D. 400, for France A.D. 800 to 1926, and for Germany A.D. 700-1932.

The second half of Sorokin's third volume was devoted to the facts and statistics on outbreaks of revolutionary violence and war, both subjects of obvious sociological interest. Again, as in most of the other fields investigated, Sorokin reported the impossibility of making a fully satisfactory study, simply because of the lack of precise and adequate information. No subjects have attracted more attention, but most historians in the past have been singularly remiss in their accounts of them. Information is often non-existent or unsatisfactory on such elementary matters as: the number of people involved as participants and victims; the number of battles and the sizes of the armies engaged; numbers of killed, wounded, maimed or taken captive; the number of revolutions, internal disturbances and social upheavals and the precise weight to be assigned to each. Again Sorokin with all due caution used what information he could glean, certain only that he was presenting much more than that hitherto collected. In fifty statistical tables illustrated and summarized in fifteen graphs, he presented his results for many countries and many periods from the Ancient World to modern times.

In brief outline, such were the fact-finding explorations undertaken by Sorokin as a prelude to the study of sociology in the manner in which, in his opinion, it should be undertaken. Before proceeding to a summary of the new sociology to which this vast enterprise has led, it will be very desirable for the reader again to pause and to consider Sorokin's method. Were the subjects to which Sorokin gave so much time, thought, and heavy labor appropriate to sociology? If not, which could safely be omitted? What additional subjects ought Sorokin to have included as throwing a better light on sociology than those on which he concentrated? Can it be alleged fairly that all Sorokin's questions reveal a sinister bias showing that he was not truly concerned with pure sociological knowledge resting upon the values and forms of society which men have created in the past, but that, instead of this scientific purpose, he was merely seeking to put over some preconceived doctrine of his own under the guise of a scientific sociology? If so, what is that bias? Furthermore, can the critic alleging such bias give reasons for supposing that Sorokin or anyone else could have foretold what all the answers to all the many questions would be?

Here it is important to distinguish preliminary hypotheses, upon which all sciences depend, from a pre-formed ideology. Sorokin's questions are surely too diverse, too numerous, too clearly designed to elicit sociological facts, for any such suspicions of preconceived bias to arise. They were genuine hypotheses. If there are lingering doubts upon that point they will disappear when Sorokin's statement of his findings and results is examined.

These questions by the reader will, it is believed, dispose of much of the criticism to which Sorokin has been exposed by people who either have not studied his methods or have failed to understand them. So far as it is known, no such critic has attempted, by answering them to devise another and a superior approach to sociology. There has been uninformed criticism by those who shrink themselves from the toil and trouble of propounding any general conclusions of their own; there has been sniping on minor points; there have been valuable corrections in details and, what Sorokin valued even more, philosophic reflection about some of his conclusions which help either to modify them, to reformulate them, or to carry them further. As Sorokin's concern was the advancement of knowledge, he was his own best critic when it comes to assessing the adequacy and validity of the factual basis for his theories. Like any other investigator who seeks light from the past, he faced the inevitable alternatives — — either he must pass the problem by, however important it be, in order not to take chances of making too many, or too great, blunders, or he must go ahead and take these chances. In this latter case the study would be of value only if he would try to be as careful and as unbiased as possible in the study of the facts. The relevant facts he collects must be at least as complete as, or more complete than, those in any other study hitherto made. He should not claim the privilege of infallibility or the validity of his results, but should simply say, "Let us study the relevant facts as well as possible and then see what the results will be, without certainty as to whether they are accurate but with confidence that they are more reliable than purely inspirational theories or ones based upon only fragments of the existing data."* He must put 'all his cards on the table' in the sense of stating his assumptions Finally (and here speaks the prophetic voice of the pioneer, well aware of the normal reception of advances in sociological knowledge today) he must be ready normal reception of advances in sociological knowledge today) "he must by ready crowd of waiting critics, from ignorant journalistic 'snipers' and politicians, pacifists and militarists, up to the finicky and meticulous scholar accustomed only to a study of little narrow topics and to the art of straining at gnats."

In this faith, and with a determination such as only loyalty to the truth can inspire in any author, Sorokin first collected and then reviewed the results of a vast assemblage of information on the nature of the beliefs, behavior, achievements, and actions of humanity from the earliest available records up to modern times. All the facts bore upon specific cultural and social subjects on which they often threw more light than

---

*P. A. Sorokin, *Social and Cultural Dynamics* (New York, Bedminster Press, 1962), Vol. II, pp. 268-9.

Sorokin would have believed possible. They also called for many revisions of generally accepted notions. Sorokin had not been a student of the history of ideas for half a life-time without acquiring a reasonably adequate orientation in history. Yet, as he observed, "Like many others somewhat acquainted with history, I held certain preconceived ideas of the kind generally accepted. . . . . . . When however the results were studied, they sometimes quite contradicted my preconceived ideas. In such cases I naturally felt that I must find out whether the figures were not playing me a trick and giving quite misleading results. So I proceeded to check and recheck the results. After sufficient study I had to recognize that in most cases the figures were right; while the ideas that I had drawn from textbooks, journalistic articles, historical novels, prevalent opinions and propaganda in various forms were wrong."* This statement alone is the best commentary upon the notion that Sorokin framed all his enquiries in such a way that they would give him the answers he desired. It also indicates that those whose inclination is to question or oppose his views had better arm themselves with sources superior to the "hunches" and general impressions by which he confesses himself to have been misled.

To fully assimilate the enormous amount of material he had assembled was another colossal task. At the same time it was fruitful and exciting in the vistas of unsuspected trends and unanticipated correlations which it revealed. Clear patterns began to emerge for certain periods, fortunately sufficiently enduring, cohesive, and consistent, to be beyond the bounds of mere chance occurrence. Other periods were less well-defined.

Before long Sorokin was able to work out and to present both his facts as indicated (all too briefly) above and some of the conclusions which he drew from them.

When the results were published in the first three volumes of *Social and Cultural Dynamics* in 1937, the appearance of many tables of statistics, percentages, averages and graphs appears to have had the same effect upon some readers as would quotations in Greek or Hebrew. Sorokin has been accused of attempting to quantify qualities, of indulging in "astro-physics" and so forth, all of which is plain nonsense. He has done no more than to count and try to assess on a comparative scale the products, events, and thoughts which everyone who writes upon cultural history has always attempted to assess. The only difference between them and him is that he has tried to assess more openly, more thoroughly, and more accurately.

Ibid, Vol. III, p. 287.

Some of his countings and assessments may contain errors, but this is true of all human efforts to count and measure. Every year, for instance, for many a decade, the British Government has published an annual report full of measurements and maps showing the annual distribution of rainfall over the British Isles. These figures, being "scientific" and "official," are never questioned. Yet everyone who has ever collected and measured rainfall knows that there is a margin of error. Sometimes the observations are delayed. There may have been evaporation. There may have been some accident to the apparatus resulting in the loss of one or more periodic observations. There may have been a plain error in reading from a calibrated scale or in the pen and ink entry on the returns sent in to the Meteorological Office. Despite checking, some errors may have been made by some junior clerk in copying, or in additions, or in calculating averages. Over the country as a whole, such minor discrepancies are not regarded as serious. The accuracy of the rainfall returns is never doubted.

Analogous errors may mar Sorokin's figures, but if so there is a remedy which is not available to anyone who is skeptical about the validity of *British Rainfall.* The cultural skeptic can go over all the ground traversed by Sorokin and count again and assess again what Sorokin has counted and assessed. Fields which Sorokin did not explore can be added and new calculations made as a check upon Sorokin's work. He would have been the first to welcome any such undertaking.

Such was the spirit in which Sorokin undertook what must be the most vast enterprise ever to have been contemplated and executed by any sociologist. It is a gigantic monument of industry and application, recalling some of the pioneer work of great nineteenth-century scholars who single-handedly set themselves similar heart-breaking tasks which remain to astonish posterity, men such as John C. Loudon, G. R. Porter, or Thorold Rogers.

Methodology & Sorokin's
Social & Cultural Dynamics

Description and Explanation

Like all great works, Sorokin's *Social and Cultural Dynamics* carries conviction by its own weight of fact and argument. It is able to do so by effectively marrying fact and theory, to yield more facts and a refinement of theory from their fertile union. The brief, summary description of the range and content of the work which follows will, it is hoped, be seen to be sufficiently stimulating to lead any who read it directly to Sorokin's own works for inspiration. At the outset and at the risk of some repetition, which may however assist the argument, an indication will now be given of some of the key-concepts which emerged from it and are used in it to provide the central ideas of Sorokin's sociology.

Most history is a record of what happened and no more, or very little more. It is full of ideas about origins, changes, developments, often of vivid, concrete images and living portraits of personalities and events. These ideas try to hold up a mirror to the past. Such descriptive ideas Sorokin, following Windleband, calls 'ideographic' or pictures of forms of the real.* Sorokin mentions by way of illustration the work of great historians such as Herodotus, Thucydides, Polybius, Gibbon, Mommsen, Fustel de Coulanges and Rostovzeff as examples. History as they wrote it was largely ideographic. From time to time these great historians also throw in a few ideas which go beyond mere description, ideas which suggest that what is said about some events or people may have a wider application than to the events or persons to whom they are referring. They may not go so far as to suggest that they are proclaiming principles which will be valid when applied to periods of history other than those with

*W. Windelband, *Präludien* (Mohr, Tübingen, 1921), Vol. II, p. 145.

which they have been dealing, but that is what average readers will probably suppose. Such generalizations heighten the interest of the narrative. Most people cannot remember all the thousands of characters, events, dates and other solid facts of history. Amid so many crowded facts they find relief in some stimulating general truths. So the few "wise saws and modern instances" they encounter, stick in their memory. They are something which readers can "take away with them." They keep alive the works of many a historian, in spite of the way in which the growth of knowledge through research may have made his historical record out of date. Many of Gibbon's "asides" are memorable, such as "the principles of a free constitution are irrevocably lost, when the legislative power is nominated by the executive." Macaulay was remarkable for such general statements: "the essence of war is violence, and moderation in war is imbecility"; "the reluctant obedience of distant provinces generally costs more than the territory is worth." Few of those who have struggled as schoolboys or undergraduates with the Latin of Tacitus are likely to forget those sparkling phrases which he distilled from the bitter waters of affliction to remind humanity of its folly and stupidity: "it is human nature to hate him whom you have hurt" – *proprium humani ingenii est odisse quem laeseris;* "that human propensity to follow readily but not to lead" *–insita mortalibus natura propere sequi quae piget inchoare,"* and "the more ready to credit what they do not understand – *obscura libentius credendi.* Many are the occasions upon which such gems of apparent wisdom can be trotted out to clinch an argument. Yet general maxims of that sort may often be questioned or contradicted by others which seem equally valid. This can happen so often that another of Macaulay's maxims was "Nothing is so useless as a general maxim." It is a useful caution for sociologists. The orthodox school of academic historians invariably regards with suspicion all who are addicted to them or to generalizing about history, rather in the spirit of Disraeli who advised "read only biography because that is life without theory." When sociology is looked at from this point of view, the inadequacy of trying to develop it with none but ideographic descriptive notions alone is plainly evident. To go beyond them, and to frame "maxims" or statements which can be applied to more than one social group and to more than one period of time, becomes essential if sociology is to have any pretensions to be regarded as a science. The knowledge sociology should provide ought to be in the form of generalizations or statements about uniformities that have something of the character of scientific laws. In contrast with the "ideographic" word-pictures, Sorokin revives a word little used in English since the seventeenth century to describe these more developed, more precise general statements as "nomothetic" or "law-giving." Only from them can explanations be derived.

The Lack of Valid Explanations in Sociology

A clear path through the large and growing tangled thorny thicket of contemporary sociology has still to be made. As it is today, countless unfortunate students may well despair in their efforts to follow the convoluted thought of eminent professors as they learnedly pursue the "foundations of sociology" with potted versions of the ideas of Machiavelli, of Hobbes, of Locke, tracing the fate of various notions through the works of Adam Smith, Malthus, Rousseau, and others, down to Darwin, Spencer, Sir Henry Maine; assessing, after a fashion, the weight and influence of each, all of whom have also somehow to be related to Kant, Hegel, Comte, Marx, Durkheim, Max Weber, Freud and as many other writers as can be thrown in as make-weights. As it is usually impossible to guess whether and how far any one of these writers was really influenced by any of his predecessors, and if so to what extent, the whole exercise is reducible to a parade of book learning. Not until all the various notions examined are caught up, instead of being left unrelated, and exhibited as referable to some inclusive general principle, as Sorokin has done, will all the authors of the sociological classics cease to be so many puppets pulled out of a professor's magic box. Sorokin shows them as real persons, the sons but also the guides and innovators of their age, by no means always consistent or always exponents of the whole range of social ideas of their time.

Even sociology's professional practitioners weary as their contemporaries propound new sociological concepts and claim to be in possession of new "tools" of research and analysis, which, however, fail to achieve the advances they were supposed to make possible. Meanwhile aspirants for a certificate of competence in sociology may be expected to show a ready skill in dealing with "ideographs" such as "integrative functions," "pattern maintenance," "structure of action," "societal inputs and outputs," "roles," "goal attainment," "goal gratification," "resource processing," "socialization of motivational capacity," "value specification (legitimation)" "institutionalized permissiveness in processes of social control," "exogeneous and endogenous sources of change," "pattern-variables." To be sure, those who succeed in manipulating all this bogus coinage to the satisfaction of their examiners are likely to possess more nimble wits than those who fail, so the curriculum which imposes such a task has as much to be said in its favor as Macaulay's words about the Cherokee language, when he defended the practice of examining the ability of students to write Greek and Latin verse. "If instead of learning Greek we learned the Cherokee, the man who understood the Cherokee best, who made the most correct and melodious Cherokee verses, who comprehended most accurately the effect of Cherokee particles, would generally be a superior man to him who was destitute of these accomplishments."* Cherokee is at least likely to be superior to sociological name-dropping and *Kategorienwirtschaft*, the dance of bloodless categories, in one important particular: it would at least have some evident relationship to the things of this world.

When readers encounter in the ensuing summary of Sorokin's contribution to this tangled sociological scene such words as "ideational," "idealistic," "sensate," "principle of immanence," "principle of limits," "logico-meaningful integralism," they may be liable to conclude that these also are no more than mere additions to the sociological junk-pile of professional verbalism. Not only is this untrue but the understanding of these simple half-dozen terms, none of them really difficult, will open the door to an easy grasp of a vast range of social phenomena which have eluded the pursuit of sociologists in the past. They will also enable everyone to shut the door upon a mass of obsolete, useless notions. In the way that Linne (or Linnaeus) brought order into botany and Darwin brought it into biology, Sorokin's achievement clears up an immense confusion and sets the stage for far more rapid progress.

Sorokin's advance, as theirs, is sure, because it emerges from a thorough study of and a power to master a vaster world of facts than that with which any previous sociologists had dared to grapple. While they were still inventing new technical words and writing glosses upon the works of others, Sorokin went straight to the facts. From them he derived his half-dozen guiding principles. With their aid he was able to put the whole subject into a new perspective because his reading of the facts yielded far more than another set of verbal "ideographs." Sorokin's new concepts stand as shorthand expressions for a rich assemblage of ideas, but they owe their power to the fact that they do more than this. They point to valid generalizations over huge areas of fact, and they yield formulas of

*G. O. Trevelyan, *Life and Lectures of Lord Macaulay* (London, Longman's, 1909), pp. 585-6.

uniformity which can be successfully employed within that vast area of fact, which are especially illuminating as explanations of changing sociological valuations.

As Sorokin points out, the discovery of such explanatory 'nomothetic' notions is the result of an intuitive, reflective process of a mind grappling with a vast welter of facts. Such ideas are never provided by the facts themselves. Had they been, humanity would not have had to wait for Linnaeus or Darwin, because the facts of botany, embryology, morphology and geological succession were known before they applied their minds to such studies. Once glimpsed by intuition, nomothetic generalizations in sociology must be elaborated by logical thought, using where possible, all mathematical and statistical techniques. Finally, the developed hypothesis must be tested by all the relevant empirical facts, again using as many statistical and other methods of empirical verification as possible. Inasmuch as true experimentation is beyond the resources of sociology, it is necessary to rely upon the logical method of concomitant variations and the theory of probability in order to establish genuine correlations and explanatory principles. Often even these resources are also beyond scientific sociology simply because sufficient facts, particularly those relating to past periods, do not exist. As a result of the best possible use of all available resources, the nomothetic hypotheses, as well as the phenomena whose uniformity is to be measured and tested against the relevant facts, must all be clearly defined. The slow, halting progress or virtual stagnation of sociology as a source or science of nomothetic, generalizing concepts complained of above, results from the failure of sociologists to meet these methodological requirements.

Discarded Explanatory Principles in Sociology

One by one the magic formulas which were proposed as the mainspring of social science and as solutions to sociological problems have had to be discarded. Take the opposing theses of the schools of Spencer and of Marx. According to the one, the individual should be entirely free to pursue his own economic destiny. The answer of the other would be, "So he has been and the result could be seen in the poverty and misery of masses of people in the 19th century." There were of course other explanations of that poverty, principally the population explosion, but the Marxists would be correct in saying that unrestrained liberty for able, aggressive, acquisitive individuals did not, in the nineteenth century, produce an ordered social system which the masses would accept. On the other hand complete totalitarian control according to a strict Marxian creed is death to individual liberty. This is no mere theoretical pronouncement because it is abundantly evident that State-communism has frequently caused hardship, destruction and death.

What has sociology to propose which will explain, if it cannot resolve, such classes of sociological principles? What sociologist has proposed a "political constant" which might be expected to emerge from and resolve the reciprocal relations of freedom and control? Unfortunately none. Other general ideas which have been suggested as explanatory principles have also been found to be inadequate. Among them have been "family relationships," "small groups," "social action," "the institutionalization of action," "social structure." The authors of almost every one of the many treatises in sociology adopt some such "principles" of their own. Adequately explained, some of them may throw a little light upon some aspects of sociology to provide absorbing reading for anybody fascinated by descriptions of social phenomena, but they do not yield that synoptic, synthetic grasp which the subject needs if it is to become a science. For too long, sociology has had a notorious lack of such general principles.

Testimony to the weakness of sociology abounds on all sides. An attempt, for instance, to explain the blight of specialized jargon described as "sociologese" said that "if a general theory of social behavior ever came to be established, then its terminology would no more be regarded as jargon than the terminology of economics or demography (or chemistry or physics). But there isn't yet such a theory." Apparently despairing of ever achieving any broad unifying concepts able to account for social behavior, the attack went on to doom sociology as irremediably "an aggregate of unsuccessful or provisional attempts to talk more precisely about individual behavior."*

An initial and insuperable obstacle to the acceptance of explanations proposed hitherto exists because all the facts identified and described as sociological, are variables. An accurate sociological description of, say, "city life" today is virtually irrelevant as an aid to understanding town life in the Middle Ages. Historians may not be much troubled by such differences, but sociologists should be. This challenge provided by historical change was one of the provocations to which Sorokin's sociology is the response.

*W. G. Runciman, "Sociologese," *Encounter,* 1965, Vol. XXV, No. 6, 46-7.

Changing Values, Changing Social Life.

"History relates the aim at ideals," said Whitehead.* Everybody has long been well aware of the pronouced shift which took place in the broad pattern of human values between pagan and early Christian societies, and between those societies and our own times. The Christians martyred in the Colosseum by pagan Romans, the monks, nuns, abbeys, and cathedrals, the 'schoolmen,' the power of the Popes, the Crusades, all represented a way of life which was very different from that of today. The people who then set standards of behavior were guided by other-worldly considerations which, in time, came to be less and less influential. Before long, people came to be more concerned about the things of this world and inclined to "have a good time," which usually meant self-indulgence instead of pious asceticism. The contrast can be seen today in the absorbing interest in food, drink, sex, leisure, and entertainment. Striking as is the difference between a life governed by other-worldly considerations and one given up to the pleasures of the world, it is not one into which all sociological facts can be neatly fitted, and Sorokin was not so naive as to suppose that they could be. Yet the contrast was strong enough to provoke reflection and research. At least two fundamentally different ways of life provided a standing challenge to sociology.

What was the precise nature of these contrasting human ways of life? How long did they last? When did they change? Were the immediate consequences temporary or lasting? And what in turn has been their history?

The historical record of such changes, springing as they must from the nature of man, suggests that they have their basis in, or correspond with, broad human traits. Some meanings, values and rules make a more immediate appeal to some people than to others. Fundamentally there can be two and only two main classes of meanings and values from which, or from combinations of which, the whole vast, rich pattern of cultural life can arise. In order that ambiguous terms such as "meaning" and "value," upon which much of Sorokin's work depends, are not smuggled into the argument without a clear understanding of their purport, it may be said here that *meaning* is used in the simple basic English sense of "using words with the sense that," of "being a sign of", of "conveying sense, purpose or point." Similarly *value,* an especially significant word, stands for "the

*A. N. Whitehead, *Modes of Thought* (Cambridge University Press, 1938), p. 142.

quality of being of use, being desired, being looked upon as good." "Values" thus open the door to the whole universe of purposive human action, because, as Whitehead was to point out, "our experience is a value-experience" and "our enjoyment of actuality is a realization of worth, good or bad."* If this is not the true world in which sociology has its place, it would be interesting to learn in what other world it could be conceivably found.

Sorokin's fact-finding expeditions into history were directed at the discovery of the meanings and values implicit in, or generating, human activities. He found many. He certainly did not claim to have discovered them all, but those which he did find were sufficiently comprehensive and suggestive to be able to bring others within the range of his vision also.

First, how do meanings and values ever arise? Either they could be predominantly those given by the senses, or they could be derived from religious tradition, priestly authority, a sacred book, and result indirectly or directly from intuition, mystic illumination, or reflection.

Many of the questions about the nature of human activities, thoughts and creations to which Sorokin tried to find the answers were designed to throw more light upon the way in which, throughout the past, mankind had relied upon these two sources of ideas and values – experience or intuition; worldly interests or other-worldly influences. Had they really been effective? Could their influence be plainly detected not merely in one or two branches of human activity, where they might be expected to be powerful, such as art and philosophy, or could they be seen to influence other branches also, such as law or music – in fact the whole world which sociology should explain? Did they exhaust the matter? If not, what other sources of ideas and values were revealed in the historical record?

As the results of the researches of many of his investigators began to arrive, Sorokin was able to see more clearly into these questions. By the time all his material had been received and digested, four years had elapsed. In those years Sorokin achieved a new approach to sociology which was, in time, not only to revolutionize the study of that subject, but to bring new interpretative principles to history, philosophy, aesthetics and all other humanistic studies. Through Sorokin's work, in other words, sociology may at last be said to have come into its own as a philosophy able to explain much about the nature of all human striving and achievement – in short as the Proper Study of Mankind.

*Ibid, 150, 159.

Logico-Meaningful Cultural Systems

Sorokin was able to achieve such a Copernican revolution in sociology
after he had discovered the existence and the vital force of coordinated,
well-articulated, self-consistent patterns of cultural values. For it became
apparent, when he had worked over his results, that during long stretches
of time, men had been guided by scientific, philosophical, aesthetic, moral,
legal and social principles, all of which mutually fortified and sustained
each other. At one period such a congruence of values and polarization of
energies to realize them went on under the aegis of religion or
other-worldly interests. Reviving a seventeenth century word, which the
Oxford English Dictionary relates to "the formation of ideas of things not
present to the senses," Sorokin calls it an "ideational" period. It might be
described as the Age of the Gods in contrast with another way of life
which also achieved a unification of a common congruous set of values but
under the aegis of the kingdom of this world, the Age of Man, described
by Sorokin as "sensate," a word defined by the *Oxford Dictionary* as
"perceived by the senses." Such periods had alternated more than once
within historical times. Each lasted long. Developing these preliminary
insights, he was able to work out his major interpretative concept, that of
"Logico-Meaningful Cultural System" to describe the true quality of each
period. Sorokin was dealing with human societies and their way of life.
For him therefore "meaning" is the decisive quality for it divides the
human from other forms of life and being. Paper, ink, printing, cloth
bindings, may make an organic product, but if that product is the Bible,
Aristotle's *Politics,* or the works of Shakespeare, it becomes a cultural
object. It is charged with meanings, it becomes a "value" object for
reasoning human beings. "Logico-meaningful" applied to a set of
meanings, indicates that they are bound together in a manner which
implies that each contributing element is compatible with the other
elements with which it is in alliance; that they all make up a whole which
is greater than, but consistent with, the parts, upon each of which it
confers a significance which the part would lack in isolation. Such a
tightly-knit, triparte concept of organic unity Sorokin also found in St.
Thomas Aquinas.

Sorokin's investigations had yielded clues to explain the way in which
what he called the "values, meanings, norms" of different periods of
history could be seen to have become integrated so as to provide
consistent, coherent, ways of life to the men and women who lived them

and yet give way to quite other ways of life which became, for a time, equally satisfactory to later generations. A deeper understanding of values, of culture, cultural history and consequently of sociology of "socio-cultural" life, was thus made possible. And not only that, because "logico-meaningful" implies for the individual the possibility, indeed the necessity of integrating aspirations, aims, activities, to attain a consistent unity of being, nature, and purpose. When such a coordinated, cohesive character is achieved it may be described as 'integral.' An "integralist" is one who is able from the multitude of available values to select and assimilate all those which are compatible and mutually self-supporting, whose appropriation and exercise involves the least derogation from the highest values realized in the past, as well as the possibility of fruitful progress in the future.

These concepts, "logico-meaningful" and "integral," are more than the "Ideal Types" of Max Weber; they are the sociological or philosophical standards or criteria which sociology has hitherto lacked. These standards do not merely aid sociological vision in the aquisition of greater definition, precision, and range; they also point to and encourage revision of all partial sociologies in such eminently practical and urgent matters as education, racial prejudice, and social policy generally.

The Principle of Immanent Change and the Principle of Limits

Granted the possibility of detecting the existence of such logico-meaningful cultural systems, it still remains to explain why a seemingly well-constructed, tightly-bound, coherent system of meanings and values should not last forever. As it will be seen in the sequel, true logico-meaningful cultural systems have been dominant for many centuries. Nevertheless the continued practice of activities directed to any one end, noble as it may be, is more than humanity has been able to stand. Some values once honored begin to lose their appeal; responses become stereotyped and unreal. Almost all human experience testifies to such a development.* Sorokin describes it as a Principle of Immanent Change. It explains why sociological changes occur. It is a development which reaches its culmination when no further prospect of progress upon the old lines can be foreseen, when humanity tires and seeks new ideals. Sorokin

*It is the essence of the celebrated Hegelian dialetic.

describes such a culmination as occurring according to his Principle of Limits. That explains the "when" of cultural change.

After these preliminary introductory observations upon Sorokin's general line of approach, a summary account now follows of the results of the investigations which he planned, showing the way in which they contributed to the building up of his new sociological synthesis.

Values in Social Theory

Sociology is fundamentally a study of values. Sociological theory rests upon a theory or scheme of values. If no sociologist, not even Sorokin himself, has said so in so many words, his outstanding contribution has been to make plain the all-important part which values play in the life of human societies. He has done so by making an exhaustive survey of the record of the major achievements of humanity in the past, as a result of which he found that they could be understood and explained only in the light of the values they served. This historical study was essential because by its means alone is it possible to discover how values have worked out in practice in the past and how they change over time. Not until worlds of different values are discovered is it possible to see clearly that values lie at the base of all social activities today. By these contrasts, thrown up by history, the true nature of contemporary values comes to light. Then we see them molding our social ways of life; then we can get some idea of the manner and direction in which they are likely to change.

This long chapter is therefore the most significant of this whole book. Upon the view taken of the findings it reports the claim must rest that Sorokin has revolutionized the study of sociology by subordinating it to values as the mainspring and motive force in human society. Here will be found the answer to the question "What does Sorokin mean by values?" He uses the word in its ordinary meaning, already defined, but he is able to bring out its rich and deep significance by his vast, factual, historical survey. He shows what beliefs, ideas, and things have been valued in the past. This is a demonstration all the more rewarding because never before has anything like it been provided upon so comprehensive and scientifically ordered a scale. The music of Terpander, the philosophy of Boethius, the architecture of the Parthenon, the mural paintings of Giotto and Piero della Francesca, Newton's theory of light, the music of Mozart and Beethoven, and thousands of other manifestations of the inner nature of the life of human societies in the past rarely, if ever, get much space in sociological treatises. All are, as Sorokin shows, essential elements which must be accounted for if the true nature of human society is to be understood. Before summarizing the main outline of Sorokin's work a firm preliminary caution is necessary. Sociologists committed to a scientific and impartial study of human value-judgments cannot easily smother their own personal preferences. Sorokin certainly did not conceal his, which was for an "integrated" or idealist system of value. He was apt, especially in his popular lectures, to denounce in his own vigorous language any marked deviation from that harmonious balance which he favored between the extreme forms of the two major "polar" systems of ideational and sensate values. Because in his own lifetime sensate desires seemed to be running wild, he seems loudest in his denunciation of sensate excesses manifest, for example, in an exaggerated eroticism, in an immense increase in pornography and obscenity in writing, in stage, screen, and other displays. Some of his pages are apt in consequence to seem more heavily loaded with invective than a "scientific" appraisal would warrant. He sometimes gives the impression that the word "sensate" is a term of abuse rather than the strictly accurate label to be used for all forms of gratification mediated directly by the senses and common therefore in greater or lesser degree to every sentient human being.

His invective is nevertheless in order whenever a value system is false to its own principles or premises. A sociologist may condemn sensate excesses when they defeat the basic assumptions of a sensate system of values supposed to ensure the maximum enjoyment of sensual desires. Indulgence in alcohol, tobacco, or drugs which dulls aesthetic receptivity, which causes ill health and shortens life; sexual indulgence which leads to premature debility, impotence, or disease; devoting time to pornographic and erotic literature which incites to sexual excess while depriving its readers of the satisfactions to be obtained from the world's literary masterpieces — all such activities can be seen to be bad from a purely sensate point of view.

Similarly, on ideational grounds, a sociologist may hold vulnerable to criticism certain religious practices such as over-elaborate ceremonies and ritualistic observances, originally intended no doubt to augment the fervor of the faithful, if they develop to the extent of obscuring the pristine purity of the religion they are supposed to serve.

Criticism of sensate values on ideational grounds or sensate rejection of ideational principles is misplaced because, by definition, they are incompatible. Sensate condemnation of religious austerity and ideational abhorrence of sensate excesses are unnecessary because such antagonisms arise in a self-evident way from the basic assumptions of either system. Fasting, hair shirts, cold monastery cells, vows of silence, hours of prayer and the repetition of religious formularies, the renunciation of all but religious reading matter, naturally repel sensate mentalities because the whole purpose of the ideational way of life is firmly to subordinate or to reject sensate ways of life. Men and women do not enter monasteries or convents in order to have time for erotic literature or to see sex films and nude shows. Not least among the advantages of Sorokin's sociology would be the clarification it brings to the whole presentation of value and value judgments. Much confusion and argument at cross purposes could be avoided if the true nature of such mutually antagonistic major value-systems were firmly kept in mind.

Sculpture, Painting, Architecture

The written word is a poor vehicle by which to convey ideas about the arts, particularly to describe and contrast their developments through the ages. It would be much easier to examine, explain, illustrate, question, or defend Sorokin's findings by a conducted tour through some of the principal museums and galleries and in one or two of the cities of ancient culture than to attempt to give a convincing summary of them in one short chapter.

Nevertheless the main contrasts which Sorokin reported can be grasped by the aid of one or two illustrations, and by reference to works of art which many readers will have seen either in their original form or in reproductions. It must be repeated that Sorokin's theories are advanced as a guess, or hypothesis, for study, reflection, and further refinement and amendment.

His notions about the two chief, "polar," kinds of culture, the ideational and sensate, were largely suggested by the works of artists past and present, that is to say, by styles of painting, sculpture, music, architecture, literature, and drama. Sorokin found that in their light it was easier to understand the true inward nature of the art of any particular epoch and to be helped therefore to understand more thoroughly those epochs themselves. His views provide a clue to the way in which now one form or style of art and now another rises, becomes dominant, and then declines. They offer an explanation of the relationship between the changes in one form of art, in painting, for instance, and in other forms, such as architecture, music, and literature. To provide a satisfactory account of the rise and fall of different schools of art is however but the beginning. In order to understand a culture thoroughly in the 'logico-meaningful' sense described in the previous chapter, it is necessary to discover the wider relation of its art to its science, philosophy, law, economics, politics and religion. The findings in the world of art are therefore preliminary and it remains to be discovered whether they are capable of being related to other aspects of social life, particularly if they succeed in suggesting uniformities in social and cultural sequences and changes.

Never before have so many questions about the true nature of social activities and of cultural change been raised and answered as by Sorokin. There have of course been a vast number of earlier theories; many of them have been stimulating and suggestive, as Sorokin is very ready to acknowledge. Yet efforts such as those of Auguste Comte, Herbert Spencer and Oswald Spengler to discover stages of development, laws of progress or of evolution in all fields of culture, including art, have not yielded much more than facile and oversimplified analogies between cultural development and the development of individuals from childhood, adolescence and maturity to old age and death. Spengler's much vaunted work has no deeper basis than this. "Cultures are organisms," he says, "and world history is their collective biography. Every culture passes through the age-phases of the individual man... Each has its childhood, youth, manhood and old age." *(Decline of the West,* Vol. I, pp. 104-108, London, Allen and Unwin, 1926)

Without quarrelling with the self-evident idea that cultures appear, blossom and decay, Sorokin points out that merely to say this adds nothing to our knowledge, while the claim that the forms of art in all cultures show the same or similar patterns of development of childhood, maturity and senility is meaningless as long as concrete evidence of the essential characteristics of art childhood, art maturity and art senility is lacking. Unfortunately this is just what such authors fail to provide in any satisfactory form. We are never able to point to unmistakable evidence of such qualities at specified epochs of all the various cultures, so the pretended explanation is never more than an empty analogy or a figurative expression. It is not an operative concept; not a real tool or means whereby new knowledge or new insight can be gained.

More serious efforts have been made to show that art develops in a sequence of "archaic," "classical" and "decadent" forms. Such notably have been in sculpture and painting the views of W. Déonna *(L 'Archéologie, sa valeur, ses méthodes,* 1912) and Frank Chambers *(Cycles of Taste,* 1928; *The History of Taste,* 1932); in literature and music, E. Bovet *(Lyrisme, Epopee, Drame,* 1911), Charles Lalo *(Equisse d'une Esthétique musicale scientifique,* 1908). The themes of these writers, being based upon a deeper insight into the nature of the arts, are more impressive, but Sorokin shows that they do not fit all the facts, notably the facts about the development of Egyptian, Chinese and Hindu art.

Sorokin sums up his criticism of the various views hitherto advanced as explanations of the nature of social and cultural change by saying that they impose a complete uniformity where it either does not exist at all, or exists in a much more limited form than is claimed. Human activities are much more variable and creative than such limited views allow. Yet it cannot be denied that sequences, recurrence, and repetition of various types, modes, or forms of art do in fact occur, although their nature is not fully explained by such descriptions as "archaic," "classical," "modern," "decadent" and so forth.

Sorokin shows that they can all be broadly explained as aspects of the repetition and fluctuation in space and time of the ideational, the sensate (visual), the idealistic, and of other mixed styles in all their varieties and with all their minor secondary characteristics. Many essential traits of art in a given period, which otherwise would appear as meaningless unconnected fragments, then become comprehensible. More important still, the mentality behind the art, the true inner nature of the society and the culture from which it springs, can be grasped by the aid of Sorokin's principles, which then become real aids towards a fuller sociological understanding. He seeks to present in one study a comprehensive account of the changes through time in the ideas men have formed about the source and nature of the beautiful, the true and the morally right or worthy.

What, then, in art, are the characteristics of these new terms or categories by which the rise and fall of human cultures can be described and understood?

The ideational style in its finest form, Sorokin said, is purely symbolic, making no attempt to copy the visual or sensory appearance of objective reality. Examples of such an art are to be found in the Christian pictures in the Catacombs — an anchor, a dove, an olive branch, etc. — which symbolize religious ideas or signify ideational phenomena quite other than these objects themselves.

The sensate style in its finest form, on the other hand, gets as near to real objects as possible in the actual form in which they are offered to our sense perceptions. It is, Sorokin asserted, purely empirical and material, and the rendering is purely impressionistic, that is to say it tries to be illusionistic. A good camera snapshot and the most completely impressionistic pictures are the best samples of the purely visual style.

For artists of this school, such as Manet, Monet, Pissaro, Sisley, Courbet, Gaugin, Cézanne, Saurat, Renoir, Degas and others, the only reality is the visual appearance of the objects. Behind it and beyond it there is nothing. The choice of subjects is vast, because it does not matter at all what is depicted. What matters is the extent to which the illusionistic effect is caught. What above all is necessary is a good eye and a good coordination between the eye and the painting muscles. Hence he holds that impressionism was not only anti-intellectual but was radically sensate. No thought, no directing idea, no ideationality is present or required for it. It just 'snaps' or 'shoots' the visual surface of empirical objects.

One outstanding quality of this sensate art is its dynamism, due to a restless striving to catch a passing moment in the ever-fugitive appearance of the visual surface of the everyday world, the impression of change, of becoming. Another of its qualities is described by the untranslatable German word *malerisch,* used to denote the rich "paintlike" quality of a work of art in which patches of different colors, light and shade merge imperceptibly into one another. Rembrandt and Rubens are outstandingly *malerisch,* and Rubens admirably shows the dynamism of the sensate school.

The purely ideational and the purely sensate or visual forms of art contrasted in the above paragraphs are extreme forms at each end of a wide scale. Between these opposite and completely incompatible poles are a wide variety of subclasses and mixed forms. Sorokin admits that there may be such a mixture of the elements of both styles that one cannot recognize in it either the ideational or the visual and is obliged to put it into an intermediary mixed or ideational-visual style.

The ideational style admits of fewer subclasses, but Sorokin recognizes as an impure ideational style that used by artists trying to embody some visual resemblance of spiritual or super-empirical reality, such as allegorical figures of Virtue, Vice, Patience, Temperance, or the Muses, and pictures of Paradise, Inferno or the Last Judgment. There is also a less familiar form found, for example, in the geometric designs of primitive peoples, such as the Red Indians, symbolizing buffalo, snakes, hunting and fishing, and other objects and activities giving meaning to their lives.

Two mixed or "impure" varieties of the sensate or visual style call for special mention. The first occurs when some general idea or non-visual element is introduced into a visual or sensate work of art, as for example in the production of a 'character' portrait or picture in which emphasis is given to what is thought to be the essential, dominant nature of the subject at the expense of its purely momentary appearance.

Again, the subject may not be the ordinary everyday matter-of-fact things of this everyday world, which form the staple topic of sensate visual art. Despite the fact that a purely realistic empirical treatment may not be possible, the subject is nevertheless treated in a matter-of-fact way. Most of the religious pictures by the Italian masters of the Late Renaissance are in this class, for, although their subject matter was often not of this world, they rendered it in a most worldly way, giving personages, such as the Virgin, or St. Anne, the likenesses of their friends, wives, or mistresses.

It may sometimes be difficult or impossible to decide whether a mixed or impure style of art is preponderantly ideational or sensate. However, one such mixed category is sufficiently outstanding to be easily recognizable as a separate class. This is the "idealistic" style. Simultaneously, ideational and visual, it was a remarkable blend of each. The "idealistic" form of culture is most strikingly exemplified by the Greek art of the fifth century B.C. and the religious art of Western Europe in the thirteenth century A.D. It merits the name "idealistic" because it modifies, typifies, transforms, and idealizes visual reality in conformity with its ideas and ideals. The subjects of the idealistic style of art are, moreover, always carefully selected and are never debased, vulgar, ugly, immoral, or eccentric. Decay, senility, death, imperfection, or any excess of emotion or passion are excluded. Seeking no mere photographic reproduction of reality, it presents instead a beautified, re-created, idealized manifestation. Sorokin describes in detail how he discriminates between idealistic and sensate or visual styles in art.

The idealist style, like the sensate but unlike the ideational stayle, is, he points out, always a self-sufficient, aesthetic value created for its own sake, but it is always more than this. Here it differs from the sensate, because it expresses, teaches, and propagates an ideal. Ideal values lie outside art. To the extent that it serves religion, moral or civic virtue, or other ethical ends of a non-aesthetic character, as idealistic art usually does, it is always more closely correlated with the ideational than with purely sensate visual forms.

The sensate, visual style, on the other hand, is much more likely to be art for art's sake. It serves no values other than artistic values. It is therefore, says Sorokin, often associated with aestheticism in a particular sense, with that period in art history when art for art's sake appears, with its crowds of aesthetes, connoisseurs, collectors, professional critics, theorizers of beauty, and professional artists who want to be artistic and nothing more. Links with religion, public safety, decency and moral well-being are spurned by the extremist sensate school. Here Sorokin interjects a moral note by pointing out that such supposedly realistic and free art is in reality the victim of its own illusion. In fact it becomes also a servant, but a servant of other masters than those served by idealistic or ideational art. Sensate art is dedicated to the Golden Calf; to the empirical visual reality, to sensate needs, (eudaemonistic, hedonistic and utilitarian); to the sensual fancies of the Epicureans, the rich, the powerful.

Idealistic art is akin to ideational art in that it also serves purposes beyond itself, but these are the ideals or values of a genuine collectivity. The artist's own personality, needs, and ambitions are of no account in his creations. Indeed idealistic artists are usually anonymous and unknown, as are those of the creators of many medieval Gothic and Romanesque or Byzantine cathedrals.

Sensate art, on the other hand, is jealously prized as a means of personal distinction, so it is individualistic to a high degree. A further clear distinction between the two styles is found in the choice of subject matter, which artists of sensate cultures always take from their own everyday world, made up of familiar individual objects, persons, events, historical scenes, and landscapes. It is rare for idealistic art to illustrate such themes, just as it never chooses scenes of common or low life, the drunkard, criminal, street urchin, or pretty faces or erotic figures which are staple subjects of sensate, visual art.

While sensate art strives after a dynamic effect and is charged with emotions and agitated by passion, idealistic art is quiet, calm, serene, immobile, and at peace. Its products partake of the same quality. They endure as ever-present sources of spiritual and aesthetic satisfaction, whereas the products of sensate art are incessantly changing in form and style in a desperate search for novelty and effect. Sensate art deals in "best sellers," in "hits and sensations." The effort to create a sensation need not of course always be made upon established sensate lines and a number of other mixed forms may arise, which do not merit the name of idealistic art but which are nevertheless not wholly sensate.

Cubist and futuristic art present one such special type which, Sorokin points out, has no ideational character except to the extent that it seeks, by reaction against sensate, impressionistic art, to restore the peace of mind and thought which sensate art rejects. For the most part, however, such modernistic art does not seek to represent a super-empirical, non-materialistic world, but tries to find new ways of presenting the solidity, weight, spaciousness, movement, and other properties of the material world. Sometimes it seeks to attract attention merely by being different. Then the artist may be credited with some new insight or new ideas, despite his inability to say coherently what they are.

What seems a mere juxtaposition or mechanical union of sensate and ideational styles occurs in Egyptian sculpture, even from the Old Kingdom, which yields examples of a mixed style in which clear and beautifully rendered portrait heads of a pronounced visual sensate type are combined with what, from the sensate standpoint, is a quite unnatural rendering of the rest of the body, particularly its anatomy and posture.

These few examples by no means exhaust the wide variety of mixed styles observable in the long course of the history of human art. Their value lies in illustrating the chief principles and major concepts by means of which Sorokin not only interprets the forms of artistic creation so far achieved by mankind, but also explains their inner nature and shows the manner in which they have been developed and transformed. The result is both a useful clue to the history of art and a most suggestive guide to the history and progress of human culture in all its spheres. For he went on to discover that the essential values manifest in the art of a given period of culturual development can be seen also in other and very different branches of the cultural life of that period as a whole.

Sorokin's classification of styles in art into the three main groups — ideational, sensate and mixed — identifies the predominant mentality shown in each style. It uncovers the essentials of the *Weltanschauung*, i.e., the general philosophy of life of the artist and of his society; it can be shown to stand in the closest relationship with the characteristics of other aspects of a given culture; its science and philosophy, religion and morals, forms of social and political organization, and the nature of social relationships — in brief with all the essential traits of the given culture and its mentality.

To substantiate such theories was a large task. Sorokin was able to show how they provide new and satisfactory canons of historical interpretation and explanation. To vindicate the claims of this theory completely would involve rewriting the entire history of painting, sculpture, architecture, music, literature, drama, and all other human arts and sciences. It is obviously a colossal task, beyond the unaided powers of any single individual to achieve in its entirety. Sorokin enlisted specialist helpers and with their aid he succeeded in presenting a very thorough survey, if not of the entire history of human artistic achievement, at least of its most notable forms, whose nature and influence any theory of art must attempt to explain.

Sorokin begins at the beginning with prehistoric art, whose manifestations, particularly in paintings of mammoths, buffaloes, bison, deer and other game animals in rock and cave dwellings of palaeolithic and neolithic man, have been brought to light in recent times to astonish the world. Surprise at the remarkably realistic life-like achievements of some of these primitive artists has no doubt provoked this reaction, since other primitive peoples do not seem to have given evidence of any comparable skill. On the contrary their work often seems crude and clumsy, lacking the maturity of the artist of the early stone age. The explanation of the apparent mystery, Sorokin holds, is that these palaeolithic peoples were predominantly of a sensate type whose art was naturally visual. The art of the later stone age peoples in the neolithic period was, on the contrary, much less visual and much more ideational. The idea that it is strange to find what seems to be a 'mature' art in the earliest period results from our mistaken belief that our own art, which is also visual and sensate, is a fine flower of human endeavor and 'evolution' which time has conspired to realize, and that therefore anything resembling it must be "modern."

Sorokin does not merely take a revolutionary view of changes in art-forms in upsetting unreflective current assumptions, but he also establishes the important principle that there is not, as popular expectations would seem to indicate, any straight line of progress in art *from* ideational *to* visual sensate forms. Indeed, to the extent that his description of sensate art as lacking any profound intellectual content or reflective power is true, it seems plausible to believe with Sorokin that it is not strange to find that visual art precedes ideational art in these earliest centuries of human existence. To have established at the outset the possibility of a "modern" visual form of realistic pictorial art developing among primitive people helps also with the study of Egyptian art.

Sorokin considers that a marked fluctuation, in the nature of a relative increase or decrease of ideational or sensate elements, is observable during the long course of Egyptian culture. Its four main epochs were:

Old Kingdom, to about 2700 B.C. — Non-sentimental depiction of a sound material world in a mildly ideational style, containing elements of naturalism and visuality, increasing from the fourth dynasty and manifest in portrait sculpture representing private and ordinary persons.

Middle Kingdom, from about 2400 B.C. to about 1600 B.C. − The art, mainly sculptural at the beginning, is much less visual, but in the thirteenth dynasty a visual style becomes much more pronounced, manifest particularly in art depicting the everyday life of the common people, houses, gardens, musical parties, baking, brewing, fishing, and so on.

New Kingdom, from about 1600 B.C. − A notable turn to ideationalism and idealism occurred in the time of Akhenaten (c. 1377-1358 B.C.).

A sharp turn towards intimacy, picturesqueness, dynamism, to the visual and baroque occurred in the period of Tutankhamen (1358-1349 B.C.), after which there was a gradual shift once again toward ideationalism. The fourth epoch of the history of Egyptian art is obscured by alien invasions in the early seventh century B.C. and by Assyrian and Persian domination. It was not until Egypt came under Greek kings and Greek inspiration (from 332 B.C.) that there was some revival. Sorokin believes it possible to trace similarly alternating cultural patterns under the Ptolemies and in the Roman period.

Chinese culture flowed in two main streams, the ideational, represented by Taoism (and later by Buddhism), and the mixed, represented mainly by Confucianism. A purely sensate mentality was also always present, Sorokin holds, but it was a minor current.

These two streams are characterized by their products. The subjects of Buddhist art are essentially super-sensate and super-empirical. The invisible inner world and its values are depicted by visible symbols. The great artists of the Han period attempted in this way to reveal the inner character, the spirit or soul of things, and so did their successors during the growth of Buddhism in the Transition period and in the early T'ang period beginning in 618 A.D., especially during the Sui dynasty which preceded it (about 590-618 A.D.). The same is true of the later period of the five dynasties down to the Sung period (907-960 A.D.).

The topics for the most part are supersensory, such as the figure Kuan-yin, of Bodhidharma the first Buddhist missionary, the tiger and the dragons and other symbolic designs.

Divergencies towards visualism accompanied periods marked by a decline or persecution of the Taoist-Buddhist believers. Orthodox Confucianism or passive Epicureanism in the Middle T'ang period characterized the second part of the reign of Ming Huang, which witnessed the rise of an Epicurean humanism. The beauty of the everyday world then furnished the subject matter of art. The court-painters, such as Wu-Tao-Tzi, with their mastery of perspective and fidelity to natural appearances, produced pictures possessing an extraordinary power of illusion.

Ideational art concentrating upon religious subjects was not given up, but it appears to be the style of a minority, as it was again in the period of the Northern Sung (960-1126 A.D.), particularly at the end of it with the reign of the Emperor Hwei Tsung (1101-1126 A.D.), himself no mean painter.

Few styles of art have been more consistently ideational for a longer period than has the Hindu. Sorokin has no difficulty in quoting eminent authorities who stress this other-worldly aspect of Hindu art, pointing out that it has no counterpart in 'modern' (i.e. visual, sensate) European art. Sanskrit lacks a word for art in the sense it is used in modern European languages. Art for Hindu peoples is life as it is interpreted by religion and philosophy. Art for art's sake is consequently unknown. Instead a symbolism was created to express the various qualities of the Supreme Soul in imaginary superhuman figures. In this way arose the designs of many-headed gods and goddesses with many arms. Incomprehensible to the average uninstructed spectator trained to recognize and to like modern Western European art, they may not become more comprehensible by being labeled "ideational." However, the first advantage of such a label is that it points to the fact that in Hindu art such a spectator is in touch with the products of a civilization which is radically different in kind from his own, based upon different presuppositions about the nature of reality and of the values to be put upon the things of this world.

After this first awakening, the spectator can be led to enquire in what other qualities also Hindu civilization is distinctive and from that, if Sorokin is correct, to an understanding of a way of life which in its innermost essence is entirely foreign to our own.

With the earliest manifestations of human art in the Mediterranean world, a very different civilization comes in question. From the twelfth to the ninth century B.C. a form of art flourished in the isle of Crete which was markedly visual in character; at times extremely impressionistic, with excellent renderings of animals and human figures based upon a mature knowledge of their anatomy. Slender, pretty, voluptuous feminine figures, flowers, picturesques, drama, dynamism and sensuality are marked features of this Creto-Mycenaean art, which may have begun in the sixteeth century B.C.

The Archaic period of Greek art (about 900-500 B.C.) which appeared after the disappearance of Creto-Mycenaean art, is fundamentally different. Simple geometric patterns, characteristic, as often said, of an uncultivated race, but actually entirely different in meaning and purpose, were used by the early Greeks, in striking contrast to the vigorous and life-like representations of the Cretans. Vase painting at this time in Greece was purely linear, at first using merely one tint or color, resembling drawing rather than painting. Beginning in the sixth century B.C., a change becomes observable. Efforts were then made to render subjects somewhat more visually. Visual or sensate art began to rise in favor, ideational art to decline. Then came the miracle of the Greek achievement of the fifth century B.C., when in Sorokin's words, the descending curve of ideationalism and the ascending curve of visualism cross each other, during a marvellous blending in the form of sublime idealistic art. The predominant figure of the period — and of all time — in sculpture was Phidias (c. 490-417 B.C.), but there were other famous names, such as Polycletus (452-405 B.C.), Agoracritus, Colotes, and Callimachus.

The subjects of this fifth-century sculpture are gods, heroes, or ideational entities such as Victory or Nemesis. But the perfect technique is visual. The same can be said of painting in which Polygnotus (c. 475-447 B.C.) won a renown as great as that of Phidias.

The characteristics of this great period of Greek art have often been described, and they will be briefly summarized here as the supreme examples of what Sorokin means by his "idealistic" mixed category or of cult or class.

The idealist artists of the fifth century B.C. used their excellent knowledge of human anatomy to depict human beings in their ideal or perfect form. There are, Sorokin reports, no realistic portraits, no ugliness, no defective traits or types. Before us are immortals or idealized mortals; old age is rejuvenated; the baby is depicted as grown up; the women have little that is specifically feminine but appear like perfect athletes; there are no landscapes. The postures and the expressions are free from any violent or debased or too human emotion and distorting passion; they are calm, serene, imperturbable like the gods. Even the dead shine with the same calmness and serene beauty. All the statues have a 'Greek' profile; not because all the Greeks had such faces, as Winckelmann thought, but because it was the profile thought to be perfect. The hairdress is simple but well ordered; the drapery is perfectly adapted to the body, simple and marvellous in its orderly beauty. Eyes are natural and perfect, and shine with calmness and serenity; the lips and mouth are ideally cut; the postures are dignified and idealized. As Pliny pointed out long ago, it was an art which sought to make noble men still nobler. It is not that the artists could not or would not depict the lower passions, for these are shown on the vase paintings when the subjects are the creatures of lower and inferior orders, such as slaves, centaurs, fauns and animals. Finally, Greek idealistic art was deeply religious, patriotic, instructive, moralizing and educative. It was created not only for its own sake, but also as a means for just such instruction and education. It was not separated from, but was the partner of religion and of civic and social morality. After the resounding victory of the Greeks over the Persians, there was a universal upsurge of national spirit, an ardent and enthusiastic desire to exalt their religion and their country; hence the unity, harmony, and marvel of the art of the period. Its horizons lay beyond common ordinary persons and objects, for it strove to create universal types of eternal and not merely of temporal value.

This great outburst of idealistic art was not sustained by more than about two generations of artists. By the end of the fourth century B.C. it had been replaced by the conspicuously sensate or visual style of Hellenistic art. From the historians of Greek art, Sorokin has summarized the main important characteristics of this later sensate Hellenistic art. Because the qualities he enumerates are also found in later period characterized by the sensate mentality, they strongly support his general theory of cultural development.

In sensate art:

1. The figures of young women, which before were rare, became quite common subjects of sculpture and painting, and they are represented as voluptuous, seductive, sexual figures often set off against realistic figures of old women.
2. A similar change occurs in relation to the figures of men.
3. Portraits of individual persons, especially of rulers and of patrons, become more common.
4. Real landscapes and dramatic historical scenes become more common.
5. Everyday life, crowds, mobs, the common run of people, especially pathological types, criminals, beggars, street urchins more and more replace heroes and ideal men, so that the emphasis is placed upon mortality instead of upon immortality.
6. Human postures and expressions lose their idealized patterns and become realistic; serenity and calm are replaced by the pathetic, by passion and emotionality, including suffering, sorrow, pain, fear, agony

and distortion. Dynamism and violent movement replace static immobility. There is no reticence about nudity or sex.

7. 'Art for art's sake' becomes the rule in order to give merely sensuous pleasure to the sensate man. No other ideal or value exists behind the art object.

8. Compensation for lack of quality is sought in mere hugeness, mere mass. The bigger a statue or building can be, the more impressive and the better it is supposed to be.

Roman artists fell so completely under the sway of the excellent Greek masterpieces that any native development they might have achieved was inhibited. There are unfortunately few extant examples of the earliest native Roman products, but there is some evidence that Italic art, the first source of Roman inspiration, was rather ideational. The second source, the art of the Etruscans, was predominantly sensate or visual by the time the Romans fell under their dominion. This is not true of earlier Etruscan art.

If this was the true state of affairs, it probably helps to explain, although Sorokin does not make the point, the intensity of early Roman distaste for the Etruscans and Greeks. By the time the Romans encountered them, they were already in what he would describe as a sensate decline which appeared deplorable and shocking to the stern and more ideational moralists of the Roman Republic in the second century B.C. Hence the resistance to Greek influences of Romans of the old school such as Cato the Censor and his contemporaries, among whom was the grandfather of Marcus Tullius Cicero. It endured long after the Romans had freed themselves from all fear of Etruscan or Greek military power.

Sorokin classes the whole of Roman sculpture and painting from the first century B.C. to the fourth century A.D. as being predominantly visual (sensate) although he allows the Augustan period to be pseudo-idealistic. It was not a real idealism spontaneously springing from deep sources, it was rather a change of fashion, of the pattern for imitation, as a reaction against the imitation of the archaic Attic and of the overripe Hellenistic patterns of the preceding century.

Augustan pseudo-idealism barely survived Augustus when it was succeeded by a more extreme visualism, which endured until a change of style in the fourth and fifth centuries A.D. paved the way for the Christian "ideational" style.

The monumental remains of Imperial Rome furnish the evidence upon which this view is based. The Ara Pacis, the Arch of Titus, the Column of

Trajan, the vast palaces and colossal statues, the "boudoir mythology" of Roman painting at Pompeii and elsewhere, all tell the same story of an overripe sensate visualism in art.

Then, in the fourth and fifth centuries of our era, a curious thing happened. All the artistic skill of the preceding centuries seems to have vanished. Instead we have in sculpture very rough "blocks" cut apparently without any skill, very primitively, without showing any ability to render the individual traits of the persons rendered or even the anatomy of the head and other parts of the human body. The earlier supremely beautiful letter forms of inscriptions become crude and displeasing.

The usual explanation of this state of affairs is that it represents the decay, degeneration, death and end of Roman art. But, says, Sorokin, this is to judge the matter by a very subjective evaluation, based on a mere assumption that there can be only one real style of artistic performance and that is the visual.

The development of sculptural art in our own day illustrates Sorokin's views. Many of the works of modern sculptors, Eric Gill, Henry Moore, Epstein and others, may have a crude and unformed appearance. They are anything but visual. Yet nobody can doubt that such masters of their craft could produce excellent works in the traditional visual manner if they wished. The same may well have been true of the sculptors of the fourth and fifth centuries A.D.

Just as many centuries before, the highly-developed Creto-Mycenaean art was succeeded by ideational Greek art, so now the Christian ideational art began to replace the sensate pagan visual art of the Roman Empire. Christianity was an ideational cultural stream from its very emergence. Hence it necessarily gave rise to an extreme form of the ideational art, as any such culture must if it is truly integrated. And, indeed, the earliest Christian art, that of the Catacombs, was practically pure ideational art: symbolic and transcendental in form as well as in content. Symbols of a dove, an olive branch, an anchor, a fish, the cross, a good shepherd and a few others comprised its subjects. They did not mean a fish or an anchor but referred to a transcendental value quite different from these visual signs. They were the visible signs of the invisible world; in brief, it was "otherworldly art" because Christianity itself was based on an "otherworldly" mentality. In spite of that, it was still a form of art profoundly influenced by its Graeco-Roman and Oriental past. Appearing in a small stream in the total Graeco-Roman visual art, with the growth of Christianity it grew more and more, until in the fourth and fifth centuries it became practically a major stream. In this process of ascending to domination, Christian art lost something of its initial ideational purity by admitting an element of visualism. This ideationalism continues, however, throughout the subsequent centuries to the Middle Ages, almost up to the thirteenth century. Remaining examples of ideational painting are relatively few. The ninth century *Book of Kells* is one of the most remarkable.

During the period of this ideational otherworldliness with its extreme asceticism and radical puritanism there were numerous prohibitions against any art and any representation of religious topics in painting or sculpture, both in Byzantium and in Western Christianity. Any admixture of sensate visual art was felt as a taint, so that even the use of icons and iconography was very sharply discouraged. Sorokin quotes a typical pronouncement on this matter from a declaration of the Synod of Bishops in 754 A.D. in Byzantium:

"The sinful art of painting is an insult to the fundamental dogma of our salvation, Jesus Christ. . . The ignorant painter, moved by the sacrilegious motive of profit, depicts what should be believed by the heart only. . . Christ was simultaneously God and Man."

It was doctrine of this type which led Ruskin to make the plausible but misleading generalization that "the religious passion is nearly always vividest when the art is weakest." The Fathers of the Church, the Christian Orders and institutions who followed them, did not weary of protesting against or prohibiting any art or any element in it that might contribute to sensuous enjoyment. This does not mean that they were indifferent to beauty. For them, beauty was essentially an object of intelligence. "The beautiful," said St. Thomas Aquinas, "is the same thing as the good, differing only conceptually." Whoever seeks the good by that very act also seeks the beautiful. An ideational culture is not therefore likely to bequeath a rich variety of art forms to posterity.

In Byzantium, with its peculiar synthesis of the Graeco-Roman and Syriac-Egyptian styles, the development of the arts was also deliberately arrested. After the sixth century A.D., its (ideational) images were standardized and deviation from them was prohibited. Their characteristics have been described as "iconographic idealization of attitudes; general kindness of the expressions of the visages; painting even the old faces rosy; exaggerated gracefulness of the body; forceful energy of movement and gesture, especially that of the foot stepping aside . . . poetically dishevelled head of hair (*chevelure*); 'prophetic' or 'Old Testament' lips; locks of small beards; an inspirationally directed look and a pupil turned profoundly to the corner of the eye."

For five or six centuries at least this style was maintained. Nevertheless, after the ninth century, some sensate visual elements crept in, so that again a rare and harmonious synthesis occurred between the ideational and sensate elements, giving rise in the thirteenth and fourteenth centuries to Byzantine idealistic art. Akin in such respects to the art of Greece in the fifth century B.C. and to European art of the thirteenth, this new form has been styled the Byzantine Renaissance. Before it could develop into a more full-blooded sensate, visual art, the Byzantine Empire fell before the onslaught of the Turks in the middle of the fifteenth century.

The ideational character of Western European art during the same period was also strongly in evidence, although it took a slightly less uncompromising form, remaining more Greek and less affected by Egyptian and Syrian influences than was the art of Byzantium.

Sorokin suggests that it was this indirect Greek heritage, which had no important rivals, that helped to maintain in Europe a closer contact with the affairs of this world through the encyclopedic learning of the medieval schools of Europe based upon the seven liberal arts, the trivium — Grammar, Rhetoric, and Logic; and the *quadrivium* — Music, Arithmetic, Geometry, and Astronomy.

From about the ninth century also, as in Byzantium, sensate, visual tendencies became apparent, in the Carlovingian Renaissance for example, but ideational characteristics continued dominant until the end of the twelfth century.

Then one of those rare moments in the development of human culture again occurred. The rising tide of visualism and the ebb of ideationalism resulted, in the thirteenth and partly in the fourteenth century, in one of those sublime blends of both styles in the form of a supreme idealistic art, an art in all its essential traits similar to the great idealistic art of Greece in the fifth and part of the fourth centuries B.C.

One of the most interesting of Sorokin's conclusions from the wealth of material he had gathered, was this evidence that such an idealistic art appeared when the dominant ideational style was declining and the moderate visualism was rising. Idealistic art does not appear when ideational art begins to replace sensate art. Instead there are fumblings for something new and strange to replace overripe visualism which may materialize as modernistic incongruities; cubism, futurism and other mixed "isms" which are neither the fish of ideationalism nor the flesh of visualism; nor are they a harmonious blend of both styles. Sorokin illustrates this generalization by reference to the transition from

Mycenaean art to the Archaic Greek art of from the overripe Hellenistic Roman art to the Christian art of the fourth and fifth centuries A.D. and to the art of our own day in Western Europe.

Whatever may be the reliability of such an apparent principle, Sorokin has no difficulty in establishing the singular correspondence in quality between thirteenth century Western art and that of Greece of the fifth century B.C. Both were ages of faith, refusing to derive their central values from this world or from earthly life. Thirteenth century art was not an art for art's sake. Its grand Gothic cathedrals have often been described as the Bible in Stone. Its statues, in their postures, gestures, expressions, appearance, are all lighted by the sublime serenity of the religious and moral ideal. These great creations were anonymous collective works expressing a collective ideal. As in the Greek art of the idealistic period also, this new Western European form has calm and quiet and a lack of dynamism (the Platonic ideas do not change); there is no show and nothing *malerisch;* there is no patheticism, no sentimentality, no emotionalism and no disorder. It tended to convince but not to disturb emotionally.

But, and again as in Ancient Greece, this period of idealistic grandeur was short. Already at the end of the thirteenth century the 'optimum' point was left behind, and the art of the fourteenth and fifteenth centuries already represents the period of transition from a waning idealism toward a full-blooded visualism.

The chief characteristics of sensate visual art, already described above, virtually all became manifest in a new setting and under different conditions. Sorokin's new theory is thus able to account for the development of Renaissance art, the rise of Baroque and Rococo styles leading to the Impressionism of more recent times. He has no difficulty in supporting his own description of these art forms by quoting from the writings of historians of modern art and by reproductions of outstanding examples of the craft of painters and sculptors of the various schools and fashions which have succeeded one another since the fourteenth century.

Following one strand in the earlier period of transition from the idealistic to the visual sensate trend, he shows how for example the figure of the Virgin, who, in the thirteenth century, was always shown as a noble lady, begins to be represented in more homely guise. Other writers have, of course, also drawn attention to the way in which the Virgin was given more of the nature of common humanity. Before long she was shown smiling at the gambols of her infant, and then as an ordinary peasant woman dandling or suckling her quite ordinary babe. She might also be depicted lightly veiled. Before long the execution of pious imagery assumed that commercial and industrial character it has not yet lost.

As idealized figures became more mundane, greater efforts were made to depict them as the victims of emotion, feeling, and human passions. Unflinching faith having been lost, Sorokin says, and man being thrown upon himself, emotionality, passionateness, dolor, pessimism, suffering, side by side with the attempt to see salvation in pleasure, seized the Christian world. With the previous world (which seemed unshakable) falling to pieces and a new world not yet assured, such dolor and despair are rather comprehensible. Should we wonder that exactly at that time such themes as Death in its Ugliness, the dance macabre, corpses (including Christ) in all their reality, become as it were epidemic? Sorokin illustrates the matter by pointing to the fact that, beginning in the fifteenth century and continuing in the sixteenth, religious art became more theatrical, the images of corpses and death's heads and skulls multiplied in the churches, on church glass windows and in pictures.

Religious art, moreover, not only ceased to be the whole of art exclusively, but steadily fell away from being the main form of art. Secular art steadily became more visual, more realistic. Vasari boasted of having painted a strawberry plant so successfully that a peacock tried to eat the berries, thus paralleling the well-known story which testified to the greatness of the painter Xeuxix (c. 420-380 B.C.) by recording that one of his works was so realistic that a bird tried to pick up a grape he had painted. Both stories testify to the unquestioning acceptance of purely visual-sensate values in art. Generalizing, Sorokin says that when we study the change of technique, moving from the thirteenth century to the "Primitives" of the fourteenth and fifteenth centuries, and from them to the "Classics" of the Renaissance, and then to the baroque of the seventeenth century, we are immediately aware of the movement from less illusionism to greater, from the linear style to the *malerisch* style of painting. Sorokin's views absorb and complete those of other art historians rather than conflict with them.

Wölfflin, for instance, enumerates five fundamental pairs of the representational forms of art:

Linear	versus	*Malerisch* (painterly),
Plane	versus	Recession,
Closeness	versus	Openness,
Multiplicity	versus	Unity,
Clearness	versus	Unclearness.

Sorokin regarded the first elements of all these pairs as being mutually interconnected, and also the second. Wölfflin's first categories approach the ideational, while his *malerisch* with its related forms is nearer the sensate, visual style. Now the linear appeals to the sense of touch; the "painterly" *(malerisch)* to the eye only. In fact, as Sorokin pointed out, generally the shift from the ideational to the sensate, visual art (and culture) is marked by a great stress on the value of the *eye* among the organs of sense, and of the sight among all the senses.

These considerations, he held, make it easy to understand how European painting and sculpture from the time of the Renaissance passed from the clear-cut linearism of the Primitives of the fifteenth century, through the Classics of the sixteenth century, to the pronounced baroque of the seventeenth which is *malerisch* art — that is to say, from linear classics, like Leonardo da Vinci, Piero della Francesca, Botticelli, Dürer, Raphael, Holbein, Michelangelo (partly), etc., to the more *malerisch* Frans Hals, Van Dyck, Rembrandt, Velasquez, A. van der Velde, Bernini, Rubens, Vermeer, Ruysdael and so on.

Despite marked individual differences in style among the various painters and sculptors in the fifteenth century in various countries of Western Europe, the trend toward visualism is common to almost all of them and to all countries. Sorokin did not, of course, maintain that ideationalism and the tradition of the Middle Ages were completely replaced, but that their influence was waning. Instead there was a growth of individualism, dynamism, emotionalism, and of portrait and *genre* painting. A secular spirit rises both in subjects and in manner. As in Greek art of the fourth century, sensualism, voluptuousness, eroticism make further headway. The pretty woman begins to become more and more a common subject of art; even the saints were depicted nude.

It was against developments of this type that reformers such as Savonarola raised their voices, but in vain. Sensate art continued to advance despite individual painters like Fra Angelico (1387-1455), who in the seclusion of their cloisters were more faithful to the earlier idealistic style. Piero della Francesca (?1416-1492) maintained it in the following generation. So revolutionary has been the change in aesthetic values since he painted, that an art critic broadcasting in 1966 had to work hard to convince the public that Piero della Francesca's art could be properly understood only when it is realized that he painted from religious conviction and was not merely concerned to exhibit his mastery of composition, line, color and design.

Sorokin puts the complete triumph of sensate visualism in the sixteenth century. The Flemish school, beginning with the two Hubert van Eyck's grew in visualism and became entirely visual, and undilutedly naturalistic. As Taine pointed out, art fell from heaven to earth and began to serve human affairs almost to the exclusion of the divine. The Dutch school, as everybody who has visited the art galleries of the world will know, confines itself, again to quote Taine, "to reproducing the repose of the bourgeois interior, the comforts of shop and farm, outdoor sports and tavern enjoyments, all the petty satisfactions of an orderly and tranquil existence."

No other country went so far as the Low Countries in this respect, although the classic painters of Italy kept close to an earthly idealism of the empirical world and of the sensory human body, of landscape and of visual form generally. The main thing in the art of design, according to Cellini, was to fashion cleverly a naked man or woman. Other countries, France, Spain, Portugal and England, midway, some of them, between the Italian and Flemish types, showed the same tide or rising visualism.

The Reformation and the Counter-Reformation may appear to have produced a reversal of this trend but, Sorokin holds, sensate visual art was in reality gaining all the time. Protestantism in its iconoclasm would not and did not have a religious art, a few religious pictures notwithstanding. After the Council of Trent of 1563, the Catholic Church imposed a stricter censorship on religious pictures and sculpture, but it proved powerless to resist the trend of the times. At best a simulated religiosity, a more or less mechanical standardization of the figures, postures and scenes depicted was all that was achieved. Such artificiality is easy to distinguish from the depth of genuine belief by which the best idealistic art is obviously inspired. Sorokin points to several factors which help to illustrate and explain the contrast.

In the first place the violence of the politico-religious struggle with the Protestants meant that the spirit of calmness, untroubled faith, and serenity was gone from Catholic art. Then, as an index to the pronounced sensate visual nature of such art, he points to its pathological, sadistic, and terrifying emotionalism. Religious pictures show the tortures and sufferings of martyrs, while secular art reveled in imagining the most violent scenes of ancient history. There is a great multiplication of the scenes of death and of death itself. The skull of death is a common adornment of tombs, rendered with a terrifying naturalness.

Particularly noteworthy also is the change from the use of symbolism in the Middle Ages to that of the sixteenth century. Dante followed St. Thomas Aquinas in believing that the visible universe and human society were images in the mind of God. The persons in his poems are actual, but they symbolize some invisible form of existence. By the sixteenth century this was changed. The persons or actors were for the most part hypostatized intellectual abstractions — Justice, Prudence, Memory, Intellect, Liberty, Friendship, Sleep, and so on — usually with an effort to make the meaning of the allegorical figure not only naturalistically and intellectually justifiable but pleasant and sensually enjoyable as well, in a way quite foreign to the transcendental symbolism of an ideational epoch. As often as not, the allegories of the sixteenth century failed to achieve their purpose and remained strange, artificial, and cold.

Religious art in the sixteenth century was now being dwarfed by the more extensive secular art, a change which became yet more pronounced in the seventeenth century. Sorokin collects from the art historians of Western Europe a string of adjectives used to describe the conspicuous visual art of this sensate period collectively labeled, as a style, baroque: "theatricality, illusionism, illusionistic artificiality, showiness manifest in the ostentation of art, sumptuousness, pomp, luxury, overabundance of decoration, impurity, latent or open sensuality and sexuality, paganism, dynamism, patheticism, twisted and convulsive exaltation of ecstasy, and other strong emotions, imitative, purely cerebral and chilly academism, pseudo-idealism." Particularly notable in the exterior of baroque buildings, these qualities are present inside also, gluttony for mirrors, damask flowers, gilt, stucco, garlands, even pretty angels which are hybrids between the angels of religion and vulgar cupids. In complete contrast with the ideational or idealistic styles, baroque is at once recognized as the world of theatrical and ostentatious visualism, as a purely illusionistic world created only for the eyes as a mere show but with the intention to pass this show for a genuine world.

The somewhat later rococo style of the eighteenth century is the direct outcome of the baroque and belongs to the same family of theatricality and show, but the decorations are changed for the sake of variety. The rococo world is the same illusionistic, artificial world of seen surfaces and appearances, but they are now made in an effeminate, enfeebled, idyllic pastoral, coquettish fashion. It is the "boudoir" world with artificial and illusionistic rocks, waterfalls, gorges, fountains, idyllic shepherds and pastorals, cupids and nymphs, with other exotic freaks and illusionistic devices of an enfeebled, weary, bored, overripe culture. Such art, originating in France, penetrated and became dominant in Germany, the Netherlands, Italy, Spain and Portugal; only England escaped its influence to any considerable degree, probably because of the heritage of the Puritan outlook.

In discussing other aspects of eighteenth-century art, Sorokin deals with the series of waves of imitation of other forms of art, a phenomenon also observable in the Hellenistic, sensate period of Greek art and in Roman art from the Augustan era onwards. In this sequence of various fashions and imitations, the previous idealistic form was never successfully achieved, all the imitative waves remaining generally in the sensate stream and the change consisting in modifications of essentially sensate form in spite of the efforts to attain a real idealistic or even ideational art.

How visual and sensate ecclesiastical art could be at this time is shown by the reproduction in Plate of a female head then added to the altar in the Cathedral at Chartres.

Sorokin saw that when, during the Renaissance, men began to copy the art of Greece, they had as models examples of the ripe Hellenistic and Roman art. They produced, he said, a brilliant but pseudo-classic and pseudo-idealistic visual art. Then as a reaction came the purely naturalistic visualism of the Flemish school, the baroque of the Italian with academism as its offshoot and as the second imitative, pseudo-classic wave. In spite of their differences, they were all not less, but more sensate than the art of the Renaissance. Toward the end of the seventeenth and the beginning of the eighteenth century, the baroque as well as academism were worn out, giving place to the rococo style on the one hand, and to the Flemish "sweetened" naturalism on the other. Both by their very nature are fully visual and sensuous, each in its own manner.

About the beginning of the second part of the eighteenth century, the rococo style was practically worn out, and again, for the third time, there were signs of a return to classicism. This return was an accomplished fact in France at the end of the eighteenth century, with painters such as David and Ingres. Thus, within one century, art made a whole circle. That domination of the third imitation of classicism was short, however; around 1825 it was almost over, and it was soon replaced by the romanticism of the second quarter of the nineteenth century, typified in the works of painters such as Daumier, Millet, Corot, and the brothers Maris. Romanticism did not last longer; within one-quarter of a century it was also outmoded. It was replaced by something like "naturalism," and several other currents, one of which developed into the colorful impressionistic school of the last quarter of the nineteenth century, led by Manet, Monet, Renoir and others. In it visualism reached its most extreme and purest form: there was, and there is, no possibility of going farther along that line. The triumph of Impressionism was again short, and, toward the end of the nineteenth century, its fashionableness was already on the decline. "Expressionists," and especially "cubists," "futurists," "symbolists" appeared as the opponents not only of the impressionistic school but of the visual style itself.

Sorokin adds to this summary account the following remark upon the art of our own times. At the present moment, we have a most diversified conglomeration of many schools and currents, among them those ready to challenge the visual style generally, and the first symptoms of the search for something akin to an ideational style. But these symptoms as yet are weak; the searchers look, but have not yet found what they desire. It is clear from the often heated controversy which such efforts arouse, that innovation in style, particularly in the sensate visual style, is not merely difficult but also a most ungrateful task, rarely rewarded by sympathetic encouragement. Here, probably, is a fundamental reason why the position of the artist in contemporary life is felt to be a social problem.

It is important to note that Sorokin worked over the material which he had collected about the development of art through the ages from several directions. Otherwise it might be suspected that the results were inevitably predetermined by the way in which the material was classified and presented. If, for example, all pictures had been placed in three or four well-marked classes: sensate, ideational, idealistic and other mixed styles, it would not alone prove more than that such a fourfold classification could accommodate a number of paintings. Other classifications might serve to group paintings also and then seem to support the value of a different classification. Sorokin's facts themselves first establish the necessity for his threefold classification at the same time as they demonstrate its value as an interpreter and guide.

The following brief statement summarizes the findings relating to European art as a whole, beginning with the Creto-Mycenaean and Graeco-Roman cultures and ending with the present day. Accompanying them are two charts giving in diagrammatic from some of Sorokin's statistical findings upon the decline of ideational and the rise of sensate art, reproduced here as Figs. 1 and 2.

Period	Dominant Style of Art
B.C. 12th-9th centuries	Visual art.
B.C. 8th-6th centuries	Ideational with a possible transitory nonvisual but not ideational reaction in the ninth century.
B.C. end 6th-beginning 4th centuries	Marvellously mixed idealistic.

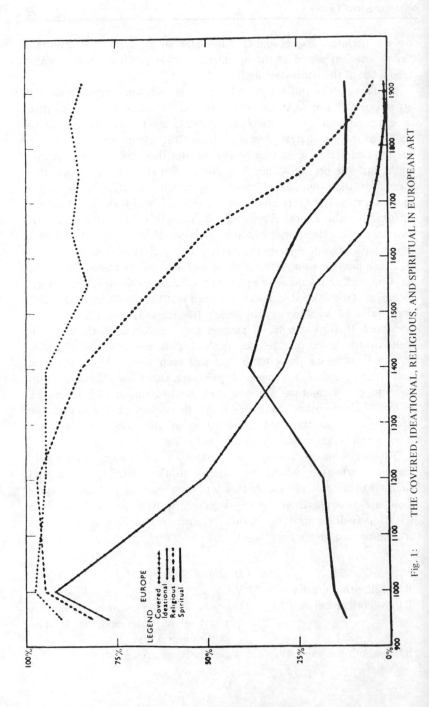

Fig. 1: THE COVERED, IDEATIONAL, RELIGIOUS, AND SPIRITUAL IN EUROPEAN ART

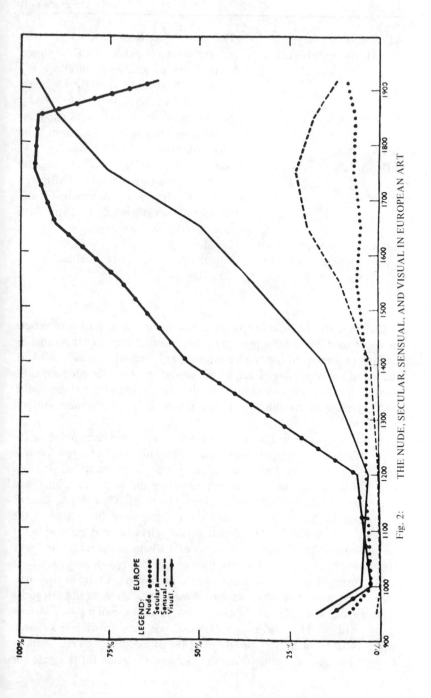

Fig. 2: THE NUDE, SECULAR, SENSUAL, AND VISUAL IN EUROPEAN ART

LEGEND: EUROPE
Nude ●●●●●
Secular ——————
Sensual — — — —
Visual ——◆——

B.C. end 4th century to A.D. 4th century A.D.	Hellenistic and Roman visual art with several smaller, shorter and shallower ripplings of ideational, idealistic and visual fluctuations upon the long-term tide of the main style.
A.D. 4th-6th	Non-coherent, anti-visual reaction looking for something new and different from visualism but not having found it.
A.D. 6th-12th	Ideational, with several slighter fluctuations: slight return to visualism in Carlovingian Renaissance and rigorous ideationalism in 10th, 11th and early 12th centuries.
A.D. end 12th to early 14th	Idealistic.
A.D. 14th-20th	Visual with secondary fluctuations.
A.D. 20th	Reaction against visualism.

On the basis of this study, of its development and succession of various forms of painting and sculpture, Sorokin was encouraged to think that by holding resolutely to his "logico-meaningful" method of study, and with the aid of his integrating principles of the ideational and sensate mentality, it was possible to contribute usefully and practically to the better understanding of the history of one branch at least of human cultural activity.

If this is true, he had already gone a long way towards establishing the value of these concepts of "ideational," "sensate" and "idealistic" as true operational concepts. That is to say, they are able to group and classify a whole range of sociological facts whose nature and necessary connections would be imperfectly understood without their aid. They help to "place" a work of art in its period; they throw light upon the nature of the mentality or outlook on life of that period. The clues they provide to the various distinctive characters of works of art help to show how and why they are related and in what way they change. By establishing such facts about forms of art, they do not merely place works of art in their true class or category, but they also show how far those classes and categories are coherent, well-knit, distinctive wholes with their own proper style and characteristics. They help, says Sorokin, not only to discern between which variables in art we should expect the functional-causal relationships to exist but also to establish them in fact and to decide the integrated or unintegrated nature of a given compartment of culture — in this context, the compartments of art in painting and in sculpture.

Architecture

It remains to apply the scheme so developed to other branches of human endeavor. Sorokin next takes architecture. Here, however, he provides no charts or statistical tables, but it is clear that he has used a large body of facts in framing his theory. The best illustrations and the most detailed source of reference to the facts of architectural development which he describes are to be found in any good history of architecture.

Briefly, Sorokin's findings are that Egyptian architecture throughout its history was predominantly ideational. It was mainly religious architecture producing pyramids and temples. Internally, therefore, it served ideational purposes. Externally, on many of its buildings there is not the slightest ornament. There were, it is true, waves of visual art. Under the Fifth Dynasty and towards the end of the Old Kingdom there appears a circular column with palm leaves already notably complicated and ornamental. It will be recalled that in the later stage of the Old Kingdom its paintings and sculpture seem also to have become more visual.

There were similar incursions and regressions of visual art at later periods. The beginning of the Middle Kingdom shows a very simple style of column which became more complicated later. Under the New Kingdom or Empire, there were the inverted bell-shaped columns which were followed, particularly in the Saito and the Roman periods, by overloaded decoration and a mixture of various architectural styles. It was then that a new type of capital with a human head beneath each face of the abacus appeared. This movement towards greater and more fanciful ornamentation and decoration became much more marked under the Ptolemies and the Romans. The form and especially the size of buildings over all these succeeding periods also showed corresponding changes from ideational to visual styles, or the reverse, in their painting and sculpture.

Similar developments occurred in Greece, where the architecture was predominantly ideational up to the fifth century B.C. The Doric order was an ideational style; simple even in details, modest in size, with a minimum of sculptural ornament. In the fifth century B.C., and for most of the fourth century B.C., idealistic styles with the Ionic order are characteristic. The buildings of this period, of which the Parthenon at Athens (447-432 B.C.) is the most renowned, were distinguished by marvellous harmony and proportions, striking just the right balance between ideational otherworldliness and visual beauty. Ornament was indeed by no means shunned, as the eternally famous sculptured frieze of the Parthenon so well demonstrates.

At the end of the fourth century B.C. a long period of visualism set in, lasting until the fourth century A.D., although shallow, short-lived reactions and minor fluctuations occurred, not however affecting the main stream. The 'visual' revolution affected the inner character of buildings no less than their external appearance. Great size, profusion of ornamentation, luxury, costliness, visual magnificence, increase of illusionary devices, mixtures of all styles are among the characteristic marks to which Sorokin calls attention in the architecture of this sensate period. The Corinthian order and still more the composite columns and capitals of the later Roman style, notably such examples as those furnished by the Arch of Titus (A.D. 81) and the Arch of Severus (A.D. 204), provide good illustrations of the visual style as it developed in the Roman Empire.

The few extant ruined remains make it possible to imagine the sense of grandeur and magnificence with which these buildings were designed to impress the onlookers. Until the heyday of Augustus and the Emperors who succeeded him, Rome had not been notable for architectural splendor. Under the Republic it was indeed a dull and somewhat mean city until the first century B.C., when the increase of wealth and new ideas of building brought about a change.

Augustus boasted that he had found a city of brick and had left a city of marble, but the change had begun before his time, and it would probably have occurred without his intervention. Had there been no Emperors; the houses of Rome's leading citizens might yet have come near to rivaling the huge imperial palaces built on the Palatine Hill of Rome, whose ruins yet remain to suggest something of their vast scale.

Apart from a temporary reaction toward simplicity and austerity under Trajan and Hadrian (A.D. 98-138), the sensate wave gathered momentum and carried everything before it. The Great Temple (about A.D. 131-161) and the Temple of Jupiter (A.D. 273), both at Baalbek in the distant Syrian valley, the colossal baths of Caracalla in Rome (A.D. 211-217) and the baths of Diocletian (A.D. 302), are among the many mute but exceedingly effective witnesses to the strength of visualism in late Roman imperial times.

The downfall of the Roman Empire in the fifth century A.D. meant the eclipse not merely of the sensate style but of architecture as well. Where it survived, as it did in Byzantium, it took a notably different course. There the wave of ideational Christian architecture was indeed based upon Graeco-Roman skills and traditions, but it did not follow their styles. The manner in which external decoration disappeared from Christian architecture is one striking sign of change. The basilica and the Byzantine dome show their technical antecedents clearly enough, but their manner leaves no doubt that their true nature and purpose was something radically different from that of the buildings on which they were modeled. The difference was further accentuated when the Romanesque and Gothic styles were elaborated. Sorokin points out that exteriors were plain, but ample compensation for the dull exterior of the basilica was made by the gorgeous polychromatic decoration of the interior for the greater glory of God. Quite as important as the decoration was the symbolic form of the Christian churches. The great dome of the basilicas was regarded as representing Christ, the four adjacent domes were the four Evangelists. The later churches were built in the shape of a cross, facing eastwards towards the Holy Land.

Sorokin points out how in medieval towns and cities, the great cathedrals and churches dominated the skyline, completely overshadowing the civic buildings, the houses of the wealthy, or the palaces of the great, as some of them, notably the Cathedral at Chartres, still do. It was not until the fifteenth century that the grand architecture became more and more secular. The palace, the *Rathaus*, the mansion, the commercial edifice, the parliament buildings and so on then began to command attention by their size and magnificence.

Before that occurred, there was the marvellous blend between the visual and ideational elements which reached its climax in the second half of the thirteenth century, after having inspired and created cathedrals such as those at Noyon (about 1157-1228), St. Denis (1144), Sens (1144-1168), Notre Dame at Senlis (1155-1185), Chartres (1194-1260), Reims (1212-1300), Amiens (1220-1288), Beauvais (1225), Canterbury (1174) and Salisbury (1240).

These glories were not sustained as the spirit of the age continued to change from ideationalism to a sensate character. From the end of the fourteenth century until the Renaissance, Gothic architecture became more decorative and flamboyant. By the sixteenth century there seemed no hope of further progress from this style of building and decoration, and it was then that some effort was made at the Renaissance to revive the older styles. Columns, pilasters and entablature were revived in Roman fashion, but for decorative rather than for structural purposes.

Despite an effort after simplicity and its very considerable success at the hands of a genius like Brunelleschi, it remained a new wave on the strong sensate tide which was sweeping all before it.

That is to say emphasis continued to be put on appearance rather than upon structural merit. In the seventeenth century, possibly as one result of the attempt to combine classical with Gothic styles, or as a reaction against a narrow interpretation of the canons of Vitruvius, Western architecture assumed the so-called baroque style. All the emphasis went upon visual, illusory show; the search for effect through the arrangement of light and shadow; a taste for contrast and movement; a search for theatrical effects and a distinct appetite for the colossal. It was a quest by no means unrewarded, as anyone can testify who saw Dresden before it was obliterated.

The rococo in architecture as in painting was still more visual, erotic, futile, reduced almost entirely to puerile decorations. Sorokin calls it a confectioner's sweet and toyland architecture.

In the late eighteenth and in the nineteenth centuries, several waves of neo-classic, romantic and classic architecture with attempted revivals of Gothic and Renaissance prototypes followed one another, but none succeeded in creating an ideational style, or any original style at all.

Sorokin will not lightly concede that skyscraper architecture represents a new and real style. It is, he admits, undoubtedly a trend toward structural simplicity but hardly ideationality. It resembles modern cubist painting in being a reaction against extreme visual art. It is not ideational, because nearly all its buildings are secular. They do not pretend, says Sorokin, to symbolize any transcendental reality. They serve instead the most material, the most commercial, the most empirical and the most visual needs. Among the merits claimed for them are that they are "functional." They are machines in which to live and work. Desperate efforts are made to combine maximum size with maximum profits and dividends. Hence they are too cerebral, mathematical, commercial, scientific and planned, being all quite regular and almost deadly correct.

On the basis of his rapid survey, Sorokin is able to amplify the provisional conclusion resulting from his study of art-forms, by claiming that his ideational, sensate and idealistic categories fit the world of architecture as satisfactorily as they do the two branches of the arts, painting and sculpture, which he had previously examined in much greater detail. By "fit the world of architecture" is meant not merely that buildings bear an obviously distinguishing hallmark of their age which corresponds sufficiently accurately with those categories, but that the categories themselves help to suggest the hallmark or distinguishing characteristics.

It is easy to see how such a claim might seem dangerously like begging the question in the manner many "philosophies of history" beg it, namely by imagining a "law," or a "principle," or series of "laws" or "principles" of historical change and then looking for facts to "prove" the laws; such inescapable facts that seem either not to fit or indeed to disprove the laws are then either ignored or given some special interpretation to make them fit the theory. Nobody has more trenchantly exposed this inherent fallacy in the writings of others than Sorokin. It will occur at once to every reader that he also faces this pitfall. He avoids it by his strenuous efforts to look at each main branch of human activity separately, assessing the facts by as objective an interpretation as possible and seeing whether they conform fairly to the ideational-sensate-idealistic hypothesis.

This is the task he sets himself throughout, and it remains to see how far he succeeds with it. At the outset he has established his three main logico-meaningful cultural mentalities — ideational, sensate (visual) and idealistic — by a very full statistical sampling of thousands of paintings and many sculptures. Without any similar statistical enquiry he has given a summary survey of the main trends of style in architecture which fits plausibly into the pattern provided by the history of painting and sculpture.

He has shown how his interpretation of the history of art brings order and sequence into art history over many ages and epochs in a way that challenges and supersedes all previous theories on the subject. The proposal of Sir Charles Holmes, for example, in A Grammar of the Arts (1931), to divide all art into representative art, decorative art, and constructive art can at once be seen to be inadequate. Sorokin mentions some, but does not by any means survey all these rival theories. The inadequacy of many of them, already revealed by the succinct survey of Ogden, Richards and Wood in the *Foundation of Aesthetics* (1925), will, it is believed, be shown with greater clarity when they are again reviewed in the light of Sorokin's principles which, as the following chapters will show, are by no means merely views about art, but relate, as rival theories seldom pretend to do, to the entire range of cultural life as a whole.

Will the history of the other human arts and sciences confirm or upset Sorokin's provisional conclusions?

Music, Drama, Literature, Criticism

Is there such a thing as ideational music or sensate music? To the
majority of those who have been trained by long familiarity with the great
tradition of music developed in Europe since about the middle of the
eighteenth century, this may well sound a strange question. Music for
them probably means the production of outstanding and renowned
composers, such as Bach, Handel, Mozart, Beethoven and their successors
up to our own time.

It is true that some new kinds of music bearing scant resemblance to the
works of those classic composers are now apparently giving satisfaction to
many, but for the most part these novelties are little better understood or
appreciated than are similar efforts to create new styles in painting,
sculpture, and architecture.

In the Middle Ages music was also something very different from either
classical music or the works of modern composers. There is a definition of
music by the philosopher Boethius at the beginning of the Middle Ages
which Sorokin quotes to bring out this difference: "Human music is that
which is understood by anyone who descends into himself or sinks into
himself." By these mysterious words, Sorokin considers that Boethius
thought that a knowledge of music should impart to the mind an
understanding of its true principles, and that this was very much more
important and valuable than the mere practice or performance which
brings music to the ear. It is merely another example of the general
principle that the mind is superior to the body. Consequently the real
musician is the man who knows a chant by force of reason, not the man
who has learned it by practice. The testimony of the ear, in other words, is
of no significance and should be ignored.

Such a doctrine, which sounds so strange to us, was, however, the
theory supported by most of the Greek philosophers. It was supported by
the thinkers of the Middle Ages, and it reigned supreme for almost one
thousand years. Strange as it is, it is no stranger than the concept of
ideational painting. By it Boethius and his famous predecessors and
followers meant what Sorokin styles the ideational or symbolic form of
music, in contradistinction to the sensately audible. Just as in ideational
painting, the visual impression through the eye plays a secondary role, and
the aim of the picture is to give the idea of the object as it exists in the
mind, so in ideational music, the main thing is not how it sounds —
pleasant or unpleasant — but the power of being able to grasp that which is

beyond the sounds and for which they are mere signs and symbols. This hidden meaning beyond the sounds is only to be grasped by intuition, reason or mind, by "descending into oneself," as Boethius put it. Such music need not be harmonious, pleasant or enjoyable; indeed the combination of sounds perceived by the ear may be ugly, but if to the mind it means something great for which it is a mere symbol or "symbolic" stimulus, then it is great, "heavenly," ideational music.

Sensate music, on the contrary, is judged by its sheer "audible beauty," regardless of any hidden meaning. It takes sounds at their face value and it is an end in itself. In more detail, Sorokin analyzes the difference between the two classes under the following main characteristics. Ideational music tends to be "inner." Like the silent communion of the soul with God, it employed the simplest means: no orchestra, no musical instruments. The voices sang in unison. There was no polyphony and the melody was all within one octave. At the time of St. Gregory, the Roman school had only seven singers. In all the luxury of the Sistine Chapel, there were but thirty-seven, and this number was reduced to twenty-four in the year of Palestrina's *Mass of the Pope* (1565). This, however, was one of the early monuments of polyphony. Sensate music tends to be theatrical and external. It has to be interesting, enjoyable, entertaining, successful and popular. It seeks effect by the massing of voices, from their wide range, their modulations, by all kinds of consonances and especially dissonances, chromatics, contrasts of rhythms and of intensity. It demands enormous choruses and concert halls. With the aid of commercial advertising and publicity, it seeks to be the richest, loudest, and biggest in the world.

Ideational music tends to be and is comparatively pure in style. Sensate music is not and cannot afford to be pure. Sorokin refers briefly to some of its adjuncts: the lowest forms of vaudeville and musical comedy with their mixed styles, including everything from classical music to jazz, dancing, athletics, comedy actors, complicated by light effects, scenery effects, and sound effects. As though the spectacle were not enough, it is accompanied by the sale of ice cream and sweets for the unoccupied mouths of the audience. Not, of course, that this is a nineteenth century novelty, for Aristotle observed two thousand years ago that the sale of sweetmeats in the theatre was greater if the performance was poor. More developed and involved, but essentially similar in type, is the musical drama of Richard Wagner with its mixture of music, poetry, dancing, stage, popular topics, and legends, which Sorokin describes as the most magnificent incarnation of impurity, in the noblest forms of sensate art.

Ideational music, in complete contrast, consists of audible signs for great inaudible values which are and have to be the values of a collectivity. The values of an individual are too weak, fragile and uncertain to become those of a collectivity. Ideational music, therefore, requires a fairly well-knit homogeneous society to sustain it. Sensate music does not need such support. It is music for the buyer, and it satisfies heterogeneous societies. Ideational music, as self-communion or communion with God, has no pride of authorship. Sensate music has to be individualistic, and its author is concerned to protect his rights and to insure that his name and authorship figure as prominently as possible in public performances.

Ideational music does not give rise to any special aesthetic theorizing by critics. It is controlled by religious and moral censors whose concern is with its relations with the values lying behind the sound symbols. Sensate music, by its nature, calls for a criterion of its beauty and perfection, and hence stimulates theories of beauty and aesthetic theorizing by musical critics.

The principal mixed class of music, the idealistic type, seen in the works of Palestrina, Vittoria, Orlando di Lasso, Bach, Handel, Mozart and Beethoven, also has a considerable purity of style, but it is not so pure as that of the ideational epoch. Yet its values are perfectly blended with sensual beauty. Sorokin holds that the beauty of the music of the great composers of the idealistic period is immediately appreciated by all who hear it, and that it stands in no need of critics to bring forward reasoned proofs that it is great and beautiful or to tell people to admire it.

So much for preliminary definition and description of the three main contrasting forms of music. Have they historically the reality which Sorokin supposes? He points out that just as ideational and sensate painting are found in most primitive as well as in most civilized cultures, the same is true of music. After referring briefly to some other views of musical development, he says that it is reasonable to suppose that primitive peoples sing when they are excited, when they have an abundance of energy or merely because they enjoy it, because music and singing are pleasant and biologically useful. All such chanting and singing are merely forms of sensate music. Side by side with it there is an ideational form. It has two main varieties, the music of magic and that of religion. Both of these forms are in their essentials ideational music, not sensate. The use of music in performing magical acts and in religious societies is universal and is found even among the most primitive societies. But it is not confined to primitive peoples nor need it be assumed that all primitive peoples practice it. Those that do so believe that with the magic chant everything is possible. Incantations exist for various vitally important purposes, for obtaining rain or fine weather, for appeasing evil spirits, or for curing disease in men or animals. The sense and the importance and influence of such music, therefore, derives not from its sounds as such, which may to the sensate ear be repellent, but to the magical, mystical or religious value lying behind them.

Ideational symbolic music has existed in Egypt, China, India, in Greece, Rome and in Europe during the Middle Ages. It was because of its mystical or symbolic meaning that it became one of the most important responsibilities of government, and this is why the sages, thinkers, and statesmen, such as Confucius, Pythagoras, Plato, and Aristotle, gave so much time and thought to it.

The difficulties of illustrating changes in the vogue of ideational, sensate and idealistic music are very much greater than those arising from the similar treatment of painting and sculpture. Sheer lack of knowledge makes it impossible to trace the exact way in which changes occurred in the predominant music of Ancient Egypt, Assyria, China, India, and Palestine.

Sorokin believes that both the ideational and the sensate forms existed and that one form followed the other in the history of most of these lands, and that the same is true of the earlier period of Graeco-Roman music and of Creto-Mycenaean music, despite the fact that not a single note of music has survived from these early periods, nor unfortunately from the period of Terpander, his contemporaries and successors of the eighth, seventh and early sixth centuries B.C., when Sorokin considers ideational Greek music reached its highest development. Some of the musicians are known, and the forms and styles of their music are indicated by surviving references. It was a grand music, bound up with religious ceremonies and religious civic performances which took place in temples and religious theaters. Being an integral part of important public functions, it was jealously protected. From a speech of Demosthenes of 349 B.C. against Midias, it is evident that the death penalty could be demanded as late as the fourth century B.C. for a supposedly unlawful interference in the functions of the man in charge of the chorus in the festivals. The terms used in referring to this music all indicate its religious character. *Nome* meant a religious chant in honor of one or other of the gods of a given province; *dithyramb,* a lyric hymn to Dionysos; *paean,* a chant to Apollo; other terms like the *prosody* the chants of the march of the religious cortege to the temple, and the *threnody* are equally of religious or magic significance.

It was an essentially simple music. The instruments were poor and must have lacked variety of *timbres;* the performers were few, since sixteen to twenty-four voices at most made up the chorus in the lyrical dramas of Greece.

Sorokin believes that in the course of the sixth century B.C. the sensate form of music began to be heard. Towards its end and in the fifth century B.C., roughly speaking, the decline of ideational music and the rise of sensate music balanced to produce the marvel of the idealistic music of the fifth century. This idealistic music seems to have reached its point of maturity or a perfect equilibrium between religion and pure art in the music and, associated with it, in the poetry and drama (tragedy and comedy) of Pindar, Aeschylus, Sophocles, Euripides (partly), Aristophanes, Simonides of Klos, Agathocles, Melanippides of Melos (master of counterpoint), Bacchylides, Damon, and others. In its essential parts it still remained ideational and kept the forms of the hieratic music and drama demanded and sanctified by traditional beliefs. But elements of sensate music began to creep in. If the tragedies of Aeschylus (525-456 B.C.) exhibit these but slightly, they are already in considerable evidence in the works of Euripides (485-406 B.C.), and this is the reason why most of the thinkers who immediately succeeded him, like Plato, take Euipides as the boundary line of what they styled decadence.

Sorokin summarizes the characteristics of the transition from ideational to sensate music and drama with which music became increasingly involved as follows:

(i)   Progressive abandonment of the purely sacerdotal art in favor of music to please.

(ii) Increasing substitution of destiny for the gods and other meta-physical abstractions.

(iii) Complication of the technicality of music intended to make a greater impression and to please more.

(iv) Increase of the purely 'human' theme of music and drama associated with it.

(v)   Increase of the comical, satirical, and sarcastic veins in ridiculing and satirizing human affairs and events and relationships (Aristophanes and the increasing number of comedies).

(vi) Decreasing role of the chorus and increasing role of individual performers. Likewise an increasing individualism characterizes the authors also. They begin to be more and more individualistic and less and less ready to sink their own personality in the anonymous collectivity.

(vii) Progressive permeation of the profane spirit in art.

(viii) Progressive loss of calm serenity in music in favor of its increasing passionate, pathetic, individual emotionality.

(ix) Introduction of the feminine element on the stage.

After the fourth century B.C., sensate music, already strong, continued to grow and to dominate the ideational music of the preceding period. The marvellous balance of the fifth century was disrupted in favor of sensate music.

Euripides, Melanippides, Phrynis and his disciple Timotheus of Miletus were denounced as the corrupters of taste, but their successors, such as Philoxenes of Cytherea (436/5-380/79 B.C.), Telestes (*b.* 420 B.C.), Agathon (*d.* 401 B.C.), and a crowd of parodists continued this tendency. The essential traits of this music are its increasing profane, sensual, human, individualistic interest, its increasing striving after effect through greater mass and quantity, and its new professional character. Then began the monster concerts with hundreds and thousands of artists and the craze for the biggest building, the biggest orchestra and chorus and the greatest noise to be achieved by the power of instruments, by contrasts of consonances and dissonances and the concentration upon pure technique generally.

The status and functions of the music-maker also underwent a fundamental transformation. From being a moral and social leader, a prophet, magician, or priest, he became a professional and an individualist seeking personal renown, fame, and fortune by his art. Through it he sought to make his living — and a most luxurious one — to be famous, to be popular, to be the idol of a crowd of emotional and half-hysterical followers. The cult of many of them, says Sorokin, was hardly less than that of Richard Wagner with the enormous crowd of half-crazy Wagnerian devotees throughout the world. The cities of Greece vied for the honor of having a famous musician among their citizens; some of them were named after artists; statues were erected to composers; enormous sums were paid for their concerts. In brief, the popular musician was a manufacturer of an important sensual pleasure, and as such he was paid well by sensual values, from applause and fame to wealth and sensual and sexual love. In this way the situation continued, with slighter ups and downs, until the victorious ideational music of Christianity put an end to this sensual music, great in a way in its initial stages, but, Sorokin believes, completely degenerate during the Alexandrian, Pergamene and Roman periods.

Roman music suffered, as did other forms of Roman art, by being completely eclipsed by the earlier maturity of the Greeks. Early Roman music was probably of a rather low-grade ideational form, but, before it or a Roman sensate music could develop, the Roman world was flooded by what Sorokin describes as the superannuated and overripe sensate music which was imported from Greece. The intermediate stage, the classical miracle of idealistic music was almost unknown to Rome, as it was unknown in painting, sculpture and architecture, except by imitation. By the end of the first century B.C., the Roman world was avid for musical festivals on a gigantic scale. Music to be sure was by no means the sole attraction at these spectacles, but it was nevertheless tremendously popular as a source of social distinction. Nero and his lyre may typify the popularity of music from the emperors to the *bourgeoisie*. Children were taught music, which became a lucrative profession, and great was the vanity of its virtuosos. There were also many critics and theorizers about music.

In such a period of sensate art, there appeared, says Sorokin, a crowd of grammarians, rhetoricians, philosophers and art amateurs, art critics, art reviewers, evaluators, and educators, most of whom neither were artists nor knew anything about art except beggarly superficialities. But they invaded the stage, became noisy, influential, authoritative, and they wrote innumberable texts and compendiums, not to mention articles, in which and through which they crushed many talents and created successes out of nullities. Even when a moralizing voice like Plutarch's is heard in this noisy crowd, it is a voice crying in the wilderness. Moreover, his preaching is not spontaneous, not otherworldly or mystic or ideational, but entirely reasoned, rationally calculated and based not so much upon ideational principles as upon very earthly, very utilitarian, noble but sensate considerations.

With the Middle Ages in Europe, the scene is entirely changed. During almost nine hundred years, from about the fifth century A.D. to the fourteenth century, music was either exclusively ideational or predominantly so, and the ideational nature of this music was of the purest and most sublime character. Its central form was the Gregorian chant which, says Sorokin, from the standpoint of a sensually audible criterion, is no music at all but something queer, unenjoyable, primitive, and dry, lacking what we now consider to be the elements of music; for it has neither measure nor harmony nor polyphony and it divides words without any regard for their sense and unity. Its predecessor, the Ambrosian chant, was yet more extraordinary, having had as many as 332 notes to one syllable. It was music intended not for listeners but for performers, and all those in church chanted it. Its value arose solely from its symbolic nature. We may be helped to appreciate this fact by remembering music which we ourselves value not for its aesthetic quality, which may indeed be poor or absent, but for its association and meaning. Sorokin enumerates school and college songs and national anthems by way of illustration.

The religious grand music of the Eastern Church was very similar to the Gregorian chant, which consisted roughly of about three hundred introits and communions, one hundred graduals, one hundred Alleluias, twenty tracts, and one hundred offertories, all characterized by a spirit of gentleness, humility, and resignation, and possessing a curiously ethereal, static, timeless quality.

It was not achieved as a whole all at once, but represented the results of continuing efforts by the Fathers of the Church over two centuries, notably by St. Augustine, St. Benedict, St. Jerome, Clement of Alexandria and others who opposed instruments and instrumental music, which were excluded from churches after the fourth century.

The classic expression of ideational music in the Byzantine Church occurred in the fifth, sixth, and seventh centuries. Sensate elements began to creep into the grand religious music from the tenth to the twelfth centuries, gaining in power and influence to produce the great idealistic music of Byzantium in the thirteenth, fourteenth, and fifteenth centuries, somewhat earlier therefore than in the West.

There, the first signs of its mixture with the sensate style occurred in the twelfth century with the rise of the troubadours, *trouvères* and *Minnesinger*. Slowly, secular motets, madrigals, and symphonies grew from these beginnings. In spirit and character this music was different from the chants heard in the churches. Love and the affairs of this world are its themes. Its monodies were sentimental and gallant with instrumental accompaniment. No doubt the new style perpetuated a traditional secular folk music which continued during the great period of ideational music, never however enjoying such prestige or respect among the leaders or 'the bearers' of the predominant culture. Nevertheless it and the songs of the troubadours continued to be much influenced by the ideational music of their age, and they were not fully sensate in quality.

Profane love and worldly affairs were still idealized. A modified idealistic Platonic spirit reigned. Gradually the sensate trend showed itself in new developments. After the thirteenth century music became measured, it developed polyphony, produced and developed counterpoint, which reached its Golden Age in the fifteenth century. A richer variety of rhythms was introduced and cultivated. Harmony and 'vertical' scoring instead of 'horizontal' marked another major development, and new complications were introduced by varying the volume and intensity of sound: *piano, forte,* for example. The use of chromatic consonances and dissonances were mastered and perfected and so was instrumental music, which was blended with the human voice. It then remained to develop choruses and orchestras, and to enlarge their scale and finally to combine the sound impressions, thus rendered infinitely more varied and expressive, with visual impressions through form, color and motion. This trend was general in Western culture, particularly in France, Flanders, Italy, England, and Germany from the thirteenth to the sixteenth centuries.

It is, of course, unfortunate that, over the vast period from the ancient World to the Middle Ages, hardly a note of music has survived. Sorokin's conclusions, like those of all who write or speculate on the nature and development of early music, are necessarily hypothetical, supported solely by literary references. Statistical evidence to illustrate such conclusions is therefore entirely lacking for the major part of musical history. From the sixteenth century onwards, Sorokin was able to use the two collections of statistics already mentioned, one of the number of composers and the second of the number of their works, each being divided according to whether the composers and compositions were religious or secular.

Sorokin recognizes that it is impossible to get a completely accurate picture from either of these sources. Are the Gregorian chants, for example, to be counted as one work? Is a madrigal of a few bars to be regarded as quantitatively balanced by a complete Mass? Are composers of many works such as Palestrina to be equated with those of more slender output? These are the elementary difficulties of any effort to apply quantitative measures to cultural history. All that can be established by such inquiries is the direction of the main trends of development. Imperfect as the results may be, they at least claim to be based upon as complete a survey of the whole field of effort as it is possible to make. To that extent they are not less reliable than casual summary judgments based upon varying degrees of familiarity with musical history. On the contrary, they are probably more reliable than the best critical opinion which had not also attempted a smiliar quantitative comparison.

It is, at any rate, in the light of such a survey, and on its authority, that Sorokin's main conclusions on musical evolution since the sixteenth century are based. The broad trend, as would be expected, is one in which the proportion of religious music tends to decrease, while that of secular music tends to increase.

In the sixteenth century, the number of known musical works (those mentioned in the standard histories of music) were 44 per cent religious and 56 per cent secular. The number of religious composers was 53 per cent; of secular, 47 per cent. In the nineteenth century, the religious composers accounted for 24 per cent, the secular 76 per cent; while the religious compositions were only 21 per cent against 79 per cent of secular works.

Statistics of this sort do not show how the ostensibly religious music of the later periods became itself increasingly secular in character. If some parts were religious in spirit, says Sorokin, the other parts were sensate, the music of opera or symphony.

During this change, from ideational to sensate music, which became increasingly evident between the sixteenth and nineteenth centuries, there again occurred a manifestation of the mixed or blended idealistic type of music. What is remarkable is that, in comparison with painting, sculpture and architecture, the idealistic form in music seems to have been delayed until the sixteenth, seventeenth and eighteenth century. Here Sorokin encountered the first striking discrepancy or lack of synchronous correlation in the development of forms of art; for the perfection of the idealistic phase of European sculpture and architecture occurred in the thirteenth and fourteenth centuries. At its greatest period, with Bach, Handel, Mozart, Beethoven, there is little difference in style between idealistic religious and secular music. It was music still inspired by sublime ideals and idealistic values, although these influences had waned in other cultural fields.

From the time of Palestrina (A.D. 1524-1594) up to Beethoven's Ninth Symphony and his last quartets, music reached great heights of purity, nobility, idealism and sensuous perfection. Some muddy streams of lesser music, no doubt, are also to be found during this long epoch, but they were of small account in comparison with the prevailing tone. At the outset, during the period of Palestrina-Vittoria-Lasso-Bach, religion continued to provide the inspiration and main value of music. In the development from Lulli-Rameau-Gluck-Mozart-Haydn, although the religious quality is less evident, the music, Sorokin observes, is a fresh, pure, spontaneous song of youth; idealistic, imaginative, with silvery laughter, without any burden of sin or tragedy or worry or 'dirt of daily vulgarity.' The idealistic period culminates with the music of Beethoven, the music of a sage to whom all the ecstasy of wisdom and all the tragedy of reality are known; its pain and pleasure, its noble and its vulgar aspects.

He has fathomed all this and has not been seduced by it.

The steady growth of sensate music during these centuries is shown not merely in the relative decline of religious music, but in the increasing theatricality of music, oratorio, opera and comic opera. Richard Wagner epitomises this evolution. Sorokin quotes with approval a description of him as "neither a musician who made poems, nor a poet who made music, but a theatricalist who made both whenever he wanted them."

By Wagner's time, another mark of sensate art characterized music also; the growth of colossalism. Monteverdi's *Orpheus* (1607) was scored for about thirty instruments. Orchestras did not get very much larger until after the end of the eighteenth century. Bach and Mozart wrote for orchestras of thirty to sixty instruments. By 1830 the *Fantastic Symphony* of Berlioz was scored for more than a hundred instruments. At the same time there was a steady increase of the brass, woodwind and percussion instruments in orchestration. This sign of rising sensualism is emphasized in what Sorokin calls the field of vulgar music, where it appears in the domination of the brass band and the saxophone, which have driven out the more delicate music of the strings of the eighteenth and previous centuries.

Then there has been the complication of the texture of music and the deliberate creation of technical difficulties. It is a feature, Sorokin thinks, of decadent periods, whether in art, science, or religion, to look to technique to make good the absence of genius.

The increasing professionalism and individualism of composers is another aspect of the same degenerative process, and so also is the enormous development of musical education, musical criticism, musical discussion and musical aestheticism. These characteristics have often been explained as being due in whole or in part to the fact that sensate art is created for a market. Artists are, therefore, inevitably tempted to adapt their work to the prevailing taste of the largest class of consumers who will usually also be the poorest. This leads directly to the danger that art, being forced to search for cheap sensation, will become vulgar and commercial, subject to incessant change under the continuing pressure for increasing variety and the effort to popularize new and contrasting fashions. Sensate music, like sensate art in general, is therefore committed to a search for all that is striking, extreme, exotic, picturesque, and monstrous. Its themes thus tend to be perverse and dramatic, as will be seen to be especially true of literature and drama. The rise of musical comedy, which was quite unknown in a period of ideational art, further emphasizes the ridiculous, stupid, perverse, and criminal aspects of life.

Another source upon which sensate music relies for novelty is also one neglected by ideational art: that of ordinary everyday life. Examples are musical compositions on themes such as the railroad and aeroplane by Honegger, the factory by Molotov, Noises of London by Elgar, and the *May First Symphony* of Shostakovitch. More popular themes, however, are those portraying life as something exotic and, like cocktails, detective stories and thrillers, providing a contrast with the habitual routine of life. They are usually woven around sex. Sorokin lists *Samson and Delilah, Aida, Oberon* and the whole Wagnerian series of the Ring, *Tristan and Isolde* among many examples of this type of sensate music.

He points also to a general tendency running through all sensate art, including music, towards pathos, dramatism and emotion, of which he notes "moronic and sentimentally sad crooning" as a recent example in the field of contemporary vulgar music. He points also to the rising proportion of music written in a minor key. From Aristotle onwards, the minor key has generally been considered sad, dolorous, and lamentable. In the sixteenth century it was still regarded as something painful and abnormal. Since that time it has been increasingly used. Sorokin has made a calculation showing that from the eighteenth century, when about 22 per cent of the works of the main composers were in the minor key, the figure increased to 25 per cent from 1800 to 1850, and to 38.5 per cent from 1850 to 1900.

From the same sources, Sorokin provides a rough index of the types of musical composition according to their content divided into seven main classes. These are:

Mythology and Pseudo-history, e.g., the operas of Lulli, the aristocratic operas of the Venetian School, and the *galant* operas of Rameau, the *Prometheus* of Beethoven, the *Oedipus* of Stravinsky, etc.

Comic and *Genre* Music, e.g., classical comic operas: Rossini's *Barber of Seville,* Smetana's *Bartered Bride.*

Revolutionary and War Type, e.g., Tschaikovsky's *1812,* Beethoven's *Leonora* and *Fidelio,* Rossini's *William Tell.*

Animalism and *Paysage,* e.g., Debussy's *Clouds,* Rimsky-Korsakoff's *Scheherazade,* Wagner's *Siegfried's Idyll.*

Historical e.g., Moussorgsky's *Boris Godunoff,* Wagner's *Meistersinger.*

Exoticism, e.g., Beethoven's *Ruins of Athens,* Weber's *Oberon, Tourandot,* Strauss's *Salome.*

Urbanism and *Nature Morte*. These are works reflecting industrial, urban, mechanized or still-life phenomena, examples of which by Honegger and others have already been quoted.

It is significant that, until the eighteenth century, musical themes were apparently drawn solely from the first two of these seven classes, and that no more than eleven works were devoted to war and revolution during the eighteenth century, while those eleven works all date from 1780 to 1800. The remaining four classes were yet slower in developing. Sorokin's statistics are summarized as follows:

Table 1:   TYPES OF MUSICAL COMPOSITION

Period	Mythology Pseudo-History	Genre Comedy	Revolution War	Animalism Paysage Folk Legend	Historicism	Exoticism	Urbanism Nature Morte
600-1700	123	24	—	—	—	—	—
1700-1800	112	97	11	—	—	—	—
1800-1820	14	26	3	—	—	—	—
1820-1840	14	14	5	2	4	—	—
1840-1860	14	12	4	16	5	8	—
1860-1880	9	40	15	20	10	13	12
1880-1900	12	14	3	25	8	20	8
Total 1800-1900	63	106	30	63	27	41	20
1900-1920	15	15	6	19	6	11	20

From his analysis of musical history in the light of his general principles, Sorokin sees little hope for contemporary music. Inner emptiness and the most complicated and brilliant technique are the destiny to which it is doomed until it is replaced by the ideational music which has still to appear, but, he thinks, will probably grow eventually. Sorokin detects the first clumsy signs of it in some of the modern "isms." In the works of composers like Stravinsky and Honegger, he sees the modernism or "cubism" in music and a revolt against sensate music, notably similar to the reaction of the anti-visualists in painting. Such modern composers, he holds, are still searching, but they do not know what they are looking for, since they remain the product of a sensate age, discontented with, but unable to transcend its sensate mentality.

This brief and necessarily imperfect summary survey of the history of music indicates that, despite minor fluctuations in style, there seem to have been major "tidal" waves of ideational and sensate music. They do not correspond point by point with similar movements in painting, sculpture, and architecture. Music became classically ideational in the fifth and sixth centuries A.D., while the ideational period of painting, sculpture, and architecture began two or three centuries later. The idealistic phase of music lagged in comparison with that of the other arts, all of which had attained it by the thirteenth century. The idealistic phase of music dates from the fifteenth to the beginning of the nineteenth century.

Literature

It will be unnecessary to devote much space to a description of the nature of ideational and sensate literature, because the preceding summary characterizations of similar forms in painting, sculpture, architecture, music and drama should have indicated their quality sufficiently.

Sorokin provides fewer statistics for this aspect of his study, which is devoted to a brief summary of the evolution of literary forms in a few of the chief countries of the Western world, confined to those inheriting the cultural traditions of Greece and Rome.

Regarding as ideational those literary works dealing with superempirical and transcendental matters and the invisible world, and as sensate those concerned with empirical phenomena in their sensory aspect, where words and images have nothing but their empirical meaning, Sorokin lists productions ranging from hymns, dithyrambs, prayers, odes, narratives, proverbs, incantations up to Dante's *Divine Comedy,* as examples of ideational literature, and the purely realistic and naturalistic novels, dramas, plays and lyrics as typically sensate literary productions. He acknowledges that, in a rough or highly developed form, both of these types of literature seem to have coexisted in virtually all cultures at all periods. They occur, however, in different states of purity and in different proportions.

Among primitive folk, both forms, and especially the ideational, are to a large extent impure, with the ideational and sensate elements interwoven. Most of the early epics are of this class, such as the *Mahabarata* and

Ramayana, the *Gilgamash* epic, parts of the Bible, the *Iliad,* the *Odyssey,* the *Edda,* the song of *Beowulf,* or the Russian folk epics about the great heroes, Iliya Murometz, Dobrynia Nikititch, Sviatopolk and others. Nevertheless it is probable that, to those who first heard them, these epics appeared very much more symbolic than they do to us today. Some were idealistic in Sorokin's meaning of the word.

The question therefore arises: are the ideational-sensate-idealistic values as evident in the history of literature as they have appeared to be in the history of sculpture, pictorial art and music? Sorokin holds that they are. It is possible to distinguish different proportions of the two extreme types, ideational and sensate, at a given moment in literary history, and he further holds that these proportions do not remain constant but fluctuate in a manner closely paralleling similar fluctuations in the fields of painting and sculpture. It is a view which emerges from a comparative study of the leading histories of literature and of literary criticism, beginning with the earliest surviving literature of Greece.

The exact dates at which Homer and Hesiod wrote are unknown, but it was possibly in the eighth century B.C. To the Greeks before the fourth century B.C., the *Iliad* and the *Odyssey* were regarded as religious, moral, and educational works rather than as works of art. What, however, is more significant of the predominantly ideational trend of the literature of that period is the fact that most of it was practically inseparable from music and was religious, magical, and symbolic in character. Such was the Doric choral lyric of religious nomes, dithyrambs, paeans, prosodies, and threnodies.

Side by side with the ideational stream, there was sensate literature, especially the Ionic stream represented by Theognis, Sappho, Anacreon, and the Sicilian comic but moralizing poets of the sixth century B.C. It was a minor and subordinate current permeated also by ideationalism and idealism. The sixth and fifth centuries B.C. were the period when the great ideational-idealistic literature of Greece flourished, in which both sensate and ideational values were marvellously balanced, in content and in form. With Pindar, Aeschylus, Sophocles and to some extent Euripides and Aristophanes, the literary art of Greece reached its peak.

The increasingly sensate character of the values evident in the literature and literary criticism which followed this period, particularly after the end of the fourth century B.C., is indicated by all the symptoms already noted as characterizing Greek painting, sculpture and music. The chief are:

Less religious and more secular subject-matter.

Gradually heroes and even gods are depicted as mortal, while common, vulgar, sub-social and picturesque types become more popular as themes.

Description becomes more realistic and scientific.

Symbolism practically disappears.

Tragedy gives way to comedy, to satire, to burlesque and to the picaresque.

A false archaism in the attempted revival of archaic forms in more "modern" guise.

Increasing sensualism, eroticism and concentration upon pleasure as the only objective.

Development of "art for art's sake," aestheticism, art criticism, art education, art appreciation.

Growth of individualism among writers, with an emphasis on their professional character, mannerisms, vanity and influence marked also by improvement of their social and material position.

All these changing values are seen in the progressive evolution of Greek literature. The Old Comedy with Aristophanes, which developed after the death of Euripides, was in its origin and early stages also religious; but as the Middle Comedy and New Comedy succeeded it with Menander and Philemon, the gods and heroes disappeared, and with them went all mythological, religious, and heroic quality also. Surviving fragments indicate that practically all these later comedies dealt with very ordinary people; morality was at a low ebb and sexual themes were frequent.

With the later literature of the Hellenistic period, the sensate type reaches its extreme point. Its main characteristics are compactly summarized by Sorokin as including imitative epics in which contemporary potentates and patrons assumed the place of the gods and heroes in whom all belief had vanished; pedantically learned and super-scholarly poetry of the rococo type, thoroughly technical and scientific and therefore perfectly mediocre even in the works of its greatest representatives, such as Callimachus, Apollonius of Rhodes; bucolic and pastoral poetry of Theocritus, with his sugary shepherds and shepherdesses; mystery stories, epigrammatic and satirical literature, the extravagant rhetoric and riddles in the poetry of Lycophron and others; and the whole permeated by notorious Alexandrian eroticism and indecency.

Literary Criticism

Sorokin finds his views confirmed by the development of literary criticism among the Greeks. Other writers have been surprised that there were no literary critics before Plato and Aristotle, and some have concluded that the Greeks had no aesthetic consciousness or feeling for and appreciation of beauty until the Peloponnesian War.

Plato's attitude is characteristic. All readers of the *Republic* will recall the striking passages in which he proposes to censor poetry and to banish artists in order to ensure that literature should serve religious, moral, social and political values. Aristotle also, although he does not ally himself uncompromisingly with such views, is, as Saintsbury said, "doubly and triply ethical" in his appraisal of artistic effort.

After Aristotle, the development of rhetoric and the rise of the sensate school of literary critics is marked. Menander, Theophrastus, Pausanias, and Athenaeus are among the best known, but there were dozens of guides, manuals, and text-books, and scores of professional critics during the third and second centuries B.C., especially in the Pergamene and Alexandrian schools. Commentary after commentary was compiled on the classical works of Greek literature, such as those of Homer, which were analyzed from every conceivable point of view. As the mass of verbal criticism and technical rhetoric grew, so creative ability declined. There are few better illustrations than that provided by the literary productions during the late sensate age of the truth that artistic perfection is not a thing in itself, not something to be pursued in abstraction, but rather a quality achieved in devoted self-forgetful search for other values, desired for their own sake. The art of this later period of Greek literature, says Sorokin, became separated from other values — religion, morals, idealism, and philosophy — and, freed from their tutelage, turned into a mere source of sensual pleasure. Nothing was produced that was comparable with the works of Homer or Hesiod, Theognis, Pindar, Aeschylus, Sophocles, Euripides, Aristophanes, or even of the lesser creators in literature.

He might have added that aesthetic values are not singular in this respect. There are others which share the fate of aesthetic values if they are consciously pursued as ends in themselves. Beauty, peace, happiness and other great qualities are like the bloom on the peach. They have no existence apart from that of the healthy organism by which they are sustained. They are, as it were, a by-product generated by the organism's own health-giving activities which are undertaken usually with little or no consciousness of self-seeking, but always with reference to some ends or values transcending the self with which the self can be identified and submerged. Health, happiness, love itself are among those abstract qualities which, like literary creativity, elude the over-eager pursuer.

Roman literature, like Roman art in general, as Sorokin has already pointed out, suffered from an irresistible invasion relatively early in its own development by the whole weight of the Greek artistic and literary tradition, comprising almost all the works of all the famous Greek painters, sculptors and writers from the early ideational period, as well as those of the later sensate decline. The full splendor of this tremendous heritage, available to the Romans in its entirety instead of in the fragmentary form in which it has reached us, must indeed have been overpowering. Efforts were made by the Romans, as late as the middle of the first century B.C., to protect their native culture, but in vain. Cato the Censor (c. 234-149 B.C.) and Cicero's grandfather have been mentioned as typical of the strict Republicans who, throughout their lives, had set their faces against Greek influences. How completely the situation had changed by the first century B.C., in two generations, may be seen in the activities of Cicero himself. Nobody strove more energetically than he did to introduce Greek civilization and culture into Roman life. He was able to do it openly without apology or the danger of censure, from which, in an earlier generation, men as renowned and as able as Scipio Africanus and Caius Gracchus had by no means been immune.

Until the influence of Greece carried everything before it in Rome, art and literature remained archaic but sincere and predominantly ideational or idealistic, being mainly religious, magical, and moral. At the same time there was a strong undercurrent of rugged naturalism and rough but subdued sensatism which must have been immensely stimulated by the impact of sensate Hellenistic models. For this reason the idealistic period of Roman culture was cut short. It was compressed into the first century B.C. and the beginning of the first century A.D., and it is exemplified in the writings of Cicero, Sallust, Lucretius, Livy, Seneca, Virgil, and, to some extent, of Horace.

The strength of the purely sensate stream, Sorokin says, is evident in the idealistic materialism of Lucretius, and still more in the poems of Catullus and Ovid. Sorokin rightly omits any reference to Plautus and Terence, despite the fact that their plays antedate the works of these later writers, because they were but translations and adaptations of the Greek comic dramatists. He might however have referred to Ennius as an example of the early Roman ideational period. By the second half of the first century A.D. Roman society had become highly literary and aesthetically-minded, as the works of Persius, Petronius, Seneca the Younger, Juvenal and Martial show. There were many bookish aesthetes like Pliny the Younger and his friends. Quintilian well illustrates the vogue of criticism and the refinements of aesthetic theory. Despite the intensity with which it was cultivated, literary inspiration eluded the Romans in the most flourishing centuries of their vast Empire, the greatest and best organized that the Western European world has ever known. Aulus Gellius, Macrobius, Statius, Longinus are surviving examples of the barrenness that then pervaded life.

The most virile and cultivated literary form was that of satire, represented by Petronius, Juvenal, Martial, Persius and others. Tacitus was perhaps the greatest of them all, and he was as much a mordant critic of his age as he was a pure historian. Toward the end of the fourth and the beginning of the fifth centuries A.D., the sensate wave of Graeco-Hellenistic art had run its course and was dead. A sterile aestheticism lingered into the following century, of which Sorokin quotes one specimen provided by an extract from a letter of Sidonius Apollinaris, bishop, count, poet and critic, complimenting his friend Claudian on a new book he had just produced.

"O book multifariously pollent. O language, not of a thin, but a subtle mind! He feels like Pythagoras! He divides like Aristotle!... He 'suades' like Cato, dissuades like Appisu, persuades like Tully . . . He is instructive like Augustine. He soars like Hilary, and abases himself like John, reproves like Basil, consoles like Gregory" and so on.

It was from a low ebb such as this that the ideational Christian literature rose. Despite some survivals of the outmoded, outworn and artificial sensate style, the ideational stream was dominant by the end of the fifth century A.D., and it remained dominant for the following seven or eight hundred years. When again sensate cultural values gained in vigor in the thirteenth and fourteenth centuries, there was first a mixed idealistic style, soon swept away by a marked sensate literature which has endured with minor cross-currents until our own times.

In Italy, France, Germany and in England before the thirteenth century, there is practically no writing of consequence that was not devoted to religious themes. The rare exceptions are heroic poems like the *Hildebrandslied* in the ninth century and *Beowulf.* All the literary effort of these centuries went into the production of commentaries on the sacred books, the lives of saints, religious poems such as those of Cynewulf, and translations such as those of Bede, Orosius, Boethius, and St. Gregory.

Sorokin calls attention to the way in which symbolism during this period became a fundamental category of human thought dominating all the thinking and writing of the early Middle Ages. The Fathers of the Church — Gregory the Great, Dionysius the Areopagite, Cassiodorus, Boethius, Scotus Erigena, Isidore of Seville, Bede, and other writers, all show a determined search to find, expound, and interpret hidden meanings, whether in the Bible or in the works of pagan writers such as Cicero and Virgil. Everything in the world was forced to serve as symbols, signs and imperfect indications of the real world, the World of God, lying beyond and above this world.

The writers of such a period reveal in their choice of themes and manner of treatment the same exclusiveness that has already been mentioned as characteristic of the painting, sculpture, and music of an ideational age. Sorokin points to another feature distinguishing ideational literature in general that is also apparent in medieval literature, namely, its lack of perspective or sense of historical space and time. This feature, so strangely evident in the medieval treatment of classical and biblical figures who were regarded apparently as belonging to the same epoch as contemporary or recent medieval heroes and heroines, appears also in the highly ideational Brahmanic writings of India. The reason for it, says Sorokin, is evident. Ideational literature deals with and is moored to the eternal unchangeable world of Being, not to the fleeting and changing world of Becoming. History, as we know it, as a separate branch of thought and learning, cannot develop in a highly ideational society, as will be explained in more detail in the section on Being and Becoming.

Just as Sorokin has noted that great attention to literary techniques and the elaboration of critical standards are characteristic of a developed sensate age, so he remarks upon the absence of literary criticism during almost the whole of the Middle Ages. This is no new discovery of his. What is new is his analysis of what he regards as the main forms of human culture. Lacking any such comprehensive historical perspective of changing values and the rise and fall of systems of culture, other writers have sought to account for this lack of literary criticism in the Middle Ages by advancing various theories, some of which seem plausible and true up to a point. Some explain the matter by reference to the rule of the Roman Church "having imposed the fetters of religious dogma on the medieval mind"; or by biological analogy "the age being one of intellectual childhood, it was incapable of detachment and reflexion which all critical thought demands"; or by "the intellectual isolation of the Middle Ages and the prevailing ignorance of much that was best in the teaching of antiquity." These quotations are not from Sorokin but from J. W. H.

Atkins' review of the problem in *English Literary Criticism: the Medieval Phase,* Cambridge University Press, 1943.

The manner in which the early medieval ideational form of culture was succeeded under the growing impulse of sensate influences, first by a mixed idealistic phase and subsequently by unmistakably dominant sensate styles, will be evident to all acquainted with the nature of the national literatures of Western Europe. A brief summary survey listing some typical works is all that Sorokin attempts, and it is necessary to abridge it still further here.

In France, Germany, and England the proportion of religious among major writings, which was about 95 per cent in the ideational period, fell in the thirteenth and fourteenth centuries to about 30 to 55 per cent. The growing secular literature was however still permeated by the religious point of view so that it remained heroic, positive, ennobling and moralizing. In France, *La Chanson de Roland, Tristan et Iseult,* the *Roman de Renard,* the histories of Joinville and Froissart and the *Roman de la Rose* are outstanding. In England, there were the Arthurian romances and epics, and Langland's *The Vision Concerning Piers Plowman,* leading at the end to Chaucer and the dawn of a new age. To deal in any detail with the special characteristics of national literatures would upset the scale on which Sorokin had to plan his work. Its broad scope and universal range compelled him to deal in generalities which may not always fit particular epochs and specific countries. It is as though he is mapping whole continents: others must fill in the provinces and the counties. His readers will be able to compare his general analysis with that arising from their own reviews of the infinite detail of national cultures and national literatures.

English literature, for example, provides a special case in the survival of an English prose style of remarkable beauty and power until the fifteenth century, preserved and developed in the devotional literature of the English people during a period in which Norman French was the language of their rulers. Both because this is an aspect of English literature which has only recently received adequate recognition, through the work notably of G. R. Owst and of R. W. Chambers, and because it aptly illustrates the theory advanced by Sorokin, it deserves mention as one aspect of literary history and of the vitality of a culture; in this case the ideational value-system of pre-Conquest England.

If one work had to be selected as a pre-eminent example of the idealistic literature of medieval Europe, it would undoubtedly have to be Dante's *Divine Comedy*. Although it is still read and studied, it is not surprising to find it regarded today, in a new and very different age, as being among the waning classics. During 1950, for example, it was prominently placed, with other products of ideational and idealistic periods, in a list of boring works by students at Columbia University, New York.

The transition to the more sensate style is typified in the *Roman de la Rose*, probably the most popular work of its period. Sorokin points to the difference between the first and the second parts of this work. He considers that the first part, by Guillaume de Lorris, provides an allegorical treatment of sensate love at its sublimest, noblest, most decent, in a most delicate and most romantic form, according to the chivalric code of love. Somewhat later, Jean de Meung composed the second part, more fleshly, more sensate, partly cynical, erotic, and scoffing. He satirizes chastity, the clergy, kings, nobility and the monastic orders. He provided the motto *Fais ce que tu voudras* taken over later on by Rabelais. From a literature in which the sex of a saint is regarded as immaterial, to one in which a woman is distinguished sharply from man but reverenced and idolized, we move in the fourteenth and fifteenth centuries to a *bourgeois* attack on women as untrustworthy, sensual creatures, a necessary evil and a pest. Chaucer, who died in 1400 A.D., typified this transition for English readers, notably in his *Canterbury Tales*, in which the contemporaneous existence of ideational and grosser sensate value-systems is admirably portrayed. Romance and romantic love, the farce and comedy of everyday life, belief in magic, are portrayed together with a reverence for things holy which typify a mixture of cultural influences and indicate at the same time that new influences and tendencies were abroad. Later writings accentuated this development. Sorokin reports that an (unpublished) study of the number of occasions in which adultery or illicit sex relations are described in the literature of the period, indicating whether they are condemned, praised, or left without comment, gives statistical confirmation of the trend indicated. Similar results are forthcoming if search is made for other traits of sensate culture. The economic argument, for example, which has today become so much of an obsession that it is sometimes supposed to be a kind of key able to solve all problems of art, philosophy and social science, is virtually absent in literature before the twelfth century. In the idealistic period, it comes out in a religious guise, in complaints against moneylenders and, in the fourteenth century, antiquity." These quotations are not from Sorokin but from J. W. H.

especially after the Black Death, in references to the evils of avarice and speculation, the shortage of labor and the overtaxation of the laboring classes.

Another theme is that of duty *versus* revolt, the obligation to persevere even in painful and uncomfortable conditions, in ways of life recognized as obligatory. Ideational literature invariably regards religious and moral duty as absolute. Homage was still given to this requirement in idealistic literature, but some measure of flexibility in its observance was regarded as excusable in particularly difficult circumstances. At the same time patriotic and chivalrous duty began to be recognized, and to weaken proportionately the emphasis upon religious duty. In the fourteenth century, self-interest and material convenience grew much more powerful at the expense of a sense of duty — one clear symptom of an increasingly sensate cultural system.

Other symptoms include greater attention to the affairs of everyday life, to landscape and nature, to the common man and the lower classes, to real historical persons and the adoption of an increasingly dramatic, emotional and pathetic tone. Ideational literature is simple, serene, calm in an unfaltering faith in God and His providence. By the fourteenth century, a very melancholy, sad and pessimistic tone becomes evident, particularly in France. In England also the *Vision of William concerning Piers the Plowman* by a contemporary of Chaucer, the later *Piers the Plowman's Crede* (about 1393), and the works of Wyclif testify to an increasingly sombre outlook on life.

So it almost always happens, says Sorokin, when one major cultural system comes to an end and the next has not arrived. When the new form has come, the sadness will be replaced by the most optimistic assurances of progress and by a refreshing joy of life. If Sorokin is right, then it is wrong to suppose, as many critics and historians of literature have done, that a sufficient explanation of the cultural climate or temper of an age is to be found by reference to purely material conditions, though they are as catastrophic as the Black Death of 1348-9. Sorokin holds that it is the cultural temper that determines the manner in which material things exert any influence. His theory seems to have greater reason and plausibility than the view he contests, for if the melancholy tone of literature during the last half of the fourteenth century is to be attributed to the Black Death, it would be natural to suppose that all such calamities would always provoke a similar melancholy. But this is not a sequence which can be uniformly detected in history.

The transition from the ideational to the idealistic phase of culture is seen, Sorokin claims, in literature when symbolism yields to allegory. Sorokin is careful to emphasize the significant difference between the two. Symbolism attempts to indicate, by signs taken from the actual everyday world, the transcendental realities of the world beyond the senses. Allegory tries to endow abstractions, mostly taken from the sensory world, such as love, beauty, youth, liberty, hope, reason, purity, innocence, and so on, with a semblance of existence as though they were persons. In the *Roman de la Rose,* for example, such characters abound: Dame Leisure, Sir and Madame Wealth, Liberality, Frankness, Courtesy and Youth and others. Such a strange outmoded literary style is easier to understand if it is regarded, as Sorokin suggests, as a compound of the sensate and ideational aspects of reality, and typical therefore of idealistic art.

Interesting also is the suggestion that as this allegorical literature broke down, it survived in modified form in morality plays (such as *Everyman*) and mystery plays, but degenerated in the sixteenth century into euphuism and other artificial literary mannerisms which lingered on until the eighteenth century, when allegory practically disappeared.

The idealistic period was also the beginning of literary criticism, although it by no means attained any great development; Dante's *de Vulgari Eloquentia* and some parts of the work of St. Thomas Aquinas are probably the most notable critical works of this period.

Sorokin dates the domination of sensate literature and criticism from the fifteenth century up to the present time. He allows for minor ideational and idealistic fluctuations, but holds that they were merely ripplings upon a fairly continuously rising tide of sensatism that showed no signs of being halted until the end of the nineteenth century.

This trend is first noticeable in the increasingly secular nature of literature. Religious writing declined in quantity. For France, it may roughly be regarded as 100 per cent of all literature up to the twelfth century, 55 to 30 per cent from the twelfth to the fourteenth centuries, 25 to 20 per cent in the fifteenth century, 25 to 35 in the sixteenth, seventeenth, and eighteenth centuries, and about 10 per cent in the nineteenth, and twentieth centuries. Ten per cent of the literary production of the nineteenth century meant, of course, vastly more works than 55 per cent of the total product of the fifteenth century. More significant than this pure percentage decline, which is obviously a merely relative and not an absolute measure, is the far more important qualitative change in the nature of religious writing which became increasingly controversial, and, in the eighteenth century, increasingly irreligious. The quarrels between Protestants and Catholics, the quarrels of Protestant sects among themselves, the search for a more empirical matter-of-fact view of religion such as that undertaken by the Deists, not to mention the skeptical undermining of religion by the Encyclopedists and the openly ironical, satirical and slanderous attacks on asceticism, otherworldliness and religion and the priesthood, must all be included under the general heading of books on religious matters, but their style and content are quite foreign to that of an age inspired by ideational values.

Merely to mention some outstandingly popular works illustrating these tendencies would require many pages. Boccaccio's *Decameron,* de la Salle's *Cent nouvelles Nouvelles,* many of the works of Rabelais, Molière, Diderot, Swift, Lesage, and Voltaire may stand as typical of an outlook which was later to be perpetuated and accentuated in France alone by writers such as Zola, Flaubert and Anatole France among the better known.

Love as a theme of literature has shared the fate of religion in being progressively stripped of its idealistic character in order to be exhibited in a more sensual guise. The transition, says Sorokin, was from the idealistic love of Dante for Beatrice, to Petrarch's love for Laura, still delicate but permeated by sensate motives, to the sensual gallantries of Boccaccio, and thence to the obscenities of Aretino, Beccadelli, Lorenzo Valla and the buffooneries of Poliziano.

Where the tendency did not run to extremes, as in some of the works of the authors just cited, and when reticence and deference to etiquette are better preserved, as in the works of Castiglione, Poggio and others, there is little trace of idealism, still less of ideationality. In brief, says Sorokin, love as it is treated in literature changed within two hundred years from a purely platonic, almost ideational form devoid of sensuality, to a mere bedroom affair of crude sex physiology, not unmixed here and there with perversity. Logically and in practice, there can thereafter be no possibility of going farther along this road, the end of which had already been reached in Italy and France at least by the sixteenth century.

All that could be attempted by way of a search for novelty thereafter was to apply the same treatment to more and more classes of society on a wider range. It was a development aided by the technical improvements in printing and publishing which continually cheapened production and put books and periodicals within the reach of vaster masses of people whom compulsory free education was teaching to read and write.

The result, seen notably in French literature of the nineteenth and twentieth centuries, says Sorokin, was that sensual and sexual love, both normal and pathological, became the dominant theme: love of the old and the young, of the poor and the rich, love bought, love granted, love in this way and love in that − but love always hovering near the bedroom and rarely, if ever, idealized and never ideationalized. Chateaubriand, Mme de Stael, George Sand, A. de Musset, Stendhal, Balzac, Hugo, Merimée, Baudelaire, Zola, Maupassant, Verlaine, Daudet, France, Flaubert, Goncourt are among those included in his comprehensive enumeration of the sensate school from which their admirers will be hard put to extricate them. Sorokin is not, of course, concerned, as his language may suggest (for he makes no secret of his preference for idealism, if not for ideationalism) to draw up an indictment on puritanical lines, such as Robert Buchanan's well-known attack on 'The Fleshly School of Poetry' in England in the 1890's. His purpose is to place the writers quoted in the broad context of cultural development to which he considers them to belong.

He admits that he may overstress his case in the interests of brevity and clarity, and he realizes that all countries do not show the same developments at the same time, although the tendency in all of them is to move in the same direction. In England, for example, he does not allow Chaucer's *Canterbury Tales* any trace of ideational or idealistic inspiration, which seems rather hard on the Prioress and the clerk of Oxenford, although he acknowledges that Gower, Sir Thomas Wyatt and Roger Ascham, among others, maintained the earlier quality. It would not be difficult to add names, such as those of Sir Thomas More and others, to these perpetuators of idealistic traditions.

Preoccupation with economic questions is another unmistakable sign of sensate culture. Certainly it has developed on an increasing scale since the fifteenth century. Almost entirely absent during the ideational period, economic considerations and problems emerge in the idealistic period when, however, they receive scant treatment and are by no means to the fore. By the nineteenth and twentieth centuries, the most important themes of literature were either economic questions or economic interpretations of almost all forms of human endeavor. Love itself was not immune. Economic matters, such as food, drink, and material possessions, make the strongest appeal to all the organs of sense, so it is self-evident that the more the sensory nature of reality is emphasized, the more prominently will economic interpretations and considerations seem self-sufficient as a key to human thought and behavior. It is easy to see why literature became increasingly preoccupied with the generosity or wickedness of the rich, with the exploitation and the wrongs of the poor, with crimes attributed to the poverty, greed, hypocrisy, unfaithfulness, and self-seeking of all manner of people in various social groups.

The further and deeper that authors were able to carry such analyses, the greater was the degree of insight and wisdom attributed to them. Hence not literature alone, but psychology and other human and social studies were invaded in the nineteenth and twentieth centuries by attempts to provide an economic interpretation for every manner of human activity.

It is in the light of considerations such as these that Sorokin's explanation of the rise of capitalism is more satisfactory, because it is a more fundamental explanation than that provided by writers such as Max Weber, Ernst Troeltsch, or R. H. Tawney who have tried to find the impetus for the nascent economic enterprise of the sixteenth and seventeenth centuries in the theological and religious doctrines of the Protestant reformation. Without in any way detracting from the sound scholarship and great learning of these writers, Sorokin is nevertheless able, by relating both economic capitalism and Protestant ideas to the newly emerging sensate culture, to supersede the argument which sought to establish some cause-and-effect relationship between the two. This is a striking example of the scientific economy of his theory.

A third great distinguishing mark of a rising sensate literature is that the classes of people whose activities, thoughts and aspirations are made the themes of literary efforts in the sensate age include as broad a range of the common run of everyday folk as possible. The wide canvas filled by Chaucer has continually been enlarged, so that, after the fourteenth century, merchants, peasants, courtiers, artisans, servants, rogues, criminals, prostitutes, failures, derelicts, and the wretched become the subjects of literature; and to these are added, as time goes on, other plainly pathological types: murderers, swindlers, exploiters, hypocrites, scoundrels, profligates, idiots, and any other picturesque personalities. In this way among others, a sensate cultural epoch becomes an Age of the Common Man.

Shakespeare is a writer whose standing in Sorokin's scheme of cultural standards many readers will wish to have explained. Sorokin does not specifically include Shakespeare as a sensate writer, although he quotes others who have pointed to Shakespeare's naturalism. There are other unquestionably sensate qualities in his poems and plays, yet it is impossible to deny the idealistic insight and inspiration that characterize his work and are among his enduring titles to fame as an unrivalled interpreter of humanity. Sorokin recognizes Shakespeare's idealistic character by pointing out that his heroes, like those of most Elizabethan dramatists, are in the main truly heroic figures.

The same is true of the epic poems and romances, whose heroes in the fourteenth, fifteenth, sixteenth, and part of the seventeenth centuries were still drawn on a grand scale, paying little heed to the mediocre, the vulgar, the everyday and the banal. Ariosto's *Orlando Furioso,* Tasso's *Jerusalem Delivered,* Camoens' *Lusiad,* Ronsard's *La Franciade,* Spenser's *Faerie Queen* and Milton's *Paradise Lost* are outstanding examples of the vitality of the idealistic tradition in epic poetry.

Romances and novels, particularly those such as Malory's Arthurian romances and the innumerable *Amadis* stories, flourished until the seventeenth century, despite the gibes of Rabelais *(Pantagruel* and *Gargantua,* 1535-1552) and Cervantes *(Don Quixote,* 1605-1615). These stories of more exalted personalities and their adventures, which can often seem exceedingly boring and tedious to a modern reader, lost their popularity in the eighteenth century, when tales about heroes and heroines of a very much more matter-of-fact and everyday type rose in popular favor. It is not difficult to add to Sorokin's general account of the progress of this tendency in Western Europe a few details of its development drawn from the history of English literature.

There was no lack of idealistic influences in seventeenth century England after the death of Shakespeare, and it is not necessary to do more to establish the fact than to add to Sorokin's general review the names of some pronouncedly idealist writers, such as Henry More (1614-1687), George Fox (1624-91), John Bunyan (1628-88), Sir Thomas Browne (1605-82), Izaak Walton (1593-1683), Jeremy Taylor (1613-67), Richard Baxter (1615-91), John Milton (1608-74), George Herbert (1593-1633), Richard Crashaw (? 1613-49). Nevertheless such men stood out in strong contrast to many writers of the time. The underlying sensate culture evident in other aspects of life is made plain by careers such as those of John Donne (1573-1631), whose later piety and religious devotion atoned for a youth in which such qualities were very little in evidence.

After the Restoration of Charles II, the comedies of Aphra Behn (1640-89), William Wycherley (?1640-1715), William Congreve (1670-1729), Sir John Vanbrugh (1664-1726), George Farquhar (1678-1707), and Thomas Shadwell (?1642-1692) gave the most convincing evidence of the profoundly sensual character of the stage before Jeremy Collier delivered his attack on plays and playwrights in his famous pamphlet *A Short View of the Immorality and Profaneness of the English Stage* (1698).

Sorokin draws attention to another fundamental difference between sensate and ideational literary forms which is revealed most clearly by the drama. Sensate drama is essentially a show, an illusion, a temporary substitute for some reality. The ideational mystery and miracle plays were not of this order. They were not frequently performed and never for mere entertainment, amusement or pleasure. The very development of the theater is in itself a highly important symptom of the growth of the sensate culture. It therefore helps to explain why the reaction against the theater was so violent in a society loyal to ideational standards.

The forty years which separated the end of the Puritan regime in England from the beginning of the eighteenth century were sufficiently full of vigorous life and thought to render hazardous any attempt to sum up or to label the true characteristics of the period, so varied and so complex were it manifestations in many spheres of life. The *Mayflower* expedition to the New World in 1620 may symbolize the Puritan reaction to worldly excesses which remained a vigorous force in the minds of men for many generations after it seemed to have lost the battle politically and socially. It is not surpising, therefore, that the Puritan tradition survived to guide the life and conduct of vast numbers of men and women who were not born until long after it had apparently vanished away. Vital as this tradition has been and indeed yet remains, both in the United Kingdom and in the United States of America, it did not survive unblemished. It is sufficient to recall the prevailing temper of the age revealed in the lives of Charles II and his Court, in which characters like Samuel Pepys could pass as exemplary by comparison with the majority, to realize the increasingly sensate nature of English society. Sensate influences had far less opposition after the disappearance of the Revolutionary generation of Puritans. "Never before in this country," says a historian of English literature, "had men written so much about religion and practised it so little" as in the eighteenth century.

The rise of the English novel dates from this period. Daniel Defoe (?1661-1731), " a pioneer novelist of adventure and low life," was the first to write entertaining fiction about the lives of soldiers of fortune, pirates, prostitutes, and a deaf and dumb conjurer. It will be unnecessary to follow the development of the novel up to our own times through the work of Samuel Richardson (1689-1761), Henry Fielding (1707-54), Tobias Smollett (1721-71) and Laurence Sterne (1713-68) (remembering that Sterne was a priest of the Anglican Church) in order to add a few more English examples to illustrate Sorokin's conclusions. Today the majority of bookstalls and lending libraries with their high proportion of best-selling thrillers, detective stories and novels notable only for their more or less skillful variations upon the themes of sex, sadism, and violence, offer a daily incontrovertible demonstration of the victory of sensate cultural standards.

Stage entertainment has followed a similar course to arrive at the same end. The theatre critic of a London newspaper, *The Evening Standard,* on July 21, 1950 summed up the character of a popular stage show then running as "another example of the ruthless technique of Broadway in which a formula is rigidly prepared and relentlessly carried out. The basis of the play is Sex, Sadism and Sentimentality. To this is added some adolescent humor, a spice of idealism, a drop or two of patriotism and a quart of pretended innocence," concluding that "we are passing from art to photography while the undiscerning mob shout their joyous approval." At about the same time in 1950, another stage entertainment was being advertised by a single word coined by the same critic and triumphantly repeated in bright red letters by those promoting the show: "Sexcess."

The annual reports of the Public Morality Council provide chapter and verse about these persistent sensate trends, notably in its complaints about nudism on the London Stage. Since the first publication of my summary account of Sorokin's views in 1952, the failure to maintain the prohibition on the unexpurgated version of D. H. Lawrence's *Lady Chatterly's Lover* represented the virtually final defeat of a censorship which had until then maintained the traditional British reticence about the open discussion of sexual intercourse in the language of coarse, uneducated people.

Not merely has this concentration upon abnormality and low life characterized the novels and drama of the nineteenth century, but, Sorokin contends, it has effectively killed the capacity to depict heroic, positive social types. They have to be sought now in queer and abnormal personalities, such as Tolstoi's Pierre Bezoukhy or Dostoevsky's Raskolnikoff and Prince Myshkin, most of Ibsen's and Hauptmann's characters, the heroes of Zola, Maupassant, or even the best types of Charles Dickens. The alternative is to create what he describes as quite unreal purely "paper-made" synthetic *resonneurs* like Romain Rolland's *Jean Christophe* or to present a positive social type of a very cheap, very ordinary or doubtful quality like some of the proletarian characters of socialist-communist literature.

The reason, says Sorokin, is plain. The sensate, realistic mentality concentrating upon sensory perception sees human beings empirically as solely bioconscious, physiological entities moved by instincts, reflexes, complexes, and drives, often of the lowest animal order. Any attempt to

soar from this low level to introduce socioconscious controls serving some
value, or to create heroic characters, is frustrated. Sensate writers have
their wings clipped and are forced, says Sorokin, to crawl over the surface
of the earth. Earthbound, their vision is limited to very ordinary and very
evanescent mortal beings. The vogue of the satirical, ironical, and comical
in literature in general, and in novels, stories or plays in particular, is
another aspect of this same prevailing tendency. As we move into the
eighteenth, nineteenth, and twentieth centuries, the range of such satirical
writing has widened to include all the fundamental values of the ideational
and idealistic cultures until, Sorokin concludes, there is nothing left which
it has not slandered, ridiculed or debased. Religion, God, the saints, the
Virgin, angels, devils, sacraments, Paradise, Inferno, the Creed, the State,
the Government, aristocracy, nobility, talent, genius, sacrifice, altruism,
marriage, the family, asceticism, idealism, chastity, faithfulness, loyalty,
science, philosophy, moral duty, property, order, truth, beauty,
righteousness, man himself; everything and everybody are slandered,
satirized and defiled. Not a single value, Sorokin concludes after this
comprehensive list, has escaped.

The "debunking" biography, a relatively recent innovation, is
symptomatic of the same trend. Froude's *Life of Thomas Carlyle* (1884)
was an early precursor of a style that has attained a great vogue in recent
years, particularly since the First World War. Lytton Strachey (1880-1932)
led the way with a brilliant set of essays on four very diverse characters of
the generation before his own, whose only common quality, significantly
enough, was their outstanding attachment to religious experience and to a
quest for spiritual certitude which dominated their lives, as it also
dominated the lives of very many of their contemporaries, in a period
which clearly showed an idealistic reaction or ripple upon the prevailing
sensate tide. Strachey's four "Eminent Victorians" were the first martyrs
of an acid bath in which less skillful imitators have sought to devour
established reputations. Hardly any intimate or shameful details have been
regarded as irrelevant by this new school of biographers dismissed by
Sorokin as "dirt painters."

They may stand as examples of the tendency of literary criticism to
follow the same sensate evolution as literature itself. The lack, in an
ideational period, of criticism as an independent intellectual exercise
valuable in its own right has already been stressed. Using the findings of
historians of literary criticism, such as David Sauvageot and George
Saintsbury, Sorokin shows how its rise occurred in the fifteenth century

and how by A.D. 1600 it had become a recognized department of literature. Criticism then, as between the fourth and third centuries B.C. in Greece, still had religious and moral values as well as purely aesthetic standards as its criteria. With the sixteenth and subsequent centuries, the non-aesthetic ideational criteria became progressively less relevant. By a writer like Montaigne, literature and art are viewed chiefly as a means of amusement and enjoyment, and only partly of knowledge. In some countries, in France particularly, an effort was made through academies to codify the principles of aesthetic criticism which, had they been long respected, might have delayed the free development of sensate attitudes.

Sensible, moderate, rational, even scientific, this academic authority was powerful in the seventeenth century, and it survived into the eighteenth century, particularly in France, to sustain the fading light of idealism for two or three generations. How important criticism became is evident from the standing in the world of letters and of polite society of figures such as Addison, Johnson, Pope, Voltaire, Lessing, Diderot, Goethe, all of whom were notable for their critical opinions. The social and literary standing of the professional critic is now well established. Sorokin thinks that now, as in Rome during the later Roman Empire, most of their criticism is empty, ignorant, thoughtless, and negligible so far as its inner content is concerned, although it is powerful in other respects. For it is able to exercise a great influence upon the taste of the general public toward the good or bad, and to determine the success or failure, fame or tragedy, the poverty or fortune of artists and writers. He notes also the inevitable tendency towards linking critical opinions with the quantitative success of the work criticized so that books which sell in large quantities or plays with long runs are those praised by critics. At the same time these great successes have a short life, the best seller of one season being rapidly replaced by another. These conditions are reacting upon criticism itself, which is being replaced, Sorokin thinks, as an effective agency for creating public demand for books, by merely commercial forces: the skill of advertisers and public relations experts who are able to help publishers in the fierce competitive scramble for markets. Such agencies symbolize the bankruptcy of contemporary criticism, being anonymous and merely profit-making, not always administered by critics or connoisseurs of art or literature. Sorokin had contemporary tendencies in American publishing in mind, but similar complaints are not lacking in the British Isles. At the occasion of the Edinburgh Festival in August, 1950, Sir Stanley Unwin called attention to the danger that the same pressures might produce the same results in England also. Criticism of the critics by futurists, symbolists, surrealists and other modernists provides additional evidence of the crisis in sensate criticism, although it does not yet point to paths leading to a new and greater kingdom of art and literature and criticism. It will be evident that Sorokin's theory of the kinds of cultural activity briefly summarized above is based in the main upon the history of Western European civilization. He is chary of claiming that it is also adequate as a key to the art of the Middle and Far East, although he believes that it will be found to be equally useful as a guide to their cultural development.

Sorokin's analysis of the evolution of artistic and literary values has the merit not merely of providing a workable historical frame of reference, according to which changes in style can be grouped and explained, but of illuminating some difficult problems of aesthetic philosophy. He is able by its means to resolve the question whether "pure art," "art for art's sake," is or is not the true aesthetic ideal, superior to the opposite notion that art is only art if it worthily serves some purpose other than that of providing mere aesthetic satisfaction. The answer is plain. Those who champion "art for art's sake" have really been fighting for the sensate form of art, the direct and main function of which is to give sensate gratification, delight, pleasure, joy. To the extent that art is thereby separated from great values of society or of culture it may be said to have been "freed," but it is then simultaneously enslaved to sensations. So the true difference between "pure" (sensate) art and "impure" ideational art consists not in the fact that the one is free and the other is not (because it is the "handmaid of religion" for example), but in that they are subordinated to two quite different masters: one to hedonism, to emotions and sensations; the other to the ideational and idealistic values of religion, morals, civics, science, and philosophy.

The apparently greater freedom of the sensate artist is, moreover, an illusion as long as he is dependent upon finding someone to hire him and to give him the highest material or money value for his work. In a free market, or to use Sorokin's words — which however have become almost an abusive slogan — in a capitalist society, the highest bidder will be the rich and the powerful, the captains of industry and commerce. In a totalitarian society, everything must obey the dominant gangsters, whether military, demagogic, fascist, nazi, or communist. These classes are able to dispense with bids for support; all they need do, and they usually do it fairly quickly, is to silence, eliminate, or liquidate any writers or artists who do not support them. The sickening sycophancy of the tolerated performers with the brush or pen who remain and are allowed any activity in such a community is a quality vastly different from the genuine single-minded devotion of ideational and idealistic artists.

The ostensible servitude of artists in an ideational society is not felt as subservience, since no consciousness can arise of the separation of art from the other values which that society cherishes. Religion, philosophy, science, morals, civic patriotism, art, were organically one in Greek culture up to the end of the fourth century B.C. The same was true of the ideational medieval period in the West. Sensate culture can also be an integrated culture, despite its principle of diversity and the independence of its main values and activities. Its aesthetic category for instance seeks to be autonomous and separate from the other categories of truth, wisdom, religion, and moral principles. The task of integration is therefore doubly difficult because it is not felt to be essential.

Sorokin's account and analysis of the slogan "art for art's sake" is another example of the way in which he is able to offer wider, more inclusive, yet self-sufficient, standards of judgment than any provided hitherto in the history of art. He also has the merit of being able to show the strength and weakness, the degree of validity and effectiveness of the views and theories of other writers upon the history and appreciation of art. He briefly examines some of them. The theory of the German writer, Paul Ligeti, in his book, *Der Weg aus dem Chaos,* for example, is shown to be fallacious, because it attempts to see what Sorokin describes as ideational art•only in architecture, idealistic art only in sculpture and sensate art only in painting. Frank Chambers attempted, in his *Cycles of Taste* (1928) and *History of Taste* (1932), to account for the lack of art education, aesthetic theory, and art criticism in Sorokin's ideational period of Greek and medieval art by supposing them to be times when aesthetic consciousness and the appreciation of art did not exist, a supposition which Sorokin considers to be indeed strange if it is to explain Homer's *Iliad,* the Parthenon, or the Cathedral at Chartres with its ten thousand pieces of sculpture. Not only, he holds, is such a view clearly untenable, but the theory deduced from it, that creativeness in art falls as the development of art appreciation and art criticism rises, is equally false. There were critical standards in the days of Phidias, and before him, and also among the Fathers of the Church, but they were concerned with the extent to which art-forms were in agreement with, and able to express the main non-aesthetic ideational values. Saintsbury is nearer the truth when he wrote that "no constant ratio exists between periods of creation and periods of criticism."

Sorokin considers the correct view to be that which recognizes different forms of art, ideational and sensate, each with their masterpieces.

With some reservations he claims that one of the greatest periods of creativity in art usually occurs in the idealistic periods, when art is not yet divorced from the ideational world, and at the same time dresses itself in the noblest forms of sensate reality. So it was in the fifth century B.C. in Greece and in the thirteenth to the fifteenth century A.D. for architecture and sculpture; to the seventeenth for painting; and to the eighteenth and nineteenth centuries for music.

The strength of Sorokin's position in comparison with previous attempts to describe and explain the development of human culture clearly rests upon his insistence that it is essential to regard the main cultural systems as independent, unified entities. When this fundamental doctrine is accepted, a great number of earlier views become untenable. They can be seen to be the source of errors which Sorokin is able to avoid, because he refuses to use criteria appropriate to one cultural system in appraising the value of another. The fact that the ideational mentality is absolutist and centered upon a fixed value, makes it inevitably opposed to diversity and variety. For this reason it appears from a sensate standpoint, to be monotonous, poverty-stricken and boring. Those condemned to endure it are pitied as creatures living in the Dark Ages, as though, as Charles Lamb objected, they were crawling about in a world which knew no sunshine. It is more probable that they were, or many of them were, illumined by an inner light, since vanished from the earth.

The one cultural system cannot, therefore, yield principles by which the other can be condemned or praised, because the strong and marked differences between them are fundamental and cannot be brought into relation by terms common to each. Their basic major premises, says Sorokin, are incommensurable. They are therefore described in this work as cultural parameters.

The English philosopher R. G. Collingwood, whom Sorokin does not quote however, held that the analysis which detects absolute presuppositions may be called metaphysical analysis, that all metaphysical questions are historical questions, and that all metaphysical propositions are historical propositions. This insistence that metaphysical systems, as they succeed one another in the history of philosophy, must be understood as wholes and within their own frames of reference is a view common to both writers despite their differences in other respects.

Sorokin's provisional conclusion, therefore, that there can be two or three equally valid solutions to the problem of aesthetic values may stand until the history of other forms of cultural life, science, philosophy, law and ethics, and of forms of social, political, and economic organization has also been reviewed. On them also Sorokin has new insights to offer.

Philosophy

If the nature of any historic period of social life is to be understood as a whole, it is obviously impossible to stop short after reviewing its paintings, sculpture, architecture, music, drama, literature and criticism, despite the evident fact that many eminent students and investigators would consider it to be a very considerable performance to provide half as much, or less. After his comprehensive survey of all these subjects, Sorokin proceeds to devote a further volume of some seven hundred pages to the main trends in the development of philosophy, logic, scientific knowledge, ethics, legal systems, and the theory of the State in the history of Western European culture from its early Graeco-Roman foundations to our own day.

Again his conclusions rest upon the extraordinary amount of laborious research already described. The doubts and criticism excited by any effort to apply statistics to the history of art and literature are likely to become very much more serious when their subject matter is philosophy, ethics, and law. Yet it must be repeated that just as the refusal to be interested in the philosophy of history is itself a philosophical position, so the refusal to attempt to give greater precision and clarity to ideas about degrees of influence or philosophical importance, size, quantity, and number, relying instead upon rough estimates or vague guesses, is also to make value and quantitative judgments, although they will probably be crude, unreliable, and not really very enlightening.

A great deal depends obviously upon the philosophical ideas selected for study. The only way in which Sorokin has found it possible to bring so vast a field as philosophy, religion, and science under ordered examination in this way has been by selecting as the basis for his comparative study one or two of the critical major themes or special topics upon which philosophers and thinkers have generally been divided in successive cultural epochs in the history of Western thought.

These themes are idealism and materialism, being and becoming, realism, nominalism and conceptualism, society and the individual, the nature of personality in law, determinism and indeterminism, the idea of progress, optimism and pessimism, crime and punishment, the nature of space, time, number and causality, and of scientific thought generally.

Sorokin's main findings in this vast field of human speculation will therefore be reviewed and summarized.

Theories of Knowledge — There can be few more critically revealing aspects of the inward nature of any period of cultural development than the doctrine of knowledge and truth adopted by each system as the ultimate guide or goal. For it is clear that unless religions, philosophies, and sciences acknowledge the same standards of ultimate truth, there cannot very well be any presumption that they belong to the same type of culture. When, however, such common standards of truth distinguish two or more cultural systems, or their component elements, those systems are linked in a very definite manner. For Sorokin, such a common property is evidence of "a basic logico-meaningful identity."

Now to hold that there can be more than one logico-meaningful cultural system is to assume that there can be more than one standard of knowledge and truth. This is an assumption which does not occur naturally to the great majority of people, who accept without question the values and norms they find ready-made by the society or the culture into which they are born.

Sorokin arrived at the idea that there can be two or more systems of knowledge and value as a result of his study of the evolution of styles of painting and other arts. This conclusion may be provisionally accepted as basis for Sorokin's descriptive analysis of the main cultural systems in the expectation that an effort will later be made to review and reformulate it. On this provisional basis, in order to discover what are the main systems of knowledge and truth, he raises the further question, "Are the categories 'ideational', 'idealistic', and 'sensate' relevant to knowledge and to truth generally?"

It is logical to expect that the knowledge given by the organs of sense will be most unlikely to play a dominant or important part in an ideational culture in which the truth of faith inspired by God through revelation, intuition, or mystic experience will be thought to be the sole valid and certain guide.

A third possible source of knowledge and truth is that to be gained by human reason and logic. Those who put their faith in human reason are willing to examine both the evidence of the senses and what is offered as the testimony of revelation or intuition, trusting that the human intellect will succeed in judging how far each is valid. This mixed ideational-sensate outlook is characteristic of the idealistic culture.

There are, as Sorokin has been careful to emphasize, several other forms of mixed cultures beside the idealistic. There is the attitude of extreme skepticism and unbelief, and also the despairing state of mind which desperately wants to believe but cannot, which Sorokin describes as Fideism.

The three main systems with some samples of the subject matter of each and the way in which each considers truth to be attainable are summarized by Sorokin as follows:

Ideational Truth of Faith

Subject Matter: Supersensory and superrational: God, devil, angels, spirits, soul, immortality, salvation, sin, redemption, resurrection, purgatory, paradise, inferno.

Sensory and empirical phenomena are studied incidentally only, not for their own sakes, but as visible signs of the invisible world, as symbols of supersensory reality.

Theology is the supreme study. Exposition of the truth is based upon general principles (apodeictic) and is symbolic.

How Truth is Reached, or the Method of Validation: By reference to the sacred source or Scripture with which statements must be in accord. New truths must be shown to be due to the same divine inspiration or, in less theological language, to intuition. Purely logical reasoning and the testimony of the senses have a merely subsidiary role and are allowed only insofar as they do not contradict the truth of the revealed Scripture. Otherwise they are rejected as invalid or inspired by the devil, when they become heresy, blasphemy, or black magic.

Idealistic Truth of Reason

Subject Matter: Partly supersensory, partly sensory and empirical. Knowledge about sensory reality is not so highly valued, but it is sought and included as far as the scientific development of the time allows, and it is embodied in a total system of knowledge which usually takes the form of idealistically rationalistic philosophy. The ultimate reality is thought of as knowable, to be reached by reasonable argument based upon self-evident or agreed foundations or premises (i.e., the exposition is dialectic and deductive).

How Truth is Reached, or the Method of Validation: Mainly by logical reasoning but also by reference to the testimony of the senses. The findings both of reason and of sensory perception are supported by reference to sacred writings and revealed truth with the aim of including them all in an harmonious body of knowledge.

Sensate Truth of the Senses

Subject Matter: Mainly the world revealed by sensory perception. Any matters not easily reducible to sensory-material forms (such as thought, feeling, values) are dealt with either by concentrating upon their sensory aspect (e.g. as in behaviorism) or by disregarding their non-material aspect, which may be treated as subsidiary, irrelevant, unknowable, or non-existent (e.g. as in agnosticism, positivism). The natural sciences are then regarded as providing a pattern for the study of all other subjects.

Truth is to be reached by concentrating upon the facts, especially those to be reached by experiment (e.g. exposition is inductive).

How Truth is Reached, or the Method of Validation: Mainly by reference to the testimony of the senses reinforced by their extension through instruments or apparatus, such as microscopes, telescopes, and balances, supplemented by logical reasoning, especially in statistical and mathematical forms. All such findings remain provisional as hypotheses and are not accepted as proved until tested by the sensory facts. Hypotheses contradicted by the facts are unhesitatingly rejected. Sacred writings and faith in revelation have no place and are rejected as superstitious and as valueless. They are dismissed in much the same way as the findings of the senses are ignored by those who uphold an ideational system of knowledge.

This summary of the specific characteristics of the three main logico-meaningful cultural systems from the standpoint of their system of knowledge and truth arises from the historical record and the evidence provided in the works of the leading thinkers in Graeco-Roman and Western cultures from 580 B.C. to A.D. 1920.

Sorokin is careful to point out the inevitable limitations of this historical investigation. The sheer lack of information about the actual opinions of the great majority of people on such questions in the Middle Ages and in ancient times is the first, most obvious, and critically serious of these limitations. The problem of how to use what information we do possess is particularly difficult, because it is not a question of merely counting up the expressions of opinion on the nature of truth but of attempting some assessment of their relative influences.

Sorokin, with the aid of two leading Russian professors of philosophy, set about this task. They adopted a scale of "marks" or "credits," and sought to credit every known thinker with his appropriate rating or weight in this scale. It is not a question of assigning marks according to the scientific or any other value of the various thinkers, but solely of the extent to which their work and example influenced others. Everybody who writes or reflects upon the history of thought is led to make such estimates. Sorokin seeks to make them as thoroughly and as scientifically as possible by boldly trying to devise a scale of magnitude to show such influences. The history of culture obviously has much to gain from a sound judgment in this first step of judging the relative *influence* of leading thinkers. The criteria used in preparing this rough measure of the comparative influence of great philosophers are listed as the following:

a. The number of special studies or monographs devoted to a philosopher.

b. The approximate number of times the philosopher's name has been mentioned in the works of his contemporaries and later philosophers and thinkers.

c. Whether he was a founder of a school of philosophical thought.

d. Whether his name is mentioned in elementary textbooks on the history and the theory of knowledge.

e. The number of his disciples and followers.

f. Whether his works have been translated into foreign languages.

g. Whether his works have been frequently republished.

h. Whether he was the creator of an original and complete system of philosophy and epistemology.

Sorokin and his collaborators claim to have considered almost all the relevant facts under the above eight headings. After doing so, they assigned to each thinker the value between one and twelve which seemed to them to adequately indicate his status and influence in the particular branch of the history of human thought they were attempting to review. The merit of such a procedure is to reduce the influence of subjective elements in estimating the standing of thinkers. Some sample valuations of the thinkers listed under their various schools of thought will best illustrate the procedure followed. Sorokin's lists contain many more names than those given in the following pages, which merely list some of the better-known writers.

RATIONALISM, 560 B.C.–A.D. 1920

Anaximander	5	Thomas Aquinas	12	Tillotson	2
Heraclitus	7	Copernicus	8	Kant	12
Pythagoras	8	G. Bruno	8	Swedenborg	4
Parmenides	7	Descartes	8	Lessing	6
Zeno	5	Comenius	7	Goethe	8
Socrates	9	Pascal	7	Hegel	8
Euclid	3	Malebranche	7	V. Cousin	4
Plato	12	Guelincz	6	Whewell	6
Aristotle	12	H. More	4	Rosmini	6
Alcuin	4	Leibniz	9	Boole	4
Photius	3	Spinoza	8	Bradley	7
Adelard of Bath	2	Cudworth	5	Bosanquet	4
Abelard	4	Bossuet	6	Michelet	2
R. Grosseteste	4	Fénelon	6	McTaggart	5
Albert the Great	8				

MYSTICISM, 360 B.C.–A.D. 1920

Plato after 385 B.C.	12	Comenius	7	Schelling	8
Xenocrates	3	H. More	4	Schopenhauer	8
Nigidius Figulus	4	Malebranche	7	W. Blake	4
Philo Judaeus	8	Arnauld	4	Hegel	8
Plutarch	8	Nicole	4	Shelley	6
Plotinus	12	Cudworth	5	Schleiermacher	4
Macrobius	4	Shaftesbury	5	Schlegel	4
Maximus Confessor	6	A. Collier	5	Emerson	6
John Scotus Erigena	8	Berkeley	8	Ruskin	6
Anselm	7	J. Edwards	1	J. Erdman	4
Bernard of Clairvaux	5	Sam Johnson	1	Bergson	8
Eckhart	8	Rousseau	8	M. Eddy	4
Thomas à Kempis	4	MASONS:		Michelet	2
Paracelsus	4	English Masons	4	Dostoevski	8
St. John of the Cross	4	French Lodge, The		Hartmann	8
G. Bruno	8	Great East	4	Bradley	7
Cardan	6	Russian Masons	4	Soloviev	6
St. Theresa	6	Jacobi	6	Steiner	4
Jacob Boehme	6	Herder	6	Tolstoi	8

| Pascal | 7 | Fichte | 8 | Nietzsche | 9 |
| Spinoza | 8 | | | | |

FIDEISM, 400 B.C.–A.D. 1920

Antisthenes	5	Seneca	8	Jacobi	6
Diogenes	5	Lucius Cornutus	4	Fichte	8
Crates	4	Musonius Rufut	5	Lammenais	4
Zeno	8	Epictetus	6	Hamilton	6
Cleanthes	5	Dio Chrysostom	6	Mansel	2
Menippus	5	Marcus Aurelius	6	McCosh	4
Chrysippus	7	Peter Damian	3	Khomiakov	4
Panaetius	5	Loyola	8	Gratry	1
Q. Mucius Scaevola	1	Pascal	7	Cousin	1
Posidonius	7	Reid	4	Sigwart	5
Cato	2	Beattie	2	Renouvier	7
Cicero	8				

SCEPTICISM, 460 B.C.–A.D. 1920

Protagoras	8	Sextus Empiricus	6	Diderot	6
Gorgias	5	John of Janduno	3	Hume	8
Critias	3	Nicholas of Autrecourt	4	L. Feuerbach	6
Thrasymacus	3	Montaigne	6	J. Stuart Mill	8
Hippias	4	Charron	2	Kierkegaard	4
Aristippus	6	La Rochefoucauld	1	Renan	6
Pyrrho	6	Glanvill	2	Nietzsche	9
Timon	3	Bayle	6	Pierce	1
Carneades	5	D'Alembert	5		

EMPIRICISM, 580 B.C.–A.D. 1500

Thales	4	Lucretius	8	Manichees	3
Anaximenes	2	Asclepiades of Prusa	4	John Chrysostom	5
Diogenes	3	Celsus	1	John of Salisbury	3
Empedocles	6	Galen	7	Alexander Neckham	2
Democritus	8	Tertullian	6	Roger Bacon	6
Xenophon	7	Longinus	2	William of Ockham	8
Epicurus	8	Diogenes Laertius	3	Buridan	2
Apollodorus	2	Eusebius	3	Nicolaus (Oresme)	2
Zeno	2				

EMPIRICISM, A.D. 1500–1920

B. Telesius	6	Brown	4	Helmholtz	6
Bacon	7	D. Stewart	4	Hamilton	6
Herbert of Cherbury	4	Gauss	4	Du Bois Reymond	5
R. Boyle	4	James Mill	6	Galton	6
Newton	9	Bentham	6	Binet	4
Locke	8	Cuvier	8	Baldwin	5
Leeuwenhoek	5	H. Spencer	8	de Roberty	3
Hooke	5	J. S. Mill	8	Brentano	4
Buffon	6	A. Comte	8	Meinong	3
Voltaire	7	Purkinje	6	Tönnies	4
Montesquieu	6	Buckle	5	Croom Robertson	4
Hutcheson	4	Lafitte	5	G. Gompertz	4
Condillac	6	G. Grote	2	Masaryk	4
Reid	4	C. Darwin	8	Mach	6
Pestalozzi	8	Liebig	4	W. James	7

The above, it must be repeated, are merely a selection of some names according to one of the many classifications used by Sorokin. His full lists occupy seventy-five pages of small print in double columns.

Such catalogues obviously present a very plain target for criticism, and long arguments might range around almost any of the valuations, apart from any questions about the validity of the basis on which they are made. That Rousseau, Locke, Fichte, and Darwin should be equated in their influence, for example, may seem a surprising result. So is the equation of a world figure such as Voltaire with the relatively little-known Renouvier both with credits of 7. The temptation to dismiss all the elaborately constructed tables of evaluation all because of disagreement over a point or two in the marks or ratings of various individual thinkers, may appeal to critics in a hurry to discredit a novelty, but to yield to it would be to overlook the fact that discrepancies of this order of magnitude have little or no effect on the broad trend and cumulative results. Like the multitude of small dots which collectively make up each pictorial illustration in a daily newspaper, the individual ratings contribute to a general effect which would not be noticeably different even though here and there one or two, when seen through a magnifying glass, may be slightly larger or smaller than they should have been. The rating assigned to some thinkers varies with the classification under which they appear. Thus Jeremy Bentham, whose influence may have seemed undervalued by being listed as 6 among empirical thinkers, is given a rating of 7 when classified among the upholders of the theory of determinism. Samuel Johnson, assigned only 1 as a mystic, gets 6 as an upholder of the ethics of principles. Despite the length of the lists and the large number of thinkers included in them whose names will be unfamiliar to any except specialists, there are one or two omissions of which the more notable for English readers will be Richard Rolle of Hampole (1290?-1349); Joseph Butler, on whose famous *Analogy of Revealed Religion* (1736) generations of English clergy have been trained; William Law who through his *Serious Call to a Devout and Holy Life* (1728) has also had a wide influence; and William Wordsworth (1770-1850). This is a small matter in comparison with what has been included to illustrate Western cultural development by showing as concisely as possible the influence of any given thinker, the number of thinkers in a given movement of thought, and the strength of that movement.

Sorokin recognizes and emphatically rejects the objection that cultural matters cannot be weighed and measured in this way. The very people who object do it themselves all the time, but they do it vaguely and without committing themselves too far. They use such generalizations as "it was the epoch of the rise and triumph of . . . materialism . . . nominalism . . . socialism . . . or the Gothic style of architecture;" "Kant was one of the greatest philosophers;" "the period was marked by an increase in riots, revolts and disorders." Statements of this kind, used to give some rough indication of the comparative influence, popularity, magnitude, value, size, frequency, or the increase or decrease, growth or decline, rise or fall of various cultural phenomena, may be called *verbal quantitative* propositions in contrast with Sorokin's resolute effort to substitute *numerical quantitative* propositions for them. There can be little doubt that, as well as being vague, the *verbal quantitative* description is a lazy way of comparing magnitudes. One of the dangers of trying to substitute numerical quantitative descriptions for it arises from this laziness of readers who may be tempted to take on trust and without examination the hard work of others, such as Sorokin. It is a danger increased by the natural inclination or the necessity to make some numerical estimate upon what may often be inadequate grounds. The figures might then seem to lay claim to greater precision and certainty than the real state of knowledge would warrant. The aim must be to guard against such dangers without giving excuses to those who would prefer to cover up their disinclination to grapple with a tough problem by adopting an attitude of general skepticism about the possibility of achieving any reliable estimates at all.

The search for clear and distinct ideas in this field cannot be held up by such fears and hesitations. Sorokin would be the first to welcome greater precision, and his work remains a standing challenge to those able either to prove its invalidity or to organize co-operative research so as to investigate with greater intensity and accuracy the rise and fall of systems and types of human culture in whose detailed history and quantitative assessment he has sought to pioneer. The first task was to assess the individual contributions of distinguished and representative thinkers and writers on a scale of significant influence from 1 to 12. Then Sorokin grouped the thinkers in their various schools of thought to indicate the fluctuations in the main systems of truth. Here he expands his broad three classes of the truths of faith, of reason, and of the senses, using instead the following six classes:

A. Empiricism: the truth of the senses.
B. Rationalism:
    a. Religious or ideational rationalism, the truth of faith.
    b. Idealistic rationalism, the truth of logic; of the human mind, its laws, categories and concepts.
C. Mysticism: a less rational and more esoteric brand of the truth of faith than religious rationalism.
D. Scepticism: methodical doubting of the possibility of human knowledge.
E. Fideism: logically connected with scepticism in that it believes that the truth of the most important principles and facts cannot be obtained through mere cognition, empirical or rational, but is to be achieved through the act of volition, the will to believe or instinct. Related to mysticism, and not merely negative like scepticism.
F. Criticism or Agnosticism: contends that the phenomenal or empirical world alone is accessible to our knowledge, while the ultimate or transcendental reality, whether it exists or not, is inaccessible and need not be known. It thus occupies a somewhat middle position between empiricism, rationalism, and skepticism, but is closer to empiricism.

On the basis of his numerical assessments already described above, he then calculates the way in which the influence of these six main systems of truth has fluctuated between 580 B.C. and A.D. 1920. The results are shown first in a table of changes for every twenty years, and secondly in another for every hundred years in these twenty-five centuries. They have also been shown in graphic form on page 127.

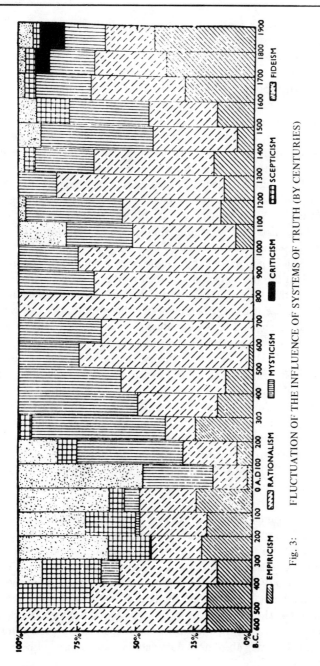

Fig. 3:   FLUCTUATION OF THE INFLUENCE OF SYSTEMS OF TRUTH (BY CENTURIES)

Sorokin draws attention to one or two conclusions suggested by the results of this statistical study.

The first is the absence of any single line of advance or progress. None of the main systems has steadily increased, decreased or remained constant. The popular notion, therefore, that there has been a progressively increasing acceptance of the empirical truth of the senses at the expense of a continually declining loyalty to the truth of faith (religious rationalism, mysticism and fideism) or to the truth of reason (idealistic rationalism) is shown to be false. Such a movement is indeed characteristic of the last five centuries and is additional evidence of the predominantly sensate character of their culture. It is evident that a similar progress of empiricism was not maintained after its early beginnings in the sixth century B.C., when it grew only to decline once more in the third century B.C., thereafter remaining almost non-existent from the fifth to the eleventh century A.D.

The notion popularized by Comte that mankind passes from the theological to the metaphysical and then to the positive stage, which has been called the law of three states, does not fit the facts. It seems plausible, because it gives pre-eminence to the empirical sensate system in which we are living and to whose values therefore those of the theological and metaphysical stages appear as preparatory and inferior.

Similarly, Herbert Spencer's theory that society and culture move from a less differentiated and integrated to an increasingly differentiated and integrated system is also contradicted. Since the Middle Ages it is true that such a development has occurred, but the Middle Ages themselves showed, says Sorokin, a recession to simplicity after the complex society on whose ruins they were established had passed away. Spencer might conceivably have retorted that his theory stands up a good deal better if continuity in the history of the Middle Ages is looked for in the story of the Germanic tribes who broke the Graeco-Roman cultural pattern. The fact that the pattern broke would, however, remain to indicate the occurrence of fundamental change or of weaknesses of which many other symptoms abounded, all of which demand explanation. This is a question which will call for further consideration in studying Sorokin's views about the nature and causes of fluctuations in cultural systems.

The difficulty of measuring cultural trends is illustrated at the outset of Sorokin's historical survey of the first of his six systems of truth and knowledge. On the basis of the work of but one thinker, Thales, about whom very little is known, it might be concluded that the period from 580 B.C. to 560 B.C. was absolutely dominated by empiricism, although there are plausible grounds for regarding him as very similar to the religious rationalists, idealists, and believers in a divine providential control of the universe. Later Greek thinkers about whom more is known show that up to about 460 B.C. the truth of faith, represented by ideational or religious rationalism, amounted to about 90 per cent of all the systems of truth. Thereafter the truth of the senses, empiricism, grew, remaining strong with minor fluctuations. From 460 B.C. to 400 B.C., the nature philosophers, Empedocles and Democritus, the Sophists and others, brought about the development of the natural sciences in Greece which were further developed, especially between 320 B.C. to 260 B.C., the period of the Epicureans and the disciples of Democritus.

It was a movement which had its echo in Rome, particularly between 120-20 B.C., the epoch of Lucretius, the Graeco-Roman materialists and Epicureans. In Rome also there were some discoveries in the natural sciences at this time. The empirical way of thinking then seems to have weakened and remained low until about A.D. 200-360, the time of Gallienus and the Peripatetics, as well as of some of the empirically inclined Church Fathers and Manicheans. Then it flared up and remained comparatively high until about A.D. 480. After about A.D. 540 it disappeared, submerged by Christianity's rising truth of faith, and it did not again come into evidence until about A.D. 1100. Gaining influence fairly steadily in the twelfth, thirteenth, and fourteenth centuries, empiricism was not yet dominant, and indeed it disappeared in the first half of the fifteenth century. The following notable short upward waves of empiricism occurred around

A.D. 1100	Roscellinus and others;
1180	John of Salisbury, Alfred of England, Alexander Neckham;
1220	Michael Scott, Roland of Cremona;
1230-1250	Bartholomew Anglicus;
1260	Roger Bacon;
1320-1340	William Ockham, Buridan, Nicholas of Oresme, Albertus of Saxony;
1460-1500	Gabriel Biel

After about 1460, when empiricism re-emerged, it rose rapidly, especially in the sixteenth century and, after minor fluctuations, reached the extraordinary and unique indicator of 42 per cent for the whole of the nineteenth century, and the still higher figure of 53 per cent for the first twenty years of the twentieth century. High as these percentages are, many readers will probably be surprised that they are not very much higher. Sorokin does not, however, belong to the "all or none" school of sweeping generalizations, and his method reveals the complex nature of the reality he seeks to portray.

Recessions in the forward surging wave of empiricism occurred in the second half of the sixteenth century, in part of the seventeenth and at the beginning of the nineteenth century.

Discoveries and Inventions — Sorokin supports the conclusions arrived at by his statistical survey of the number and influence of empirical or sensate philosophers and thinkers by an independent investigation of the number of discoveries and inventions in the natural sciences. Not merely were the computations upon which this second investigation was based taken from entirely different sources, but they were provided by another set of workers who were unaware of the first enquiry. Not surprisingly, they found that the development of natural sciences and of inventions aid each other and therefore occur at the same time. Both are products of a sensate mentality.

Using as a foundation the co-operative chronological survey provided by twenty-six German scientists in Darmstädter's *Handbuch zur Geschichte der Naturwissenschaften und der Technik,* Sorokin and his collaborators constructed statistical tables to show for nine main branches of science (mathematics, astronomy, biology, medical science, chemistry, physics, geology and technology), the number of inventions in each by 100-year periods from 800 B.C. to A.D. 1500 and by 25-year periods from 1501 to 1908. From these tables, a series of graphs were drawn, of which that reproduced as Fig. 4 may be regarded as summarizing the main conclusions reac

Lack of data unfortunately makes it impossible to extend the chart to include Egypt and the ancient civilizations of the Near East.

When the study is pushed into an investigation in greater detail of the contribution of various countries to the sum total of inventions and discoveries in more modern times, it becomes evident that no continuous or single line of development has occurred in the progress of discovery. This fact is interestingly brought out by Sorokin in another chart not reproduced here. By these means, Sorokin succeeded in showing that there has been a positive correlation between periods in which the truth of the senses was dominant and a correspondingly high rate of discovery and invention.

He is also able to show that the domination of the truth of faith is negatively correlated with the progress of discovery and invention, as a comparison of Fig. 3 and Fig. 4 will show, despite the combination in Fig. 3, under the heading "rationalism," of both ideational and idealistic rationalism. Looking at the evidence respecting the dominance of religious

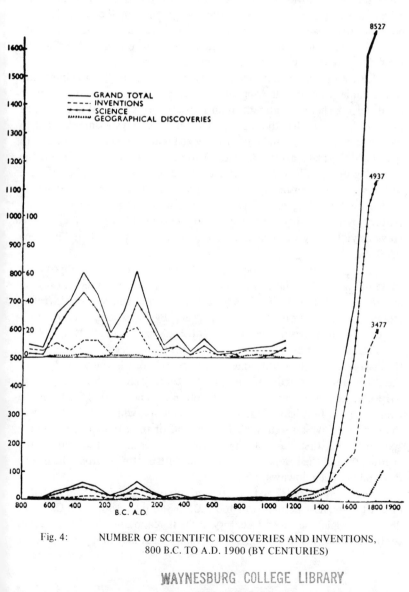

Fig. 4:   NUMBER OF SCIENTIFIC DISCOVERIES AND INVENTIONS,
                   800 B.C. TO A.D. 1900 (BY CENTURIES)

or idealistic rationalism, mysticism, and fideism, it is evident from Fig. 3 that throughout the period from the beginning of our era to the end of the fifth century A.D. these three currents of the truth of faith were dominant. Mysticism and fideism were then strongly in evidence, as they were not before the fifth century B.C. or after the sixth century A.D., when the pure ideational truth of faith completely dominated the scene, driving out empiricism and scepticism and so removing the main source of both mysticism and fideism. In the sixteenth century the last desperate effort was made to maintain the influence of the truth of faith before the steady decline set in which has continued ever since.

Neither mysticism nor fideism is a movement likely to achieve any considerable popular following, and it seems rather unnecessary to single them out for special treatment in an introductory survey. It is interesting to note, however, that the main periods in which mysticism appeared to provide a satisfactory source of truth were about the middle of the fourth century B.C. (Plato after 385 B.C., Xenocrates and others); around the beginning of the Christian era (Philo, Nigidius, Figulus, and others); the fifth to seventh centuries A.D.; the ninth century; a high point in the twelfth century (Erigena, Maximus Confessor, and others); the fourteenth century, remaining high in the sixteenth century although not so high as previously. There were slight crescendos from 1660 to 1720 and between 1780 and 1840.

Atheism may logically be expected to show movements opposite to those of the truth of faith, but parallel with the truth of the senses. Thus before the fifth century B.C., there is scarcely one atheist, but thereafter criminal condemnation of impiety appears. By the second century A.D., the decrease in atheism becomes evident. It disappears in the Middle Ages.

Idealistic rationalism was prominent between 540-450 B.C. (Pythagoreanism, Heraclitus and the Eleatic school); in the second half of the fifth and first half of the fourth century B.C. (Socrates, Plato, Aristotle, and others); again about 200 B.C.; about 80 B.C.; from the twelfth to the first half of the fourteenth century, which was its climax in the history of Western culture; the first half of the fifteenth century; the sixteenth and first half of the seventeenth centuries; the end of the eighteenth, and the beginning of the nineteenth centuries, after which time its trend has been downward.

It remains to note that scepticism, although not a system of truth, reached its highest points from 460 B.C. to 380 B.C., 180-120 B.C., about 20 B.C. and in the second century A.D. It reappeared in the sixteenth century, since when it has existed as a minor stream of thought, especially notable in the periods 1520-1540, 1560-1600, 1740-1780. Scepticism therefore emerges when the truth of faith declines and the the truth of reason, and particularly truth of the senses, find more followers. As empiricism triumphs, scepticism retreats; but not to vanish as it does when the truth of faith is dominant. When scepticism fades, so also does fideism, since fideism is the desperate reaction which scepticism provokes. Looking ahead, some connection may be noted between the growth of scepticism and social upheavals.

Criticism, as a distinct development in philosophy, was a late manifestation at the end of the eighteenth century, seen especially in the work of Hume and Kant. After a temporary recession it resumed its growth after 1860 to become, next to empiricism the most powerful current in philosophical thought. Its movements, being almost opposite to those of skepticism, suggest to Sorokin that it fulfills functions which scepticism is unable to perform at certain periods in the history of thought.

Summing up the totals provided by his system of indicators for the whole period studied, he records the following relative weights. It may here be pointed out that the combined totals of the "weights" of influence of all the thinkers in the various schools of thought corrects the bias shown by the percentages of such thinkers at any one time, such as that noticed on page 127 Thales produced a record of 100 per cent for materialism in the period 580 to 560 B.C., but this contribution to the total weight of that school is only 4.

Truth of Faith,

　　composed of mysticism, fideism and religious rationalism　. . . . 1650

Truth of Reason　. 1292

Truth of Senses, composed of empiricism　. 1338

Scepticism and Criticism　. 476

From these results Sorokin concludes that religious and idealistic rationalism has so far been the most powerful system of truth, empiricism being next in importance. The record suggests, says Sorokin, the principle of self-regulation of cultural processes and their automatic tendency to balance one another. Possibly also, he thinks, each form of truth has its own part to play in the life of the mind and of society and that each may be equally necessary. Such in outline are the main features of Sorokin's views on the main trends in one significant aspect of the history of philosophy. His many quotations illustrating his conclusions cannot be reproduced here, but may be followed in the second volume of *Social and Cultural Dynamics.*

Every reader will no doubt test Sorokin's theories for himself in the light both of his own conceptual framework, resulting from his own independent study, and of his own detailed knowledge of special periods in the development of human thought.

Idealism and Materialism — Before leaving philosophy and the history of thought, Sorokin examines the varying fate of other first principles or fundamental concepts during the time that has elapsed since they were first discussed by the Ancient Greeks.

The first such additional principles are the well-known opposing schools of thought of idealism and materialism and the mixed theories based on each. Idealism maintains that the ultimate or true reality is spiritual; that it is God, spirit, soul or mind, or Platonic ideas. According to these views, reality is immaterial, spiritual, or psychical in essence. Two main types of idealism may be distinguished. *Monistic Idealism* regards all individual and separate systems of immaterial and spiritual reality as being but the temporary manifestation of one ultimate, all-embracing spiritual being, whether it be thought of as God or the Absolute: Absolute Idea for instance; Mind or Spirit. *Pluralistic Idealism,* still believing in the immaterial nature of reality, views it as being made up not of one fundamentally simple system but of a multitude of independent centers or systems of spiritual reality, such as souls, spirits, or monads, which together constitute the ultimate reality.

In striking contrast with the two types of idealism stand the many varieties of materialism. Sorokin singles out two as the main and most important types. The first form regards ultimate reality as living matter capable of sensation, of striving, and to some extent of possessing consciousness. This form he calls *Hylozoistic Materialism.* Hylozoism, from two Greek words meaning "matter" and "life," was a word used by Cudworth in the seventeenth century. The second form, *Mechanistic Materialism,* is materialistic in a more thorough-going way, since it regards spiritual and immaterial phenomena, if indeed they can be said to have any true reality, as a passive product of matter and of mechanical motions of material stuff or particles.

Mixed forms of idealism and materialism include skepticism, agnosticism, and critical philosophy.

In order to assess the relative influence of these various attitudes towards fundamental reality, Sorokin and his collaborators again classified all the thinkers who have written about them, assigning to each an appropriate weight on the scale of 1 to 12, in the manner already described in the treatment of the various systems of truth. The results have been embodied in a series of statistical tables which are shown in graphic form in Fig. 5.

Sorokin again explains that the years 580-540 B.C. are misleadingly classified as completely under the sway of hylozoistic materialism, owing to the fact that only two names, Thales and Anaximander, are known. The probability is that the period was in fact predominantly idealistic. Making due allowance for this necessary adjustment, Sorokin is able to show that idealism is correlated closely with the truth of faith and materialism with the truth of the senses. If not in all the minor fluctuations, then at least in the main waves, the empirical system of truth of the senses shows itself as being positively associated with materialism. The truth of faith is similarly associated with idealism, especially in its pluralistic form. The truth of reason is linked less with religion and more with dialectical idealism, especially with monistic idealism. Significantly enough, reliance upon the truth of reason began again to manifest itself in the thirteenth century. Sorokin describes the more intellectual, argumentative, idealistic systems of the twelfth and thirteenth centuries as dialectical, to distinguish them from the simple, purely religious idealism of earlier centuries.

It follows that the empirical system of truth, materialism and scientific discoveries are closely associated. They are negatively related to the truth of faith and to pluralistic idealism. Such results are not very surprising, and indeed are, as Sorokin points out, logically to be expected. They reinforce the view already become familiar, that the predominant form of culture in Greece in the sixth, fifth, and fourth centuries B.C. was mainly ideational and idealistic. In the centuries from the third to the beginning of our era, culture was mainly sensate. From the first to the sixth centuries A.D. there was a decline in the sensate and rise in the ideational culture. From the sixth to the twelfth centuries, the ideational culture prevailed virtually to the total exclusion of all other forms. The twelfth, thirteenth, and fourteenth centuries were mainly idealistic, but the tide of sensate culture was rising. A desperate reaction against its onset was made during the fifteenth century, but it did not succeed in damming back the sensate tide which has steadily gained, with minor fluctuations, ever since it again began to rise in the sixteenth century.

Sorokin's views may be illustrated by the contrast at the end of the seventeenth century between the newer materialism and the older idealism summed up in the controversy between John Locke and Leibniz. The mind, said Locke, is a blank until actual experience imprints impressions

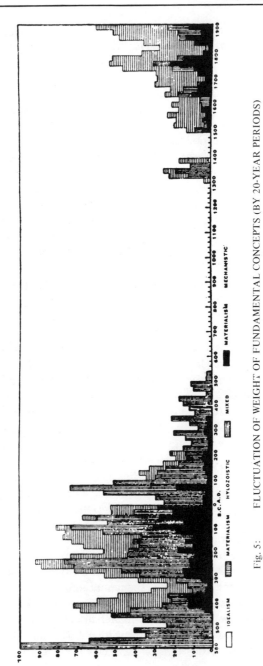

Fig. 5:   FLUCTUATION OF WEIGHT OF FUNDAMENTAL CONCEPTS (BY 20-YEAR PERIODS)

upon it. He believed the old maxim *nihil est in intellectu quod non prius fuerit in sensu.* Leibniz also admitted the truth of this remark as far as it went, but he pointed out that the senses do not receive external impressions in the form of ideas. The active work of the mind is necessary before external sense impressions can create internal ideas. Leibniz therefore vindicated the idealist view by adding to that maxim the deeply significant words *nisi ipse intellectus* to emphasize the all-important creative activity of the human mind in building up knowledge. But the work of Leibniz, which he was too generous to publish after Locke's death, was little known, and for two generations it lay buried among the mass of his manuscripts at Hanover.

The sensate tide rolled on. It is manifest today in the contemporary tendency to interpret man, culture and history mechanically. It is to be seen in the emphasis put upon reflex actions, upon the influence of endocrine glands, upon psychoanalysis and upon economic conditioning as determinants of behavior. Spiritual, idealistic influences are rarely allowed any operative power. Far otherwise was the situation over the many centuries in which ideational and idealistic forms of culture prevailed. Yet, as Sorokin notes once again, neither the ideational nor the sensate cultural stream can claim continuous development. There are no periodic or wave-like movements. There are no rises or falls every hundred, three hundred or six hundred years, as some writers have plausibly tried to suggest. Likewise there is no adequate evidence to support famous theories of constant, cumulative cultural progress, based upon Hegel's three-beat rhythm of "thesis-antithesis" and resulting "higher synthesis."

Being and Becoming — Other philosophical first principles, in addition to the notions of idealism and materialism examined by Sorokin, are the twin notions of being and becoming, or of permanency and change. He describes these as the eternalistic and temporalistic mentality, and he points out that they are the basic principles underlying hundreds of more specific theories in science, philosophy, and religion.

The philosophy of pure Eternalism was predominant in the thought of Brahmanic India and of Taoism in China. It has characterized the thought of several Western philosophical systems, such as those of Parmenides and Zeno. The famous paradoxes of Achilles and the tortoise, and of the arrow, by which Zeno sought to prove that motion and change are unreal, are outstanding examples of the philosophy of being. Although not part of the religious thought of the Middle Ages, it reappeared in Christian literature with Pascal. Among others holding such views, Sorokin notes Cervantes and J. Boehme, and among relatively very few modern thinkers, Schopenhauer.

The opposite school of thought regards reality as a constant state of becoming. It holds that everything is in a state of incessant change and flux. The little that is known of the pre-Socratic philosophers of Greece already shows the force of this thought at an early age. The often-quoted remark of Heraclitus that "all things are born through opposition, and are in flux like a river," is typical. In our own time, the same doctrine has had powerful advocates in David Hume, Diderot, Feuerbach, Bakunin, J. S. Mill, Renan, Nietzsche, William James, Vaihanger and Spengler.

Mankind has found, however, that neither pure being nor pure becoming can alone satisfactorily explain their world and their experience. Those who attempt to rely solely on one of these theories have always failed, for they have been compelled to bring in, however surreptitiously, the other to help to give their doctrine a semblance of truth. The idea of process must seek meaning from the idea of being, whether it be in the form of "the ultimate reality," cosmic rays, matter, energy, God, the Universal Spirit, or the Unknowable.

The effort of idealistic thought to realize and express the truths of the notions of being and of becoming has taken various forms. Among them, Sorokin enumerates the atomic theories of Leucippus and Democritus. According to this view, matter is regarded as stuff whose ultimate nature consists of unchangeable atoms. From the ever-changing combinations of these atoms the opposite notion of becoming is derived. In our own time, atoms are replaced in the theory of being by electrons, protons and neutrons, and yet more refined concepts far removed from the old idea of matter as "stuff."

Another form of the theory attempting to explain both being and becoming is that of Plato, of the Neo-Platonists, partly of the Peripatetic school, and of most of the medieval thinkers from St. Augustine, St. Thomas and the Scholastics to Spinoza. These thinkers regarded the realm of being as the supreme ultimate reality. The realm of becoming for them is that of the empirical world of sense perceptions subject to generation and corruption, process and change. This view Sorokin calls eternalism-temporalism, and he finds that by far the greatest number of thinkers incline to it. Outstanding are Plato (12), St. Thomas Aquinas (12), St. Augustine (10), Luther (8), Loyola (8), Spinoza (8), Berkeley (8), Hegel (8). The numbers after each name indicate Sorokin's estimate of the relative influence and importance of the thinkers mentioned from the standpoint of the development of this doctrine of eternalism-temporalism.

Sorokin notes a variant on this theme in which reality is graded into three or four classes; on a scale of an increasing "being," and a decreasing "becoming," as the lower forms of existence are overshadowed by emphasis upon the higher forms. He does not mention the remarkable monadic theory of Leibniz in this connection, although he awards him a score of 9 out of 12 among the thinkers who sought to achieve an equilibrium between the two schools of eternalism-temporalism and of temporalism-eternalism. The few thinkers whose influence he rates about as high or higher in this respect are Pythagoras (8), Socrates (9), Aristotle (12), Zeno (8), Chrysippus (7), Cicero (8), Plutarch (8), Nicolas of Cusa (8), Leonardo da Vinci (8), G. Bruno (8), Kepler (8), Descartes (8), Galileo (8), Kant (12).

Yet another variant of the mixed types is that which concentrates upon the relationships of things, picking out the uniformities, regularities, and causal relationships between them, which it then attempts to state as laws according to which changes take place. These laws then become the immutable, constant, and unchanging factors in the universe. The whole effort of science becomes concentrated upon these uniformities and causal laws, so that a tendency arises to regard science and the scientific statement of laws as an end in itself, perhaps even as the refuge of immutable being.

Social science, as well as natural science, has also become a field in which uniformities and laws are sought, but this has been a relatively late development in Western thought. G. B. Vico was a pioneer in the search for what he regarded as "the ideal universal and eternal laws along which proceed all nations in the cycles of their appearance, development, decadence and end." His words had very little immediate influence and, despite other beginnings on different lines, such as those of Montesquieu, it was not until the nineteenth century that the search for uniformities and laws invaded history to create a new branch of thought, the philosophy of history. From the standpoint of Sorokin's theories, the history of history as a separate branch of thought is specially revealing, since it can only develop during the prevalence of the sensate-temporalistic mentality. Hence it is not surprising that the Hindu ideational mentality failed to develop any historical sense or any reliable chronology. The same deficiency characterizes the Middle Ages in Europe and the heroic periods of Greece and Rome. History, in the modern sense of the word, did not properly emerge until the fifth century B.C. in Greece (Herodotus and Thucydides) and not until the second and first centuries B.C. in Rome. In

European culture, history, as distinct from chronicles, such as the
Anglo-Saxon Chronicle and others, first appears with Joinville nd
Froissart in the fourteenth century A.D., after which it steadily grows
until, in our own time, every subject is treated historically. Life itself is
controlled by time measurements. "We cannot live without a watch," says
Sorokin. "We go to bed winding it; we get up at the command of the
hands or alarm of a clock, we move, work, act, eat, sleep, love, quarrel,
study, pray, live by a watch and controlled by watch time." This is all very
new in the age-long experience of humanity.

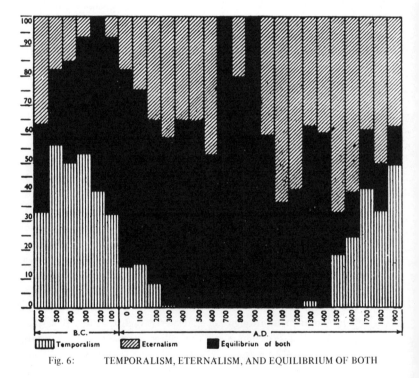

Fig. 6:   TEMPORALISM, ETERNALISM, AND EQUILIBRIUM OF BOTH

There are therefore five main groups of theories on the subject of the nature of things as either process or reality or both. Sorokin lists them as:
1. Pure Eternalism.
2. Eternalism-Temporalism, where the aspect of becoming is present but is greatly overshadowed by the aspect of permanent being.
3. Pure Temporalism.
4. Temporalism-Eternalism, where the aspect of becoming is far more stressed than that of being.
5. Equilibrium of Eternalism-Temporalism, giving equal importance to both aspects which are regarded as equally important modes of reality.

In a statistical appendix of eleven closely-printed pages, Sorokin lists and classifies the various thinkers in these five main groups, giving each thinker a numerical indicator of his relative influence on a scale rating of 1 to 12 (*Social and Cultural Dynamics,* Vol. II, pp. 663-675).

After reviewing the various theories of being and of becoming, Sorokin summarizes his detailed findings in a series of statistical tables and in graphic form in Fig. 6.

The comparative strength of the various systems is set out in the following statistical table, which brings out the predominance of the idealistic mixed eternalism-temporalism variety of eternalism in comparison with pure doctrines of being (eternalism), or of becoming (temporalism). At the same time the results testify to the continuing vitality of apparently quite outmoded ways of thought, showing once again the qualifications necessary before any age can be labelled purely sensate or ideational.

Table 2:   FLUCTUATIONS IN THE DOCTRINES OF BEING AND BECOMING

Period	*Eternalisms*		*Temporalisms*		*Equilibriums*
	Pure	Mixed	Pure	Mixed	
600 B.C.- A.D. 100	18	75	179	136	317
A.D. 100-600	0	194	29	11	341
600-1500	0	284	0	4	324
1500-1900	149	1337	131	767	481
1900-1920	47	268	37	382	109
	214	2158	376	1300	1572

All Eternalisms **2372** *All Temporalisms* **1676** *Equilibriums* **1572**

Realism and Nominalism — More striking still is the illustration Sorokin brings to his study of philosophical development by analyzing the relative importance and the number of thinkers who, at various epochs, took opposite sides on another fundamental theme. This is the great question started by Plato, about the true nature of the definitions, generalizations, and concepts of human thought. Is it true that there is nothing in the real world that corresponds to our general abstract ideas about such subjects as society, the State, or justice, or about classes of things such as the horse, as the Nominalists believe, or are those abstract ideas themselves the true reality, the eternal truths, as the Realists such as Plato said they are? Or is the third possibility correct, that concepts exist in the mind only and are real to the extent that we think with them and operate with them, but that they do not exist in their own right outside the mind, as the Realists contend they do? This third view is that of the Conceptualists.

The three schools of thought had several variants but they can be roughly summarized with the aid of a few Latin prepositions. The philosophical Realists took the view that general ideas (or in Latin *universalia*) refer to the supreme realities of which all earthly things are mere partial reflections. These general ideas, "universals," being timeless and eternal, exist before and apart from their manifestation in actual concrete form, *ante rem,* that is, before the things of which they are the generalized expression. Such was the view of transcendental realists, as Plato and those who followed him are often described. They believed that there is some real, common element in every individual far more fundamental than any specific superficial differences they may exhibit. That basic common element could be thought of as an archetypal form existing in the Divine mind as a pattern for creation. Thus Realists suppose that beyond brown horse, black horse, and white horse, there is the universal horse without which horse A or horse B could not be put into the class of horse. Plato called such a generic essence the Idea of a horse.

Such philosophical "realism" believing that *genus* and *species* are real, existing things was too metaphysical for many people. Aristotle accepted the reality of a "universal," or Idea to the extent that by its nature it has a fitness or capacity to be in many, or be predicated of many. He and those who followed him were immanent Realists believing general ideas to be present in or immanent in the individual objects of the physical world, *universalia in re.*

Some philosophers, such as St. Thomas Aquinas and his followers, accepted both the transcendental realism of Plato and the immanent Realism of Aristotle, adding the further notion that general ideas or universals can be formed in the light of experience as the mind abstracts and compares them, *universalia post rem.* Such philosophers are known as Conceptualists. Universals for them are concepts in the mind, and theirs is a logical or psychological theory. In the process of thinking about general ideas such as horse, a special non-sensory, but not supersensory, cognition of them enters in and transforms the singular impressions and images into abstract concepts.

The position of the nominalists is simple. They do not believe that there is anything in the external world corresponding to generalized concepts of *universalia.* Likewise they hold that there are no real concepts in the mind, but only individual images and impressions. The notion that we have concepts in our minds arises, they say, because we are deluded by words, because we use the same word or symbol for many single impressions of similar things. We experience white horse, brown horse, black horse, and then fallaciously assume that there is something real corresponding to the word "horse." Because philosophers of this school of thought argued that it is a vain quest to look for any reality beyond the words or names, *nomina,* they were called nominalists.

Sorokin emphasizes the fact that the battles between realists and nominalists are by no means things of the past. The truth of his contention is evident in the controversies occasioned by logical positivism which were being vigorously debated when he wrote. On a more popular level were works on the newly-christened subject "semantics," such as that of Stuart Chase, on the nominalist side, *The Tyranny of Words.*

Again relying upon his statistical method, Sorokin and his collaborators classified all the main philosophers according to their stand upon this greatly debated question of the status of the general concepts, with the results shown in the diagram reporduced as Fig. 7.

Once more it is probably desirable to refer to the various limitations by which the accuracy of these statistical estimates and of their diagrammatic representation must be qualified in order to make it clear that minor adjustments may be thought necessary by some readers, who may object to some of the classifications (e.g., the inclusion of Abelard among the nominalists), as well as to some of the assessments of relative influence relating to certain philosophers. Nevertheless the broad result is probably very similar to that which any other independent survey would produce.

The results show that realism is the doctrine of the ideational culture, conceptualism that of the idealistic culture, and nominalism that of the sensate culture. Again there is no clear progress in one direction or

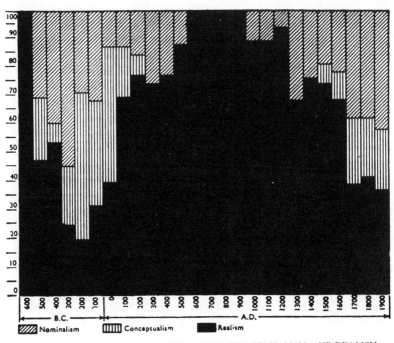

Fig. 7:   MOVEMENTS OF NOMINALISM, CONCEPTUALISM, AND REALISM

unilinear evolutionary trend. Again the results show how the influence of
any one system of truth depends upon the prevalent culture, rising and
falling with that culture. It is the rise of the sensate culture which has
given nominalism its "scientific" and convincing quality. Knowledge, or
what appears to be truth to any individual human being, cannot be
understood except as a manifestation of the culture in which it arises and
functioons.

Theories of the State – Philosophical debates about the nature of
knowledge, particularly when they sound so technical as these discussions
of "the nature of universals," may seem remote from practical realities.
Nevertheless they can and do illuminate difficult or baffling problems of
everyday life. Further illustrations of the manner in which men's views
about the true nature of universals have been reflected in their opinions
upon many other subjects will follow.

One such is the relation of the individual to society. Must the individual always be sacrificed for society, or should the claims, rights and welfare of the individual always be put first? Already, before the World War of 1939-45, Sorokin could write that thousands of lives have been sacrificed and hundreds of thousands mutilated in the struggles resulting from passionate determination to uphold one way or another of answering such questions. The prison-state of the Fascists in Italy or of the Bolsheviks in Russia was followed by its atrocious development in Nazi Germany, and we have by no means yet seen the end of the menace they represented. To be sure the Bolshevik, Fascist, and Nazi doctrines about the nature of society were the hastily improvized rationalizations of political gangsters seeking to disguise their self-seeking, power-grabbing acts of violence with a respectable cloak of pseudo-philosophical doctrine. They were not based upon philosophical principles nor upon those old political theories which regarded society as the true and primary reality and which thought of the individual as something altogether secondary and derivative. Sorokin labels that way of regarding society as *universalism*. Those who hold it are logically bound to regard society not only as the fundamental true reality, but also as the source of values for mankind, so that corresponding to the philosophical idea about the true nature or being of society (the ntological aspect of the matter), there is also an ethical view, namely, that of ethical universalism. These are among the results of regarding human society as the realist philosophers do, and of believing that society is one of the "universals" which has a reality of its own which cannot be reduced to the individual existences of which it is composed.

In complete contrast stands the view that the individual is the true and primary reality. Society is then of value only to the extent that it provides the individual with a richer life and helps him to achieve a fuller realization of his self-seeking impulses. This is the ethical singularism. Clearly it is the view the nominalists must take of the matter in opposition to the ideas of the realists.

An effort to harmonize universalism and singularism can be made by regarding individual and social interests as two aspects of the same value, resulting in the doctrine of ethical harmonism. The philosophers and thinkers who have written on these questions do not, however, fall neatly into these three broad divisions of universalism, singularism, and harmonism. Some writers did not always think or write consistently on the subject. After a patient analysis of their work, Sorokin distinguishes the three following main groups: singularism, with three sub-groups;

universalism, with two sub-groups; and the view believing in the mystic unity of individuals. The three types of singularism are:

Pure Individualism or, as Sorokin describes it, extreme or consistent sociological singularism. For this view the individual alone is real, he alone must be the source of value and his rights should be paramount. Social values are at best derivative, because society is of value only in so far as it serves the life and happiness of the individual. Extreme hedonists and anarchists are its products as well as moral individualists such as Stirner. This atomistic view of society as a mere aggregate of individuals is, of course, a sociological form of nominalism. Among some of the better-known writers listed by Sorokin as exemplifying this way of regarding society are the following, together with the index number or "marks" indicating their approximate importance and influence in the history and development of thought.

Thrasymachus (3), Epicurus (8), Diogenes (3), Lucian (4), Mandeville (4), Rousseau (in his *Discours* only) (8), Diderot (7), Godwin (4), Proudhon (6), Bakunin (4), Dühring (6), Fourier (5), Carlyle (5), Nietzsche (9), Tolstoi (8), Stirner (6), Kropotkin (4).

Moderate Sociological Singularism. Logically believing that none but individuals are real, this less extreme form of singularism is willing to look at the sum of all individuals, or society, as a supreme value, along with individual value. Sorokin gives a relatively short list of the writers and thinkers who have taken this point of view, including Sir Thomas More (6), Campanella (7), Fénelon (6), Saint-Simon (4), Robert Owen (4), K. Marx (8), Engels (6), L. Blanc (3), W. Morris (4), Jaurès (5), S. Webb (4).

Collectivistic Sociological Singularism is a form of singularism in that it does not regard the nature or essence of society as being anything more than the sum of the individuals it contains. Nevertheless it differs from the two more extreme forms of singularism in that it regards the whole body of individuals banded together as more important, or as ethically more valuable than any individual alone. In this sense it may be said to give priority and superiority to the collectivity and not to individuals. The welfare of the group is the supreme law. The utilitarian doctrine of the greatest happiness for the greatest number best characterizes this form of singularism, and the liberalism of the nineteenth century was its best expression. In our own times, the Bolsheviks, Fascists, and Nazis have taken this point of view with the utmost violence and in complete disregard for individual human rights, not for theoretical but for practical reasons. If those in control can pose as some sort of collectivity, as representing the "proletarian class," the Communist party, the Fascist, or

Hitler party, the nobility, or the religious collectivity, it pays them to adopt a theory which subordinates all other individuals to themselves in their collective disguise. This subordination can be of the most complete and drastic kind, involving the silencing or extermination of all who criticize or oppose the group that has taken it upon itself to decide upon the ethical or other purposes which the collectivity is to serve. These purposes can often be nothing more than the crudest, purely materialistic form of the ethics of happiness. Among the better-known of the writers and thinkers, whose doctrines support such a singularistic-universalist view, Sorokin lists, with the indicators of their relative influence on his 1 to 12 scale of ratings:

Socrates	9	Montesquieu	6	James Mill	6
Democritus	8	Voltaire	7	J. Stuart Mill	8
Empedocles	6	A. Smith	6	H. Spencer	8
Thucydides	8	Hume	8	Buckle	5
Protagoras	8	Burke	4	de Tocqueville	2
Xenophon	7	Tom Paine	4	Cobden	3
Demosthenes	4	Helvetius	6	Grote	3
Carneades	5	Quesnay	6	Darwin	8
Horace	6	Condorcet	6	Freud	4
Ovid	6	Gibbon	6	Tarde	5
Dion Chrysostom	6	Bentham	6	Gobineau	4
Marsilius of Padua	4	B. Constant	6	Simmel	5
Machiavelli in his		Sismondi	4	Westermarck	4
Discorsi	6	Malthus	6	Galton	5
Locke	8	Ricardo	5	F. W. Maitland	5
Bayle	6	J. Adams	3		
Hutcheson	4	A. Comte	8		

Needless to say these men would have shrunk from the lengths to which twentieth-century totalitarian states have gone in perverting their theories by bending them to their own ends.

Sociological Universalism is based upon an entirely different idea of the nature of society, which it regards as something existing in its own right beyond and apart from the mere aggregate of individuals of which it is composed. Society, according to this view, has its own organic life which cannot be reduced to any expression in terms of the existence of individuals. It is therefore from society, and not from individuals, that supreme values are to be derived. Such a doctrine is obviously one which would come naturally to anyone who believes in the true reality of supersensory phenomena, in other words, to the realists rather than to the nominalists.

Sorokin distinguishes two classes of the main varieties of sociological universalism.

Moderate Sociological Universalism, which while still maintaining the independent existence and value of society as its first principle, nevertheless recognizes some reality and value in the individual. In practice, therefore, although certainly not in theory, this moderate form of universalism approaches the doctrine of collectivistic sociological singularism just reviewed above. The following are some of the principal writers and thinkers adopting this theory:

Pythagoras	8	Abelard	4	Kant	12
Heraclitus	7	Roger Bacon	6	Schiller	8
Aristotle	12	Duns Scotus	8	Fichte	8
Chrysippus	7	William of Ockham	8	St. Simon	6
Polybuis	4	Wycliffe	3	Fournier	5
Nigidius Figulus	4	Petrarch	3	Macaulay	4
Cato (Utica)	2	Gerson	4	A. Comte	8
Caesar	6	Calvin	6	Lassalle	5
Varro	5	Zwingli	4	Renouvier	7
Virgil	8	Knox	4	Emerson	6
Philo Judaeus	8	Althusius	4	Le Play	7
Tacitus	4	H. Grotius	6	Fabian Society	7
Apuleius	6	Milton	7	Gierke	6
Clement of					
Alexandria	6	Harrington	4	Renan	6
Pelagius	3	Pascal	7	Tönnies	4
Dionysius the					
Areopagite	8	Comenius	7	Durkheim	5
Gregory the Great	4	Spinoza	8	Sombart	5
		Rousseau *Contrat*			
Bede	3	*Social*	8	Stammler	5
Alcuin	4	Beccaria	6	Max Weber	5
Lanfranc	3	Herder	6		

Universalism, the complete expression of the realist idea of society, in which the individual is nothing and society or the state is everything, is exemplified by many others of whom some of the best known are:

Anaximander	5	S. Thomas Aquinas	12	Bossuet	6
Parmenides	7	Raymond Lully	5	Fénelon	6
Plato	12	Dante	8	Vico	6
Tertullian	6	Luther	8	Wolff	7
St. Augustine	10	Machiavelli (Prince)	6	Hegel	8
St. Anselm	7	Bodin	6	Schopenauer	8
Gregory VII					
(Hildebrand)	6	Campanella	7	Carlyle	5
Peter Lombard	4	Francis Bacon	7	Ranke	5
John of Salisbury	5	Hobbes	8	V. Soloviev	6
Albertus Magnus	8	Leibniz	9	Dostoevsky	7

Apart from these two major and opposite theories of singularism ana universalism, there is a third way of looking at the problem. Sorokin calls it *Sociological Mystic Integralism,* because it tries to find an harmonious synthesis between the two conflicting theories. It provides more subtle and difficult ideas than the shrap-cut alternatives of singularism and universalism at the cost of a somewhat mystical and metaphysical elaboration of the main issues involved. The individual is regarded as the incarnation of society; society is the universal reality permeating every individual as his generic essence. Society and the individual represent two different aspects of the same value. Neither can be given a secondary or derivative value or be made the mere means of the other. Sorokin's list of thinkers taking this developed philosophical position includes fewer names than can be cited under singularist and universalist thinkers. Among the better known are:

Cicero	8	Macrobius	4	Milton	6
Seneca	8	St. John Chrysostom	5	Shaftesbury	5
Plutarch	8	Proclus	8	Rousseau	8
Epictetus	6	Maximus Confessor	6	Kant	12
		St. Bernard of			
Marcus Aruelius	6	Clairvaux	5	Schiller	8
Justin Martyr	5	St. Francis of Assisi	6	Fourier	5
Plotinus	12	Hus	3	Emerson	5
Origen	8	Nicholas Cusa	8	Dostoevsky	7
Porphyry	7	Thomas More	6		
Bruno	8	Komensky	7		

It will be noticed that some of these names, such as Milton, Kant, Schiller, Emerson, are also included among the less extreme forms of universalism, which is not surprising since, in some of their writings, they exerted a notable influence in favor of a universalist view of society, even though it did not always extend to a thorough-going mystical view. It is also evident that some writers on political theory were by no means consistent in their views in all their works. Rousseau is a notable example of a man whose opinions changed very considerably from those he first expressed in his *Discourse on Inequality* (1754). Sir Thomas More can be listed as a mystical integralist and also as a collectivist. Summarizing the broad development of human thought about the true nature of society in its relations to the individual, in so far as it is revealed by the number of writers in the various schools and their influence as they are assessed by relative weights on the scale of 1 to 12, quoted after their names, Sorokin arrives at the following composite estimate:

Table 3:   CURRENTS IN SINGULARISM, UNIVERSALISM, AND INTEGRALISM

Period	All Singularisms	All Universalisms	Mystic Integration
600 B.C.-A.D. 100	288	300	30
A.D. 100-600	37	253	166
600-1500	13	400	82
1500-1900	766	1002	97
1900-1920	228	184	0
Total	1332	2139	375

In the light of his findings, he concludes that the domination of the sensate culture favors the doctrine of sociological singularism which in such a period is alone considered to be truly scientific. Thus he points out that the textbooks on sociology appearing between 1880 and 1920 almost invariably adopt the standpoint of moderate, even of extreme, singularism. They reject as metaphysical and unscientific any attempt to look upon society as a primary reality. They will not regard any social organism as a mystical body which it is impossible to explain, to express, or to reduce to the individuals of which it is composed.

Quite otherwise were the thoughts of men during the greater part of their history, for they all regarded the body social, whether it be Church or State, as more real and more valuable than the individuals in it. All such universal views, characteristic of an ideational or idealistic culture, were discredited by the nineteenth-century insistence upon the supreme necessity of sticking to what were said to be 'the facts' and of avoiding theories and speculative generalizations. To believe that insight and explanation can be achieved merely by collecting and contemplating vast accumulations of facts is, as Sorokin asserts, quite unjustified. The delusion he attacks might perhaps be illustrated by saying that those who accept it seem to regard the process of acquiring knowledge as being rather like the way the Hungarians were said to make the rarest Imperial Tokay wine; namely, heaping up great piles of grapes and collecting the juice which runs from them without recourse to a wine press. Sorokin certainly does not ignore or despise facts, for all his theories arise from a most exacting and thorough preliminary survey and classification of the thought and influence of the great philosophers. His view might be summarized by saying that facts are infinite, and that a fact is not a fact in any branch of knowledge unless it is a relevant fact, the operative word here being *relevant*. To decide what facts are relevant is to make a judgment about their value, and that is something which the facts themselves do not provide. Value in turn arises from the need to find some concept or theory by which the facts can be incorporated into an illuminating body of knowledge which should not only explain them adequately but which ought also to serve as a clue to further knowledge.

Sorokin has made a chart to summarize the results of weighting and counting the various contributions to the theory of society and social life which is reproduced here as Fig. 8, p. 152.

Here is a new way of surveying the long record of speculation in the Western world about the all-important question of the true nature of human life in society, based upon the notion that all such views are the expression of one or other form of the philosophical ideas men have held about the reality and validity of their thoughts upon the true nature of general ideas.

Political and sociological theories are thus related directly and intelligibly to philosophical theory of which they can at once be seen to be a particular expression. Political theories themselves are shown to be capable of classification according to a comprehensive all-inclusive cultural scheme. Armed with such a detailed analysis and description, students of political and sociological theories have a guide to the assessment of all

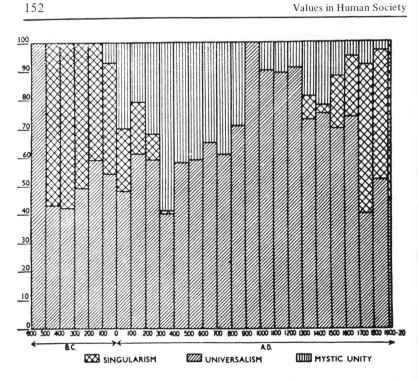

Fig. 8:   MOVEMENTS OF SINGULARISM, UNIVERSALISM, AND MYSTIC UNITY

notions on the subject and are correspondingly less likely to fall easy
victims to the first theory presented to them with plausibility and force, as
the unfortunate Germans succumbed in their millions to the half-baked
crudities of Herr Hitler, and as millions of others have been deluded by
ingenious speculations purporting to develop the teachings of Karl Marx
and the ethical and economic doctrines of Communism.

Personality in Legal Thought — Sorokin reinforces his general attack upon
the problem of society as a whole by a closer analysis of a more detailed
aspect of it, that is of the nature of associations or societies in the sense of
limited groupings and collectivities active on a smaller scale and more
restricted in their scope and operations than is society or the State as a
whole.
      The views that legislators and lawyers take of this question of the
reality of the juridical personality, of corporations and institutions, may

seem a highly technical and specialized matter. Yet, as Sorokin points out, it is a very practical and pertinent matter, for the property, liberty, and very life of thousands of persons have depended and will in future depend upon whether one or another view is taken of it. A juridical personality in law means any body consisting of one or more individuals regarded by the law as a unit and usually endowed with the right to perpetual succession and to act as a single person. Relatively clear and simple as this idea may seem, it has been the subject of every kind of contradictory theory and hypothesis. Using again as his guide the broad philosophical concepts of realism and nominalism which he employed in reviewing the history of metaphysical and political philosophy, Sorokin reduces broadly the various conflicting theories about the true nature of juridical personalities to three main types, recognizing however that each of the three has several sub-divisions.

These three classes are those of Realism, of Nominalism, and of the mixed conceptions of juridical personality. Among the varieties of the Realist's conception he distinguished:

1. Transcendental realism, which puts the reality of the juridical personality in some supersensory essence or being. The best example is the way in which the early Christian Church united and dissolved everything in God.

2. The more mundane form of the realistic view which regards the juridical personality as a real organism with a character of its own over and above that of the individuals belonging to it, having its own body and its own system, partly corporeal and partly psychological. This view, labelled by Sorokin "Empirico-organismic realism," was held by some German theorists of law, such as Bluntschli and in part by Gierke.

3. The psychological realism which finds the reality of the juridical personality mainly in some psychological essence over and above the reality of individuals, for example "public opinion," "the group mind," "common will," "group aims," or "group interest."

4. The more naive functional realism is content to see the reality of the juridical personality in its functional unity which seems a reality in its own right distinct and apart from that of its members. According to such views, there can be a collective or individual responsibility or collective and indivisible honor of the group different from the honor or the responsibility of its members. From this point of view, as in all the realist points of view, the group comes first and the individuals second. The feelings evinced towards a football team by its supporters or towards a regiment by those who have served in it might be examples.

In contrast to all these realist views stand the various nominalistic conceptions of the juridical personality which view it as a legal fiction and regard the individual members of groups as the only real elements in it apart from the various sensory objects (property, buildings, etc.) attached to it artificially. For the lawyer and statesman of this school of thought, a corporation is a legal fiction, an aritificial device with no independent powers of action apart from those of its members or representatives. In a few interesting pages, Sorokin attempts to indicate the main periods in the trend of thought on this matter, concluding again that there has been no constant trend. The ups and downs of the realistic conception of the juridical person correspond, however, closely enough with those of general philosophical realism, with belief in sociological universalism and with the truth of faith.

Legal history unfortunately does not possess adequate sources relating to the legal thought of Greece on this subject, but such evidence as there is supports Sorokin's suggestion that, up to the fifth century B.C., the Greeks took a predominantly realist view according to which the individual then had no rights except by virtue of his membership of the state or of social bodies. He thinks that there is some evidence, admittedly not very much, that a more nominalistic view prevailed after the fifth century B.C.

The evidence is more abundant about the Roman view of the matter which began, like the archaic Greek, by being strictly realist. The distinctive character of life under the Roman Republic was the extent to which the Romans were at first enrolled into a large number of clans and tribes, in which they were closely bound together in kinships or family groups. Later in the history of the republic, the artisans of Rome are found associated in corporations or clubs, but not for political purposes. Each such grouping operated as a real unity and was regarded as such. The responsibility of the members and their property could not be distinguished from that of the corporation. At the end of the republic and under the Roman Empire there was a marked change. Many associations or unions of working men were abolished by the Senate in 64 B.C., and, although they were revived for political purposes by Clodius, a tool of Julius Caesar, their rights were very soon curtailed and they did not recover their former status. Thereafter, and until the time of Justinian in the sixth century A.D., a definitely nominalist view was taken of corporations which, from the lawyer's standpoint, became legal fictions.

.Meanwhile the rise of Christianity was powerfully promoting an extremely realist view of social organization, according to which all the values, rights, duties, and property of the believers were merged into those of the Church. In the Middle Ages this movement was further strengthened by the naive realistic mentality of the Germanic peoples. Roman law of the Imperial period survived, however, to influence thought on this subject, so that by the twelfth and thirteenth centuries a distinctly nominalistic note began to be heard. It developed, however, without entirely supplanting the earlier realism.

As late as the fifteenth and sixteenth centuries, realistic elements continued to be mixed with an increasingly nominalist outlook in Germany, England, Italy, and France. Legal theories of the seventeenth and eighteenth centuries, with their development of the medieval doctrine of natural law, did not mark a complete swing-over towards nominalism, despite the pronounced form of nominalism evident in the characterization by writers such as Althusius and Hobbes of corporations and collectivities as mere collections of individuals. The tendency thereafter was all in favor of individualism, atomism, and singularism, which became more evident in the nineteenth century when the influence of France spread Napoleonic legislation widely throughout Europe. Savigny, whose great work on Roman law was published in 1840, achieved a commanding authority by his renowned expression of the nominalistic theory of the "legal fiction" doctrine which had its antecedents in Roman law of the Empire. Another interesting precursor was Innocent IV, the Pope who, in the middle of the thirteenth century, had developed a conceptualist view of the nature of corporations which served as a basis for the more thorough-going nominalism of his successors.

A realist reaction did not become manifest until the end of the nineteenth century, despite some mixed and not very clearly defined universalist and collectivist notions, such as those of Auguste Comte, Herbert Spencer, Durkheim, and others. It was von Gierke who raised the standard of realist revolt against the strongly nominalist principles evident in the proposed revision of the German Civil Code. When the new code appeared in 1900, it was apparent that his objections had not been in vain. Political thought slowly began to turn against the full-blown nominalist conception to give greater emphasis to the power, prestige, and right of collectivities at the expense of those of individuals. Communist, Fascist, and Nazi doctrines depended upon a half-baked and distorted realism for what shreds of respectability they could muster as thoroughgoing theoretical explanations of the true notion of society and of political parties and of the relation of the individual to them.

Sorokin compares the semi-developed pseudo-philosophies of

Communism and Fascism to the cubist movement in art. Neither are satisfactory doctrines in their own right. Their significance lies solely in the fact that they represent a fumbling revolt against the prevalent extreme nominalism of their time.

His conclusion is that just as the realist way of thinking about corporations and societies was prevalent in the ideational cultures, so nominalist doctrines in law become evident as sensate cultures rise, and they weaken as such cultures decline. During their relatively short reign, idealistic cultural systems are characterized by mixed, eclectic, and conceptualist theories of the juridical personality.

Unless these theories, and indeed the subject as a whole, are viewed within their wider cultural setting, Sorokin urges, they will never be intelligently understood, but every manner of fortuitous association with miscellaneous economic, religious, scientific, even geographical factors will be suggested as their proper explanation. This general defense of his main position as a historian of social philosophy is, of course, one he can use in support of all his summary surveys, but it appears specially forceful and apposite when applied to limited special problems such as that of legal philosophy in relation to collectivities.

Determinism and Indeterminism—The next "First Principles" of social theory which Sorokin examines are those of the conflicting theories of determinism and indeterminism.

Again, with the co-operation of others, an independent review was made of the theories of the principle writers who, implicitly or explicitly, developed a theory illustrating these conflicting opinions which men have taken of their power to shape their own destiny.

Determinism denies that man has such power. Just as in the material world every effect or event has its cause, so in the human sphere, everything, including the minds as well as the actions of men, is regarded as the product of its cause. Indeterminism denies this necessary invariable relationship between phenomena and rejects especially the idea that men lack free will or the power of choice to modify their own fate.

Between these extreme and opposite views, there are several mixed theories. Some indeterminist theorists allow freedom of the will, but believe, nevertheless, that many of man's actions are conditioned; some determinist theories are so qualified by special reservations, limitations and exemptions that they amount almost to indeterminism.

Other writers, such as Cicero and Plutarch, were not consistent, adopting determinism as a general principle, yet refusing to believe in

fatalism as a general creed. Cicero, following the writers of the New
Academy, tended in speculative matters to regard probability as the only
rule of life, but he did not carry over this view into his ethical writings,
where he stuck much closer to the Stoic doctrines and the ethics of
principle, which were, of course, more consonant with the old Roman
ideational position. Other later writers deliberately combine both views, as
Immanuel Kant tried to do with his theory of man's completely
conditioned behavior in this world of phenomena, but complete freedom
in his real essence as a 'noumenal' being. Writers such as he and
Malebranche used arguments which can be made to support both sides of
the question. There are a large number of writers who cannot easily be
classified under either of these two opposite schools of thought, and these
Sorokin has necessarily omitted in constructing his estimates of the
respective weight and opinion to be assigned to each class. Examples of the
principal supporters of these contradictory points of view, selected from
Sorokin's longers lists giving the names of its principal thinkers and their
place in the scale of influence from 1 to 12, are:

DETERMINISM

Pythagoras	8	Heraclitus	7	Panaetius	5
Plato	12	Zeno	8	Varro	5
Cicero	8	Nigidius Figulus	4	Epictetus	6
Plutarch	8	Marcus Aurelius	6	Luther	8
Wycliffe	3	Leonardo da Vinci	8	Calvin	6
Zwingli	6	Melanchthon	5	Kepler	8
G. Bruno	8	Bacon	7	Hobbes	8
Galileo	8	Jansen	6	Pascal	7
Guelincx	6	Spinoza	8	Malebranche	7
Mandeville	4	Hume	8	Voltaire	7
Helvetius	6	Holbach	6	Priestley	6
Diderot	7	Kant	12	Bentham	6
J. Mill	6	A. Comte	8	Spencer	8
K. Marx	8	Engels	6	Tolstoy	8
Bradley	7	Democritus	8		

INDETERMINISM

Aristotle	12	Grosseteste	4	Glisson	3
Theophrastus	7	Albertus Magnus	8	Berkeley	8
Epicurus	8	St. Thomas Aquinas	12	Kant	12
Lucretius	8	R. Lully	5	Vico	7
Philo Judaeus	8	M. Eckhart	8	J. Edwards	6
Justin Martyr	5	Dante	8	Rousseau	8
Apuleius	6	Gerson	4	Condillac	6
Origen	8	Nicolas of Cusa	8	Fichte	8
Tertullian	6	Erasmus	5	Schiller	8
Plotinus	12	Loyola	8	Herder	6
Porphyry	7	Cardan	6	Goethe	8
St. Basil	6	Campanella	6	Whewell	6
St. Augustine	10	Gassendi	7	Schelling	8
Gregory I	4	Descartes	8	Carlyle	4
Maximus Confessor	6	Cudworth	5	Lotze	5
Alcuin	4	Leibniz	9	Hartmann	8
St. Anselm	7	Malebranche	7	Dostoevsky	7
St. Bernard	5	R. Boyle	4	J. S. Mill	8
Abelard	4	Locke	8	Rickert	6
Peter Lombard	4	H. More	4	W. James	4
John of Salisbury	3	Bossuet	6	L. Stephen	7

It will be noted that, for the reason given above, Malebranche and Kant appear on both sides.

Summarizing the resulting balance of forces or influences, Sorokin arrives at the following table.

Table 4:   INDICES FOR DETERMINISM AND INDETERMINISM

Period				Determinism	Indeterminism
580 B.C.-A.D. 100	..	..		678	212
A.D. 100-540	..	..	..	239	557
540-1500 ..	..	..	..	73	519
1500-1920	..	..	..	1302	1339
				2292	2627

In more detail he has constructed the following graph based upon the analyses of changing views by twenty-year periods over the same long stretch of time. His statistical tables, giving the detailed basis for this graph, are not reproduced here, but may be found in Volume II of *Social and Cultural Dynamics.*

Generally it is evident that determinism fluctuates with the fluctuations of other manifestations of sensate cultural forms, whereas indeterminism accompanies those of the ideational culture, the truth of faith, realism and idealism. The mixed view indeterminism-determinism is characteristic of periods of idealistic culture.

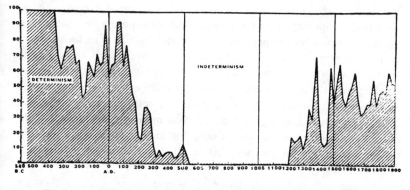

Fig. 9:   FLUCTUATION OF DETERMINISM AND INDETERMINISM

Looking at the predominant opinion on the matter in our own times, Sorokin finds that the "iron determinism" characteristic of most scientists and thinkers in the middle of the nineteenth century has softened considerably. No longer is mankind thought to be driven on by an inexorable, inevitable necessity. There is now a tendency to substitute the idea of probability for rugged determinism.

The Idea of Progress — Allied to the ideas of determinism and indeterminism, as fundamental explanations of the nature and destiny of human development, are other general notions on the subject of the progress and development of mankind. The idea of evolution stated by Charles Darwin in 1859 was a scientific statement which many took to be a complete proof of the reasonableness of that belief in progress which was then already widely shared and was being popularized by many writers, notably by Auguste Comte and Herbert Spencer. The doctrine of evolution has so completely colored thought on the entire question of human development that the earlier theories it supplanted seem strangely remote, antiquated, and obsolete.

As Sorokin's own theory of historical change in itself attempts to explain the nature of the progress of history, it is not surprising to find that he is specially interested in the various notions on the subject which have influenced past ages. Apart from his largest work, *Social and Cultural Dynamics,* which presents the basic historical evidence from which his central ideas are developed, he has also returned to the subject in later books, such as his *Society, Culture and Personality* (1947), and *Social Philosophies of an Age of Crisis* (1950).

Attempts to account for the nature and direction of change in human cultural development have mostly proceeded either on the assumption that the change is always in one direction, whether for better or for worse, or on the assumption that the whole process follows a cyclical movement. Most people in the Victorian era believed that humanity was progressing steadily along the line of more freedom, democracy, and increasing wealth. Such views are usually to be found in sensate cultural systems. In earlier classical antiquity, on the contrary, it was more general to believe the earlier traditional view that things were developing for the worse; that the Golden Age was in the past and that mankind was steadily departing from it.

In contrast with such linear theories are the cyclical theories. Sometimes they also characterize a sensate culture, particularly at a time when it is beginning to lose its hold on the loyalties of mankind. Oswald Spengler's long book on *The Decline of the West,* which had great renown for a short while in Germany after 1918, attempted to popularize a somewhat imaginatively drawn but essentially crude and subjectively conceived cyclical process. Efforts to explain cultural changes as purely mechanical uniformities either are the product of a sensate outlook or arise at a time of mixed culture. Ideational theories of cyclical or endlessly recurring changes depict them as manifestations of inner transformations experienced by the ultimate or true spiritual reality, whether it be God, Brahma, Providence or Tao.

The ideational Hindu and Chinese cultures provide particularly striking cyclical theories. The Hindu theory of the cycle of world creation and dissolution regards it as occurring in four ages incessantly repeating themselves within the period during which the sun, moon, and planets return to the state of conjuction in which they began, which the Hindus estimated to be 4,320,000 sidereal solar years. These four ages are: the Kreta or golden age (1,728,000 years), during which the creation of the world occurs; the Treta or silver age (1,296,000 years); the Dapara or bronze age (864,000 years); and the Kali or iron age (432,000 years), the age of decline and dissolution, which bears all the marks of Sorokin's sensate culture and which began, according to the *Vishnu Puránâ*, in the fourteenth century. At the end of the Kali age, a Brahman with supernatural powers appears to destroy inquity and re-establish the age of purity, or the Kreta age, when the cycle recommences.

In China all the fluctuating processes of human affairs are regarded as but the special varieties of the eternal rhythm of the Yin, or negative essence, and Yang, or positive essence, each of which has its root in the other, and both of which make up the alternating rhythm to be observed, as the Chinese thought, in the fate of dynasties and of mankind. Sorokin characterizes this predominant Chinese view as being in the main that of a mixed culture. The ancient Chinese and Taoist cultures were, however, mainly ideational, while the later Confucianism was a more sensate culture with a doctrine of progress in three stages, beginning with the anarchy of a primitive epoch, the Disorderly Stage, to which a small capitalist society succeeded; the Stage of Small Tranquility; that in turn giving way to the Stage of Great Similarity, marked by social order, mutual benevolence, and reverence.

In Western European civilization, Sorokin draws attention to the uniformly cyclical theories of the sixth and first part of the fifth centuries B.C. in Greece, and their prominence in the fifth and fourth centuries, also with a more complicated period succeeding from the third century B.C. In the fourth century B.C., some ideas of progress began to appear along with a revival of older ideas of retrogression, which can be detected in early writers such as Homer and Hesiod before the sixth century B.C. Before Christianity had won any real influence, a new version of the cyclical conception was favored by Stoics and Neo-Platonists. In all these confused streams of thought, Sorokin detects one expressing the still-lingering optimism of the decaying sensate culture, especially from the third century B.C. to the first century A.D., another more pessimistic stream portending its decline, and a third, a definitely cyclical view, foreshadowing the generation and growth of the succeeding ideational culture, which was to last almost unbroken up to the thirteenth century A.D. From then up to the sixteenth century, a newer note can be discerned. The ideational inheritance, shot through with more sensate impulses, produced the idealistic color of the Age of the Renaissance.

The general belief in astrology maintained the vogue of cyclical theories which endured with or without such support through the fifteenth and sixteenth centuries, although writers like Bodin, G. Bruno and Campanella contributed notably to a change in favor of the progressively linear conception of human history. The modern "idea of progress" had its origin unmistakably in the seventeenth century. From then onwards it suffused men's thinking in literature, science, philosophy, political and social theory. Those like G. B. Vico, who continued to advocate cyclical conceptions, were little heeded. Fontenelle, Montesquieu, Voltaire, Adam Smith, Priestley, Herder, Kant, and others, helped to establish ways of thought which prepared the path for the application by Herbert Spencer, Lamarck and Darwin of the idea of linear evolution in biology and in the social sciences.

It was not until the twentieth century that mankind awoke to the realization that belief in the idea of progress itself was a very recent faith and that it has had historical antecedents of a very different character. In the nineteenth century, as Sorokin points out, the prevalent opinion took some linear, and usually a progressively linear, conception of change as the chief topic or main ordering principle in the social and humanitarian sciences. Anthropologists, sociologists, historians, economists, political and social philosophers, and theologians have all popularized some type of the theory of progress, whether it be progress from ignorance to science, from instinct to reason, from despotism to liberty, from inequality to equality and so forth — sometimes regarding the development as progress in a straight line, sometimes as progress by stages, such as Comte's three states, theological, metaphysical, and positivist. Now, however, such views are no longer blandly accepted as the unquestionable pronouncement of scientific discovery. In biology, in which the doctrine of evolution received its classic statement, it is still the dominant philosophy. Nevertheless a new interest is being given to cyclical and undulating pulsations in the phenomena of life. The social sciences have thrown overboard the notion that all human societies pass through a uniform sequence of stages in their course of development. Economic theory is no longer concerned so much with the economic stages of development to which German economists especially devoted attention in the last half of the nineteenth century, but it now concentrates more upon cyclical, recurrent, and fluctuating aspects of economic phenomena. Nothing more strikingly illustrates this reversion to interest in cyclical theories than the great vogue of Spengler's *Decline of the West*. There has been no work of comparable influence supporting the older linear view of social development since 1914.

From such considerations, Sorokin concludes that it is probably correct to hold that the idea of a progressive linear evolution in the development of mankind and society is associated with a rising sensate form of culture, and that it is not found in the predominantly ideational culture, where cyclical theories are more generally favored.

It is impossible to leave this topic without pointing to the obvious fact that Sorokin's own work is a resolute effort to demonstrate and to justify a pronouncedly cyclical view of historical development. He does not, of course, disguise the fact, and in the fourth volume of his great work, *Social and Cultural Dynamics,* he analyzes, more thoroughly than any other writer has so far attempted to do, the broad philosophical and sociological ideas and concepts involved in a thoroughgoing cyclical theory of history. There he faces the question of how cultures change, examining in turn such problems as the extent to which cultural systems change as a whole or in parts, the rise and diffusion of sociocultural phenomena, the ways in which changes in cultural forms synchronize, and the extent to which it is possible to detect rhythm and phases in such movements, resolutely attempting to identify two-three-five-phase and still more complex rythms.

Not content with his demonstration of the nature of cultural change, Sorokin goes on to seek for reasons to explain why changes occur, and to found his own views upon the self-generated internal origin of such changes, which he describes as the principle of immanence of cultural change. These views will be described more fully later.

Science

Sorokin's review of the historical development of the guiding principles of human thought and philosophy extends to include a survey of some fundamental principles of modern science and therefore of other more specialized general principles analogous to those of determinism and indeterminism already examined above. Such are the basic elements or categories of human thought concerned with time, space, number, and causality and the general scientific theories to which they make an essential contribution.

While it is true, as Kant pointed out, that knowledge cannot be had unless the mind is able to think in terms of cause and effect, or of space, or of time, nevertheless, Sorokin observes it is equally clear that different minds at different times have used these inescapable notions, these fundamental *a priori* categories, as Kant called them, in very different ways.

Theories of Causation – Both the ideational and the sensate mentality make use of the indispensable category of causation, because both believe that everything in the world results from some cause or may be explained by some reason. But whereas the sensate mentality regards the relationship between cause and effect as constant and invariable, such an idea is by no means characteristic of the notion or category of causation in an ideational cultural system. The prevalence of indeterminism in ideational epochs has already been described, and the ideational notions of causality not surprisingly are those of indeterminism. The explanation lies in the fact that the ideational mentality seeks in the world beyond the senses – in God, Brahma, Tao, Providence, or the devil – the true cause of all happenings and events. The sensate mentality will not look beyond the world of sense perceptions or the sensate world for such explanations. Idealistic and mixed mentalities will look for them both in the supersensory and in the domain of the senses. These logical expectations derived from a bare consideration of the nature of each dominant cultural system are confirmed, Sorokin holds, by a survey of the views expressed on the question by writers in various epochs.

In India, for example, the Hindu's conception of causality in the Vedas and in the Upanishads was predominantly ideational. The course of nature and of the world were regarded in these works as manifestations of the supersensory Brahma or other power. In China, however, Sorokin considers that a more mixed view of causality prevailed. Nevertheless, as he points out, all changes were accounted for by Chinese sages not by causality or special causes but in the first place by Tao, the Principle of Order that rules the world, and then by the derivative principles of Yin and Yang. Such notions seem just as wildly remote from the scientific atmosphere of modern Europe as do those of the Hindus, since they also seek explanations of things and events in a world beyond the senses, in an imaginary framework compounded of fantasy or of dreams. To dispense with the notion that every effect must have a cause and to look for all explanations of happenings in the world to such notions as order and harmony as the Chinese and Japanese are said to have done, is to live in a different universe from that of Western European culture. Yet the nature of Chinese civilization makes it clear that, whatever may have been their underlying philosophy, the Chinese were capable of close attention to concrete things in medicine, in chemistry, and in agriculture.

In Western European thought, the ideational and sensate views of causality fit neatly enough into the broad trends of development for which cumulatively impressive evidence has already been produced. Before the fifth century B.C., as the writings of Homer and Hesiod and as Greek religion and mythology make clear, the Greeks considered happenings in the sensate world to be caused and controlled by supersensory agents. Beginning with the second half of the sixth century B.C., and lasting throughout the fifth and well into the fourth centuries, these earlier supernatural notions were mixed with more sensate views in the idealistic conception of causality best illustrated by the philosophy of Plato and of Aristotle. In the *Phaedo* and *Timaeus,* Plato develops his view of the supersensory idea as the real cause of observed facts. Aristotle gives a more developed theory in his doctrine of the four classes of causes: formal, efficient, material, and final. Of these, the material cause or matter, and often the efficient cause, belong to the sensate world, but the formal cause and especially the supreme final and first cause, or God, belong to the ideational world. Aristotle clearly seeks to relate in one system of thought the mundane with the transcendental, mechanism with finalism, and the sensate world with the ideational world. His influence, like that of Plato, endures to this day. After the fourth century B.C., his views were soon reduced by the Stoics and Epicureans to a sensate dead level in which the efficient cause alone was considered to provide all that a theory of causation required. From the beginning of the Christian era until the fourth century A.D., the most diverse views — ideational, sensate, and mixed — are all found, but the trend was towards a rise of ideational theories of causation, not only with Christianity but in the Neo-Platonic thought of writers such as Plotinus. This trend ended in the fifth century A.D., in a complete victory for Christian ideational views of causality. They endured almost to the end of the twelfth century A.D. During these long ages, the will of God was generally accepted as a sufficient ground or explanation of all forms of change. From the end of the twelfth to the fourteenth century, a change is noticeable which resulted in the replacement of the ideational conception of causality by the mixed and particularly the idealistic idea. The time was at hand for a revival of the mixed Aristotelian doctrine of fourfold causality, to some extent accompanied also by the simpler Platonic idea.

These revivals of Greek idealistic thought are evident in the works of such men as Thierry de Chartres, Gilbert de la Porré, Alexander of Hales, Robert Grosseteste, Roger Bacon, and others, ending with Albertus Magnus and St. Thomas Aquinas. After the fifteenth century the ideational conception of causality steadily lost ground before the rising sensate views. It was a tendency powerfully aided by the works of Copernicus, Galileo, Gassendi, Pascal, Kepler, Boyle, Newton, and above all by Descartes and the Cartesian philosophers from whom indeed the origin of modern philosophy is commonly dated. A generation later it culminated in the radical denial of the validity of any non-experimental inferences in the doctrine of Hume, who maintained that we could not observe more than the contiguity and succession of pheonmena, and that the idea of any necessary connection in their sequence was added by our mind. From this view, Kant's theory that causality is an a priori form or category of the human mind was a logical development, as was also the modern scientific habit of regarding causality as a mere routine of perception, best expressed perhaps mathematically as a purely functional relationship, without further enquiry into its nature or fruitless speculation as to what might lie behind the observed purely quantitative uniform relationships.

The idea of a necessary connection between a cause and its effect, which survived in the philosophy of Hume, has since been given up by many thinkers and in its place nothing remains except the idea of probability. A causal bond is considered to exist when it is possible to establish the existence of a high degree of probability in the uniformities observed to occur. The teachings of such well-known men as H. Poincaré, Mach, K. Pearson, Cournot, Clerk-Maxwell, Pareto, Planck, and Einstein have powerfully aided this purely mathematical approach.

The result, Sorokin holds, has been a plunge into chaos. The attempt to base all knowledge upon a theory of probability, to reduce the notion of causation to a routine of perception, is to destroy the boundary line between science and non-science, truth and falsehood, the causal and the incidental. When there is nothing to choose between one causal law and another except expediency or the purely pragmatic test which finds that one proposition is more convenient than another, the world and reality become something liquid, frameless, uncertain, and fantastic.

In scientific theory, as in other fields, the sensate cultural system has worked itself out by developing a scepticism about science and empiricism itself, thus sapping the very foundations of its own knowledge.

Sorokin goes on to illustrate this development by referring briefly to the variations in other fundamental concepts of scientific knowledge, especially the notions of time, space, and number.

Time — There are the ideational theories of time looking for absolute time in another world than ours, and there are the sensate theories for which time is a phenomenon relative to the movements of the world of the senses. Writers such as Poincaré and Mach reject absolute time and space as metaphysical and useless because they cannot be measured. For them, as for thousands of scientists, that alone is real which is measurable. The properties of time, therefore, are nothing but those of the clocks, and the properties of space are but those of the instruments of measurement. Number also plays an entirely different role in an ideational cultural system from that which it occupies in a sensate system. The use of numbers as symbols, the belief in magic numbers, is characteristic of the "numerology" of ideational thinkers and is entirely foreign to the scientific mathematics of our sensate age for which quantitative knowledge alone is real knowledge. Sorokin does not deal in any detail with the history of mathematics, but he refers in a footnote to the fourth volume of his *Social and Cultural Dynamics* (page 752) to the somewhat discouraging results of the efforts of the anti-intuitional mathematicians and symbolic logicians to prove anything and everything in mathematics without any recourse to intuition, as Whitehead and Russell sought to do in *Principia Mathematicaa,* for instance.

Atomic Theories — When these first principles and categories of human thought show such marked fluctuations, it is to be expected that general scientific theories, to which they contribute and in which they are somehow held together, should also change. Sorokin illustrates the argument by briefly tracing the history of the atomistic theory, the theory of light, and the mechanistic and vitalistic interpretation of the phenomena of life.

    In doing so he corroborates the expectation that atomism, as a form of materialism, should develop in association with the empirical system of truth, with mechanistic materialism and in general in a sensate cultural system. In Greek tradition the atomic philosophy was traced back to a Phoenician, but its sudden vogue at the hands of Leucippus and Democritus in Greece at the end of the fifth century B.C. was shortlived. The idealist movement under Socrates, Plato, and Aristotle had no use for atoms. Epicurus almost a century later attempted to revive the outcast theory, but had no noticeable success. Asclepiades in the first century B.C., from whom Lucretius learned, was almost alone in following atomic philosophy, and Lucretius himself (99-55 B.C.), who first brought the doctrine prominently before the Romans, did not succeed in popularizing it. After the death of Galen in 200 A.D., atomism disappeared from Western Europe for a thousand years, although some acquaintance with it survived, through Byzantium, among the Arabs. In the twelfth century, however, atomic ideas made a hesitant reappearance, as the writings of

Adelard of Bath and William of Conches testify. These few and faltering beginnings found little echo. In the thirteenth century, Roger Bacon took the prevailing view against atomism. Despite the partial recovery of the Greek and Roman classics, particularly of Lucretius (in 1418), it was not until the seventeenth century that atomic theories began to come into their own, particularly through the works of Francis Bacon and Gassendi.

Without attempting to follow in detail the various views of the ultimate nature of reality expounded by Descartes, Boyle, and Newton, to whom Sorokin refers, or by Francis Glisson and Leibniz, whom he omits, it is clear that the seventeenth century launched scientific thought upon an atomic conception of matter which was notably developed a hundred years later by Dalton, Lavoisier, and Gay-Lussac. In the twentieth century, however, the firmly held belief that atoms are physical realities came under attack. The sequel may perhaps be best indicated by Eddington's statement in 1928 that "the physical atom . . . . is a schedule of pointer readings." Since then ideas about the constitution of the universe have become far more complex.

Sorokin's brief and compressed historical review, necessarily much further abridged here, indicates clearly enough that atomism is positively associated with the empirical system of truth and with sensate culture, and that it owes its vogue and popularity to the type of mentality supporting them.

Biological Theory — Similar assertions can be made about the development of biological theories, particularly the association of vitalistic theories with ideational culture and of mechanism with materialism and sensate culture. Sorokin illustrates these matters by a brief reference to doctrines about the origin of life itself, showing that in an ideational cultural epoch, such as the Middle Ages, most people believed in the spontaneous generation of life (abiogenesis), whereas in our modern sensate culture such a view is completely rejected in favor of biogenesis on the ground that it alone can be experimentally justified, regardless of its logical inability to contribute anything to the baffling problem of the origin of life.

Theories of Light — Theories about the nature of light may not seem explicable by Sorokin's theories, yet he points out the interesting fact that the three main theories about the nature of light are associated with the main cultural epochs. They were first, that light emanantes from the eyes, the visual-ray theory; second, that particles are detached from the surfaces of all bodies which are impressed on the eyes, the corpuscular theory; and lastly, the wave theory, that light is an impulse propagated through a pellucid or diaphanous medium such as the modern luminiferous ether.

That the corpuscular theory should be associated with atomic theories is plausible enough. In ideational periods very few people bothered themselves about the nature of light, but the general.tendency was to believe the emission or visual ray theory.

In idealistic periods there were mixed views, with the visual ray theory and the undulatory or wave theory predominating. From the sixteenth to the twentieth centuries, the visual ray theory gave way to the more sensate undulatory theory and still more to the corpuscular theories. The twentieth century again shows a reaction against the nineteenth century views, Sir William Bragg going so far as to say in 1921 that "on Mondays, Wednesdays and Fridays we use the wave theory, on Tuesdays, Thursdays and Saturdays we think in streams of flying energy *quanta* or corpuscles."

Sorokin's investigations into scientific theories do not extend as deeply as those into the history and forms of art and philosophy; and he does not contend that all scientific theories and the oscillations in their prestige and credibility can be demonstrated to have a tangible connection with the changes in ideational, idealistic, and sensate forms of culture. Nevertheless the critical and fundamental concepts he has detected in the long history of scientific thought seem to establish adequate grounds for believing that, in the field of science as in that of art and philosophy, his main cultural systems may afford a frame of reference and interpretation capable not merely of holding together and illuminating the rise and fall of various activities, fashions, and theories but of emphasizing, in a manner never before realized, their essential interconnection and fundamental unity. Their utility in this respect will stand out all the more clearly if they are compared for example with other efforts to discover plausible cultural and sociological correlations of scientific thought, especially those purporting to explain everything by a single factor such as geography, climate, or economic or political thought.

Ethics, Law

From scientific and philosophical thought and speculation, Sorokin turns next to human endeavor and conduct and to the theories men have elaborated about them. Between the theory and the practice of morality there is often a great gulf. Men often see and approve the good, but follow evil to the extent that they are not restrained by law and the police.

Sorokin accordingly distinguishes the lower level or the "moral minimum" which society demands of all its members, expressed in its purely juridical norms and values; and the moral and ethical values which in a developed, integrated ethical system represent the developed human conscience, the peak of the moral mentality of the society. In this spirit Sorokin reviews the long history of men's thoughts and speculations upon the grand questions of right and wrong and on the ground and source of all value. His aim, once again, is to arrive at some reasonably precise estimate of the principal types of ethical theory and of the relative influence and importance of those who have thought and written about such problems.

Theories of happiness range from the more inclusive and philosophical class which regards the aim of human conduct as the attainment not merely of the maximum of sensual pleasures, but of the more noble, lasting and more refined non-sensual pleasures as well. This is the philosophical doctrine usually referred to as eudaemonism. There is a second less inclusive branch of the ethics of happiness which is content to regard the desirable and the good in life as the sum of separate, singular, sensual pleasures. This type of ethical theory is more carnal than eudaemonism and is satisfied with short-term results. It is the doctrine of hedonism. Utilitarianism, the third form of the ethics of happiness, emphasizes in Sorokin's opinion, the means of obtaining happiness rather than explaining what happiness itself is.

The ethics of absolute principles are contrasted with the ethics of love, as in the purer Christian tradition of St. Francis, for example. The ethical principles of some other ideational societies, however, seem to have been of a very different order, involving human sacrifices and other harsh, inhuman practices. The nobler forms of eudaemonism are sometimes associated with the ethics of principles.

Sorokin lists in tabular form the lists of thinkers and the results of his analysis of ethical theory, the ethics of love, the ethics of principles, and the ethics of happiness. The main trends are indicated in graphic form in Fig. 10.

From these diagrams it is apparent that the ethics of happiness was of small account up to the second part of the fifth century B.C. Moral values were held sacred. They were regarded as the commands of the immortal gods, not to be called in question or doubted by mortal man. In the second half of the fifth century B.C., and in the fourth century, there is a great and sudden change. The ethics of happiness in a noble and eudaemonistic form then appears, and before long the more sensate ethics of the Sophists. Both Plato and Aristotle are placed by Sorokin in the ideational-idealistic class as men who believed in the ethics of principles,

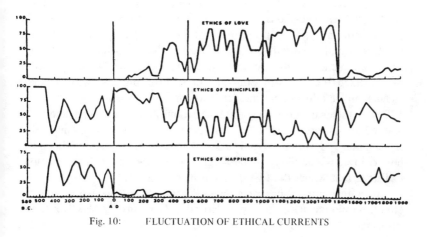

Fig. 10:   FLUCTUATION OF ETHICAL CURRENTS

although Sorokin holds that Aristotle is nearer to the sensate school as Plato is to the ideational school.

Throughout the fourth, third, second, and first centuries B.C., the ethics of happiness was in the ascendant, declining in the first century of our era and going underground in the fourth century A.D. Then, from the fifth century A.D. to the end of the fifteenth century, ideational values seem to have dominated men's thoughts. To learn the will of God and to obey His commandments was then the supreme rule of conduct. All sensate considerations, such as individual happiness or enjoyment, were held to be of no account in comparison with holiness and devotion of the whole life to God. Thousands of men and women sought to accomplish their vows of poverty, obedience, and chastity as monks or nuns in seclusion from the world.

Although no writer before the end of the fifteenth century can be found to expound a sensate system of ethics in opposition to this otherworldly philosophy, a considerable change in the climate of opinion begins to be observable from the end of the twelfth century onwards. A place begins to be found in the works of such writers as Peter Abelard, St. Thomas Aquinas, Roger Bacon, Dante, and Petrarch, for a note of sublime eudaemonism, allowed always only in so far as it does not contradict the commands of God. All such writers had an ideational training and a religious outlook. Nevertheless the same idealistic tendency noticeable in the literature of the period can be detected in their works.

The sixteenth century, the time of the Renaissance and Reformation, saw a sudden enormous increase in sensate systems of ethics. The seventeenth and eighteenth centuries witnessed a slight reaction, but in the nineteenth and twentieth centuries sensate ethics in a frankly utilitarian and hedonistic form dominated, and not merely progressively subordinated the ethics of principles or of love, but also weakened the eudaemonistic ethical doctrines. It is worth while to compare Table 5, p. 175 with the chart illustrating the fluctuations in the view taken about the nature of universals. (Fig. 10 on page 171), for it is evident that single-minded devotion to universal or general concepts, such as duty, honor, love, is not likely to be so general among nominalists as among realists, a fact which the two diagrams help to show.

In a few interesting paragraphs, Sorokin again relates his views of ethical development to those popularized in Germany by Max Weber and Ernst Troeltsch and in England by R. H. Tawney on the subject of religion and the rise of capitalism. Sorokin agrees with these writers in their views about the ways in which the reforming theories of Luther and Calvin, and of the other dissenting creeds, undermined ideational ethics by justifying, glorifying, and sanctifying a utilitarian sensate mode of life. He completely rejects, however, their theory that Protestantism was in any real sense the cause of modern capitalism. Both the rise of Protestantism and the rise of capitalism and of modern economic practices were really manifestations of the great underlying movement of cultural life away from ideational and otherworldly values towards a sensate, mundane, carnal system. The same essential transformation, although in a different form and degree, took place within the Catholic doctrines and in the moral teachings of these centuries. To regard, therefore, the Protestant Reformation as the cause of capitalism is about as logical as to regard the growth of whiskers on a man's face as the cause of his growing from boyhood to manhood. This short reference indicates how Sorokin's theory of cultural development is able to set in a new and illuminating perspective an exceedingly plausible and well-established sociological theory of economic development which, however, must now be given up in the terms in which it has hitherto been stated.

As the high periods of the ethics of happiness, Sorokin notes 1560-1620, 1760-1780, and finally from 1880 to our own day. He considers that most of the sensate systems have since become more sensual and subjective, more earthly and more carnal than they were during the greater part of the history of Greece and Rome. Certainly he finds little difficulty in illustrating this view by reference to certain aspects of contemporary life with its elevation of utility and hedonism into the guiding principles and dominant traits of life and behavior. He points to the way in which almost anything is now turned, if possible, into a source of monetary gain, whether it be titles, religious preaching, the birth of quintuplets, quadruplets, or fame in sport, politics, or crime. Money-makers tend to be accepted as the natural leaders of society. Socialists and communists who make a violent denunciation of this state of affairs part of their stock-in-trade, have, on a final analysis, no better principles to offer. Their aim also is money and material satisfaction, but they want it for larger social groups and for the masses, not forgetting themselves.

Lenin quoted Marx on "the fundamental principles of materialism" from Marx's *Contribution to the Critique of Political Economy:* "The mode of production of the material means of life determines in general the social, political, and intellectual processes of life. It is not the consciousness of human beings that determines their existence, but, conversely, it is their social existence that determines their consciousness."* There was sufficient plausibility about such a theory to build upon it the thesis that all spiritual results of man's historical activity are in the long run determined by the material forces of production, tools, and machines, together with natural resources and the skill to operate them. Such a rejection of "spiritual results" and the cultural values to which they led was much less plausible. As though he sensed this, Stalin seemed to bring back some of the despised "bourgeois" values.

Stalin's *Dialectical and Historical Materialism,* for instance, has a passage to the effect that "far from denying the significance and role in history of social ideas, theories, views and political institutions, Historical Materialism emphasizes the role and importance of such factors in the life of society, in its history .... their significance lies in the fact that they facilitate the progress of society and is the greater, the more accurately they reflect the needs of development of the *material* life of society. New social ideas and theories indeed arise only after the development of its *material* life has set new tasks before society. But once they have arisen, they become a most potent force which furthers the *material* progress of

*V. I. Lenin, *The Teachings of Karl Marx,* reprinted in *A Handbook of Marxism,* E. Burns, ed. (London, Gollancz, 1935), p. 543.

society. It is precisely here that the tremendous organizing, mobilizing and transforming value of new ideas, new theories, new political institutions becomes manifest."

The key word in the above quotation has been put here in italics to indicate how its whole doctrine illustrates Sorokin's theories of the sensate cultural development of our times. Judged by that standard, one high priest of the new creed had no new insight to offer. Indeed, like Aaron of old, he set up a Golden Calf because that is what the people demanded, or what he thought they would demand. The appeal such a doctrine might have made to the depressed, illiterate, and poverty-stricken masses of Russia and elsewhere would not be difficult to understand. Had it gone no further there would be less cause for complaint. What is historically and scientifically untenable on Sorokin's principles is the attempt to put forward such a doctrine as a basis for a new social theory and as a general principle of ethical validity.

The essential hollowness of a pseudo-religion, openly and for long very violently anti-religious, that has no other principle than the pursuit of material welfare is, however, becoming generally evident. Moral atomism, relativism, and nihilism are its inevitable outcome, for it has no absolute principle. To that result add the rule of force and coercion in the relations of individuals and groups. Sorokin published this verdict two years before the outbreak of World War in 1939, with its long record of almost unbelievable horror and barbarity and its aftermath of crime and unrest.

In the light of Sorokin's principles, it is not difficult to see the moral bankruptcy of Fascist, Nazi, Communist, or other Prison States. For such systems serve no moral values transcending individual or national self-interest narrowly conceived as an increase of wealth or of power. Ask to what good ends the wealth and the power are to be devoted and there no answer – except more wealth and more power.

The outcome of the ethical section of Sorokin's work is to establish once again that throughout human history the ideational cultural systems had greater comparative strength than the sensate cultural systems. Summarizing his statistical conclusions on this aspect of his survey, Sorokin presents the totals in table 5.

Relating his findings to the concepts suggested by his investigations in other branches of thought, art, and science, Sorokin can establish that ethical systems can readily be classified as ideational, sensate, or idealistic. The commands of an ideational ethical system are absolute, as is to be expected from its nature and purpose. Its nature is usually determined by its origin in the will of God or of some supersensory power. Its purpose is

Table 5:   TOTALS OF THE INDICES OF RELATIVE INFLUENCE OF ETHICAL DOCTRINES

Period			Ethics of Happiness	Ethics of Principles	Ethics of Love
540 B.C.-A.D. 100	..		239	356	—
100 B.C.-A.D. 600	..		28	305	120
A.D. 600-1500	..	..	3	71	307
1500-1900	..	..	799	1061	228
Total	..	..	1069	1793	655

to bring its followers into unity with that supreme and absolute source of value. There can be no question of its principles being used as a means for anything and anybody. An ideational ethical system cannot be intended merely to increase the sum of sensate happiness, comfort, pleasure and utility. Consequently any notion of expediency or subjective relativity is ququite foreign to it.

A sensate ethical system, on the contrary, is a series of man-made rules, justified and deserving of respect only to the extent that it increases the total amount of happiness, comfort, utility, and pleasure enjoyed by man, either individually or as a group. Such a system is essentially relativistic, since the rules change if conditions change and they lose all their force if they cease to produce the happiness, pleasure, and other tangible practical ends for which they were designed.

An idealistic ethical system occupies a position midway between the ideational and sensate systems. It derives its main principles, which are absolute, from the command of God or of some other supersensory, supreme authority, but it acknowledges secondary principles such as the commands of reason. These are relative and therefore changeable. So also its aims are service to the absolute ethical value, or God, and are therefore transcendental, and at the same time they are related to conditions of the everyday world, since the system holds that happiness in this life is the reward of those who serve God.

Criminal Law – After a fairly comprehensive investigation of the changes which have occurred in men's theories about right and wrong, Sorokin proceeds to a yet more detailed examination of the practical action men have taken in their criminal codes to give effect to their views. For these codes indicate not merely what forms of conduct are considered wrong in a given society, but how wrong they are thought to be.

Never before has any historian of comparative law undertaken so laborious a study and analysis of the content and its change in time of the main criminal codes of France, Italy, Austria, Germany, and Russia. It was not possible to include Anglo-Saxon criminal law in the survey because it has not been codified.

After the period of the Barbaric Law up to the twelfth century, Sorokin analyzes codes of law to discover how ideas have changed about crime and punishment from the twelfth to the fourteenth century, from the fourteenth to the eighteenth century, in the eighteenth century, in the nineteenth century, and in the twentieth century. Just over one hundred criminal acts typical for all time and all societies are classified in nine groups. They are crimes against:

Physical person

Moral person

Property

Religion and religious values

The family

Sex crimes

The certainty of evidential means and documents (*e.g.,* forgery, perjury)

Social-economic customs and habits

The state and political order.

Sorokin's summary review of the history of the criminal codes of the five countries establishes how the types of punishable actions fluctuate from one period to another. He shows that it is not true, as it is commonly believed to be, that in the course of time the number of the types of action punishable by criminal law increases. They change, and the changes are similar to those followed by all compartments of culture, a reminder, if one were needed, that criminal law also is an inseparable part of an integrated culture. Sorokin's investigations show that when a culture passes from the sensate to the ideational form, a series of actions not regarded as criminal in the sensate period are included in the criminal class. They are mostly crimes violating ideational values, particularly religious values, and action is taken against them with little or no regard for mere individual or social utilitarianism, hedonism, or eudaemonism. New forms of punishment of an ideational nature are also introduced, such as interdiction and excommunication. The punishments tend to be more severe than those provided by normal sensate criminal law, probably because the ideational period succeeds one in which sensate impulses have run riot, with the result that the human personality is deeply demoralized and disorderly. Ideational values, moreover, have the task of restraining the natural inclinations of sensate man, and that naturally requires greater pressure than sensate law would apply. It is hardly necessary to point out that this is not to affirm that severe punishment is necessarily a sign of an ideational culture.

The contrary change from the ideational to the sensate form of culture eliminates almost all ideational crimes from the class of criminal actions. Other crimes are revalued from the standpoint of minimizing penalties upon such ideational actions as remain punishable and of penalizing especially actions endangering the hedonistic, utilitarian values of the society, and especially those of its commanding and controlling groups. This is a result which might be expected on philosophical grounds also, because in a sensate age, a nominalist philosophical outlook is unlikely to believe in the reality of the general principles or universals which an ideational realist age wishes to foster.

Insofar as it is possible to generalize upon the comparative severity and amount of punishment in codes of either ideational or sensate inspiration, it seems that the governing factor is the extent to which the predominant type of culture is deeply rooted and established. If it is firmly planted, then punishment tends to be mild and moderate. When, however, cultural forms are changing, then penalties tend to become more severe. It is a tendency seen in the cruelty of settlers conquering new lands from native populations whose ethical ideas and practices are widely different from their own. It appears with astounding force in times of social revolution. Sorokin cites in evidence the cruelties in the Roman Republic in the first century B.C., in the Dutch Revolution of 1566, and in Cromwellian England. The cruelties of the Roman Catholic Inquisition, with its fierce persecution of heretics, are another example. But never have cruel penal laws or pseudo-laws exerted a more disastrous influence than during the French Revolution after 1789, or in the Russian Revolution after 1917, which eclipsed all previous records of butchery and oppression not merely in magnitude, but in duration also.

Sorokin sums up these tendencies by quoting one of his earlier generalizations to the effect that whenever differences and conflicts arise within groups about standards of conduct and their observance or, as he describes it, whenever the ethico-juridical heterogeneity and antagonism increases, then the amount as well as the severity of punishment imposed by one part of a group on the other tends to increase. Other things being equal, the greater the differences and the antagonisms, the greater such increase will be. As they diminish, so the quantity and severity of the punishment tends to diminish also.

So brief a summary is necessarily inadequate upon a theme so vast that Sorokin himself was forced to omit from his volumes the extensive and detailed analysis of the mass of data upon which his conclusions repose.

Social Relationships, Politics, and Economics

It remains to be seen what relationship, if any, exists between cultural life and the story of wars, revolutions, and social relationships generally.

Because Sorokin approached history as a sociologist, he was concerned especially with problems of society. In the third volume of his *Social and Cultural Dynamics* he selected three main sociological problems for analysis: social relationships, including the family, village, guilds, church and state, and economic conditions; war between states; and finally internal disturbances within states.

Social Relationships – The first of these themes, social relationships, does not lend itself to statistical illustration, and, while this is not true of the second or third, unfortunately adequate statistics are not to be had relating to wars and revolutions, particularly in earlier times.

From a review of literature illustrating the history of social relationships, Sorokin draws a series of conclusions about their nature and development, of which merely a bare outline can be given here. For a fuller description and analysis, together with a list of the sources on which his studies were based, the reader must be referred to Sorokin's own works. The third volume of *Social and Cultural Dynamics* and his *Society, Culture, and Personality* are the chief, but his earlier work on the sociology of revolution and his joint works with Zimmerman and Galpin, *A Systematic Source Book in Rural Sociology* (Minneapolis, 1930), and with Zimmerman, *Principles of Rural Urban Sociology* (New York, 1929), are also relevant.

Sorokin selects for historical study the Franco-German Carolingian and feudal periods, reviewing in turn the nature of relationships in the feudal state, the Church, the family, guilds, *Bunde,* corporations and other associations, village communities, and urban communities. These were the main groups of which medieval society consisted. Their predominant characteristic in the early Middle Ages, up to the ninth century A.D., was that they were each held together by familiar bonds of various degrees of purity and intensity. *Fidelitas,* loyalty, is the keyword, for it supplied the most general bond, the common and universal form of social relationship in the Middle Ages. The subjects of the king were his *fideles.* It is true that *fidelitas* was established by a solemn ceremony which might be regarded as being in the nature of a contract, but it would be wrong to hold that the relationship once established was contractual in essence. It was much more akin to relationships within a family.

Compulsory relationships likewise were not absent from medieval societies. They were inevitable in the military organization. Apart from that, their main role was to link the serfs, the unfree, and the semi-free classes to the free upper strata of society. Sorokin dates the first initial weakening of this early, predominantly familial relationship at the end of the eleventh and at the beginning of the twelfth centuries. The change then foreshadowed was in the direction of increasing contractual relationships at the expense of the familial relationship and to some extent of the compulsory relationship also.

Thereafter the trend was to become more pronounced, although from the thirteenth down into the sixteenth centuries the picture is very complex and somewhat contradictory. The transition began to show itself in a disorganized system of social relationships which was provocative of unrest and disturbances. It is clear that contractual relationships and compulsory relationships in particular both grew at the expense of familial relationships, and that this trend continued through the seventeenth and eighteenth centuries with the marked ascendancy of absolute monarchies typified by Louis XIV and Frederick the Great. They did not survive unchallenged. In the nineteenth century and up to 1914, contractual relationships triumphed at the expense of compulsory relationships and, to a lesser degree, of the already weakened familial relationships.

Now, however, there are signs of a change. Compulsory relationships are replacing contractual relationships, and pseudo-familial relationships are being developed. Of them Sorokin gives a pessimistic account. The Prison-States and other dictatorships cannot establish a real familial relationship, even if their rulers and sycophantic entourage wished to do so. They are able to arouse some temporary emotion in the masses by attacking and vilifying those whom, rightly or wrongly, the masses have regarded or have been induced to regard as their enemies. This is no way to create a family spirit, and indeed it was not long before the new rulers began to treat the masses as though they had conquered them. The bosses of the Prison States are described by Sorokin as "dictatorial wrecking companies," who are not builders of the future but mere wreckers of the past. Sorokin reaches this conclusion after following the story of the developments in social relationships in some detail as they are manifest in the history of the State, the church, the family, village and urban communities, corporations, guilds, and confraternities, in the bonds between the free strata of society and those between the free and unfree strata. Sorokin's own sketch is necessarily much shorter than he would wish it to be on a theme so vast that volumes would be needed to do it justice. To present its bare outlines in so summary a fashion is to do it less than justice, but they will suffice to prepare the way for the first broad conclusion Sorokin draws, namely, that there has been no uniform trend in the processes analyzed. It is only necessary for him to tabulate the broad main pattern of relationships for this fact to stand out clearly.

> Eighth to twelfth centuries – Familistic, compulsory, contractual.
> Thirteenth to sixteenth centuries – Weakened familistic, contractual, compulsory.
> Sixteenth to eighteenth centuries – Compulsory, familistic, contractual.
> Nineteenth century to 1914 – Contractual, familistic, compulsory.
> 1914 onwards – Compulsory, familistic, contractual.

Whatever may be thought of Sorokin's analysis, it at least has the merit of going deeper into the question than any previous theories have done.

For example, Sir Henry Maine's well-known generalization that, in Western society, social relationships have developed from status to contract seems merely a rough approximation when contrasted with Sorokin's more precise statement of the matter. Similarly, it is impossible to agree with those who consider that there has been a trend or progress towards increasing sociality, solidarity, altruism (familism), or the reverse. Nor is it true that history shows ever-increasing compulsions and antagonisms between men and their fellows.

To state the course of development in human social relationships aright is but the first part of Sorokin's aim. He next wants to know what are the reasons for the fluctuations, to what extent are the sequences he describes likely to be found in the history of societies other than those of one part of Western Europe and, finally, how do they relate to his concept of ideational, idealistic, and sensate societies.

Why then, in the first place, does one form of social relationship weaken and give way to another? Sorokin answers this question by invoking his principles of limits, according to which there are relatively few possibilities of innovation in basic social forms and processes, and by invoking also his theory of immanent changeability. If it is asked whether he means anything more by these impressive words than that things change because they do change, the answer is that he is able to give a deeper, richer content to his theory than such a reduction to tautological nullity implies. This is a claim to be more fully vindicated in the sequel. The essential aspect of the matter is that forms of social relationship, like all sensory phenomena, belong to the world of becoming. Change is the law of life, biologically, psychologically, culturally. Not merely life, but the material environment in which men live, act, and feel is constantly changing also. Friendship may, therefore, give way to aversion or hatred, devotion to contempt, and familism into contractualism or compulsory exploitation. That such an explanation does indeed exhaust the matter may be seen more clearly when it is put into concrete terms. A leader, warrior, lord, or priest, may by his inherent qualities sustain and inspire genuine familial relations with lesser folk who depend and are willing to depend upon him. But it is not likely that all his successors will exhibit the same qualities, neither is it probable that his subject peoples will continue forever to perpetuate a form of relationship when its ground or essence no longer exists. The formal relationship between the leader and his followers may no doubt survive for some generations, but it is then probably no more than a shell of its previous reality. The shell will easily become brittle and break in such circumstances. The search for a more secure and satisfactory relationship becomes inevitable.

Contractual relationships, which seem to promise to make good the deficiencies of the familistic system, before long reveal inadequacies that are felt to be intolerable. Sorokin illustrates the situation by referring to the replacement of the serfdom and villeinage of the Middle Ages by free and relatively free labor contracts. It was, he said, a great and noble achievement. In time, however, conditions changed. Suppose, he says, that hungry but free workers, with hungry families depending upon them, confront employers who are in no such economic difficulties. Then the freedom of the workers is nominal and the contractual relationships they may be forced to make are in reality of a compulsory nature.

In the nineteenth century a crisis overtook the contractual wage relationship which could not be continued, or was not continued, except by driving hard bargains at the expense of the weaker party, which were inevitably felt to be inhuman and unjust. Here conditions again had changed. Sorokin does not pursue his analysis. It would, however, seem that the crisis in contractual relationships was in reality a direct outcome of vast and unprecedented increases in human population, which we have now learned to attribute less to a sudden and reckless increase in the size of families than to improvements in health and sanitation which enabled children to survive who would inevitably have died in the inferior conditions of previous centuries. The result was that the labor marked was flooded with the offspring of parents who were quite powerless to bring about the necessary expansion in the national economy which would alone have provided them all with a living. To contemporaries it may have seemed that the fault lay with the parents, who, through ignorance or improvidence or both, were unable to rear their children and to launch them into the world as their parents and grandparents had on the whole contrived to do. Many employers, large numbers of whom had risen by fierce energy and determination to survive from the ranks of this huge surplus population, so used the contractual system that it became in effect a form of compulsion. On the whole, they made the system work by securing the necessary expansion of national wealth, enriching themselves by employing labor that was cheap for the same simple reason that anything is cheap in a free market if the supply of it exceeds the demand for it. Any of the "downtrodden workers," as social reformers called them, might, with equal energy and initiative, have become employers themselves. But what was the alternative at such a time, except starvation for the workers? The "industrial revolution" rescued them from this fate. In later days also, new forms of economic compulsion arose, when millions became unemployed, not because they were faced with harsh contractual terms but because they could obtain no contract of any kind and were forced to rely upon public or state aid for survival. Juridically, says Sorokin, men were still free to accept the contract or not; but factually, in such overwhelming economic crises, there is no contractualism any more. It had to be replaced by something even worse; compulsorily imposed work with a small compulsory remuneration. The shell stays, the content is changed.

What happened in the former freely-operating contractual wage relationship has also occurred in other fields where, through changing conditions, contractualism has completely changed in character. Earlier liberties of speech, press, meetings, unions, and political suffrage continued to exist in law. In fact, says Sorokin, in some countries they became monopolized by various private and public agencies. Before long the masses ceased to believe in their fictional freedoms and fell a ready prey to demagogues who openly slandered and vilified their liberties and the whole social system in which those liberties were supposed to exist.

Hence the ascendancy of Communism, Fascism, and Hitlerism.

In the relationships between nations, there has also been a breakdown. The old doctrine, held as sacred in Roman law, that contracts should be fulfilled, *pacta sunt servanda,* has given way to expediency. The Germans, who broke their promise to respect the neutrality of Belgium in 1914, not surprisingly were not more likely to honor their signature of the Treaty of Versailles. Since 1919, the lack of honor among nations unhappily has all too many tragic illustrations, and new examples continually occur. When expediency replaces strict regard for the sanctity of contractual obligations, the road to cynicism and nihilism becomes short and it will inevitably be taken. A thorough-going nominalist can take a short way with notions such as honor when self-interest drives him to do so. The compulsory relationships which the Prison-States are imposing can provide no remedy for the consequences of refusing to honor contractual obligations and, in Sorokin's view, they are inevitably doomed. To withhold freedom, as they do, before long kills the chained and exhausts the chainers.

In this way, Sorokin expounds what some careless and hasty critics have mistaken for a self-evident tautology that the causes of change in social relationships, so unmistakably recorded in history, are self-generated or immanent in the social process itself. At the same time, he makes it clear that there are strict limits to the forms of social relationships, so that, when one form is exhausted or worked out, there are no more than two other forms which may replace it.

From the nature of the change, at which the very few examples quoted above can merely hint, it is not difficult to see the answer to the second major question that Sorokin poses, namely, whether there is anything inevitable in the sequence of such changes as can be observed in the history of Western European society. From the nature of the case, there is clearly no reason why the observed sequences should be universal and not merely one among others that are possible. How do the observed changes fit Sorokin's ideational-idealistic-sensate universal and not merely one among other that are possible? How do the observed changes fit Sorokin's ideational-idealistic-sensate classifications of social and cultural phenomena?

It seems that the more ideational any culture is, the more conspicuous are its familial social relationships. The more sensate it is, the more those relationships are likely to be compulsory and especially contractual. Sorokin does not state the connection more positively, for he realizes that a definite answer is hardly possible to the question whether the apparent association of familial and ideational culture is merely a coincidence or whether it has a deeper significance and is of a logical and functional character.

There are indeed, he thinks, good grounds for supposing that the association is more than merely coincidental. Ideational values, being those of absolute and religious principles, inhibit the sensual and carnal desires of those who are loyal to them. Consequently the urge to drive hard bargains is swamped by a fraternal spirit towards fellow brothers in God or in Spirit. A more fundamental reason is that in an ideational society it is the group, or the ideational principle of brotherhood in God, the *corpus mysticum*, which it is supposed to enshrine, that alone is real. The individual does not count, except insofar as he makes up the collective oneness of the society in which all are dedicated to a higher purpose. Such a view of the matter conforms to the findings about sociological theories of universalism and singularism and the to a highter purpose. Such a view of the matter conforms to the findings about sociological theories of universalism and singularism and the philosophical theories of realism and nominalism.

Abstract considerations of this sort are, of course, proposed by Sorokin as no more than a general guide in interpreting the actual events of the Middle Ages in Europe. The social and cultural world of that time was not *purely* ideational, a caution stressed at the beginning of this study. There was, for example, the institution of slavery which the leaders of the Christian society inherited from the age-long tradition of the pagan world and which, despite their aversion to it, they could not quickly liquidate, although they proved to be the main agency first to mitigate it and later to abolish it. In this way, Sorokin attempts to account for the considerable development of compulsory relationships at this time in the shape of slavery and its medieval form as serfdom. He also draws attention to the fact that the familial relationships were sharply limited by the extent of the ideational society supporting them. Outsiders were unable to participate in its benefits and were indeed often treated with the utmost cruelty. Sorokin's thesis can be illustrated by the strife between the patricians and plebeians in the early Roman republic, by the ferocity of the Christian crusaders, and by the medieval treatment of the Jews and others regarded as heretics.

It is easy to see why a sensate society with its nominalist philosophy, not believing that groups or collectivities have any supersensory or transcendental reality, substitutes contractual or compulsory relationships for those of a familistic type. Not merely does a sensate culture put all the emphasis upon the independent existence and the desires and values of the individual, but those values themselves are thought of in sensory terms as denoting material commodities, objects, and wealth. Consequently all men free to pursue their own way are almost certain to seek the same things. Competition and the struggle for existence cannot be much softened by appealing to the competitors to respect human brotherhood, the *corpus mysticum,* because it is of the essence of the sensate mentality to deny meaning to such mystical entities. An idealistic society is required to soften and to control these extreme self-seeking drives and appetites. In the thirteenth, fourteenth, and fifteenth centuries, Sorokin considers that social relationships showed that mixture of the familistic, contractual and compulsory forms which is one of the distinguishing marks of an idealistic culture.

The emergence of sensate man in the sixteenth century caused a tremendous explosion which rent the older fabric of social relationships. Violent, emotional, and greedy, he was not to be restrained by the word of God or by his own bond. Physical compulsions alone could control him, and hence it was that the sixteenth, seventeenth, and eighteenth centuries saw a new growth in compulsory relations and a notable increase in the real powers of central governments. The lesson was learned, and by the nineteenth century, after the French Revolution, sensate man was becoming more balanced and reasonable and more ready to settle down. He developed, says Sorokin, into a solid contractual citizen who wanted to bargain instead of to fight, to live and let others live. Hence the recent age of contractualism, the mature form of the crystalized and balanced sensate culture.

How this apparently stable state of affairs gave way in the twentieth century, and was followed by a greater amount of compulsory relationships than the world has ever before seen, is a matter of contemporary experience. Sorokin has alluded to what he regards as some of its causes. He characterizes recent efforts to devise some alternative to the contractualism that has broken down as being analogous to the efforts of the cubists to find new art forms. The result, which has taken the form of Hitlerism, Communism, and Fascism, is not familism or altruism but the collectivism of the hard labor prison, with its hatred and its coercion. It is a regime fundamentally opposed to familism and anything like it. The dictators successfully destroyed contractualism, but replaced it mainly by compulsory and mechanical slavery: soulless, mirthless, companionless, largely devoid of real altruism, real familism, real solidarity. It has created so far only the pseudo-solidarity of the executioners among themselves and the forced and pathetic alliance of their victims. During the years which have elapsed since this apt description appeared, the most fearful events have confirmed its deadly accuracy, not merely in Germany and the countries overrun by the Nazis, but in Russia, in Eastern European nations overrun by Communists, and now in China and Africa.

The results have been clearly destructive of human relationships as they have been developed in the course of Western civilization. How to build anew among the wreckage left by the hordes of modern spiritual huns, vandals, and mongols, who have devastated the human heritage, bringing disasters far worse than those caused by their earlier prototypes, remains the problem to which Sorokin could merely point in 1937.

Political Theory — Forms of government and leadership have obvious links with the question of social relationships in general, but they are usually discussed independently of the broader social and cultural environment in which they arise. It is one of Sorokin's many merits that he refused to regard the two problems apart from each other, and that, before dealing with the political, juridical, and ethical questions of the forms of government, he first considers the broad sociological background against which governments and leaders of governments are operating. His findings are simply stated. Ideational cultures breed theocracies; sensate cultures give supreme power to the rich, to the military, or to groups which physically dominate society, whether they be the organizers of economic or other empires, inventors and scientists or various manipulators and bosses down to powerful leaders of criminal gangs.

Idealist societies have a political regime and leadership, partly theocratic and partly secular, of the type of sensate societies. Stated as a logical deduction from his general principles, this thesis is illustrated by supporting examples. The Brahmanic Buddhist, Tibetan, and Taoist parts of Chinese culture have been essentially ideational, and their aristocratic and sociopolitical regimes have been theocratic in their essentials. The two thousand year ascendancy of the caste of Brahmans of India was such that although, formally, they did not rule, they were able, through their prestige and superiority, to make India in effect a decentralized theocracy. In Tibet there had been an age-old centralized theocracy under the Dalai Lama, until it was overthrown by Chinese communists.

Western civilization shows similar characteristics. Before the sixth century B.C., Greece, then with a predominantly ideational culture, was governed by a king-priest. Already, before the time of Solon (c. 639-559 B.C.) Athens had, however, come under the domination of the rich and physically powerful. Ideational motives continued to exercise their influence, as may be seen in the poetry ascribed to Solon. Later, in the theories of Plato, with his advocacy in *The Republic* of the rule of philosopher-kings, a pronounced idealistic doctrine was developed, but it is clear that fully sensate views were then already current in the doctrines of Gorgias or of the sophist Thrasymachus whom Plato combats. Aristotle also took an idealistic stand in opposing the sensate forms of government, tyranny, oligarchy, and mob rule, and in praising instead the three good forms of government: monarchy, aristocracy, and polity. His warning that, above all, every state should be so administered and so regulated by law that its magistrates cannot make money was certainly not much heeded by the later sensate societies.

Rome shows a very similar development. The traditional account of the kings of the sixth century B.C. shows them to have been regarded as religious leaders. Their sacred duties survived the creation of the Republic in 510 B.C. A chief priest, *pontifex maximus,* then inherited part of the kingly religious powers; but the chief secular magistrates, the two consuls, were also invested with sacred powers and they performed sacred duties. All three, however, were elected by the people. It is well known how these awe-inspiring functions gradually paled in the light of common day. At the beginning of the first century B.C., a *pontifex maximus* was brutally assassinated by the political gangster, Marius, and a generation later that same exalted office was secured purely for personal political ends by a free-living, free-thinking, dashing political adventurer, Caius Julius Caesar, then only thirty-seven years old. The later Empire, despite the foundations so carefully laid by Augustus, who was declared to be a god, failed to restore any ideational character to Rome's supreme leader, upon whom some pseudo-idealistic prestige was conferred which the notoriously despicable characters of many of the succeeding emperors made difficult to sustain.

A very different state of affairs resulted from the increased power of Christian ideationalism towards the end of the fourth century A.D. Before long, Christian leaders, such as St. Ambrose, spoke and wrote as though the emperors were under their tutelage, a position which some emperors seemed content to accept. From the fifth to the thirteenth centuries, Europe had a predominantly theocratic regime precisely at the time that its culture was ideational.

Signs of a changed outlook begin to be discernible at the end of the twelfth century, when the first efforts begin to be made, by Marsilio of Padua and others, to claim some greater weight for the secular arm, reconciling, after the manner of idealistic theories, in one system both the spiritual and the secular power. As though conscious of the impending danger, Pope Boniface VIII, in 1302, issued his Papal Bull *Unam Sanctam,* declaring, "I am Caesar, I am Emperor." The subsequent arrest of the Pope and the removal of the Papal See to Avignon were sufficient answers to such a boast, providing conclusive signs that the days of theocratic government were over. The Babylonish captivity lasted from 1309 to 1377, and it was followed by the Great Schism in which two Popes, one in Avignon and another in Rome, disputed the heritage of St. Peter until the middle of the fifteenth century. It is unnecessary to pursue the story in detail. The collapse of theocratic government before the end of the Middle Ages in Western Europe is a matter of common knowledge. It may, however, be permissible to add to Sorokin's account a brief reference to the survival into the nineteenth century of the States of the Church in Italy with their antiquated, inefficient, and corrupt administration, contrasting so unfavorably with a reformed state system such as that achieved in England. All who have read Sir George Trevelyan's *Life oj Lord Macaulay* will recall the pungent language in which that doughty liberal idealist castigated the effete theocracy which he encountered during his first visit to Rome.

Bad as that regime clearly was, the results of contemporary decay in the leadership of sensate societies in Germany and Russia were more horrible. Sorokin catalogs the major activities, up to about 1936, of the minority parties who within living memory seized power in those countries; how they tore up the law of the land, stifled criticism, prohibited religious, moral or scientific beliefs deemed unfavorable to themselves, developed large-scale propaganda agencies in the effort to make themselves respectable and to manufacture that public support they knew themselves to lack. Along with all their crimes against the freedom of the human spirit went strict control and perversion of the educational system, monopoly of all the means of communication and the terrorism and brutality of the police. He might have added that little better demonstration is needed of the consequences of complete lack of principle among large numbers of the population of a sensate society than the evident fact that such gangsters were able to recruit all and more of the thugs and bullies they needed to staff their censorships, their secret police, their concentration camps, and their firing squads. That men can be so easily found for such brutal work was a sufficient indication of the moral values of the society in which they lived. The numbers of those with a sufficiently robust faith in liberal principles and in the absolute values of the human spirit, in the right and good, who accepted exile or death sooner than submit to the gangsters, armed as these were with the most formidable powers most brutally executed, were indeed large. Far larger were the masses whose loyalty to principle was too weak to ensure that the subversive movements were brought to nought.

Lest it should be thought that the words "ganster" and "Prison-State" are used here and elsewhere in this work as mere expletives, hate-words, or animal growls in the same way that Communists shout "Fascist beast," enemy of democracy," "enemy of the people," and "imperialist lackey" at those they wish to destroy, it may be as well to amplify Sorokin's arguments a little. A gangster is one whose dominant motive is a hatred, which he is prepared to back with the utmost violence, terrorism and brute force, of anything limiting his arbitrary power to use for his own personal satisfaction, in complete disregard for the principles of natural law and the rule of law, the possessions, the persons, and the lives of other men and women, obviously without their consent. Political gangsters create Prison-States from which their victims cannot escape and often try by some lying pronouncement uttered in the name of "the people," the Reich, the Party, or "the people's democracy," or by the trickery of fake elections, to simulate the willing assent of their victims to the swindle by which they are robbed, despoiled, starved, or murdered. A gangster, therefore, is not merely uncivilized. He is the active enemy and wrecker of civilization.

Edmund Burke, who witnessed the first outbreak of gangster-rule to occur in modern times on a scale carrying a threat of mortal danger to European civilization, recorded his astonishment that the mobs of the French Revolution were able so easily to loot, rob, murder, and to exult in murder. Contrasting this triumph of what he called "the swinish multitude," with his own no doubt over-idealized picture of the way of life they sought to destroy, he provided in imperishable language an obituary of a ruined culture. "Ancient opinions and rules of life," he said, were being taken away "to be replaced by a barbarous philosophy which is the offspring of cold hearts and muddy understandings." "The age of chivalry," he lamented, "is gone. That of sophisters, economists and calculators has succeeded; and the glory of Europe is extinguished for ever."

The melancholy future for Europe proved infinitely worse than he dared to imagine or that Sorokin dared to forecast in 1936. Bad as the violence and brutality of the French Revolution undoubtedly was, never in its most lurid moments could it have been believed that, after another hundred and fifty years, careful plans would be made, buildings and equipment would be provided, and a personnel recruited and trained to operate slaughter-houses for the extermination of men, women, and children by the hundred thousand. Would Edmund Burke or any of his contemporaries, including those who professed such indignation at his contemptuous reference to "the swinish multitude," have dreamed that among the fruits of another century and a half of civilization would be the concentration camps and mass-murder installations of the German Nazis and the vast slave-labor camps of Russia and Central Europe in which hundreds of thousands would be condemned to toil, to starve, and to die, beaten and tortured more brutally, more consistently, and more persistently for far longer than the worst sadist could continue to ill-treat animals? When merely to be able to flee home and country, destitute, to escape such a fate, as Sorokin himself was extremely fortunate in being able to do in 1922, would be regarded as a boon? Those like Tom Paine who attempted to answer Burke by saying that he pitied the plumage but forgot the dying bird certainly could not now repeat their question-begging sophistry. The decay of a sensate political system, horrible as its results have proved, is upon Sorokin's theory only to be expected as the full consequences of sensate political theory and the sensate way of life are worked out in practice. Like all deep cultural movements, the course of politics and government follows its own immanent development. The destruction of Fascist and Nazi governments, which has occurred since Sorokin described them in their heyday as evidence of the decay of sensate political life, could only be regarded as an inexorable immanent consequence of their own inevitable road to ruin if it is believed that it was their own immanent development which brought about the war in which they were overthrown. *Deus quos vult perdere dementat prius:* those God wants to ruin he first drives mad. The total result is therefore intelligible from the standpoint of Sorokin's claim that his theories provide keys to a better understanding of the past.

Once understood, they help to make comprehensible and even predictable scores of details about any given political system. A single quotation from the Code of Hammurabi or from a speech by Moses would, for example, be likely to indicate that it relates to an ideational society from which it is permissible to expect a theocratic government; the statement of laws as absolute commandments or taboos of supersensory powers; supernatural sanctions against offenders *(sacer esto,* excommunication, expiation of sins or crimes, etc.); a legal system employing supernatural techniques (ordeals); laws protecting ideational values of no direct interest or concern from a utilitarian, hedonistic point of view; education strongly influenced by theology; the inclusion of oracles, saints, and seers in the political structure in which its leaders themselves undertake sacred duties, little development of contractual relationships, and no great position of influence or authority reserved for the rich or physically powerful.

Such are some of the clues to historical understanding which Sorokin's theory provides, relating to one limited aspect alone of the subject-matter of the present work. Amplified as they might easily be by references to earlier sections stating the characteristics of ideational art, literature and philosophy, they are of cumulatively impressive significance. There will be scholars here and there to whom they may bring little that is new, especially in relation to their own narrow, specific areas of history in which, indeed, they may need modification and restatement. But for the great majority of those with a general interest in the course of broad, sweeping social and cultural developments in past ages, Sorokin's theory delivers keys that open a multitude of doors and hidden passages in history.

Such claims should be judged not alone by the extent to which Sorokin's own scheme provides a reliable clue to the past, but also by the extent to which it shows up the inadequacies of earlier efforts, a study best pursued in the light of his *Social Philosophies of an Age of Crisis.*

Liberty – The degree of freedom enjoyed by any individual in society is clearly an aspect of his social relationships and of the nature of the political authority to which he is subjected. It is also an aspect of that individual's own character or nature. Sorokin insists particularly upon this subjective aspect of the matter, since he argues that the only meaning human liberty can have arises from the relationship between human wishes and the means of satisfying them. Anyone who has many more aims, ambitions, or wishes than he can attain with the resources at his command, inevitably feels limited, frustrated, and not fully at liberty. Another person possessing the same resources, but with very much weaker desires and ambitions, will not be conscious of any lack of freedom. This last type of freedom is the inner type of freedom characterizing ideational societies. In the familistic social relationships described above, the apparent restraint imposed on its members is not felt by them as a restraint, because it provides them with a free realization of their wishes and desires.

Sensate freedom is not regarded in the same way as being capable of attainment through a limitation of desire. All the emphasis is put upon the external means of satisfying desire and upon the possession of those means by the individual. Sorokin points to the fact that sensate man cannot understand ideational liberty, which for him appears to be at best self-illusion and at its worst a self-seeking doctrine making use of high-sounding phrases and ideas in order to exploit and enslave other people. Similarly, men devoted to an ideational culture look upon sensate freedom as a miserable subjection to external material conditions, and they consequently regard those exposed to it as playthings of blind material forces. A multi-millionaire will not feel free if his vast wealth does not enable him to gratify every whim or fancy. A stern ascetic, whose aspirations for union with God are satisfied, will not regard his sparse diet of bread and water as a deprivation.

Sorokin's evident preference was for the mixed form of freedom characteristic of the well-balanced, "integrated" personality in whom the satisfaction of sensate desires is controlled by respect for worthy ideals.

Thus Sorokin is able to take one of the time-honored topics of prudential morality and to relate it easily and intelligibly to a broad general historical philosophy. It is easy to see, for example, why the demand for political and civil rights does not develop in an ideational society whose kingdom is not of this world. A new light is thrown upon the story of the struggle for human rights and fundamental freedoms when the effort to achieve them is seen to occur in sensate societies. The first theories about them in the field of political freedom appeared in Western Europe in the twelfth and thirteenth centuries. Not all classes of society were directly and equally involved at first in the social disturbances which led to the production of documents such as Magna Carta (A.D. 1215). The movement then begun in England has since steadily extended to encompass all classes, both sexes, and all ages, as the long history of English constitutional law and the feminist and youth movements and nursery schools of modern times attest. The French Revolution in 1789, inaugurated by the Declaration of the Rights of Man, showed how deeply the sensate trend had affected all classes in France. The widespread unrest throughout Europe in 1848 was yet another symptom. Now, however, as in other cultural and social developments, marked changes have occurred in the attitudes of several countries towards personal liberties and political freedoms.

The Communist regime in Russia dismissed them as bourgeois prejudices. The Fascists of Italy and Hitler's Nazis, for ostensibly different reasons, followed the Communists' example. Other dictatorial regimes have done the same. In countries still on the whole faithful to the doctrine of liberty and individual freedom, there have been, since Sorokin wrote, the most tremendous increase, although often under constitutional forms, in the powers of central governments. Brought into being under the stern necessities of a war for survival against the avowed enemies of liberty, these constitutional restrictions on free enterprise nevertheless have not lacked support, especially from the advocates of national planning or social engineering. In England, where Lord Keynes was perhaps more influential than any other man in disturbing traditional views, there has been a striking clash between the views of political and economic planners and those who mistrust them. Attacks on state control, such as those by Professor von Hayek in *The Road to Serfdom* or by Professor Jewkes in *Ordeal by Planning* and others, succeeded in capturing public attention, while more balanced and factual studies of the real nature of the process of social organization, such as those provided by the works of Professor C. E. Merriam, by Professor Herman Finer, and by Richard Warner's *Principles of Public Administration,* have been little heeded.

In seeking an explanation of the change from ideational to sensate ideas of liberty and freedom, Sorokin again neglects the influence of external forces, and puts all the emphasis upon his doctrine of immanent change. Each system breeds its own decay. There is a limit to the extent to which the most ascetically-minded ideational man can suppress the satisfaction of his bodily needs. The great masses of mankind are far less ready to suppress such desires than a saint would be. When they are denied physiological, psychological, or social satisfactions, they will try to get them. If they cannot obtain them peacefully, they will resort to violent means. Disorders, riots, and revolts thereupon arise to gravely undermine society. If the process is not stopped, there will be a serious loss of vitality, followed by emigration, suicide, or death.

That sudden change, relentlessly imposed upon traditional culture can cause the decline and death of whole tribes and communities is, Sorokin considers, proved by the fate of many primitive peoples, Melanesians, Polynesians, and Fijians, for example. The conventional explanation that exposure to unaccustomed infections brought by white races and that their consequent proneness to disease accounts for their decline, is, he holds, disproved by the fact that other primitive tribes, similarly exposed, have not died off as long as their ways of life were not interfered with seriously. The contrasting fate of the aboriginal Indian tribes in North and South America and of the Maoris in New Zealand in the last hundred years illustrates the point.

Sensate liberty is possibly more rapidly self-destructive than ideational liberty because of the well-known speed with which repeated sensations pall. The need to satisfy any particular sense, that of hunger, for example, can be fairly easily met. But as long as sensory needs rule, the satisfaction of one of them merely tends to increase the demands of others. The more sensate men have, the more they want, while it becomes impossible to find the means to satisfy them all, because economic resources cannot be expanded fast enough. When it has been possible for a limited number of very wealthy people to command everything they need, the result not only for them but also for the society in which they live, has often been demoralizing, devitalizing, and disintegrating. Such was the fate of the Roman aristocracy during the decline of the Republic. Driven by desire, they exhaust themselves in the search for new sensations until they may become, like Dorian Gray of Oscar Wilde's story, the oversensual seekers for perverse pleasures, which soon debilitate body and mind, spreading a trail of corruption wherever they go. Sorokin denounces in vigorous language the lengths to which sensate indulgence can go in offending idealist and ideational standards, but such excesses are better rejected on sensate grounds alone for the reason explained at the beginning of this chapter; "better" because sensate and ideational values are incompatible by definition. Then it becomes evident that any organized society must control such disintegrating forces or perish. Sorokin here did but repeat the wisdom of Aristotle who in his *Politics* 2000 years earlier had said that "it is of the nature of desire not to be satisfied" and that "he who bids man rule adds an element of the beast, for desire is a wild beast." Sorokin did not quote Aristotle, whose remedy however was essentially Sorokin's also, namely, respect for idealist or ideational principles. "He who bids the law rule," said Aristotle, "may be deemed to bid God and Reason rule." There must be self-control and the limitation of desires if society is to survive, but this leads necessarily to some form of idealism or ideationalism. In this way Sorokin demonstrates the immanent nature of the breakdown of sensate forms of liberty and of the rise of ideational liberty and order.

Government and Administration – This discussion about the various kinds of social relationships, political systems and liberty has been in predominantly general terms. Sorokin's factual studies had analyzed the distinction between such systems on the basis of the number of social relationships involved in each. From that point of view social systems can vary almost infinitely.

The simplest system contains only one social relationship, a society whose members have but one link, for example, that of collecting Nicaraguan postage stamps. An "Association of the Collectors of Nicaraguan Stamps" is a social system or group that regulates only one relationship out of hundreds of others which its members possess. If that were really the only link between people in society it would be an example of a perfect *laissez-faire* system. The complete opposite to this simple system would be a fully totalitarian system in which there were no free individual activities but all behavior was controlled and regulated. Instead of one link between individuals, a dense series of links would then characterize the social network. In practice it is virtually impossible to point to absolute totalitarianism or to an absolute *laissez-faire* system. Some social groups multiply the fibres of the network of relationship and therefore tend more towards totalitarianism; in others, or at other periods, regulatory and regimenting rules are given up so that many fibres drop out of the network which thus moves towards *laissez-faire*. Such fluctuations are a constant feature of social and political processes.

History can be looked at again, in order to detect these periods of the decrease or of the intensification of social relationships or of the contraction and expansion of governmental control. Such a study does not merely simplify an otherwise confused and tangled story, but it shows up at the same time the thoughtlessness and superficiality of an enormous literature on socialism, communism, capitalism, and liberalism, and political organization generally. Instead of presenting the study of human societies as a clash of warring "isms," it reveals the common basis of all of them, at the same time as it explains their variations on the basis of the varying number and complexity of their internal network of links, the number of fibres in each social network making up the relations of rulers and ruled, and of authority towards its subjects. The reality of sharp differences and the fierce opposition between extreme types of the unorganized and the highly organized community are certainly easier to understand in the light of such an attempt to describe their true nature scientifically and dispassionately.

From this standpoint of the degree of government control, it is possible to understand the similarity which makes recent Communist, Fascist, and Nazi systems species or classes of the same genus or large class of totalitarian states among which are to be found the state systems of ancient Egypt, Peru, Mexico, Japan and of China, especially in the eleventh century; of Rome under Diocletian, of Byzantium, and of other systems of government in East and West. In all such states, the government controlled almost all economic life, much of family relationships as well as religious, educational, military, and other activities. Like a spider's web, the network of the state system was so closely woven that the individual was hardly able to take a single step without touching it and bringing it into action. These early forms of totalitarianism were, Sorokin considers, more totalitarian than the Western state systems of the nineteenth century. Without attempting any statistical presentation of the rise and fall of totalitarianism, Sorokin briefly notes some of the more prominent fluctuations.

The Roman Empire, beginning at the end of the third century A.D. and especially under Diocletian, became very markedly totalitarian, and so it remained until it fell in the fifth century. Merovingian and Carolingian Empires had a far less totalitarian form, while the feudal states, which followed, dropped an enormous number of relationships from the state network. Sorokin adds that some of the dropped functions were taken over by other organizations. Although his remarks are true of the central government, they should not, therefore, imply that the individual was liberated from external controls. With the decline of feudalism and the rise of national state systems, under rulers such as Louis XIV or Frederick the Great, the network of governmental control once again became denser.

By the end of the eighteenth century, *laissez-faire* liberalism had swept away many of the mercantilist controls and ushered in an era of private enterprise in which individuals were very largely left to manage their own affairs, usually on a contractual basis. Their freedom, although large in relation to what had been attainable hitherto, was by no means complete. The first encroachments upon it, admittedly in a very modest form, occurred before 1850. The first signs of the growth of the Welfare-State of modern times may be seen in Bismarck's policy of state insurances in Germany. It is unnecessary to list all the forms of state interference, beginning with the protection of women and children in industry, the creation of a police force, the inspection of factories, mines, workshops and ships, the enforcement of public health and sanitary rules, compulsory education, and many other extensions of state activity, all of which began in England and in some other countries before the year 1900. They point to a trend which, as Sorokin says, made a tremendous jump with the World War of 1914-1918 and another jump, since he wrote, with the World War of 1939-1945. His conclusion, in 1937, that the present is an age of sharp rise in totalitarianism and of an increasing interference of the state government in all affairs has been shown to be correct.

At the same time it is permissible to point out that, in our own times, far more conscious attention is being given to the administrative problems implicit in these developments. The rise of the administrative Welfare-State under responsible parliamentary government makes the close network of relationships encompassing the individual today a very different affair from that in which he was enmeshed in earlier times. It has, for example, been argued (by Richard Warner, *Principles of Public Administration,* London, 1948) that the modern welfare state system can be regarded as the logical way of giving fuller effect to the grand principle of the division of labor upon which the efficiency of all social life must clearly depend. Sorokin adopts a similar standpoint when he points to the fact that social organization is not a mere matter of State organization, but that it includes also the organization of churches, voluntary societies, and other bodies. The striking thing about the development of the modern Welfare-State has been the transfer to the central or local government of any social activities undertaken by these non-governmental agencies. The Church has formerly been the chief victim in many countries of such revolutions in modern times. It has ceased, for example, to be the sole social means of providing educational facilities or to be the sole registrar of births, death, and marriages. However, qualitative distinctions of this sort in no way weaken the very evident truth of Sorokin's contention that the sheer number and complexity of the relationships between governments and peoples have most notably increased during the first half of the twentieth century.

Turning to the question whether ideational or sensate cultures are more likely to strengthen than to weaken the links between government and peoples, Sorokin finds that *logically* there is no direct or very close relationship except in the following respects.

Ascetically ideational cultures care little for State or government, so that no strongly marked totalitarian system is likely to be found when they prevail. Their lack of organization leaves them particularly vulnerable to foreign invasion. This logical expectation is verified by the history of the predominantly ideational Hindu culture in India.

Actively ideational cultures tend to create strong governments, usually directed by the paramount religious organization, so that they should lead to totalitarian theocracies. This, in fact, occurred to some extent in the Middle Ages. The theocratic rule of the Calvinists in Geneva, and especially in Scotland (strikingly documented by H. T. Buckle), affords another example.

Sorokin finds rather more difficulty in explaining the fluctuations in totalitarian systems in the sensate societies of the last four centuries. Why, after the powerful central controls developed by the early national States, was there so pronounced a swing away from their totalitarian tendencies in the eighteenth and early nineteenth centuries? Sorokin puts it down to the "overripeness" of sensate society occurring in a time of relative peace and security, a state of affairs abruptly shattered in the twentieth century by wars which have stimulated, as they always do, a new totalitarianism.

War is not the only disturbance which, in ideational as in sensate cultures sternly compels societies to organize and discipline themselves if they are to survive. Economic calamity, whether caused as in earlier times by famine, flood, or other natural disasters, or as in our own time, by catastrophic economic depressions, such as that in the United States after 1929, can have similar results. Illustrations abound in the measures taken by authorities to save the lives of peoples threatened by such calamities. In ancient Egypt, the great power of the Pharaohs rested on such a basis. In China also, at a very early period, government control of production, distribution and consumption had to be accepted as the only means of fighting famine.

In ancient Greece and in Rome, the story was much the same. As the needs of the growing population outstripped local resources, the state was forced to organize relief measures. In Rome the trend is remarkable, particularly around the time of Tiberius and Gaius Gracchus, whose Corn Law of 123 B.C. represented a most thorough-going effort to apply, for the first time in Rome on a large scale, the rational spirit of the Greeks in the interest of organization and material efficiency. These were but slender and unsuccessful beginnings. Centuries later, the failure of the Romans in the later Empire to achieve a successful economic and social organization culminated to produce, under Diocletian, a most thoroughgoing state-socialist organization of industry and labor.

For the Middle Ages, Sorokin lists the famine years in France and in England, all of which provoked increased governmental interference in economic relations. It should perhaps be added that the interference was not always very effective, since the absence of an adequate administrative service made the actual achievements of government intervention of much smaller practical effect than was intended. To the list of famines might also be added that of plagues – notably the Black Death of 1348-9.

There is probably little need to add to Sorokin's long list of examples to show how sudden catastrophes tend to provoke governments to devise remedies. His theory of the basis of social organization may, however, be a little further developed. If, he says, all human beings were wise, moral, exceedingly social, and altruistic, government of a compulsory nature would be unnecessary. They would themselves, of their own will, do all that was needed. As this happy state of affairs is notoriously not realized in practice, the necessity for government arises, as the sages of all ages have proclaimed, from the iniquity of mankind. Social life is, therefore, in a state of permanent emergency because there must be compulsory direction if the energies of lazy and unworthy men are to be directed to socially desirable ends, such as the need to save mankind from food shortages and famine. A society of none but wise and good men faced by sudden calamity such as war or a natural catastrophe might be presumed to organize voluntarily, so that the execution of each individual's task would not be felt as a threat to their freedom or liberty. Whenever the less wise and good overwhelmingly desire an increased measure of common effort, they must put up with the administrative means, the government regulation, the thick network of planned and ordered relationships without which that common effort cannot be effective. They also would not then feel conscious of the loss of liberty as an evil. Totalitarianism as such would have no terrors for them. Such, it may be added, was the state of mind of the overwhelming majority of the British people when, in 1940, they alone stood against the victorious Nazi aggressors. No love for totalitarianism as such inspired their resolve to accept the most thoroughgoing restrictions and controls upon the food they should eat, the clothes they might wear, or the work they should undertake. It was because they loved liberty more than life that they were willing to accept any sacrifice. They did not interpret liberty according to a narrow nominalistic standard or by any cool economic calculus of cost and advantage. It was not merely that they had to save their lives. Most of them might have done so by surrender. They were inspired by devotion to a purpose transcending their own immediate security, by devotion to the idea of a free society and a free world and a hatred of the bullies and aggressors who were destroying freedom. Here surely was the secret of their strength and a reason for their survival. The same spirit will inspire the stand all free peoples are ready to make against current communist or any other forms of totalitarianism. Writing before 1937, Sorokin declared that the harshness and brutality of those totalitarian regimes marked them in his opinion for inevitable decay. They will, he said, either be killed by the peoples subject to them or vanish by enfeebling and destroying the peoples they oppress.

Economic Fluctuations — Sorokin concludes his review of peaceful change in society, as distinct from changes caused by war and internal disturbances, by a review, made in cooperation with five other scholars, of economic fluctuations. He is easily able to show that the majority of writers on this subject, however sharply they disagree on many points, all accept the idea that there must be close links between the cultural and the economic aspect of life. Some, like Marx, regard economic conditions as determining the forms of cultural life; others take a contrary view and subordinate economic activities to the broader cultural conditions, including the religious outlook, of any given period of history.

What then is the true relationship, if any, between the fluctuation of economic conditions and cultural life? Factual studies of this great problem are beset by enormous difficulties. The bare facts about the realities of economic life over vast stretches of history are either woefully inadequate or altogether missing. When some few facts exist, it is almost impossible to extract much from them. What, for example, was a good, poor, or average standard of living at the beginning of each of the last twenty centuries, and how did one compare with another? It is obviously impossible to answer such a puzzle with any pretension to scientific accuracy. To do so would involve some reasonably secure estimate of a whole series of factors: quantity and quality of goods produced and consumed per head of the population; the more elusive gratification derived from power, prestige, freedom, contentedness, health, morality; and the outlets for directive and creative abilities.

The evident objection that it is impossible to derive a clear-cut definition of economic well-being from such nebulous general notions as these does not deter Sorokin from the search for the best estimates he can make or from criticisms of much contemporary social science, which he regards as fundamentally fallacious, because it attempts to proceed as though in possession of clear-cut ideas of such concepts as economic welfare or well-being, which, by their nature, cannot be clear-cut or definite. Tested by his own notion of economic well-being, the inadequacy of many attempted definitions based on income-and-expense accounts is clearly evident.

Many contemporary business barometers, made up of such factors as steel production, building construction, power consumption, and so on, are of no greater utility. They cannot be projected backwards into the past. Instead of attempting to proceed by means of such inadequate notions, Sorokin and his colleagues have tried to use a ten-point scale of values in assessing past economic conditions. It is as follows:

10 excellent economic situation of the highest prosperity
9   very good
8   good
7   very satisfactory
6   satisfactory

5 fair
4 almost fair
3 rather bad
2 bad
1 very bad

Many who study and write about the past are probably able to form some such judgments about the state of economic activity at the various periods of history in which they are interested, although not all formulate their standards of appraisal in such methodical detail. Still less do they consciously analyze the long list of symptoms of prosperity and depression, eighteen of the most important of which were listed by Sorokin and used as guides in the studies undertaken by his collaborators. They are:

1. Mention by contemporary chroniclers of the existence and increase of economic enterprises.
2. Contemporary testimony about poverty and prosperity.
3. Appearance and growth of comparatively large individual fortunes.
4. Evidence of the growth or decline of agricultural enterprises and agricultural populations.
5. Evidence of the foundation, growth, and increase of cities and city buildings.
6. Opening and development of new trade routes by land, water, and air.
7. Evidence of the rise of labor movements.
8. Expansion or shrinkage of colonizing activities.
9. Population movements, growth or decline in size or density, the increase or the decrease in mortality-rates.
10. Epidemics and deaths from disease.
11. Direct evidence about the standard of living, prices, wages, employment, unemployment, and the accumulation of wealth.
12. War and peace.
13. Flourishing or decay of the arts, philosophy, and science; the creation or importation of art objects.
14. The building of temples, monasteries, cathedrals, and other religious centers; their adornment and enrichment or decay and dissolution.
15. The growth or decline of schools and other institutions of learning.

16. Political unification or disintegration.
17. Internal peace or disturbance.
18. Political expansion or decline.

Such being the main criteria and standards of evaluation, it remains to consider how they are to be applied both in breadth (that is to say, over how wide an area of any country or empire) and in depth (that is to say, to how many of the various classes of society the evidences of economic conditions may be regarded as applicable). Sorokin and his colleagues have made a gallant attempt on the basis of this comprehensive series of ideas to survey the economic history of the ancient world. As a result they present a series of charts which are reproduced here.

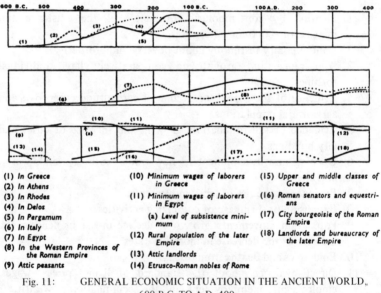

(1) In Greece
(2) In Athens
(3) In Rhodes
(4) In Delos
(5) In Pergamum
(6) In Italy
(7) In Egypt
(8) In the Western Provinces of the Roman Empire
(9) Attic peasants

(10) Minimum wages of laborers in Greece
(11) Minimum wages of laborers in Egypt
   (a) Level of subsistence minimum
(12) Rural population of the later Empire
(13) Attic landlords
(14) Etrusco-Roman nobles of Rome

(15) Upper and middle classes of Greece
(16) Roman senators and equestrians
(17) City bourgeoisie of the Roman Empire
(18) Landlords and bureaucracy of the later Empire

Fig. 11:   GENERAL ECONOMIC SITUATION IN THE ANCIENT WORLD, 600 B.C. TO A.D. 400

The broad general conclusions drawn from this analysis, which, it must be emphasized, is no more than the best provisional estimate that can be made in the lack of adequate data, may be stated in summary form. Economic prosperity characteristic of sensate cultures, making happiness and well-being their aim (eudaemonism), is not found in periods of ideational culture, but occurs in association with sensate cultures at the period of their ascendancy and before their decline. Such, for example, seems to have been the situation in Greece. Economic prosperity was not very high in the ideational sixth century, but it rose considerably with the rise of the sensate culture in the fifth and fourth centuries. It was more pronounced in Athens than in the rest of Greece, and still more marked in centers of Hellenistic culture, such as Rhodes, Pergamum, and Alexandria.

These improvements were not equally enjoyed by all classes of the population. In the earlier periods the predominantly familistic form of social relationships ensured that economic benefits were more generally shared by all classes. The development of a more sensate culture, by giving full rein to the greed and egotism of its leaders, replaced those familistic bonds by contractual and compulsory relationships, which were no longer protected by religious and moral checks. The exploitation of the poor by the rich in turn provoked revolt and rebellion and caused a general decline in economic prosperity of the society as a whole.

In Rome, the laboring classes also failed to enjoy the sudden rise in economic well-being of the senators and business classes (equestrians); but in the first, second, the third centuries A.D. they seem to have benefited by a considerable improvement which put them in a much better position than, say, the laboring classes in Egypt at the same time. Sorokin also notes the interesting fact that the economic position of the Etrusco-Roman landlords suffered a decline as the ideational culture of earlier times began to give way to the more sensate culture of the sixth and fifth centuries B.C. Later, however, the landlords, together with the bureaucracy, began to improve their position when the sensate culture declined and the ideational culture rose in the third and fourth centuries A.D. Sorokin explains this state of affairs by saying that the landlords with the priests were the main organizers of the social, moral, and economic order in the ideational society before the sixth century B.C. As a rule, any class charged with this task of organizing a social system of values, including economic values and activities, almost inevitably improved its own economic status at the same time.

Additional support for such a theory is forthcoming from a study of the situation in France and in Germany, the main results of which are also summarized in two charts. Looking first at the chart of general economic conditions in France from 800 A.D. to 1926 (Fig. 12), it is at once apparent that in the ideational Middle Ages the situation was "very bad" or "rather bad," and at its best no better than "almost fair."

After the eleventh century and up to the second quarter of the fourteenth century, a period of predominantly idealistic culture is

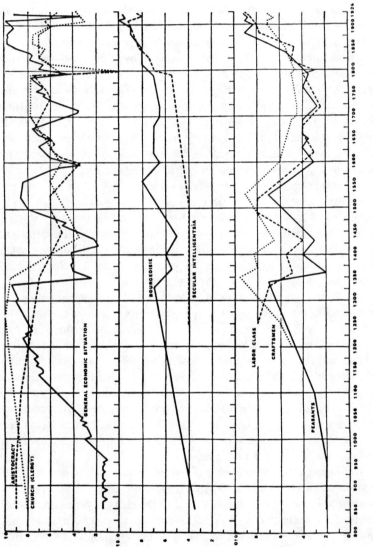

Fig. 12:   GENERAL ECONOMIC SITUATION IN FRANCE, A.D. 800-1926

associated with very marked improvements. The subsequent decline was in large measure due to the devastating results of the Black Death in the middle of the century. But, despite this disaster and the Hundred Years' War which France was fighting with England, sensate culture and society soon began to recover, quickly reaching a relatively high level of economic prosperity. A temporary decline occurred at the end of the sixteenth century, mainly as a result of the wars of religion. These religious wars were, like the Reformation by which they were provoked, themselves an immanent expression of the developing sensate culture and mentality. Recovery was fairly rapid, and after some fluctuations, of which the chief were caused by the economic disasters and unsuccessful wars at the close of the reign of Louis XIV, the Revolution, and the Napoleonic Wars, the curve of prosperity steadily rose until the war of 1914 again brought down the standard of living.

A specially interesting feature of the chart is the separate particulars provided for the chief classes of French society. The clergy, aristocracy, and landowners, as the chief bearers of the medieval ideational culture, enjoyed relatively their best position in the Middle Ages. The popular notion is that they continued to improve their position by grinding the faces of the poor, until the poor, unable any longer to endure their miserable condition, were forced to revolt. The facts are rather the opposite. Contrary to commonly accepted ideas, the aristocratic classes declined relative to the general economic levels; indeed, Sorokin considers that the aristocracy never fully recovered their relatively greater advantages after the setbacks of the Crusades and the medieval communal movements. The Revolution for 1789 finally almost destroyed them, and their place was taken by the new types of great landowners, not, however, before they had loaded the fair land of France with their magnificent *châteaux* and their gardens in the seventeenth and eighteenth centuries.

The bourgeoisie and the intelligentsia rather than the nobles and the clergy were the main bearers of the sensate culture, and the manner in which they improved their position relative to the other classes of French society is sufficiently evident from the chart.

The laboring classes, the peasants and craftsmen, reached what was relatively the highest point in their economic fortunes during the idealistic culture of the thirteenth and early fourteenth centuries. Social and moral principles were held sufficiently in reverence to ensure that these classes then shared in the increasing national wealth and income. The succeeding sensate centuries deprived them of this moral protection, and it was not until the great scientific and technological discoveries of the nineteenth and twentieth centuries had so markedly increased national prosperity that the relative economic welfare of the laboring and artisan classes again registered a notable improvement.

In Germany, a somewhat similar general development occurred, with, however, not quite the same marked contrast as that observable in France between ideational poverty and sensate prosperity. The charts, which are self-explanatory, emphasize the calamitous effects of the Thirty Years' War on German economic life. Central Europe and Austria are included as part of Germany up to A.D. 1500.

The German landed aristocracy and clergy, as the main bearers of the ideational culture, enjoyed relatively their best economic situation in the period dominated by ideational culture. The lay intelligentsia, the bureaucracy, and the capitalistic bourgeoisie rose relative to the other classes with the rise of sensate culture. Sorokin has not estimated the economic consequences of the introduction of the welfare state which, on his principles, may plausibly be regarded as an effort to recover some of the virtues of a familistic order of society.

Owing to the longer survival of the aristocratic tradition in England and in Scotland, where it is reinforced by the solidarity of the clans, hopes may be brighter for the success of such a task than they might be in other countries which have either violently broken with such tradition or indeed never known it. Nevertheless the effort to re-create familistic altruism in contemporary industrial society by a compulsory redistribution of the national income has given rise to many doubts. One of the chief is the fear that the policy of depriving people through taxation of many benefits they could otherwise secure for themselves may end by greatly weakening the initiative springing from self-interest, yet fail to generate a true altruism of a familistic society, if indeed it was ever hoped to produce it. The more usual view no doubt is that the fuller material life which the welfare state should secure for each individual member of it will endow them with abilities and resources able to lift the national income and everybody's share in it to new levels, high enough to overcome any adverse effects upon individual enterprise which otherwise would prove a serious menace, both internally and in relation to the competitive position of the country in international trade.

Sorokin's view of general economic history, based upon his review of trends revealed in the records of the past, is a more thoroughgoing attempt to get to grips with the problem as a whole than anything produced by his predecessors. It has affinities with the findings of some of them, Max Weber, for example, but it is broader and deeper.

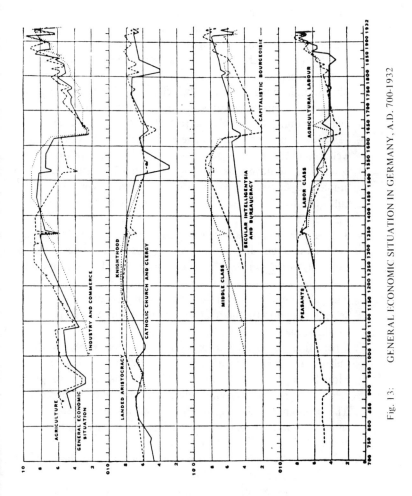

Fig. 13:   GENERAL ECONOMIC SITUATION IN GERMANY, A.D. 700-1932

Summarizing the results of his investigation, his main conclusions about the course of economic history are as follows:

1. The economic situation of a country or nation, or of any other large or small social system, does not remain constant, neither does it show any uniform trend but it rises and declines.
2. There are short-term and long-term fluctuations.
3. The economic level of ideational societies tends to be lower than that of sensate cultures.
4. Idealistic or mixed cultures, which arise as ideational cultures decline and sensate cultures advance, normally show a relatively high economic level in relation to that of ideational culture.
5. Sensate cultures provide relatively the highest levels of economic welfare, but a peak is reached after which the culture breeds conditions unfavorable to its continued existence. These immanent consequences of the full development of sensate culture adversely affect all its values, including its economic values.
6. The above relationships between economic conditions and predominant cultural types may be obscured or destroyed by external forces, such as plagues, famines and wars, but, apart from such calamities, they conform to and are explicable by the basic differences in behavior and mentality of ideational and sensate man and by the relatively greater harmony and balance of idealistic man.
7. Where there is no integration of a culture as a whole, or where a culture and economic life are not sufficiently well related and brought together, it is not possible to discern or to predict relationships of the type indicated in the preceding paragraphs.
8. The economic well-being of the various classes of people in the same economic or cultural system does not vary uniformly for them all.
9. In each of the main cultural systems, one or more classes are its main bearers, agencies, and integrators.
10. The main bearers of ideational cultural values are the sacerdotal class (priests, clergy, Brahmans, Lamas, etc.) and the religious landed aristocracy.
11. The main bearers of sensate cultural values are the capitalist-commercial bourgeoisie, the secular bureaucracy and

the independent, free-thinking, scientific, artistic, intelligentsia, and professional classes.

12. Peasants and agricultural laborers are very rarely the main bearers of any type of culture, because it would seem that they rarely attained the relatively high degree of mental development and integration needed for such a role.

13. The classes which integrate a culture are immanently destined to rise socially and economically as it rises, and to decline as it declines. Self-evident in relation to the leaders of sensate culture (No. 11 above), it may be less obvious why leaders of ideational culture (No. 10 above) should ever become wealthy. The fact is, however, that such men cannot escape the responsibility of exercising political, economic and social power and authority nor the privileges by which such responsibility has traditionally been accompanied and rewarded.

14. The growth in the wealth of ideational leaders undermines the ideational regime.

15. Sensate culture is also undermined by its own immanent developments. One example is the conflict between the secular intelligentsia and the moneyed bourgeoisie. Both are children of the same sensate culture, and their fate is inevitably bound up with its fate. Such conflicts occur as the sensate culture begins to decline, and they are suicidal. The capitalist class, attacked as it were from within by a relatively leisured class of intellectuals who could not exist without it, seems to lose its energy, virility, determination, and self-confidence and especially its self-respect. Sorokin might have illustrated this point by a reference to the career of George Bernard Shaw among others, who, after undermining the foundations of capitalist society by his vigorous, witty denigration of its leaders and a simulated, insincere advocacy of socialism, left a large personal fortune, despite his vigorous protests at a scale of taxation which was the logical consequence of the ideas he had espoused.

16. The economic fortunes of the laboring classes do not fluctuate as widely as those of the classes who lead, direct, or integrate cultures. In an ideational culture, the incomes of the working classes are usually low because the general economic level of such a culture is itself low.

In idealistic cultures, the general level tends to rise, because, in the dawning sensate culture, a greater attention to the good things of this world stimulates desires and improves economic efficiency. At the same time, however, ideational cultural forces remain vigorous and able to restrain and control the increase of greed and to delay the decrease in the familistic feelings and the decline in the sense of justice of the leading classes. Moral scruples about accepting the payment of interest upon loans are evident in attacks upon usury, which seem incomprehensible to a sensate mentality.

As a result the growing wealth tends to be more fairly shared and the laboring classes benefit to a relatively greater degree than they do later on, when sensate forces are fully released and victorious sensate man puts his own gain first and cares much less for social justice than did his idealistic or ideational predecessors.

Nevertheless, technological progress in a fully efficient sensate culture is such that it raises the general level of economic welfare to so high a pitch that all classes benefit, including the laboring classes, who are very much better off than their forefathers, despite huge increases in their numbers.

17. When a sensate culture declines, the general economic level declines, and the position of the laboring classes also worsens. Such a decline may be hastened by war, revolts, revolutions and a sharpening of the class struggle, as is happening in our own time, despite appearances to the contrary, due, in part, to monetary inflation.

18. There is a definite, although not close, association between the rise and fall of economic well-being and the dominant type of culture. Economic processes and activities are more subject to the influences of the external world and of nature than are cultural processes, and they may therefore be subject to considerable changes which are unrelated to the immanent development of the cultural life in which they occur. However, it is not true, as the extremist adherents of the materialist or economic interpretation of history assert, that the association between economic conditions and cultural activities is such that any change in these economic conditions is immediately reflected in cultural life also.

What is said above relates to the levels of prosperity and economic well-being of societies, that is to say the quantitative aspects of economic life. Equally marked differences are observable in the qualitative aspects of economic activities in the contrasting cultural forms. Ideas about production, distribution and consumption, the forms of social relationship in the various cultural systems, opinions about capital, property, profit, usury, price, almgiving — all show the most marked differences in ideational, idealistic and sensate societies. So much so that Sorokin affirms that contemporary economic theory, arising as it does in a purely sensate society and frame of reference, cannot be applied in any intelligible way to the economic life of an ideational society. This is an aspect of the history of economic life and theories which, says Sorokin, is badly in need of study.

It will now be evident that, on his principles, the study of social forces and of society, which is the subject-matter of sociology, is but another aspect of the study of the forms and types of culture in history. There is, therefore, but one reality for the sociologist and historian alike and that is what he describes as the socio-cultural world, one and indivisible. Nothing but the inherent complexity of so vast a world and difficulties of presentation are responsible for the separate treatment of cultural and social movements. That is neither new nor surprising. What is new in Sorokin's work is his determined attempt to deal as exhaustively as possible with each and to attack with the utmost resolution the task of demonstrating the nature of the mutual inter-relatedness of each.

Wars and Revolutions

The Fluctuation of War — Up to this point the historical changes studied by Sorokin have related in the main to ideas in the minds of men, their nature, sequence, and fluctuations. They are ideas which have governed or influenced the actions of individual artists, poets and philosophers, of large groups of men and women, or of whole societies and peoples. With the study of economic change, the social aspects and applications of Sorokin's theories became increasingly prominent. From theories of economic relationships and activities he proceeds to investigate human behavior in the raw as it is exhibited in wars and revolutions.

With great justification, he claims to be among the very few pioneers in the methodical study of war. It may sound a strange, presumptuous claim to make when, for several generations, there has been continual complaint that too much attention has traditionally been given in historical works to wars and the records of wars. The trouble is that it has not been sociological attention. Much of the literature on the subject has been inspirational rather than accurate, consisting of the prejudices and interests of the authors rather than an accurate history of the wars they describe. National campaigns and small skirmishes receive a great deal of attention in the county or district in which they occur, so that scales of magnitude of wars in the minds of children between, say, the Napoleonic Wars and the Battle of Bunker Hill get all awry and men and women consequently grow up with as false a set of ideas upon the relative magnitude of wars as they would get upon the comparative sizes of the moon and of Jupiter by looking at the sky at night.

To correct such false perspectives completely is an impossible task. However great may be the desire for true, objective, scientific knowledge about the exact incidence of war upon the social life of past ages, the amount of trustworthy information on the subject is too fragmentary to allow reliable conclusions to be drawn from it. Such is the poverty of our resources that, until the second half of the seventeenth century, it is exceptional to find even roughly accurate reports upon essential aspects of wars: the size of the fighting forces, the number of lives lost in fighting and among the civilian population, and the economic cost. Those reports which survive are frequently grossly inaccurate, such as the estimate of Herodotus that the Persian army contained a million men. The true duration of wars is also often in doubt. A state of war may have existed without much fighting having occurred; or there may have been many skirmishes and local clashes of which no record survives. The Hundred Years' War between England and France in the fourteenth and fifteenth centuries, if measured in actual fighting time, would prove to be of much shorter duration than the World War of 1914 to 1918.

When an effort is made to extend the study of warfare by relating it to the broader social groups or countries from which the armies were drawn, further complications arise, because there is no accurate knowledge of the size of their populations. If the study is carried over several centuries, there is the additional complication that the size and extent of the territory of those countries does not remain constant any more than do their populations. These difficulties are further aggravated when wars are waged by coalitions of several countries together, or when, as in the Middle Ages, wars were fought with the aid of mercenary foreign troops.

Having faced this formidable list of difficulties, Sorokin cannot be accused of undertaking lightheartedly the tremendous task of attempting to weigh and measure the incidence of warfare in Western civilization since the dawn of recorded history. He confines himself to three obvious and outstanding quantitative elements in war and he presents his conclusions as no more than a study of the variations in those three quantities. They are the strength of the army, the number of casualties, both killed and wounded, and the duration of the wars in which they were involved. All other aspects, such as economic costs, or the diseases and deaths caused to civilian populations, are ignored.

Almost all the important European wars, about nine hundred and sixty-seven in all, were studied on this basis, as they occurred in the history of Greece (24 wars), Rome (81), Austria (131), Germany (24), England (176), France (185), Netherlands (23), Spain (75), Italy (32), Russia (151), Poland and Lithuania (65).

The wars of Germany, Spain, the Netherlands and Italy are fewer, because they are studied from the sixteenth or seventeenth centuries and not from the tenth or eleventh centuries, as are the others, except of course Greece and Rome. Sorokin is content to claim no more for such an analysis, based as it is upon an exhaustive study of the best authorities, than that it very probably more nearly approaches reality than the mere guesses, incidental and fragmentary statements, and *ad hoc* theories which have generally done duty in this field in the past.

Without entering further into questions about the statistical techniques used, the sources and their conflict and agreement, all of which can be studied in detail in Sorokin's work, the results of his enquiries are reproduced in graphic form (see Fig. 14).

Such is the broad picture based upon as exhaustive a study as the facts of history allow. It stands in marked contrast with the many partial, conflicting, and imaginative theories set forth from time to time by astrologers, numerologists, astro-physicists, sunspot theorists, climatologists, geographers, and others. Many other illusions dissolve and disappear when confronted with this record. Elaborate notions about the cyclical appearance and disappearance of wars, ideas about a constant trend leading to the reduction and elimination of wars or their constant and steady increase are alike shown to have no basis in history. All that can be said is that the curve of war in history fluctuates. Consequently all attempts to predict the inevitable recurrence of wars are made in vain. Wars are not the main or general cause of scientific progress, neither are they necessarily manifestations of exuberance or of the vital and cultural effervescence of any society. Wars are likely to occur in periods of prosperity or of depression; under autocratic and under democratic regimes; in literate or illiterate societies; in agricultural or in industrial societies; in communities of every variety of political and religious belief.

Sorokin holds that it is a waste of time to pursue an enquiry into the causes of wars on the basis of such conditions as those noted above. He suggests instead that, because war involves essentially a breakdown of the organized relationship between states, the investigation should concentrate upon searching for reasons for the breakdown. This is, of course, often undertaken, but the investigators frequently make the mistake of seeking to explain the breakdown by one principal factor or operative variable. It may be that the principle or variable proposed is the size, density or growth of the population; or changes in the means and techniques of production; or variations in prosperity and depression; or changes in political regimes. Whatever the main factor may be, it can never account for more than some local and secondary traits of war, because it can always be shown that the variables supposed to cause wars are also to be found in peaceful societies. Neither does Sorokin consider that trends of wars or peace can be accounted for directly by his own main factors of historical change, the alternation of ideational and sensate cultures. The most that he would claim is that these factors account satisfactorily for some aspects of the nature and trends of war and peace. Among them he selects the following for special mention.

Sensate wars rarely have religious or ideational color. They are fought for economic, imperialistic, utilitarian ends, although they are presented to the world in much more high-sounding language.

In a dominant ideational culture or period, wars are more generally fought for religious or other ideals. In the Middle Ages, for instance, most wars were religious in nature, and the religious motive endured, still strong, until the eighteenth century. Partisans of the economic interpretation of history, who uniformly fail to understand that sensate economic motives have little relevance as an explanation of conduct in an ideational culture, are reduced to extraordinary expedients in their efforts to prove that their theories can account for the causes of ideational wars, such as the Crusades, for example.

Whatever may be thought of Sorokin's general philosophy of history, it is evident that his demonstration of the essential relativity of the various factors or canons of interpretation, such as this economic factor, is of fundamental and far-reaching importance, not merely for history but for the social sciences generally. It completely demolishes, for example, the Marxist materialist interpretation of history, which it once more shows to be practically irrelevant throughout vast stretches of time involving more than half the recorded history of mankind.

Sorokin next observes that neither in logic nor in experience are there any grounds for believing that ideational culture is more peaceful or more belligerent than sensate culture. The militant forces making for war and

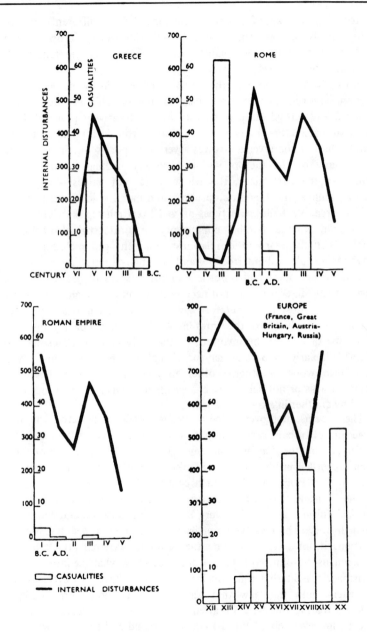

RELATIVE WAR MAGNITUDE, BY CASUALTIES AND INTERNAL DISTURBANCES

inhibitory forces making for peace in each may be very different but they can be equally strong. Thus predominantly ideational Europe of the twelfth century and predominantly sensate Europe of the nineteenth century had comparatively few wars.

Sorokin's own theory is that wars notably increase in periods of transition from one main cultural phase to another. This may be because crystalized and settled cultures tend to be comparatively peaceful if no strong external factors intervene. A transition from ideational to sensate cultural values or the reverse involves severe disruptions which weaken or remove many of the factors within a society making for order and stability. In the first place, the whole system of values — religious, scientific, philosophical, artistic, juridical, and moral — loses much if not all of its force. Next the main types of social relationship associated with either system, whether familial, compulsory, or contractual, also begin to crumble. Then also many other relationships are changed, including forms of government, ideas about freedom and about government regulation, all of which further upset and unsettle established ways of life. Of course, changes of this description do not necessarily occur at the same time in all states and societies. It is therefore necessary to take into account the possibility that only one of the states involved in war may be in transition, or that two or all may be involved, or that only parts of states may be changing. Similarly, one state may be changing from an ideational to a sensate form, while the other or others may be changing from sensate to ideational forms or not subject to change at all, as when a stable society is invaded by another in a transitional state.

There seems, moreover, to be a time lag between the rate of internal change and disturbances and the outbreak of wars between States, a fact brought out by the diagrams on page 215. Attempting to interpret the findings recorded in his diagrams, Sorokin looked at the chart of war and disturbance in Rome. In the fourth century B.C., the Roman Republic had, he considers, a firm, strong, crystallized, and predominantly ideational culture. The third century B.C. was the most militant century in Roman history. The reason cannot be found in internal disintegration or transition. It must, therefore, be the result of external attack by the Carthaginians. Sorokin says that he does not know what the internal state of Carthage was at that time. Such hints that we have, however, are not inconsistent with the view that Carthaginian culture, with its highly developed trading and agricultural enterprises, was predominantly sensate. There is, however, no doubt that, in the second and first centuries B.C. society in the Roman Republic was undergoing a radical change. The old, stern ways of life were giving place to a sensate concentration upon the good things of this world. Wars against Rome's neighbors in the Mediterranean became also vast booty hunts. Internal disturbances became more acute. The Gracchan efforts at reform were shortly followed by the devastating social wars, and these in turn were succeeded by the civil wars. Then followed an era of comparative peace at home and abroad. The new sensate culture had crystallized, and a period of stability ensued, until it also waned and was replaced by a new and vital ideational culture. Again wars and internal disturbances increased, although the lack of reliable date makes it impossible to indicate their magnitude with any precision.

Sorokin's reading of the history of ancient Rome has the great merit, which so many popular manuals on that subject lack, of pointing to the profoundly different character, culture and outlook of the Romans of the early Republic from those of the early Empire. By drawing attention to the correspondingly great cultural changes in the fourth century A.D., Sorokin's emphasis upon the self-generated immanent changes in social life in Rome throws new light upon customary notions about the causes and the nature of the decline and fall of the Roman Empire, and indeed of that Graeco-Roman civilization of which the Empire and its culture were the latest manifestation.

Throughout almost the whole of the ideational period of European history after the fall of the Roman Empire, and until the period of change which began to become apparent in the twelfth century, there are no sufficiently reliable records upon which any valid calculation of the extent of war during those centuries could be based. Using such information as exists, Sorokin supposes that these centuries, with their crystalized ideational culture were, comparatively, not very belligerent.

The transition to the very different sensate culture was, however, marked by steadily increasing outbreaks of warfare until that sensate culture itself became dominant and crystallized in the eighteenth and nineteenth centuries. Wars by no means came to an end, but their toll upon human society became somewhat less deadly than before. As in turn the sensate culture began to weaken and decay at the end of the nineteenth and in the twentieth centuries, the curve reflecting the scale and intensity of war again soars.

Whether or not Sorokin has found the right way to explain the incidence of wars, it should at least be clear that he is not wrong in asserting that most of the popular theories about the causes of wars are fallacious. He regards the many political groups which have advocated one policy after another to prevent wars as little better than quack doctors or medicine men. Referring to some of the remedies suggested, he mentions preaching birth control to reduce the density of the population; advocating a certain political regime, whether communism, fascism, or democracy, as a panacea against war; clamoring for limitless prosperity as the surest means to eliminate war; staging big demonstrations with energetic red-flag waving as an organization of peace; transferring the manufacture of munitions from the private firms to state bureaucrats. None of these devices touch the main cause, and all have been and will remain essentially impotent. Writing, as he did, before 1937, that the endless efforts to promote these panaceas have not prevented wars but have resulted in the development of intensive war-psychology and sinister preparation for future wars on an appalling scale in all countries, he clearly showed a degree of insight into the subject which was not so evident amongst the holders of the views he criticized.

Sorokin's conclusion is that the main weapon against war is the crystallization of the system of cultural values and of social relationships.

Riots and Revolutions — Internal disturbances in the relations between social groups are another social and cultural phenomena studied by Sorokin, and again his historical, statistical method of approach reveals the inadequacy of many currently held notions on the subject.

Accurate scientific ideas about social disturbances should, he considers, provide some general measure to determine at least four or five essential aspects of any social disturbance. In the first place, the proportionate extent of the area of the disturbance must be known. By this Sorokin does not merely mean the number of square miles of territory involved but the number and kinds of cities, villages and other settlements in which the disturbance occurred. Secondly, the proportion of the population taking an active part in the disturbance, for or against it, must be known; thirdly, the duration of the disturbance; fourthly, its relative intensity or the amount and sharpness of violence; and lastly, the importance of the effects of the disturbance — all these must be assessed. Unless the study of social disturbances is reduced to some kind of order on these lines, it is impossible to get any coherent idea of the true nature and effect of social unrest.

Sorokin's five factors also enable comparisons to be made between the extent of social disturbances between nations differing widely in size and population. As he points out, a disturbance created by 10,000 people is a very different matter in a population of 10,000,000 from what it would be in a population of 100,000,000. His five factors make it possible to register the fact clearly, for they would only show as disturbances of equal significance those involving the same *proportion* of populations, social areas, degree of violence, and duration.

In attempting to measure disturbances in various countries by these four scales, Sorokin again encounters the difficulties met with in attempting to measure wars. The recorded facts are lamentably fewer and less adequate than scientific precision demands. Moreover, the assessment of internal disturbances involves a greater exercise of judgment, since there is less measurement of numbers killed and wounded and more guesswork in determining the violence and effects of disturbances. That is to say, the subjective element is a greater source of probable error.

Once again Sorokin does not claim more for the results he presents than that they are based upon as complete a survey of the whole subject as he found it possible to make. He has investigated some seventeen hundred major social disturbances, a far larger number than any other student of unrest and revolutions has yet surveyed. After experiment with various scales and procedures, he and his collaborators adopted one which he claims reflects this aspect of social relations in history in all essentials without serious distortion.

The manner in which he constructed his scales of assessment is this: the scales adopted are based upon the following estimates of the factor involved. It is important to remember that Sorokin neglects minor disturbances in order to concentrate upon the important upheavals. The social areas of the disturbances are weighted from 1 to 100 according to the following scale and as the disturbances occur in:

1   A rural county or similar limited area.

3   Several rural counties or a small town.

5   A larger town.

10 Several towns of medium size or one important city, or a small feudal region, or a small province.

20 A larger feudal region or province or in a small part of a capital city.

40 Several large provinces or the whole capital city.

60 The capital city and several provinces.

80 Almost the whole country.

100 The entire country.

Clearly these are strictly proportional gradings. A town or province may vary very much in size at different periods but proportionately their relation to the social area as a whole will probably be much about the same.

The duration of disturbances is measured on the following scale:

1   Momentary or short-term shock.
3   Longer disturbance.
5   Lasting several months.
10 About a year.

For every additional year up to 5 years, add 5 to 10. Thus a disturbance of 5 years gets a value of 30. From 6 to 15 years, add 4 to every year above the 5 years with their value of 30. Thus a disturbance of 15 years gets a value of 70. Over 15 years, add 3 for every year above 15. A disturbance of 25 years gets a value of 100. Add 3 for every year above 25.

The intensity of the disturbance is assessed in five classes. The weight assigned to each is given in parenthesis after each.

1   Without violence (1).
2   Slight violence (3).
3   Violence on a considerable scale, fights, murders, arson, looting (5).
4   Still greater violence and overthrow of the government in various centers, but without serious and lasting social and political effects (7).
5   Still greater violence with the irrevocable overthrow of the central government and with deep and lasting consequences (10).

The masses involved in each disturbance are assessed in five classes also, according to whether they involve:

1   A few individuals, in plots and murders (1).
2   A small group (3).
3   A large social class (5).
4   Larger masses of the population, including several extensive social classes (7).
5   Practically all the active and adult population (10).

These last two classes are combined in one scale by Sorokin, resulting in a composite weight for every combination of each of the two sets of five grades as follows:

Table 6:   VALUES GIVEN TO INTERNAL DISTURBANCES

By the Masses Involved	By the Amount of Violence and Effects				
	I.	II.	III.	IV.	V.
I.	1	3	5	7	10
II.	3	10	15	20	30
III.	5	15	25	35	50
IV.	7	20	35	50	70
V.	10	30	50	70	100

There are thus three numerical values assigned to each disturbance: social area, duration, and a combined figure to include the masses involved, together with the amount of violence and its effects. The geometric average for each of these three values was then calculated as the indicator of the disturbance to which they related. The sum of the geometric averages of all the disturbances in twenty-five year and hundred-year periods was then calculated, and the movement of disturbances in the history of the country from period to period shown. It remained to allow for the varying sizes of different countries when the disturbances in all of them are grouped together, as, for example, when it is desired to show one curve of disturbances for all the European countries. Sorokin allowed the following weight values to different countries at different periods of their history:

Byzantium: up to the middle of the seventh century (the period of the loss of most Asiatic possessions and of Egypt), 5; up to the end of the twelfth century (the conquest by the Crusaders in 1204), 3; thereafter, 1.

England: up to the middle of the eleventh century (the Norman Conquest), 3; thereafter, 5.

France: 5 throughout.

Germany: up to the end of the eighth century, 3; thereafter, 5.

Italy: 5 throughout (a relatively high figure, due largely to location of the Roman Catholic See in Rome).

The Netherlands: up to the end of the sixteenth century, 1; for the seventeenth century, 3; thereafter, 1.

Poland and Lithuania: up to the end of the fourteenth century (time of unification), 3; up to the middle of seventeenth century (period of great power), 5; thereafter (until partition of Poland), 3.

Russia: up to the middle of the thirteenth century, 3; thereafter 5.

Notwithstanding the shortcomings and imperfections of his results, Sorokin can claim with justification that they are likely to have far greater precision and accuracy than the merely verbal attempts to convey some idea of the magnitude of social disturbances which they render obsolete and replace. Most languages have but six words for comparison: small, smaller, smallest; and great, greater, greatest. Unattracted as Sorokin professes himself to be by the effort to describe events in numerical terms, he was forced, in the interests of clarity and distinctness of ideas, to adopt his system of numerical indicators in preference to a verbal scale of merely six quantities, all of them imprecise.

Whatever doubts he might have had about the reliability of his methods and results, they were removed, he records, after he had arranged through a prominent scholar for two anonymous critics to read and comment upon a preliminary draft of his work. One tried to tear it all to pieces, describing it as an absurdity and nonsense; the other thought it a complex and cumbersome procedure for proving what every qualitative historian already knows and accepts. Sorokin's conclusion, after two such contradictory verdicts, is that there is no hope of progress except by retaining his own method of quantitative measurement and by using it as far as possible more accurately than he has succeeded in doing. The facts upon which his curve of disturbances is based may be found listed chronologically in an appendix to this third volume on *Social and Cultural Dynamics,* where they occupy over forty pages of small print, where the authority describing the disturbances is given and where each disturbance is classified as falling under one of five classes:

Political disturbances mainly directed towards changing the existing political regime.

Social and economic disturbances.

National and separatist disturbances.

Religious disturbances.

Disturbances with specific objectives, such as some personal change in government, resistance to a specific law or tax, and disturbances without any single dominant objective but with two or more equally strong objectives. This latter class includes the many disturbances which lack any marked predominant specific objective.

After these preliminary explanations, Sorokin's various charts will repay study.

The curve of internal disturbance in Greece is given Fig. 15, p. 223.

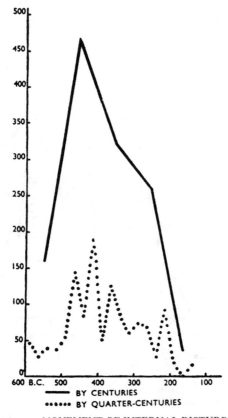

Fig. 15: MOVEMENT OF INTERNAL DISTURBANCES
IN ANCIENT GREECE

The most turbulent centuries in Ancient Greece were, like the periods
of maximum war activities, not those of decline, but the times when Greek
culture reached its peak in the fifth and fourth centuries. The most
common and frequent disturbances were predominantly political; then
came the nationalistic, social and economic disturbances. The latter were
most frequent in the fifth century B.C.

The curve for the Roman Republic and Empire, unlike that of Greece,
shows that there is no uniformity in the movement of the curves of social
disturbances and of war. (Figs. 14 and 16, pp. 215 and 224).

During the desperate Punic Wars, internal dissensions almost
disappeared, but in the first century B.C., when internal disturbances
reached unpredecented heights, war also was at a high level. At first the
disturbances in Rome had predominantly political and socio-economic

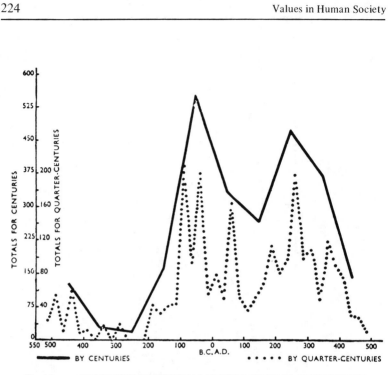

Fig. 16:   MOVEMENT OF INTERNAL DISTURBANCES IN ANCIENT ROME

causes. After the second century B.C., Rome was already an Empire, so a
number of separatist, nationalist, and regional movements appeared and
these persisted until the fourth century A.D., when their place was taken
by religious struggles.

Byzantium again shows a curve distinct from those of Greece or Rome
(Fig. 17). Less a naturally evolving cultural system than a mature system
transplanted from Greece and Rome, it is not surprising that its earlier
evolution should differ from that of a spontaneously and gradually
growing culture. The brilliant sixth century, which includes the reign of
Justinian (A.D. 527-565), had few disturbances; the periods of decline in
the seventh and eighth centuries had a high rate of disturbances, whereas
the twelfth and thirteenth centuries, which were also periods of decline,
had a low rate. The ninth, tenth, and eleventh centuries, when Byzantium
was on the whole prosperous and flourishing, had a mixed record of
internal peace and considerable unrest. The great majority of the
disturbances in Byzantium fall into Sorokin's fifth class of those due either
to mixed motives or to the pursuit of some single specific objective. They

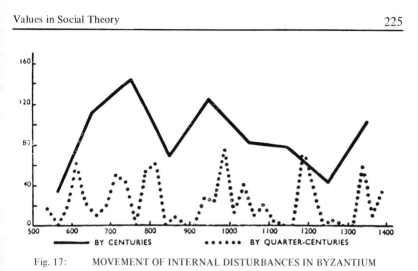

Fig. 17:   MOVEMENT OF INTERNAL DISTURBANCES IN BYZANTIUM

were not predominantly of a marked political, economic, or religious type.
Once again no immediately obvious causal connections are apparent.

In France also the record gives no possibility of connecting internal
disturbances with periods of prosperity or of decline. Neither does it
support any notions of a universal persistent social trend (Fig. 18, p. 226).

France also shows many disturbances of the mixed type. These and
political and socio-economic disturbances predominate, with, however,
conspicuous religious disturbances in the sixteenth and seventeenth
centuries and to some extent in the thirteenth century also.

In Germany and Austria there is a similar lack of correlation between
internal disturbances, war, social, economic, or cultural blooming or decay
(Fig. 19, p. 226).

Most of the recorded disturbances were of the "mixed" type,
although religious disturbances dominated during the fifteenth, sixteenth,
and seventeenth centuries. Nationalistic and separatist movements were of
some importance in the tenth and eleventh, and for a short time at the end
of the eighteenth and beginning of the nineteenth centuries.

The curve of disturbances in England again shows no continuous trend
and no periodicity (Fig. 20, p. 227).

It will be of interest to quote, in addition to reproducing Sorokin's
chart, the indicators of the relative magnitude of social disturbances, in
order that readers familiar with English history may consider how far their
own estimate of the relative magnitude and importance of the various
upheavals in English national life is reflected in Sorokin's arithmetical
assessment.

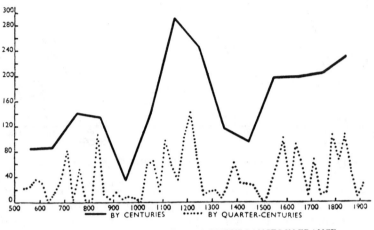

Fig. 18:   MOVEMENT OF INTERNAL DISTURBANCES IN FRANCE

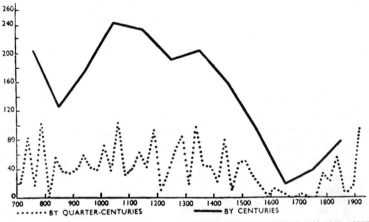

Fig. 19:   MOVEMENT OF INTERNAL DISTURBANCES IN GERMANY AND AUSTRIA

The most turbulent quarter centuries in English history were:

A.D.   751-775 (94.50)   1451-1475 (122.24)
        776-800 (85.78)   1476-1500 (97.81)
        801-825 (83.47)   1626-1650 (104.88)
        1051-1075 (110.03)

The largest single disturbances are:

A.D.   692-694 (27.16)   1381 (24.10)
        1066-1070 (55.22)   1455-1483 (34.74,
        1138-1153 (49.20)   43.75, 43.75, 38.28)
        1215-1217 (41.21)   1641-1649 (77.27)
        1265-1267 (22.91)   1650-1662 (27.16)
        1297-1300 (25.94)   1688 (25.59)

Sorokin characterizes the disturbances from the fifteenth to the eighteenth centuries in England as markedly religious; he notes that nationalistic, separatist disturbances have played a tangible role, but that the majority of other disturbances were of the "mixed" type.

The Italian peninsula, judged by Sorokin's indicators, seems to have been one of the most turbulent regions in Europe, an experience which Sorokin suggests may have some relation to the location there of the Roman Catholic See, the focal point where antagonistic interests of most of the European countries converged and clashed (Fig. 21).

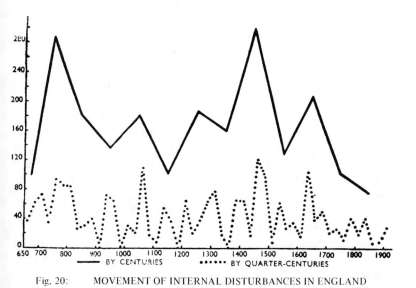

Fig. 20:   MOVEMENT OF INTERNAL DISTURBANCES IN ENGLAND

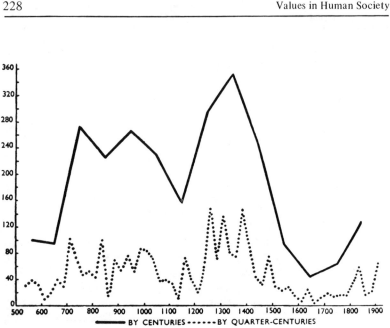

Fig. 21:   MOVEMENT OF INTERNAL DISTURBANCES IN ITALY

The majority of Italy's upheavals were of the mixed type, purely religious disturbances playing no marked part.

Sorokin's interesting statistics and charts relating to the internal disturbances of Spain, the Netherlands, Russia, Poland and Lithuania are not reproduced here, but they may be seen in the third volume of his *Social and Cultural Dynamics.*

The composite chart for the internal disturbances in Europe as a whole appears as Fig. 22 on page 230.

Summarizing the results of his long and exhaustive studies, Sorokin draws attention to some of the more important conclusions and deductions to be drawn from them. In the first place, the occurrence of important social disturbances in the life of social bodies is so frequent that these recurrent outbreaks, like tensions and sickness in individual human organisms, or storms in nature, must be regarded as a normal occurrence in the life of any social group. On an average, for all the countries studied, there has been one significant disturbance for every five years of peace.

Sorokin has worked out the average ratio of years without disturbances to those with disturbances with the following summarized results:

Table 7:   FREQUENCY OF IMPORTANT SOCIAL DISTURBANCES

Country	Number of Years Studied	Number of Disturbances in Period	Average Occurrences of Disturbances in Years	Number of Years with Disturbances	Average Ratio of Years without to Years with Disturbances
Ancient Greece, 600 B.C.-146 B.C.	454	84	5.4	122	2.7
Rome, 509 B.C.-A.D. 476 ..	985	170	5.8	219	3.5
Byzantium, 532-1390	858	49	17.5	89	8.6
France, 531-1933	1402	173	8.1	246	4.7
Germany and Austria, 709-1933	1124	150	7.5	204	4.5
England, 656-1933	1277	162	7.9	247	4.2
Italy, 526-1933	1407	251	5.6	365	2.9
Spain, 467-1933	1466	242	6.1	424	2.4
The Netherlands, 678-1933	1255	103	12.1	263	3.8
Russia, 946-1933	987	167	5.9	280	2.6
Poland and Lithuania, 1031-1794	763	78	9.8	146	4.3

Such a record disproves the fairly commonly-held opinion that some nations are inherently orderly and free from social convulsions, whereas others are by nature disorderly.

Are some nations more prone to violence in their upheavals than others? Sorokin has worked over his materials to show the intensity of revolutions in five classes from pure and bloodless disturbances down to the most violent, cruel, and blood-stained outbreaks. There is little to choose between the nations studied in this respect. Practically all of them have shown a tendency towards devilish, inhuman cruelty. He gives no comfort to those who plan or hope for bloodless revolutions, the chances of which, on the basis of the existing record, are about five to one hundred. So he regarded as naive the people whom he had heard declare, "If Communism would come to our country, it would certainly be free from its Russian excesses and terror and bloodshed and other barbarisms." The history of Eastern Europe since Sorokin published these words in 1937 sufficiently documents the correctness of his prevision.

Another calculation enables Sorokin to show that as far as the average duration of major social disturbances is concerned, the majority of them, like sicknesses in the lives of individuals, come and pass their acute stage within a period of a few weeks. Disturbances with a duration of more than a year have accounted for about 15 per cent of the total. About 80 per cent of all disturbances lasted less than a year. It is also remarkable that the magnitude of the disturbances fluctuates from century to century

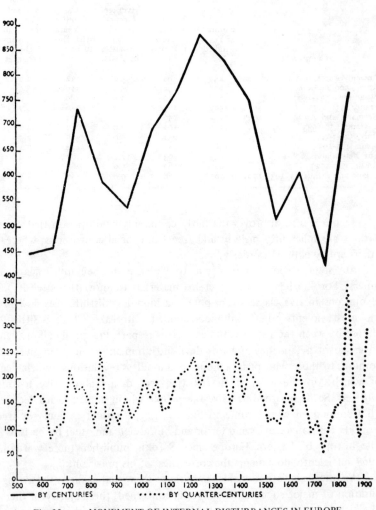

Fig. 22:   MOVEMENT OF INTERNAL DISTURBANCES IN EUROPE

much less than is commonly supposed. Some compensating reaction seems to be released to damp down the growth of disturbances or to prevent their complete elimination. At the same time, and perhaps for the same inherent, immanent reasons, it is not possible to point to any continuous trend either towards orderly peaceful progress or towards ever-increasing disorderliness.

The ups and downs of major internal disturbances do not occur with wave-like regularity. Despite some ingenious theories to the contrary, among which Sorokin selects those of the Italian thinker Guiseppe Ferrari, there is no recurrent definite periodicity. Ferrari's theory was that four successive generations completed a cycle. The first generation are the "predecessors," the men of thought who analyze, describe, and criticize the existing order of things without attempting to overthrow it. Building on their knowledge and ideas come the next generation of "revolutionaries," the men of action, who destroy the existing order in favor of a new and improved state of affairs at which the predecessors merely hinted. Extreme and fanatical, they succeed on the whole in making things worse. New problems arise, as the old ones remain unsolved, so that the excesses of the revolutionaries provoke the rise of the "reactionaries," who prove just as unsuccessful in the attempt to put the clock back and to repair what the revolutionaries had destroyed. They also fail, and the unsoundness of their plans, matching the failure of the revolutionaries, provokes a middle way which the fourth generation of "accomplishers" promote. Free from fanaticism and coming on the scene when many problems are ripe for solution, this lucky generation succeeds in restoring order, prosperity and social well-being. The cycle is complete, but the relative good fortune of the new age allows a fresh set of theorizers and academic critics to arise who again provoke a new generation of revolutionaries to be succeeded again by reactionaries until the cycle is closed once more by a new generation of accomplishers. Ferrari accompanies his ingenious theory by a series of historical data substantiating it in the experience of several European and some Asiatic countries. His material, however, is arbitrarily selected and arranged according to his own subjective principles. When the facts about revolutions and disturbances are comprehensively collected and weighed objectively, they are not found to support the notion that outbursts and disturbances recur every 115 to 120 years as Ferrari supposed. This is but one of many theories of historical change, none of which have yet produced a satisfactory explanatory scheme able to fit the facts. And yet it has been Sorokin who has been accused, by critics who clearly could not have studied his methods or his results, of imposing a preconceived pattern on the factual record of history.

Such being the state of affairs in accounting for the past, Sorokin concludes that attempts to predict the future are equally unreliable. All the ingenious folk who busy themselves with forecasting, planning, social engineering, or controlling the course of socio-cultural processes are victims of delusions, mistaking their own wishes for reality. For the pleasing notion that nature does not make leaps is a delusion. There are indeed gradual changes, but accompanying them are many abrupt, sharp, and sudden turns which make nonsense of any attempts to prolong the curve of change and revolution beyond the point it has so far reached.

The theory of orderly progress was a typical product of the capitalist regime at its height in the last quarter of the nineteenth century. Two generations of English students of economics trained on the well-known *Principles of Economics* of Alfred Marshall, will recall that he put on the title page of his book, first published in 1890, the words *Natura non facit saltum*. And with reason, for it is more evident now than when Sorokin wrote in 1937 that the capitalist regime Marshall described was one of the most orderly of social systems, giving the greatest assurance of internal and external peace, of sensate liberty and of individual freedom. A not dissimilar impression of that period was given, after it had collapsed, by another Cambridge economist in the opening pages of *The Economic Consequences of the Peace* (1919).

Sorokin also thought that to replace a liberal political regime and free market economy by any of the totalitarian systems, whether socialism, communism, fascism, or Hitlerism, would increase the chances of war and disturbance as well as greatly reduce individual liberty. On the basis of his statistics up to the year 1925, Sorokin reported that the twentieth century was on a rising tide of internal disturbances and that so far it had been the bloodiest period, one of the cruellest and least humanitarian, in the history of Western civilization and perhaps in the chronicles of all mankind. Those optimists who in 1937 treated this verdict with scorn must seem very foolish now.

Another deduction from Sorokin's results is that the movement of internal disturbances in the countries studied does not coincide with the outbreak of international wars. The two movements do not synchronize, neither does there seem to be any positive or negative association between them. Sorokin worked over his results several times before arriving at this conclusion, since in the history of Greece, Rome, and Russia there seemed to be some slight indication that disturbances tended to occur most frequently during and around years of war. He was, however, forced to conclude that the relationship was neither simple, uniform, nor close. He tried again by investigating the plausible notion that there is a positive association between unsuccessful wars and big disturbances, and again between successful wars and the absence of such disturbances. Despite some impressive examples of just such connections, the weight of all the evidence does not confirm that they are the general rule. The connection in fact is not a necessary one, but it arises because the onset both of wars and of internal disturbances are each related to a more general factor, that of the transition from one cultural system to another.

It is here that Sorokin states his own explanation of the origins of great social disturbances. Other conditions being equal, they occur during the periods when the existing culture, or the system of social relations, or both, undergo a rapid transformation. When that culture or system is strong and crystallized, internal disturbances tend to decrease and stay at a low level. The record he produces (Fig. 22) shows that there have been three main peaks in the fluctuating occurrence of major internal disturbances, the eighth, the thirteenth and fourteenth centuries, and the nineteenth and twentieth centuries. All three were periods of transition, either in the system of social relations of Europe or in that of its entire cultural system. These were the greatest turning points of European history.

The eighth century, the period of the Carolingian Renaissance, did not, it is true, involve the replacement of the predominant ideational culture by a sensate culture, but it did usher in some great changes in the system of social relationships and in the forms of social, economic, and political organization.

The thirteenth and fourteenth centuries were those of the greatest transition, for then it was that European culture began its radical change from an ideational to a sensate culture; from the feudal to the modern system of social relationships, that is to say, from predominantly familistic to coercive and contractual relationships; from theocracy to secular government; from ideational freedom to sensate liberty.

The nineteenth century was preceded by the final liquidation begun by the French Revolution of the post-medieval relationships of social organization in Europe, the sweeping away of coercive relationships, and the establishment of predominantly contractual relationships. By the middle of the nineteenth century, this process was virtually completed and Europe settled down to its new contractual, free-market system.

The main and indispensable condition for an eruption of internal disturbances, therefore, is that the social system or the cultural system or both shall be unsettled. Other popular theories attributing internal disturbances either to growing poverty and hard material conditions or, on the contrary, to increasing material progress, are sharply contradicted by the facts. The economic, materialist interpretation of history is again proved inadequate, limited, and quite unable to yield the scientific, intellectually satisfying explanation of the trend of human affairs which its devotees, particularly the Marxists, so stridently claim it has provided. Sorokin notes in passing that an explanation of the conditions markedly similar to his own, provoking men to commit suicide has been conclusively demonstrated by Emile Durkheim, who pointed out that they are to be found in any destruction of social and cultural networks (*anomie*) which has the effect of demoralizing and isolating an individual.

It is quite unrealistic to ascribe increases in criminality to illiteracy, mental deficiency, poverty, and low standards of living. Many countries suffering from such conditions have relatively fewer criminals in their midst than has the United States, whose steadily rising standards of life have not banished or reduced the toll which criminals annually level upon American society. The virtual abolition of chronic poverty and the general diffusion of well-being in Great Britain by the 'Welfare State' has been accompanied by a heavy toll of crime, violence, and juvenile delinquency. The circumstances provoking suicide and crime are precisely those which produce riots and revolutions — the difference between them being merely one of scale, between single individuals and social groups.

Sorokin does not claim to be able to explain all the ups and downs in the record of disturbances by assigning them to periods of profound cultural change, but he regards these periods as one of the most important causes, perhaps even the most important cause, always present and inherent in all disturbances, their presence or absence, increase or decrease. His explanation of the conditions in which internal disturbances occur is therefore the same as that which he offers for the increase of war.

On the same grounds, he would expect that the forces generating disturbances rarely, if ever, work in one country alone. In fact they seem to work in many countries simultaneously, for the direction of the curves of the indicators of social disturbances between the countries studied is identical, although in no two countries were the curves parallel; neither did they have the same direction in all centuries. The significance of this common experience is that acute revolutionary disturbances can rarely be isolated and confined to one country; they are, and should be, of general concern.

They are, in fact, social and cultural phenomena and they cannot be satisfactorily explained on any other basis.

Personality and Behavior

The cumulative evidence from the preceding sections strongly supports the idea that the dominant system of values molds the type of mentality of the vast majority of human beings who are born and live in it. Other conditions being equal, a person's mentality will be ideational if he has had no contacts except with those of a pure ideational culture. If his contacts are with the sensate culture, he will have a sensate mentality. A person in contact with different types of culture will have a mixed cultural mentality. Close association with nothing but an unintegrated culture, or with a multitude of cultures of contradictory character, will produce unintegrated personalities, unless by happy, although unlikely chance, the perfect balance between an ideational and sensate culture is struck to produce the integrated unity of the mixed idealistic culture. Such exceptions are rare and they are hardly ever perfect.

Value systems or cultural mentality are one thing. Actual concrete behavior by no means corresponds closely to it. It is a common everyday experience to find that prosaic, selfish, ugly, inhuman acts are justified by their perpetrators to the world, apparently sincerely, by high-sounding language as deeds of the utmost nobility and grandeur. It is not, therefore, true that ideas directly rule the world in the literal meaning of those words.

The differences between the thoroughgoing sensate and ideational mentalities, themselves rarely if ever found in their pure forms, are considerably reduced when the actual behavior rather than the beliefs of their exponents is studied. Elementary biological needs ensure a common minimum of similarity between both types. Members of ideational societies, such as ascetic monasteries, have not always mortified the flesh to the same extent as their founders and conspicuously holy brethren have succeeded in doing. Failure to live up to high ideational standards is then apt to be excused, justified, or glorified by specious pretexts of one sort or another. Murder and savagery have notoriously been permitted or encouraged in ideational cultural societies as long as unbelievers or infidels are the victims. Various forms of sexual license and the accumulation of riches have also found indulgence in manifest contradiction with the essential principles of the ideational way of life. In these and other ways, Sorokin allows for the influence of external circumstances of life upon cultural change. Such aberrations are exceptions, and however persistent or impressive they may seem, they should not be allowed to obscure the essential quality and the reality of the ideational mentality and of the ideational way of life. Differences between the bearers òf the ideational and sensate cultures are less great in their respective conduct and personality than in their mentality; nevertheless they are real differences and they may readily be perceived.

To the very great, although not very clearly definable, extent that mentality or cultural outlook finds outward manifestation or expression in behavior, it is inevitable that there should be striking contrasts between the acts of the predominantly ideational and the basically sensate cultural types. If the present book has not succeeded in indicating the reality of this difference, Sorokin's own works accumulate ample evidence, adequate to establish the truth of the fact that strongly contrasting productions in the arts, in science, philosophy, religion, in moral systems, systems of law, in forms of political, social and economic organization, result from general value systems or patterns of culture not only divergent but themselves forming coherent systematic wholes — cultural super-systems, as Sorokin calls them.

These artistic and cultural manifestations are themselves a form of behavior. To build the Parthenon or the cathedral at Chartres, a modern laboratory, hospital, cinema, theater or law-court, involves the capital and labor, in other words, the activity of hundreds of men over a very long period. By their fruits they are known. They are also known by what they leave undone. It may be concluded, therefore, that the dominant type of culture conditions the forms, the stimulation, and inhibition of certain actions and reactions, and it conditions also the activities closely related to the satisfaction of elementary biological needs. The key-word clearly is *conditions,* for it is not claimed that the relationship between the type of value system or culture and type of conduct is everywhere as complete or as close as is the relationship between the type of culture and its related mentality.

In an effort to test these conclusions by another statistical survey of history, Sorokin presents the results of an investigation made by an independent research worker.

The accounts of individuals mentioned in the ninth edition (1875) of the *Encyclopaedia Britannica* were analyzed and classified as belonging to the sensate, ideational or mixed cultural classes. The number of lines given to each in the *Encyclopaedia* was regarded as a rough indication of each person's relative influence. Then geometric averages for the total number of persons and of lines in each 50-year period from 950 B.C. to 1849 A.D. were computed. The sum of the geometric averages for all the personalities in each of the three classes in every fifty-year period was regarded as 100, and the percentage of each of the three types in every period was established.

The results are given in Table 8, p. 238.

These figures show, Sorokin concludes, that within every fifty-year period except five, for which data will probably always be lacking, all three types, ideational, mixed, and sensate, are to be found coexisting. The ideational type is less frequent than the sensate and mixed, as would be expected for the reasons just explained. Despite erratic movements, there are definite long-term waves in the relative rise and decline of each type, and these agree broadly with the conclusions reached on other grounds relating to the prevalence of each cultural system. For instance, the period 950 B.C. to 851 B.C. appears dominated by the sensate type of personality, which is consistent with what is known as Creto-Mycenaen culture.

850-801 B.C. is a transitional period.

800-501 B.C. shows a notable increase in the percentage of ideational types, as would be expected from what is known of the early history of Greece.

500-451 B.C. seems well balanced, with a slight domination of ideational types, which tallies with the idealistic culture of Greece at that time.

450 B.C.-A.D. 1 shows a decisive change; sensate and mixed types grow at the expense of the ideational.

A.D. 1-249 indicates a sudden but unstable spurt of the ideational type, characterizing a period of violent transition.

250-899, notwithstanding erratic fluctuations for a few fifty-year periods, the record shows a perceptible trend towards an increase in the ideational types.

900-1199 and 1200-1399, a decline in ideational types followed by their rise in the next period.

1400 onwards shows a steady trend in favor of either the mixed of the sensate type.

Table 8:   GEOMETRIC AVERAGES FOR TYPES OF HISTORICAL PERSONS,
950 B.C. TO A.D. 1849, INCLUDED IN THE ENCYCLOPEDIA BRITANICA (1875)

PERIOD	Ideational		Mixed		Sensate	
	Number	Per Cent	Number	Per Cent	Number	Per Cent
950–901 B.C.	0	0	0	0	17.9	100
900–851	13.7	12	0	0	102.7	88
850–801	0	0	18.0	100	0	0
800–751	21.6	53	0	0	19.2	47
750–701	53.4	76	11.8	17	5.2	7
700–651	9.8	34	11.1	38	7.9	28
650–601	21.5	22	35.6	37	38.6	41
600–551	69.6	38	61.0	34	50.7	28
550–501	120.4	40	67.5	22	114.2	38
500–451	124.6	37	107.6	33	100.9	30
450–401	68.6	11	228.9	38	306.2	51
400–351	79.6	13	326.0	56	180.7	31
350–301	43.2	7	279.9	45	290.1	48
300–251	33.1	12	192.1	70	59.7	18
250–201	12.6	5	85.3	35	148.1	60
200–151	12.5	5	96.3	39	145.1	56
150–101	0	0	43.6	45	51.8	55
100–51	16.9	4	112.4	24	333.8	72
50–1	69.4	11	224.2	35	339.1	54
0–49 A.D.	179.9	31	119.3	21	272.9	48
50–99	46.0	9	219.2	43	240.7	48
100–149	100.0	26	208.4	55	72.0	19
150–199	23.7	7	238.4	76	54.7	17
200–249	121.5	43	133.5	47	29.8	10
250–299	102.7	56	32.8	18	46.9	26
300–349	78.0	23	126.2	37	139.0	40
350–399	204.7	40	190.2	38	111.7	32
400–449	80.4	22	165.2	45	123.7	33
450–499	22.8	11	113.4	52	80.4	37
500–549	77.9	28	84.6	30	115.9	42
550–599	45.6	30	58.6	39	48.0	31
600–649	58.5	40	45.2	31	42.2	29
650–699	29.6	45	19.0	29	17.2	26
700–749	43.1	44	15.3	16	38.7	40
750–799	33.8	48	12.6	18	23.6	34
800–849	57.0	36	74.1	47	26.3	17
850–899	91.0	37	76.6	31	76.8	32
900–949	16.8	14	51.7	42	54.5	44
950–999	18.1	10	75.6	42	87.2	48
1000–1049	38.2	15	75.0	29	148.5	56
1050–1099	24.4	6	145.6	37	218.7	57
1100–1149	72.5	17	176.6	41	177.3	42
1150–1199	74.8	15	210.9	41	228.0	44
1200–1249	66.1	15	166.9	36	231.3	49
1250–1299	172.0	33	185.9	35	167.0	32
1300–1349	91.4	26	181.7	51	81.2	23
1350–1399	144.6	23	152.5	24	330.4	53
1400–1449	141.4	18	322.7	42	302.1	40
1450–1499	240.9	15	602.1	38	730.9	47
1500–1549	543.4	17	1037.5	33	1543.1	50
1550–1599	485.9	14	1429.7	41	1528.1	45
1600–1649	537.0	12	1861.5	42	2023.5	46
1650–1699	949.4	19	1641.8	34	2179.0	47
1700–1749	724.0	17	2014.4	44	1534.0	39
1750–1799	901.6	10	3566.6	41	4329.9	49
1800–1849	1460.0	9	7301.1	50	5870.5	41

This empirical study was made independently by a student unaware of the main conclusions to which Sorokin's other work was pointing. It provides historical evidence that there is an association between the type of dominant value system or culture and the frequency of the type of conduct and personality. Sorokin supplements it by a survey of the types of Roman Catholic Popes and of the monarchs of France, Russia, Austria, and England. The Roman hierarchy would not be expected to yield many sensate characters, but Sorokin's statistics show that conspicuously ideational types disappear after about A.D. 942, except for the century 1045-1144. From 942 to 1044, and especially from 1342-1549, a slightly sensate type of Pope dominated. Kings, on the other hand, can hardly be expected to be ideational types. Apart from the English kings, they were indeed of increasingly sensate types as Western culture expanded. Nevertheless from 1250-1399 the ideational type of monarch increased. In England this period was longer, from 1216 to 1413.

A final calculation is based upon the number of men active in the field of business, on the one hand, and of religion on the other. These contrasting types probably reflect well the contrast between sensate and ideational behavior. Again, as would no doubt be expected, business did not become an avenue through which historical importance could be achieved until the late Roman Republic. Thereafter it again fell away, but reappeared between A.D. 1100-1149, and began, after minor fluctuations, to grow and maintain itself. Sorokin considers that this evidence established that there are indeed ideational, sensate, idealistic, and mixed, including the unintegrated, forms of behavior and types of personality, and that each type occurs most often in respectively the ideational, sensate, idealistic, or mixed society.

The Nature of Cultural and Social Change

The survey undertaken by Sorokin does not end with a few often tentative and imperfectly elaborated generalities. His conclusions are specific, and he uses them as a basis for a new approach to the study of sociology, or the life of mankind in groups and societies.

With this aim, he followed the publication of the first three volumes of *Social and Cultural Dynamics* in 1937, after further prolonged reflection and after considering all the many criticisms and comments they have provoked, with a fourth volume in 1941. In it he studied in detail three main groups of problems arising from his earlier findings and theories. He sought to analyze in more detail the nature of a true system of values or culture, of what he calls a socio-cultural system or supersystem; to distinguish it from mere chance mixtures of an unsystematic, unrelated kind that he describes as socio-cultural congeries, as well as from the miscellaneous collections of cultural systems and these congeries found in any one place, which he describes as the structure of the total culture of an area. He next discussed how value systems change, and finally asked why they change. Inasmuch as the answers to these problems will to some extent at least have emerged from the preceding sections, there will be some risk of repetition in returning to them here. Nevertheless it should prove useful to recapitulate and round off the historical survey by directing special attention to the main deductions to be drawn from it.

An immediately striking fact about Sorokin's views on the nature of value systems is his insistence upon their complexity. Many, if not most historians have, of course, been so impressed by the complexity that they refuse to believe in the possibility of detecting any order, still less any system, in the apparently haphazard, chaotic, and purely casual chance sequence of events. History on these assumptions never repeats itself. Neither does it fit any pattern or follow any plan.

Such a view, which Sorokin describes as "socio-cultural atomism," dismisses any search for uniformities as unwarranted, and thereby denies the possibility of building up any broad system of knowledge about social life or of constructing any form of sociology as a science of socio-cultural uniformities. Despite the vehemence with which this atomist view is often held, the very people who propound it may often be found introducing general ideas at some stages of their work without, however, giving any adequate definition or elaboration of their meaning.

A completely opposite doctrine is maintained by many historians and sociologists, who regard the whole mixed bag of miscellaneous aspects of social life of every kind or the total culture of any area as something which can quite properly be discussed as though it were a whole, a single thing, self-contained and complete in itself or, as Sorokin describes it, entirely integrated as a single functional system. A number of anthropologists have fallen victims to this error in discussing the total culture of areas, such as the Trobriand or Samoa Islands, or of the Melanesians or other groups, primitive or not, as though they were necessarily completely integrated, static wholes. Sorokin regards the twenty-one civilizations, Hellenic, Western, Sumerian, Egyptiac, Far Eastern, Indic, etc., of A. J. Toynbee's great work *A Study of History* (1934-39), as another example of the same mistake. These integralist theories are mistaken because they simply mix the causal, meaningful, or mixed relationship which a true cultural system must exhibit with all sorts of purely chance occurrences, not really essential parts of that culture but consisting instead of other inessential factors derived from mere adjacency in space and time.

Between the cultural atomists and· the integralists there are many other currents of sociological and anthropological thought, such as those popularized by the diffusionists, for example, who regard a culture like that of Egypt as a completely integrated whole, but yet imagine in some obscure way that various elements of it could separate themselves from the rest of the system and diffuse, each in different directions, to take root in the various cultures to which they had emigrated.

All such theories fail to do justice to the real nature and wide range of cultural and social value systems which any true culture must include and integrate. Sorokin lists language, science, religion, fine arts, ethics as the main cultural systems of mankind. Each of these systems (except language) has many sub-systems to include, for example, literature, music, theater, architecture, sculpture, and painting under fine arts, and law and morals under ethics. In addition there is a large number of mixed value systems, all of which are either composites or derivatives from the first five named, being combinations of their sub-systems. The main such derivative systems are religion-law, science-art-ethics, and systems of philosophy, of economics, and of politics.

Over and above these purely *cultural* or value systems and these sub-systems stand the *social* systems, and the men and women composing them, who act as bearers or agents through whom the cultural reality finds expression. They may be the bearers of one or two specified kinds of cultural values if they are associations for definite and limited artistic, religious, economic, or other purposes, or they may be bearers of a whole collection or encyclopedia of cultural values. The family, the university, or the state are examples of this omnibus social class.

The overwhelming majority of earlier efforts to frame a general, all-inclusive view of this vast field of cultural and social systems and sub-systems try to find a nomothetic theory or explanation of them by selecting some chief or prime factor, variable or principle, as a kind of central axis on which all the cultural and social systems depend and by which they are conditioned. The unity of the cultural system is thus made to result from the all-embracing power of the selected chief principle or central axis. Looking again at some of these ideas in the light of Sorokin's work, it will be seen that the many great principles which have been put forward as the clue to historical development, to serve as this "central axis," fall into two broad groups, those which regard the axis as some compelling force existing in its own right outside the culture or society and those which select one of the factors or systems existing within the culture or society itself as the axis.

The chief *external* integrating or governing principles occur in the geographic theories, including climatic and cosmic theories, such as those about sunspots and the influence of the stars, and the biological theories which stress the supposed controlling influence of factors such as race, heredity, pressure of population, or the evolutionary struggle for existence.

Among the factors or systems selected from within the various cultural systems and sub-systems as the key to the operation of human development as a whole have been:

the economic: Marxism and others
the technological: Marxism, T. Veblen, and others
the religious: F. de Coulanges, A. Comte, Hegel (partly), Max Weber
    and others
family forms: LePlay and his school
customs, habits, folkways, *mores:* Sumner
science: De Roberty and others.

These few examples by no means exhaust the list.

Popular as the search for a single explanatory principle has been, there have also been other theories suggesting that there are but two main systems which between them can explain everything. Thus the universe has been studied under the aspects of civilization and culture, or divided according to its material and non-material aspects, or its technological and ideological aspects. All the variegated thoughts and achievements of mankind then have to be compressed into one or other of the two all-embracing factors. Whatever may be thought of Sorokin's own historical analysis outlined in the preceding chapters, it should at least have made evident the inadequacy of these and all other simpler or more arbitrarily drawn efforts to explain the nature of cultural development. He has, moreover, thrown down a very clear challenge to those who assume that no general philosophical explanations are possible. In sharp contrast with the oversimplified schemes of sociological interpretation briefly alluded to above, Sorokin concludes that the total culture of an individual or of a society is neither an incoherent maze of unrelated uncoordinated peculiarities, or "congeries," nor is it ever likely to be one perfectly integrated system. To the extent that a considerable part of the total culture of a society or an individual is unified into one of a few great super-systems, it may be said to be rational, logical, consistent, and "integralist." It shows a system of meanings as its central and absolutely essential characteristic. To the extent that a people's culture consists of congeries, either parts of systems or of single cultural values, they are non-rational, non-logical, inconsistent creatures.

To contend that man and society are perfectly rational and logical, as the philosophers of one main idea or the totalitarian integrators do, or to believe, like those who consider, as the atomists must, that man and society are completely non-rational and non-logical are both equally wrong. The truth is that at any given moment there are to be found in man and society rational and logical together with non-rational and non-logical opinions and behavior; super-systems coexisting with congeries; consistency with contradiction; integration with disintegration, both synthesis and the accumulation of disunited and undigested values. Sorokin emphasizes the fact that the number of unintegrated, eclectically mixed cultures is enormous. Nevertheless, amongst the welter of confused and confusing cultural phenomena, he claims to have detected and described three great super-systems which have for long periods in the past successfully polarized most of the activities and beliefs of very large numbers of people and of many societies.

After charting the existence, growth, development, and decline of these ideational, idealistic and sensate cultural super-systems, it is possible to get a new insight into the character of past civilizations and cultures.

By demonstrating the manner in which each of these super-systems successfully integrates their various component values into a truly unified culture, so that their arts, science, social and economic philosophy are seen to have an interrelated common style peculiar to each and not shared by the other two, Sorokin makes possible a new encyclopedic grasp of the nature of past cultures so as to deepen and also to extend historical knowledge.

How the discovery and description of his cultural super-systems succeed in providing operational concepts for cautious use in historical interpretation becomes clearer after he has explained in the light of his facts and his theories how cultures and cultural systems change in space and time.

How Changes in Social and Cultural Life Occur– Does the total culture of a given area change all together as one system, or do its various elements change atomistically and independently from one another?

Sorokin answers this question by making several important distinctions.

If a cultural system is closely integrated, it changes as a whole, in togetherness. The greater the integration and interdependence of the system, the greater the togetherness of the change.

If it is not closely integrated, none but considerable changes in the most important parts of it will be interconnected and able to lead to a change of all the important compartments of the culture as a whole.

If a given culture is a mere spatial congeries, any part of it can change without involving any change in the rest of its elements. When, as usually happens, a given total culture is made up partly of coexisting single congeries and partly of several systems, some but not all of which are subordinated and united into larger value systems and super-systems (some being coordinated with one another and some being congeries to one another), then such a culture will change differently in its different parts. All its important elements united into a super-system change together. Its congeries all change independently and at a different rate from that of the super-system.

There is a further complication which Sorokin does not fully analyze, resulting from the fact that cultural value systems and sub-systems themselves evolve according to their own immanent principles, thereby influencing the super-system also. Marxist economics is perhaps one of the most striking examples of such an immanent development, for it has exercised a tremendous influence upon contemporary life and culture, although it has been shown to be an influence still within the framework of a sensate super-system.

It may seem that such an interpretation does not explain very much and that the atomists, who think that everything is a matter of chance, are not far wrong. Certainly Sorokin does not blink the very great difficulties of going beyond the scepticism of the atomists. One immediately obvious practical difficulty is of deciding which elements are mere congeries and which are truly parts of one system. Although real, the difficulties, Sorokin holds, are not insurmountable. He is at least able to dispose quickly of a vast number of false clues. He points out that a moment's reflection upon these very numerous and complex fundamental patterns of change will soon explode all the single-factor, monistic theories of cultural change, such as Marxism, geographical, technological, or biological determinism, all of which, in so far as they purport to explain the whole history of human cultural development, Sorokin describes as hopelessly dead.

In the ideational-idealistic-sensate value super-systems and their related social elements, on the other hand, it is possible to embrace satisfactorily not all but a far larger number of systems and sub-systems than any other rival theory so far propounded can hope to do. Proof of the fact becomes all the more impressive as the review proceeds of other general problems of the nature of cultural change. One of them is to discover, when systems change together, whether they do so through space. Aristotle long ago demonstrated that no motions or changes, whether of number or kind, can occur without local displacement or movement in space. Space change can happen independently of other forms of change, but these cannot occur without it.

Physical as well as social space is involved in the migrations of cultural phenomena. The steam locomotive, communism and the designs of motor cars, jazz and lipstick, Beethoven's symphonies and the theory of evolution move from one country to another, from one class to another, from city to country communities.

Movement in social space, although one of the simplest forms of cultural change, involves a multitude of fascinating problems upon which all too little light has so far been shed by students of history and social life. The routes by which cultural objects and phenomena have travelled can also form an absorbing study. It involves knowledge of the direction of the streams of the cultural elements, an investigation of the importers and earliest recipients of new cultural values, an explanation of the lag in the entrance of the finished products into the culture of the rural classes, lower classes, and less civilized peoples. It leads to studies of the shifting of great centers of culture, and therefore to an inquiry why certain cultural systems and values multiply and spread successfully while others do not. Of them all, it may be asked, which cultural values penetrate and are first to diffuse, the material or the non-material, and how are cultural objects and values transformed in the process of migration? It is a question of migration not merely from place to place, but from upper class to lower class, or, what usually occurs only in periods of cultural decline, from lower class to upper class. (Sorokin often uses the word "class" in its conventional, descriptive sense, and not "scientifically" as a sociological reality.) Difficult as it is to answer these questions — impossible upon the basis of single factor or monistic theories of cultural change — they become more tractable as soon as a systematic use is made of the concept of a total culture of any people or community as a conglomeration of systems, super-systems, coordinated systems, and congeries of systems and single elements.

Cultural changes occur not merely from one area to another, and from one social class to another, but also from one period of time to another. The four theories of this temporal aspect of cultural change maintain:

1. That when all varieties of cultural phenomena change, they all change at the same time.

   This theory will not bear examination, particularly in the absence of any agreed time unit as the measure of change, e.g., is it a year, a generation, or a century?

2. Some classes of cultural phenomena always lead in the change, while the others lag in a certain uniform order.

   One of the best-known varieties of this theory is the Marxist notion that changes in the technique of economic production precede and determine changes in the structure of society which in turn precede and determine changes in the political, social, and intellectual forms and life of society. Material culture is supposed to lead in the process of change while the non-material lags. Apart from the great initial difficulties over which Marxists and non-Marxists have wrangled as to the exact meaning of the "material factor" — whether, for example, it is to include technique which, as a form of knowledge, is essentially a non-material factor — the theory of the primacy of the economic or technological factor in cultural change is simply and plainly contradicted by the historical record of the movements of discoveries and inventions in technology and natural sciences, philosophy, humanities, fine arts, and social science. Sorokin concludes that all the known varieties of a uniform cultural lag theory are fallacious, inasmuch as they elevate a partial case into a general rule.

3. All cultural phenomena change but in no uniform order and in merely haphazard sequence.

   This view also is contradicted by the evident links and connections between the systems within cultural super-systems.

4. Some classes of cultural phenomena change at the same time, others at other times, but uniformly in a settled order of change; while there are yet others which show no uniformity at all in their changes.

Sorokin's findings confirm that the main forms of art or science or philosophy, law and ethics, united into one system, broadly speaking, change together, causally and meaningfully, and in time, whether this time is a year, a decade or a century.

While this is true of the composite super-systems, there is hardly any invariable uniformity about the times of change of the minor movements of all these variables, such as painting, music, and literature.

The important thing is to grasp that the system as a whole changes. It is not true that one of its components, the economic, for instance, starts the change in the first place and the other components follow.

Variations in the Creative Achievement in Different Cultural Fields — Relying again, as far as possible, upon as objective a series of facts as he was able to collect, Sorokin, with the aid of a collaborator, presented an analysis of the relative importance of all the historical persons mentioned in *Encyclopaedia Britannica* (9th edition) who have contributed to each of the following fields of culture over each period of fifty years: religion, statesmanship, literature, scholarship (humanistic, juridical, and social sciences), science (including technology), philosophy, business, fine arts, and miscellaneous.

He does not place a greater value upon the results of this survey than its obvious limitations permit. Such qualities as editorial omniscience, the perfect objectivity of contributors to the *Encyclopaedia,* or the complete adequacy of their historical knowledge, for example, are not assumed. Over-emphasis upon British and English-speaking people must also be allowed for, as well as the necessary absence of any personal record matching the great achievements of anonymous artists and collective enterprises in the ideational and idealistic periods, all of which must be recognized as additional shortcomings. The results shown are therefore somewhat distorted, but the distortion is not catastrophic. No better information is readily available, while that which Sorokin provides is, as he claims, the fullest, most systematic, and most impartial data so far given by any theory of culture and cultural change. It at least is not the type of fact so often used by so-called scientific writers whose facts are purely and simply illustrative, descriptive shreds of pseudo-facts, quite unable to support scientifically, as they are supposed to do, the generalized propositions they are brought in to sustain.

The numerical indicators produced as a result of this study give for each fifty years the geometric average of the number of persons mentioned in each field and the number of lines devoted to them in the *Encyclopaedia Britannica.* The quantitative-qualitative assessment of each eminent person's historical achievement thus results from the amount of space devoted to him. An arithmetical average of all the geometric averages in the last column gives a rough index of the total creativity of each fifty-year period in all ten fields of activity, the table summarizing his general results.

Sorokin also presents the results (omitted here) from the following countries separately: Greece, Rome, France, England, Germany, Austria, Hungary and Bohemia, Russia and Poland, United States.

The main deductions drawn from these findings are:

1. That in all fields of culture, both in the non-material subjects (religion, literature, art) and in the material subjects (science and technology), cultural achievement is accumulative.

2. The direction of the process is naturally linear, if only because of this accumulative addition of cultural achievements over time.

3. The creativeness of various periods fluctuates enormously and violently. Some periods have no achievements of any kind. In other periods there are great explosions of creative activity.

4. Religion and statesmanship provide a more continuous stream of creative historical persons. Creativeness in economic and business achievements is most fragile, the least continuous and most apt to dry up and disappear. Again it is entirely false to claim that historically, technological, economic, and scientific inventions or creativeness are more continuous or accumulative than the religious, political, or humanistic activities.

5. Religion and statesmanship provide historical persons and creative achievements earlier than any other field. Literature comes next. Business is the last to develop. Philosophy, fine arts, science, and scholarship all appear at about the same period. Social, political, and military organization are the earliest paramount necessities for any group.

6. Religion and statesmanship are not merely the first to emerge; they remain the most important fields.

7. The manner in which the ten cultural systems, summarized above, emerge and decline is in accord with what has been found about the succession of ideational, idealistic, and sensate cultures. The record in relation to business and religion affords the best evidence of the mutual incompatibility of the ideational and sensate cultures. Reduced to the most summarized formula, it seems to show that it has indeed been found that man could not, over the centuries, serve both God and Mammon.

8. Literature, fine arts, and music for the writers of the *Encyclopaedica Britannica* meant, for the most part, the idealistic and the sensate forms of those arts. Partly for this reason, but

above all because, in their ideational forms they are largely collective or anonymous productions, the indicators of influence and leadership in them are greater in sensate than in ideational periods.

9. Science is predominantly a sub-system of sensate culture, and the statistical indicators show that it rises and falls with sensate culture.

10. Scholarship and philosophy can flourish in ideational, idealistic, or sensate periods as the indicators show.

On all these grounds, Sorokin bases his claim that his division of culture into super-systems of value with their qualitatively different dependent systems is an analytic procedure superior to that so far provided by any other classification. He also claims that it provides a historically valid, easily understood explanation of cultural changes.

His theory fits the facts; and by the facts he means, if not all the facts, at any rate vastly more of them than any previous writers on the subject have thought it necessary to collect. At the same time, he recognizes that there are not by any means as many facts as could be desired, particularly relating to ideational epochs.

Rhythm and Phases in Cultural Change — Sorokin next takes up the question whether the cultural changes show any rhythm in their movement. Rhythm, tempo, periodicity cycle, oscillation, and fluctuation are all terms that have been used very frequently in the social sciences, but rarely with any precision. Sorokin devotes some pains to their elucidation.

Among the many previous rhythmical theories, Sorokin calls attention to those in pairs, or dyads, such as war/peace; order/disorder; the Chinese Yin and Yang; the Hindu alternation of the materialization of the spiritual unity (Brahma) and its dematerialization; the Babylonian rhythm of the destruction and recreation of the world; the eternal struggle between strife and love of Empedocles; Campanella's alternation of religion-atheism; Saint-Simon's rhythm of "critical and organic periods"; Fourier's anarchy-unity; A. N. Whitehead's intuition-scholarship; J. L. Lowe's convention-revolt in poetry and literature.

There are very many others. In the social sciences, writers have called attention to such dual sequences as rapid population increase followed by slow increase or stationary condition (G. Schmoller, R. Pearl, G. U. Yule); alternation of concentration of wealth and its more even distribution (G. Schmoller, V. Pareto); expansion and contraction of government regimentation (H. Spencer, P. Sorokin); rise and decline of aristocracy (Aristotle, Plato, Ibn Khaldun, Vico and others); challenge and response,

Table 9:   HISTORICAL PERSONALITIES MENTIONED IN THE ENCYCLOPEDIA BRITANNICA (1875)

Geometric Averages of the number of lines devoted to each.

Period	I Religion	II State	III Literature	IV Scholarship	V Science	VI Philosophy	VII Business	VIII Misc.	IX Fine Arts	X Music	Arithmetic Average
B.C. 4000–3951	—	8.4	—	—	—	—	—	—	—	—	0.8
3000–2951	—	6.4	—	—	—	—	—	—	—	—	0.6
1500–1451	—	—	—	—	—	10.0	—	—	—	—	1.0
1050–1001	39.0	48.3	—	—	—	—	—	—	—	—	8.7
950–901	17.9	—	—	—	—	—	—	—	—	—	1.8
900–851	13.7	21.8	44.6	—	—	—	—	—	—	—	7.9
850–801	—	18.0	—	—	—	—	—	—	—	—	1.8
800–751	10.6	19.2	10.9	—	—	—	—	—	—	—	4.1
750–701	53.4	18.2	—	—	—	—	—	—	—	—	7.2
700–651	9.8	—	19.3	—	—	—	—	—	—	—	2.9
650–601	36.2	21.7	34.8	—	—	—	—	—	—	—	9.3
600–551	69.5	39.2	25.7	—	—	41.0	—	—	6.6	—	18.2
550–501	42.3	104.4	12.8	—	—	122.7	—	8.7	7.6	—	29.9
500–451	30.8	96.7	105.8	5.9	—	64.8	—	2.8	26.9	—	33.8
450–401	3.6	168.0	144.4	80.3	—	110.4	—	9.3	48.4	—	58.8
400–351	2.8	175.0	26.3	57.4	3.8	214.3	5.5	5.2	27.1	—	52.2
350–301	—	281.7	32.1	31.2	14.1	145.3	14.3	—	50.6	3.1	54.4
300–251	—	70.4	51.7	1.7	10.3	91.6	—	—	—	—	26.0
250–201	—	155.0	42.7	5.8	4.4	8.5	—	4.6	—	—	24.6
200–151	6.7	111.7	81.0	38.6	30.9	13.0	—	—	—	—	
150–100	5.6	37.5	12.3	5.4	33.6	11.4	2.2	—	—	—	8.6
100–51	13.1	265.9	95.2	23.2	12.9	14.8	—	26.0	15.3	2.2	43.8
50–1	—	216.0	219.5	128.1	7.5	4.0	—	—	2.8	—	61.9
A.D. 0–49	253.4	125.6	41.3	41.1	23.2	55.3	—	18.5	—	—	54.9
50–99	36.4	170.7	159.8	55.1	8.4	46.8	—	—	3.7	—	48.7
100–149	132.3	37.3	54.1	71.7	14.1	2.2	—	11.2	—	—	34.7
150–199	97.3	70.4	68.3	34.4	38.7	38.6	—	—	2.6	—	32.2
200–249	155.2	77.3	16.7	15.2	10.3	19.6	—	—	—	—	28.4
250–299	135.6	36.6	3.8	1.7	4.3	—	—	—	—	—	18.2

A.D.											
300– 349	200.0	75.8	—	29.5	9.4	22.9	—	5.7	—	—	34.3
350– 399	307.9	78.7	41.9	34.7	15.0	18.0	—	3.3	3.3	—	50.0
400– 449	197.3	83.7	33.8	50.6	—	—	—	—	—	—	36.5
450– 499	35.5	86.8	—	53.1	4.7	20.1	—	—	—	—	19.6
500– 549	56.4	119.3	11.9	58.8	7.4	28.6	—	—	—	—	28.0
550– 599	80.3	40.6	22.4	15.2	4.1	—	—	—	—	—	16.6
600– 649	199.4	52.0	44.2	7.2	—	—	—	—	—	—	30.7
650– 699	78.5	1.7	14.6	—	12.0	—	—	—	—	—	9.5
700– 749	54.0	34.1	—	12.2	—	—	—	—	—	—	11.2
750– 799	34.4	55.2	—	8.1	—	—	—	—	—	—	9.8
800– 849	76.3	60.8	4.6	24.1	—	—	—	—	—	—	16.6
850– 899	129.8	80.4	—	45.0	8.9	16.6	—	—	—	3.1	28.4
900– 949	80.2	54.0	7.8	15.5	3.3	9.7	—	2.4	—	8.0	18.1
950– 999	59.1	59.1	48.0	19.7	—	5.8	—	—	—	—	22.6
1000–1049	94.6	129.3	14.3	8.8	29.2	—	—	—	—	10.5	28.7
1050–1099	195.1	211.6	23.1	25.5	6.3	28.3	—	—	—	—	49.0
1100–1149	152.6	132.7	20.0	110.0	—	29.7	3.0	—	—	—	44.8
1150–1199	222.4	182.0	63.9	54.4	18.9	56.3	—	4.5	—	—	58.4
1200–1249	136.9	195.1	41.4	62.6	13.2	8.8	—	8.6	4.7	—	47.7
1250–1299	156.3	156.3	47.2	64.4	8.8	21.4	16.9	—	35.8	—	54.0
1300–1349	108.7	185.0	108.2	53.1	14.8	34.3	15.0	5.0	78.1	—	58.7
1350–1399	195.8	180.8	142.5	32.5	4.6	—	29.5	14.3	36.6	—	65.1
1400–1449	231.9	193.8	56.0	90.8	—	33.2	40.1	29.0	157.7	—	78.0
1450–1499	393.4	222.0	120.2	213.5	12.1	8.9	100.7	116.6	442.1	12.1	156.4
1500–1549	805.8	504.4	409.2	220.3	96.3	65.3	82.3	149.2	790.4	10.8	310.1
1550–1599	626.6	782.3	782.1	363.9	187.0	49.1	70.0	138.2	262.3	75.9	334.8
1600–1649	512.6	927.0	828.9	441.7	295.0	328.5	71.7	57.7	686.0	38.4	426.8
1650–1699	901.1	1063.1	942.8	389.3	420.7	303.2	68.1	181.2	560.1	78.1	478.4
1700–1749	634.2	786.4	842.6	527.7	451.0	318.8	77.9	397.3	249.0	149.1	421.8
1750–1799	452.4	2329.9	1666.5	995.2	1318.0	404.5	271.3	530.2	597.9	295.8	872.9
1800–1849	944.6	3201.0	2765.0	2022.2	2042.2	535.3	692.7	—	1327.7	390.4	1445.1
Totals	9287.3	14937.4	10406.2	6646.4	5199.4	3361.6	1561.2	1726.2	5423.3	1077.5	5962.9

withdrawal and return, rout and rally, apparentation and affiliation societies, schism and palingenesis, growth and decline of civilizations (A. J. Toynbee, O. Spengler); centralization/decentralization (Brooks Adams); technical-materialistic phase and spiritual-religious and ethical phase (L. Weber); culture/civilization (Spengler); binding and loosening (*Bindung und Losung* of K. Joel).

This long catalog by no means exhausts the list of various dyads or two-phase rhythms which have been proposed as clues to the processes of history. Three-phase rhythms, or triads, are yet more popular among social and philosophical thinkers, and they can undoubtedly be detected in many social and cultural phenomena. Examples are synthesis of meanings (conception) / incarnation into vehicles (objectification) / acquisition of human agents (socialization). invention / imitation / opposition (G. Tarde); appearance / growth / decline; ideological phase / organizational phase / power phase in social movements (R. Mayreder); breakdown / disintegration / dissolution of civilizations (A. J. Toynbee); architectural / plastic / pictorial phases in art (P. Ligeti); lyric / epic / dramatic in literature (V. Hugo); ancient / medieval / modern (Herder, Hegel, Ranke, Comte, Dilthey); age of gods / of heroes / of men (G. Vico); three stages of disorderly / small tranquility / great tranquility (Confucius); theological / metaphysical / positive states (A. Comte); thesis / antithesis / synthesis (Hegel).

Four-phase rhythms are also discernable. The alternations of the seasons, the biological rhythm of childhood / adolescence / maturity / old-age, morning / afternoon / evening / night all set a pattern which has been widely adopted. Florus, who flourished around A.D. 200, thought he detected such a rhythm in the history of Rome, and Spengler in our own time applied the pattern of childhood / youth / manhood / old-age directly to the explanation of historical change. Four-generation rhythms were adopted by Ibn Khaldun, by Machiavelli, and by G. Ferrari.

An example of the more complicated six-phase rhythm is the well-known cycle of Polybius, monarchy / tyranny / aristocracy / oligarchy / democracy / mob-rule, which he thought was eternally repeated. Sorokin regards the division of the week into seven days as evidence of yet more complicated rhythms of which the month and the year are others. He suggests that magic numbers, such as 3, 7, 9, and 12, bear witness also to the reality of rhythms in social life. In one of his earlier works he analyzed, classified, and criticized the views of other writers who had studied fluctuations, rhythms, and cycles of social processes. (*Contemporary Sociological Theories*, 1928, pages 728-756.)

Having established the reality of rhythmical change in social and cultural affairs, Sorokin points to the insatiable desire of the human mind to seek to establish and to explain the major rhythms of human history. The thinkers who have sought to satisfy this desire, from Confucius, Lao-Tse, Plato, Aristotle, St. Augustine, Erigena, St. Thomas Aquinas, Ibn Khaldun, Vico, Machiavelli, Hobbes, Descartes, Montesquieu, Adam Smith, to Kant, Hegel, Comte, H. Spencer, Marx and others, are still eagerly studied and discussed, while hundreds of less ambitious, fact-finding studies are neglected and forgotten.

For his own suggestion that the three-phase rhythm of ideational / idealistic / sensate cultures provides a valid and useful clue to historical change, he does not claim more than that it may unquestionably be discerned in the history of Western culture and that, in addition to disclosing one of the most all-embracing, long-term or tidal movements which has twice recurred, it also points to a number of smaller rhythms in the main fields of culture, indicating their interrelations with one another.

Sorokin does not claim for his theory, as Spengler and others did for theirs, that it is universal and applicable to all other cultures as well as to that of Western civilization, despite some evidence for it in Egyptian, Hindu, and Chinese history.

The rhythms which may be discerned in the passage of Graeco-Roman and Western culture from a dominant ideational phase to idealistic and sensate phases have already been described. They may be summed up as follows:

1. Ideational-idealistic-visual (sensate) rhythm in painting, sculpture, architecture.
2. Ideational-idealistic-sensate rhythm in music, drama, literature, and art criticism.
3. Ideational-idealistic-sensate rhythm in the systems of truth and knowledge; in religion, philosophy, science.
4. Rhythm of stationary, increasing and rapidly-growing discoveries in the natural sciences and in technological inventions.
5. Ideational-idealistic-sensate rhythm in the systems of ethics and law.
6. Familistic-contractual-compulsory rhythm in the field of social relationship.
7. Theocratic-idealistic-secular rhythm in the field of political regimes.
8. Rhythm of the rise and decline of sensate economic well-being.

9. Rhythm of the rise of war and internal disturbances in the transitional periods from one phase to another; and decline of such outbreaks in the periods of crystallization and domination of ideational and sensate phases.

10. Rhythm of leadership and domination of religion in the ideational phase, and of business and other sensate activities, in the sensate phases.

11. Rhythm of the rise of the ideational type of historical persons in the ideational phase and of the sensate type in the sensate phase.

12. Rhythm of ideational-idealistic-sensate forms of liberty.

13. Tidal rhythm in increase and decrease of totalitarianism and *laissez-faire.*

14. Rhythms of idealism / materialism, of eternalism / temporalism, of nominalism / conceptualism / realism, of ideation / idealistic / sensate conceptions of time, space, causality, and of other first principles and fundamental categories of human thought.

Relationships of Meaning and Causality in Cultural Life in Both Their Static and Their Dynamic Aspects. – The wealth of material studied and presented by Sorokin in each of these fourteen main cultural sub-rhythms of values has been indicated above, together with brief summaries of the way in which their true nature has been classified and rendered more comprehensible by the account of the main embracing rhythm of the super-system of values, the ideational, idealistic and sensate. An understanding of the nature of the super-system of values gives a firm grasp of the nature of the sub-systems in the same way as the branches and leaves of a plant may be identified from the main stem. This is a bold claim, for it cannot be made on behalf of other theories of cultural development because, Sorokin says, they all look in the wrong places for the order of change throughout time. He summarizes the point by claiming to have discovered both a static and a dynamic meaningful-causal relationship between an enormous number of socio-cultural phenomena and socio-cultural processes with their rhythms and phases. This summarized statement contains a wealth of meaning, inviting some clarification and further thought.

"*Static* meaningful-causal relationship" may be explained as the relationships in which, where A is given, the B C D are meaningfully-causally connected. Thus if the essential character A of a sensate super-system is known, it is possible to say that, if A is given, then such and such additional qualities and characteristics B C D E ... N will also be given. For example, it can be predicted of such a system A that its art B will be predominantly visual, with all the essential characteristics of such an art $(B\ C\ D\ E\ F,$ etc.); that its system of truth C will be predominantly empirical, with concentration on the natural sciences and technological inventions; that $D,$ supersensory religion, will play a very modest part; that its ethics and law, $E,$ will be predominantly utilitarian, hedonistic, expedient; that its government, $F,$ will be secular, led by military, or rich, or professional groups; that its literature, $G,$ will be predominantly realistic, sensual, in part erotic, with a common type of people instead of gods and heroes as its main personages.

Similar schemes can be drawn up for the ideational and idealistic cultural systems. Given the nature of the value super-system, there is thus a clear and tangible possibility of predicting a large number of the forms which would be assumed by its art, philosophy, religion, ethics, social organization and so on; since the A and its $B\ C\ D\ E \ldots N$ are connected causally and meaningfully.

It may be objected that this is a circular argument since A is only known as A by the character of the sub-groups $B\ C\ D\ E \ldots\ N.$ The inadequacy of such a superficial objection may, however, be seen from the fact that the meaningful-causal relationship exists not merely between A and its $B\ C\ D\ E \ldots N;$ but also between B with $C\ D\ E \ldots N,s,$ between C and $B\ D\ E \ldots N$ and N with $B\ C\ D\ E$ and so on. The organic unity of the whole can be further shown from the fact that if A is given, $B\ C\ D\ E \ldots N$ will be there; if A is absent, $B\ C\ D\ E.\quad.\ N$ will be absent.

"*Dynamic* meaningful-causal relationship," the second half of the claim here made for Sorokin's theory, means the type of relationship which exists between A and B if, when A varies, B also varies. In the scheme just given, it means that if A varies, not only B but $C\ D\ E \ldots N$ also vary. Such a dynamic relationship exists when an ideational cultural system, A moves to the idealistic phase, $A1.$ Then all the other sub-systems, $B\ C\ D\ E \ldots N$ and their related systems also move. Furthermore, if it is known what kind of fundamental transformation is being experienced by B or C or $N,$ it is possible to foresee with considerable probability the kind of transformations which $D\ E$ and other embraced value systems, with their rhythms and phases, will be undergoing. A complex net of dynamic relationships of interdependence is thereby discovered, not only between the main cultural process with its super-rhythm — the passage of the super-system from A to $A1$ for example — but between the embraced processes and their rhythms.

Sorokin illustrates the theory by assuming that our culture is at present in transition from a dominant sensate phase to a more ideational phase. It would then, he holds, be probable that wars and revolutions will increase, that economic prosperity should decrease, that most sensate values should decrease, beginning with money and the prestige of wealth; that the increase in scientific inventions and discoveries would be at a slower rate; that supersensory religion should find more followers in all its varieties accompanied by increasing mysticism, religious rationalism, fideism; that utilitarian and hedonistic ethics should lose ground; that visual, sensate, sensual, and erotic forms and contents of the arts should also decrease.

These changes are probable, not certain. Sorokin does not claim that the sequences he thinks he has discovered are universal and eternal. They have, however, been fairly typical and general. The fact that the sequence ideational-idealistic-sensate appears only to have occurred twice in the history of Western civilization is not, he thinks, a valid statistical reason to doubt the reality and necessity of connections he describes, for their strength lies more in their logico-meaningful interconnections than in the statistical number of their actual recurrences. His theories certainly do not lack empirical foundation. Indeed, he has handled more relevant empirical facts, and handled them with more care, than all the guardians of empiricism in sociology taken together. Despite the accusations of some of his critics, Sorokin is less concerned with securing credit for the originality of his views than with demonstrating the way in which they carry further, amplity and correct earlier views tending in the same general direction. This book will have failed if it does not show Sorokin to have woven his theories out of the very stuff of history.

Theories of Periodical Social Change — After establishing that cultures change and that rhythmical patterns may be discerned in those changes, Sorokin next examines various theories which have sought to demonstrate the existence of periodicity in cultural change.

This review takes him far afield into a study of some strange and fantastic notions advanced not merely by mystery-mongers of various kinds, but also by profoundly original thinkers, such as Plato and Aristotle. These fanciful imaginary speculations, lumped together by Sorokin as meta-empirical, are to be found especially among ancient Hindu theories, as well as in many others, including Chinese, Aztec, and Arab speculations. The true nature and significance of Plato's mysterious perfect number of time which completes the perfect year, when all the eight revolutions of the seven planets and the sphere are accomplished together and they again meet at their original point of departure, have continued to baffle his commentators and interpreters. It may be taken as a more exalted sample of the many obscure outpourings of astrologers, soothsayers and numerologists whose activity by no means came to an end at the close of the Dark Ages. No less a genius than Sir Isaac Newton was much given to such speculations, some of which are to be found in his *Observations upon the Prophecies of Daniel and the Apocalypse of St. John,* published after his death in 1733. Nietzsche and Herbert Spencer in more recent times indulged in views with no better factual basis than those of the most wildly speculative theories of much earlier times.

All may be dismissed, Sorokin concludes, as curious and ingenious, perhaps, but incapable of providing any serious or tested knowledge. Many of them, for example, propose such long term periodicities that there is no means of checking their validity.

Cosmic theories of periodicity in historical change are mainly astronomical, astrological, and meterological. The idea that the course of human affairs is very closely linked with the movements of the heavenly bodies is of the greatest antiquity. One of the oldest of such varieties of cosmic theories of periodicity had its origin in the ancient Babylonian development of astronomy and astrology. The great cycle, the *annus magnus* or the world's year, was thought to be completed when all the stars assume again a position they had before, a period variously estimated at 432,000,000, 720,000 and 480,000 years. The idea persisted, as the reference above to Plato's views indicates. It was kept alive by the Pythagoreans and, in varying forms, is quite commonly found in Greek and Roman writers. The Gnostics and the Fathers of the Church took over similar ideas, which were also kept alive by the Arabs. The early scholastic writers, such as Abelard, William of Conches, Alexander Neckham, Adelard of Bath, were full of astrological theories and prognostications. Similar views persisted throughout the Middle Ages, as the works of Bartholomew of England, Robert Grosseteste, Albertus Magnus, St. Thomas Aquinas, Dante, Peter of Abano, and Roger Bacon all testify. Sorokin also quotes many later views, down to works of similar import solemnly put forth in our own time. Considerably less fantastic and more closely tied to mundane events are theories of the geographic type. So also are those of the bio-organismic type of cosmic periodicity, of which that interpreting social rhythms and periodicities by the idea of generations in human life is chief. Sorokin has little difficulty in demonstrating the fallacious nature of these cosmic and biological explanations of cultural change.

That social happenings cannot be regarded as perfectly independent of the cosmic and biological conditions in which they occur is so obvious that it may readily be admitted. But it does not follow from such an admission that the dependence of social and cultural life on cosmic and biological sources is so close that any change in those sources must necessarily be tangibly reflected in social and cultural life. Any careful study of the facts is sufficient to show that the number of changes in social and cultural life which go on independently or directly contrary to cosmic and biological forces is legion.

Any reliance upon such theories must, moreover, be seen to be unjustified when it is discovered that periodicities in such matters as sunspots, the life of a generation, rainfall or climate generally, are no true periodicites at all but statistical averages, mean, mode or median, dressed up to look like periodicities. It becomes, therefore, statistically impossible to verify the periodicities in social and cultural life alleged to be based upon cosmic and biological forces. Many of the theories purporting to expound such periodicities are perfectly naive and fantastic. Sorokin will allow no better status to the business cycles with which recent economic literature is so full. They again are purely statistical averages, not identical with a true periodicity, and their description varies from author to author, from country to country, and from period to period. The truth is that they are averages based upon fancifully varying intervals.

The root of the fallacy in all such cosmic and biological theories is, says Sorokin, that they look for periodicities in the wrong place, that is to say outside and not inside the world of social and cultural phenomena itself. Inside that world there are indeed periodicities, but they represent intentionally or unintentionally established social conventions. Many are of an hourly, daily, weekly, monthly, or annual occurrence. There are still longer periodicities running over several years, such as the four-year term of office of an American president. All such conventional periodicities are essentially relative to the country or society in which they occur.

The application of measures of time to describe change in social and cultural life presents many difficulties which Sorokin examines, including some of the better-known efforts to deal with them, such as the so-called law of acceleration which asserts vaguely that everything in the universe tends to change faster as time goes on. For some writers this view is based upon such facts as that the Stone Age lasted longer than the Iron and Bronze Ages. But the use of stone continued with the use of iron and bronze, and both are still used today. For this and other reasons, Sorokin concludes that little is to be gained from such notions. He offers, instead, his own view that, when a super-system of culture passes from the ideational to the idealistic and then to the sensate phase, the rates of change in time of the quantitative, qualitative, and spatial changes of the super-system, and of all its main systems and sub-systems, tend to become faster. The opposite occurs when a super-system passes from a sensate to an ideational phase, for then the rate of change tends to become slower. Within the sensate phase of the super-system the rate of change tends to become particularly fast in its later, overripe stage. Without enumerating all the arguments and considerations Sorokin advances in support of these conclusions, it will be sufficient to note that they are not merely logically consistent with the nature of the super-systems in question; they are also borne out by the facts presented in the preceding chapters. They also fit the observed sequences of events better than any other theories so far offered. They can, for example, explain retardation as well as acceleration which the so-called law of acceleration is forced to ignore. Besides being very definite, they also have the advantage of relating together the rates of change in large numbers of social and cultural processes. This study concludes Sorokin's review of the nature of change in social and cultural processes. It remains to consider how and why such change occurs.

Why Cultures Change: The Principle of Immanent Change in Social and Cultural Life and the Principle of Limits — Relentless becoming instead of everlasting permanency was no doubt recognized by mankind as the law of life long before Heraclitus, at the dawn of Greek philosophy, proclaimed that all things are in a state of flux.

Logically, three answers are possible to the question how change is brought about in value systems. Change may be caused by forces or factors that lie outside the social and cultural system itself. Pressure of the environment, coupled with mechanistic and behavioristic theories of mental and social activities, have been widely regarded as an all-inclusive and sufficient explanation of social and cultural change. The fundamental principle, according to such a view, is that of stimulus/response. Current thinking is deeply impregnated with these notions so that the explanation of many social evils, such as crime, the defectiveness of social institutions, political or economic organization, is looked for in external causes.

The opposite solution is the immanent theory of social and cultural change, which holds that social and cultural systems change by virtue of their own forces and properties. Those who hold this view do not place all their hopes for reform or for the improvement of life in some rearrangement of external conditions. They view social and cultural life as an integral self-contained system, and they would not expect to change an old system into a young one, any more than a doctor would expect to transform an eighty-year-old man into a youth of twenty. Hegel is considered by Sorokin to have arrived at the most consistent and universal conception of immanent change ever created in the history of human thought. Aristotle's theory, although only derivatively immanent, is also one of the most systematic, complete, and all-embracing theories of change in general and of socio-cultural change in particular. These are but two examples, analyzed in greater detail by Sorokin, among at least four main types of theories of immanent change.

A third possible explanation attempts to combine both the external and immanent factors. Where a truly synthetic or integral principle arises from such a combination, it may suggest a satisfactory solution. Too often, however, real integration is not achieved. Then, although lip-service may be paid to the idea of joint influence, in practice no definite solution is achieved, but merely vague suggestions are given with some emphasis perhaps upon a single external or immanent factor.

Sorokin considers that the true source of change must be sought within a social and cultural system, although external factors may also play some part under certain conditions and limits. Change is from within, is immanent, because it is an inevitable consequence of the very existence of the cultural system as a going concern. The alternative to change is static equilibrium, a state fatal to any organism, since it spells stagnation, atrophy, and death. Change is the law of life. The environment is relaitvely unchanging. To look for the source of change in the environment instead of within the process of life itself is therefore demonstrably illogical. Extreme externalistic sources of change are thus ruled out unless everything is attributed, without any further attempt to find a rational explanation, to God or the Prime Mover. Mundane material external causes cannot offer a satisfactory explanation. They usually lead to a mere postponement of a solution. Sorokin gives, by way of example, the attempt to explain changes in American family life in the last fifty years (A) by some external factor (B), say a change in industrial conditions. Then the question naturally arises, "Why have industrial conditions changed?", so that a new theory (C) is brought in to explain (B). It may be the theory (C) that there has been a change in the density of population. But then why has (C) come to be? In this way the suggested explanation is pushed back until some remote notion connected with climatic change or sunspots or other possible cause is reached. All are equally unsatisfactory, because the inevitable question must soon be asked of whatever external cause is chosen, "Why is it capable of changing itself and of starting changes in the others?" The question is impossible to answer, especially if some material aspects of the environment, such as climate or geology or geographic factors, are proposed as the solution, because that leads to the extraordinary hypothesis that the least changing factors of all are brought in to account for the most rapidly changing of all phenomena — those of life itself.

If the search for purely external causes of change is abandoned in favor of some one of the elements of cultural life itself, such as the means and modes of production of Marxism, the mystery is by no means solved. How is it possible to demonstrate that some elements in social and cultural life, such as the family, religion, or science, cannot change themselves, while others, such as the methods of production, density of population, art or social customs, can do that?

To believe instead that the true principle of change is engendered within the cultural process itself is not to believe that external forces have no influence in producing cultural change. The family or any other social system, for example, changes immanently, but being in interaction with the State, with business organizations, the Church and other social systems, each of which also changes immanently, the changing family is subject to influences and pressures from them as well. Sorokin likens the total situation to a constellation of immanently changing systems. Change in one member of the constellation is facilitated by changes in the others. Sorokin advances the somewhat paradoxical view that the external, biological, or cosmic forces operate in a somewhat similar way. When plague germs or some natural catastrophe attack a cultural system, they provoke a reaction from a living organism itself in the process of change.

Among the many practical results of adopting Sorokin's view of the matter would be to introduce a much more cautious note in history text-books where, for example, they seek to expound the so-called causes of great historical events, such as the decline of feudalism, the emancipation of serfs and villeins, the Peasants' Revolt, the Crusades, the Reformation and the Renaissance. On Sorokin's view the crude inadequacy of much that has passed for historical insight into many of these great themes will at once become apparent: the notion, for example, that the Revival of Learning was largely stimulated by the expulsion of Greek scholars and their books when Constantinople was captured by the Turks, or the even more desperate efforts which have been made to find some plausible theory on the lines of the economic interpretation of history to explain the Crusades.

Instead, therefore, of regarding historical phenomena as an amorphous lump occasionally disturbed or lifted by one or two magic levers, whether economic or bacteriological or climatic, Sorokin depicts history as a field of forces developing according to their own internal principles of evolution, and interacting not in a mechanical but in a truly dynamic fashion. Not only upon general political history does Sorokin cast fresh light. His account of various theories about economic fluctuations, particularly theories about business cycles, is also illuminating. Some of these theories look for the causes of business fluctuations in forces external not merely to the business system but also to the social system of which business is a part. There are, for example, geographic theories of climatic changes, rainfall, sunspots, or other cosmic influences used by various writers to explain the matter. On the other hand, many business cycle theories are of the clearly immanent type, seeking their explanations of recurrent booms and depressions in the process of saving and investing, in building and construction work, in changes in tastes, and therefore in the quantity and quality of production, in banking operations or in the economic system as a whole. Others offer immanent explanations, but only after insisting that the economic sphere must be regarded as part of the larger social system. Others again collect a number of factors, some immanent and some external, social, psychological, biological and cosmic, often apparently without realizing that a mere mechanical juxtaposition of various factors mostly incommensurable with one another mixes things which cannot then be understood in their comparative roles or in their working together.

To elaborate the consequences of Sorokin's conception of the nature of the forces producing cultural change extends the analysis beyond the realms of history and far into the field of sociology. He shows that there is no incompatibility between the two. On the contrary, history, as the record and explanation of social and cultural change, must inescapably contribute to sociology and be influenced in turn by sociological theories. Sorokin's own work gives probably the most detailed and thoroughgoing demonstration of this historical nature of sociology and sociological nature of history, not merely in the four volumes of his *Social and Cultural Dynamics,* but in his system of general sociology best summarized in his *Society, Culture and Personality, their Structure and Dynamics* (1947). It must, therefore, suffice here to report Sorokin's own summary of his conclusions upon "the why and the how" of social and cultural change.

1.   The reason or cause of a change in any socio-cultural system is in

the system itself, and need not be looked for anywhere else.

2. The external environment which is mostly composed of the immanently changing systems is an additional reason for a change of system.

3. Any socio-cultural system, changing immanently, incessantly generates a series of immanent consequences, which change not only the environment but also the system itself.

4. The destiny or life career of any socio-cultural system represents mainly an unfolding of the immanent potentialities of the system itself which are the main factor in its own destiny.

5. External forces cannot fundamentally change the immanent potentialities of the system and its normal destiny, but they may crush the system or stop the process of unfolding its immanent potentialities at one of the early phases of its existence. They make also slow down or hasten, help or hinder, strengthen or weaken, the process of realizing those potentialities.

6. So far as the system, after it has emerged, bears in itself its future career, it is a determinate system and in this sense deterministic. So far as the future of the system is determined mainly by the system itself and not by external agents, such a determinism is indeterministic or free, flowing spontaneously from the system itself according to its own nature.

7. The main direction and the main phases of the unfolding are predetermined by the immanent forces within the system, but a considerable margin for variations remains free so that many of the details of development are free and become an unforeseen and unpredictable matter of chance environment and free choice.

8. The relative action of environmental factors and of self-control in shaping the destiny or life career of any system is not constant for all socio-cultural systems, but the more perfectly the system is integrated, the more powerful its self-control will be.

9. A socio-cultural system will have greater power in molding its destiny and be more independent of the forces of environment:
   a. the greater its membership;
   b. the better the members of the system are, biologically, mentally, morally, socially;
   c. the greater the wisdom, knowledge, and experience of its members;
   d. the better the system is organized;

e. the greater the total sum of the means of influencing human behavior and controlling the forces of nature at the disposal of its members;

f. the more consistently the system is integrated and able to achieve solidarity.

Any attempt to look further into the nature and ground of historical change encounters very obvious and considerable difficulty. If it is asked, for example, why the observed rhythms occur or why social and cultural developments have taken the course they have done, it is not possible to advance beyond the plain and simple empirical position that such are observed facts and there is not more to be said.

Recognizing that many will want some answer to the question, "Why is it so empirically?" Sorokin reviews several sociological attempts to provide answers and reaffirms his own Principle of Limits, to amplify, correct, and supplement them. Among various efforts to account for periodical movements and rhythmical changes in social and cultural developments, he examines various mechanistic theories, all of which he rejects, including all efforts made to apply the idea of equilibrium in the social sciences.

His views, summarized as the Principles of Limits, are as follows:

1. Identically recurrent socio-cultural processes are impossible.
2. Eternally linear socio-cultural processes are impossible. Any process that appears to be such is in all probability a long-time linear process which in its complete life is likely to be a non-linear process.
3. A linear trend limited in time is found in almost all socio-cultural processes. Its duration is different for different processes, but is shorter than that of the whole existence of the system.
4. It is impossible, both factually and logically, for any socio-cultural processes to have unlimited possibilities of variation of their essential traits. Therefore "history is ever old and repeats itself."
5. Apart from the essential traits, there is a wide, almost unbounded possibility of variation of the accidental properties of a system. Exhausted systems may be replaced by new ones, again giving almost unlimited possibilities of variation. History is therefore ever-new, unrepeated, and inexhaustible in its creativeness.
6. Since practically all the socio-cultural systems have limited

possibilities of variation in their essential forms, it follows that all systems that continue to exist after all their possible forms have been exhausted are bound to have recurrent rhythms. Recurrence in the life process of such systems is therefore inevitable.

7. The recurrent rhythms will be more frequent, conspicuous, and easier to detect and understand in proportion as the possibilities of variation of main forms are more limited.

8. Failure to grasp any recurrent rhythm will result from the process of the socio-cultural system having comparatively large possibilities of variation which empirically prevent the infrequent rhythm being noticed. Or the process may have too short a life span, dying early before it has had a chance to run through all its forms. Or the coexistence and mutual interference of several contemporaneous and different rhythms in the same system blur the rhythm of each, so that, to the observer or listener, they appear as unrhythmical "noise." Or there may be an excessively long duration between the recurrences. Or the rhythm may be exceedingly complex and many-phased.

9. In the light of the considerations in the preceding paragraphs, it is possible to assert the truth of the apparently contradictory statements that history ever repeats itself and never repeats itself.

10. Alternative views of history excluded by these considerations include the strictly cyclical, identically recurrent conception of the socio-cultural process; the linear theory of unlimited movement in one direction; the "unicist" view of the unique nature of historical phenomena that denies the existence of any recurrent rhythms in the socio-cultural process in favor of the idea that all happenings are brand new and unique in the totality of their traits and properties at any moment; the static conception that there is no change and that the socio-cultural world ever remains strictly identical with itself. All such views are untenable. The valid view is that of an incessant variation of the main recurrent themes which contains in itself as a part all these views and, as such, is much richer than any of them.

Insofar, therefore, that the broad trends of Western culture have been manifest in fully integrated cultural patterns explicable as movements of three great cultural super-systems, the ideational, idealistic, and sensate, it seems clear that none of these three can help changing, rising, growing, existing full-blooded for some time, and then declining.

The possibilities of change for these fully integrated systems are strictly limited. There can hardly be more than five fundamental answers to the chief problem of all, the true nature of reality, two of which are negative. That is to say, for a fully integrated cultural system, reality must be either supersensory (ideational premise) or sensory (sensate premise) or it has both aspects inseparably (idealistic premise) or it is entirely unknown and unknowable (premise of scepticism) or it is known only in its phenomenal aspect while its transcendental aspect, if it has such, is unknowable (premise of criticism and agnosticism). Each of these several premises may, of course, show many varieties differing in detail. Similarly there cannot be more than five or six integrated systems of truth: the truth of faith, of reason, of the senses, of their idealistic synthesis, or an integrated skeptical and agnostic or critical system. Art styles also must be ideational (symbolic), visual (sensate) or idealistic (integrated symbolic-visual). More detailed patterns of art, such as classic and romantic, idealistic and naturalistic, conventional and revolutionary, linear and *malerisch,* find their development within these three fundamental forms. So also in ethics, in social, economic, political, and other relationships, all, insofar as they are integrated, have limited possibilities of change.

What is said above, Sorokin is careful to emphasize, applies merely to *integrated* cultural systems. The number of unintegrated, eclectic, and mixed combinations of the ideational and sensate cultural elements is enormous, but by their nature they cannot serve as a major premise of integrated systems of culture. They are characteristic particularly of transitional periods.

Such considerations, arising from the Principle of Immanent Change and from the Principle of Limits, pointing to the strictly limited possibility of the main forms of change, help considerably, therefore, to throw more light on the nature of cultural change and represent a major contribution to dynamic sociology.

Sorokin pursues the analysis yet further. Given the three main super-systems of ideational, sensate, and idealistic culture, it is clear that each may be either completely true, completely false or partly true, and partly false.

If any of the three were entirely true, it could be expected to endure forever, for it would give an adequate knowledge of reality, it would permit its bearers to adapt themselves successfully to their environment which they would fully understand and thereby ensure a better social and cultural life than could be attained by any system based on error.

If any of the three were entirely false, none of these satisfactory results would be possible and none of them therefore could have dominated millions of human beings for centuries as they did. Moreover after they had disappeared, it would, on such a hypothesis, be unlikely that any of them could have recurred, as they did.

The third possibility, therefore, seems inescapable, and it is necessary to conclude that the observable super-rhythm of alternating sensate-ideational-idealistic cultural super-systems is explicable only on the assumption that each is partly true and partly false, partly adequate and partly inadequate.

The vital part in each of these great cultural systems gives their bearers the possibility of adaptation and survival. Their invalid part, existing side by side with their valid part, leads their bearers away from reality. As any one of the three systems grows, emphasis is increasingly put upon its own special and partial aspects of reality; it becomes monopolistically dominant and it tends to drive out all other systems of truth and reality with the valid parts they contain. Validities are increasingly lost; falsities develop and multiply. Society and its culture, built upon such a basis, becomes more and more empty, false, ignorant, inexperienced, powerless, disorderly, and base. The society of its bearers must change its major premises unless it is to perish. Change having been forced upon the society and culture in this way, the process recommences with the new system which has replaced the old and discredited system. Such is the nature of immanent change in a cultural system. It is a dialectical process rather than an organic process. That is to say, Sorokin did not rely upon biological analogies in an attempt to show that cultures die as it were of old age. He seeks to demonstrate that their failure results from the working-out of their own presuppositions or inner natures in such a way that the majority of people no longer derive a satisfaction from them comparable with the enthusiasm engendered by their early promise.

Despite the cogency of such an anlysis, it seemed to Sorokin to need further defense, particularly perhaps because of the evident claim it makes on behalf of the truth of faith derived from sources such as those described as intuition, inspiration, revelation, extra-sensory perception, mystic experience, and so on. No honest investigator can, he thought, deny that from some such force great contributions have been made to science, art, philosophy, religion, ethics, technology or even to economic and practical creative values. Some kind of intuition is at the very base of the validity of the systems of truth, of reason, and of the senses. Intuition has been one of the most important and fruitful starters of an enormous number of scientific, mathematical, and philosophical discoveries and technological inventions. The greatest artistic, religious, and ethical systems of culture have been inspired by religious and mystical intuition. Sorokin had no difficulty in illustrating these contentions from the history of human thought, from the literature of artistic, musical, and poetic creation, or from the lives and autobiographies of scientists and technicians.*

The Theory of Knowledge — It is in the light of such considerations as these that Sorokin sought to transcend his provisional assumption that there may be not one but several, indeed, six possible systems of knowledge and truth. Such an assumption may seem difficult to substantiate. By what standards could it itself be pronounced true or valid? No ideationally-minded thinker would concede that truths of the senses enjoy an equal validity with the truths of faith. No man born and bred in a sensate culture would be likely to admit that his science based upon sense impressions has no better title to credence than the pronouncements of intuition or of religious and ideational thought. The sceptical, agnostic, or critical positions are by their nature unlikely to yield positive standards of truth. Nevertheless, as will be shown in Chapter 9, it is an important gain to have established the relativity of knowledge to two or three great principles. Even if they are themselves variables, they stand as parameters of values of which their derivative values, themselves variable, are functions or modes.

There is, therefore, one way only of avoiding the complete relativity of judgment which would inevitably result from the acceptance of five or six standards of truth, and that must be by extracting from each such system of knowledge, or parameters, any valid elements which can be combined, supported, and verified by elements of other systems.

Far from being a despairing eclecticism, such a conjoint standard of validity is that which has in fact been used to achieve all the major advances in knowledge. That is to say, empirically, intuition, for example, has been found to make an indispensable contribution to discovery. Of course, Sorokin does not commit the wild error of saying that because some intuitions have been fruitful, every intuition is therefore valid. On the contrary, he believes that most intuitions have probably been

---

*When Sorokin, in 1937, stressed the immense significance of intuitions as the source of creative inspiration, recognizing at the same time that they can often be the source of grievous error, it was not the commonplace it has since become (see Koestler, A., *The Act of Creation,* London, Hutchinson 1964, pp. 211, 261 *passim*).

productive of error. However, the same verdict must be passed upon many pronouncements of the senses, as well as upon many of the conclusions arrived at by the most rigorous logical reasoning or by dialectical argument.

It has not been by mere attention to the findings of the senses that modern knowledge has been secured. Mankind possessed that resource for millennia without deriving great insight from it. The sensory acuteness of many primitive tribes is notoriously much greater than that of civilized man, but it does not confer his knowledge upon them. Sense impressions without the ordering activity of the mind, its intuitive and reasoning powers, are sterile. To the ancient saying that there is nothing in the mind that was not first in the senses, Leibniz made the profound addition "except the mind itself," to emphasize the impotence of sensate findings alone to understand the world.

Yet mere logical argument, bereft of other control, is also sterile, as the schoolmen of the Middle Ages labored to prove to all eternity.

Intuitive insight, logical reasoning, empirical verification must therefore all play their part in establishing integral truth, which may therefore be described as being three-dimensional. It is not identical with any of the three forms of truth, but it comprehends and includes them all.

It does not follow as a matter of course that integral truths attainable in this way are in fact able to comprehend the whole of reality. Almost certainly they cannot, for truth is finite, reality is infinite. All that can be said is that the resolute search for integral truth represents the best that the limited minds of finite men are able to accomplish.

Sorokin's own theories depend essentially upon such an outlook and procedure. His intuitive grasp of the real character of the great cultural systems that explain the fluctuating character of the history of civilization and his logical deductions based upon them have been derived from and carefully chedked and tested against the recorded facts, that is to say by the methods of sensate science. He can therefore offer his results as an attempt to attain integral truth, since they transcend the truth forthcoming merely from intuition, logical reasoning, or accumulations of facts. At the same time he does not claim to have solved all the problems or to have removed all difficulties.

Sorokin's patiently elaborated theories are likely to be greeted as was the discovery of America by Columbus, with the retort that they were already known. It may for instance be said that nobody in their senses would ever try to be anything except an integralist in his sense of the word, but the failure of each of the main great super-systems of culture to achieve such integration or to attain conscious realization of their own limitations and imperfections disproves such a claim. For that reason they proved unable to survive. The truth, the whole truth, integral truth, was not in them. To refuse to accept such a verdict would be to impoverish needlessly the vital cultural and spiritual heritage of mankind.

Misunderstandings and Criticism

An account of the reception of Sorokin's work in the world of learning would itself make an interesting chapter in the history of ideas. It would illustrate the conservatism of many academic minds and a time-lag in the spread and development of new ideas unexpected among communities who are popularly supposed to be alert and eager to follow wherever the scientific argument seems to lead. Sorokin has not complained on this score, trusting with a scholar's instincts that his duty is done when his findings and theories are made known, and that sooner or later they will find their own level, being accepted or rejected by the dispassionate, informed judgment of posterity. Certainly his ideas, like all ideas, will prosper only to the extent that other minds can take them up and make them their own, a process which may easily become a fertile source of misinterpretation. With profound insight, Leibniz stressed this autonomy and unique character of the individual "windowless" monad, developing as far as its own innate capacities allow, receptive of "influences" only to the extent that its own quality makes possible. So it is not merely Sorokin's personal experiences and the range of books and periodicals in many languages that he had read, greatly exceeding that of many who chose to ignore or criticize him, but his insight and creative powers of analysis and synthesis operating upon such materials over the years, which have resulted in his reformulation of sociological methods and problems. Of all the barriers which Sorokin's message has to surmount, the most formidable in Great Britain was the general climate of philosophical opinion at the time when *Social and Cultural Dynamics* appeared. Such was the hostility to all attempts to work with generalized concepts or abstract ideas that words such as "ideational socio-cultural supersystem" were immediately liable to be suspect and condemned by those who did not bother to examine or understand their empirical foundation. The deep distrust of the Anglo-Saxon mind when confronted with any effort to treat sociology or history philosophically was of longer standing. It was the age of Logical Positivism. Much of the heritage of philosophical thought and discussion was written off as meaningless.

It is strange that no one saw how, by faithful adherence to empirical, scientific methodology, Sorokin had cut the ground away under pedantic semanticism. While not in any way minimizing empirical fact-finding because his whole historical survey had been nothing else, he also vindicated the claim of intuition to be, as all philosophy and all literature implicitly, if not explicitly, showed it to be, the mainspring of thought. It is indeed and always has been an essential guide without which empiricists are a mere disorderly mob unable to rise above the drudgery of verbal analysis and logical manipulations from which all vital human quality and values are necessarily missing. By restoring a conceptual framework built out of facts and values jointly, Sorokin is able to create a theory of value which rescues sociology and all other humanistic studies from that sterile semanticism which threatened to drain them of all life, movement, and vital significance.

The fact that Sorokin's analysis shows semanticism to be the product of a decaying sensate culture did nothing to recommend his work; neither did his prediction of troubles ahead. He had foreseen during his lectures in the 1930's and in *Social and Cultural Dynamics*, an era of violence and the likely outbreak of a gigantic conflict with immensely powerful weapons and explosives vastly more destructive than anything yet suffered by humanity. The year 1937 when *Social and Cultural Dynamics* appeared had already been made ominous by persecution and great international alarm.

In the United Kingdom more directly exposed to the threat of war than the United States, there were other obstacles at that time to the reception of a large American treatise in three volumes with such a title as *Social and Cultural Dynamics.*

Because *Social and Cultural Dynamics* was a sociological study created out of the fabric of history, it was immediately regarded as another contribution to the "philosophy of history." Indeed it is, but it would be unfortunate if it were looked upon as no more than that. For the philosophy of history has few sponsors and had long been regarded by orthodox academic historians with suspicion and dislike almost as though it were an emanation from the lunatic fringe. The result was that Sorokin was classed as a successor to Spengler and as a companion or rival to his friend Dr. Arnold Toynbee. Spengler and Toynbee had both set out as historians and their contribution to sociology was incidental. With Sorokin it was the other way round. He sought to establish sociology by building with material quarried from history. The facts collected for him were chosen not in order to support a theory, but in order to provide the materials from which a theory could be constructed. The result for the philosophy of history as for sociology and other humanistic studies is profound. Unfortunately it has been delayed by unnecessary misunderstandings and mistakes.

As an example of the way in which Sorokin has been misrepresented through failure to grasp his method, the criticisms of Professor W. Stark may be cited. He objects to Sorokin's work because Epicurus and Bentham are wrongly "thrown into the same basket." Bentham, said Stark, although he was "certainly an Epicurean of a kind" is not elucidated by this "vaguest of all vague labels." The label however is Stark's, who also complains that Kant and Bentham are "thrown into different baskets" by Sorokin although they both "shared a common social background" and both believed in liberty and equality. The first comment on these criticisms is that Sorokin, as he made clear, was not assessing persons. His aim was to attempt to arrive at some estimate of the influences their works have had in favor of certain specific sociological ideas. He did not assume that every writer could be given a label committing him to wholehearted support of one or two schools of thought. He was concerned especially to make estimates which would be more precise than the usual impressionistic comments made on a basis of subjective personal preferences and limited therefore by the extent of one man's reading, outlook and prejudices. On a scale of relative influences in favor of various ideas exerted by different writers, Sorokin's investigators and he arrived at the following estimates of the respective contributions of Kant and Bentham to the following classes of ideas. ("Degree of influence" is estimated on a scale of 1-12.)

	Kant	Bentham
Empiricism	0	6
Nominalism	0	6
Conceptualism	12	0
Temporalism - Eternalism	0	6
Equilibrium of Temporalism - Eternalism	12	0
Singularism - Universalism	0	6
Universalism - Singularism	12	0
Mystical Unity of Singularistic Persons	12	0
Determinism	12	7
Indeterminism	12	0
Ethics of Happiness	0	6

Ethics of Principles	12	0
Pluralistic non-religious Idealism	12	0
Mixed Philosophies plus Skepticism - Agnosticism, Criticism	12	6

(The inclusion of Kant as a determinist arises from his concept of man as part of a "phenomenal" world, as an indeterminist because man in his "noumenal" essence is free.) Sorokin did not investigate contributions to a belief in "liberty" and "equality", and it would be interesting to learn how such an inquiry should be attempted and what the worth of any results might be expected to be.

The relative importance throughout history of the contributions of Epicurus and Bentham are estimated as follows:

	Epicurus 300-260	Epicurean School 60 BC - 360 AD	Bentham 1820-1840
Empiricism	8	1	6
Mechanistic Materialism	8	1	0
Temporalism-Eternalism	8	1	6
Nominalism	8	1	6
Extreme Singularism-Individualism	8	0.5	0
Determinism	0	0	7
Indeterminism	8	1	0
Ethics of Happiness	8	1	6

Such a comparison shows how slap-dash and misleading it would be to regard Epicurus and Bentham as in "a common basket."

Since Sorokin was attempting to assess the relative importance in various ages of values such as those illustrated above, Stark's comments will be seen from the above details to have missed the point. His argument that Bentham and Kant "shared a common social background" and to this fact "precisely" was due their "community of preoccupations" is an excellent illustration of the imprecise, slipshod sort of judgment into which even an eminent scholar can on occasion lapse. It demonstrates the immensely superior concern of Sorokin to detect and assess as objectively, as clearly, and as accurately as possible, the influences behind certain approaches to broad general problems which have recurred in historical times. When it is remembered that Sorokin lavished the same concern on every thinker known to have contributed to the problems here illustrated and many more as well, it will be possible to get some idea of the immense range of his enquiries and his patient attention to detail.

Stark unfortunately is not content to criticize on detail for he proceeds to say that "our criticism. . . . is one of principle. Sorokin's procedure assumes *a radice* the possibility of quantifying what is qualitative and this is almost like supposing that it is possible to square the circle. . . . there is really nothing that can be counted."

It is of course abundantly clear that Sorokin was not "quantifying" the qualitative but, as emphasized above, using numbers in an effort to give greater precision to ideas usually expressed by vague phrases such as "little influence", "considerable influence," "very great influence." Nevertheless it is satisfactory to read that Stark considers Sorokin as "essentially an all-round sociologist" and a "true sociologist of knowledge."*

*Ibid p. 238.

Sociology and the Theory of Value

A New Empirically-based Theory of Value

It would be a mistake to leave the impression that the predominant reaction to *Social and Cultural Dynamics* was critically hostile. Reviewers may have the first word, and a few are apt to scorn new ideas offered by authors whom they feel they can attack with impunity. Sorokin has some amusing examples of his treatment by such incompetent critics. At first the professional sociologists who reviewed for the *Journal of the American Sociological Association* made common cause against him. It would be idle to suppose that such hostility was without influence, but powerful though it might be supposed to be, it failed to dissuade scholars beyond the academic world of American sociology from showing an immediate and growing interest in his work. This response has been positive, assured, and greater than that bestowed internationally upon the work of any other American sociologist, alive or dead.

Nevertheless the full import of Sorokin's achievement through his *Social and Cultural Dynamics* has still to be realized. What follows therefore does not merely echo his words or what he has said, but seeks to indicate something of the promise which his work holds for the future of sociology. It does not seem too much to claim that with *Social and Cultural Dynamics* Sorokin had reached a watershed in his own sociological progress. Several reasons suggest that it is a watershed of sociological thought also. The fertilizing streams that flow from it will swell to irrigate many arid zones of the sociological world, and indeed in the world of history, education, aesthetics, law, government and elsewhere. The findings contained in *Social and Cultural Dynamics* have this power because they bring within one conspectus the whole vast world of human values. As a survey and inventory of a very varied range of human activities it is soundly based upon firm fact, insofar as facts are available.

Unlike many empty abstractions of conventional academic sociology, Sorokin's value principle is not another example of a mere conceptual creation, another excursion into the *Kategorienwirtschaft* of abstract sociology. He does not exhibit sociology as the field in which "sensate" or "ideational" ways of thought "direct" or "command" human activities. Those abstract nouns are not the subjects of verbs but mere shorthand symbols used to sum up whole classes of human activities down the ages which were enumerated and reported upon in Social and Cultural Dynamics. Their nature has unfortunately also been misunderstood by Stark who says, correctly, about Sorokin's theories, that "the basic philosophy of a period is, to some extent, granted a higher ontological status than that of all other contemporary ideas," but, incorrectly adds that this basic philosophy (that is to say Sorokin's cultural supersystems: ideational, idealistic and sensate) "is in some degree hypostatized, perhaps even reified." However he seemed uncertain of the true nature of Sorokin's findings for he qualified the tentative suggestion in such a way as virtually to withdraw it, by adding "though to what extent is uncertain and cannot be discussed here."* More's the pity, because Sorokin's work radically amends *The Sociology of Knowledge* which now needs rewriting because now for the first time, sociologists, philosophers and historians have a reliable guide to the principles and opinions latent in the activities which many of the human race have pursued over the greatest part of recorded history. The consequences are incalculable, for they necessarily reach down into every area of human activity.

If his "logico-meaningful socio-cultural supersystems" are soundly based, Sorokin has virtually amalgamated sociology and the theory of value. If they are not soundly based then Sorokin will have been guilty of overlooking some vitally important social value manifestin the past or in the present, but excluded from his "logico-meaningful socio-cultural super-systems." Unless critics can point to such an omission, they must concede that, theoretically and empirically, Sorokin's scheme of values is all-inclusive.

The critic just cited, despite his admitted uncertainty about the true

*W. Stark, *The Sociology of Knowledge* (London, Routledge & Kegan Paul, Ltd., 1958), p. 226.

nature of Sorokin's classification of forms of value as they have been manifest in history, nevertheless attempted to dismiss them on the ground that they "are far too wide to fit the culture content of any concrete society."* They are indeed as wide as a cultural supersystem is likely to be. To say that they are "too wide" can only mean that they would fit more than one society or culture. They do not. It is impossible to describe the early Roman Republic or Early Christian Europe as sensate societies. It is impossible to regard Rome under Nero, or Edwardian England, as indifferently describable as ideational or idealistic or sensate. Of course it is possible to detect surviving ideational and idealistic streams of influence. Sorokin was not painting a black and white, all-or-none picture of the historical past. Who is so naive as to believe that to be possible? He was concerned with detecting major trends and influences. Of course differences can be observed in the nature of an ancient sensate society such as the age of Nero and, say, Restoration England. But they were not "very great" differences, as are the differences between a sensate and an ideational or idealistic cultural system. Their resemblances are more significant than their differences.

Sorokin's interpretative categories might be refined in the light of further exhaustive historical investigations, but it is believed that such an enquiry conducted upon any likely alternative hypothesis would produce much the same conclusions. Take for example some of Max Scheler's interpretative supersystems which Stark regards as most pormising. One of them like so much continental speculation since Marx, is doomed at the start because it is the conventional division between "lower class" and "upper class." Irrelevant for such an enquiry because it is meaningless as a cultural distinction over huge stretches of history, it is also empty of content. "Class" can become significant in sociology only by having some value-content pumped into it, and any values that may be used for such a purpose are better defined, classified, and applied by Sorokin's principles. Elsewhere Scheler offer another classification according to which culture-complexes or supersystems differ as they are led by scientists, philosophers, or religious men. Again Sorokin's analysis is more detailed and refined than this rough and ready division, which is easily absorbed by Sorokin's three categories, to emerge with far greater point and precision.

Greater justice had been done to Sorokin's contribution to the

*W. Stark, *op. cit.*, p. 280 .

sociology of knowledge by a Belgian scholar, Professor Maquet, some
seven years before Stark's criticisms.* From it Sorokin's work emerges
clearly, despite some critical reflections and disagreements, as "a definite
contribution to the problem of the social conditioning of thought" which
proves "the existence of a logical relationship between the fundamental
and philosophic aspect of the ensemble of a culture's mental productions,
and the position concerning the nature of reality adopted by that culture."
Maquet shrewdly noted that Sorokin "does not pay very much attention
in general to the epistemological consequences of his sociology." Maquet
sees some important consequences, which Sorokin himself does not stress,
of his integralist theory of culture and personality, notably the solution it
provides for the apparent paradox that the truths of the senses, of reason,
and of intuition and faith, although apparently incompatible, are each
valid in their own spheres. But Maquet does not stress the additional
consequence of Sorokin's views which is emphasized in this book, that
they merge sociology and the philosophical theory of value.

Value and Culture

To assert that Sorokin has provided a new theory of value may seem
hazardous, for Sorokin himself makes no such specific claim. In order to
test it, it is necessary to know what is expected of a theory of value and
then to consider how far Sorokin's ideas go to provide a satisfactory
answer. There have been many spurs in modern times to pursue such an
inquiry, one of the most pointed being provided by Laird when he wrote
that "Value *may* prove to be the key that will eventually release all the
human sciences from their present position of pathetic, if dignified
futility."** Whitehead also said "all ultimate reasons turn on values."†
The obvious initial difficulty of stating what the concept "value"
should convey may be partly eased by noting how the word has developed
from its original Latin root with its predominantly physical significance of
strength, health, efficiency to the more abstract concept of "merit" or

---

*J. J. Maquet, *The Sociology of Knowledge. Its Structure and its Relation to the
Philosophy of Knowledge. A Critical Analysis of the Systems of Karl Mannheim and
Pitirim A. Sorokin,* trans. by J. F. Locke (Boston, Beacon Press, 1951). Stark refers
to the French original of this work in a few notes.
**J. Laird, *The Idea of Value* (Cambridge University Press, 1929), p. *xix.*
†A. N. Whitehead, *Modes of Thought* (Cambridge University Press, 1938), p. 184,
and *Nature and Life* (Cambridge University Press, 1934), p. 24.

"worth." Thus anything or any action deemed of value stands, for the person by whom it is so regarded, in relation to some standard of distinction or excellence which that person has adopted. The notion of the subjectivity of values thus arises at once. One of the main obstacles to the progress of the philosophy of value has always been this fear that all statements of liking and disliking, of holding dear and holding cheap, are inevitably "subjective," so that there has always been insuperable doubt as to whether excellence can be held to be "objective." If it is not objective, no philosophy or "science" of value can arise because the very essence of a claim that an object or an action has "value" is that it should be regarded as more than merely a personal expression of pleasure or satisfaction. In order to transcend such subjectivity, some philosophers have had recourse to metaphysical arguments. Others have argued that action of the valuing human subject in striving to achieve or to give effect to preferences gives logical evidence of a sense of obligation or duty. It is then a short step to extract a standard from that sense of dury which may be held to be "objective" rather than "subjective," particularly when it is found that the valuing individual is not alone in behaving or thinking as he does. The world of value is thus built out of the beliefs or opinions of all who share similar attitudes or relationships to whatever things, events, relationships or persons they unite in prizing or valuing. Some thinkers stop at that point, holding that value subsists in or is conferred by such a relationship; that it does not inhere as an eternal property or quality of the phenomena that are valued. But such phenomena tend to become credited with the possession of such eternal qualities, so that other thinkers take this further step and hold that there are absolute values, the objective reality of which compels general recognition and acknowledgment, as, for example, mathematical truths must do, always and everywhere. Among the distinguished philosophers who have recently supported this ancient, Platonic, idea of the objectivity of values, such as Nicolai Hartmann and others, Max Scheler is probably the most eminent. He points to the need for historical research into what he calls the *Ethos auch die Anschauungs-weisen der Welt, die Welt-anschauung d.h. die Struktur des erkennenden Welterlebens wie es aller Urteilsphare vorausliegt.* * Only by such means, as he saw, would it be possible to transcend the limits imposed by one's own scheme of values and world view and hence also to

---

*M. Scheler, *Der Formalismus in der Ethik und die materielle Wertethik,* (Halie, a.d.S. Niemeyer, 1921), pp. 312-313. (French trans. by de Gandillac, *Le Formalisme en Ethique* [Gallimard, Presses Universitaires, 1955.])

surpass the historical relativism with which values are regarded. Scheler did not complete the study he had promised of this historical background of varying world-views, but from the brief note in which he referred to his plans (p. 312) it would seem that he proposed to give special attention to linguistic developments. As it is, his historical references, as one would expect from a great scholar, are many and are pertinent. But they all suffer from the fatal defect of being selected as apposite illustrations of his point of view. They are not the fruit of long historical research, undertaken to discover all the facts about the cultural outlook of earlier times, but useful bits of history culled from memory which happen to support his arguments. Of how many writers on social theory, except Sorokin, is not this equally true?

Whatever may be thought of Sorokin's results, they were not obtained by such an arbitrary selection of none but suitable facts, chosen to confirm some pre-determined sociology or philosophy. He therefore gave practical effect to the general notion towards which many thinkers were converging. In Germany, the work of Rickert and Meinecke' has been mentioned. In England the lone voice of R. G. Collingwood at Oxford in favor of a strictly historical treatment of metaphysics was little heeded.*

Sorokin carried out that historical investigation which Scheler and Collingwood, among others, saw to be necessary. Although Sorokin did not say so in these terms, he then discovered that with the central concept of "value," which is what his "meanings-norms-values" imply, he was able to account for an immense number of sociological facts.

The superior power of Sorokin's presentation over all alternative schemes so far proposed is due to the fact that it is soundly based upon an understanding of the implications of the concept of culture. Developing his ideas in this respect, the present writer has endeavored already to state their essence and from it to distill a definition of "culture" as an operational concept.** Allowing for differences in terminology, that account, as Sorokin's, is in harmony with the wisdom of the Greeks. They regarded the world of value as being made up of activities resulting in the discovery of truth, the achievement and appreciation of beauty, and the

---

*It has indeed been declared to be "too riddled with contradictions. . . . to be salvaged" (A. Donagan, *The Later Philosophy of R. G. Collingwood* [Oxford University Press, 1962], p. 279), a criticism energetically and successfully rebutted by D. Rynin "Donagan on Collingwood" in *Rev. of Metaphysics* (1064), Vol. XVIII, pp. 301-333.

**F. R. Cowell, *Culture in Private and Public Life* (New York, Praeger, 1958).

observance and realization of worthy moral behavior. The autonomous spheres of these three great value-categories, the True, the Beautiful and the Good for the interpretation of cultural activities, have been illustrated often enough already, and need not be argued here.

Transcending Cultural Relativity

As an inclusive theory of value, Sorokin's scheme has the great merit of resolving the supreme difficulty upon which other theories of value have floundered. Constructed in a sensate age, for application to sensate preferences, their standards were of little use when they had to appraise the cultural achievements of an ideational age. Realization of this weakness infected all value judgments, which were inevitably regarded as "subjective," and consequently as out of place in rigorous thought. Hence the pride with which scholars proclaimed the necessity of keeping "scientific" subjects such as economics, sociology, history, law and so forth free from value judgments, *wertfrei*. As soon, however, as it is seen that, just as all scientific work has an inescapable *a priori* element derived from the questions, concepts and theories of scientists, so also value judgments depend upon a logico-meaningful cultural super-system, and are variables or functions of that supersystem, which serves them as a parameter, the fact that such a supersystem is itself a variable can then be readily accepted. Another parameter serves the different set of values of a different logico-meaningful cultural system, some of which may conflict with some of the variables of the first parameter. Those that do not so conflict may seem to qualify doubly as values which humanity holds in special honor.

The mathematical analogy by which Sorokin's cultural supersystems are here referred to as parameters, does, it is believed, effectively establish the type of relationship found between them and their dependent values. What other concept provided by sociological theory can be designated as a standard of judgment or parameter of other sociological phenomena in this sense? Not "roles," "class," "action" or "structure;" not, it is believed, any other value-free idea.

It will be evident that Sorokin's theory of value centers upon the idea of logico-meaningful integralism. Any values that are not so integrated lie beyond as "congeries," that is, as unintegrated or partially integrated values. But these are not excluded or left as unexplainable. Sorokin's theory enables them to be seen for what they are, as partial value-systems.

Obviously partial values can be sources of intense satisfaction, reward, and consolation to many people. The strength of mind of the "man of one book"; the whole-hearted devotion of one who "lives for music," "for painting," or with any other single cultural value absorbing all their energies, is notorious. Yet to the extent that such people forego participation in other cultural values or are forced to live in a cultural system no better than an unintegrated hodge-podge of minor or discordant values, their lives are subject to privations and probably frustrations, by which they would not be so vexed in a well integrated logico-meaningful cultural system, in more of whose values they might share. Here again it is a matter of degree, for it may be doubted whether any perfectly coordinated logico-meaningful cultural system has ever existed. Sorokin's investigations revealed clearly enough the partial cohesion of his main supersystems, the best of whose leaders may have fallen short in some particular. Nevertheless their collective contribution was able to give a quality and tone to their era which was more "of a piece" and able to qualify as an integrated pattern of mutually supporting cultural values than were other periods characterized by relative cultural confusion. Such periods have been less significant over vast stretches of history than the integral cultural systems, but they are not on that account mysterious or destructive of the concept of logico-meaningful integration. Sorokin's principles have the merit of separating them from more integrated cultures and of providing a standard, the standard of logico-meaningful integration, by which they may be assessed. If such a statement appears to beg the question in favor of the logico-meaningful system, it is only necessary to try to extract standards of judgment from the congeries or from any other source and to charge them with the task of acting as standards, a task for which they are plainly inadequate. A part cannot be a reliable test of the quality of a whole.

Value in Anthropology

The utility of such a discrimination between partial and logico-meaningful cultures may be seen over the whole realm of cultural life. It may be illustrated in relation to many of the so-called "cultures" of anthropology. Often, it would seem, so little is known about the way of life of people of ancient times whose existence is surmised from archeological discoveries that the use of the word "culture" in referring to them cannot be given the meaning it has in sociological theory. "Beaker culture," "Chassey culture," "Windmill Hill culture," "Bell-Beaker culture" and countless other such labels do not seem to the uninitiated to be more than convenient titles for museum exhibits. When anthropological field workers make a careful report of the way of life of primitive tribes many facts are thrown up of great interest, but they do not usually greatly aid cultural development. While in theory it may be desirable to be ready to regard all patterns of life which mankind has imposed on the raw materials of existence as equally valid, sociologists want some criteria or standards by which they can be evaluated. To apply critera which it has taken the civilized world thousands of years to develop would clearly be out of place, yet other valid methods of assessment are so far wanting.*

Sorokin's "integralist" standard of cultural development demands an equal concentration upon and devotion to the values of knowledge, of aesthetic appreciation, and of moral worth. To call for such harmonious integration of the highest cultural values realizable at any one time may seem a counsel of perfection. Humanity can have no grounds for desiring less, because anything less spells privation in some significant respect and therefore imperfection.** When primitive tribes favor — as some of them appear to have done, practices inimical to life such as cannibalism, head-hunting, ritual mutilation and so forth, those practices cannot be regarded as valid patterns of life, for it is not life that they serve. In sociology on Sorokin's principles, "facts" cannot fruitfully be studied unrelated to a standard of value. In the history of science a similar conclusion was reached by Sir Lawrence Bragg, a Nobel Prize winner: "The essence of science lies not in discovering facts, but in discovering new ways of thinking about them.† Other practices which may qualify as cultural but which cannot be integrated into a cohesive, logico-meaningful pattern of culture are less valid than those which can be integrated in support of such an integral pattern. Many of the facts collected and cherished by anthropologists or social historians as equally valid can

---

*A. L. Kroeber and C. Kluckhorn, "Culture, A critical Review of Concepts and Definitions," *Peabody Museum Papers*, XLVII, 1952, is a candid survey by two eminent American anthropologists of what they called "this lack of clarity and precision" in the use of the word "culture" by anthropologists. It was discussed in the light of Sorokin's views by F. R. Cowell in *Culture in Public and Private Life* (London, Thames and Hudson, 1959), pp. 333-340.

**B. S. Sanyai, *Culture: An Introduction* (Asia Publishing House, 1962) gives an excellent statement of the idea of "privation" as a criterion for distinguishing levels of culture.

†A. Koestler, *The Act of Creation* (London, Hutchinson, 1964) p. 234. A. N. Whitehead's general standpoint is also relevant.

therefore now be segregated as variables of greater or lesser significance according to their possibilities of contributing to a potential logico-meaningful cultural supersystem, that is of being elements of a distinct and characterful whole. That whole is precisely what a philosophical theory of value ought to be able to elucidate and explain. Its full attainment must remain an ideal for society and culture even although it is rarely achieved in practice.

Value in Sociology

Anthropology is but one of the disciplines which will profit by revision in the light of Sorokin's principles. Miss Ruth Benedict has shown that it is a discipline which can greatly fortify sociology.* Every subject in which value judgments have a place is capable of similar reformulation, and none more so than sociology itself. Where sociologists employ value judgments, Sorokin's contribution has immediate use. Where attempts are made to eliminate such value judgments on the mistaken ground that sociology should deal with 'facts' and not 'values,' Sorokin's theory can come to the rescue. In this spirit he avowedly subordinated many of the themes which often occupy a very prominent place in the textbooks, such as "class" and "role" to value-theory in a far more forthright manner than other writers have done. Divisions of society into "classes" or "groups" can only pose as scientifically "factual" if value-concepts are somehow imparted to, or imported into them. What these values are, or may be, history alone can say. It will usually report changes of such magnitude that the terms exhibit no common meaning or social significance.

To say that from a sociological point of view the meaning of "classes" such as priest or ploughman was very different in the thirteenth and nineteenth centuries from what it is today would be regarded as so obvious a remark as to be hardly worth making. Yet such a truism is the best vindication of Sorokin's insistence upon the primacy of value theory in sociology. Economic factors can often account in modern times for the relative ease of access of members of any society to the values and value-forming and sustaining activities by which that society is guided. But this is something very different from the idea that there are specific

*Ruth Benedict, *Patterns of Culture* (Penguin Books, 1934, 1946). This excellent study concludes on the note, "Social thinking at the present time has no more important task before it than of taking adequate account of cultural relativity."

concepts or values with which 'classes' are identified. The great efforts made by a few 'intellectuals' in the 1920's to work up a tremendous sentiment among 'the working classes,' which was to constitute a distinctive working-class or 'proletarian' culture, were uniformly unsuccessful. Far from favoring any such specious adscription to their own level, the working classes' one ambition was to live like a good 'bourgeois' who in turn was only too eager to enjoy many of the privileges of the 'aristocracy.' The so-called 'intellectuals' who ineffectively tried to raise the standard of 'proletarian' culture deserved to fail for they did not believe in it themselves. They were unable to say what a 'proletarian' culture might be. 'Class' therefore is an abstraction which has its uses as a classificatory rubric in descriptive historical sociology only where it can be given content from the prevalent values of that time.* Consequently its meaning constantly changes. It is not necessary to go back to Republican Rome, to 17th century England or 18th century France to realize this. In our own time the concept of 'Working Class' has radically changed between 1910 and today.** Sociologists who attempt to juggle with 'class' as an operative concept are therefore guilty of reifying an abstraction. Yet they have charged Sorokin's doctrines, which effectively expose their shortcomings, with making precisely this mistake. Great stress has also been laid upon the concept of 'role' as a valuable, explanatory sociological 'tool.' Even a philosopher as acute as Professor Dorothy Emmet appears to accept 'roles' as 'omnipresent in social life' in which they form its 'recognized patterns.' Rightly regarding this use of the word in sociology as a metaphor borrowed from the theatre she defines it in one place as "a capacity in which someone acts in relation to others."† She also says that "capacities are not capacities to do anything whatsoever" because they are limited by 'our kind of system' and by 'relationships which form our social environment.' This significant qualification can be effectively spelled out solely by a general theory of value, which is just what Sorokin provides. It seems strange that, after reporting her gratitude to Professor L. J. Russell

*T. H. Marshall, *Citizenship and Social Class* (Cambridge University Press, 1950) gives a sane and balanced analysis, although Sorokin vigorously rebutted Marshall's "interpretation of my position as denying the existence of social classes." It was, said Sorokin, "grossly inaccurate." See also F. R. Cowell, *Culture in Private and Public Life* (London, 1959), pp. 280-294 on the relation of economic class and culture.
**R. Miller, *The New Classes* (London, Longmans, 1966) records kaleidoscopic changes in the meaning of class such as would wreck it as a concept in any scientific discipline.
†Dorothy Emmet, *Rules, Roles, and Relations* (New York, Macmillan, 1966), pp. 13, 28, 40, 121.

for the advice never to use an abstract noun with a verb of action, she also appears to follow the prevalent sociological fashion of regarding sociology as largely a matter of people enacting roles and of role-relations. Later (p. 170) a role is described as "a name for a typical relation in which typical action is expected." It must indeed be evident that somehow the blank 'capacity' of a role must acquire a content if it is to become an operative concept. How this transformation can happen needs more explanation than sociologists are usually ready to provide. Professor Emmet herself, seemingly unconsciously, abandons the blank concept of a role as a capacity when she supplements it by the concept of a 'typical relation' expected to exhibit 'typical action.' The operative words 'typical action' are smuggled in surreptitiously. Their metaphorical derivation, from the theatre is forgotten. The process by which roles come to life in the person of fine actors and actresses interpreting words which dramatic genius has highly charged with meaning is no prototype for a passionless scientist inspecting the phenomena of human life in societies. Before long Professor Emmet gives away the sociological game of roles by her pertinent observation that "the notion of a role has built into it a notion of some conduct as appropriate" (p. 40). Unfortunately she gives no answer to such questions as surely should arise, such as how this operation is performed? or why? or when? or by whom? or, and, this is the crucial point, *what* is it that is 'built in?'

An abstract notion such as 'role' like that of 'class' has no qualities, and should not be used with an active verb. Unlike the Census classification by occupations, it becomes plausible in sociology only by having values surreptiously injected into it.

"Structure" is another sociological term, much used as noun and verb. It also is unfit for the load it has to carry. The way anything is made or put together, or any pattern of relationships having formal properties can be understood only in relation to an organization, if not a specific design, in other words to some qualities or properties which alone confer significance, importance, or value, which alone therefore give any meaning "structures" may seem to possess. Values emerge in practice in the actions and interactions of individuals, families, tribes, groups, societies, communities, associations, institutions, political parties, governmental machinery; the whole of which are fit and proper subjects of sociological description and analysis. Until such structures are endowed with values of some sort, however, they are as dead as the skeletons in museums of natural history. They are a drag upon sociology as a science of men in action and as wearisome a burden to students seeking enlightenment upon the forces that make the world go round as the fossilized bones of extinct birds and mammals can be to museum visitors. Not until some imaginative reconstruction by specialists and experts presents replicas of such creatures as they probably appeared in real life are they likely to make the impact which they deserve to do upon the imaginations of those who gaze upon them.

'Social action' and 'the structure of social action' are other empty sociological terms. An abstraction such as 'action' must be characterized before it can acquire meaning or value. It cannot derive such vitalizing power from another abstraction such as 'structure.' Both can mean almost anything. Sorokin put the emphasis on "dynamics," that is, on values in action.

Value in Art

Apart from the skill and techniques of artists, the study of art is nothing if not a study of value. It was largely from the study of art forms that Sorokin derived his interpretative ideas of ideational, idealist, and sensate socio-cultural forms. They have only to be compared with the explanatory concepts of other writers upon aesthetics and art history for their superior range and inclusiveness to become apparent. The rightly renowned theory of Wölfflin's *Principles of Art,* rewarding as are its penetrating insights, remains for many connoisseurs and critics, one of the best statements of aesthetic philosophy. Yet, as already seen in the summary of Sorokin's account of the development of art, Wölfflin's famous five explanatory concepts readily fit into Sorokin's scheme, where they gain point and clearer definition, by the use of Sorokin's 'idealist' and 'sensate' categories. Not only are Wölfflin's categories then absorbed but, thanks to Sorokin's general sociological standpoint, they are brought into relation with corresponding periods of the development of other branches of social and cultural history, a relationship which does not transpire from Wölfflin's treatment of the subject. Moreover Wölfflin's scheme omits altogether the 'ideational' category which Sorokin illustrated so convincingly. Byzantine art for example, the art of the 'Middle Ages' of Europe, of ancient Egypt, of Ancient Western Asia, of India, China, and Japan, all lie beyond Wölfflin's scope. He could no doubt have provided an illuminating account of them, but his splendid talents were concentrated upon European 'Renaissance' and 'Post-Renaissance' art. He was not concerned with providing a 'sociology of art.' This is what Sorokin has done. So anyone who accepts Wölfflin's ideas, as Sorokin did, has already accepted some of those of Sorokin. By accepting Sorokin's scheme as a whole therefore, they lose nothing, but get a very considerable plus-value of greatly deepened and enlarged sociological insight.

An Operational Theory of Value

The superiority of Sorokin's sociology can thus be seen by comparison in its success in providing those explanatory, operational, 'nomethetic' ideas which have already been proclaimed as the distinguishing feature of a true 'science' or organized body of thought in which all its constituent facts are linked and explained by a readily understandable theory. Of no previous sociology could this claim be made with such confidence in its comprehensive sweep and power. Take the most renowned, that of Max Weber. Penetrating and highly suggestive as his insights undoubtedly were, they have left no guiding principles that immediately spring to mind when confronted with sociological problems, except for a few of great generality. Weber was obsessed with the political future of Germany and sceptical about the consequences of that 'disenchantment of the world,' which, with other pessimistic principles, he may well have acquired from Nietzsche, whose powerful pronouncements so profoundly stirred German thought towards the end of the 19th century. Those more positive and fruitful insights which Weber bequeathed, his 'ideal types,' his 'spirit of rationality,' *(zweckrationales Handeln)* his 'loyalty to objective values' *(wertrational)* , can all be caught up and given clearer definition, depth of meaning, and historical explanation by Sorokin's theories. So also Weber's methodological principles, such as his 'adequate comprehension of causation' *(adaquäte Verursachung)* can be more fruitfully included in Sorokin's 'logico - meaningful' concept. To say this is not to belittle Weber's stature as one of the giants of sociology, but merely to register an advance which he would surely approve in the continuity of thought towards greater precision, clarity, and comprehension.

Without prolonging this illustration of Sorokin's contribution by citing the work of individuals, many of whom such as Nietzsche, Dilthey, Rickert, and others are very relevant, it may be taken further by contrasting the utility of Sorokin's ideas with that of other concepts currently honored as interpretative, explanatory, 'nomothetic,' or operational ideas in sociology. 'Class' and 'Structure' have already been found to be simply ideographic notions of scant utility until they become endowed with some value-content.

Can a similar judgment be made about Sorokin's 'ideational,' 'idealistic' and 'sensate' socio-cultural systems? Surely not, because they immediately recall the historical realities of which they are the generalized expression 'Ideational Art' at once recalls Byzantine mosaics, sixth century B.C. Greek sculpture, or the Carolingian Age of Europe. It does not recall the 'idealistic' art of say fifth Century Greece of seventeenth Century Europe. Still less does it evoke memories of sensate art and architecture, of the early Roman Empire or of A.D. 1900.

Let the matter furthermore be put to a practical test. Take a vanished civilization of which no more than a few artifacts remain, that of the Etruscans, for example. Suppose it is said that Late Etruscan art was 'sensate'; that the earliest was 'ideational'; and that there seems to have been a brief period in which 'idealistic' art was manifest. Anyone already acquainted with the characteristic qualities of such styles in later periods but who had never seen any examples of Etruscan sculpture, jewelry, pottery, or painting would have some idea of what to expect. Furthermore, without looking at the descriptive labels of Etruscan exhibits in any good museum of antiquities, such a novice would very likely be able to guess fairly accurately whether the objects were of the Early or Late periods. If it is objected that Etruscan art was a mere copy of the Greek, from which the 'ideational   sensate' classification was partly derived, it may be rejoined that one cultural period characterized by logico-meaningful integration would have no use for alien art belonging to a later period. The Romans of the 5th and 4th centuries B.C. were no strangers to Greek art. The southern half of Italy and Sicily were then under Greek rule. But the Romans, still in their 'ideational' stage of cultural development, spurned everything Greek, and they continued to do so for another two or three hundred years. Yet we imagine that the magnificent creations of the Greek genius have only to be seen in order to be admired. If this rejoinder is disputed, then let the experiment be made with another people, say, the Minoans before 1400 B.C. whose art flourished in Crete before the Greeks had arrived in Greece. Late Minoan art is clearly 'sensate,' and it gives rise to the expectation therefore that social life would be 'sensate' also. Not behavior alone but beliefs and laws would be expected to have sensate rather than ideational qualities. No suggestion of any such wider sociological significance can be extracted from other descriptive categories in art. Wölfflin's categories − plane or recession, closed or open form, clearness or unclearness, for example, can indeed be used in giving an aesthetic account of Etruscan or Minoan art. But having done so, no suggestion about the nature of the social life from which they emerged would transpire. They would remain as cultural variables of an unknown parameter; a shiny surface that does not reveal the diamond of Value of which they are one facet.

Sorokin's sociological principles have the merit of suggesting such hypotheses over the whole of the sociological scene just as Newton's laws were able to predict the existence of the planet Neptune long before it was discovered. For art is but one facet of the value-principle in sociology. The discovery of a stern ideational code of laws of some early civilization would similarly stimulate conclusions about the non-representational character of the art, if any, of the time when the code was compiled. Whatever that art might be, it would not on Sorokin's theory be impressionistic, sex-ridden, realistic, produced in order to gratify sensual men. Such expectations of predictable parallelisms and uniformities evident over a wide area are based upon an assumption that the culture in question has a logico-meaningful integral character. Chance exceptions, or isolated instances of personal eccentricity 'in advance of the times' or as antiquarian hang-overs from preceding cultural styles, would not upset such an expectation. If, however, they prove sufficiently numerous to upset it, then it is probably a sign of cultural confusion, of a set of cultural congeries rather than of a settled logico-meaningful culture. Prediction, or confident characterization upon Sorokin's principles is then no longer possible, although by using Sorokin's principles some guiding lines can be traced in the chaos. They will be a mixed medley of cultural values from different cultural super-systems. In the Los Angeles area, for example, around 1930 there was already a riotous mixture of architectural styles. There were idealistic forces in the churches and in the philosophical and other faculties of two Universities. There was the influence of the Huntingdon Library and its collection of urbane eighteenth century English paintings. Yet at the same time there was a confused medley — fortune-tellers, astrologers, clubs, societies, the cinematograph industry, Aimée Semple Macpherson — and many other influences all with their dependent supporting public. Their variety defied classification. Yet outwardly and predominantly the economic and cultural atmosphere generally was not markedly different from that of any other great American city during the 'sensate' era. Its cultural unity was however a brittle affair compared with the atomsphere at the same time of a town such as Aberdeen or Warsaw. In those cities, also, evidence of mixed cultural forces was not lacking.

Sorokin's 'logico-meaningful' characteristic may be thought less successful in relation to cultures in crisis than to those flourishing in their heyday. Before regarding such an admission as fatal to the claims made here on behalf of Sorokin's theories, it must be asked what alternative theory is better able to explain the phenomena observable during a period of the breakdown of a cultural super-system? None so far is in sight, which is not surprising because no sociology except Sorokin's has given a viable account of any cultural whole, whether in crisis or not. Let anyone endeavor to explain without using Sorokin's theories the sort of sociological situations just mentioned. What operative concept can suggest the nature of a society as effectively as Sorokin's concept of cultural or value super-systems does? What can any of the vaunted analytical 'tools' such as 'status,' 'role,' 'class,' 'structure,' 'action,' and so forth, contribute to the elucidation of an imperfectly known culture such as the Etruscan or Minoan? Obviously, nothing. These stock phrases of the sociological text books are at once seen to be valueless as soon as they are taken out of their ideographic, descriptive function and are put to any practical test. They are not 'nomothetic' ideas or 'tools.' As descriptive ideographs they are not worth the inordinate amount of space they usually occupy in general works on sociology.

Sorokin's service to sociology in this respect recalls the clean sweep made by chemistry and physics of the pseudo-concepts of the pre-scientific age, such as "elective affinities," phlogiston, the four "elements" — fire, air, water, earth — the influence of stars and the sky upon the generation of man and metals, animals and plants.

Cleaning up unnecessary verbiage is but the beginning of the revolutionary transformation which the development and application of Sorokin's theory makes possible. By showing how human actions came to be what they were, it enlarges understanding of the past and sets mankind free from the shackles of any determinism, thereby greatly enlarging the area of planned, purposive development towards an integrated logico-meaningful culture, defined in terms of the values to be pursued. These values are not abstractions. When culture is defined as the human activities formulating, progressively understanding, and appreciating, and actually creating, all that which it is possible to classify within the broad domains of knowledge or truth, aesthetic activity or beauty, and of moral achievement or goodness, then many branches of human activity achieve new directives. Among them are education, government, and law. The many special sociologies being put forth as sociologies of knowledge, of art, of education, and so forth, can find through Sorokin's concept of logico-meaningful cultural supersystems that common interpretative principle linking them directly with sociology which they tentatively and partially possess at present. The reason is plain. Being pre-eminently studies of human values in some form or another they are variables of a general cultural system of value. When it is a logico-meaningful system, these aspects or branches of it are cultural variables capable of being brought into relation with their 'supersystem' which serves them as parameters. They are different facets of a central storehouse of value. Value is like a great diamond stone which when cut can exhibit many sparkling colors. Special sociologies of education, of law, of thought, and so on acquire new strength and power when they are seen as facets of value-centered sociological theory. It is possible to make on behalf of Sorokin's logico-meaningful cultural sociology a claim reminiscent of Darwin's defense 'I believe in Natural Selection because it groups and explains well (as it seems to me) a host of facts in classification, embryology, morphology, rudeimentary organs, geological succession and distribution.' It must be left to specialists to work out all the ways in which the logico-meaningful concept of culture can transform all the various value-laden human studies, but sufficient may by now have been indicated to stimulate efforts to apply the idea fruitfully to such a task.

Later Development of Sorokin's Study

Explanations for the General Public

Far from exhausted by his ten years work on *Social and Cultural Dynamics,* combined as it was with his responsibilities for creating and running the Department of Sociology at Harvard University, Sorokin very soon pushed on by undertaking, in conjunction with Clarence Q. Berger, an investigation into the ways in which a representative sample of 100 white-collar unemployed spent each of the twenty-four hours of their time. Regarding the interest of the book which resulted, *Time Budgets of Human Behavior* (Harvard University Press, 1939) as being confined to psycho-social specialists, Sorokin speaks of it as "probably the most boring of all my boring works," a verdict which was not supported by critics and reviewers. It at least gave magazines and newspapers material for long articles, one of which appeared in a Sunday newspaper under the headline 'Nine Minutes for Necking.' This contribution to descriptive sociology was but an interlude, and Sorokin returned to general theory and to build it upon the foundations securely laid by *Social and Cultural Dynamics.*

In 1941 an invitation to deliver the Lowell Lectures in Boston gave him an opportunity to put the leading ideas of that great work to the general public. The trustee and curator of the Lowell Institute by whom the lectures were arranged reported that they had never seen so great an audience at previous lectures and the numbers grew as the lectures continued. That this response of the discriminating people of Boston was as merited as it was enthusiastic quickly became evident when the lectures were published as *The Crisis of our Age* (New York, Dutton, 1941). Between October 1941 and August 1945 the book went through nine editions. Translations appeared in Portuguese, German, Dutch, Czech, Norwegian, Finnish, Spanish, and Japanese, and others have been undertaken. The book was also re-published in England and New Zealand. It was hailed by the *Chicago Daily News* as a "literary thunderbolt" beside which "all other books pale into insignificance."

The Sociology of Disaster

In the following year Sorokin published *Man and Society in Calamity* (New York, Dutton, 1942). No other sociologist has ever had his qualifications for writing such a book. In it he was able to include material suppressed by the Bolshevik censors from his book, *Hunger as a Factor* published in Russian in 1921, now revised in the light of twenty years thought and study. War, revolution, famine, and pestilence were the major themes. Their effect was examined upon behavior and vital processes, as shown by death, birth- and marriage-rates; upon social mobility and social organization; and finally, upon socio-cultural life. In the seven chapters of this last division, the influence and the value of *Social and Cultural Dynamics* were plainly evident. So also was the supreme significance of the philosophy of value which, as it has been argued above, is the guiding thread by whose aid sociology can be extricated from the bewildering maze of facts, events and processes requiring elucidation.

Calamities were not chosen by Sorokin as subjects for merely descriptive and analytical study. His deepest feelings had been stirred by the ghastly experiences through which he had lived and they were further exacerbated by his broad historical survey. The record of the earlier calamities which he reviewed were all the more vivid and poignant because he was able, through his earlier personal sufferings to relive them in vicarious experience to a degree hardly possible to other sociologists. Consequently he was obsessed by the need to discover vital operative principles on which mankind could rely to diminish, if not to abolish, the load of misery which it had been forced to bear.

It seemed as though "in civilized man the nervous centers controlling our thoughts and speech-reactions have possibly become more autonomous from those that control our overt actions than in 'primitive' man." How else is it possible to explain that "we can quote by heart the Sermon on the Mount, we can write profound commentaries on Kant's *Critique of Practical Reason,* can deliver a lofty sermon on altruistic love, and at the same time, can remain aggressive egotists?" There could be little hope of progress as long as "the existing governments and leaders, and our fellow men show inexhaustible abundance of the fiercest contradiction between their noble preachings and ignoble practices."* No wonder therefore that Sorokin saw little ground for optimism as far as man-made calamities are in question. Accompanied by a ghastly amount of suffering they would sooner or later come to an end, after destroying their victims. Amid them all it is possible to discern some countervailing activity which might have reduced their catastrophic effects. Rational planning in the light of modern scientific knowledge should be able, greatly to reduce, if not to prevent, the worst effects of famine and pestilence. Revolution and war may seem less susceptible to ameliorative measures. By tracing their fundamental cause to a clash of value-systems between warring countries or to the degeneration of the value-system which plunges a society into revolution, Sorokin provided a new clue to a hitherto baffling problem. To Societies threatened by revolution, the warning and the advice in *Man and Society in Calamity* were clear. "Either perish or begin to build a new system of values binding firmly the members and groups, with a new distribution of rights and duties" (p. 303). Failure to act upon this principle explained disasters of the past, especially those of the recent past. "The activities of the statesmen, of the League of Nations, and of all the innumerable 'ousters of war and revolution' after the First World War" illustrated the troubles which result when societies and their leaders look for remedies in the wrong place. "The system of values was entirely forgotten." Instead, desperate efforts were made to tinker with mere economic and political conditions. Feverish preparations for one session after another of the League of Nations were made by the experts, the scientific, political and economic advisers who were researching and devising allegedly down-to-earth, practical measures. They did no more than tinker with economic, administrative and political matters such as inflation, currency-control, deflation, and monetary and marketing problems in general. "The result was horrible and terrible – a complete fiasco" (305-6). If Sorokin's verdict on so many years of strenuous labor by hundreds of devoted men and women seems harsh, his summary account of what happened despite so much effort cannot be contradicted. All those efforts, he held, "not only failed to eliminate war and revolution, poverty and injustice, and other calamities, they not only failed to reduce their destructive force, but they rather increased the catastrophe by making wars more appalling and world-wide; by brewing revolutions on a scale never seen before in history."

---

*P. A. Sorokin, *The Ways and Power of Love* (Boston, Beacon Press, 1954), p. 311.

The Prediction of Troubles Ahead

A quarter of a century after Sorokin wrote this book is an interval sufficiently long to estimate the worth of his ideas. He was not content, as most sociologists were, merely to register, to describe and to utter some few vague hints about desirable lines of action for the future. Such was his evident confidence in the worth of his sociological principles that he took what would be regarded as unpardonably 'unscientific' in an historian, and what is for, a sociologist, a very rash plunge. He committed himself to specific, prophetic statements about the shape of things to come. Readers will easily be able to decide in the light of what has happened since 1942 how far Sorokin's foresight has been vindicated. As he has been criticized for excessive pessimism, his forecasts made in 1942 merit careful consideration. His prophetic warnings included:

1. There will be an increase in irritability, depressive moods and mental disturbances.
2. The death toll will be enormous. The birth-rate will decline, except in countries slightly affected by calamities.
3. Voluntary and compulsory migration will increase enormously. A growing number of the population will become nomadic as refugees or human flotsam, drifting over the countries of the earth.
4. Class divisions of society will be radically changed. Formerly privileged classes will be reduced in size, importance and wealth. Ranks, hierarchies of groups and classes will be largely dissolved and replaced by different sorts of superiorities and inferiorities. Contrasts between rich and poor will be diminished without, however, preventing a few of the *nouveaux riches* becoming enormously rich. But they will not constitute a permanent class or social stratum. Striking contrasts in ways of life will diminish. The unbridgeable gap between the aristocracies of 'society' or of wealth and the lower classes will get narrower and become easier to traverse. Class differences and inequalities will not disappear but they will tend to diminish.
5. Family position, hereditary title, honesty, integrity will cease to prevail as titles to distinction. The mob will be taken in hand by active, cynical party loyalists characterized by their impressive smartness, manipulative ability, brutality towards their opponents, and indifference to human suffering as they unscrupulously fatten like vultures on the tragedy and sacrifice of others. Social change of this type resembles that caused by revolutions which are "initiated by

idealists, carried through by brutal murderers and profiteered upon by scoundrels."

6. In education, science and culture, so called 'specialists' will rise to the top, strong on detail but ineffective at generalities. Positions of power and influence will be increasingly taken by smart alecks, mediocre, uncreative managers of science, arts, philosophy, and the press. Lobbyists, politicians and manipulators will be found on the directorates of Foundations, press, syndicates, scientific councils, and artistic institutions.

7. Divorce will increase as the sacredness of marriage declines, resulting in more and more broken homes with concomitant adverse effects upon young dependent children.

8. Private educational institutions will tend to disappear, to be replaced by public or state-controlled institutions. The content of education will deteriorate as energies are concentrated upon training technicians of war, hygiene, medicine, industry and farming. In the arts 'fiction-makers,' 'verse-makers,' 'picture-makers,' 'show-makers,' and 'music-makers,' will be turned out as technically equipped 'money-makers' instead of educated folk dedicated to the pursuit of cultural values for their own sake.

9. Societies will tend to become increasingly totalitarian with increasing control, regimentation, and regulation by the State. The area of independent initiative remaining in which persons or groups are able to manage their own affairs will progressively shrink.

10. Genuinely democratic political government and with it, private property, will tend to diminish along with the general decline in freedom. Individuals will increasingly be turned into puppets, manipulated and controlled by the central Government. Excessive centralization will require growing armies of State bureaucrats to clamp its regime down upon all and sundry, so that personal freedom and self-regulation will be constantly restricted.

11. Economic levelling will result in the collapse of the well-to-do without enriching the poor, although skillful, favored individuals among the *nouveaux riches* will succeed in feathering their nests despite the impoverishment of society as a whole.

12. Suspense, uncertainty, and insecurity will infect the lives of millions to a greater extent than anything they had previously known.

13. Painting, sculpture, music, the theatre, literature, philosophy, ethics, law, and religion will be more and more obsessed by the atmosphere of

calamity. Sombreness, melancholy, pessimism, and dolor will increasingly infect the fine arts to the extent sometimes of pathetique, macabre, and sadistic expression.

14. Psychic manifestations provoked by the calamity-minded outlook will vary. Superstitious beliefs, astrology, portents, and omens will sway the minds of many. Profligates and criminals will multiply while at the other pole a sublime moral heroism will be evoked although at first among a few. Militant atheism will be answered by fervent religiosity, egotism by altruism, anti-social practices by self-sacrifice for the community, militant materialism by fearless idealism, scepticism by growing fanaticism, criticism by dogmatism. The resultant clashes may be accompanied by great suffering and martyrdom. The outcome will ultimately be a heightening of effort leading to a revolution in philosophy, the fine arts, science, and all cultural activities. A new world will be born.

Sorokin's Forecasts Twenty-five Years Later.

Having himself survived calamities in which millions perished, Sorokin has some claim to attention when he remarks that persons deeply committed to a system of values which they venerate and regard as worthy of the service of their lives are able to bear any calamity with fortitude. For they have a conviction of human dignity, a self-respect and a sense of duty ensuring true peace of mind. His message for humanity in crises therefore is plain. Society must at all cost reintegrate all its values: religious, moral, scientific, and philosophical.

When Sorokin published this book in October 1942 the Second World War was reaching a climax. German armies had stormed their way through Russia and North Africa and they were threatening Stalingrad and Egypt. The Japanese in their triumphant advance had overrun vast areas in the Far East, including Malaya, the Philippines, Sarawak, Hongkong, New Guinea, and Java. But already there were signs that the fortunes of war would turn in favor of the Allies. Victory, upon which they were resolved, would, it was not doubt thought, restore peace to the world and give the lie to Sorokin's pessimism. If the First World War had not been a 'war to end war', as optimists then proclaimed, the Second World War surely would succeed and a brave new world would emerge. Sorokin records some of the expressions of contemptuous scorn with which his prognostications, briefly summarized above, were greeted by colleagues, students, and other contemporaries in the 1930's and 1940's. Since 1942 it will suffice to write the words, "Korea, India, Pakistan, Indo-China, Algeria, Congo, Tibet, Hungary, Nigeria, Indonesia, Yemen, China, Vietnam, Czechoslovakia" as some among many possible reminders to which the reader can add from memory other areas where peace, which once reigned, sometimes under alien rule such as 'the Pax Britannica, was brutally shattered. The millions in countless villages and towns, who have suffered from tribal and religious wars, mob violence, taxation, confiscation and robbery, which the Pax Britannica on the whole once had prevented by enforcing the Rule of Law, are inarticulate. Many are dead. Many of their new leaders, who at first profited by political revolutions, have not had the happy career upon which they seemed at first to have embarked. The price of revolution was more accurately foreseen by Sorokin than by anyone else.

On the domestic front, who, in 1970 and after, can scorn Sorokin for predicting as early as 1937 the striking changes in the relations of social classes, the pressure towards uniformity, the spoliation of wealth by the confiscation of private property disguised as 'taxation,' the increase of social animosities, bad tempers, violence and crime? The triumph of demagogues, the tightening grip of State control, the ever-swelling ranks of bureaucracy, the limitations imposed upon private people through taxation, state-direction, and new compulsions, have, within twenty-five years of Sorokin's predictions, attained dimensions and force which in Great Britain alone confound and dismay even the advocates of 'socialism in our time.' For it is not that by these means everybody is becoming wealthier, wiser, more contented and better educated.

In educational and cultural affairs it is just as difficult to rebut Sorokin's forecast. In Great Britain, the pressure to enforce comprehensive schools upon unwilling and protesting parents in defiance of Article 26 of the Universal Declaration of Human Rights has avowedly been applied in order to effect social and political adjustments and to improve education as a secondary goal. The poor success of the British in retaining the services of scientists as well as the medical practitioners they have trained and the extent to which British health services depend upon doctors and nurses from other countries is but one of many symptoms of a malaise which involves the erosion of old loyalties and ways of life. Hardly a day passes but that anyone aware of the level of cultural interests and activities in the years before Sorokin prophesied their decline does not encounter evidence confirming the accuracy of his predictions.

Memories of mighty works of old and loyalty to the traditions they inspired still stimulate many to maintain their struggle to respect, and to strive to measure up to, the standards bequeathed to them by the giants of the past. All is not black, but whether the substantial accuracy of Sorokin's anticipations can be controverted over an area wide enough to be highly significant, is a matter upon which every reader will have an opinion.* Sorokin himself was in no doubt and the decline he witnessed was such that he was seriously and increasingly alarmed. Immediately however, he returned to more general sociological theory, publishing in the following year *Sociocultural Causality, Space, Time* (Durham N. C., Duke University Press 1943), but the anxieties of the age weighed heavily upon him. In this mood he wrote papers on the problem of War and in 1944, produced *Russia and the United States* (New York, Dutton, 1944) in which he sought to show, despite the Cold War, that basic resemblances held possibilities of mutual understanding which then, and for many years later, seemed chimerical and far-fetched in the extreme to some of his critics. Again relations between the Soviet Union and the West have undergone many changes since 1944. Again Sorokin was strikingly in advance of his age.

Towards a Complete System of Sociology

Despite growing anxieties, Sorokin continued his services to academic sociology. *Sociocultural Causality, Space, Time of 1943* was a prelude to the completion of a new major work, published four years later, *Society, Culture and Personality – Their Structure and Dynamics* (New York, 1947, Harper;1962, Cooper Square Publishers).   This large volume, together with his surveys of the history of sociological thought is his best, all-round presentation of the fundamentals of sociology.

Those 'structural' questions in sociology which formed so large a part of the stock-in-trade of professional sociology at that time, but which had not been given special emphasis in *Social and Cultural Dynamics* were then taken up by Sorokin, but only to be subordinated to their more significant sociocultural setting. This pronounced shift in perspective is fairly evident

---

*Sorokin's doctrines are rejected by some academic critics who registered their satisfaction with things as they are and the prevalent optimistic belief that everything will turn out all right in the end. *Cf* P. Geyl, *Debates with Historians* (London, Batsford, 1955), p. 132, and A. Stern, *Philosophy of History and the Problem of Values* (The Hague, Mouton, 1962), p. 197.

in Sorokin's view of the nature of sociology as "a generalizing science of sociocultural phenomena viewed in their generic forms, types and manifold 'interconnections'." Among such phenomena, Sorokin includes groups and institutions with their organization or lack of organization, their solidarity and antagonism: the confused medley of problems such as arise from theories about race, kindred, ethnic groups, tribes, social order, caste, and class.

Sorokin surveys all such concepts and theories in turn as a prelude to an understanding of the ways in which they work out in the real world of action. As might be anticipated, the changes which had occurred in their form and qualities down the ages excited his special interest.

Sorokin advanced the view that it is impossible to create a sociology unless personality, society, and culture were regarded as indissolubly bound together. "Personality" as the subject of sociocultural interaction; "society" as the sum of interacting personalities; and "culture" as the collection of "meanings, values and norms," and all the vehicles in which those meanings were objectified, shared and conveyed: these three are an indivisible trinity. None of the three elements can exist without the other two. The mistake of many sociologists has been to try to proceed as though such a division were possible, so that, for example, great efforts have been made to base a sociology upon essentially empty, meaningless, incoherent concepts such as the *Gemeinschaft* or *Gesellschaft* of Tönnies, or "association," "community" of some English-speaking sociologists or social "structure" and "role." "Small group" is another example of a phrase which has had a considerable vogue. As long as it has no other quality than size it lacks significance. If it is to become a "tool" of sociological research, it must be endowed with human qualities which only descriptive sociology can supply. That they are often in the form of illustrations from novels, from Jane Austen to Sinclair Lewis, shows the fictional nature of the whole enterprise.

When, following Aristotle,* every human art, every inquiry and every action and pursuit is believed to aim at some good, the notions of class and status are seen to be of minor importance in sociological theory, despite the vigor with which they are manipulated when once they have been suffused with meanings. Then, abstractions although they are, they become reified so that, coupled with verbs, they are all too often productive of conflicting emotions, of devotion, of hate or of fear. Such grievous mistakes, it may be thought, ought never to have been made after

Ethica Nicomachea, W. A. Ross, ed. (Oxford, Clarendon Press, 1925), p. 1094A.

the saner wisdom of Aristotle had served so many subsequent generations. But apart from a few oustanding sociologists, notably Sorokin, the continuity of thought has not everywhere been maintained in more recent times. Hence terms such as 'role,' 'structure,' 'class' have made their way into sociology, although they seem to be neither facts, values, nor operative concepts.

The errors to which such a procedure leads are particularly serious in the world of industry where it has been well said that "by characterizing labor disputes as group conflicts, one is in danger of conveying the impression that such disputes presuppose the existence of established and coherent groups. This impression would be wrong. . . it is more correct to say that labor-management disputes tend to develop into intergroup conflicts than that they have that character from the outset."* What is true of groups is, often, equally applicable to the ideas about 'status' and 'class.' "Discussions of different theories of class are often academic substitutes for a real conflict over political orientations."**

Sorokin's Criticism of Traditional Sociology

Sorokin criticized devastatingly the efforts of many sociologists to wriggle out of the difficulties into which they became involved through trying, by allegedly 'value-free' concepts, to describe socio-cultural action as though it were analogous to physicochemical action. Some seemed to assume that they were not using value-laden terms when they invoked words such as family, school, church, arts, and so forth (*Society, Culture and Personality* 148n). So Sorokin was justified in condemning "the gross inadequacy of prevalent definitions and conceptions dealing with the problems of organized groups, institutions, social norms, modes, folkways, customs, law and social norms" (87). His criticisms amount to a clear call to base 'structural' sociology upon an explicit theory of value. If Sorokin does not demand this in set terms, his prescription to rescue 'structural' sociology from the morass in which it is floundering clearly amounts to just that: "the law and moral norms of a group define precisely the conduct, the relationships, the possessions, the advantages and burdens,

*O. Kahn-Freund, "Intergroup Conflicts and their Settlement," *British Journal of Sociology,* Vol. V (1954), p. 193.
**S. M. Lipset and R. Bendix, "Social Status and Social Structure," *British Journal of Sociology* Vol. II (1951), p. 150.

the sayings and doings or functions and roles, social statuses and social positions of its members. All these are mere derivatives or consequences of the respective legal and moral norms of the group." (p. 89). This last sentence merits great emphasis and all the attention of all sociologists.

On the supreme importance of getting ideas straight upon this whole question of the true nature of social solidarity and social antagonisms, Sorokin wrote, "The question is one of the basic problems of the social sciences in general and of sociology in particular. It is also one of the most acute practical problems of contemporary social life." (p. 118) Sorokin accordingly dealt with it at some length before proceeding to the next range of questions relating to social differentiation and stratification within the many groups into which human beings are variously organized. By adopting the same principle and by stressing the dependence of social 'classes' upon values, meanings, norms, he was able to cut his way through the confusion in which the whole question had become bogged down in vague definitions and through the failure to see organized societies as the products of many links and bonds. By the concept of 'multi-bonded ties' he was able to accommodate many sociological facts and to point to the values, meanings and norms corresponding to the occupational, economic and legal status by which the reality of class divisions in Western society has usually been detected. In this way he was able to explain, for example, the significance to be attached to social class divisions in Western societies before the eighteenth century.

Valuable and essential as it is to clarify ideas upon the modes and forms of the interaction of individuals, sociology does not gain depth and full significance until the totality of 'meanings, values and norms' by which their interaction is explained are studied and evaluated for their own sake. The behavioral, material levels of society must be shown in relation, and be explained, Sorokin contends, by the ideological quality governing them. He criticizes the views of Max Weber and Max Scheler because they failed to take this further step. Scheler's 'real aspects of social life' − sex, hunger, climate, race, and allied biological, physical, and chemical phenomena are on another and lower level of discourse. They condition existence but do not explain its essence. They are independent of cultural factors and there seems no way of bridging the gap between the two.

Again therefore Sorokin's solution may be seen to make a theory of value the principal interpretative key to sociology. How the dynamics of social and cultural processes are explained in the second half of *Society, Culture and Personality* will be easily grasped in the light of the findings and theories reported in Sorokin's *Social and Cultural Dynamics* from which, in effect they are summarized. His new statement about them made ten years after that pioneer work, has the virtues of being written after he had reviewed the critical reception of that work and after constantly re-thinking its form and conclusions. The merits of *Society Personality and Culture* are not thereby exhausted. The book is specially notable for the exceptionally scholarly, painstaking manner in which Sorokin reviews all the leading and many other contributions to the subject. Yet Sorokin did not advance his views as dogmatic pronouncements. He has always presented them as hypotheses. Tentative although his conclusions were, they had come from a full and thorough investigation by an experienced, life-long scholar at the height of his powers with a splendid record of achievement. In the over 700 pages, clearly but closely printed in double columns, of *Society, Culture and Personality,* Sorokin set out his mature views upon the scope, nature and logical method of scientific sociology. He compared and tested his own presentation with the work of others, seeking agreement with them as far as possible, and, where this was not possible, explaining carefully and objectively, his reasons for dissent. His persistent effort to follow where the argument appears to lead, regardless of personal renown, to honor his predecessors by striving to detect and maintain the continuity of thought, are not the least of the many valuable aspects of this magisterial treatise. The wealth of references to and comments upon the opinions of sociologists, philosophers, and other writers adds immensely to the utility of the book as a guide to the development and range of sociological speculation. Sorokin himself has observed that it is a book for the mature student rather than for beginners, but there can be no doubt that beginners should be encouraged to tackle it as soon as they have acquired the necessary background and to refer to it constantly as a support and promoter of their later development.

Some Critical Reactions

As in all Sorokin's sociological writings, the reader is conscious of the work of a mastermind of exceptional sweep, range, tenacity, and critical power. It is of course true that his criticisms are framed in terms of his own assumptions about the force of 'meanings, values, norms,' a remark trite enough it would seem to verge upon the self-evident, were it not the fashion among certain critics lacking any other basis for denigration to proffer such an observation as though they had detected a circular argument. It is a pointless remark unless such critics can dispute the standing which Sorokin assigns to value and provide criteria capable of absorbing all that Sorokin has achieved.

It is not that Sorokin has lacked more acute critics than these. During more than a quarter of a century which elapsed between the publication of *Social and Cultural Dynamics* his ideas have been noticed by one or two penetrating minds and occasionally referred to in passing by perfunctory writers who had clearly never taken the trouble to examine or understand them. In 1963 when Professor Philip J. Allen produced his composite survey *Pitirim A. Sorokin in Review,* not only were considered judgments upon Sorokin's work available, but he was able to answer them. It will be especially illuminating to all who wish, with Sorokin, to follow where the argument about his central doctrine on values leads, to ponder over the critical articles in that book by Professor Ford on 'Sorokin as Philosopher,' Dr. Arnold J. Toynbee on 'Sorokin's Philosophy of History' and Sorokin's replies to them as well as to an article of evident force and insight by Daya Krishna which appeared in the *Indian Journal of Philosophy* (1960, I. 175-84). That they led Sorokin to make further explanations and some reformulation of his views is the best measure of their cogency. Nevertheless it is also equally evident that Sorokin was able to accommodate all such critical observations without abandoning any of his principal doctrines. None of the critical remarks damaged the foundations or the super-structure of his sociology. On the contrary, they brought impressive testimony to the outstanding quality and permanent value of his achievement.

Sorokin on Supraconscious Influence

One of the main points of this exchange of views was Dr. Krishna's contention that there could be no possibility of achieving the 'integralist' standpoint which is essential to Sorokin's whole system, because intuitive cognition of any suprasensory and superrational elements, upon which it depends for all possibility of real progress, cannot be verified. None but sensory and rational knowledge, he urged, is susceptible of verification, hence there can be no real link between ideational or inspirational ideas and sensory knowledge. Sorokin explained that by suprasensory and superrational intuition he was referring to those flashes of insight from which all the greatest achievements of mankind have always sprung. They constitute a specific way of cognition and creativity which is essentially different from the ways of sensory, rational, mathematico-logical cognition and creativity. He was not referring, as perhaps his critics imagined, to the oracular *ipse dixit* utterances of self-constituted sages, or prophets, or to braggart claims made by demagogic politicians and other quacks. Sorokin has no difficulty in establishing that the great geniuses of all ages, Buddha, Plato, Shakespeare, Newton, Beethoven, and others, exemplify the principle he had postulated. The intuitions by which they enriched the human patrimony brought into existence forms of being and relationships which are inaccessible or only partly accessible to sensory and rational forms of cognition or creativity. Sensory and rational methods may and must test, develop, and realize the potentialities of such great ideas or patterns given by intuitional inspiration, but they are impotent to create them. Let anyone unconvinced by Sorokin's argument on this point name any major achievements fit to set besides the insight of genius that have been won through plodding, patient perseverance, however careful and assiduous, using none but sensory and rational processes.

Sorokin instances the achievements of the greatest integralist thinkers such as Lao-tse, Plato, Aristotle, St. Thomas Aquinas, and others whose systems of thought have for millenia ranked among the greatest in the history of philosophy. Had similar powers been within reach of patient plodders working on sensory and rational lines there should have been vastly more achievements to record than those actually registered in politics and government, literature, humanism, social science, fine arts, philosophy, and music. Sorokin does not make the point, but it inevitably occurs, that sociologists themselves might have much more to show for all the immense effort that has been put into the study of sociology if patient hard work alone could achieve creative power. Available material upon which to work in America alone has rightly been claimed to be "almost limitless."* The energy devoted to its expolitation is immense, for when that remark was made in 1950 it was reported that in the United States, sociology was being taught every year by several thousand instructors to about half a million students in nearly 2000 institutes of higher learning.

Already more than one thousand higher degrees as Doctors of Philosophy had been awarded in sociology by more than 50 universities. Over 100 textbooks of sociological 'principles' had been published. Countless essays, monographs, contributions to learned journals had

---

*H. W. Odum, *American Sociology, The Story of Sociology in the United States through 1950* (London, Longmans, Green & Co., Ltd., 1951), p. 53.

appeared, several being referred to for a year or two by friends as 'classic' statements, which, together with most of the other literature, was speedily forgotten as they were swept away by the avalanche of print in succeeding years. It will be a sad comment upon a work written to extol the achievement of some generations of devoted American sociologists to record the impression which Professor Odum gives of mountains of labor productive of few and small mice. His book records for example, an analysis which shows the subjects to which over six hundred articles had been devoted in the *American Sociological Review* between its foundation in 1936 and 1950. They included Social Theory (236) Marriage and the Family (95) Social Statistics and Research Methodology (89) Population Sociology (68) Social Problems (65) Social Psychology (56) Criminology (35) Race Relations and Ethnic Groups (30) Ecology (22) Social Planning (21) Educational Sociology (18) Social Pathology (13) Teaching of Sociology (12) Housing (11) Rural Sociology (11) Urban Sociology (9). A similar analysis is provided of the subjects for which American Universities awarded over 800 higher degrees of Doctor of Philosophy in Sociology between 1936 and 1948. They covered much the same subjects with the addition of 19 degrees for studies of the Co-operative Movement. Librarians and bibliographers grapple tirelessly to list, file and shelve the resulting annual tonnage of printed matter. Since 1950 there has been a yet further expansion of student numbers, of graduates, of instructors, and a yet greater multiplication of books and articles. In 1950 however, all that was claimed was that American sociology has been "relatively impressive — in its cumulative contribution and . . . in the perfection of its science."*

Have these apparently impressive, hopeful statements been vindicated by results? If sensory and rational forms of cognition, if plodding hard work were able to create insights, there surely ought by now to have been some major advance, some great interpretive insight able to embrace and explain the myriad facts of social life and activity which were already recorded in 1950 as being available for study in limitless profusion. What has happened is, that apart from Sorokin's great synthesis, the same old subjects are being thrashed over. While much repetition is inevitable in any educational processes over the years, it might be thought by now that solutions would have been reached upon some major problems. Population levels, family and matrimonial relations, race relations, crime and violence, the direction of education, to name but a few current difficulties, might

*Ibid, p. 18.

by now have been resolved, with clear patterns or blueprints for a better world. Notoriously the situation is far otherwise. 'New' sociologies appear every other year to be hailed, celebrated, criticized, and forgotten. On all sides the complaint arises that sociology lacks its Aristotle, its genius to control, order, and expound its subject matter. The history of the subject was studied, 'influences' were traced, new technical terms were constantly being created as obscurity deepened and confusion became more widespread.

An Integral Theory of Value Needed.

The possibility that it will be through a theory of value that a great advance may be made in sociology had not escaped acute minds. A powerful stimulus to the comparative study of value as a key concept in sociology was imparted by the anthropologists E. B. Tylor, Sir James Frazer, and E. Westermarck, among the pioneers, while Ruth Benedict more recently showed convincingly how necessary it is to 'place' values in their appropriate setting or pattern which could often be far different from that of the contemporary Western world. At the conclusion of an illuminating essay, Professor Gunnar Myrdal records his sense of dissatisfaction, despite his pioneer efforts to reshape value-theory in economics. He states his conviction that "the final solution of the value problem in economics and in the social sciences generally must therefore be to set up a method by which human valuations are rationally and openly introduced into theoretical and practical research to give it direction and purpose, to make it both unbiased and relevant to life."*

The pregnant and earlier remark of the British philosopher, John Laird, made in 1929, may be repeated at this point. "Value *may* prove to be the key that will eventually release all the human sciences from their present position of pathetic, if dignified futility."

It is the contention of this book that Sorokin has achieved no less than this great revolution in sociology, and has thereby given an immensely valuable lead to all human sciences. Such was the message implicit in the pages of *Society, Culture, and Personality.* That Sorokin had not succeeded in making it sufficiently explicit was the opinion of an acute British sociologist, Professor Donald MacRae, who reviewed the

*G. Myrdal, *Value in Social Theory* (London, Routledge & Kegan Paul, Ltd., 1958), p. 260.

book on its appearance. In a critical account of what he described as "a rich and important book," he reported that he did not think it measured up to 'a system of general sociology' of which, however, he doubted the likelihood of anyone ever creating. In this he was, as he made clear, echoing Sorokin's own view, who had said that he made no claim to be able to expound the whole complex social web of action and interaction because, in the present state of knowledge, such a claim could not be otherwise than pretentious. Professor MacRae concluded: "What we now need is an account of Sorokin's social philosophy and his fundamental value system in the more philosophical English sense of these phrases."* It is partly to meet this challenge that the present book is written. The further aim and purpose here is to indicate the utility of developing and applying a theory of value on Sorokin's lines to sociology and the human sciences in general.

*British Journal of Sociology, Vol. II (1951), p. 262.

Ethics in Sociology

The Harvard Center in Creative Altruism

Mounting concern over the darkening future which he foresaw for mankind would not be driven from Sorokin's consciousness. While he was working on *Society Culture and Personality,* he records that "the relentless occurrence of calamities and the highly critical situation of mankind persistently disturbed me and seriously interfered with the book's completion." During that period he had, however, witnessed the victorious end of the Second World War, the creation of the United Nations Relief and Rehabilitation Agency, the United Nations Organization, the Food and Agriculture Organization, and especially the United Nations Educational, Scientific and Cultural Organization, all pledged to work for the preservation of peace and for the moral and material progress of mankind. His own adopted country, the United States of America, was giving its wealth to restore the broken world on a scale of generosity unparalleled in the annals of humanity. The Nazi war criminals who had survived were brought to trial. Despite the evident possibility of a new start from out of the pit of horror into which, for six years, mankind had been plunged, despite the expectation that the tragedies of those years had burned indelible memories, despite the resolve, affirmed internationally by almost all the nations of the earth, to ensure a progressive and rapid advance in living conditions, in communication, and in education and culture, despite the ideals to which all subscribed in the Universal Declaration of Human Rights, Sorokin remained profoundly uneasy. For him the war had revealed depths of human depravity to which he knew no parallel. There had been bloodstained centuries in the past. Throughout the whole of antiquity before the collapse of Rome there had probably been no bloodier century than the first century B.C. Yet the Second World

War killed more people than made up the entire population of the Mediterranean World at the time of Julius Caesar, Antony, and Cleopatra. The planned slaughter of millions of Jewish people in Central Europe revealed the lengths to which tyranny could proceed during the twentieth century. By comparison, the explosion of the first atomic bomb on August 5, 1945 was a much smaller event, for no more than some 80,000 Japanese then perished, although many more had been wounded. The reverberations of this dread event echoed long after memories of the atrocious inhumanity of invading Japanese armies had grown dim, long after the slaughter and destruction inflicted by German air raids on Great Britain and Allied air raids on Germany faded in the memories of the survivors. Thought about those past horrors might still bring a tragic renewal of grief, but the atomic bomb was more than a memory; it was an ever-present fear. Like all acute fears it provoked some to hysterical reactions which Communist States in particular did their best to foment while taking care to make vastly more destructive atomic weapons themselves. Sorokin neither organized nor joined sporadic 'Ban the Bomb' demonstrations, he sought instead to apply his sociological wisdom to infuse new vitality into the sagging morale of humanity. In 1945 he resolved upon action, as soon as his long task of writing *Society Culture and Personality* had been completed.

For a University professor to found upon his own initiative a 'Research Center in Creative Altruism,' some very unusual provocation may indeed seem requisite. Such was the action upon which Sorokin embarked, single-handed. He had no faith in any of the current antidotes to war and other forms of inhuman, bloody strife. Democracies, he knew, are no less belligerent and prone to violence than aristocracies. Education, religious 'revivals,' communism, socialism, capitalism, the United Nations, and other political contrivances, he believed, were all equally powerless to deflect man from destruction as long as they were unaccompanied by what he called 'increased altruization of persons and groups.' He set forth his view in *The Reconstruction of Humanity* (Boston, Beacon Press, 1948) in which he provided 'the minimum of evidence' for their support. In the following ten years that book was translated into German, Norwegian, Japanese, Spanish, and Hindustani.

The prospects of enlisting aid through his one-man Research Center did not daunt Sorokin. He had already proved that he was able to undertake worthwhile work without the aid of grants from Foundations or Governments, and although grateful to the U. S. Department of Agriculture and later to Harvard University for aid in completing two of his major enterprises, he was content to proceed alone. Then, without any initiative on his part, an offer of substantial financial aid came from Mr. Eli Lilly. Sorokin gratefully accepted, and the large sum of $120,000 was made over to Harvard University for Sorokin to use on his new enterprise. Such an award, of which other scholars dare not dream, was a providential stimulus to which Sorokin quickly responded. It is unnecessary here to repeat in any detail his description of the many activities and publications of the Center which are told in its publications and in *A Long Journey* Sorokin's autobiography. Something will be said, however, about his method and main lines of approach.

Characteristically, Sorokin's first enterprise was to collect such facts as he could discover, to serve as an empirical basis for further work. In two years he completed and published *Altruistic Love, A Study of American Good Neighbors and Christian Saints* (Boston, Beacon Press, 1950). Never before had some 4600 saints from the Christian calendar been the subject of a sociological investigation planned to discover, report, and discuss their age, sex, marital and family status, occupational, economic, and social position, education, intelligence, health, longevity, rural-urban and national distribution, political ideologies, group affiliations, and their path to sainthood. The changing character and numbers of saints down the ages were also examined. The altruists in the volume were a sample study of 500 living Americans. Further exploratory sample studies continued after the publication of that book, among students at Cambridge, Massachusetts, on the patients in the Boston Psychopathic Hospital, and among other individuals. Sorokin organized a symposium of 28 contributions from various experts to illustrate ego-transcending techniques, the scientific significance of Yoga and related techniques, methods of altruistic education in Hutterite and Mennonite Communities, the dynamics and etiology of friendship and enmity, as well as various techniques of transformation of inimical into amicable relationships.

Love as a Force in Social Life

In the light of all this preparatory work and his own reflections, stimulated by the obsessive pressure of deepening anxieties for the future, Sorokin wrote *The Ways and Power of Love. Types, Factors and Techniques of Moral Transformation* (Boston, Beacon Press, 1954). It will be plain from the summary account of Sorokin's own stormy past, and above all from the general tenor of his sociological studies of revolution and his description of the consequences of a break-up of a sensate civilization, with their tremendous threat to civilization, that he had every motive to promote any action that would help to avert the perils he saw to be looming ahead. Indeed it may be asked, who has not such an incentive? Yet it was a fact that the whole of this eminently practical and urgently necessary task had been virtually neglected by sociologists. An examination of the hundreds of textbooks, treatises, monographs, and dissertations on the subject revealed that it lay beyond the range of almost all professional sociologists. Had they anticipated Sorokin by basing their theories upon a well-founded integral psychology and by making a theory of value the core or backbone of their subject they could not have failed to see that the transgression and violation of 'meanings, values, norms,' precipitate urgent practical problems for any science of society. But failing to provide such a positive account over the whole range of sociology of what those values, meanings, norms might be, they were less likely to deal with the negative aspect of the consequences of destruction and denial of 'meanings, values, norms.' Among the rewards of integrating sociology with value-theory is the result that ethics becomes inseparably a constituent of the subject, not in any remote, philosophical, semantic way, but as an operative factor deciding between social health and disease, progress or catastrophe, life or death.

Sorokin was modest about the likely worth of his work, but at a time when "better brains are busy with other problems, including the invention of means of extermination of human beings. . . . with promotion of warfare. . . . . in cultivation of the intellect and tribal patriotism of their pupils, while many a religious leader is absorbed in the intertribal crusades against various enemies — under these conditions somebody, somehow, must devote himself to a study of the miracle of love, no matter how inadequate is his capacity."* At a time when far too many communities and nations are rent with discord, hate, and violence, it does not seem illogical, misplaced, or inappropriate for the 'science of society' to devote some effort to the problem of achieving concord, love, and peace. Should not a vigorous effort be mounted to wage 'this holy war' of united mankind against its eternal and implacable enemies: death, disease, stupidity, ignorance, criminality, sterile suffering, poverty and the like? To ask such a question in an academic environment was and, it is to be feared, still is productive of little except embarrassed evasion of the question as being a theological speculation, one fit only for a sermon in church,

---

*P. A. Sorokin, *The Ways and Power of Love* (Boston, Beacon Press, 1954).

because it seems remote from any 'scientific' concern. All speculative energies available for such problems were concentrated instead upon "the negative, pathological and sub-human phenomena typical of the disintegrating phase of our sensate culture."*

Sorokin's Integralist Concept of Human Personality

Once again, Sorokin went his own way, in disregard of orthodox academic opinion, as a Harvard Professor with William James as a predecessor should be able to do. His subject took him beyond the boundaries by which academic sociology was generally confined. There can be no doubt that he succeeded in presenting the best survey of altruistic devotion available in the literature of the subject. He takes up and tries to complete the penetrating analysis of Nygren's celebrated book* by showing that the duality of Eros and Agape must be resolved so that instead of standing as conflicting opposites, egocentric love (Eros) and theocentric love (Agape) are harmonized within every individual human being.

In criticizing *Society, Culture and Personality,* Professor MacRae, whose review has already been mentioned, had observed that 'personality' did not get as full a treatment as the title of the book seemed to promise. Sorokin has certainly remedied any such deficiency, for it will be evident from his case studies of saints and altruists and from the activities of his Harvard Center, that the whole enterprise turned upon personality as its theme. Once again, Sorokin's early work as a specialist in psycho-neurology is very evident. After reviewing once more the various theories about personality, Sorokin summarized his 'integralist' position after describing "the three levels of human mental structure, — the unconscious, the bioconscious and the socioconscious — " by saying that "the ideally integrated person may be defined as one whose unconscious drives, and bioconscious and sociocultural egos are in a state of mutual harmony. Such a person experiences himself as one, a unified ego. The poorly integrated person, on the other hand, is one whose unconscious drives and bioconscious and socioconscious drives are constantly at war with one another . . . such a person is likely to become a suicide, an inmate

*P. A. Sorokin, *A Long Journey* (New Haven, Connecticut College & University Press, 1963), p. 277.
**A. Nygren, *Agape and Eros* (London, S. P. C. K., 1937).

of a mental asylum, a sophisticated and cynical human animal, or a demoralized brute."* Sorokin thus makes a clean sweep of all the partial, inadequate, obscurantist notions including those of psychoanalysis. He condemns Freud's *id* because it obscures the reality of 'vital energy' or 'life' for which it really stands. Moreover he objects strongly to the ambiguity by which Freud makes the word stand now for 'vital energy' and now for "sex energy, muscular, cutaneous, genital, anal, oral." "Not a scintilla of knowledge is added through such a misleading identification of sex with life." As Freud later makes "the unconscious *id* identical with libidinal and death-destructive instincts" his whole idea about the unconscious is "a logical hash."** The simpler concept of 'unconscious drives' avoids such tendentious confusion.

The bioconscious level of personality is that registering biological tension and energy, such as awareness of hunger, thirst, cold, heat, sex. Neither the unconscious drives nor these bioconscious drives are inherently social or antisocial in character. They become such only on the socioconscious level where activities and energies "are derived from and generated by the conscious, meaningful, interaction of mindful persons in their collective living-experience and learning." It is on this level that 'meanings, values, norms' become operative and cultural arises.† Sorokin refers briefly to the many complicated influences brought to bear upon individuals forming a part of any such society, all of them different in their abilities, outlook, powers of assimilation and response. It is on this socioconscious level that conflicts, tensions, and social strife arise. It does not seem hazardous to add that it is on this level that any desirable adjustments in personality traits should be sought, for there alone can opportunities to influence them arise.

Beyond these three levels which it should be within the power of individuals and societies to realize and to control, is the fourth, the personality level of the supraconscious. As already indicated, it is from this still mysterious level that those energies and activities spring by which

---

*P. A. Sorokin, *The Ways and Power of Love.* (Boston, Beacon Press, 1954), p. 95.
**Ibid, p. 86.
†It is satisfying to be able to point to the essential agreement of Sorokin's analysis with that of Leibniz, whose concept of the monadic nature of the universe is based upon a scale of consciousness arising from *petites perceptions* (or the unconscious) to the highest rationality (G. W. von Leibniz, *Philos. Schriften,* C. J. Gerhardt, ed. Vol. VI, pp. 598-623). *Cf* J. Laird, *The Idea of Value* (Cambridge University Press, 1929), p. 165; and L. L. Whyte, *The Unconscious before Freud* (New York, Basic Books, 1960), and (Tavistock, 1962).

genius has enriched the world with new insights and "the greatest creative victories of man in the fields of truth, beauty, and goodness."

Such, in terse outline, is the general framework within which Sorokin explains the energies and the mental structure of man. He has the merit of superseding an immense amount of confusion, contradiction, obscurity, and absurdity. Anybody willing to give candid, objective, unprejudiced attention to the arguments by which Sorokin effectively routs the ideas of Freud for example, will relish his reference to 'the phantasmagoric imagination' of that author.

If Freud did not find the right key to the dark mysteries of human and social behavior, he was not alone. Sorokin makes no extravagant claims on his own behalf. In the light of subsequent progress in the analysis of personality which it will ever be Freud's title to fame for having stimulated so powerfully, it may still be possible to find a better solution than Sorokin's, but he at least does not look for it in the wrong place. Altruism, which he sees as the one thing needful, cannot emerge on a Freudian level. "The unconscious forces in man cannot serve as the fountainhead of the most intense, universal, pure, durable, and adequate love." The whole history of mankind with the record of the few supreme teachers by whom the world has been turned towards the ways of peace, Jesus, Buddha, Mahavira, Lao-tse, Confucius, show that "no supreme love behavior can occur without the supraconscious in action."

As Sorokin freely acknowledges, to invoke the supraconscious is to evoke an unknown. How ordinary, fortunate, altruists acquire their quality is difficult to discover. Sorokin dismisses as unprovable, improbable, or very doubtful, a number of conventional explanations. If the mystery of altruism is an unknown X, it does not help to explain it with an unknown Y such as divine grace, spiritual inheritance, the karmic consequences of good deeds in a previous incarnation, astrological, astro-physical, or cosmic 'forces,' pre-natal 'emgrams,' or other occult influences. Equally useless are geographic explanations such as climate, scenery, flora and fauna. There are other false trails such as those which regard altruism as in some way a product of biological heredity or of such factors as the color of skin, cephalic index, stature, weight, and other somatic qualities. More fantastic are the theories which make character turn upon practices such as swaddling infants, to which several anthropologists have attributed characteristics observable in late life. The notion popularized by Freud, for example, that frustrations provoke aggressive reactions can and has been very plausibly illustrated, but Sorokin has no difficulty in demolishing any claim that such a correlation is uniformly observable. That the contrary is true will be evident to anyone concerned with character formation by whom, in Sorokin's terms, bioconscious drives are continually being 'frustrated' or controlled by socioconscious values.

When known factors tangibly influencing character formation are investigated, the problem of explaining altruistic social conduct becomes less mysterious. Of them all, Sorokin put family influences in the first place. For this opinion he did not lack an enormous body of evidence to which he referred in support of conclusions to which many would be inclined to assent on the basis of their own experience. "The main source of children's knowledge of right and wrong is still their home and the family" (p 198). "The more harmonious the family, the better the child's moral reputation and behavior. With the passage of years, the parental family's influence tends naturally to weaken." Beyond the family circle, other groups, persons and forces with whom a child or youth directly interacts exert an influence roughly proportional to the intensity and duration of exposure to such influences. The other 'forces' may be schools, teachers, churches, priests, theatrical shows, movies, games, and radio and television programs. Incidents such as killing an animal, destroying a bird's nest, or the experience of specially impressive natural phenomena, have all been recorded as motives to altruistic conduct, a notion which will not appear strange to admirers of Wordsworth's poetry. The retroactive effect of a person's first good deed can also be potent, as anyone who recalls William James on habit or remembers Oscar Wilde's testimony, "It is quite remarkable how one good action always breeds another" will be aware. Nevertheless Sorokin does not believe that the problem can be completely resolved on this basis. Despite his refusal to accept occult forces he considers that "no supreme love behavior can occur without the supraconscious energy in action." That is to say the example of Christ, of Buddha, and of other supreme formulators of the highest moral ideals cannot be explained by the sum of all the known factors contributing to altruistic conduct. This conclusion squares of course with Sorokin's general position that the most striking examples of creative power in the history of human culture have arisen from some as yet unexplained flash of insight or superior mental endowment which mankind has so far been unable to create, attain to, or command at will. The whole question of "the altruistic formation and transformation of human beings," he reports, "is an exceedingly delicate, complex, and difficult operation" (p. 287).

Sorokin proceeds on this basis to review institutional aids to altruistic conduct, notably religious communities, monasticism, brotherhoods, yogas, mechanical drill, and the fine arts, and to give some account also of negative influences, conflicts, the trials and pains of regenerative behavior, and the problem of the control of biological drives. He lists twenty-six such distinguishable techniques, all of which may aid in stimulating altruistic activity (p. 290).

With *The Ways and Power of Love* Sorokin probably carried the study of altruism in human conduct about as far as it was possible to take it at the time. It was a pioneer effort to put a study hitherto regarded as belonging to the domain of religion and literature within a sociological frame of reference. If the Harvard Research Center in Creative Altruism had provoked no more than this exhaustive study, it would have amply justified its existence and its generous financing by the Lilly Endowment. This was, however, by no means the only product of the Center. In addition to the series of lectures, discussions, and other books and papers, the Center promoted a Research Society in Creative Altruism in 1955. A Conference convened by the Society resulted in the Symposium Volume *New Knowledge in Human Values* (1959). With the gradual near-exhaustion of the funds, the activities of the Research Center diminished, while the work of the Research Society came to an end. In the spirit by which all this activity had been inspired, Sorokin naturally continued to work. Amid his continuing contributions to learned journals both in the United States and overseas, in addition to the occasional lectures which he agreed to give out of the very many that he was pressed to undertake but had to decline, he produced two more books. The American Sex Revolution (Boston, Porter Sargent, 1957), a sociologist's commentary upon the astonishing social changes which had occurred during his lifetime, was also a vindication of the accuracy of his diagnosis of the nature and probable course of sexual morality in the decay of our sensate society. Anyone who had encountered Sorokin's social and cultural theories in the 1940's, still a time of relative decorum in comparison with the situation a quarter of a century later, and aware of what occurred during the breakdown of the sensate society during the early Roman Empire, would probably have anticipated much of what has happened and of what Sorokin had to say. His summary account of the lengths to which obsessive preoccupation with sex has gone, with its destructive physical, mental, and moral effects upon social welfare, is yet one more confirmation of the accuracy of his research and of the analytical and predictive power of his theories based upon it. Swedish, Spanish, Portugese, Japanese, Indian, and other translations of the book soon appeared. In *Power and Morality* (Boston, Porter Sargent, 1959) he, with Professor W. Lunden, made a trenchant attack upon the inadequacies of those who wield political power in the great nuclear-armed states. How to replace them by 'scientists, saints, and sages' was the problem he shared with Plato, and he may well have been resigned in advance to anticipate no better result than has rewarded Plato's smiliar hopes over the last two thousand and more years.

Was the whole scientific effort to promote a more altruistic way of life a failure? The question naturally arises, not merely from the preceding reference to the slowing up of its activities but because it is probable that most people would have expected it to fail. Why this should be so is an interesting illustration of the veracity of Sorokin's belief that the present age is one of a bankrupt and decaying sensate culture-mentality whose course towards a complete and possibly catastrophic collapse will be very difficult to arrest. Such a remark may seem to give a handle to critics who have alleged that Sorokin has invented his abstractions of 'ideational,' 'idealist,' and 'sensate' culture and has proceeded to write as though, instead of being concepts, which it is all they are, they were real entities of an operational type, fit to be coupled with active verbs; in other words that he is guilty of reifying an abstract mental construction.

In point of fact the very existence of the Harvard Research Center in Creative Altruism provided impressive testimony to the contrary. If Sorokin had believed that something called 'a sensate culture' must inevitably proceed upon its own predetermined road to destruction, he would have lacked faith in the usefulness of throwing all his energies into the attempt to halt and to reverse the process of decline. Instead of regarding a crash as inevitable, he strove with all his energies to induce mankind to take the path of sanity, away from discord, hate and violence, towards concord, love and peace. He believed fervently that by stating the alternatives clearly and by indicating the right way, it should be possible, even in a 'sensate' society, to attract a considerable amount of support for altruistic activities. He was however under no illusions about the chronic difficulty of a task rendered all the more acute by the ambivalent attitudes observable all around him. "Existing governments and leaders, and our fellow men, show inexhaustible abundance of the fiercest contradiction between their noble preachings and ignoble practices." Not 'a sensate society' therefore, but men and women of inadequately integrated personalities, prisoners of bioconscious drives imperfectly balanced and harmonized by socioconscious controls are the agents of disaster. This use of the words 'inadequately integrated,' 'imperfectly harmonized and balanced,' obviously appear to beg the very question at issue. So they do, but Sorokin has already redeemed his title to use them by having provided an account of the qualities of 'adequately integrated,' 'perfectly harmonized and balanced.' Such is the service of his concept of 'integral personality.'

Because this message seems not to have penetrated everywhere, Sorokin's 'meanings, values, norms' have been stressed here at the risk of what may appear to be a somewhat tedious repetition, as a theory of culture; that is to say as a theory of value embracing all those activities and realizations which have traditionally been regarded as modes or aspects of the *Summum Bonum* or the Good; *Bonum verum*, or truth or knowledge; *Bonum iucundum,* or aesthetic merit; *Bonum honestum,* or moral worth. To have been able, since 1950, to have created the Research Center, to have enlisted many to cooperate with him, to have published volumes of permanent worth on a neglected but vital topic can never all add up to failure. Sorokin's resolute affirmation of the cause of altruism confronted the world with a repetition of a message that should never have been allowed to fade.

Sociology and the
Philosophy of History

Sociology and the Philosophy of History

Because Sorokin, in his quest for the facts of human thought and achievement as the raw material which any sociology must explain, went to look for them in the historical record, and because of the use he made of what he found there, he is widely regarded as another philosopher of history. The title is certainly merited to the extent that he has presented a theory to explain the broad course of social development over the ages.

It is a description which will make him suspect in many academic circles today, with the result that his whole sociological standpoint may seem suspect also. This would be doubly unfair because he went to history, as it has already been shown, with as open a mind as any sociologist or philosopher of history has ever done. Moreover he used what seemed to be the facts of history upon the nature of the life of men in societies throughout the ages to frame hypotheses for sociology, not for any philosophy of history. The result was a rich harvest of ideas which he found could be organized as patterns of values. He found meaning in history. He did not seek, in the manner of some 'philosophers of history', to impose values upon history. Having in this way discovered that certain distinctive value-patterns were of dominant significance throughout long periods in societies of which records survive, having shown that those value-patterns offer a better explanation of sociological reality in its nature, organization or structure, and change, than any alternative theory had provided, Sorokin has in effect given an entirely new philosophy of history to the world. Yet, it must be repeated, it was not his aim to do this. As a sociologist, he was seeking to understand the life of man in society and the myriad forms and happenings by which that life is characterized.

As a philosopher of history, his work is scrutinized and criticized by other philosophers of history, for whom his predominant sociological motive may mean less or, indeed, little. As a sociologist, his philosophy of history may seem to other sociologists, few of whom have taken a deep concern in the subject, to be something of a redundancy in a discipline with sufficient problems of its own. To the non-specialist layman who may, by chance, encounter Sorokin's work, it may well seem, both as sociology and as philosophy of history, to be too speculative and abstract. To demonstrate the error of such misjudgments and to vindicate the striking, positive, and very practical progress in knowledge which Sorokin has achieved, is consequently a necessary, if difficult, task. In Great Britain, where philosophical interests of any kind have never been general and where indeed they have often been scorned as the futile concern of a somewhat eccentric minority, it is especially difficult, even towards the end of the twentieth century, to evoke much serious interest in the philosophy of history. The very mention of the subject in some academic historical and philosophical circles is liable to arouse suspicion. Among the general public, interest is very much greater. Writers offering any new generalities on the subject, however wide of the academic mark, such as Winwood Reade, Wilfrid Trotter, Sir Halford MacKinder, Ellsworth Huntington, H. G. Wells, Haushofer, Spengler and others, enjoyed a far wider circle of readers than many academic historians.

Some Early Philosophers of History

Sorokin's task and his achievement stand out more clearly when this very slow growth of academic philosophical, scientific interest in history and the theory of history is borne in mind. The contrast provided by the miraculous expansion of scientific knowledge in modern times has often been cited and there has been enormous interest in the thought-processes and the ways in which such an advance in knowledge was achieved.

The attempt to apply similar methods to the study of man in society and history was naturally made, but it could show no such progress. Nor is this surprising. Every human being is unique. The facts of human history are infinitely numerous, change has been the law of individual and collective life since the origin of man, the records of much of that change are non-existent or inadequate and above all there is little or no possibility of controlled experiment with human societies and human lives such as that available to the scientist. In such circumstances, it was long before curiosity over the true nature of the human past began to replace the myths and legends, priestly, theocratic, or traditional notions, which served to explain history rather in the way that old wives' tales had provided botanical and medical wisdom.

A few examples will best indicate the way the matter developed in the British Isles. In the seventeenth century, a standard work on history was the celebrated *Annales Veteris et Novi Testamenti* of Archbishop James Ussher together with his survey of the chronology of the Ancient World from the Babylonians and Persians, first published in 1650-1654 and subsequently reprinted in Paris (1673) and elsewhere. He presented the history of the world in five eras beginning with the creation of the world on October 23, 4004 B.C. The second era began on October 23, 1657 B.C. after the old world had been destroyed by the Flood, when Noah emerged from the Ark to repopulate the world after the first rainbow had sealed the new dispensation. The subsequent epochs were dated from the journeys of the Israelites under Abraham, the Exodus from Egypt under Moses; from the building to the destruction of Solomon's Temple, down to the birth of Christ. The people of Europe, according to this ancient tradition, stemmed from Japhet, who was said by Moses to have peopled the Isles of the Gentiles. Such was the state of historical learning about the ancient world solemnly proclaimed by a learned Archbishop a generation after Shakespeare. In England a somewhat more critical view about the history of Britain had already emerged in Shakespeare's lifetime but the Biblical chronology still firmly held the field for all the ancient world. "Now that the Iles of the Gentiles mentioned by Moses, were those of Europe, all learned men confesse" wrote John Speed in his *History of Great Britaine* (1611 and 1623). He was not however ready to accept the tradition that Britain had been founded by Brutus, leader of the Trojans. "The last but much applauded opinion, for the possessing and peopling of this Island (of Britain) is that of *Brute,* generally held for the space of these last four hundred years (some few men's exceptions reserved) who, with his dispersed Trojans, came in and made conquest of this Island, the year of the world's creation 2887 and after the Universal flood 1231" (p. 162). Speed spent many words controverting this idea, pleading that just as the French no longer believed in their origin from the son of King Priam, as Scotland had rejected Scotia, the daugher of King Pharoah of Egypt, Ireland, their Hiberius, and other countries their demi-gods, so the Britons might discard Brute who had murdered his parents and had "sprung from Venus that lascivious Adulteresse." Speed was a pioneer and Brutus survived his criticisms for some decades.

Scientific Philosophies of History

In such a climate of opinion anything in the nature of a philosophy of history independent from the biblical tradition was inevitably a delicate plant in the garden of history. It continued to be neglected and despised even while the garden itself was cultivated with ever-increasing vigor, so that it is little short of a miracle that it ever took root or survived. Giambattista Vico was hardly a name to his contemporaries, and later 18th century writers also ignored him. Such is the power of creative thought, however, that sooner or later original and promising ideas are detected by other vigorous minds. Michelet revived Vico. The views of Herder and Hegel were never suffered to languish in obscurity for a century or more, at least in Germany. How far they influenced thinkers outside German philosophical circles is problematic. They were little known, appreciated, or intelligently criticized in Great Britain. There, the fate of Henry Thomas Buckle (1821-1861) is symptomatic of Anglo-Saxon attitudes. He had read widely, given up his father's banking business to concentrate upon his work, which he pursued with a passion that almost exhausted him. He was independent and he sought no academic or other honors. He was no transcendentalist. He had no theories about the Absolute or the Spirit of the Age. He sought to account for the character of civilizations in history on physical, moral, and intellectual grounds. He stressed the power of natural causes, of climate and natural environment. So pragmatic an approach might be thought likely to secure him a respectful hearing in the middle of the 19th Century. But either the strength of tradition or the latent spiritual yearnings of the British revolted at theories so much in accord with their practices and so much at variance with their professed beliefs. Buckle's *History of Civilization in England* was published between 1857 and 1861 at the time of the *Origin of Species* (1859). One Darwin was enough. His weight of unfamiliar but impressive evidence and his reputation as a scientist were such that those who were most revolted by his findings were at a loss to know how to rebut them. Buckle, a young man, they thought they could meet on their own ground, so he was attacked with a virulence that recalls the odium with which eminent theologians assailed, after he was dead, the memory of Julian the Apostate. Doctrines such as these that had earned immediate fame in France, for Hippolyte Taine brought the scorn of many vocal critics when expounded by an Englishman in England. It is not difficult now to expose the uncertain bases of many of Buckle's contributions, nor is it necessary to defend all his facts and theses in order to pay him the respect due to a sincere, earnest and skilled writer who gave up a life of leisure in order to toil at the thankless task of endeavoring to detect the facts by which human destiny has been shaped. Had he lived beyond the early age of forty years, he would doubtless have continued his work and have succeeded in giving good account of many of his ideas in answer to his critics. Rejected and scorned by eminent academics and men in public life, deprived by early death of the defence and improvement he might have given it, Buckle's book nevertheless exerted an enormous influence. It was, for instance, reported to have been four times translated in Russia, where it was widely read, and several times in Germany; and it has never lacked readers in England.*

His influence may be seen in later attempts to make a 'science' out of history, provided with laws and uniformities, and in attempts to explain historical events by natural causes. Thus 'human geography' at the hands of men such as Vidal de la Blache and Sir Halford Mackinder became a valuable contribution showing how human life can be conditioned and influenced by its natural environment. The search for climatic explanations for all historical changes was however carried too far by enthusiasts such as Ellsworth Huntington. The fact is that no such single interpretative principle, whether sunspots, rainfall, population levels, economic activity, racial qualities or any other, can rise above its own limited presuppositions and frame of reference. None are equipped to cope with the whole range of human values and human destiny.** As long as nothing better was forthcoming, the philosophy of history remained very much under a cloud. The stock 'respectable' opinion about it long remained, as Mr. Raymond Mortimer testifies, quoting a remark of Bishop Stubbs, "I don't believe in the philosophy of history, so I don't believe in Buckle" to which Mr. Mortimer added "Stubbs commands my assent."†

A Bishop might certainly be expected to believe in a philosophy of history to which he was committed by the Thirty Nine Articles, notably

*J. M. Robertson, *Buckle and his Critics: A Study in Scoiology* (Swan Sonnenschein, 1895). This painstaking work of great learning admirably reveals nineteenth century attitudes to the philosophy of history in England.

C. St. Aubin's *A Victorian Eminence. The Life and Work of Henry Thomas Buckle* (London, Barrie, 1958) is a most valuable book. Based on manuscripts and other sources, it is the only full modern study of Buckle's life and work.

Bertrand Russell, in *Fact and Fiction* (London, Allen & Unwin, 1961), p. 37, records how "as a boy I read with delight a book then famous though now forgotten, Buckle's *History of Civilization."*

**F. R. Cowell, *Culture in Private and Public Life,* pp. 53-54.

†*Sunday Times* (London, February 16, 1958).

VI and XVII and the Creed of the Established Church of England. Stubbs did not disavow interest in any secular, humanist, scientific attempt to account for the course of human affairs. Mr. Mortimer had forgotten the Bishop's two lectures on the methods of historical study, for in them, although he does not mention Buckle, he does say "certainly there is a Philosophy of History which is not content with abstractions but busies itself with following up causes and following out consequences, goes behind the scenes of the drama as well as directs a microscopic vigilance on the stage." At the same time, he must be considered as committed to much the same views as Archbishop Ussher and John Speed. The Bible story was his supreme authority as it had been theirs, "The most precious of histories are those in which we read the successive stages of God's dispensations with man."*

Some Recent Criticisms of the Philosophy of History

Faith in a theological philosophy of history has continued to inspire many and it has more recently been evident in the great work of A. J. Toynbee, *A Study of History*. That this faith can be held while rejecting work such as Toynbee's has been made evident in the criticisms which his book has received from Christian scholars.** The argument can therefore proceed without theological presuppositions.

It is not made easier on that account, and to venture far with the great debate which the possibility of a philosophy of history has aroused in our own time would require a large volume in itself. To try to indicate the climate of opinion with which Sorokin's contribution had to contend and some of the critical reactions his work has provoked, will be all that can be attempted here. No other writer on the subject yet appears to have accepted his ideas wholeheartedly; but then, by none of them has his thesis been exhaustively and fairly examined. From the comments scattered through this book, evidence will be found to support this charge against most of his critics. Dr. Toynbee is an exception, but Sorokin has answered him.†

*W. Stubbs, *Lectures on Medieval and Modern History* (Oxford, Clarendon Press, 1886), pp. 83, 89.
**P. Geyl, *From Ranke to Toynbee* (Northampton, Mass., Smith College, 1952), p. 77 (citing Professor Rogier), reprinted in *Debates with Historians* (London, Batsford, 1955), p. 157.
†P. J. Allen, ed., *op. cit.*, pp. 67-94, 423, 426-436.

An impartial inquirer seeking a reasoned verdict upon Sorokin's work is perpetually conscious of an animus against it, often candidly expressed, as though the critics are thereby absolved from the necessity of following Sorokin's presentation and ideas in any detail. The summary accounts given of those ideas by such critics are moreover always brief, partial, perfunctory, and inadequate. Whether the bulk of Sorokin's volumes, the style in which they were written, their vast scope, are found forbidding; whether Sorokin's whole attitude and approach seems too antagonistic to currently fashionable philosophical and historical ideas; whether his revival of something in the nature of a cyclical theory in history was thought sufficient to brand him as obsolete; whatever the explanation may be, it is disappointingly true that in the English-speaking world the novelty of his theories has failed as yet to yield the results they promise.

It will be useful to consider his contribution in relation to that of some other men who enjoyed greater contemporary renown, such as Morris Cohen, for example, who was generally regarded as outstanding by his contemporaries. He had, it was said "both the facts and the phosphorescence of learning", set off by "rationalism, wit, clarity and style."* The philosophy of history had held a fascination for him all his life and he had lectured on the subject in New York City in 1899 to 1900 before he was twenty. He regarded his book *The Meaning of Human History* as his *magnum opus.* It was one of the last books he lived to write. It has been proclaimed that it is 'a fountainhead of ideas and methods for students of historiography, philosophy and ethics.' It is indeed full of ripe knowledge and wisdom and it is not in order to decry it or its author that it must be pronounced inferior to Sorokin's views on all critical points upon which the further progress of the philosophy of history depends. Although Sorokin's work *Social and Cultural Dynamics* had been available for some years before Cohen wrote, and although he, like Sorokin, had spent his boyhood in Russia, in humble circumstances, he nowhere mentions Sorokin although he decries Spengler and the idea of historical cycles.**

Symptomatic of the attitudes with which Sorokin's work has been approached by other writers are such remarks as "the historian who presents me with large generalizations and in the same breath tells me that he has been proceeding empirically will always arouse my distrust." The

*Leonora C. Rosenfeld, in her *Preface* to M. Cohen's *The Meaning of Human History* (LaSalle, Illinois, Open Court, 1961).
**M. R. Cohen, *op. cit.*

late Professor Geyl wrote thus with reference to Toynbee*, but the attitude persists in his short reference to Sorokin as 'a prophet of doom.' Mentioning the "immensely elaborate tables" summarizing the result of Sorokin's empirical researches, of which he says "nobody can help being awed by the immense labor that is involved" in their collection, Geyl records that "they strike me as entirely unconvincing. To me it seems an illusion to think that so complicated, so many-sided, so protean and elusive a thing as a civilization can be reduced to a bare and simple language of rows of figures. The idea that by such a device the subjective factor in the final judgement can be eliminated is the worst illusion of all."

On this basis Geyl proceeds to ask a number of questions to which he evidently considers that none but answers damaging to Sorokin's work can be rendered. In that he is as mistaken as in his assertions that that "the one point fixed and determined beforehand" was "the conclusion that Western civilization is in a decline owing to a surfeit of materialism and other evils".... "Is it not that he began with a conviction and then set out to prove it?"** It was Professor Geyl who evidently 'began with a conviction and then set out to prove it.' In a sketchy, journalistic style, in three and a half pages, he appears to consider that he has dismissed Sorokin's life work. All the criticisms which he advanced, all the pitfalls into which he alleged that Sorokin had fallen, had of course been anticipated by Sorokin during the course of the ten years labor devoted to planning and executing *Social and Cultural Dynamics*. Literary historians usually shrink from logical, epistemological, and philosophical arguments and they have little interest in geometrical averages, graphic presentation, or numerical summations, but they might be expected to master them all if they wish to attack anyone who uses such methods as aids to thought.

It is necessary here again to recall that the whole set and attitude of mind in philosophical and historical academic circles at the time when Sorokin wrote was so opposed to any generalizing activity that it was almost impossible for anyone who chose to indulge in it to get a hearing. Many practising historians believed that generalizations were a source of error, and because some had been wrong, all must be condemned. 'The facts of life do not penetrate into the sphere in which our beliefs are cherished; so Sorokin was not a likely candidate for sympathetic or impartial consideration. Symptomatic of the climate of opinion at the time was the objection, not made with him in mind, but generally against

*P. Geyl, *op. cit.* p. 76.
**P. Geyl, *Debates with Historians* (London, Batsford, 1955), pp. 134-5.

all attempts "to trace a structure in history. . . . . the one and only true pattern into which alone all the facts will be found to fit." Sir Isaiah Berlin criticized this quest with words which the majority of historians in the English-speaking world could be counted upon to approve. He condemned the task as impossible. Any inquiry along such lines was, he said, "always *a priori* for all protests to the contrary." When any such attempt is made there is always "an obsessive pattern at work," however clear from doubt the facts themselves may be. Sir Isaiah concluded that "there is no historical thought properly speaking save where facts are distinct not merely from fiction, but from theory and interpretation in a lesser or greater degree."* Here speaks the voice of 'scientific' history, reminiscent of the words of a patent researcher who, after a lifetime of toil in the Public Record Office, said that when he considered the extraordinary difficulties he encountered in trying to establish the truth about a single past event, he marvelled at the facility with which some people could describe and arrange whole epochs of history.

Yet Sir Isaiah's pronouncement is the death of history unless his words "in a lesser or greater degree" are an escape clause to let thought aerate the facts in some way. For, as he well observed five years later in another context, a historian who stuck to so rigid and restrictive a code would not get far, because "however accurate his discoveries of fact, they remain those of an antiquarian, a chronicler, at best an archaeologist, but not those of an historian."** It was an established doctrine long before he wrote, in the two standard manuals on historical method and the study of history. Professor Ernest Bernheim in his *Lehrbuch der Historischen Methode* (five editions between 1889 and 1912) and Professors Ch. V. Langlois and Ch. Seignbos in their book *Introduction aux Etudes Historiques* (1897) Paris translated as *Introduction to the Study of History* (1898-1912) were concerned to set forth the pure doctrine of 'History for History's Sake.' Both volumes were severe in their rules for the painstaking discovery, the full examination of evidence, the confirmation from other sources, the weighing of authorities, the critical appraisal of authors, scholarship, scholars, and interpreters. Professor Bernheim in particular

*Sir I. Berlin, *Historical Inevitability* (New York, Oxford University Press, 1955), pp. 69-79. E. H. Carr, in *What Is History* (New York, Macmillan, 1961), pp. 86-89, comments shrewdly upon this essay of Sir Isaiah Berlin's and disposes also of many of the arguments of Professor Karl Popper which, he points out, have added confusion to the subject by their ambiguities and lack of precision.
**Sir Isaiah Berlin, "The Concept of Scientific History," in *History and Theory,* I, (1960), p. 27.

was very thorough in establishing the independence of history and in delimiting its relations with politics, sociology, philosophy, science, art, anthropology, ethnography, and enthnology. Yet in spite of the great vigor and assurance with which all three called for reverence for the unsullied purity of the practitioners of their craft, they had to end by admitting the necessity for generalizations.

It is all very well to assert that "all historical facts have an equal right to a place in history" and that "history cannot sacrifice a single fact." For it is evident that unless historians learn to group, to co-ordinate, to subordinate and to relate, their study would crush them under its own weight. To record "all the actions, all the thoughts, all the adventures of all men at all times" is so obviously ridiculous as a target for history that nobody would attempt it.* History is not the only discipline based upon facts. The others have found their own way out of the dilemma they faced "of being either complete and unknowable or else to be knowable and incomplete." All sciences in fact abridge, condense and frame hypotheses, grouping many facts under a few classificatory concepts.

In practice, the lack of valid generalized hypotheses in history is slurred over and ignored by conventional rubrics such as 'the Heroic Age,' 'the Classical Age,' 'the Hellenistic Age' in Grecian History; 'the Dark Ages,' 'the Medieval Age' or the 'Middle Ages,' and 'the Modern Age in European History.' None of these labels are concepts, none can be adequately defined. All are of relatively recent origin and they have no better title to respect then recent conventional usage which naturally confers upon them some prescriptive prestige.** Nervous publishers and editors hesitate to accept a history in which they were flouted or ignored. Yet such conventional divisions bear about as much relation to the philosophy of history as the running titles put on the top of the right hand pages of most books, usually by a harassed publisher's editor working against time, bear to the 'philosophy' of the book's subject-matter. If it is sought to dignify them by greater consideration, they are immediately vulnerable to Hegel's jibe that the ordinary historian who thinks that he is doing nothing but faithfully recording what he finds is by no means so

---

*Ch. V. Langlois and Ch. Seignobos, *Introduction to the Study of History* (London, Gerald Duckworth & Co., Ltd., 1898), pp. 262-3. The best recent comprehensive account of this "professional" or "scientific" history, *L'Histoire et Ses Methodes* forms part of the *Encyclopedie de la Pleiade* (Paris, Gallimard, 1961).
**O. Halicki's *The Limits and Divisions of European History* (London, Sheed and Ward, 1950) voices discontent with the traditional divisions without being aware of Sorokin's reformulations.

passive. On the contrary, 'he brings his categories with him and what he sees, he sees through them.'*

To have to repeat what should be obvious a century and more after Hegel wrote, is a sad commentary upon the honor paid to the continuity of thought in the profession of history which, above all others, should honor it. Dissatisfaction with the conventional divisions of history was becoming more evident and it is significant for the subject of this book that the great Dutch historian Huizinga voiced such discontent in the course of a lecture in 1929 on 'The Task of Cultural History.'**

Given the fact that historians must have categories, they should not therefore be allowed to smuggle them in surreptitiously, but be made to declare them 'on entry.' The grand operative principle in all scientific work must be "no unexamined assumptions." What should they be declared to be? To answer this question constitutes a philosophy of history. Strangely enough the very existence of such a 'philosophy' has been proclaimed to be philosophically unacceptable.

The Rejection of the Philosophy of History — Croce, Collingwood and Oakeshott

The recent fashion of adopting a somewhat condescending, if not scornful view of the work of Benedetto Croce should not be allowed to obscure the force and value of many of his opinions. He held Hegel in high respect and he followed in the spirit of that great genius, but did not copy his ideas literally or without critical reflection. His views on history challenged many established reputations and he saw no good in the philosophy of history, which indeed he denouced in no uncertain manner. His arguments were all the more forceful for being grounded in a deep philosophical position and a mastery of logical theory. They amounted therefore to just what he denounced, a forthright and forceful 'philosophy of history'. He dismissed as pseudo-histories, the chronicles and also examples of pseudo-history which used documents and narratives and sought to improve upon the bare record by transcribing and by striving for

---

*G. W. F. Hegel, *Vorlesungen über die Philosophic der Geschichte* (1848), p. 15. This work remains a most powerful statement of the place of reason in historical writing.
**Johan Huizinga, *Men and Ideas* (London, Eyre & Spottieswoode, 1960), pp. 17-76. A somewhat astringent view of Huizinga is presented in P. Geyl's *Encounters in History* (New York, Collins-Knowlton-Wing, Inc., 1963), pp. 188-237.

literary effect. Such histories may be correct, as books of reference, but they are not true history, (richtig'e non 'wahr'). Such philological historians succeed in killing any real interest in history by their doubts, hyper-critical attitudes and remoteness from living interests.

So remedies are sought for the intrinsic uncertainty and 'cold indifference to life' of philological histories based upon chronicles and documents regarded as objective things (*come cose esterne*). As they are presented without thought or logical coherence, they cannot be corrected by the solutions usually sought, which either try to compensate for their lack of thought by sentiment or to remedy their defective logic by aesthetic coherence. Croce condemns most of the famous writers of history on such grounds – Herodotus because his story turns too much upon the goings on of the gods; Livy, he said, wrote an epic on the heroes of the Roman Republic; Tacitus wrote tragedies; Droysen hymned the strong centralized State of Macedonia, the Prussia of Ancient Greece; Grote glorified democratic institutions; Mommsen was given to Caesar-worship; Thierry celebrated the middle classes, and so forth. The element of cariacture in these descriptions may be resented, but Croce's contention that such writings could be described as 'poetical history' has some point. Such work was based upon 'philological' history but built with conjectures supplied by the imagination of the historian who smuggled his interpretation into his narrative by question-begging insinuations such as 'probably,' 'we may say that,' 'evidently,' 'perhaps,' 'it may be suggested that,' and so forth, which are not challenged, as they should be, by the question 'how do you know that?'

Rhetorical or oratorical history, devised to teach a moral, is a third type of popular history, erected upon foundations provided by philological or poetical history. Such pragmatic (*practicistica*) history has all their deficiencies with the potentially dangerous quality of being a medium of propaganda as well. Pseudo-histories of the poetical or pragmatic type may have value as poetry or rhetoric for they may be able to infuse history with values which philological history ignores.

To dominate historical material by the principle and the criterion of value is precisely the reform which philosophers have demanded but, says Croce, the values brought by poetry and rhetoric are values of sentiment, not of thought. 'Because history is the history of mind or spirit, and because spirit is value, indeed the only value that it is possible to conceive, history is always history of values. Because also mind or spirit reveals itself as thought in the historian's conscience, the value which rules over history is the value of thought.' Croce's whole life-work was dominated by such a conception, indeed it appeared in the title to the most important series of his writings which were published as *'Filosofia dello spirito'*; a contribution to 'the philosophy of mind.' Mind, Spirit or Value was, he said, the unique problem of history and he was prepared to translate this philosophical language about 'mind' or 'spirit' into the more everyday words of 'Culture, Civilization, Progress.* With such a pronouncement, Croce might be thought to range himself among the philosophers of history and of sociology, yet he scorned both. He denounced 'Buckle and the many tiresome sociologists and positivists who lament with great pomposity and no less lack of intelligence that history lacks observation and experiment and who try to reduce history to a natural science.'**

His jibes were understandable at the time when he wrote, for many a crank had tried, in books and articles long since forgotten,o to popularize personal prejudices as a 'philosophy of history' in which as many plausible illustrations as possible were included as evidence. Sociology, said Croce was one of "those branches of literary or bookish production which seem to be condemned to inferiority and to lurk in a sort of scientific 'demi-monde,' because they lack a link with anterior research and findings about the subject with which they are concerned.† He was aware of Barth's attempt to equate sociology with history but he had a theory of his own which may well have seemed superior in the then state of sociology. History for Croce was philosophy. This truth, which could not be seen as long as history was limited to chronicling or philological history, rests on the logical ground that 'the universal (the predicate) is determined in the judgment by individualizing it.'††

This cryptic utterance needs explaining. The mind can only gain knowledge by relating its notions, intuitions, or awareness of particular things and thoughts to a wider range of ideas. Everything must be seen in some perspective. The singular needs to be seen in relation to the universal. 'Universals' for Croce were concepts. They universalize intuitions, providing greater awareness of wholes. A true concept has many representations, but no single representation and no number of representations can be equivalent to the concept by which they are

---

*B. Croce, *Teoria e Storia della Storiografia* (Bari, Laterza, 1917), pp. 21-31. English translation by D. Ainslie, *Theory & History of Historiography* (London, George C. Harrap & Co., Ltd., 1921), pp. 29-41.

**B. Croce, *op. cit.,* p. 36 (Eng. trans. p. 46)

†B. Croce, *History as the Story of Liberty,* trans. by S. Spriggs (London, George Allen & Unwin, Ltd., 1941), p. 197. See also pp. 137, 141.

††B. Croce, *Teoria e Storia della Storiographia,* pp. 49-50 (Eng. trans. p. 60).

expressed. There are many beautiful things and thoughts but the concept Beauty is not exhausted by them. Intuitions, representations, are always singular and individual but concepts are always universals. Together, intuitions and concepts make up the world as it is known. They are the predicates of judgments about reality. A sentence which has a universal as subject and another as predicate such as "the will is the practical form of the Spirit" is meaningless (a good rule to set besides Professor Emmet's dictum that abstract nouns should not be the subject of active verbs). The four concepts making up the unity of the world are the Beautiful, the True, the Useful, and the Good. Each is a unity or synthesis of opposites — beautiful-ugly; truth-error, utility-worthlessness; good-evil. There is a clear parallel here between the concepts of philosophy which, on Croce's theory, are also the concepts of history and the values — meanings — norms — which, as it has been seen, are Sorokin's interpretative principles in sociology.*

Croce's scheme clearly makes a theory of value paramount. With it and by its means he equates history and philosophy. This is the same theory of value as that which constitutes the essence of Sorokin's interpretation of sociology. Croce would probably have recoiled at the suggestion that sociology might be elevated into philosophy. Indeed, he denied 'sociology' the status of a concept on the ground that society is not universal but individual, related to the groupings of certain beings which representation has placed before the sociologist and which he has arbitrarily isolated from other coplexes of being that representation also placed, or could place before him.** It is evident that the kind of sociology which Croce knew was mainly "structural," "institutional" sociology, the very type that has been subordinated in Sorokin's thought to sociology resting upon values. Had Croce applied his concept of culture to the identification of cultural patterns in the lives of the men and women of past ages, he would have anticipated Sorokin.

*B. Croce, *Logic as the Science of the Pure Concept,* trans. by D. Ainslie (New York, Macmillan, 1917), pp. 324, 149, 92, 93, 41, 77, 96.

H. Wilson Carr, in *The Philosophy of Benedetto Croce* (New York, Macmillan, 1917), provides a clear exposition of Croce's views. Croce's four concepts which are able, as universals, to serve as predicates to explain the world are also those regarded in this book as the constituents of culture, except that in cultural life the concept of utility, or vitality (as Croce also explains it), may be assumed as a conditioning factor making life and all cultural values possible. F. Battaglia's *La Valeur dans L'Histoire* (Paris, Aubier, 1955) contains a useful summary statement of the theories of Croce and Gentile.

**B. Croce, *Logic as the Science of the Pure Concept,* p. 42.

By making value-theory the interpretative principle in sociology, and by explaining values as meanings and norms which can be seen to be the same as Croce's universal concepts of the beautiful, the true, the useful and the good, Sorokin has elevated sociology into a philosophy. Croce's arguments that history is really philosophy may be matched by the assertion that Sorokin has, by his historical studies, shown that sociology is congruent with history and at the same time, by his value theory, with philosophy also. Since Sorokin's theory had emerged independently as sociology from a comprehensive factual study of history, it provides striking inductive, empirical support for Croce's philosophical acumen and insight which at the same time Sorokin extended and applied to the past as a whole. Value theory was again vindicated as a supreme interpretative principle.

Sorokin has gone further by showing how value-patterns, as logico-cultural supersystems, change over time, so providing a radically new basis for the explanation both of the quality and character of the particular representations of the value concepts and of the causes and nature of their change.

Croce's theory was not so complete an axiology because he did not give the detailed, factual accounts of the content of value systems which Sorokin has provided. Croce's theories have been strongly attacked; in particular, his equation of philosophy and history. He wrote a great deal; there have been complaints about the inadequacy of some of the English translations and much has not been translated, so his views are not available as a whole, except in Italian. Because he did not state his views with sufficient precision and because they lend themselves to cariacture, misunderstanding, and misrepresentation, Croce has been held to be a dangerous guide; dangerous because he obscures the hard, vitally necessary toil of the fact-finding historians whom he dubs philological historians. The "blight of Crocean idealism" has been offered as an explanation of the backward state of sociology in Italy.* If idealism is a blight, the implication would appear to be that positivism is its remedy. Unfortunately the crash of all such hopes shows how misplaced those hopes were. As Sorokin has convincingly shown, it is by working out ideas such as those of Croce, that progress in sociology has come. It has also been objected that Croce's equation of philosophy and history is unnecessary. To some it even seems tautologous and meaningless, in the

---

*F. Ferrarotti, "Sociology in Italy," in H. Becker and A. Boskoff, eds., *Modern Sociological Theory* (New York, Dryden Press, 1957), p. 696.

way that sentences composed of universals are, on his own showing. But so summary a statement as his 'history is philosophy' is based upon a wealth of argument which should not be written-off as meaningless. Similar considerations defend Sorokin's concepts of 'sensate' 'Idealist,' or 'ideational' because they are summary labels capable of immediate translation into a vast range of appropriate empirical facts, in the same way that labels such 'the halogens' are to those trained in chemistry.* What has not been successfully impugned however is the essential basis of Croce's contention that the mind by which history, philosophy, and all other subjects are studied, must and can only form its judgments by means of concepts, and that these concepts can ultimately be seen to be examples of four major (value) concepts: the beautiful, the true, the useful, and the good. It is with these concepts that Sorokin explains the story of men in societies, past and present.

Paradoxically also the very possibility of a philosophy of history has also been rejected by an acute critic who nevertheless, like Croce, argues with force and conviction for value-theory and for a 'coherence' theory of

---

*Amid a vast literature, Croce is criticized by:

G. Calogero, "On the So-called Identity of History and Philosophy," in *Philosophy and History Essays presented to Ernst Cassirer* (Oxford, Clarendon Press, 1936), pp. 35-52;

P. Weiss, *History: Written and Lived* (Carbondale, Ill., Southern Illinois University Press, 1962), pp. 43, 82;

M. Mandelbaum, *The Problem of Historical Knowledge* (New York, Liveright, 1938), pp. 39-57;

G. J. Renier, *History, its Purpose and Method* (London, George Allen & Unwin Ltd., 1950), pp. 41-3;

M. Cohen, *The Meaning of Human History* (La Salle, Ill., Open Court, 1961), pp. 49-52;

A. Stern, *Philosophy of History and the Problem of Values* s' Gravenhage, Mouton, 1962), pp. 22, 25-6.

J. Macmurray in *The Clue to History* (S.C.N. Press, 1938) does not mention Croce, but proclaims that "the reality of human life is action, not thought," and condemns the view that "it is the world of pure spirit alone that matters" (p. 235). On these grounds he explained the then real triumph of Hitler and Mussolini. Neither Croce nor Sorokin were devising a strategy to change the world in this sense but were seeking philosophical and sociological explanations of the nature of the world of human societies in historical times. To credit two such enemies of humanity as Hitler and Mussolini with qualities drawn from "the world of pure spirit" would be repugnant, but millions of their supporters were deluded into following them by belief in their propaganda. That propaganda made its appeal inevitably to the supposed interests of its audience, upon a low, emotive, level. Nazis and Fascists were eventually overthrown by "action," which was certainly inspired by the "world of pure spirit" of another and "purer" kind.

truth. "Without valuation there is no practical judgment, no activity," wrote Professor Michael Oakeshott; "the criterion by which we determine the truth or falsehood of our judgments of value, is not correspondence with some external standard, but the coherence of the world of value itself." So also of truth, "practical truth conforms to the general character of truth; it is the world of practical experience as a coherent whole, the world of practical fact." Published four years before *Social and Cultural Dynamics,* such ideas have clear affinities with Sorokin's standpoint and notably the principle of logico-meaningful cultural systems. Whereas Sorokin was to carry his ideas forward as the foundation of an integral sociology and as a philosophy of history, Professor Oakeshott did not do so. Instead he rejected the possibility of a philosophy of history in two short pages. Such a philosophy, he said, would be bound to fail. It might try to discover general laws, which however would 'involve the complete destruction of history.' It might assume the possibility of taking "a view of finite existence from some standpoint outside the actual course of finite life," but then "nothing recognizable in history remains." Finally it might purport to "discover and elucidate the plan or plot of History," and that would either be a skeleton or general plan without details, which might be philosophy, but would not be history; or it might mean "a selective simplification of history based upon some assumed notion of general significance, such as Hegel's, when it is indistinguishable from history itself." Then it fails for the same reasons that, in Professor Oakeshott's opinion, 'the attempt to find the world of unqualified reality in the world of historical events' must fail.*

The writings of Croce and Oakeshott powerfully influenced the philosophical views of Professor R. G. Collingwood at Oxford who did much to make them better known in the course of his own independent philosophical work. For that he has not had the recognition which he deserves. In the present context his views on the nature of metaphysical thinking are especially significant. By using them as an explanation of philosophical development, he also suggests a philosophy of history which has affinities with Sorokin's conclusions, of which however he does not appear to have had any knowledge. He said, for example, that "metaphysics is the attempt to find out what absolute presuppositions have been made by this or that person or group of persons, on this or that

*M. Oakeshott, *Experience and its Modes* (New York, Cambridge University Press, 1923), pp. 274, 278, 267, 154-5. This opinion was later confirmed in his essay, "The Activity of Being an Historian," in *Historical Studies* (Cambridge, Bowes and Bowes, 1958).

occasion or group of occasions . . . how the groups are organized; whether different absolute presuppositions are made by different individuals or races or nations or classes . . . or whether the same have been made *semper, ubique, ab omnibus."* "In metaphysics as in every other department of history the secret of success is to study the background."*

On this basis, which is essentially that of Sorokin, Collingwood was able to carry the matter beyond Croce's and Oakeshott's paradoxical conclusion that the facts of history must be present facts and that the historic past can only arise out of ideas in the present based upon evidence existing in the present. According to that view, very closely argued and retained by Croce, the historical past, in so far as it can be known, is not past at all. It is not even something surviving into the present, it is the present. It is true that the historian carefully and critically thinks about the past as past, but the historian and his thought live in the present.

This paradoxical statement has naturally been criticized and denied for the same reasons that the similar statement of Berkeley, *esse est percipi,* has been controverted on the ground, for instance, that it asserts no more than the tautology that we cannot think of anything existing except when we do think of it. The essence of this belief that 'to exist' means 'to be perceived' by some mind can be applied to history as easily as to everything else. History for Croce is an àct of thought, it is 'the form in which the full reality of existence is presented to consciousness. Knowledge of a past fact can only arise in relation to some present living interest, not to a past interest. To hold that "the past did exist while the present does exist," is not a sufficient reason to distinguish the past from the present. It seems to fly in the face of common sense, yet this is what Croce's theory of the identity of history and philosophy involves.** It has been assailed by such a question as "To what does the historian refer when, in the present, he thinks about what he regards as the past?" If he has to re-create that past in imagination, whence does he derive that which is to be re-created? The word implies that something existed, otherwise it could not be re-created. Such arguments distinguish the historian's past events from the present state of mind by which he contemplates them and they may be shortly stated as, 'If no past, then surely, no history?' Since neither Croce nor Oakeshott were ready to abolish history, there must, thought Collingwood, be a third alternative and this, he suggested, was "a

*R. G. Collingwood, *An Essay on Metaphysics* (Oxford, Clarendon Press, 1940), pp. 47, 191.
**H. Wildon Carr, *The Philosophy of Benedetto Croce* (New York, Macmillan, 1917), pp. 193, 194, 199.

living past which, because it was thought and not a mere natural event, can be re-enacted in the present and in that re-enactment (be) known as past." History then becomes not a 'mode' of experience in Oakeshott's word, "but an integral part of experience itself."*

That Sorokin's views are able to accommodate and absorb such ideas, should be evident. The logico-meaningful cultural supersystems by which he explained the broad characteristics of past ages are, as Croce said they must be, the product of thought and not mere philological, poetical, or pragmatic notions dressed up to look like history. They satisfy Collingwood's criterion by making plain the nature of the different absolute presuppositions according to which the lives of the men of the past were organized. They provide that background which Collingwood proclaimed to be essential for success, while satisfying also the requirement that history should be its own criterion and not be supposed to depend for its validity on something outside itself. Croce, Oakeshott, and Collingwood were aware of the development of sociology which they all distrusted, possibly for the very sound reason that some of the inadequate sociologists they knew seemed anxious to provide criteria of validity to history. Croce had denounced as an absurdity, "the positivistic fiction that history can be reduced to a science. . . . . a classification and statistical table of reality. . . . by substituting colorless formulae and empty abstractions which are applicable to several epochs at once or to all times, for the narration of individual reality, a tendency which appears in sociology and in its polemic against what it calls psychological or individual history and in favor of institutional or social history."**

Collingwood, like Croce, explained the rise of sociology by describing it as a corrective for the dull, uninteresting results of the labors of historical fact-finders who had subjected vast masses of evidence to accurate and critical examination with a precision that was new in historical writing. While strictly in accord with positivist methods, their efforts do not, as the positivists assumed and hoped, yield those new uniformities upon which the laws of history might be based. Auguste Comte tried to remedy the deficiency when he used the raw material about human life collected by the historians from which he tried to discover causal connections and so to establish the new science of sociology. The sociologist would thus be a kind of super-historian, a title

*R. G. Collingwood, *The Idea of History* (Oxford, Clarendon Press, 1946), pp. 154, 158.
**B. Croce, *Logic as the Science of Pure Concept* (New York, Macmillan, 1917). pp. 305-6.

he would merit because he applied scientific thought to weight, assess, group, and order the facts, to all of which the pure empirical historian who discovered them, scared of making value judgments, gives equal weight. For an impressionable public, this is little different from no weight at all. For the time the 'sociological' approach using value judgments exerted on enormous influence, particularly when Karl Marx shaped it for his own purposes. Even so austere a professional historian as J. B. Bury could say in 1904 that 'history. . . . is subordinate to sociology.'

Yet the new approach failed. It was, said Collingwood, natural for "scissors-and-paste historians who have become disgusted with the work of copying out other people's statements and who are conscious of having brains. . . . should use them. . . . by inventing a system of pigeon-holes in which to arrange their learning. This is the origin of all those schemes and patterns into which history has again and again been forced." Collingwood did not mention such 'pigeon-holes' as 'Ancient,' 'Medieval' and 'Modern,' 'Classic,' 'Romantic,' 'Baroque' and so forth, but he did include among the offenders Vico, Kant, Hegel, Comte, Marx, Flinders Petrie, Spengler, and Arnold Toynbee. All such schemes "are the offspring of caprice" and if any of them flourished, it was not owing to their scientific cogency "but because it has become the orthodoxy of what is in fact though not necessarily in name, a religious community." Marxism in particular, he said, has had "an important magical value" for this reason.

Collingwood's own recommendation for the proper understanding of history was that "the historian must re-enact the past in his own mind" by thought and reflection; thought being both immediacy, as part of the present flow of consciousness, and mediation, when the object of historical knowledge is revived in the historian's mind. The act of thinking itself, which is the proper object of historical knowledge, is reflective thought. It is not merely immediate, liable to be carried away by the flow of consciousness. In writing history, Collingwood said, the historian "must be able to enter with equal sympathy into the essential features and values of each way of life: he must re-experience them both in his own mind as objects of historical knowledge."* That is all very well, but by what value judgments is the historian to arrange his ideas? It is surprising that Collingwood did not put more emphasis upon 'value' in his theory of history, for he was keenly interested in aesthetics. Failing to supply interpretative value systems, he was unable to provide the key to the mystery.

*R. G. Collingwood, *The Idea of History* (Oxford, Clarendon Press, 1946), pp. 128-9, 148-9, 264, 265, 300, 304-6, 308, 327.

Some German Philosophers and the Philosophy of History

In these debates the pioneer work of German philosophers was not ignored, but its impact on the English-speaking world was much less than it deserved to be. In particular, the contribution of the great German philosopher Wilhelm Dilthey (1833-1911) was not appreciated. Its bulk, its fragmentary uncompleted form, its difficulty, even for German-speaking people, and the fact that for long none of it was translated, delayed its impact and obscured the light of its vigorous, seminal, ideas. Dilthey sought, in the record of human reality in Time, to identify social and cultural trends, religions, and philosophies. He was 'historicist' in the best sense, not as one wishing to impose a pattern on history nor as one who thought it possible to make far-reaching predictions of its probable course, although he was prepared to believe that, because there is continuity, the idea of possible regularities need not be wholly excluded. For Dilthey, meaning, significance, values, and purposes were pre-eminently important. Furthermore "in the course of historical events periods can be delimited in which a unity of mental climate,"* a whole way of life, "took shape, reached its Zenith, and disintegrated again. In each such period there exists an inner structure common to them all, which determines the connections of the parts to the whole."**

Dilthey therefore recognized that a cultural system has a structure and development, although he saw no way of discovering a law of such development. He rejected philosophies of history and the then novel subject of sociology for the very good reason that nothing then available satisfied his conception of the world of mind and of values. When it is remembered that he was a young man of 24 when Auguste Comte died, that he witnessed the publication of the works of John Stuart Mill and Herbert Spencer and recalled Mommsen's arrival in Berlin, the pioneer nature of his own ideas stands out all the more strikingly. Later, as sociologists moved more in his direction he was more sympathetic; to Simmel for example. Collingwood's complaint, that owing to his interest in psychology he ended by surrendering to positivism, is too sweeping; it should not obscure the powerful impetus many of his writings gave to a

---

*H. P. Rickman, ed., *Meaning in History: W. Dilthey's Thoughts on History and Society* (London, George Allen and Unwin, Ltd., 1961), p. 155. This is a useful survey, with translations of short extracts from *Der Aufbau der geschichtlichen Welt in den Geisteswissenschaften.*
**Ibid. p. 149.

fuller philosophical approach to the problems of culture, humanism, and value.*

In Germany, despite the reluctance of Dilthey to prepare material for publication, his work was recognized by keéner minds upon whom it exercised a powerful influence. Among the many German thinkers stimulated or inspired by him were von Gierke (1841-1921), Simmel (1858-1915), Rickert (1863-1936), Windleband (1848-1915), Troeltsch (1865-1923), Othmer Spann (1878-1950), Karl Mennheim (1893-1947), and many more. Hugo von Hofmannsthal testified to his influence beyond the realm of academic philosophy: "Wunderbar die Luft um diesen alten Mann."** Dilthey's insistence upon separating humanistic studies, *Geisteswissenschaften,* from natural science struck a note which found a greater response in countries with a Latin tradition than in the English-speaking world. Upon it Croce based his philosophy of mind. In Spain, Ortega y Gasset produced many striking ideas in the light of what he had learned both from Dilthey and from the men in Germany who had profited from Dilthey's insight. In Germany more than in any other country the debate about cultural life was far more animated and profound than elsewhere and for this Dilthey deserved the main credit. To trace the manner in which *Kultur* in Germany became a keyword in the philosophy of history when both that subject and the word itself provoked, in England, abuse rather than interest, would need far more space than is available here. No German philosopher seems however to have been able to develop that heritage of thought to the point where a consistent, viable, philosophy of history emerged.† Rickert was outstanding among the successors of Dilthey. He sought to replace Dilthey's concept of 'science of mind,' *Geisteswissenschaft,* by 'science of

*R. G. Collingwood, *The Idea of History* (Oxford, Clarendon Press, 1946), p. 174
H. A. Hodges, *Wilhelm Dilthey – An Introduction* (London, Routledge and Kegan Paul, 1944)
W. Dilthey, *Gesammelte Schriften* (Stuttgart, Teubner, 1914-1938) I-X. Volume VII, *Der Aufbau der geschichtlichen Welt in den Geisteswissenschaften,* is most significant in this context.
**"There is a wonderful radiance about this venerable man."
†M. Mandelbaum, *The Problem of Historical Knowledge* (New York, Liveright, 1938) provides one of the very few short critical accounts of this development, but it now needs revising in the light of subsequent development. See also the pertinent criticism of it on many points in Charlotte W. Smith's *Carl Becker on History and the Climate of Opinion* (Ithaca, N.Y., Cornell Univ. Press, 1956), pp. 91-100. A much more comprehensive and thorough study is H. von Srbik's *Geist and Geschichte vom deutschen Humanismus bis zur Gegenwart,* 2 vols, (Salzburg, Otto Muller, 1950; München, Bruckmann).

culture,' *Kulturwissenschaft,* a development which Sorokin was to adopt
and to carry further.

History as Culture — Meinecke

Among historians, the later work of Friedrich Meinecke is especially
noteworthy. In 1928 he contributed an article to the *Historische
Zeitschrift* (No. 137) "Kausalitäten und Werte in der Geschichte," later
reprinted in his *Staat und Persönlichkeit* (1933). These dates are
interesting because he anticipates Sorokin's conclusion without having
undertaken the massive toil required in order to write *Social and Cultural
Dynamics,* which Sorokin did not publish until 1937. Describing the
search for causes and the effort to understand and to expound values as
the two great explanatory principles evident in the modern development
of historiography, Meinecke gave the first place to values. The search for
causes and the reliance upon "value" as an explanatory principle are both
evidences of mankind's age-old quest for truth. Because Truth is itself one
of the main supreme values, the search for causal explanation is, he said,
subordinate; "behind the search for causalities there is always, implicitly
or explicitly, the search for values, for that which we know as culture in
the deepest sense." History thus becomes, as it became with Sorokin,
"nothing but the history of culture, meaning by 'culture' the production
of unique spiritual values and of historical individuals." These spiritual
values are not alone those "created through effort consciously directed to
religious, philosophical, political and social thought constructions and to
works of art and science. Others grow immediately from the necessities of
concrete practical existence." In this practical, day-to-day existence, man
remains, it is true, "upon the plane of nature but with a glance lifted
upwards to the high peaks of value for guidance. In satisfying the
necessities of life he tries to do so in a way that allows at the same time
the realization of the true, or the good or the beautiful."* Sorokin, the
sociologist, and Meinecke (1862-1954), the most eminent German
academic historian of the twentieth century, are thus found to be in
agreement about the essence of history and of the life of man in society.
Sorokin does not appear to have read Meinecke's famous essay. Like his
own work, it probably needs a new generation of historians before its
influence begins to be felt. Yet the cultural interpretation of history was

*F. Meinecke, *Staat und Persönlichkeit* (Berlin, Mittler, 1933), p. 47.

'in the air' during the lifetime of both these eminent men. Meinecke quotes from what he called a "beautiful letter" written by the German philosopher Albert Dove to Rickert on January 27, 1899 trying to persuade him that the great interest in history arises not only because the past may have paved the way for, or even 'caused' the present, both of which ideas seemed then the main inspiration of 'scientific' history. There is a deeper bond as long as life has any meaning.' We leap across vast gaps in Time in which 'causes may or may not have operated,' 'by the force of simple sympathy,' in other words, because we are moved by a sense of values simply because of our common humanity. Here, a view of the deeper nature of history, made possible by a cultural interpretation, is disclosed, which is of a different order of thought from that so-called 'scientific' view based upon an analogy of historical method with the methods of the natural sciences. Meinecke, in subordinating the scientific or mechanistic approach, did not for one moment seek to abolish or neglect it. It is the historian's first task. "To begin with, the road of causality must be undeviatingly pursued to utmost limit."*

It is the first task, but it is only a beginning. What is essential is to clarify ideas about the cultural values of the past. Almost as an aside, Meinecke dropped a pregnant hint — 'Whole ages and generations can find nourishment in the cultural values of a particular period in the past which are specifically related to them.' Such a natural affinity should not of course be taken to extreme lengths so that it clouds or perverts attitudes to life as it must be lived. Fear of such danger led "a strong spirit such as Max Weber" into the opposite error, "provoking his unrealistic project of a value-free historical research for reasons themselves highly charged with values. 'I wish to see,' he said, 'how much I can endure.'" Partly because of such perplexities, but above all from their intrinsic importance, Meinecke regarded a "determination of the essence of values as the main concern of philosophy."** Instead, in England, where no echo of his words seems to have been heard, linguistic and analytical interests left no time or energy for progress along lines already indicated by Laird and others. The study of the humanities, and of sociology as essentially of the humanities, has been unnecessarily retarded as a result.

Progress in the direction of giving more weight to cultural values as the best explanatory principles in these subjects was necessarily slow by reason of academic conservatism, by the vogue of mechanistic, 'materialist' interpretations of which Marxism is the most conspicuous, and also by

*Ibid, p.33
**Ibid, pp. 40, 48, 49

false trails laid by eminent historians and sociologists who were seeking for new light and new principles. Rickert, for example, in his pioneer effort to invoke cultural influences in trying to clarify the logical and methodological difference between the natural sciences and history, was criticized by Meinecke on Platonic lines for looking upon values as in some way 'adhering to historical realities instead of being seen to be realities in their own right.' Alfred Weber, brother of Max Weber, wrote, he said, not as a historian but as a sociologist. He disclaimed philosophical competence but nevertheless saw the desirability of linking cultural history with sociology. In doing so he became a prisoner to his own prior analysis of world history as a matter of the characteristics of certain closed historical systems, *Geschichtskörper,* which he thought he could detect in the long story of human evolution. Such were the Chinese, the Indian, the Egyptian-Babylonian. They constituted man's first step, *erste Stufe.* The second step was the Persian-Jewish and Mediterranean cultural area. Then followed the third step which was taken in the Byzantine-Slav-East, the Islamic, and the Western historical systems. Within each he sought to detect similarities in social structure. Despite shrewd and suggestive remarks, to be expected from a veteran scholar of Weber's distinction, although many were concealed in language more involved than that of Henry James at his most prolix, no convincing new synthesis emerged. Sorokin studied it but he did not think that Alfred Weber had advanced matters notably by it. He paid a tribute nevertheless to the lead Weber had tried to give to the effort to get sociologists to 'attack the central problems of social and cultural life, to understand the historical processes, their meanings, their how and why in their totality' instead of resting content with the 'sterile and pedantic . . . pure study of forms and descriptions of little facts (however precise).'*

Meinecke did not develop his profound insight into a detailed exposition, but he did urge his countrymen, after Hitler's war had brought disaster to Germany, to draw inspiration from the age of Goethe, when a truer cultural way of life held great promise.

The Unresolved Problem of the Relativity of Cultural Values

The problem which none who relied upon values as a key to the understanding of historical problems could surmount was the difficulty of

---

*P. A. Sorokin, *Social and Cultural Dynamics* (New York, Bedminster Press, 1941), Vol. IV, p. 159.

getting agreement generally upon standards of value. It was seen that these standards change, thus introducing a relativism into all judgments which seemed to ruin them as standards. Although Dilthey launched the idea of cultural systems with their inner structure, no use was made of the idea until Sorokin undertook the empirical research to discover whether cultural systems could be identified and, if so, what their content might be.

One of Sorokin's very highly gifted contemporaries, Ernst Cassirer, probably the most eminent German philosopher after Dilthey whose philosophical position he shared, also came near to anticipating Sorokin's theory of the nature of culture and of cultural development. A man of immense learning, amazing memory, endowed with great power of application and energy, Cassirer recalls Sorokin's exceptional qualities, including his wide literary and artistic interests. He was working on his theory of concepts a little later than was Croce in Italy, but he took the whole world of philosophy and of cultural life as his field of action. Like Dilthey, he saw the need to "take cultural reality as given in human experience and to analyze its basic forms and the functional interrelations of these forms with one another." As a neo-Kantian, Cassirer was committed to the idea of a 'free or undetermined, creative, symbolic expression of the life process.' As he deemed Kant's ontological ideas to be inadequate, there was, as Cassirer saw, an urgent need for some theory or principles able to integrate all the sciences and humanities within a single, unified cultural perspective. Cultural values seemed the obvious source of such a unifying principle, but Cassirer was not better able than Dilthey to find a universal criterion in them because both saw that such values were relative to each age and to society. How Cassirer sought to grapple with the difficulty cannot here be pursued, but may be seen in his many writings; notably in his great work *The Philosophy of Symbolic Forms (1923-29)* and in his *Essay on Man* (1944).

Despite his splendid achievement, Cassirer failed to hit upon a theory such as Sorokin's. His functionalistic harmony of culture has been described as "purely formal," providing "no criterion for the evaluation of the content or "substance" of any given cultural configuration."* Cassirer was not alone deficient in this respect, for, until Sorokin's massive survey, the materials for such a study had not been gotten together and systematized. Immense though Cassirer's learning was, he never achieved a

---

*D. Bidney, "On the Philosophical Anthropology of Ernst Cassirer and its Relation to the History of Anthropological Thought," in P. A. Schlipp, ed., *The Philosophy of Ernst Cassirer* (Evanston, Ill., Library of Living Philosophers, 1949), pp. 500, 469.

comprehensive theory of cultural development. Another of his friendly commentators perceived this shortcoming in Cassirer's otherwise brilliant presentation of "the spirit of the Renaissance." Cassirer's statement, he said was "only an elaborate way of saying that "we 'perceive' certain common 'tendencies' running through Renaissance thought" – and he asked, "is Cassirer trying to indicate something deeper by his 'ideal types' his 'unities of direction,' his 'common task' and 'will'?"*

In the light of such antecedents, the significance of Sorokin's contribution stands out all the more clearly. Like Cassirer, Meineke and others, he was seeking deeper explanations of human culture and its development. In his logico-meaningful cultural supersystems, he has presented a fertile hypothesis by which the whole vast complex world of history could be seen to exhibit something in the nature of comprehensible patterns. By their means he was able, as it has been seen already, to accept the relativity of cultural standards while still preserving cultural values as such, as the essence, the *leit-motif,* of the sociological and also of the historical process. His is, and Dilthey and Croce might have welcomed it, a philosophical solution, grounded in a theory of knowledge, validated by an empirical discovery of correlations, and found to be explicable by universals of the greatest generality, themselves tested explanatory concepts which have been available and widely used at least since the time of Plato.

In that way Sorokin completed previous partial views, bringing into focus a vastly greater range of values and interests, by no means only those originating in the English-speaking world. There, it was tragic that Collingwood's career was cut short by death in 1943 at the early age of 52, so that he was unable to take up the question of value in history in greater detail. Croce had given very clear pointers in that direction and he was by no means alone. Concentration upon value theory as a means of elucidating history, although it was a foremost tenet of both Croce and Gentile in Italy, was perhaps sidetracked in the critical examination of that identity between philosophy and history which they had proclaimed. As developed by Sorokin, a comprehensive theory of value-patterns as a foundation for sociology now allows the subject to escape the strictures by which Croce, Collingwood, and others dismissed it. The very values which Croce proclaimed as the realm of mind have been shown by Sorokin to be the vital element in sociology. If parallels or uniformities in sociology are

---

*J. H. Randall, Jr., "Cassirer's Theory of History as Illustrated in his Treatment of Renaissance Thought," in *The Philosophy of Ernst Cassirer, op. cit.,* p. 722.

discernible in its development down the ages, they do not involve 'the complete destruction of history' as Oakeshott thought that laws in history would do. On the contrary, they exhibit history vivified with meaning. Sorokin's succession of cultural supersystems, discovered within the historical process, provides that "view of finite existence from some standpoint outside the actual course of human life" at any one time which Oakeshott regarded as destructive of everything "recognizable in history." On the contrary, the detection of the special values of a cultural system in any one period greatly assists in the recognition of its true historical quality, as the example cited above from Etruscan or Mycenaean history suggests. Finally, Oakeshott's fear that a philosophy of history would be 'indistinguishable from history itself' can be seen to lose force, and for the same reasons. It may be thought less a condemnation than an ideal to strive to achieve. If Croce considered that his four universal concepts of the beautiful, the true, the useful, and the good did in fact point to that 'world of unqualified reality in the world of historical events' which Oakeshott ruled out as impossible, Sorokin certainly showed how their varying manifestations are discernible in the broad attitude towards life which the historical record reveals men as having adopted during the course of human history.

Generalizations in History

Historians in the United States of America were as slow to take much interest in the philosophy of history as were their professional colleagues in the rest of the English-speaking world. The very idea of generalization, or of abstract thought in a subject generally supposed to be entirely factual, objective, and as 'scientific' as possible, was repugnant to most working historians. A brief account of one *cause célèbre* will indicate the general attitude they took towards the philosophy of history in the first half of the twentieth century.

In the year 1932 a slim volume appeared in the United States with the intriguing title *The Heavenly City of the Eighteenth-Century Philosophers** which was to enjoy great vogue. Its success was remarkable because it contained the text of only four lectures in which Professor Carl L. Becker ran lightly through a vast subject, making points rather than

---

*Carl L. Becker, *The Heavenly City of the Eighteenth-Century Philosophers* (New Haven, Yale Univ. Press, 1932).

presenting a closely argued thesis. Such was his wit and stylistic elegance, qualities somewhat rare among academic historians at that time, that his book survived far longer than most Foundation lectures. Twenty-five years later it was the subject of a solemn symposium, duly recorded in a book longer than his own, in which fourteen historians aired their views about its merits and failings.*

Becker had pointed out with engaging wit and urbanity that the philosophers of the Enlightenment had won their reputation for thoroughgoing iconoclasm because they sought to replace theology and the precise deductive logic of St. Thomas Aquinas and others, by concentrating the power of human reason upon the facts of natural phenomena ("the most important event in the intellectual history of modern times" p. 21). Yet, it would be a rash man who would refuse to recognize 'the extraordinary ingenuity and acumen' displayed by St. Thomas. On his own ground, his arguments cannot be overthrown (p. 11). If to reason well is to be a rationalist then St. Thomas was a rationalist. Becker was impressed by the evident fact that both Voltaire, the 'rationalist;' and St. Thomas Aquinas 'the man of faith' had "a profound conviction that their beliefs could be reasonably demonstrated." "In a very real sense it may be said of the eighteenth century that it was an age of faith as well as of reason, and of the thirteenth century that it was an age of reason as well as of faith" (p. 8). This was no paradox, said Becker, the *Philosophes* were "nearer the Middle Ages, less emancipated from the preconceptions of medieval Christian thought, than they quite realized or we have commonly supposed." (p. 29) "There is more of Christian philosophy in their writings than has yet been dreamt of in our histories." (p. 31) It is true that the philosophers of the Enlightenment demolished the Heavenly City of St. Augustine but they did so "only to rebuild it with more up-to-date materials." (p. 31) They no longer believed in the Christian paradise, but they had beliefs of another kind. "For the love of God they substituted the love of humanity; for the vicarious atonement, the perfectibility of man through his own efforts; and for the hope of immortality in another world, the hope of living in the memory of future generations."

Becker's ideas created something of a *furore* among historians. Some more hide-bound academics affected to dismiss them as a more or less literary *jeu d'esprit,* a shocking exhibit of 'the love of abstract

*R. O. Rockwood, ed., *Carl Becker's heavenly City Revisited* (Ithaca, N. Y., Cornell University Press, 1956).

speculation.' Others defended his book, while yet others raked over every statement in it to show how much there was in it that they could amplify, improve, and correct.

The whole debate, lasting a quarter of a century and more, is simply and easily put into perspective on Sorokin's principles. What Becker had discovered in 1932 was that the climate of opinion in the thirteenth century was, in Sorokin's description, an ideational merging into an idealistic cultural system. That St. Thomas Aquinas reasoned acutely from accepted Christian theological presuppositions is evident. That Locke and Hume reasoned acutely with the very different presuppositions of a sensate society to show that sense impressions and not *a priori* notions are the source of truth, is equally evident. Some of Becker's critics even accused him of equating the two cultures because he had pointed out that men reasoned in each of them. Neither the critics nor Becker saw the real point at issue, though Becker spoke of 'climate of opinion' and *Weltanschauung.* However, as soon as Sorokin's 'idealistic' and 'sensate' categories are brought into action, together with his demonstration that cultural survivals and hangovers persist long after major tendencies and trends have brought radically new cultural presuppositions to the fore, then the whole controversy sparked off by Becker's stimulating little book is at once transformed. He was too good a historian, too responsible a thinker to be easily faulted, although the plodding specialist, scared of generalizations, might call in question some of his sentences. He did not leave his theme until he had pointed to the first cracks in the proud assertiveness of the sensate philosophy. After Hume "had remorselessly exposed the futility of reason" in the matter of ultimate good and evil in the world, he said, we "experience a slight chill, feeling of apprehension. . . . . we are suddenly aware of . . . . . a faint far-off tremor running beneath the solid ground of common sense." In the face of this threat to their confident complacency the philosophers of the Enlightenment followed Rousseau's lead and "tempered reason with sentiment." (p. 68-69) They heralded the progressive weakening of sensate cultural values.

It is remarkable that throughout this controversy the key concept of changing cultural value patterns was never once overtly recognized and brought to the forefront of the argument. Latent in Becker's lectures, which were written six years before Sorokin's *Social and Cultural Dynamics,* that new interpretation had been available to Becker's later critics throughout nearly twenty years. Yet by none were they mentioned. The very idea that changing cultural value-patterns, in Sorokin's logico-meaningful sense, provided a clear, convincing solution to their problem, was unrecognized. "Value" was not mentioned as a fundamental concept in the history of human society. The work of Dilthey, Ricker, Meinecke, and others to establish such an idea had no recognition. It is to be hoped that future editions of Becker's little book will be accompanied by some recognition of the manner in which his thesis was later the subject of Sorokin's far-reaching investigations, into which, with slight adjustments, it may so easily be seen to fit.

Wide-ranging and profound ideas, involving the very essence of philosophy, sociology, and history were therefore slow in attracting interest from practising historians and academic teachers of history. It will come as something of an anticlimax to follow the views reached after six years work by the Committee on Historical Analysis of the American Social Science Research Council and reported in 1963 in *Generalization in the Writing of History*. Although presented as the report of a committee, it contains nothing but individual, signed contributions. Professor Louis Gottschalk as editor contributed a foreword and conclusion as well as the only attempt to analyze, in any detail, the nature of the generalizations in which historians are likely to deal. A quarter of a century previously, Professor Morris Ginsberg had performed a similar service for sociology in an earlier symposium volume, as one of its four editors, so it is possible to compare ideas about the scale of generalizations to be found in the works of historians and sociologists. Summarized, they are as follows:

Degrees and Types of Generalization

Professor Ginsberg's List in Sociology*	Professor Gottschalk's List in History**
1 Empirical associations or correlations.	1 No generalizations.
2 Formulations of conditions under which institutions or	2 Few generalizations strictly limited to the subject investigated.

*M. Ginsberg, "The Problems and Methods of Sociology" in F. C. Bartlett, M. Ginsberg, E. J. Lindgen, R. H. Thoules, eds., *The Study of Society* (London, Routledge and Kegan Paul, 1939), pp. 472-3
**L. Gottschalk, "Categories of Historiographical Generalization" in L. Gottschalk, ed., *Generalization in Writing of History* (Chicago, University of Chicago Press, 1936), pp. 113-4. P. Gardiner, "Generalization in History," in G. H. Nadel, ed., *History and Theory* (Middletown, Wesleyan University Press, 1964) has a more scientific list.

social formations arise.

3   Assertions that change in given institutions are associated with changes in other institutions.

4   Assertions of rhythmical recurrences or phase sequences.

5   Descriptions of the main trends in the evolution of humanity as a whole.

6   Laws stating the implications of assumptions regarding human behavior.

3   Interpretive generalizations of interrelated trends based on antecedent, concurrent, and subsequent events.

4   Comparative generalizations seeking parallels and analogies in other times or places beyond the subject matter in hand.

5   Propositions about past trends and analogies suggested as applicable to the future also.

6   Philosophies of history providing cosmic understanding of human affairs past and to come.

Both historians and sociologists, as these summary lists indicate, were seeking to get beyond the 'raw material' of their subjects. They wanted answers to such questions in history as "who?", "what?", "when?", "where?" Sociologists casting a wider net sought to account for relations, origins, change, patterns of change, and to construct philosophies of the social process able to embrace all such phenomena as well as to clarify psychological presuppositions about the nature of the human beings by whom the whole social process was set in motion and kept going. Both lists were drawn up without reference to the attempt of any writers on history or sociology to have used them in providing historical or sociological syntheses. Sorokin's hypotheses had already given ample evidence of having attempted just such a task. It is therefore satisfactory to have evidence, such as the Committee on Generalization in History provided, to show that his work both met an acknowledged need and was ahead of the general development of sociological and historical practice and theory.

Most contributors to the Report of the American Committee decisively rejected the nominalistic view which would rigorously confine history to a clear, concise, and accurate presentation of facts and nothing but facts. History in this sense, as the whole past of mankind, cannot exist. All we have is history as *the study of* the past of mankind, not a minute by minute, hour by hour, week by week repetition of everything that happened at far distant points of time. That there is a gap between history as actuality in this sense, and history as it is studied later, is evident. Nothing but trained historical sense, which is another name for controlled imagination, can substitute explanation for duplication of the historical process. At times, as every historian knows, there are gaps which are unbridgeable even in imagination.

The Committee's volume gave no evidence that Sorokin's methods or achievement were considered, although his work was casually referred to in two footnotes and his opinion of Dr. Toynbee's *Study of History* was mentioned. The Committee's report is not therefore referred to here as evidence that any of Sorokin's conclusions had been accepted by its members. It is all the more valuable therefore to be able to read in it remarks which support his independent approach to historical generalization through cultural values. Particularly relevant is the contribution by Professor William O. Aydelotte. "Facts do not speak for themselves," as he reminds those who have not followed the history of thought since Immanuel Kant explained why this should be so. "Historians must generalize if they are to say anything worth saying" (p. 151), a remark equally applicable to the whole field of learning, science included, as A. N. Whitehead pertinently observed when he said that "no systematic thought has made progress apart from some adequately general working hypothesis." A vast mass of painstaking empirical research has failed in the past for the lack of just such a suggestive lead from an inspired theory or hypothesis. None but dull or lazy minds shun the difficult art of thought in the search for such fruitful suggestions. Professor Aydelotte was ready to admit that he had been glad to profit by the new ideas and new perspective he had derived from the social sciences, although this "interest in co-operation with the social sciences" was, he said, something new in American historiography. It had been "bitterly resented by many in the profession." Historians, he reported, condemn all philosophers of history "and then we crib from them."

It is necessary to clear the ground by these brief references to the long and enduring antagonism of many professional historians to anything in the nature of a general statement about the course of history because Sorokin has undoubtedly had to make headway against it, and a very strong and adverse current of opinion it has been. The ironical fact is that Sorokin himself had in fact already illuminated the Committee's problem twenty years before it had set to work, but his contribution had evidently not come to their notice to demonstrate that history cannot ignore values, and that values are not given by events alone.

The general statements which Sorokin wished to discover and the enquiries he set going for them had also anticipated a pertinent saying in another essay in the volume *Generalization in the Writing of History* by

Professor Roy F. Nicholls that "If the writing of history is to have its greatest significance and be more than a mere narrative of events, it ought to attempt to communicate the meaning of what men have done" (p. 143). "Meaning" was another of Sorokin's keywords for he asked had all the vast endeavor of humanity down the ages any meaning? If so, what was its sense, its purpose, its point?

It was remarkable that as late as the mid-twentieth century a learned society of historians should find it necessary to reassure the world that generalizations are permissible in history. The common sense view, so confirmed at great length, was shortly and accurately stated in an engaging series of lectures by Mr. E. H. Carr, a Fellow of Macaulay's Trinity College at the University of Cambridge while the American Committee were half-way through their labors. "It is nonsense to say that generalization is foreign to history; history thrives on generalizations." The historian, he said, "is not really interested in the unique, but what is general in the unique."*

A more serried series of investigations by historians and philosophers was presented jointly at the fifth conference of the New York University Institute of Philosophy from which much support can be derived for the conclusions reached by Sorokin on the subject, although his ideas were not mentioned by the twenty-six participants. The logical analysis of history was discussed mainly in relation to the possibility of formulating "covering laws" in history and not in the more fundamental manner in which Croce had accounted for the relation between individual judgments and universals. To invoke universals would, some feared, involve those doing so in an Aristotelian metaphysic of real essences. Yet the supreme need of every advanced science for "a systematic form in which the simplest postulates entail, predict, and explain the richest theorems and most varied observations is written into the very charter of the knowledge-endeavor, and this in two ways, psychological and logical." How such a desirable result can be secured if universals are rejected is a mystery.

The symposium did not succeed in resolving the problem of the subjectivity of all historical judgments. Reference was made to "that fake objectivity that consists in multiple subjectivity, that is, of being shared with other historians."** Now the relativity of historical judgments to the cultural mentality from which they arise may not create "objectivity" in

*E. H. Carr, *What Is History* (New York, Macmillan, 1961), pp. 57-8.
**D. C. Williams, "Essentials in History," in S. Hook, ed., *Philosophy and History* (New York, New York University Press, 1963), pp. 382-3.

in the sense of attaining the reality, or "the-thing-in-itself," of history supposing that, despite Kant, this is what the word "reality" is thought to imply. To consciously relate historical judgments to a specific cultural mentality, in the awareness that a different value judgment about the same kind of phenomenon would have seemed appropriate in another and different cultural mentality may not be "objectivity," but it is different from a "fake objectivity" resting on a mere contemporary majority opinion. It is different, and historically superior, in that it affords greater insight. Socio-cultural examples emerge of behavior and ideas which derive meaning from the cultural system in which they abound. Such are the phenomena of requiring interest upon capital loaned, or the exploitation of the female form for gain in restaurants, night clubs, and elsewhere, from the elegant and expensive to the most dingy and sordid, along with other forms of commercial sexual allurement, all of which have become part of the "modern" way of life. Yet they would have been regarded as enormities in an ideational age when serfdom, if not slavery, trial by ordeal and burning for heresy, all of which would be enormities today, were regarded as part of the normal practices of the age.

So also the objection to "role" and "class" as fundamental concepts of sociology, difficult to define at any time, have to be given different meanings in different cultural supersystems if they are to be endowed with explanatory relevance. Sorokin's hypotheses have the merit of putting such matters in an intelligible historical and sociological perspective and it is unfortunate that the symposium on history and philosophy did not take them into account.* As its members did not mention either Rickert or Meinecke, and as they virtually ignored the cultural interpretation of history, their work, although in some respects admirable, did not advance the problems discussed in this book to the extent that it might have done.

*S. Hook, "Objectivity and Reconstruction in History," in S. Hook, ed. *op. cit., p.* 255 comes near to discussing the problem, but avoids it. "The conclusion is inescapable," he writes, "that what makes a historical account, not *the* truth about what it describes but *truer* than another, once the historical problem under consideration has been selected, is whether it does justice to the available evidence by means of a method and criteria of relevance which do not differ fundamentally from the way in which conclusions are formed in other fields, like medicine or geology . . . truths in history may be more difficult to obtain than in other areas of experience, they are not more relative." This statement of current practice in sound, scientific history does not fully meet the problems to which Sorokin addressed himself, which are those arising *after* historians using Professor Hook's methods have done their work. It will be noted also that he begs the question of the identity of historical and scientific methods, and also uses words such as "criteria of relevance" upon whose definition much may depend.

Analytical Philosophy of History

Is it possible to discuss "meaning" in history without invoking value concepts? This seems the aim of an "analytical" account or philosophy of history.

There is, of course, a distinction to be made between value judgments passed by historians on the personalities and events of the past, which may be highly colored, purely personal and subjective statements, and the efforts of "scientific" historians to rigorously exclude any such bias. Professors Langlois, Seignobos, Bernheim, and Sir Isaiah Berlin championed such "scientific" objectivity. Sorokin's whole work was one long effort to be faithful to the same ideal. He, like any "scientific" historian, sought the truth about the past. Yet he, more than any other historian, brought "value" into historical interpretation. But it was not his own personal value-preferences. His was the very different task of detecting, analyzing, and classifying the values latent or evident in the unrolling of events and the actions of prominent personalities in the past. There seems no reason why "scientific" historians should not have made a similar approach but in fact none of them have done so yet on Sorokin's lines. Perhaps the need to do so was not so apparent until the rise of sociology. It was to advance sociology that Sorokin undertook his massive historical studies.

Academically, the principles adopted by Sorokin of seeking value patterns in history were followed by the best historians but only for the limited periods with which they were concerned, and often implicitly adopted rather than being overtly declared. To write history without bringing values into the narrative at all would be an extreme form of the "nominalist" approach to the subject, the state of mind that has produced logical positivism, semanticism, and analytical philosophy. There certainly seems no place for values in analytical philosophies of history such as that expounded by Professor A. C. Danto. Whether he considers values entirely irrelevant is not made clear. He attacks what he calls "substantive" philosophies of history. They are not named, but he said that while they purport to give accounts of what happened in the past, they do *more* than that, they try to account for the *whole* of history. It is true that there have been philosophies of history written with this purpose, notably those founded on the Bible, but Danto does not appear to refer to them. Apart from them, the others answering his description, such as that which Buckle began to sketch, have long since been dead and buried, without benefit of the surgical skill and agonizingly protracted slow tortures of analytical philosophy. Danto exhumes the body of some unknown, buried "philosophy of history" so that he may, with the dead-pan seriousness of the slow-motion analytical philosopher, survey it from all sides before deploying his considerable armory of logical weapons, pseudo-mathematical, algebraic letters, formulas, and small diagrams, to kill it all over again. Why this was thought worth doing is the first puzzle, because already on page 5 he dismisses all philosophies of history as "crude" and "unspeakably inept." Philosophers of history, he says, are guilty of the basic error of supposing it to be possible "to write the history of events before the events have happened." Having announced his discovery, he promises, "I shall argue it is a mistake." He does, and at some length, although Schlegel had done the work for him with far sharper point and conclusion over a hundred years earlier when he said, "The historian is a prophet looking backwards."*

"Substantive" philosophies of history, Danto complains, "seek for the significance of events before the later events in connection with which the former *acquire* significance, have happened (p. 11)." Having detected this basic mistake, Danto pronounces, "I wish to maintain that we cannot enjoy a cognitive standpoint which makes such an activity feasible." In what way this portentous discovery is essentially different from the stock objections to the "philosophy of history" already quoted, such as Sir Isaiah Berlin's "obsessive pattern" or Collingwood's "pigeon-holes," is not apparent. Danto considers that "substantive" philosophies of history which purport to explain the whole of history imply the possibility of getting beyond and outside the whole context of history. By "history" he seems to imply the whole span of history and since that is still being extended, he holds that there is no possibility of transcending it. He does not allow for the fact that history is not a whole of this nature and that we have some knowledge of shorter, complete, and closed periods of history such as those of the Ancient Egyptians, Babylonians, Assyrians, Greeks, and Romans, upon which philosophies of history have been based, even if limited and partial.

Recognizing that "a certain concept of meaning" is used in philosophies of history, Danto explains what it involves by saying that the "meaning" of events has "reference to some larger temporal structure in which they are components," a view which he assimilates to the "theological" because it is seen "as bearing out some divine plan." It is a

*A. W. Schlegel, "Der Historiker ist ein rückwärts gekehrter Prophet," *Athenaeum* (Berlin), i, ii, 20.

use of the word "meaning" which he considers would be "grossly improper in science."* "Structure" upon which "meaning" turns is not defined, but later it is said that "any narrative is a structure imposed upon events, grouping some of them together with others and ruling out some as lacking relevance." To say that a narrative mentions only significant events is "to put the matter trivially."**

Why "relevance" is accepted, while "significance" is spurned, is not clear. "Significance" however is recognized as needing explanation. Certainly something ought to be said to show how "structures" come to be "imposed upon events" and why some events are "grouped" with others and some are "ruled out." The principal senses in which Danto understands "significance" are described as "pragmatic significance" which turns on "a moral point of some sort"; "theoretical significance," which is a particular narrative regarded as illustrating by example other similar narratives, such as an account of one revolution in relation to revolutions generally; "consequential" significance, in which events are described because the historian wants to make them a contributing factor to his general narrative; and finally, "revelatory" significance, which attaches to the discovery of a piece of evidence at first missing from a narrative but one which, when discovered fills the gap and makes the narrative more complete. Danto realizes that his senses of significance are "hardly exhaustive and perhaps not even exclusive."†

When "morals" are included among sources of significance, it might be thought that values in general and value-patterns could not be ignored, but Danto ignores them. He quotes with apparent approval, the view that "the difficulty with the grandiose proposals of the Marxes, the Spenglers, the Toynbees . . . can hardly be that they are history, but that they are grandiose," a remark which in analytical philosophy is perhaps equivalent to "boo! to Marx, Spengler and Toynbee," although Danto is apt, to use the word "odd" as an expression of disapproval.† Before Sorokin can be included with "Marx, Spengler and Toynbee" in such a condemnation, many considerations are involved which Danto does not invoke. It cannot be that a writer who cited philosophers such as Croce, Collingwood, Dilthey, Hegel, Kant, Leibniz, Marx, Spengler, and Vico was unaware that values have been considered as relevant in the philosophy of history, even

*A. C. Danto, *Analytical Philosophy of History* (Cambridge University Press, 1965), pp. 7-9, 14.
**Ibid, p. 132.
†Ibid, pp. 132-399.

although he did not mention Rickert, Meinecke, Troeltsch, or Max Weber. Among others, he cited and quoted with approval on several occasions, a work of Professor H-I Marrou which is, in fact, one long powerfully sustained argument against his own limited, "analytical" approach. A glance at the ".pictorial" frontispiece to Marrou's book in which the "anti-positivist" philosophers of history alone are included, and at the references commending Sorokin's work (notably 175), or at references to Marrou's sharp comments on the orthodox but strictly limited point of view of the conventional manuals of historical method (p. 105) – any or all of them might have put Danto on his guard, even if he had missed Marrou's explicit advocacy of a cultural approach to history: "L'histoire ne se soutient pas a elle seule, comme revaient les positivistes; elle fait partie d'un tout, d'un organisme culturel dont la philosophie de l'homme est comme l'axe ("History is not the self-sufficient reality imagined by the positivists; it is but a part of a cultural whole which turns upon the philosophic idea of man").* Whatever the merits of analytical philosophy, they do not warrant that description. The inadequacy of the analytical approach when confronted by the immensely complex nature of historical reality is made strikingly evident by Professor Marrou's description of the historian's task, "Comment comprendre le Métier d'Historien" on another occasion.**

It can only be supposed that Danto avoided "value" because the "analytic" method to which he was committed has so far seemed impotent to deal with it. "Analysis" therefore is too limited to allow a philosophical discussion of history or historical writing. Everything is to be said in favor of the correct use of language and for the avoidance of question-begging words which blur discourse and produce fuzzy, confused arguments. To that extent a discussion such as Danto's is valuable. As a complete philosophy of history it will not do, for the same reason that analytical philosophy will not do as a complete program for philosophy.

Sorokin made it clear that language is a cultural system, just as Meineke and he showed that history can only be understood in a cultural context. In relation to language, the point has been admirably enforced by Wilson. "Language is not an abstract activity but a form of life. It is something used by people; and not only this, much more *a part of them* than most linguistic philosophers suppose. A man's language is *only a*

*H-I Marrou, *The Meaning of History,* trans. by R. J. Olsen (Dublin, Helicon, 1966)
**H-I Marrou, *L'Histoire et ses Methodes* (Paris, Gallimard, 1961), pp. 1467-1539

symptom of his conceptual equipment." It can therefore acquire meaning and be understood only within "a framework of attitudes and values towards all aspects of human life that we meet." Since "history," even more so than language, can acquire meaning only within a framework involving human life, the inadequacy of an "analytical" philosophy of history is at once apparent. No amount of critical acumen and refinement and super-refinement about the logic of a mere narrative of events omitting all value-considerations will create a philosophy of history or a theory of culture. Analytical philosophy suffers from a fatal shortcoming "the error of supposing that only those disciplines which result in true propositions have any bearing upon truth."* From such a blinkered outlook upon the life of man in society, past and present, Sorokin substitutes a wide-ranging conspectus of the full universe of human discourse.

How do Sorokin's theories stand in relation to Danto's axe? Sorokin's 'philosophy of history' should not fear the block set up for analytical destruction. For Danto's argument has some surprising loopholes. "It is legitimate to ask for meanings *in* history" he says (p. 13). If "substantive" philosophers of history have only to claim that they aim at no more than that, many might surely claim that any general analytical condemnation should at least be postponed until their meanings are studied. Narrative histories escape. They are a *genre* of which Danto approves. He says that they throw into relief the miserable failure of "substantive" philosophies of history. It takes him the whole of his Chapter 11 and 22 pages of involved analytical argument, replete with letters small and large, 'x, y, G, t, t-2, -3, G-ness,' diagrams, formulas and so forth, the 'tools' of the "analytical" reasoner, to reach (on p. 255) the triumphant conclusion: "the role of narratives in history should now be clear. They are used to explain changes, and most characteristically large-scale changes taking place, sometimes over periods of time, vast in relation to single human lives. It is the job of history to reveal to us these changes, to organize the past into temporal wholes, and to explain these changes at the same time as they tell what happened. So much heavy labor to reach a conclusion already well known, recalls the sage remark of Mr. Weller senior in Dickens' *Pickwick Papers,* "vether it's vorthvhile goin' through so much to learn so little, as the charity boy said ven he got to the end of the alphabet, is a matter o' taste." It comes strangely from an author who

---

*John Wilson, *Thinking with Concepts* (New York, Cambridge University Press, 1963), pp. 126-141.

writes, "that most of the generalizations which cover human behavior are truisms, may be confirmed by consulting nearly any sociological study chosen at random" (p. 213).

Some analytical philosophers have still the opportunity to consult with profit Sorokin's *Fads and Foibles in Modern Sociology and Related Sciences.* For "the role of narratives in history" in Danto's conclusion, it is possible to substitute "the role of Sorokin's explanations of history," making it evident that whatever hard things Danto has said about unnamed "substantive" philosophers of history, they do not apply to Sorokin. An additional reason for believing that Sorokin's views are not damagingly incriminated by Danto's strictures is the fact, insisted upon here, that his was no quest for a "philosophy of history," substantive or otherwise. He also aimed at discovering "general facts concerning the behavior of individuals and groups in political contexts and social contexts as well."

On such lines, Danto writes approvingly of Thucydides, for the remarkable reason that he "wrote social science, not history" (p. 24). As there has in all probability never been a historian of repute who would not, with Macaulay, take Thucydides as his master, the point of the distinction is not evident. It disappears completely if, with Paul Barth, Sorokin, Meinecke, and others, history and sociology are regarded as facets of the same problem, the study of man in society. Danto is not really the fearsome Lord High Executioner which his forbidding first chapter made him appear to be. He agrees that history, no less than science, must have hypotheses and he corrects Charles Beard whom the idea alarmed (pp. 99-100). He realizes that many of the differences in discussions about the problem of historical explanation are merely quarrels "over how a certain key word is to be used" (p. 215). He is ready to admit that "there may *be* historical laws" (p. 254) and he has the same view as Sorokin about "flashes of intuition" and "intuitive creativity." When we behave creatively we often find that we have hit upon a certain thing without being clear how we did it" (p. 232). Pending Danto's verdict, the provisional conclusion may be drawn, that Sorokin's "philosophy of history" has little to fear from "analytical philosophy." For Sorokin did not "write the history of events before they happened," but he put forward hypotheses, which Danto agrees are permissible, to explain the changing patterns in social values to be detected in history as it happened. In their light he hoped to put an end to the scepticism which denies all possibility of charting the course which sociological and historical changes have taken over time. As for "prophecy," which Danto carefully distinguishes from mere prediction, there cannot presumably be any objection to the hypothesis that a value pattern discerned in history in the past may recur. The "cognitive standpoint which makes such an activity seem possible," which "analysis" demands, was for Sorokin a theory of knowledge resting upon the neurological, psychological, and cognitive nature of man together with the view that, underlying the infinite variety of human individuality, certain basic attitudes to reality, limited in number, tend to produce uniformities in the mass. The emergence of order, regularity, uniformities, and scientific laws of great precision in physics and chemistry despite the newly-discovered discontinuities and apparent random irregularities in the sub-atomic field, offers a suggestive analogy which might at least redeem from absurdity the notion that in sociology also, some greater systematization is not entirely hopeless even though no individual human characters are similar in all respects.

Whether analytical philosophy is adequate to the task of testing and evaluating such a hypothesis remains to be seen. To the extent that Sorokin was correct, there may be some hope of analytical aid, for, impotent although analysis has always been to create valuable new truths, it can often support those discovered by especially powerful, discerning minds using "substantive" methods.

The disagreements and criticism which Danto's book provokes, arise because he was mixing up two subjects, that may be described shortly as the philosophy of history and the logic of historical explanations.* His analytical method which is unable to cope with qualititative philosophical ideas, should be reserved for use in the quantitative world, in the world of abstract time-sequences and the world of logical inference and implication. In that world, problems of verification, verifiability, past-referring terms, temporally-neutral terms, future-referring terms, time-true, time-false statements, the role of covering laws and general laws and many other logical matters may endlessly be debated without their having any cogent bearing upon the general pattern of values discernible in the actions of men and women in the whole long course of human history.

Sorokin's scheme does not stand or fall according to its success in making history into a "science" in the sense of being able "to establish general laws covering the behavior of the empirical events or objects with which history is concerned, so as to connect knowledge of separately

---

*W. B. Gallie, in *Philosophy and the Historical Understanding* (London, Chatto and Windus, 1964), pp. 19-20 made this distinction not long before Danto's book appeared.

known events and to make reliable predictions of events as yet unknown."* It may well be that neither sociology nor history could be regarded as 'sciences' until such a description could be applied to them, whether or not the possibility or the desirability of such a long-term objective is accepted. It is possible to achieve meaning without such general laws, and history and sociology are able to find meanings, as other scientific subjects do. In scientific thought "sentences have no meaning apart from their relationships to other sentences in a calculus interpreted as a deductive system." In such a system "one sentence or formula cannot be interpreted as standing for a proposition in isolation from an interpretation of other sentences or formulae to stand for other logically-related propositions."** Sorokin's earlier studies of the epistemological and methodological problems involved in the "scientific" study of sociology and history had been thorough. As a result he had arrived at the same conclusion about the nature of deductive analysis. His views occupy much of the fourth volume of his *Social and Cultural Dynamics,* one sentence from which especially merits repetition. "The most general criterion of a system of meaning, in contradistinction to a congeries of meanings, is a logical compatibility and specific dependence or interdependence of each meaning-element, upon other meaning-elements, of the meaning-elements upon the whole system, and of the system upon the elements."†

Practicing historians and philosophers of history may be remote from these logical, procedural debates and the extent to which they are able to profit from them is problematic. The progress of the philosophy of history is no more likely to depend upon such procedural analyses than the progress of creative thought in philosophy depends upon pure logic – and no less. Every insight, every error that analytical thought can make plain is naturally to be welcomed, but as long as philosophy, sociology, and the philosophy of history are seen to be value-laden the amount of aid that analytical dissection can afford is unlikely to be great.

Surveying the whole problem more recently, Quentin Skinner notes that "there has been a marked trend away from accepting any strictly positivist view of the matter" but the opponents of positivism "have produced no satisfactory alternative." In looking for an alternative, it

---

*R. B. Braithwaite, *Scientific Explanation* (New York, Harper, 1960), pp. 84-84
**Ibid.*
†P. A. Sorokin, *Social and Cultural Dynamics* (New York, Bedminster Press, 1962), p. 21

would, he thought, be useful to remember that "it is a commonplace of the more advanced sciences that an explanation can be the result merely of establishing the most precise correlation between all possible variables. It is more than arguable that very precise and complete historical descriptions might stand of themselves as explanations in a similar way." But, Skinner observes, "an infinitely greater amount of historical research (especially of a statistical character and countless minor social and intellectual biographies) would be needed to [provide such precise and complete historical descriptions] ."* This is exactly the conclusion at which Sorokin arrived forty years previously when he began work which was published ten years later in *Social and Cultural Dynamics.* In their method, range, and content those volumes fit exactly the need which Mr. Skinner expressed. Available for his consideration for thirty years, they could not, unfortunately, have come to his notice, for had they done so, he could not have concluded his excellent paper by saying "it is also true that the type of research needed has in most areas of the discipline, scarcely begun."**

Philosophy of History and Theory of Value

There had been many philosophies of history, all of which were highly charged with values, but few in the English language had been accompanied by an explicit philosophical theory of value. When the subject was taken up in 1962 by the philosopher, Professor Alfred Stern, it might be thought that he would see the evident link between Sorokin's philosophy of history and value-theory.† Unfortunately, despite immense

---

*Q. Skinner, "The Limits of Historical Explanations," *Philosophy,* Vol. XLI (1966), pp. 199-225

**Amid the large literature on the logical problems involved it the construction of historical narratives, the following have aroused considerable debate before the publication of Danto's work:

P. Gardiner, *The Nature of Historical Explanation,* (New York, Oxford University Press, 1952)

W. Dray, *Laws and Explanation in History,* (New York, Oxford University Press, 1957)

P. Gardiner, ed., *Theories of History,* (Glencoe, Illinois, 1959)

S. Hook, ed., *Philosophy and History* (New York, New York University Press, 1969)

J. F. Ling, *Explanation in History* LXXV, pp. 589-91.

†A. Stern, *Philosophy of History and the Problem of Value,* (Mouton, S-Gravenhage, 1962)

industry and erudition, the connection not only was not made, not merely was it not seen, but any possibility of it was openly flouted and for no better reason than that which made Professor Geyl disavow interest also. They both disliked Sorokin's critical opinions upon the contemporary decay of sensate cultural values and his belief that mankind will correct its present almost exclusive reliance upon them by giving more weight to an integralist view which pays more regard, for instance, to supraconscious flashes of insight. As the grounds for Sorokin's views have already been stated, and as his specific diagnosis has been spelled out in detail, it is unnecessary to rebut here the criticisms which the two professors made of them. They were not reasoned criticisms, point by point, of Sorokin's formidable array of arguments, but the expression of purely personal preferences which, on the principles of both of the critics, should not be allowed to masquerade as scientific arguments.

Stern notes Rickert's failure to discover that scheme of universal values which would have enabled his "science of culture" to transcend the relativism of historicism. Although there are some "universal values" of the type Rickert sought, such as "health is better than sickness," nevertheless most values are either purely individual in character, such as preferring apricots to peaches, or collective values given by and dependent upon groups, and hence purely relative to time and place (137). It is difficult to extract a clear, coherent doctrine from Stern's work; however page 131 seems to be the core of the book.

There Stern discusses "value" in history as the purpose the historian had in mind in writing it. There can therefore be as many histories as there are values; histories, that is to say, which take their values straight from politics, fashions, arts, ideas, literature, philosophy, the sciences, technology, or political economy. All such histories are necessarily different. "Whoever tries," Stern concludes, "to reduce these different codes of values to a common axiological denominator is wasting his time." Not content with this dismissal, he adds the parting gibe: "He would do better to look for other ways to overcome his intellectual insecurity." It will be evident that Sorokin's patient empirical study of just such separate values as Stern declares to be incompatible and irreconcilable has resulted in just such common axiological denominators (in the plural) whose possibility Stern denies. Moreover because Sorokin discovered that such denominators, which are his cultural supersystems, change in quality as virtually complete wholes, he was able to transcend the cultural relativity by which Rickert was by no means alone in confessing himself to have been puzzled and balked.

If values only get into history, as Stern says, because they happen to reflect the special interests of the historiographers, it would indeed be difficult to go beyond a subjectivity of all historical judgments which he is just as anxious to transcend as was Rickert. He seeks to evade the difficulty by locating values not only in historiography or written histories, but in past events as well, in history as it occurred. There, he thinks, the urge to escape from an imperfect present to a more perfect imaginary future is one source of value. How such urges occur, to whom, how they are formulated, and why change, as such, should automatically be a source of value remain unexplained. Such a source of value, if it is admitted, is, moreover, difficult to reconcile with his other sources: "only by its relation to the directive value of a definite historiographical project is a historical object distinguished from any other real, but historically, indifferent, object." Two further considerations are urged to reinforce this dependence of value in history upon the values of the historian. The essential or unessential character of historical events is determined by a multiplicity of codes of value, "each of which owes its specific character to a definite historiographical project," chosen as "the expression" (by the historian, that is) "of an original choice of certain basic values." This choice will itself be determined by the particular social, historical, cultural, and existential conditions in which the historian lives.

While there is evidently considerable force in Stern's statement of the character of much historical writing, it by no means adds up either to a complete theory of history or to a theory of values. Sorokin's theories, which include it, are in all respects superior. It is difficult to believe that many historians could accept Stern's account of their activities. To take but a single example, we should presumably be required, on his assumptions, to believe that the values discernible in the political career of Cicero arise because they are chosen as a "historiographical project" as the result of "certain basic values" themselves determined by the cultural environment of the historiographer. What happens surely is that historians aim to give an account of the past which will reflect as accurately as possible the values of that past. When they write the history of the Roman Republic, they come across many references to Cicero, Caesar, Pompey, Octavian, Antony and others. Such men are not "chosen", they impose themselves. Their lives, particularly Cicero's, are relatively well documented. It is not necessary to import value judgments into an account of Cicero's life and work in order to describe it "philosophically"; he himself leaves the reader of his letters, his speeches, his philosophical and other writings in no doubt about them. If one historian chooses to ignore or misstate Cicero's values, he is very soon corrected by another. No "directive value of a definite historiographical project" is needed to define them; they are there. History recognizes them. None but bad historians do not.

The observation point was made by Mandelbaum who points out in opposition to "the relativists" (as he describes Croce, Dilthey and Mannheim) that "every historical fact is given in some specific context in which it leads on to some other fact" and that such facts must be real because historians who fail to mention them are criticized for such an omission by other historians. If value judgments were all subjective as the relativists claim, no criticism on such grounds would be admissible. Stern apparently does not seem to realize the damage this pertinent observation inflicts upon his desire to derive value in history from the nature of the "historiographical projects" in which history is presented.* Stern's directive value of a historiographical project can of course be seen in the work of "democratic" historians who see nothing except Cicero's opposition to one-man rule, or in the works of others who, in periods of totalitarian rule, denigrate Cicero on account of his stand for freedom. None pretends that he was successful, but of the nature of his predominant values there can be no doubt. It would not seem difficult for a cool, objective appraisal to present a balanced picture, indeed it has often been attempted. If in accordance with his other criterion, Stern accepts the general account of the course of political history during the mid-first century B.C., he may invoke his other source of values, by saying that Cicero was one of a group who affirmed positive values which they imagined to be more perfect than the conditions in which they were living, an affirmation which as he rightly says constitutes "the life blood of history as reality." He then has the task of explaining the relation between such value emerging from events with the values resulting from a "definite historiographical project." It was said above that these considerations are the central core of Stern's book, but it is so packed with miscellaneous quotations and snippets from almost everyone who has ever written upon history (the history of art being a striking exception in a book about values) that it is difficult to extract any coherent doctrine from it, so less than justice may here have been done to Stern's wide-ranging disquisition.

*M. Mandelbaum, *The Problem of Historical Knowledge* (New York, Liveright, 1938), pp. 200-202
A. Stern, *Philosophy of History and the Problem of Values* (Mouton, s' Gravenhage, 1962), pp. 78-79

What can be said with certainty is that he has not seen how Sorokin's empirical survey of values-in-action in the past has provided a clear, satisfactory philosophy of value and a philosophy of history, firmly based psychologically, (Stern still flounders with Freud's "id," "ego," and "superego"); well-grounded episteomlogically, abundantly documented and seen, by anyone willing to look at it, to rest not upon partial, subjective personal notions, but upon as complete and objective an inventory of all the facts as any one pioneer investigator has so far been able to encompass.

The Philosophy of History after Sorokin

Now that Sorokin has shown the possibility of a wide-ranging synthesis, not in sociology alone, but in all humanist studies by giving them a common axis within a cultural frame of reference, the philosophy of history gains immense new significance. Values shape the form of history in the same way that values determine, or account for, or describe, the style and quality of life today. The task of "historical sociology" or "sociologial history" or "philosophy of history" is to elucidate the nature of those values. When they can be detected, assessed, estimated, or weighed and measured by the mind, historical knowledge is greatly enriched. When, over long periods, they can be seen to possess a cohesion, a concomitance, a mutual compatibility amounting to a definite pattern or to an integral whole, then they serve as a parameter, a cultural supersystem by which whole periods may be characterized.

These cultural supersystems are of course a very general, loosely fitting frame, or rather, series of frames. Ideational, idealist, and sensate cultural supersystems are but outer frames, by no means rigid, by no means walled and dyked against the survival or the infiltration of some incompatible values. It is only necessary to recall the early discovery of the *coincidentia oppositorum* the "dialectic" immanent in all value concepts, to realize that competing, conflicting values are never far below the surface. In modern times Croce left this vital matter free from doubt. Indeed there are periods when established frames seem to dissolve, as when Sorokin recognized mixed, eclectic, types, and "congeries" instead of integrated supersystems. Moreover, none of the frameworks lasts forever unchanged although some, the ideational especially, have remarkable powers of survival. If such lack of hard and fast definition or description seems a blemish upon anything in the nature of "a science" of society, it is not for that reason to be mistrusted. The account given may not have the symmetry and precision of the laws of chemistry or physics, but the social facts from which that account is drawn are not identifiable uniformities such as make up the facts of chemistry and physics. Sorokin would be forcing a pre-arranged ideology upon the facts if he attempted to impose an arbitrary pattern upon them. Instead, he points to the periods when the cultural supersystems fade, are disrupted, or forcibly altered. Unlike many other historians, he is not without resource in explaining convincingly the nature of such cultural changes, or the qualitative side of life in such periods of breakdown.

Sorokin has therefore propounded a new and striking philosophy of society and philosophy of history in the grand manner.

It is now no longer possible to shove the philosophy of history aside with the complaint that it is an *a priori* scheme, merely an arbitrary arrangement of pigeon-holes, or a propaganda effort dressed up to look like history. Sorokin has shown how it emerges from the facts of history itself as a by-product, as it were, in the identification of sociological phenomena, at once their reality and their explanation. As for the stock accusation that he rigged his whole plan in advance, it is sufficient to retort that, well aware that he would face a charge, he took every precaution to guard against it.* There are more reasons in favor of Sorokin's methods and results. He did not put his ideas forward otherwise than as hypotheses. He does not claim that they neatly fit all the facts, although sometimes in his more "popular" summary statements and in some answers to criticism, his presentation may give the impression of a more dogmatic assurance than is to be found in his more scientific volumes. He did hold that his hypotheses explain more social phenomena in the past than any other theories so far formulated.

He furthermore believed that his theories go deeper and provide a more satisfactory explanation of more social phenomena of the past than any alternative theory. A striking instance of such superiority is the example, already quoted, of his resolution of the controversy stirred up by Max Weber's celebrated attempt to link the rise of capitalism in post-Renaissance Western Europe with the rise of Protestantism. Max Weber was too good a social theorist not to be on firm ground in

*P. A. Sorokin, *A Long Journey* (New Haven, College & University Press, 1963), pp. 245-6

J. J. Allen, ed., *Pitirim A. Sorokin in Review* (Durham, Duke University Press, 1963), pp. 383-449, 454-5 establishing the concomitant spread of capitalist enterprise and the reformed religion. In his general economic history moreover he partly anticipated Sorokin's demonstration to the extent that he saw that both these movements illustrated the rise of a spirit of rational control in many departments of life directed towards worldly interests. What Sorokin supplied was a basic presupposition which could account for the rise of a spirit of greater rationalism both in religion and in economic life. With his exposition of the nature of a developing sensate culture he was able to provide a master-concept absorbing and explaining Weber's thesis and much else as well.*

One final additional illustration will show the great advance which Sorokin's theories have made possible. In his brilliant series of lectures at Cambridge in 1961 to which reference has already been made, Mr. E. H. Carr, a working historian, surveyed the state of the debate about the nature, aims, and purposes of history. In doing so he struck many a shrewd blow for clarity, precision, and truth, challenging many a pundit with an urbanity and wit that contrasts refreshingly with some other contributions to the subject. Noting the double danger faced by sociology of either becoming ultra-theoretical or ultra-empirical, he concluded that "the more sociological history becomes, and the more historical sociology becomes, the better for both. Let the frontier between them be kept wide open for two-way traffic." He realized that "the social sciences, since they involve man as both subject and object are incompatible with any theory of knowledge which pronounces a rigid divorce between subject and object." Similar methodological problems have arisen to perplex modern science, particularly physics. Later when Carr again picked up the theme, in discussing the problem of the objectivity of historical knowledge, he rightly saw that "a new model was required which does justice to the complex process of inter-relation and interaction between observer and the thing observed." He also saw that old aspirations towards objectivity must give way to "the relation between fact and interpretation, between past, present and future." Thereafter, lacking Sorokin's fruitful hypothesis of the reality of logico-meaningful cultural supersystems which enable such a relation to be seen in due perspective, Carr is at a loss. He fails to find any new model or to emerge with anything better than an interpretative

---

*R. W. Green, *Protestantism & Capitalism: The Weber Thesis and its Critics* (Boston, Heath, 1959). It was unfortunate that an otherwise comprehensive study-guide to the controversy aroused by Max Weber's thesis made no reference to Sorokin's advance, although that had been published twenty-two years previously.

standard of significance found "only in relevance to the end in view." Since this "is necessarily an evolving end," it is no solution, so that recognition of "the impossibility of total objectivity" become inevitable. Carr seeks to console himself with ideas about "the progressive development of human potentialities. ... towards goals which can be defined only as we advance towards them." In the absence of any concrete ideal such as Sorokin's "integral personality" concept this is a vague and nebulous ambition. "Values" are mentioned with the pregnant remark that "Progress in history is achieved through the interdependence and interaction of facts and values" towards, apparently, "truth." In the final lecture the disappointing end of the quest is evident in its vague faith in "the expansion of reason," "progressive development in the perspective of world history," and the naive hope that social evils "also carry with them their own corrective." Meanwhile a mysterious essence called "the world centre of gravity" is alleged to have "shifted away from Western Europe." Whether this creative genius is military power, population, political influence, or all of them together, is not clear. What his "world centre of gravity" certainly is not, but certainly should be, is an integral scheme of creative cultural values in the sense used by Croce and Sorokin.*

Such is the evident superior power of Sorokin's theories that they will go on attracting greater attention, after the time-lag which now seems inevitable in the acceptance of new ideas by the learned world. Sorokin is but one of the many pioneer spirits who were victims of such delay. Max Weber died in 1920. The bulk of his writings were not available in Germany until after his death. The first translation of one of his books into English, *General Economic History,* was published in London in 1927, the second, *The Protestant Ethic and the Spirit of Capitalism* also in London in 1930. It was not until after the end of the Second World War that any translations were published in the United States, where Sorokin had taken the lead in making them better known since 1924. It seems that roughly a generation has to elapse before novel ideas in sociology from abroad get any very general recognition in the academic world of England and the United States. Many fare worse than Max Weber notably Dilthey, Rickert, Pareto, Tönnies and Simmel. About the only striking exceptions

---

*E. H. Carr, *What is History* (New York, Macmillan, 1961), pp. 59, 67, 114, 115, 117, 113, 125, 138, 143, 141, 142
The critical comments in the text which follow may be augmented by Professor H. P. Trevor-Roper's criticisms in *Encounter* (May 1962), pp. 69-77 — in particular, his exposition of Carr's ideas of objectivity, without, however, proceeding to the point reached in the text above.

are Spengler and Toynbee. Unless a scholar becomes an exile, to achieve fame in person in the English-speaking world, as Cassirer, Mannheim, Von Mises, Hayek, Schumpeter and others did (as well as Sorokin) the spread of their ideas there can long be delayed. The theory that many alert minds in England or the United States, well-equipped with at least French and German, rapidly assimilate new thought presented in those languages, is not easy to sustain. Novel and unusual ideas, especially in a subject as academically "suspect" as the philosophy of history, are especially liable to neglect. Moreover, in every branch of learning the complaint is heard that "it is impossible to keep up with the literature." Such considerations help to explain the delayed recognition of a sociological philosophy of history which must rank as the greatest single individual contribution to the subject since the publication, in German, of the writings of Dilthey, Rickert, Cassirer, Meinecke, and Max Weber.

Summarizing the development so far reached, it may be said to result from the perception that knowledge about human affairs involves the discernment of their nature and quality, so calling for the exercise of all available categories of interpretation, one such category alone being insufficient. Analytical methods serving the category, or universal, comprising all that the mind accepts as truth, are obviously essential, but they do not exhaust the meaning of the philosophy of history. Individual historical pronouncements acquire meaning when they are subjects to the universal predicate "true." An additional universal, that of utility, has often been proposed; this is the general predicate which pragmatists sought to elevate into primacy. According to their view, historical facts, like other facts, can be conceived in all manner of possible ways and they are interpreted on purely personal grounds, depending on what anyone wants to do with them. An example is given by Stern's idea of "the directive value of a historiographical project." Some historical statements may be subject to the universal, or concept, "utility," particularly in political and constitutional history, when the study of history is seen as a school for statesmen, diplomats, and others.

Such a pragmatic criterion or universal could be dangerous if it opens the door to all manner of tendentions, propaganda, histories. Many are regarded as "historians" who create "philosophies of history" on the slender basis of their interests or passing fancies.

When historians and sociologists search for a true explanation of past human behavior, it is not enough merely to find out what it was, or what purpose it served, because these dimensions do not measure the whole of human conduct. It would be false to history and to sociology to leave out of account all those human activities for which no other explanatory predicate, or universal, can be found than that which pronounces, or once pronounced, them to be of the class which yeilds aesthetic satisfaction, or beauty; or of the class which pronounces, or once pronounced, them to be of the class of actions which are morally worthy.

Is Sorokin's Argument Circular?

Any sociology or philosophy of history which fails to invoke the main interpretative categories, or concepts, or universals must, on this view of the matter, be deficient, not because Sorokin said so, but because they alone in sociology and the philosophy of history meet the requirement that the generalizations, necessary if those subjects are to be intellectually rewarding, should succeed in explaining a greater variety of facts and ideas than any competitive explanations. If they are valid generalizations it will not be possible to overthrow them by adducing facts or ideas which they cannot explain. Sorokin was ever on the watch for negative instances by which his theories could be rebutted. Wars and violence seemed to him to be one such negative example because they occur in all his major cultural systems. To the extent that they are the manifestations of elementary human passions, they may be said to lie outside the sphere of cultural interests with which he was primarily concerned. They may be assimilated to those "crude physical conditions and necessities of life" of which Meinecke wrote, when he too excluded them: ". . . the soil and the sun, hunger and love . . . all of which the non-materialist historian takes for granted as causal presuppositions."* Sorokin's views are not without resource, even in these domains of basic necessities and passions, most of which take on a special quality from the dominating cultural system in which they are manifest. Hunger, food, and drink, although "pre-cultural," are different phenomena in an ideational age than in an idealistic cultural system, although in neither was the basic animal necessity of the savage then dominant. Absent also was a refined search for qualities and flavors characteristic of the later sensate age of late Republican and early Imperial Rome, or of our contemporary quest, regardless of expense, for "two-, "three-, and "four-star" restaurants. So also, the purposes for which wars were fought, the manner and conventions in which wars were waged, the uses and consequences of victory or defeat, have shown marked

*F. Meinecke, *Staat und Persönlichkeit* (Berlin, Mittler, 1933), p. 31.

differences which are compatible with Sorokin's theories and are therefore able to confirm them.

Supposing Sorokin's theories to have survived criticisms so far, there yet remains the objection that Sorokin derives his interpretive principles from history and then uses his principles to explain history. Apart from the difficulty of seeing where else a sociologist or cultural historian is to derive his principles if he does not get them from history, there is the pertinent reminder available that, although derived from a reasonably full study of history, there are parts of history which Sorokin did not include, but his principles nevertheless will be found to apply to them also. Such an answer does not entirely dispose of the charge that, fundamentally, Sorokin's argument is circular.

Circular Reasoning and the Relativity of Cultural Values

Few arguments in the armory of the destructive critics who abound in our decayed sensate culture are wielded with greater relish for their presumed annihilating power than the accusation that a theory of art, of history, or of morality is circular; that their authors tacitly assume principles which they illustrate by citing examples that are then held to establish the principles. Then, again, some critics seek an easy victory by showing, for example, that an idealist treatment of morality, politics, or of art is incompatible with the predominantly sensory principles upon which the critic chooses to take his stand until he has to deal with a more sensate account of morality, politics, or art, when he denounces it for its undue neglect of idealist values.

In a more profound sense, Sorokin's work may be said to show that arguments about values in the humanities and social sciences are always circular. Indeed, upon his principles, they are bound to be circular, because all component values whether of knowledge, aesthetics, or morality must, in any truly integral cultural supersystem, reflect or translate the basic presuppositions of that cultural system. In any such system the facts to which greatest emphasis is given as well as arguments about their significance or value will be relevant within the "radius" of that cultural supersystem of which they are at the same time the tangible evidence and support. Since Sorokin's analysis has detected more than one such integral cultural supersystem with distinctive component values, there is more than one such circle.

Sorokin vigorously and successfully defended himself against the charge that in formulating his classifications of cultural supersystems he had been guilty of tautology or circular reasoning.* He pointed out that analytical arguments of the type A is A are tautological, but that synthetic arguments of the type A is B are not because they enlarge knowledge by enriching the predicate. After the discovery that A is B, that knowledge can, of course, be used tautologically in analytic arguments, but that does not detract from the original discovery, which may have taken centuries to achieve. Sorokin's own discoveries in his *Social and Cultural Dynamics* are of this synthetic, non-tautological character. Spengler, on the other hand, in order to establish his idea that civilizations are like human beings inasmuch as they pass through the stages of childhood, maturity, decay, and death, did no more than select such facts from history as might seem to support his argument. Sorokin's types of cultural supersystems, as already explained, were not pre-formed in this way, but were arrived at after the history of human culture had been surveyed in great detail under other and very different sub-groups and classes of cultural phenomena. It is only within the circle or parameter of each of those separate major cultural supersystems that arguments about values become circular. But since all value systems can be shown to be included in Sorokin's scheme, arguments using them as parameters or circles must also all be circular. The findings reported in Chapter 5 establish the truth of these contentions which illuminate an immense variety of problems in sociology and the history of ideas. At the risk of possibly wearisome repetition a few examples now follow to illustrate the view that value arguments are necessarily circular.

Ethics

It has always been evident that the rules for right living followed by true believers in the great religions are those set down in holy books, the will of God or the commands of the Prophet. Such are the Ten Commandments of the Hebrew Old Testament, the Sermon on the Mount of the Greek New Testament, or the injunctions in the Koran. A secondary source comes from priestly or learned texts purporting to explain such rules. From them it is always possible to appeal to the primary source, the Word of God or of the Prophet, as religious reformers or innovators have always tried to do. The circularity of all ethical arguments so derived can never have been in doubt.

There are other ethical rules which may not claim to be the word of

*P. A. Allen, *op. cit.,* pp. 475-478.

God but are nevertheless put forward as principles of conduct from which there should be no deviation. Such is the prudential maxim, examples of which abound. Thus Phaedrus, anticipating to some extent the Golden Rule of the Gospels, proclaimed that it is right and fitting that those who visit evil upon others should suffer the same evil themselves.* Kant's famous "categorical imperative" was an *a priori,* formal, absolute, and unconditional principle requiring everyone to behave so that their action could be made a universal rule to be obeyed by everyone else as a law of Nature. To this he joined the command that in all their actions everyone should respect both themselves and others as ends-in-themselves and never allow any human being to be used as a means whereby they or others attained their own selfish purposes, aims, or ends. These moral laws within, said Kant, filled him with the same awe as that with which he contemplated the starry heavens above. It was an apt comparison. Morality should be timeless, predictable, and the subject of awe and reverence, just as is the movement of the heavenly bodies.

Any ethics of principles, whether formal or material, clearly has to rest for the vindication of its precepts upon those principles which do not themselves invoke or need other or "higher" authority. Neither can they make concessions to sensate urges and inclinations incompatible with their strict observance. Hence the asceticism and willing martyrdom of the devout and faithful.** An ethics of principles is more specifically moral than are the traditionally honored rules of primitive tribes whose religion, law, and ethics cannot be distinguished or spoken of in isolation, but this does not mean that all such rules can be established otherwise than by a circular process.

Natural Law

Kant's categorical imperative was the product of his own philosophical reflection or intuition. It is plausible to believe that a more generally acceptable system of moral rules may be put together out of the millenial experience of mankind in the course of which much wisdom should have been learned so that firm distinctions could be drawn about

---

Quod voluisti alteri intendere, aequum est ipse ut sustineas malum. Fables III 6, 10-11.
**P. A. Sorokin, *The Ways and Power of Love* (Boston, Beacon Press, 1954), pp. 105-114, where supraconscious intuition is held to be the source of ethical (and other) cultural principles.

the difference between right conduct and wrong. That a Natural Law or Law of Nature can arise spontaneously as an expression of the best instincts or inclinations of human beings, wherever they are found, was part of Stoic philosophy, popularized notably by Cicero, among others. Long eclipsed by the commandments of Christian doctrine, the idea that such a Natural Law can serve as a guide to conduct was kept alive by memories of Cicero's words, to be revived in sensate cultural times by Grotius, Hobbes, Spinoza, and others. Cicero had not proposed it as a substitute for religion as the true source of morality, neither did they. Some christian theologians saw no difficulty in accepting it; "for the law of Nature is nothing but the law of God given to Mankind for the conservation of his nature and the promotion of his perfective end" wrote Jeremy Taylor, quoting one of Cicero's many remarks to the effect that "it was God that gave justice to Mankind: he made justice by his sanction. *Est recta ratio a Numine Deorum tracta, imperans honesta et prohibens contraria.*"*

With the spread of scepticism during the rise of sensate culture Natural Law shared the fate of religious commandments. Lawyers will have nothing to do with it. Their craft is bounded by legislative enactments and legal precedents. When, in 1917, Harold Laski wrote to Justice Holmes to tell him that "we are witnessing a revival of 'natural' law and the 'natural' is the purely inductive statement of certain minimum conditions we can't do without if life is to be decent," he was trying to find some valid, objective standard upon which to base his political theories, more especially those which would lend support to his efforts to champion the cause of "the working class today." That "Natural Law" might serve in this way as a statement of elementary human rights in the sphere of economic life is a doctrine for a sensate age. It did not arise in such a form in ideational times, so "Natural Law" cannot provide that fully objective standard Laski hoped that it might.

Mr. Justice Holmes had certainly given Laski no encouragement – "I understand by human rights what a given crowd will fight for successfully," he bluntly told Laski, and he had better grounds for believing that his view rested upon a "purely inductive statement" than Laski could produce to support his wishful thinking.**

---

*J. Taylor, *Ductor Dubitantium* (London, 1676), p. 177, F. R. Cowell, *Cicero and the Roman Republic* (London, Penguin Books, 1968), pp. 350-5.

**M. deW. Howe, ed. *Holmes-Laski Letters* (London, Oxford University Press, 1953), pp. 116-117.

Since the Second World War the most impressive attempt to state Natural Law in Laski's sense of a basis for the justification of a "decent" way of life has been the Universal Declaration of Human Rights of the United Nations in 1948. A "statement" it remains, cynically disregarded whenever politicians in power in the signatory States find it inconvenient to honor their country's pledges. An attempt to make its provisions mandatory was a signal and pathetic failure. On a more limited regional basis the Council of Europe has, however, agreed to such a declaration and has established a Court to try to give it effect.

How vague the content of Natural Law is in fact was shown by Sorokin's "purely inductive" inquiry to discover "what types of actions tend to be viewed as criminal throughout all periods and all countries studied." Out of over a hundred actions viewed in some of the legal codes as criminal, less than twenty were found to be "absolute crimes" included in all the codes studied from barbaric times until the modern world after the First World War. Such deeds as murder, theft, rape, swindle, insult, violence, treason, were such as could be "fairly universally and fairly perpetually. . . qualified as criminal or wrong." So Sorokin concluded that "partisans of 'the natural law'. . . in Cicero's sense . . . are not essentially wrong."* Indeed, to the extent that "what is believed always, everywhere and by everybody" (*quod semper, quod ubique, quod ab omnibus creditum est,* in the classic phrase of St. Vincent of Lorins) can confer authority, there is a firm nucleus to serve as a statement of Natural Law. It will not so serve, however, unless there is a general willingness to observe an ethics of principles. Criminal statistics everywhere today show that in the most "advanced" countries such willingness is largely absent. Sensate lusts and desire do not stop short of theft, violence, rape, and even murder.

Casuistry

Sorokin's principles find an illustration in the topic of casuistry which, although he did not deal with it, is worth stressing both because it is usually neglected in the philosophic discussion of ethics and because it provides one more illustration of the cogency of his theories and their explanatory power.

Not until an ideational cultural system begins to give way before

---

*P. A. Sorokin, *Social and Cultural Dynamics* (New York, Bedminster Press, 1962), Vol. II, p. 577.

growing sensate demands is any possibility of flexibility in ideational rules
allowed by their upholders. Symptomatic of such a change in Christian
Europe was the development of casuistry. "Casuistry has appeared in
history," wrote Professors W. R. Sorely and R. M. Wenley in 1901, "when
external law, as opposed to ethical principle, has been taken as the
ultimate guide of conduct."* As Sorokin's more inclusive theory suggests,
the rise of sensate culture not only explains why and how external law
could arise to conflict with ethical principle, but it points to general
sociological influences having the same effect, by no means all of which
found expression in law. At first casuistry was developed to provide
guidance when Christian duties were found to be in apparent conflict. For
centuries it was a recognized branch of theology. By the seventeenth
century sensate influences in Spain and France were already sufficiently
strong to become apparent in the topics discussed by the casuists and
therefore to provoke dismay among orthodox and more puritanical souls.
Such were the Jansenists in France. They incited Pascal to attack certain
Jesuit writers who seemed to them to discuss everyday life, particularly in
its sexual aspects, with a freedom bordering upon the prurient. In
comparison with the latitude taken in more more modern times by certain
no doubt well-meaning clerics, the offence so given to religion and
morality was slight indeed. In the early seventeenth century, however,
orthodox sensibilities were very much more acute. Pascal's onslaught was
terrific. From that time onwards "casuistry" acquired that sinister smear
relegating it to the theological demi-monde that it has never since
succeeded in shedding. In England a "casuist" got the meaning of an
expert at twisting words in an argument. In vain Jesuits sought to reassure
Pascal by protesting the strictness of their own life and the necessity that
forced them "to go somewhat out of their way to meet sinners if they
were not to lose them entirely, such then already was the corruption of
morals."** The freedom with which absolution was bestowed upon
notorious sinners as part of this policy was so scandalous, said Pascal, that
"it broke the most holy Christian commandments and completely
overthrew God's laws. By compounding with wickedness in this way they
must have forgotten St. Paul's words that not only those who committed
crimes were worthy of death but so also were those who connive at their
wrong-doing."†

In the light of Sorokin's principles it seems probable that a rewarding

*J. M. Baldwin, ed., *Dictionary of Philosophy and Phsychology* (New York and
London, Macmillan, 1901). **B. Pascal,
**B. Pascal, *Les Lettres Provinciales,* 6th (1656)
†*Ibid,* 10th (1656); Romans I. 32.

study might be made of the development of casuistry not only in Christian theology but also in that of Buddhism and other great religions. In particular it would be interesting to know whether such an evolution of thought had anything in common with the idealist philosophy of Aristotle. Already in his lifetime in the fourth century B.C. a markedly sensate quality was being given to that essence of moral well-being which, on his principles, arose as a by-product of wholehearted service to those grand ideals of Socrates and Plato, the pursuit of truth, beauty, and moral worth. A life so lived would, he thought, be productive of personal felicity or blissfulness, which he accepted as desirable.

A generation later, Epicurus (342/1-271/270), simplifying the otherwordly, other-regarding element in Aristotle's eudaemonism, made it a more self-regarding satisfaction in which personal feelings and desires left less or little place for devotion to objective principles. Such feelings and desires were not the active, fleshly lusts of a purely sensate man but were of an almost neutral quality, being for a life free from pain and fear. A serenity of mind ensuring peaceful enjoyment and impertubability was his ideal. More active, energetic folk soon considered that the happiness desired by Epicurus ought to have a more positive quality and that it merited more energetic pursuit.

Hedonism

Personal or egoistic hedonism of the Epicureans who transformed the teaching of Epicurus simply made pleasure the chief good or aim in life. It is an ethical system that has always had vastly more practical than theoretical followers and exponents. Yet it does no more than follow the sensate system of cultural values to its logical conclusion. That everyone should put personal pleasure as their first and foremost consideration in all their activities was a conclusion so far in conflict with traditionally honored ideational and idealist values as to be hardly respectable. Apart from that, there is the insuperable difficulty of defining "pleasure." As long as one man's meat is another man's poison, Bernard Shaw's contradiction of the Golden Rule is relevant: "Do not do unto others as you would they should do unto you. Their tastes may be different."

No serious thinker was more forthright in proclaiming egoistic hedonistic pleasure to be the end and aim of action than Jeremy Bentham. In his *Rationale of Reward* of 1825 he said, "the utility of all arts and sciences — I speak both of those of amusement and curiosity — the value which they possess, is exactly in proportion to the pleasure they yield. Every other species of pre-eminence which may be attempted to be established among them is altogether fanciful. Prejudice apart, the game of push-pin is of equal value with the arts and sciences of music and poetry. If the game of push-pin furnish more pleasure, it is more valuable than either."* Shelley, Keats, de Musset, de Lamartine, Schubert, Beethoven, Mendelssohn and other famous poets and musicians were among Bentham's contemporaries, but he was right in believing that the majority of British and French found their pleasures elsewhere than in reading their poems or listening to their music. So they do today, despite the spread of literacy and the growth of leisure. Yet, whatever their amusements may be or the amount of pleasure derived from them, whether jazz music, television, detective stories, crossword puzzles, bingo, or betting; great poetry and music are likely to be regarded as the more "valuable."

When Bentham, one of the clearest-headed of men, could utter such an opinion, there is clearly need for a theory of value which would not rate a child's game above the creations of genius. Some way had to be found, even in a sensate society, to play down the element of private pleasure if hedonism was to be made plausible as a guide to conduct in society. Utilitarianism in ethics, politics, and economic theory were the most promising lines, and Bentham followed them. From egoistic hedonism he moved on to universalistic hedonism as the most vigorous exponent of "the greatest happiness or the greatest felicity principle." His "principle of utility," which gave rise to the label "utilitarian," merely approves or disapproves of every action whatsoever according to the tendency which it appears to have to augment or diminish the happiness of the party whose interest is in question.

Before hedonism in its egoistic or universalistic form can serve as a basis or principle in ethics, some clear meaning must be given to the "happiness" it purports to promote. To say with J. S. Mill that happiness is "pleasure and the absence of pain" merely moves the problem on to the need to define "pleasure." Without a generally accepted standard or measure of "happiness" or "pleasure," hedonism cannot provide a valid moral principle. That the "good" is the "pleasurable" involves a circular argument having a very short radius, limited to the personal points of view being canvassed or debated at any one time. Can economics give utilitarianism greater plausibility and generality by providing better notions of "utility" and of public welfare, even if not necessarily of "happiness" and "pleasure"?

*J. Bentham, *Works,* J. Bowring, ed. (Edinburg, Tait, 1943) Vol. II, p. 253.

Economics

Economic theory could not be and was not developed until the rise of the predominantly sensate culture had gone sufficiently far to stimulate reflection about the methods by which economic life, economic thought, and sensate living generally could become more effective.*

Economic theorists readily argued from the major premise of their increasingly sensate culture, according to which constantly developing material satisfactions were deemed to be able to provide mankind with highly desirable and very important values. Economic psychology became a matter of self interest and competition, of desires and their satiation, of the elasticity of demand and the marginal theory of value. Economists concentrated upon their analyses of the production and marketing of desirable goods; upon the study of the means of producing such goods, classified as land, labor, capital or equipment, and upon the laws of supply and demand by which the monetary values of those means and the monetary value of all that they produce are alike determined. From such beginnings the whole vast structure of economic theory has grown together with the whole vast structure of modern industrial and commercial civilization. Yet it remains essentially a sensate philosophy, building upon simple sensate presuppositions; a vast process, therefore, of circular argument. That this is so is seen when the sensate presuppositions are not fully accepted, as when Carlyle, enamored of vigorous creative "personalities" flayed "Dismal Science," in which vivid characters became colorless Benthamite "individuals"; when Wordsworth complained that "getting and spending we lay waste our powers"; or when Ruskin demolished Ricardo and J. S. Mill by arguments leading to his grand idea, printed in capitals, "THERE IS NO WEALTH BUT LIFE. Life including all its powers of love, of joy, of admiration." There was no genuine debate, no dialectic between such apostles of idealism and the bankers, traders, manufacturers, and their advisors. Ruskin has been falsely accused of neglecting to study the literature of economics. He knew it well enough, but his circle of thought and that of the economists were not concentric. Economists could not controvert him, neither could he influence them. His basic major premise was not sensate but predominantly that of an idealist culture.

To believe that is not to assume that sensate values, which of course

*J. A. Schumpeter, *History of Economic Analysis* (London, Allen and Unwin, 1963), pp. 73-107 shows how little interest was taken in economic theory by scholastic philosophers even after Aristotle's writings had been recovered.

Carlyle, Ruskin and the poets shared, are to be condemned. Their lives were relatively comfortable while all around them was the most appalling distress. For centuries however, an ideational tradition in ethics and aesthetics had subordinated considerations of human physical sufferings and pleasures alike in a grand scheme of a transcendental nature in which spiritual satisfactions were believed to be of supreme and superior concern. During centuries of poverty and physical suffering of an intensity unknown to modern civilization in time of peace, human effort and human wealth was lavished upon the building of churches, abbeys, and cathedrals. In relation to the economic gross national product at the time, such an expenditure was probably a greater economic burden than is the cost today of sending men to land on the moon. The Christian ethic of loving kindness and mercy did not indeed neglect the sorrows of the poor, the sick and the helpless. Church revenues, supplemented by the bounty of the well-to-do, created infirmaries, hospitals, schools, and other charitable institutions on a scale unknown in previous history. Nevertheless the ills to which flesh is heir were regarded as inevitable in the scheme of divine providence by which the world was deemed to be ruled. It is an attitude which is by no means unknown in many parts of the world today. Theoretical economists thought that large-scale intervention to remove the evils of poverty might do more harm than good.

Yet a directly contrary doctrine was being insistently proclaimed. The followers of Karl Marx were inciting poor men to rise against the rich. No ideational or idealistic ethical considerations stirred them to their revolutionary task. It had one aim and one only, to increase the sensate satisfactions of the masses. With such force was this aim pursued, so completely were all other human values subordinated or ignored by one pretense or another that Marxism was embraced by some ardent spirits with an energy almost religious in its single-minded devotion. Marxism was anything but religious in reality because it completely lacked any transcendental reference. Marxism puts no faith in the unknown or in any reality beyond the reach of the senses. For Marxists, all philosophy, all religion, all art, all history must undergo a "materialist" interpretation. Marxist doctrines in all their forms are inevitably functions of a sensate parameter and all are circular arguments with sense-satisfaction as their radius. It is impossible for them to be otherwise without ceasing to be Marxist, just as it is, or should be, impossible for Christians to condone gluttony, drunkenness, sexual debauchery, and all the other indulgences of a sensate cultural supersystem.

Karl Marx was vastly more influential than Ruskin or Carlyle because he talked the same language as the economists whose fundamental principles he pushed to what seemed to be their logical conclusion. More important still, his ideas were likely to make a powerful appeal to the sensate masses, many of whom existed in pitiable conditions of poverty, misery, and squalor at a time when many more energetic, more capable, or more fortunate folk were steadily getting richer.

The Communist Manifesto of 1848, the gospel of the Marxists, committing "the Communists everywhere (to) support every revolutionary movement against the existing social and political order of things," might seem to declare war on conventional economic ideas but in fact it was but another sub-section of the sensate economic doctrine. Its purpose was to rob existing owners of wealth by transferring their property to others collectively described as "the proletariat," who were also labelled, for the greater power and profit of their Communist manipulators, as "the State." It is unnecessary here to argue about the respective merits and deficiencies of theoretical and practical Communism or of the former "free market" economies in their common pursuit of the goals of an economic science dedicated to the greatest possible production of goods and services. Both claim great advances. It is not much more than a hundred years since a beginning was made to liberate most of the population of Russia from serfdom. Although many hundred years had then elapsed since the last serf was liberated in England, almost half the women and one-third of the men of England were unable to read or write in the world of Charles Dickens. The miseries depicted in his novels, such as *Oliver Twist* (1837-8), have been swept away by the rapidly expanding sensate economy, although they are provided as descriptions of contemporary England for Russian children. It has taken longer for such progress to transform Russia. Lenin, it has been said, was "conscious of the primitive level of the economy and the lack of 'culture' in the masses of the population" while Stalinism, which succeeded him, was "rooted in a society and a tradition which carried too many marks of primitive barbarism not yet outlived."* Nevertheless the same sensate forces are at work in Russia also. Progress there would have been greater if millions of the more enterprising and more able Russians had not been liquidated and others thereby discouraged from coming forward. Stalinism, although denounced by Khrushchev in 1956, is by no means dead. Yet some limited release of individual initiative has sporadically occurred.

In the Western world where private enterprise capitalism supposedly

Times Literary Supplement, London, December 18, 1969, p. 1453.

has free rein so that the "economic man" (that fiction of Political Economy) is able to pursue his own selfish interest, sensate, self-seeking endeavor has steadily been reined in and curbed. The grasping capitalist of Marxist propaganda has been fettered by the power of Trade Unions, impoverished by "unofficial" strikes, cramped by Government rules and regulations often enforced by inspectors, compelled to spend untold hours compiling returns and reports on his activities, and in addition heavily taxed on his earnings and profits to support a huge national scheme providing health services, retirement pensions, and unemployment pay. At the same time the business once run by private enterprise in such matters as the supply of coal, gas, electricity, communications, and public transport, has been taken over by public bodies and corporations. Free market economies are thus approaching somewhat nearer the totalitarian State-managed economies of the Prison-States with the very vital difference that in the Western world workers are free to change their employers while those employers do not possess the controlling or coercive powers at the disposal of all the directing ranks of the Communist States.

Whether to preserve such freedoms or for other reasons, the Marxists' advice to "the proletariat" to wipe out the "bourgeoisie" by revolutionary action made very little appeal in the British Isles or in the United States of America, although it made a good deal of noise and excited some alarm. Nevertheless, most of the ambitions proclaimed in the ten-point program at the end of Part II of the Communist Manifesto of 1848 have largely been realized in Great Britain. The result has not been to abolish the "bourgeoisie." It might rather be said to have abolished Marx's "proletariat." In fact, neither has been abolished because neither existed except as re-ified "ideal types" in the minds of Marx and Engels. The sociological reality, as Sorokin's sociology demonstrates, is not a story of "bourgeoisie" versus "proletariat" as "classes," but of some relatively richer sensate men and some relatively poorer sensate men most, but not necessarily all, of whom were always striving to become richer.*

Despite their success, which is quite amazing when seen against the background of economic conditions a century ago or even half a century ago, neither capitalism nor communism has yet succeeded in satisfying the

_____

*How obsolete Marxian social philosophy had already become in Western Europe was convincingly documented by an active and ardent but disillusioned Communist worker, Henri de Man, in 1927 in *Au delà du Marxisme,* translated as *The Psychology of Socialism* in 1928. *Cf* F. R. Cowell, *Culture in Public and Private Life,* pp. 280-294.

aspirations of mankind. That, despite great advances, much of the prevalent discontent is voiced upon economic grounds, vindicates the wisdom of Aristotle that "it is of the nature of desire not to be satisfied." In 1937 Sorokin already foresaw the probable outcome of the working-out of sensate desires. A generation after he wrote his grim prophecy of troubles to come, its vindication may be read in the record of unrest, strikes, and seen as well in the spread of robbery with violence that has made many American cities unsafe at night but which is of small account in comparison with the profits of an illicit trade in death-dealing drugs and the racketeering by which it is accompanied. A sensate society is ill-equipped to grapple with so many social maladies, aggravated appallingly as they are in the United States in particular by discord thought to be engendered upon "racial" grounds. Because of its sensate premises, remedies of a sensate order are sought. If some means could only be found of raising living standards, it is urged, many of the troubles now afflicting society would disappear. Earlier sensate societies, as Aristotle observed, had been disappointed by their faith in this circular argument. Sorokin held that a sensate society and its opposite, an ideational society, were both liable to collapse as overweening trust in their respective premises was found, after long experience, to be misplaced. That more is required than sensate remedies follows from Sorokin's sociological theories. He is not, of course, by any means alone in advocating a broader than sensate basis for civilized life.

Today it is highly significant that young theorists brought up to regard Communism as the only answer to all social problems have discovered the impossibility of reconciling Marxism and moral philosophy. When all human actions are believed to be causally determined, there is no place for moral ethical principles. As the product of "methods of production," they lack moral authority and moral power to change the world.*

Orthodox Marxists are logical in their denunciation as "revisionist" of all who seek to dilute the pure materialist value system with any such tinctures derived from an idealist or ideational cultural supersystem. That is why Communist parties, as soon as they have been able to seize power which they always do by ruthless violence, immediately deny all freedom of expression to writers, artists and others, and forbid all contact with any external influences likely to question Marxist presuppositions or to expose their psychological and philosophical shallowness and inadequacies. Theirs

*L. Kolakowski, *Marxism and Beyond,* trans. by Jane Z. Peel (London, Pall Mall Press, 1969).

is a sensate system so it is sternly upheld by sensate sanctions of physical punishment and suffering for the recalcitrant and by material rewards and minor luxuries for the docile. Where, as in Russia or China, the overwhelming majority were ill-educated, unreflective, sensate and unenterprising individuals, such methods succeed easily enough for the dominant party machine to maintain its tyrannical rule.*

Universalistic hedonism, utilitarianism, and economic theory alike fail to provide a sound basis for ethics and hence of sociological theory as well. They, in common with all subjective sources or guides to behavior such as "common sense," "moral sense," or even "conscience" are vulnerable to Samuel Johnson's criticism: "If a man pretends to a principle of action of which I can know nothing . . . . how can I tell what that person may be prompted to do? When a person professes to be governed by a written ascertained law, I can then know where to find him." ** So his settled view was that "we can have no dependence upon that instinctive, that constitutional goodness which is not founded upon principle." †

Conflict of Ethical Principles

Sorokin's theories thus present the ethical systems of the past, of which economic science is a branch and offshoot, as more or less self-contained and logically coherent universes of discourse, all being founded upon different and frequently opposing principles. Many examples illustrate the frequently tragic consequences when such diverse systems come into conflict.

Ideational societies in the past were logical in their denunciation as "heretical" of all who sought in any way to dilute or amend doctrines that the ruling hierarchy deemed to be orthodox. Without possessing anything like the formidable propaganda machinery, secret police, spies, and informers of the Prison-States, the Holy Inquisition was able to maintain unquestioned authority in Spain by suppressing Protestants and expelling not merely Moslems but Moors converted to Catholicism. Besides this ruthless assertion of Catholic supremacy at the beginning of the seventeenth century, the likewise ruthless expulsion of protestants from

---

*"Russia is an instance of the ease with which a new direction can be given to the opinions of a whole people." J. Bentham, *Works* (Edinburgh, 1843), Vol. II, p. 260.
**J. Boswell, *Life of Johnson*, G. B. Hill and L. F. Powell, eds. (Oxford, Clarendon Press, 1934), Vol. II, p. 126.
†*Ibid,* Vol. I, p. 443.

France at the end of the century was a minor matter. Both examples of stern intolerance were soundly based upon premises or dogma which were anything but sensate in intent. Indeed, both expulsions are regarded as so damaging to the economic or sensate prosperity of Spain and to a lesser extent of France that Spain has never fully recovered while France was gravely weakened throughout the century which followed, when it was smitten by the disaster of the Revolution of 1789. Catholic Europe, like Communist Europe, was limited with circular arguments based upon premises which did not ultimately succeed in responding to all the demands or aspirations cherished by those forced to live under their rule. After such experiences it is not surprising that others who have studied or witnessed the results of such rule are resolute in their determination not to become themselves its victims.

It should be experience and knowledge which would be able to force sociological thought to realize the nature of the circular arguments within which life has in the past been governed and, in the light of such realization, to study ways of transcending the limitations which such circularity imposes. In practice, in the freer lands where cultural life has not been shackled by Marxist-Leninist ideology or by theological dogma, and where men have not been restrained by strict secular laws, the utmost diversity is apparent. Since Sorokin forecast the likely development of sensate societies, more restraints have probably been cast aside than even he would have deemed possible within so short a time. Pornography, obscenity, homosexuality, abortion — all of which were taboo during most of his lifetime — no longer attract the penalties or the stern disapproval by which they were formerly suppressed. In his view they are symptoms of the breakdown of what he described as an "overripe" sensate culture. If they are merely concessions to an unrestrained sexuality and eroticism, they are understandable upon sensate premises. It is not possible to relate them to any principle other than that of a sensate cultural system. On Sorokin's theory of sociology they are condemned as elements in an "overripe" system. How is "overripeness" of a cultural system to be understood?

In his short book *The American Sex Revolution* (Boston, Porter Sargent, 1956) Sorokin was writing for a popular audience so his discussion was largely in terms of traditional prudential morality. He showed how "sexual gluttons and gourmands" were just as likely to be prone, if not more prone, to premature debility, disease, and death as are the victims of excessive eating and drinking. That is to say that sexual excess defeats the sensual major premise to which alone its practitioners could have recourse if they sought any theoretical basis for their activities. It may be added, in the light of what has been said above, that fierce religious persecution in the name of Christianity is a horrid blasphemy against a religion of charity, forgiveness of sins, and spiritual love. So such persecution also contradicts the major (ideational) premise to which alone it can appeal for justification. Criticism of the burning of heretics on sensate grounds is unnecessary, but of course is usually the main ground in a sensate age. Cultural systems thus become "overripe" by generating internal conflict. Since cultural values of any system have strong powers of survival, it is more likely, after a long historical evolution such as that which has occurred in most old civilizations, for conflict to develop between the partisans of more than one distinct cultural system.

Religious questions lie beyond sociology unless they arise directly from social problems. Such is the current debate upon the legitimacy of deliberate limitation of an increase in population. Sorokin describes how Bolshevik Russia, following sensate, Marxist principles, had no scruples in permitting abortion. "Free love" was encouraged also, and its leaders "deliberately attempted to destroy marriage." Moral and social chaos resulted on such a scale that in 1944-45 "the government was forced to reverse its policy" so that "Soviet Russia today has a more monogamic, stable, and Victorian family life than do most of the Western Countries."*

In other lands where sensate cultural values were in the ascendant, the Soviet example by no means encountered universal disapproval. A sensate morality approves methods to ensure that the pleasures of sexual intercourse do not invariably entail the risk and heavy responsibility of having to bear, rear, and support children. Powerful support is given to the idea that families should be limited through "family planning" because of the appallingly rapid increase in world population which, left unchecked, would seem likely to lower progressively the amenities and the standard of living everywhere. Consequently, a tremendous controversy was occasioned by the Encyclical issued by Pope Paul VI on July 25, 1968 on the illegitimacy of birth control by chemical and medical methods.

To oppose birth control in such circumstances upon religious or ideational grounds is liable to cause intense opposition, fortified by such arguments that the acute frustrations caused by such a ban are liable to cause such psychological stress and strain that possibly the health of many men and women would suffer. Nevertheless an ideational value system must subordinate sensuous pleasures to its own ideational standards. The

*P. A. Sorokin, *The American Sex Revolution* (Boston, Porter Sargent, 1956), pp. 114-115.

Pope could not make concessions. "A reciprocal act of love which jeopardizes the disponibility to transmit life", he said, "is in contradiction with the design constitutive of marriage and with the will of the Author of Life." (art. 13). He made it clear that he had considered all the arguments in favor of birth control, notably the "rapid demographic development" which led to the fear that "world population is growing more rapidly than the available resources." Many considerations (of a sensate nature) "greatly reinforced the temptation" to resort to "radical measures" (art. 2). Nevertheless the Pope maintains what is essentially an ideational principle, that "in relation to the tendencies of instinct or passion, responsible parenthood means that necessary dominion which reason and will must exercise over them" (art. 10). He observed also that "the young who are so vulnerable on this point have need of encouragement to be faithful to the moral law, so they must not be offered some easy means of eluding its observance" (art. 17).

So prevalent is the sensate mentality that many people apparently neither understood nor would tolerate such a flat rejection of practices elaborated after long scientific research. A typically crude "modern" reaction was widespread and immediate. A letter to a London evening newpaper for example, declared that "the Papal edict is a piece of claptrap straight out of the Dark Ages. It fully deserves the ridicule it will doubtless generate." "Can anyone in his right mind," the writer asked, "suffer misery simply because an ignorant and anachronistic man, celibate and lacking basic knowledge of marriage, tells him that it is the will of God?" In more temperate language very many other people, including many Catholics, questioned or rejected the Pope's ruling. Many, who accepted the Pope's ruling as being intended to restrain a mere indulgence in animal passion, might have considered that conjugal relationships of a more idealist kind were permissible without resigning that "necessary dominion of reason and will" which the Pope was concerned to maintain.

Reductionism and Confusion in Eclectic Value Theories

When the clash between incompatible sensate and ideational social philosophies is not so overt as that evident in the controversy over birth control shows it to be, efforts to achieve some compromise falling short of an idealist integration often fail to provide coherent doctrines. They are vulnerable either to sensate criticism on the one hand or to ideational idealistic objection on the other hand.

Ethical discussions about "my station and its duties," for example, which seemed admirable on idealist presuppositions, would be dismissed in a sensate society as propaganda, or as "emotional" rationalizations, because such a sensate society cannot believe in any principles except its own. If it has to give any attention to ideas controverting such principles it may do so by the pretense that their authors are really sensate too, although they hypocritically try to appear idealistic. Idealists, like Bradley, in turn assume that their idealism should make an instant appeal irrespective of the sensate inconvenience in which it may involve other people.

Not merely is every cultural supersystem a vast circle of related, cognate values, but those within each usually assume that theirs is, or should be, the only circle, so that anything apparently beyond its circumference must somehow be brought within it by one device or another. Where "rationalization" or "self-deception" fail as arguments to effect such integration, efforts are made either to exhibit alien values as antiquated and obsolete, or to endeavor by specious special pleading to reduce them to something more congruous.

Sorokin's criticisms of Freudian emphasis upon sexual feelings as determinants of thought and behavior are a good example showing up the mistake of an attempt to reduce, illegitimately, theories of human motivation. In many arts and sciences similar excessive confidence in a single factor or value judgment has often been evident. Historians often confine themselves to narrative in their effort to avoid hazardous misrepresentation of the motives and actions of human beings in the past, as the discussion in the previous chapter will have indicated. Yet even the best narrative historians cannot always resist the temptation to expound or explain. Macaulay painted an unforgettable picture of the advancing prosperity of England since the seventeenth century upon the basis that "in every experimental science there is a tendency towards perfection. In every human being there is a wish to ameliorate his own condition." Upon such a belief in "progress," he was able, with the aid of his swift, graphic style, to carry general conviction among a vast reading public. His success was earned because he was describing the progress of a society still becoming more sensate in which his two great principles are undoubtedly evident.* He did not concern himself with the vast stretch of time from the Roman Republic until the rise of the alchemists, when there was no

*More than a hundred years later Professor J. H. Plumb sought to base social and historical theory upon the idea of progress in *The Crisis in the Humanities* (London, Penguin Books, 1964).

experimental science, nor with the history of those monastic institutions to which men flocked because they were uninterested in a progressive amelioration of their worldly condition in the sense in which he and his readers understood such words. His business was to narrate. He did not need a philosophy of history to make his story supremely well told. He was too well-read, too great a scholar and too discriminating in taste and judgment to believe that the material, sensate progress he extolled was accompanied by similar progress in cultural life generally. For him Thucydides remained the supreme historian, unrivalled in later ages. He revered Aeschylus and Sophocles, Shakespeare and Milton, believing that no such commanding literary geniuses had since surpassed them.

The Thought and Character of William James may serve as another example of the difficulty, without a general theory, of validating social and cultural values and preferences. His philosophical interest was deeper than Macaulay's, so he was incited to wrestle with ethical and aesthetic problems. James became a powerful influence in the latter part of the nineteenth and early part of the twentieth century because of his clear-headed "no nonsense" approach to a great many questions and his ability to write about them in an interesting way.

He was sufficiently idealistic in Sorokin's sense of the word, to reject egoistic or universalistic hedonism, but he never seems to have elaborated a fully thought out system or theory of value. At one stage he wrote that "of all the proposed *summa genera,* pleasure and perfection have the best claim to be considered."* He did not say what he meant by either "pleasure" or "perfection," nor did he consider the possibility that it might not be very easy or even possible to enjoy both simultaneously. Ten years later he said, "the great use of life is to spend it on something that outlasts it."** Another of his maxims was that "happiness of mankind should be the great cause to which life should be devoted."† His biographer said that he was a "heated moral partisan" with a "strong distaste for anything he suspected of being decadent" and a belief in "consistency or a respect for authority." James shared the outlook of most of his seriously minded contemporaries and like them gave no very clear or consistent explanation and defense of his ethical or aesthetic beliefs. In one of his more persistent efforts to justify them he said "that act is the best act which makes for the best whole, the best whole being

---

*R. B. Perry, *The Thought and Character of William James* (Cambridge, Mass., Harvard University Press, 1935), Vol. II, p. 255.
**Ibid, p. 256
†Ibid, p. 254

that which prevails at the least cost, in which the vanquished goods are least completely annulled."*

Such a formula, like the Hegelian "Absolute," or Ruskin's "Life as a whole" may resume and try to condense an immense wealth of thought and feeling possessed by its author but it conveys nothing to those ignorant of the long train of thought leading to its formulation. James at least had the merit of realizing that the "best whole" could only be achieved at the cost of eliminating or subordinating some values. Sorokin's empirical study of the values from which any cultural supersystem is built up shows that there are exceedingly many of them and also that they may and in fact do conflict with the values of another cultural supersystem as the music of Wagner, Franz Lehar, or the latest pop record jibe with the Gregorian Chant or the melodies of J. S. Bach. The whole rich field of human aesthetics, even more than of ethical interests is reduced to a colorless blank by having "the Absolute" or "Life" as their source, or as the ultimate criterion of their worth. Never was the total cultural environment more complex and confusing than it is today. It is plausible to see the root of much contemporary malaise in the absence of cohesion, lack of direction, and consequent perplexity and uncertainty about cultural values. If they are correctly described as able to give meaning and value to human lives devoted to their pursuit or service, then anything which seriously disturbs or shatters value-patterns is bound to enfeeble or blunt human interest and endeavor because it is liable to deprive those lives of meaning and value. Durkheim's Greek name for the absence of law and organization or an understandable pattern in life, *anomie,* was also his explanation of sociological malaise often leading anyone so deprived to suicide. Sociology therefore has the strongest reason to follow Sorokin in making values and culture a central and guiding theme. If such an argument needed reinforcing, then reference may be made to the relatively equable, contented, and serene lives lived by the fortunate few who succeed in discovering a cultural interest able to "polarize," "harness," or direct their mental energies. They did not wait for a sociology and Sorokin to lay out the whole vast map of culture but took their own path, often by chance, to pursue their special, the therefore necessarily limited sphere of interest. Some became botanists, others physicists, biologists, chemists or specialists in other branches of science. Others were active in music, the theatre, architecture, sculpture, painting, poetry, and literature generally

*Ibid, p.264.

and in all the other humanistic pursuits so reflectively and engagingly surveyed by Alain in his *Système des Beaux-Arts** and weighed by Sorokin in his *Social and Cultural Dynamics*. All such specialists, connoisseurs, and critics develop refined powers of appreciation and a wealth of knowledge within their own specialty. Alive as they are to an infinitude of facts and nuances, they do not always relish efforts such as Sorokin's to map the universe of culture as a whole. For the inevitable errors, shortcomings, omissions, over- or under-emphasis they can often detect in such general surveys, they rarely have more than an amused tolerance while they may also exhibit an impatience, lack of sympathy, or positive detestation. "Do speak ill of that accursed Spengler, Decline of the West," wrote Mr. Justice Holmes to Harold Laski, "It is not lawful to know as much as he assumes to know."** His was but a sham exasperation because his real opinion, that which drove him to read Spengler, was summed up by him most admirably as "everything in the universe is as interesting as anything else if you are able to see it as a coherent part of a possible coherent whole — and if you don't see the universal in your particular, you are a manual laborer and it doesn't matter."† It must have been in that spirit that Spengler attempted his great panorama, that Hegel pursued the "Absolute," Toynbee the study of History, and Sorokin the study of historical sociology. Among the profits of seeing things as a coherent whole is that of seeing some of the specialists in a wider perspective than their own. "The relativity of criticism, as soon as you note what environment the critic lived in simply leaps to the eyes."†† Why this should be and why the cultural environment should change are among the problems which Sorokin sought to elucidate. In a period of great cultural confusion where the search for "a coherent whole" to give it form and intelligibility becomes urgent, it is not at all surprising that reductionism should be rife. Sorokin's work itself might, and probably will be regarded as reductionism, even if it is admittedly on a grander scale than most such attempts. If he is to be criticized on that score, it should be remembered that his method of establishing his generalizations was the reverse of the method of reductionists. As so frequently stressed in this work (and yet one more repetition here is to be excused because of the persistence of

---

*Alain, *Système des Beaux-Arts* (Paris, Gallimard, 1926).

**M. deW. Howe, ed., *Holmes-Laski Letters* (London, Oxford University Press, 1953), p. 1384.

†*Ibid*, p. 1208. ("... if you don't *try* to see the universal" would be more charitable.)

††*Ibid*, p. 715.

error on the point) Sorokin did not start with a formula or defined hypothesis as the reductionists do, but with a vast survey of the total field to be explained, as explained it has to be if sociology is to be shown to be relevant to the problems of humanity as a whole. If he is so criticized, moreover, his critics must make sure that they do not "reduce" his thought to their formula.

The Need for An Integral Culture

In the confused world of either jarring, competing, or harmonious and co-operating ethical and aesthetic values, Sorokin's guiding lines or polar points of reference introduce some principles of wider understanding and hence some possibility of order, coherence, and intelligibility. He offers no single Absolute after the manner of neo-Hegelain philosophy. His two or three main networks of values or "socio-cultural supersystems," serve as parameters or general co-ordinating principles for more than one whole series of values. Each is a kind of "solar system" round which gravitate cohesive, cognate values. Values of the sensate supersystem have one orbit. Those of the ideational or idealistic systems have another.

Unlike unitary theories, whether invoking pleasure, the "Absolute," or some other transcendental principle, Sorokin's scheme does not seek to force a single label or theory upon all values. He does not, like Clive Bell for example, seek a magic formula such as the expression of emotion or ecstasy through "significant" form as an explanation of all genuine art. Sorokin's cultural supersystems do not rest upon any metaphysical assumptions or require any justification other than that to be found in human nature and human experience. The irremediable relativity of some values is neither glossed over nor explained away. On the contrary, Sorokin accepts and emphasizes the stark reality of contrasts, differences and fundamental incompatibilities. He shows that all efforts to play them down or to reconcile them must inevitably be doomed to failure, because neither of the conflicting views is really able to understand the other. Integration by invoking a superior principle to which both parties can agree offers the only hope of progress.

In the supreme task of sociology to show how to bring about a better social system Sorokin's sociological principles are very suggestive. In the educational world they immediately show up the shallowness of the claims of so-called "modern" studies to replace or to subordinate older humanistic and classical disciplines. Because life itself as well as education must have an assured material foundation and an adequate economic basis, there can be no question of neglecting the natural sciences, technology, economics, law, and accountancy and all that go with them. It is equally evident that the immense values derived from such "modern studies" depend directly upon the sensate network or parameter, while any ethical and aesthetic values they may yield arise, if at all, indirectly. To limit study, training and curiosity to them alone would be to limit and to stunt the growth of the human spirit. Great as were the merits of Jeremy Bentham, Karl Marx and other prophets of the "modern" age, they and their works are no substitute for all that the greatest creative minds have achieved in the service of ideational and idealist values. The educational problem is to find effective means of stimulating growing minds to discover their bearings within both the sensate and idealist networks or parameters so as to be able to seek their own higher synthesis. Above all, they must never presume to try to judge the values of one parameter exclusively in terms of the other.

In the educational world also, virulent student antagonism to academic and public authority is symptomatic of the breakdown of a sensate cultural supersystem. In a reasonably well integrated and flourishing cultural world there is no "student problem" beyond the normal effervescence of animal spirits of the young and immature, whose passing fancies have never been taken seriously. Trouble arises today because, with the breakdown of sensate culture, those who once had the courage of their convictions no longer seem to have convictions about which to be courageous. Inevitably, therefore, there is uncertainty and insincerity about the values which should enhance life with meaning and purpose. If the young are insolent and impudent because they scorn a society which fails to provide them with principles they can respect, their resentment is understandable. But they remain merely derogatory and destructive as long as they fail to come forward with constructive ideas likely to aid the discovery of new and superior values. They will be self-defeating and destructively anarchical until means are found of transcending the closed circle or parameter of sensate values. Sorokin, who brings the problem into better focus by his analysis of the value framework within which reform is possible, does not minimize the gravity of the task. Denouncing the "inconsistency between our avowed moral standards and our actual conduct," he wrote in 1956: "especially confused are the minds and actions of the younger generation born in this atmosphere of near anarchy . . . the high rate of crime among teenagers, the astounding wantonness, senselessness, and cruelty of some of their deeds are but the inevitable consequences of the cultural confusion in which they were born and educated." He was referring to the United States as it was in 1956, where the situation stirred him to the strongest condemnation of "these human animals." Their "bestial deeds," he said, were "motivated by sheer cussedness, by cynicism, sexual debauchery, and a lust for excitement – all the fruits of undisciplined growth in an environment of disorderly morals. If this confusion continues, then delinquency, debauchery, and other mental and moral diseases will continue to spread among the youth and the adults alike, and the results will be utter anarchy."* Since he published this fiery polemic on the sexual excesses of a sensate society, the situation has further dangerously degenerated among certain sections of the world's youth by their addiction to poisonous, habit-forming drugs. It remains true that delinquent youth is a very small proportion of youth as a whole. Abnormality, however, is news in a "popular" newspaper press avid for "human stories," whereas it is difficult to get a "story" about teenage normality.

Sorokin's own "principle of limits" suggests that excess in any activity may stimulate a halt or a reversal before catastrophe supervenes.** Sociological experience which he records in such detail also suggests that it is rare for a lone reformer to secure a great audience willing to heed his words. Rare, but not impossible when that leader has charismatic magic. Although Sorokin was a prophet of woe in this respect, he was not despondent. Belief in the inventive genius of the more highly gifted and those with "supraconscious" intuition saved him from fatalism or determinism of a material, mechanical kind.

Now that social and cultural life has been fragmented as never before, not one of Sorokin's broad classes of cultural phenomena, ideational, idealistic, and sensate can alone fittingly be applied to the cultural life of the past hundred years.

Far from invalidating Sorokin's interpretation of the past, such failure confirms his view that it is our fate to live in a world of cultural chaos characteristic of the decline and fall of loyalties to a settled, traditional cultural system. A vast number of cultural values surviving today can, of

*P. A. Sorokin, *The American Sex Revolution* (Boston, Porter Sargent Publisher, 1956), pp. 140-1.

**At the end of 1969 a young proprietor of a menswear shop in fashionable Chelsea, London, described as "trendy" and as catering to the young, was reported as saying: "people aren't trying to be desperately masculine or desperately feminine any more; they're not worrying about their sexual roles as much as they used to." (David Elliott interviewed by Judy Innes, in the *Daily Mail,* London, December 29, 1969, p. 8).

course, be related to once prevalent cultural supersystems. Millions of the faithful members of Churches, monasteries, and nunneries are still devoted to millenial ideational values, remaining aloof from the efforts of a minority to "modernize" them in a way deemed likely to make them more acceptable to lukewarm, predominantly sensate natures. Faculties of philosophy, classical antiquity, literature, and art perpetuate that striving for a harmonious, integrated culture begun at the Renaissance and characteristic of an idealist culture. In the last half century, with the highly significant exceptions of the Second World War and subsequent wars in the Far East fought (like that war) in order to prevent the victory of totalitarian power and to ensure the self-determination of peoples, sensate values have never been so assiduously developed or more energetically pursued since the unrestrained sensuality of the early Roman Empire. Statistics of thefts of every kind of property; silver, jewelry, furs, radio sets, motor cars, lorries, and their cargoes; statistics of crimes of violence, of drug addiction, and of divorce, are merely a few of the consequences of sensate scorn for principles which would limit sensate lusts.

In the desire to find a way out of this prevalent cultural confusion, art and literature are eagerly but vainly scanned for the first signs of some emerging trends which may lead to a new cultural synthesis. As yet, most novelties in art, music, painting, sculpture, architecture, and literature fail to interest more than a few coteries. Certainly this could also be said about some past innovations before their intrinsic merits won general recognition, but it would be bad logic to conclude from that fact that failure to win instant recognition is an infallible sign of genius. Many immensely popular successes of the moment are soon forgotten. Literature and even philosophy do not seem immune from short-lived enthusiasms usually associated with the world of pop-singers, pop music, or fashions in women's clothing.

It is impossible to reflect Sorokin's thought without referring to his frequent and often strident denunciations of much of the evidence of the low standards in the cultural life, notably that of the masses, of today. Because of his idealist standards he has even been accused of rewriting history in order to condemn contemporary culture. It would be more honest if such critics would say what it is that they applaud among the long list of things he thought deplorable. From 1937 onwards he has said what they are, from his *Social and Cultural Dynamics* to his *The American Sex Revolution* of 1956 and later. There is usually one stock defense of "mass" culture, "pop" art, and music, and it comes down to no more than "they want it." It is generally regarded as the complete and final answer, as of course, it is, as long as human quality, education, training, amusements, facilities for travel, recreation, housing, publicly provided amenities, mass media, social and cultural tradition remain what they are. Until present levels in all these sources are raised there seems no hope of improvement, but the first requisite before standards are likely to rise is a method of inciting people, particularly children and young people, to take an interest in some subject or subjects which will lead them along the path of progress. Then they will educate themselves, as indeed they must, because it is a task which nobody else can perform for them.

A cultural sociology such as Sorokin's must allow for the possibility, for whatever reason, of an *anomie* implying a life without faith in or direction from any cultural values. As this would be a life outside society, it might be regarded as beyond the scope of sociology as a science of social life. Nevertheless it illustrates Sorokin's theory of the consequences of the breakdown of a cultural way of life. It is no new experience. Over two thousand years ago a weary and disillusioned man in Palestine calling himself the Preacher recorded some of the consequences of a life of pleasure-seeking. "I have seen," he said, "all the works that are done under the sun; and, behold, all is vanity and vexation of spirit."* What he had himself achieved — his houses, vineyards, orchards, gardens, his servants, and his maidens, the children they bore him, his cattle, gold, silver, and other treasure — pleased him no better. He "looked on all the works that my hands had wrought, and on the labor that I had labored to do: and, behold, all was vanity and vexation of spirit, and there was no profit under the sun."** Despairingly he asked, "who knoweth what is good for man in this life," but he failed to find an answer, "therefore I hated life . . . yea, I hated all my labour."†

A sociologist may echo the Preacher's words on many points and as far as social values are concerned, seek an answer to his question, "Is there anything whereof it may be said, See, this is new?" *Aonmie,* as his words show, "hath been already of old time, which was before us."††

So today, *anomie,* indifference to all values, which has been put forward as an explanation of suicide, may also find illustration in the use, which has increased in certain circles since Sorokin's work, of

---

*Ecclesiastes, 1 14.
**Ibid, 2, 17, 18.
†Ibid, 5, 12.
††Ibid, 1, 10.

hallucinatory and stupefying drugs. In nineteenth century industrial and commercial England it used to be said that to get drunk was the quickest way out of Manchester. Drug taking may seem a quicker way out of conditions of life which by lack of character, poor training, or grievous misfortune, the addict can no longer tolerate. It is well to remember, however, that many of thy inhabitants of Lancashire found another way of escape (and it was more to their credit for courage), by cultivating a sense of humor so that the county produced some of the most popular English entertainers. Wit and humor unfortunately are not notable qualities in sociological treatises, while in literary studies they are not often treated sociologically. It is a subject on which the Preacher was ambiguous, for although he said that "sorrow is better than laughter" and that "the laughter of the fool is as the crackling of thorns under a pot"* yet in a more serene mood he bade his hearers "go thy way, eat thy bread with joy and drink thy wine with a merry heart",** a good example of clash of ideational and sensate cultural values which two thousand years of human experience has hardly yet shown mankind how to reconcile.

These few examples illustrating the ways in which Sorokin's sociology puts current problems in a wider, better integrated and therefore intelligible framework help to clarify the human predicament. By revealing the closed circles within which ethical and aesthetic values must seek support and justification, Sorokin cuts through a mass of confused prejudice and argument; not least by showing the dangers and pitfalls arising when there is a "confusion of the categories"; when, for example, value judgments of an ideational or idealistic nature are assessed or criticized by criteria drawn from a sensate value system or parameter and reciprocally.

The Search for Valid Fundamental Concepts common to all Cultural Systems.

To try to force all judgments and all ideas about social and cultural life into a predominantly sensate pattern or an ideational pattern is a form of illegitimate reductionism — illegitimate because such patterns are incommensurable. To try to turn one into the other is to destroy it. To

*Ibid, 7, 3, 6
**Ibid, 9,7.

remain within the values offered by only one closed cultural circle or attached to one parameter is to forego possibilities for a fuller life. Hence the attractiveness of the idealist pattern, because the mutual antagonism and opposition of the ideational and sensate cultural points of view can only be resolved by integrating or harmonizing them in a higher synthesis of a more Hegelian form, but it is only possible to achieve such a balanced, integrated view when there is a willingness and an ability to recognize and accept elements in each capable of fusion in a worthier whole. Such ability is the distinguishing quality of the creators of an idealist culture. If that were possible, Sorokin could not be accused of reductionism.

Would he not then still be vulnerable to the change of circularity? Insofar as his arguments are dependent upon his concept of idealist social and cultural life his social philosophy is of course as circular, as dependent upon a cultural major premise, as is any other argument about values in humanistic studies. All analytical arguments of any kind must be circular and the insight of Leibniz is correct. Long reflection upon the sources, conditions, and validity of human reasoning led him to assert that in every proposition in formal logic all predicates are included in their subjects. He also saw that mathematical reasoning is essentially tautologous or circular, a resounding discovery which Wittgenstein was to make later to the dismay of himself as well as of some of his very eminent readers.

If this is so, humanity is faced with the task of ensuring that the circle in which thought is to revolve is as vast, as all-embracing as it is possible to make it. Sorokin's integralism parallels the untiring advocacy of harmony by Leibniz. Not merely has the circle of thought to be vast, but its center, upon which the whole fabric of knowledge rests, must be secure. In an idealist culture, such validity seems to be achieved when undoubted, unquestionable sensory facts have been empirically tested and subjected to reasoning guided by intuition. Natural science certainly appears to provide just such assurance through its microscopes, refractometers, molecular models and other apparatus as well as by its power to explain and to predict. Even so, idealist science is loth to claim finality for its discoveries. To suggest that all that is known in chemistry, physics, astronomy, biology and other sciences provides nothing but circular arguments founded upon some relatively simple fundamental principles would not only seem absurd, but if true, would rob "circularity" of its terrors. Yet those who before Einstein regarded Newtonian physics as virtually a divine revelation of the nature of reality have subsequently had to modify their beliefs.

Today when ultimates such as the speed of light may be transcended, when thought about the structure of "matter," the nature and origin of life and similar fundamental matters are being subject to constant revision, the search for an irrefragable factual foundation of knowledge cannot be said to have reached finality.

Sorokin's principles can therefore greatly enlarge the dimensions of philosophical speculation by accommodating other philosophies within his own wider frame of reference. He is not limited by having to take a stand upon one central idea, sensate or ideational. His discovery of the virtual autonomy of distinct great cultural supersystems with their conflicting, often mutually exclusive values, provides a factual basis which does not confine his own ideas within one circle. His sociology can understand Ruskin as well as Ricardo without superficially dismissing the clash between them as merely a confusion between the aesthetics, ethics, and economies of a single culture. It is not a clash to be disposed of as a "semantic" problem.

A hope that certain deep-lying factors may condition judgment in each cultural supersystem by appealing to some fundamental inclinations of mankind gets some encouragement from the discovery, for example, that the Golden Section is revealed by the analysis of the proportions observed, intuitively, or naturally, it would seem, by artists, architects and others who have created masterpieces such as the Parthenon and innumerable other works of art, including many splendid pictures.* Similarly the Fibonacci sequence observable in natural forms and in agreeable tones in music seems to make a direct appeal to human susceptibilities. In morality, generally recognized standards of worthy behavior such as the golden rule as well as the basic elements at least making up the idea of Natural Law might similarly qualify.

If the possibility of discovering adequate underlying concepts of such a universal nature fails, and if spontaneous common assent cannot be won to an integrated idealist scheme of values, the outlook for humanity may seem bleak at a time when the development and the acquisition of the weapons of death creates hazards never yet faced by man. In the absence of such agreement the best that can be hoped for will be a realization by everyone that cultural values are essentially relative and that cultural differences springing from principles other than their own invite curiosity and understanding rather than opposition, hatred, and destruction.

*cf. Ghyka M.C. *Esthétique des Proportions dans la Nature et dans les Arts.* Paris.

Some Other Attempts to Characterize Contemporary Culture

In the effort to find a general title able to characterize such a fragmented scene, the "Age of Humanism" clearly fails for generations which have seen two World Wars and enormities such as Belsen, Auschwitz and others too numerous to catalogue. The "Age of the Common Man" may seem more appropriate because the "common man" is currently deemed to be a predominately sensate creature and contemporary conditions are those of a decaying sensate culture. The "Age of Technology" calls attention to some cultural features beyond the competence of "common man," now that rare inventive genius has produced computers, hovercraft, space-craft, and all the other marvels which sever the world of today from the world of the past. Amazing although the miracles of science and technology undoubtedly are, cultural life includes values that artifacts cannot confer.

The "Age of Nature" would recognize the apparent subordination of human interests to a greater concern with natural phenomena such as has been evident in poetry since Wordsworth, in painting since Constable and Turner, in the immense development of gardens and landscaping and national parks, in new activities such as mountaineering, arctic exploration, pot-holing and space travel. Such trends are new, stimulating and inappropriately included as satisfactions of sensual impulses in a sensate age. Nevertheless they do not amount to a mass movement of sufficient scope and intensity to vindicate the "Age of Nature" as an apt description of social and cultural life as a whole throughout the past century or more. Like "modern" art with its "abstract," non-human shapes and sizes, architecture, music, dancing and so forth, they represent that aversion from the worn out values of a great sensate cultural supersystem and that groping for alternatives which Sorokin regarded as a characteristic reaction to what he called the "overripe" sensate period.

It is worth noting that of the alternative categories here considered, Humanism, Science, or Nature cannot plausibly be applied to either ideational or sensate periods. The "Age of the Common Man" may seem to fit a sensate period, but not in all cultural periods has the "common man" been completely sensate, despite Marxian theory. In the early days of archaic Greece and Rome, in early Byzantium, in India, for instance, the label would be wrongly applied.

Integration in Practice

The number of values common to all cultural systems is not very large and such congruence would still not provide a foundation extensive enough for a generally accepted culture. Such a universal culture was described as "integrated" and "idealist" by Sorokin. lived and the most fragile. Perhaps it is essential to share his enthusiasm for the cultural achievements of Athens in the fifth century B.C. or for those of Renaissance and seventeenth century Europe in order to see the full force of his recommendation. It was then, he thought, that a cultural patrimony was created upon which the world has since drawn, and yet continues to draw with profit. Both followed upon the decline of an ideational culture when it, too, became "overripe," as Sorokin believed contemporary sensate culture to be. Chaos, not idealism, is the usual sequel when sensate cultures decline. The best hope after the great misery such a collapse occasions is for the return of an age of faith. For faith arises when hope is dead. Yet Sorokin's advocacy of "integration" suggests a way of escape from cultural antagonisms which may perhaps serve to rescue humanity, desperate although the human predicament may seem to be.

from cultural antagonisms which may perhaps serve to rescue humanity, desperate although the human predicament may seem to be.

The best statement of that "integration" which Sorokin desired is that made by an American lady in 1924, but he does not seem to have seen the excellent book in which she described her meaning of the word. It was the result of her study of philosophy, particularly that of Hegel, which she developed in the course of her professional work in human relations in industry. Her philosophy is just as relevant in the resolution of cultural conflict as it is of antagonisms in the fields of industry and business management. She defined her objective as the search for a way by which conflicting desires could be made to interweave. " . . . the confronting of diverse desires, the thereby revealing of 'values,' the consequent revaluation of values, a uniting of desires which we welcome above all because it means that the next diversity will emerge on a higher social level – this is progress."* Her advice, tested by her own work, was that apparently irreconcilable conflict should be overcome by finding a new and more inclusive value capable of being embraced by each antagonist yielding each advantages which they can welcome with enthusiasm so that both could thenceforth work together for that "higher" common end. Miss Follett assumed that a creative mind (her own was) would be able, by intuition or inventive genius, to find the new integrating elements or factors, necessary if any synthesis or integration is to emerge. Here is integration as opposed to bare compromise which requires both parties to

---

*M. P. Follet, *Creative Experience* (London, Longmans Green, 1924), p. xiv.

a conflict of views to give up something they value without acquiring a plus-value which integration yields. Miss Follett called this plus-value "the compound interest of all genuine cooperation." "Integration might be considered a qualitative adjustment, compromise a quantitative one," she wrote, in the effort to explain and defend a technique which she had worked out in practice.* Attractive as her presentation of the matter is, the real question remains, "how is integration to be achieved?"

Sorokin's idea of an integrated, logico-meaningful culture as the one thing needful to save civilization presents sociology with a new challenge. So formidable is it that doubt will arise at the outset whether it is within the power of limited, short-lived man ever to attain anything like a full integration of all values within only one of several cultural supersystems. Our vast universe of values is the creation of specialists, all of whom complain that it is no longer possible for any single individual to master merely one specialism, whether it be history, philosophy, chemistry, biology, or any other discipline devoted to the acquisition of knowledge, which is only one of the major values making up any single, integral, logico-meaningful culture. That art is long while life is short is a very ancient discovery, so that in striving to create beauty the artist has little time to pursue the search for truth. To be active in these two fields and to achieve a morally worthy life, so serving the third main class of cultural values should not be an impossible task.

Any success achieved within any one of Sorokin's major cultural supersystems still leaves out values created in other and possibly alien systems. Yet they satisfied the aspirations of mankind for hundreds of years so they cannot be written off as worthless or be ignored by any who are loth to regard anything human as alien. If former ways and beliefs now deemed old-fashioned and obsolete are rejected, new recruits to the world of learning will be instructed by historians with no more than hazy schoolchild notions of ancient history, philosophers ignorant of the writings of medieval scholastics, art historians whose world begins with the Renaissance, political theorists and sociologists who have not pondered the fate of ancient Greek city-states or the fall of the Roman Republic. All are elements in that wider, universal cultural whole within which everything can be seen with equal curiosity and rewarding interest. Then, as Ortega y Gasset put it, and only then is it possible to "live at the height of the times."

Sorokin's work, in common with that of the sociologists of his day,

*Ibid, p. 163.

was descriptive, historical, and analytical in the main. Becoming dismayed and disillusioned by what he saw around him, relatively late in his career he turned to the practical task of reforming the ways of his fellow men. Reference has already been made to the Harvard Research Center in Creative Altruism which he established in 1949, the first major effort by any academic sociologist to give practical effect to theoretical knowledge in the reformation of human conduct. As such it was criticized by a distinguished social scientist on the ground that "moral goals are foreign to science."* Sorokin did not desist. It would, he thought, have been a dereliction of duty to remain silent in view of the probable outcome of cultural trends obvious to all which his empirical studies had shown to presage disaster.

If the work of Sorokin's Research Center cannot be said to have made any considerable, immediate impact, it is also evident that the continuing efforts of vastly larger and better equipped institutions still fall far short of their aims. Christian churches in the West and Buddhist missionaries in the Far East have for centuries striven to reform mankind, yet crimes and misdemeanors, wars and revolutions, have not only occurred but have grown more violent and sinister. If social science has nothing to say about such pathological manifestations except by way of description and analysis, it will be regarded by the majority of mankind as on a level with the study of palaeobotany or Egyptian hieroglyphs.

Sorokin certainly did not lack the courage to proclaim moral goals or to urge their pursuit as part of his duty as a responsible social scientist. Every individual, he said, should be scrupulous in performing his cultural and social functions. Nelson said much the same thing to the British Fleet before the Battle of Trafalgar in 1805 in a famous signal that has never been forgotten. Perhaps the high drama of a desperately hazardous occasion and a renowned and charismatic commander, as Winston Churchill's example was to show in the Second World War, are necessary before moral exhortation can electrify its hearers. In Sorokin's eyes, humanity faces a dangerously hazardous situation. His supreme task was to try to brace moral and cultural energies to avert the threatened catastrophe. "This is the paramount problem of humanity at the present time," he emphasized.** Individuals must tone up their moral fiber; cultural and social institutions must be organized through groups,

---

*C. Gini, "How Gini of Italy Assesses Sorokin," in P. J. Allen, ed., *op. cit.,* p. 312.
**P. A. Sorokin, *The Reconstruction of Humanity* (Boston, Beacon Press, 1948), p. 234.

associations, and federations with the object of increasing knowledge and wisdom, of discovering and propagating techniques to make human beings more noble and altruistic. He realized that "our knowledge, wisdom and techniques in this field are exceedingly deficient."* The aim, at least, was clear. "All that is necessary is the supreme mobilization of our available mental and moral forces, control of subconscious drives by the conscious and superconscious factors and unflinching determination to meet courageously all the difficulties of the pilgrimage."**

To proclaim the need for a change of heart and to point the way to salvation are rarely effective, as the experience of a line of prophets, sages, and moral leaders over thousands of years makes only too clear. Miss Follett, whose work has already been cited, had made this plain in 1924, at the same time pointing out why it should be so and how anyone should set about winning the active support of people for a new line of action. Like Sorokin, she had seen that "the task of conveying information is still an unsolved problem." Mere programs for reform are never effective. The fate of President Wilson's famous Fourteen Points in World War I showed, she said, "the futility of the formal acceptance of principles." Such statements are not operative alone because "the real problem is not how we can bring about the acceptance of this idea, but how can we get that into the experience of the people which will bring about new habits?" It is no good expecting to be able to influence the behavior of people by getting their passive assent to the plans and ideas prepared by experts. "If we consent to the will of the expert it is still the will of the expert or official. The people's will is found only in their motor mechanisms or habit systems." Ideas can only unfold within human experience, and not by their own momentum apart from experience.† Sorokin also had realized this when he advocated continual exercise in altruistic activity; it had indeed been a psychological commonplace since William James gave the same advice to cultivate good new habits in his *Principles of Psychology.* Nearly two thousand years earlier it had been proclaimed by the Founder of Christianity in the Sermon on the Mount which, Sorokin agreed, could not be improved upon as a counsel for a morally worthy life.††

To live "at the height of the times" obviously is impossible without worthy moral conduct, but integrated culture demands more than that.

*Ibid, p. 241.
**Ibid, p. 243.
†M. P. Follett, *op. cit.,* pp. 198-200, 211, 273.
††P. A. Sorokin and W. Lunden, *Power and Morality* (Boston, Porter Sargent, 1959), p. 169.

Long before William James or Miss Follett wrote, many discovered that practice must be continuous if perfection is the aim in any walk of life. Paderewski is quoted as saying that if he did not practice on the piano every day, he noticed a falling off in his performance; if he left it for two days, his enemies noticed it; while after the third day, even his friends noticed it also. It is not only love that has to be conquered afresh every day. Clearly therefore, mankind must be content with cultural standards more modest than full integration requires. Education cannot do much more for growing minds in this respect than to arouse interest in the life of the mind, out of which culture arises and progresses, to equip new recruits to learning with a desire to continue to educate themselves, and to leave them with sufficient knowledge to be able to know where to look for further aid. Samuel Johnson's well-known principle is very relevant, "knowledge is of two kinds. We know a subject ourselves, or we know where we can find information upon it."* In other respects than the acquisition of the habit of learning and the desire for it, some place must be found, as it manifestly is not always found, for moral instruction and the acquisition of habits of good conduct. Home and community life are more often potent influences in this respect than school.

Indeed, schooling may turn out more knowledgeable, more resourceful criminals if under the magic rubric "education," too often proclaimed as the cure-all for all social evils, no place is found for effective moral education. Edifying discourse and sermons in school assemblies and chapels, as Miss Follett's work well shows, are likely as long as they are made up of nothing but exhortations and the statement of principles, to be virtually useless.**

If sociology is to broaden its basis to include the study of all the factors which must contribute to individual, and therefore to social well-being and at the same time study, explain, and suggest remedies for the evils which currently retard the advancement of human welfare, even Sorokin's vast canvas would be too restricted. If sociologists are asked why it is that angelic children turn into the choleric, liverish, bad-tempered and even criminal adults who are all too numerous in any modern society, then more than a study of class, economic status, success or failure, "roles,"

---

*J. Boswell, *Life of Johnson,* G. B. Hill and L. F. Powell, eds. (Oxford, Clarendon Press, 1934), Vol. 2, p. 365.
**In *Power and Morality* (Boston, Porter Sargent, 1959, p. 166) P. A. Sorokin and W. A. Lunden record that a case study of over 163,000 individuals (criminals) failed to reveal any connection between morality or crime and education and intelligence..

personality adjustment, and so forth may well be necessary. More also than the question of cultural norms and cultural integration, because incorrect diet, vitamin and mineral deficiency, lack of fresh air and exercise, depressing physical environment, may also contribute to social malaise.

Since Sorokin wrote, new threats have arisen to aggravate sociological problems. Employment, whether under capitalist or totalitarian state direction, will be a grave problem, at least in the short run, because of the redundancies in jobs as a result of automation and the use of computers. A generation ago H. G. Wells considered humanity to be engaged in a desperately dangerous race of progress against catastrophe. Perhaps the elderly in every generation develop such alarming fears, forgetful of the surge of eager endeavor with which they faced an unknown and also potentially dangerous future in the days of their youth. Survivors of two World Wars, not to mention terrible economic slumps and depressions, may be excused if they reflect with some complacency that future generations will live by their wits, as they themselves had to do. To sharpen these wits by such wisdom as they can contrive after long experience and reflection is a natural ambition to all who wish to contribute to the science of society. Sorokin made no apology, nor does he need defense for the leadership he gave during a long lifetime to all enrolled in such a cause.

Whatever may be the difficulties, perplexities, and dangers, sociology must follow Sorokin's lead and give much more attention to the philosophy of value if it is to be able to contribute anything fundamentally useful by way of guidance to social living and social welfare. It cannot resign that duty without losing its standing as a science of man in society. If it is to fulfill that duty, the need for some scale of values becomes apparent, if only because the cultivation of any one set of values or any single value involves the subordination or even the elimination of others. Some cultural privation being inevitable, everyone should wish to choose with the knowledge at the same time of what that choice will deny him, not so that he should view what he neglects or rejects with scorn, but so that the universe of cultural life becomes for him a vital actuality and his own relative position in it becomes clear. Max Scheler's list and hierarchy of values seemed over complicated, too personal and involved, but a clear and simpler scheme was proposed by Radhakamal Mukerjee in his deeply reflective, learned and altogether excellent short survey *The Dimensions of Values, A Unified Theory.** His

*(London, Allen and Unwin, 1964) pp. 36, 78.

hierarchy runs all the way from the values contributing to the maintenance and enhancement of life, through the values assuring social integration and harmony up to the values of self transcendence which comprise the values of truth, beauty, and moral worth, harmony or holiness which are all "spiritual" in essence. Within so broad, inclusive a framework it is not difficult to place the ideational, idealistic, and sensate values of Sorokin's cultural supersystems. From many sides, value studies are gaining increasing attention. Dr. Mukerjee remarks, in his work cited above (p. 68) that "the world of values and value orientation belongs *par excellence* to the social scientist as the world of technology belongs to the natural sciences. But it is from the latter that the physicalist outlook has now spread, expelling human values and meanings from all social disciplines and rendering values themselves futile for changing the world." To Sorokin belongs the credit for his pioneering work in cultural history which effectively challenges the physicalist, materialist attitude by presenting values in their wider setting. He set out the merits of and the need for integration of cultural values and he outlined the quality of mind and disposition which would result from its achievement. In view of the obvious difficulties of full integration it will be useful to consider the nature of integration at various stages or levels.

Degrees of Integration

Perhaps the simplest and toughest form of integration is that of intellectually alert people who accept without question the values of an ideational value system. They are ready to sacrifice themselves, if need be, rather than to renounce the fundamental principles of their belief. In pagan, sensate Rome the early Christian martyrs went, sometimes joyfully, to their death. In Western Europe during the Reformation and Counter-Reformation sectarian divisions within the Christian Church found many ready to endure dreadful tortures and a horrible death sooner than abandon points of doctrine and practice which they considered to be essential. Conflict on that scale and for such reasons would indicate, on Sorokin's principles, a weakening of the ideational system.

Integration around sensate values does not breed such inflexible resolution. It has been found a satisfactory way of life, particularly by those who have not been awakened to reflect and reason upon their experience. Pleasurable reactions to sense stimuli can be experienced afresh from day to day, provided that they have not been prematurely dulled to virtual extinction by gross over-indulgence, until they diminish or pall with age. Then nemesis overtakes sensate man for there comes a time, in the words of the Preacher cited already above, when "desire shall fail."*

By clarifying the basic principles of both ideational and sensate culture, the central focal points upon which all argument and discussion about either must turn and to which they must return in a circle of longer or shorter radius, Sorokin's historical analysis shows also that human nature has not found it possible to rest forever content with either. In both, the urge of human nature for self-realization through self-assertion has made men fond of fighting. In ideational times the duty of Christian charity, loving kindness, and forgiveness failed to disarm feudal robber barons, murderers, and robbers. Not history alone, but daily experience in many a home, office, and factory shows that mildness of disposition and an affectionate regard for others by no means always elicits a response in kind from them. On the contrary, it can stimulate a hard selfishness and a domineering attitude, as Aaron Hill's jingle had it:

> Tender-handed stroke a nettle,
> And it stings you for your pains;
> Grasp it like a man of mettle,
> And it soft as silk remains.
> 'Tis the same with common natures,
> Use 'em kindly, they rebel;
> Be as rough as nutmeg graters,
> And the rogues obey you well.

A sensate culture which disbelieves the Christian doctrine of "original sin," which relaxes school discipline, trusting to the inborn good nature of young children, and which shrinks from punishing evil doers, may seem in need of such a reminder in view of its youth problems and steadily rising rate of crime.

Most people who know only the values of the culture in which they live, whether ideational or sensate (if it is integrated), do not feel cramped or limited. Ignorance and lack of curiosity about an alternative to their way of life, combined with an immense variety of interest available within the circle by which they are confined, usually suffice to engage their interests continually. Within those circles, new intuitions, new "slants" or apercus, open new perspectives, based, however, always upon the major premise or assumptions on which each culture relies. There is a huge religious literature written throughout many centuries by theologians,

*Ecclesiastes 12:5

commentators, and expositors, all of it based upon the relatively few and seemingly simple ideas of the New Testament, supplemented by the Old Testament.

Difficulties arise when an effort is made to combine some of the values of an ideational culture with some sensate values in a way that falls short of integration. Examples abound in an era of cultural confusion such as that of the twentieth century. They are especially evident in the many efforts that have been made to relate economics and ethics and economics and theology. Sorokin's principles make it clear that the economic society of today is a manifestation of the values of a sensate society, of egoistic and, in a "Welfare State," of universalistic hedonism. It is essentially a world in which values are and must be determined by the principle of supply and demand, however much the full effects of that principle may be modified by monopoly, combination through trade unions and trade agreements and by State-imposed taxation and regulation. Ethical value or disvalue arising from this interplay of forces and influences is imposed upon a sensate society. It does not arise spontaneously as it should from an ideational or idealistic society which do not have hedonism as a basic premise, but put moral worth or goodness among their fundamental postulates. Efforts to extract moral principles from the economic principle of supply and demand are reminiscent of the gentleman in *Gulliver's Travels* who "had been eight years upon a project for extracting sunbeams out of cucumbers."*

Over a hundred years ago, Matthew Arnold strove to win sympathy and help for the "multitude of children" whom he witnessed in his work as Inspector of Schools in the East End of London "eaten up with disease, half-sized, half-fed, half-clothed, neglected by their parents, without health, without home, without hope." He made an eloquent and certainly very powerful attack upon the complacency with which Christian Victorian England tolerated such evils. It was, he said, "a world of an aristocracy materialized and null, a middle class purblind and hideous, a lower class crude and brutal." He blamed "the mere unfettered pursuit of

---

*D. L. Munby, *God and the Rich Society* (London, Oxford University Press, 1961) is a recent example of the confusion arising when there is not a clear realization of the different basic assumptions, principles, or parameters between a sensate and ideational (Christian) cultural system, but an effort is made nevertheless to effect some junction between arguments based upon each which falls short of integration. Mr. Munby hoped for a few new professorial chairs of Christian Social Ethics (p. 164) and "a set of advisory committees and church leaders" (p. 169) would be equal to the task which baffled him.

wealth" which, he said, had created "those vast, miserable, unmanageable masses of sunken people, to the existence of which we are . . . . absolutely forbidden to reconcile ourselves." He wanted what was essentially Sorokin's solution of an integrated idealist culture, which would bring more "sweetness and light" into the Victorian scene. His desperate cry from the heart was dismissed by a newspaper writer in the *Daily News* who plainly told him that "the alternative is between a man's doing what he likes and his doing what someone else, probably not one whit wiser than himself, likes."* There was, in one short sentence the basic idea, philosophy, or principle of a sensate culture. Most of those who read it probably thought it a complete answer to Mr. Arnold.

Everyone with five senses has a natural urge to derive from them as much pleasure as possible. It was an urge made respectable by British philosophers from Locke to Bentham. Other people may be presumed to have sensations also, but nobody can experience their sensations as his own. There cannot be vicarious experience, except in imagination which it is impossible to verify. If the feelings of others should be taken into account, some mental activity must take place, such as the "sympathy" which Adam Smith invoked so as to bring some moral influence to bear upon the world of sensations. In an ideational or idealistic culture, on the other hand charity and love (in the meaning Leibniz gave to it — joy through another's bliss) were duties enjoined by divine command. In a sensate world, the fact that some people may sympathize with the sufferings of others may be undoubtedly true, but sensate principles provide no basis for holding that they ought to feel such sympathy or to condemn them if they do not. On those principles also, there is no authority for supposing that a "moral sense" is, or should be, general enough to be brought in as a moral principle able to influence or to control the behavior of sensate man. Such a man has only to say that he does not feel any such power telling him that he must not do what he wants to do in order to free himself from the promptings of a "moral sense." To the extent that "moral sense" was a hangover from the Christian "conscience" or a pale reflection of the idea of Natural Law, it represented the ghost of an ethics of principles. As such it had no place in a sensate philosophy of life, or sensate culture in which every sentient being, as the *Daily News* told Matthew Arnold, does as he likes.

A sensate culture is thus faced with the problem of maintaining social

*M. Arnold, *Culture and Anarchy* (London, Smith Elder, 1869) pp. 151, 152, 83. *Essays in Criticism,* 2nd series (London, Macmillan, 1888), p. 202.

cohesion and of creating an acceptable existence for all without being able to count upon sympathy, moral sense or other regulatory principle. All arguments about right or wrong, good taste or bad taste are circular, just as are similar arguments in an ideational or idealistic society. There is the difference however, that whereas in those societies all arguments have a basis in some principle, the basis or "center" of all arguments in a sensate culture are individual preferences, so that the circle in which they revolve is the unknown and often unpredictable set of preferences of each sensate individual, whose feelings and views may change from day to day. When, in philosophy, Leibniz faced this problem, he said that uniformity, good actions and bad, in the behavior of all the myriad doings of men was the result of the "pre-established harmony" which was part of God's creation of the world and of all the distinct individuals in it, not one of whom was exactly like another. He was forced to take such a point of view because he recognized, as sensate cultural thought must also, that the world is made up of independent, self-activating beings. He differed from the sensate point of view by refusing to believe that the senses alone determine conduct or provide knowledge. His universe was one in which the greatest differences in the quality of life were emphasized. For him, sensate man and the life of sensation was almost the lowest form of human existence, inferior in quality to various grades of reflective, rational, reasoning man. His philosophy was idealistic, not sensate. Lower than sensate man in the scale, or great chain of being, were animals; below them, plants; below them inanimate objects. All he called "monads." Leibniz's pre-established harmony found no support, indeed it has been regarded as ridiculous although modern thought has found no other explanation for the uniformities observable in all branches of natural science from the revolutions of the planets down to crystallography, molecules, protons and neutrons.

Mandeville, with his thesis that private vices conspire to produce public good, and Adam Smith with his idea that the division of labor and competitive enterprise in economic life were guided by a "hidden hand" to advance human welfare, were both naive versions of the philosopher's "pre-established harmony." Neither Mandeville nor Adam Smith provided any basis for moral principle. They did no more than offer one mystery to explain another. Leibniz had a far more philosophical approach to the problem, which he saw as insoluble unless the idea of a hierarchy of qualitatively inferior and superior moral and intellectual individuals is accepted. Each one integrates its own experience. The higher the individual of "monad" is in the great chain of being, the more complete and the richest in content is its integration. They exemplify the standards, intellectual, moral, and aesthetic, by which all the rest are assessed.

One of the reasons for the collapse of sensate cultures put forward by Sorokin in his doctrine or principle of limits was the psychological truth that sensations too long repeated not only become dulled and boring, but may also be nauseating. From a sociological point of view, it is also clear that social cohesion is much less well assured by a sensate than by an ideational or idealistic cultural system both of which play down the importance of the individual members of society in favor of the cultural ideals to which all dedicate themselves. A sensate culture, on the contrary, exalts the individual. What, then, holds a sensate society together?

A traditional community life derived from ideational times provides an enduring social momentum to sustain national solidarity in countries of ancient civilization, creating institutions and modifying them in the effort to adapt them to changes in the cultural climate. Sometimes "new" countries, "new" in the sense that they are suddenly emerging into ever close contact with "old" but now sensate cultures, copy these institutions without having had the experience which led the "old" countries to create them. The export of British parliamentary procedure to former British African and other dependencies is an example, but there are many others, such as the use of national flags, national anthems and other symbols. Some doubt about their effectiveness is inevitable when sensate influences within the countries that created them has eroded much of the passionate loyalty they once inspired, so that the Union Jack in Great Britain or "Old Glory" in the United States, probably no longer stir the deep emotion with which they were formerly regarded, an emotion which carried many to victory in war as it had done long ago when Roman legionnaires flung themselves at their enemies behind the Legions' silver Eagle.

As the conserving force of tradition wanes and as life becomes more complicated, every individual's dependence upon the cooperation of others for sensate satisfactions might be thought to deepen a sense of social solidarity. It seems however that the intellectual effort necessary to comprehend and to act upon such knowledge is too much to expect from a sensate society, which is continually liable to disruption as workers go on strike to wrest a greater reward for their labors. So characteristic has this maneuver become that in England in 1969-70 when school teachers went on strike for higher pay, they were said to be taking "industrial action." A strike however is the negation of industry, amounting to economic civil war, and it can be very extensive, as in England in the General Strike of 1926 and more recently in France and Italy.

As individual desires become more insistent, sensate societies may collapse in revolution, shattering traditional patterns, including the social hierarchies, (now spurned as "the Establishment" in certain circles) which had previously given such moral, social, administrative, legal and cultural direction as the society would tolerate. Eventually, out of the ensuing chaos, a new hierarchy has to be created to restore organization, order, and to grapple, if it can, with the task of reforging social solidarity. If the chaos has gone on long enough to make peace and security seem boons worth any sacrifice, then anyone who can establish himself as an undisputed leader has a relatively easy task. In such circumstances Octavius was able to create a new order in Rome and to rule in peace as Augustus, the first Roman Emperor. (31 B.C. - A.D. 14). After the French Revolution, Napoleon recreated a unity in France with the aid of his foreign conquests. Later dictators have relied to some greater or lesser extent upon creating a fear of real or pretended enemies such as the "imperialist aggressors" of communist propaganda, in order to stifle unrest and to whip up support. Such action is not very effective in the long run as a substitute for a genuine morality based upon ethical principles, so internal propaganda is brought in as well. Efforts to find settled principles by which millions of unruly individuals can be reduced to conformity if not to the spontaneous unanimity of an ideational or idealistic ethics, were seen in the frenetic, stage-managed operations of Hitler's Goebels. In Russia a Marxist-Leninist ideology has been put together as a new orthodoxy but it is apt to vary by being reinterpreted according to the wishes of the Communist Party leaders of the day. They in turn have been virulently denounced as heretics by Chinese Communist leaders professing the same ideology, so the rest of the world may be excused some uncertainty as to its precise significance. If Marx were alive today he might still find the British Museum more agreeable than life in either Marxist Russia or Marxist China. Sycophantic reverence is also given to the pronouncements of a dictator such as Stalin and, more recently in China, to the *Thoughts of Mao*. But the real pressure towards obedience to authority comes not from such works, but from fear of the arbitrary power of their authors and the henchmen by whom they are served. Physical violence, prisons, concentration camps, forced labor camps, ill-treatment from which starvation and torture are not excluded; such are among the other means by which a potentially self-assertive or rebellious individualism is curbed to produce the simulacrum of social harmony in a prison-state, or in any other tyranny. In the more or less free-market economies, fears and anxieties can also act powerfully to stimulate efforts to win social approval and the economic resources or income which usually depend upon admission to and the favorable judgment of some social circle or another, whether of employer or senior colleagues in some enterprise or in public employment. Such stimuli are of course also at work in prison-states.

Social solidarity, or the appearance of it, induced by fear or terror is a more fragile form of cohesion, much less apt to inspire loyalties than did the ideational society Shakespeare had in mind when he wrote of

> This happy breed of men, this little world
> . . . .
> Renowned. . . .
> For Christian service and true chivalry.

With his analysis of the multibonded links which can be found in any large community or society, Sorokin reveals the elements of its organization in the same way that the nerves, sinews, and bones of the human body are uncovered by dissection. It still remains to explain the nature of the living force by which such complex organisms are animated; for it is clear that a genuine social solidarity within society as a whole is something more than the sum of loyalties to miscellaneous bonds such as those of school, university, church, profession, office, workshop, or voluntary society. Cumulatively, they should help to instill a strong community sense in their participants, but taken singly, the loyalty each inspires may be somewhat brittle and prove unequal to withstanding the great strains which a true solidarity is able to survive.*

Sorokin saw the supreme need for an inspiration sufficiently powerful to hold society together and to infuse it with vital purpose. "The spirit of a good family in which every member is honestly doing his work, according to his ability, and where nobody thinks of a superiority and inferiority, is a rough approximation to this spirit of the culture and society necessary for the elimination of tensions, revolutions, and wars."** It will be evident that this solidarity, characterized by the familistic relationships described in Chapter 5, gets its strength from emotions of loving self-sacrifice, the agape of the New Testament. Such cultural values as are felt to be worth living and dying for can alone produce the solidarity at which sociology should aim. To extend the range and application of this familistic spirit beyond the family circle to the rest of humanity was the duty laid by Christ upon his disciples and followers.

*P. A. Sorokin, *Society, Culture and Personality* (New York, Harper, 1947), pp. 119-124.
***Ibid.,* p. 518.

The upshot of Sorokin's life work was to show that sociology could not improve upon this simple teaching. "To this conclusion," he wrote, "may be raised the objection that the new socio-cultural framework is itself unrealizable and utopian. If such an objection were valid, it would mean that an enduring peace is impossible. In that case all rational persons should stop fooling themselves and others with the utopia of a mankind without war, bloody revolution, and crime, and should resignedly accept them as inevitable in the same manner in which we accept death."* Because Sorokin rejected such pessimism, he looked for practical ways of stimulating creative altruism.

When ideational societies fail to maintain a generous, spontaneous loyalty to their principles against the pull of sensate indulgence, and when sensate societies with no respect for principles are found to lack inner cohesion, then orderly social life and personal security are in jeopardy. In these circumstances Sorokin's integrated idealistic cultural system alone offers a better hope. In it sensate urges are not rigorously repressed as they would be in an ideational society while the cultural ends to which sensate self-seeking is subordinated serve to polarize personal energies into the service of ideals recognized to be worthy and of more lasting value. Such are the pursuit of knowledge for its own sake and the creation of aesthetically satisfying objects, not in a mere commercial service of ephemeral fashions, but as an expression of the innermost aspirations of artists who work intensively to achieve a perfection of form, line, color, shape, and design. Such also is a respect for the need of service to humanity, for the Rule of Law, and generally for principles which can impose a sacrifice of self-regarding impulses on behalf of ideals such as fair-play, chivalry, social harmony, and well being. Human nature being what it is, established institutions in industry, commerce, and government being what they are, there may well be justifiable scepticism about the possibility of ever creating such a society. Until a general realization of its desirability can be diffused that possibility will certainly not seem very bright, as Sorokin clearly recognized with his reference to the Sermon on the Mount in the preceding paragraph.

Within an integral idealistic value system all arguments about good and bad will also be circular, but their variety and extent will be greater than in either ideational or sensate value systems; the "radius" of the circle will be longer and able, therefore to embrace within the circle, or circles

*Ibid, p. 520.

far more of the rich variety of life. That there will be more than one such circle follows from the threefold nature of idealistic culture, with its devotion to the cultural value ultimates, shortly described as truth, beauty, and moral worth. By far the greatest amount of philosophical and literary discussion of cultural and sociological topics belongs to the idealistic type of culture system, but that is because it demands an intellectual effort, skill and training which the great majority of those who lived under an ideational cultural society or system did not need to acquire. Surprise has often been expressed at the often meager inventories of books particularly manuscripts of the classical writers, known to have been housed in many of the great monastic foundations of the Middle Ages, and the miserable condition in which Renaissance scholars found many of them. They were not there because there was no need for them. Throughout the ages, sensate man predominated in sheer numbers, according to Sorokin, but not in influence unless those who led the society, the "Establishment" of the times, were sensate also, or sufficiently sensate to express, or allow to be expressed, the sensate nature of the mob or masses, few of whom were literate enough to expound or defend their way of life. In Ancient Rome, the story of Trimalchio by Petronius is an example of such literature, which was relatively very scarce until the modern sensate age made it into "best-sellers." Widely as it is now circulated in our "permissive" society (that is, one which places few if any barriers to human animal behavior or descriptions of it), it is defended as unlikely to harm morality, although the conclusion is not drawn that literature generally, whether good or bad is without influence. Unless it is denied that there is nothing so powerful as ideas, it seems hazardous to suppose that evil communications do not corrupt good manners. "Evil" in this context is referable to an idealistic cultural system which might say, with Hamlet, "What a piece of work is man. How noble in reason. How infinite in faculty . . . in action how like an angel; in apprehension how like a god." — Hamlet, who said also, "Give me that man that is not passion's slave."

Sketchy and hasty as this brief glance at the history of human value-judgments in some of their distinctive forms has been, it will have been justified if it opens new perspectives upon social and cultural theory and, by so doing, gives pointers to further and more fruitful work. Now that a new world of investigation is opening with the continuing development of electronic computers, it may be that the circularity of argument and discussion in the general and particular philosophies of value will suggest refined methods of analysis which such mechanical aids can employ with profit.

From many sides, responsible expert opinion stresses the need for conceptual thought able to grasp and to interpret mountains of fact accumulated by advancing research. Such new insights or intuitions will come from idealistic, integrated thought, as it for the most part always has done. "Those things that distinguish man from animals and are responsible for man's civilization, art, literature, and science, were achieved by less than one per cent of human population, by those in the upper tail of the curve of human variation in inventiveness, imagination, perseverance, and ability to think clearly."* In the light of Sorokin's researches, many would consider the figure of one per cent to be much too high, but whatever it should be today, it is urgently desirable that it should rise steadily hereafter. Not intellectual progress is at stake, but the well-being of humanity as a whole, especially of that vast multitude which there is every reason to believe, are most unlikely to be able to make any great positive contribution in response to the grim challenges now threatening mankind. For, as Sorokin might have said, "the integration of society is identical with the integration of value systems."**

The Validity of Value Judgments

To try to validate a value is rather like the philosophical inquiry into the meaning of meaning. It cannot be done unless some standard of judgment can be proposed, and it is not easy to see how there can be any standard other than that of value itself, which is the very question at issue. The problem can be handled only within a wider setting. Sorokin found it by locating value within his idea of the total capacity and possible range of action of man and, in turn, within reality as a whole. That, he thought, although infinite, must be regarded under three aspects: empirical-sensory, rational-mindful, and suprarational-supersensory. It must be so because these are at once the true nature and the limits of human capacity. A complete, or "integral" man is first a vital animal organism with an "unconscious," reflexological-instinctive mechanism. He is also, or can and should be, a rational, logico-mathematical thinker with a developed

*R. Mayr, "Biological Man and the Year 2000," *Daedalus* (Proceedings of the American Academy of Arts and Sciences) Vol. 96, 1967, p. 836. Many other papers in this volume (pp. 639-988, "Toward the Year 2000") are very relevant to the themes discussed in this book.
**R. Mukerjee, *Dimensions of Values* (London, Allen and Unwin, 1964), p. 71.

conscious mind. More than these qualities have distinguished some men and women whose sudden inspiration has brought new ideas, even new ways of life. By no means have all such intuitive, inspirational notions stood the test of reason and experience; many have provoked terrible disaster, despite the confident assurance and enthusiasm with which they were launched upon the world. On the other hand there have been intuitions and new ideas which have been among the greatest inventions and discoveries in the history of civilization. No view of thought, action, and reality which leaves any of these three qualities, characteristics, or dimensions out of account can be adequate.*

All thoughts, and therefore all values, arise within this framework of possible actions and ideas. In referring such actions and ideas back to that framework for their explanation and validation, any explanation or validation will perhaps seem to involve a circular argument. But it is a circle from which it is impossible to escape. There is no other resource available to mankind than that afforded by his biological, rational, and imaginative nature. There can therefore be no other standard by which the validity of values can be assessed than these, or by a combination of each or of elements of each. When a stand is taken upon any one of these values alone, the resulting valuation is not an integral judgment, and the presumption will be that it is therefore imperfect and inadequate. By the same argument, a stand can be taken upon any one of the three main components of personality and reality in order to criticize and refine, if necessary, the judgment or suggestions contributed by the other two. Anything short of an integral validation would involve a deprivation because the whole is greater than any part of it.

Sorokin's integral philosophy and sociology will, it may be hoped, be sufficiently clear from what has already been said in this book, but, if only by way of recapitulation, it may be illustrated here by returning to the problem of sex in sociology. As Sorokin's short book on the question already referred to was highly polemical (it was, as he explained, an expanded version of an article he had contributed to a popular magazine), he did not write it as a specific or scientific exposition of his integral philosophy, although of course he wrote in the spirit of that integralism he was concerned to vindicate.** In most of its manifestations, what Sorokin called the "sex revolution" was prominent in his description of

---

*P. A. Sorokin, "A Quest for an Integral System of Sociology," in *Memoire de XIXe Congrès International du Sociologie* (Mexico, D. F., 1961) Volume III.
**P. A. Sorokin, *The American Sex Revolution* (Boston, Porter Sargent, 1956).

contemporary cultural life as sensate and overripe. Certainly, in comparison with the manners and conventions of less than half a century or even of a generation ago, his word "revolution" is not excessive. Topics that were taboo then — homosexuality, abortion, birth control, the sex act — are openly discussed in newspapers and radio programs. Much of the once surreptitious traffic in pornographic and obscene material now goes on unchecked, while a great outcry is raised whenever an effort is made to ban any of it. Often lip-service is then paid to the life of the mind by getting people of presumed high standing and objective judgment to testify to the "educational," literary, artistic, or other merits of the object in question, whether book, film, stage show, or other form of entertainment. Probably the vast majority of the inhabitants of the large capital cities in which such sexual excitements are so·freely available take little or no interest in any of them or in the sex-sodden fringe of society which not only does take great interest in them but continually seeks new stimulation from them. Most people still regard the whole business as disgusting and degrading without having any very clearly formed theory of value to justify their condemnation beyond a traditional view, inherited from idealistic or ideational times, that such practices are impure or "immoral." To the partisans and creators of an overripe sensate society, by whom words such as "pornography" or "obscenity" are declared to be meaningless, such a stand is at best "old-fashioned" and at worst hypocritical and dangerously provocative of frustrations, complexes, and other psychological evils. Proposals to limit the traffic in sexual provocation are denounced in high-minded tones as a shocking return to censorship and as imposing shackles that are quite intolerable in "modern" times upon the freedom of speech and opinion.

Sorokin's integral scheme of values can put the conflict into perspective. It is seen then as the need to meet the demands of mankind on the biological as well as on the rational level with the aid of an inspired, intuitional insight capable of raising the whole matter to a new level from which both parties can realize that their point of view fails to include all that true humanity requires in relations between sexes, and between members of the same sex. Then man is no longer passion's slave; neither is his native hue of resolution sicklied o'er with the pale cast of thought, as Hamlet feared, but he is to be found among those whom Hamlet envied:

> bless'd are those
> Whose blood and judgment are so well commingled
> That they are not a pipe for Fortune's finger
> To sound what stop she please.

Correcting the excesses of biological or animal passion and infusing vitality into the cool pronouncements of rational thought, very necessary although it is to do so, does not automatically ensure all the positive action for good of which humanity is capable. A great step forward has, however, been made when that stage has been reached. Periodically popular newspapers report that some young celebrity in the public eye, made rich by public esteem, announces as a startling novelty that "love is more than sex." How much more is not discovered by reason and passion alone, or in combination, but by insight and intuition. Western civilization owes the most resounding statement of what a positive, creative love can achieve to the New Testament, particularly to the first of two letters sent by St. Paul to the people of Corinth in Greece. The spiritual force or heavenly virtue by which he said all human relations, including sex-relations, should be directed, *agape* in Greek, was translated as "charity" in the Authorized Version of the Bible, and was later rendered as "love." Greek had another word *eros,* which St. Paul used for sexual attraction or love in its prevalent modern sense of sexual desire. To distinguish "love" in St. Paul's sense from sensate eroticism, there is no better short definition of love than that of Leibniz, already quoted as "joy through another's bliss." It can integrate sacred and profane love by emphasizing the generosity and self-sacrifice which is the great quality of *agape,* but is absent from the sensate notion of love as desire. Although Christianity gave by far the most effective expression to the idea of love as active benevolence, and first used *agape* as a noun in this sense, the idea behind it was not unknown to classical antiquity, as is evident from Cicero's use of the word *amicitia* for friendship and benevolence.

While it is clear that such an integral solution for the greatest problem in human relationships should prove completely satisfactory, its attractiveness is dimmed by the realization that it has been before the world for two thousand years; and yet it seems almost as far from practical realization as ever. Nevertheless, many individuals have acted, and many now still act, according to the principle it enshrines; but the majority do not and probably have never done so. In nineteenth century England, for example, when there was a remarkable revival of religious observance, when churches and chapels were being built all over the country, when Bible reading had never been more general, when the country had never enjoyed such prosperity and the thought of progress was in everybody's mind, scenes of poverty, squalor, and misery were tolerated by the majority, though they revolted a sensitive humanist such as Matthew Arnold, whose blistering denunciation of his fellow-countrymen has already been quoted. A generation after his attack, an invalid American lady, sister of Henry and William James, settled in England. She and some of her fellow Americans found individual English people agreeable enough but "taken *en masse,* their bullying brutality made them simply odious." In comparison with her native Massachusetts, she was struck by the British working man's excessive beer-drinking, his laziness, "the absence of grit in all classes, and the construction of life on a week-kneed basis." She, too, found the "vast seething problem of poverty" to be intolerable. "The whole system of things," she said, "is hideous and to be swept away." Amid her stories of a man dropping dead of starvation and an elderly couple reduced to poverty who drowned themselves together rather than be segregated into different workhouses, she recounted how a child of fourteen, hired by "a lady" to look after her six children for one shilling a week, had no change of underclothes, but after a severe talking-to for her "graspingness" was grudgingly allowed one on loan for a year, subject to good behavior.* That was in 1890, when the "lady" in question and most other English people were thoroughly familiar with the majestic language in which St. Paul had told them that, though they spoke with the tongues of men and of angels but had not charity they became as sounding brass or a tinkling symbol. Bidden every week to show forth their faith not only with their lips but in their lives, they could walk out of church as indifferent to the misery around them as they had entered. Miss Follett was right when she spoke of the futility of the formal acceptance of principles.

Fellow feeling for those in distress seems more intense in a sensate than in an ideational or even idealistic society, in both of which men set their sights upon the things that are not solely of this world. It is indeed only within the last two hundred years that a new idea has gained momentum, until it has become an international orthodoxy, powerfully championed by the United Nations, the Food and Agriculture Organization, The World Health Organization, and the United Nations Organization for Education, Science, and Culture, among very many other international societies, the idea being that slavery, poverty, starvation, illiteracy, and disease are intolerable afflictions anywhere in the world, and that they can and should be abolished. Christian charity in ideational times did, of course, recognize the duty of aiding the poor and duly made some provision for it. Today, however, it has become, by comparison, a mass

*Edel. L. London, ed., *The Diary of Alice James* (London, Hart-Davis, 1965), pp. 79, 191, 202, 83, 116, 205.

movement, although the vast majority of people take no hand in it. Sufficient recruits are forthcoming and sufficient international cash is forthcoming to pay them so that the task has entered the experience and formed the habit of many who have worked "in the field."

Futility is also the fate of most laments about the non-acceptance of principles, a fact illustrated by many reactions to recalcitrant youth. That problem in the 1960's and later adds point to Sorokin's call for personality integration as the vital element in cultural integralism. Personality traits and characteristics ought, in his view, to integrate individual bioconscious drives of the elementary instincts of hunger, thirst, the need for warmth, shelter, sex relationships, and so forth, with socioconscious controls by values, guided and refined by intuitions and supraconscious inspiration. On such a basis, an integral value-system or culture would be firmly founded, if indeed it did not automatically ensue. As has already been made clear, a lifetime is not long enough to achieve all that integralism demands, so it is inevitable that in the earlier career of any individual, great progress has yet to be made. Lacking in knowledge and socioconscious awareness, the young are unlikely to have intuitions or inspiration as sound or as fruitful as those developed by older people with far greater knowledge and experience. Youthful contributions to the rational, logico-mathematical and intuitive, supraconscious constituents of thought and reality, while deserving consideration, cannot in the nature of things often be of much consequence. Whatever they evolve had probably best be retained by them for further consideration and testing in the light of their experience of life, which was never more complex than it will be now. Wisdom was not entirely absent from the old maxim, now derided, that children should be seen and not heard. When they may be heard as well as seen with profit is upon the affective, emotional, reflexo-instinctive level.

Adult vagueness, uncertainty, and lack of courageous firmness in upholding and translating into their own habit systems, as well as those of the young, a coherent pattern of values leaves growing minds with little direction in the very spheres in which they need it most, because they are the very spheres in which young people cannot have been active long enough to acquire sufficient insight. When emotional, sensate urges are not controlled by rational, logico-mathematical knowledge, the way is open for such aberrations as experiments in drug-taking, tobacco smoking, sexual promiscuity, wild "demonstrations" with all their destructive consequences. Integralism offers the only hope of overcoming such evils, to which the majority of the young are not willing victims.

The fear remains that possibly the greater part of the human race is still long destined to remain culturally on the biological, animal plane of reflexological-instinctive activity, little touched by rational argument and discussion, and indifferent or incredulous where any suggestion of intuitive or inspirational wisdom is concerned. If that is true, there is no hope of any general resort to Sorokin's integral solution. Anything less than that solution would not, according to his theories, allow cultural life and civilization to develop, particularly now that political power and, with it, the general direction of social life in democratic Western countries resides with the masses. Beyond that fear there is also the evident fact that many who can see that they have a duty to defer or sublimate their sensate urges in an integral cultural solution nevertheless realize that they are incapable of it, as Ovid testified when he said that he saw the better course and knew it to be better, yet he followed the worse (*video meliora proboque; deteriora sequor*). On that level humanity is, in the lapidary phrase of Anatole France, *en proie à la necessité maîtresse des hommes et des dieux,* driven by basic urges and unable to escape their predestined fate. Sooner than accept so pessimistic a conclusion, sociology can but present it to parents and educators as a challenge which sociology can reveal but they must meet.

Optimism is not encouraged when one of the arguments for free nursery schools in England is the inability of most children whose schooling begins at the age of five to deal with concepts. There are many more indications in press, radio, and television that three generations of parents, after a hundred years of free and compulsory education, are not much given to conceptual thought. They do not lack false guides who tell them not only that concepts do not matter but that they are a drag upon insight into reality. "Revelation is of thing, not theory," asserts Professor Marshall McLuhan, who believes that it is possible to deal with 'thingness' "without dealing with concept." On this basis and by an equi-vocal use of the term 'percept,' McLuhan discards organized conceptual thought, as in his remark that "theology is one of the games people play, in the sense of theorizing; but in the sense of direct percept and direct involvement with the actuality of a revealed thing, there need be no theology."* When 'biology,' 'chemistry,' 'geology' are put instead of 'theology' in that sentence, its bogus claim is exposed. One such a basis McLuhan held that theology "should ideally be the study of the thingness, of the nature of God," a question-begging assumption which the age-long quest of

*"Electric Consciousness and the Church," Marshall McLuhan talks to Hubert Hoskins. *The Listener,* Vol. 83, March 26, 1970, pp. 393-396.

humanity into the existence and character of the divine immediately refutes.

McLuhanism is one more symptom of contemporary cultural disarray and of the need for Sorokin's integral philosophy which does not allow either sense-data or logical thought or intuition (such as McLuhan's) to claim the sole allegiance of humanity.

Intuitions providing integral solutions by fusing and amplifying man's sensate urges and rational reflections to produce an idealistic higher synthesis are particularly difficult to achieve in moral activities because of the infinite variety and complexity of individual characteristics. There are probably more examples of successful integration in the natural sciences, with the discovery of uniformities and scientific laws (which may be said to be examples of integration) based upon the collection of factual data provided by the senses made very much more sensitive by the aid of instruments and guided by logico-mathematical thought. Here again the new insights are provided by the inspiration or intuition of creative genius, a fact often commemorated by naming the uniformities after them. There are thousands of hard-working men in the laboratories for one Newton, Boyle, Faraday, Gay-Lussac, Mendeleeff, Planck, or Einstein.

Integration in the arts presents other problems. Artistic success requires the coordination and integration of manual skills with the logico-mathematical or rational power of planning and organizing the design, materials, and all components of the final product. Immense variations in artistic talent and in individual awareness of and appreciation of painting, drawing, music, sculpture, architecture, literature, and all other arts and crafts greatly complicate the tasks of discerning creative genius and of rejecting inferior work. On Sorokin's principles, successfully integrated art will be best because it involves and responds to the widest range of human capacity. Such art is the creation of integrated personalities of the highest degree of skill, and they are likely to be more numerous in periods of integrated culture than in either a predominantly ideational or a predominantly sensate culture. Every reader will judge whether such a presumption is verified by the history of art from the summary of art history as Sorokin's inquiries reported it (given in Chapter 5), from personal acquaintances with great paintings, and from the writings of art historians and connoisseurs. For Sorokin, art attained its highest achievements in Greece in the sixth and fifth centuries before our era and in the Western Europe of the Renaissance. His knowledge of Oriental art and history precluded the inclusion of Chinese art, but if his theories are correct, the presumption would be that a great period of

Chinese art, such as that of the T'ang Dynasty, was also the product of a predominantly idealistic culture. Twentieth century Western European art, on the other hand, exhibits the most striking contrasts in a markedly sensate style, following the example set by Renoir, for instance, and a markedly cerebral, intellectualistic style popularized by Picasso. At the same time, the great majority of the British public preferred the water colors of Russell Flint or the hunting scenes of Sir Alfred Munnings, despite the derision of the *cognoscenti*. Even the also despised Sir Lawrence Alma Tadema is regaining some of his renown, eclipsed as it has been during the twentieth century.

Sorokin considered many forms of contemporary sculpture, many designs in architecture, as well as the content and style of "avant-garde" painting (as already explained above) to be, at best, symptomatic of revulsion at the values of a decaying, overripe sensate culture. To those brought up to admire the works of masters of sensate and idealistic art, many productions of "modern art" seem bizarre and mysterious, if not repulsive or crazy. As a reaction against traditional styles, these new manifestations naturally attract attention as well as the patronage of many who wish to keep up with the times, including some who are attracted by the possibility of making money by investing in works of art thought to be likely to increase in value. Such support is additional to any genuine liking professed by all those who feel themselves to be in tune or *en rapport* with the motives which led to the production in question. They are also accepted by those art critics who develop a special flair and (it must be added) a special vocabulary, in their reactions to them. Some such critics have been accused of playing for safety by "backing every starter" in the race for modernity and fame. Sorokin's integralist criterion must deflate very many such modern productions because they do not cater for the affective, emotional, empirical-sensory nature of humanity upon which the majority of mankind relies in interpreting reality. They hold no mirror up to Nature upon whom indeed they seem to turn a blind eye. Sooner or later their hour will pass, as integral wisdom prevails, for, as Ruskin said, "Fine art is that in which the hand, the head, and the heart of man go together."*

Literary history will be seen in a new and rewarding perspective through Sorokin's concepts of ideational, idealistic, and sensate supersystems and through his doctrine of integralism of culture, both private and public. His classification of cultures lifts the history of

*J. Ruskin, *The Two Paths* (London, Smith Elder, 1859), Lecture 2.

literature clear of embarrassment by fictitious labels attached to writers in "periods," such as "Elizabethan," "Augustan," "Classic," and "Romantic." Sorokin's more general and more genuinely descriptive concepts, "sensate," idealistic," "ideational," and their sub-classes and mixtures are not only more accurate, but they allow and encourage close cultural bonds between the history of literature and all other arts, sciences, and cultural manifestations. In comparative literature a revision of this sort is especially valuable by reason of the international links it is able to forge between national and local divisions and comparable styles elsewhere, such as the three so-called Pléiade circles, the "Philosophes" or the Parnassienne "school" in France.*

It is not the province of sociology to rewrite literary, political, educational, legal, or any other history; but if historical sociology discovers broad cultural trends and can point to the principles behind their development leading to a new social theory of value, there is every reason for suggesting that it might benefit other disciplines. If it is then found to do so, sociology in turn is enriched and a great step forward will have been made on the road to cultural integralism.

Naturally it is not a possibility that will greatly excite specialist students of limited fields of knowledge any more than, say, a microchemist may be expected to need familiarity with the contours of the Himalayas. Yet even to specialist fields, such as Shakespearean drama, Sorokin's integralist theory can bring new light. Three quotations from the beginning of Shakespeare's *Hamlet* have been included above which show an idealist revolution against mere sensate lusts and Hamlet's longing for an integral humanity whose "blood and judgment are well commingled." Thereafter the rest of the play moves on to other themes which center around Hamlet's belief that his royal father had been murdered, a crime in

---

*Among attempts to revalue literary history on these lines, one of the best is that by R. Wellek and A. Warren., *A Theory of Literature* (New York, Harcourt, Brace and World, 1942; London, Penguin, 1963). Although the authors quote Sorokin's name in footnotes, they have not assimilated his theories. They make many points which he stated more effectively but fail to incorporate them in a general, memorable presentation; likewise they wrestle unsuccessfully with "class," "economic status," and so forth, concepts which Sorokin's dynamic presentation eliminates. That Sorokin's ideas (of 1937) had escaped their notice is the only conclusion to be drawn from their laments that "the genuine parallelisms which follow from the identical or similar social or intellectual background scarcely ever have been analyzed in concrete terms." This conclusion may indeed be drawn from the whole of their book, good as it is. See especially part 3, which would benefit from revision in the light of Sorokin's theory of value.

any society. Literary critics have plenty of topics other than that of cultural integralism to occupy their discussion of *Hamlet,* and none seems to have pursued Coleridge's penetrating comment in 1818 that in *Hamlet,* Shakespeare "seems to have wished to exemplify the moral necessity of a due balance between our attention to the objects of our senses, and our meditation on the workings of our minds — an equilibrium between the real and the imaginary worlds." A struggle for just such an equilibrium characterized the cultural climate of Shakespeare's own age, a time when mounting sensate pressure was threatening ideational and idealist values, when idealistic cultural values came into their own.

Musical history shows a similar development. In some "modern" circles today, in reaction against the emotional appeal of late sensate music, the very name "music" has virtually been refused to ever-popular sensate tunes, such as those of Lehar *(The Merry Widow),* not to mention the martial marching music of Sousa. Instead, interest has revived in long forgotten pre-sensate music such as the Gregorian chant. At the same time, as in other art forms, the strong force of tradition and training maintains large and appreciative audiences for masterpieces of idealistic music, the music of J. S. Bach, Handel, Haydn, Mozart, Schubert, Beethoven, and others, already characterized in Chapter 5 of this book. Because such musicians had the genius to compose integral music, their works, even in this sensate age, are continually to be heard on radio programs and on recordings. In comparison, some of the older polyphonic music became a mere arid abstraction, as is much "serial" music of the present century.

Already in the nineteenth century, markedly sensate music excited condemnation. Oscar Wilde is said to have remarked, "They tell me that Wagner's music is not as bad as it sounds." But the reaction against non-sensate music, ideational and idealistic, continued, later to produce sensate music much inferior to that of Wagner (who, after all, idolized Beethoven and was by no means without great moments) such as *musique concrète* and current electronic extravagances.* On Sorokin's principles, both "modern music," eschewing emotional appeal, and the vulgar repetitive jingles of formless sensate music whose purpose often seems to be merely to produce a "background noise," fail his integralist test, so

---

*I am indebted to my friend, J. M. Ross C.B.E., for his critical comments and constructive suggestions on these points, and also for calling attention to the relative novelty of the general concern, internationally evident for the first time in history, to relieve poverty and distress anywhere in the world, which I quote above.

they are also destined, with the productions of most "modernistic" painting, sculpture, and architecture, to be superseded as art in general is brought again into closer relation with life.

It remains true that the integrations achieved by genius, whether they are principles of morality, laws of natural science, or canons of artistic taste, marvelous although their discovery is rightly held to be, are all liable to share the fate of any statement of principle. Priceless aids and guides as they are to a fuller cultural life, they remain inoperative as long as they are merely contemplated as principles. The Golden Rule in morality, the idealistic definition of the essence of love in human relationships, the Golden Section in architecture and designing, Boyle's and Charles' laws on the relation of pressure and temperature and the volume of gases, Graham's or Gay-Lussac's law on the diffusion of gases, other laws in chemistry, physics, and electricity — all are examples of fundamental integralist principles. Many such, especially in mathematics and the natural sciences, were so well learned at school that the learners were able to pass examinations upon them and their consequences and applications, with high honors. Yet, forty years on, they will probably be completely forgotten unless daily work in which they are relevant involves their frequent application. Then they will, as Miss Follett sagely recommended, have entered "into the experience of the people to bring about new habits." If a principle, whether scientific, moral, or aesthetic, is to be active as more than a formally accepted statement, it must somehow be translated so that it can stimulate individual motor mechanisms and emerge in habit systems. How that is to be done, as already stated above, when the problem of discovering ways of achieving moral progress was handed to parents and educators, raises questions beyond the scope or competence of sociology. It is sufficient for sociology to survey the whole vast field of human cultural and civilized activities, to show them in relation, to indicate relevant standards for their evaluation, to point to their probable lines of development, and thereby to put men and women into a better condition to discover where and how they stand in relation to each other and in society, to their past, present, and future, so that they will be able to plot their way with greater confidence and in better hope of steadily raising the level of human existence well above the sad, soggy, and sordid state in which far too many flounder today.

Sociology in Sorokin's Time

Sorokin's Criticism of Sociology

In a candid personal impression of Sorokin's contribution to sociology written in Sorokin's lifetime, Professor Corrado Gini refers to his independence of thought and to the fact that he had heard Sorokin described by an American colleague as "a lone wolf" both because of his work "outside the prevailing currents," and because of his "authoritarian intransigence in sustaining his theories." Gini however was sufficiently sympathetic to Sorokin's approach to add, "it would be most fortunate if in modern sociology, there were more similar 'lone wolves,' particularly in America, where a slavish conformity which seems to extinguish scientific initiative, now seems to dominate."*

If Professor Gini was correct, it would seem that just as the worst enemies of Karl Marx have been said to have been the Marxists, so certain sociologists have harmed sociology. Sorokin thought so, but disarmed his victims by confessing that he also shared the guilt of some of their failures and mistakes. *Fads and Foibles in Modern Sociology and Related Sciences* (1956) documents his stern judgments. The novelty of his work, his fearless resolve to follow where the argument led, his consistency in living up to the Aristotelian maxim *amicus Plato sed magis amica veritas*, have not always had their merited appreciation. At that time it seems that his reputation and influence were making more rapid progress abroad than in the United States. His book was by no means written out of spite or a spirit of revenge. "As to the irritation and distress" which his book, as he foresaw, "is bound to provoke, especially among the devotees of the exposed half-truths and sham verities, the author must humbly confess

*C. Gini, "How Gini of Italy Assesses Sorokin," in P. J. Allen, ed. *op. cit.,* p. 317.

that he himself is also one of "the sinners." He also has been guilty of committing the blunders exposed in his book. If he criticizes others, he no less severely censures himself." In reading this, it is not easy to suggest the sins to which Sorokin confessed, for he can be cleared from most of those which he denounced. Perhaps he had in mind the specialized sociological jargon into which, as a newcomer to the United States and to American university life, he was almost certain to have been trapped to some extent. How far any deformation of language in any of his early writings can all be attributed to him, and how much of it may have resulted from the efforts of others to help him, is not evident. His Russian style is said to be clear and vigorous.

Whatever the guilt to which his own conscience may have been sensitive, his litany of the sins of sociology in general was certainly formidable. Among them he included: ignorance and disregard of previous work; obscure jargon and sham-scientific terminology, such as "social mass", "field theory economics", "social mechanics" and others, much worse; sham "operationalism;" misplaced faith in tests, particularly "intelligence" tests and projective and psychological tests; pseudo-statistical methods and bogus formulae; apeing the methods of mathematical physical, and mechanical science; reliance upon artificial constructs such as "small groups", "social atoms"; pretentious predictions, and faulty and obsolete philosophical and psychological presuppositions. As growing pains or as *déformation professionelle,* such blemishes in the world of learning are bad enough but their use in education vastly magnifies the harm they do. It would be shameful if thousands of bright-eyed lasses and lads on the threshold of adult life were compelled, in their efforts to achieve a coveted certificate of intellectual competence, to bandy such words as abience, adience, ergic, synergic, metanergic, cathexis, syntality, and phrases which charity would regard as misprints, such as "the shape of the Cathexis belief attaching the various types of goal object (arrayed along a given generalization dimension) to the gratification end of a matrix."* It would be yet more shameful, if having become able to repeat such stuff, they were deluded into believing that they have learned something.** Such phraseology evokes Wordsworth's

*P. A. Sorokin, *Fads and Foibles in Modern Sociology* (Chicago, Henry Regnery, 1956) pp. 22-30.
**Daniel Bell, "Sociodicy: A Guide of Modern Usage", *American Scholar,* Vol. 35 (1966), pp. 696-714, wittily comments on the usage to exhaustion of once fashionable words in sociology such as "alienation", "charisma", "establishment", "existential", "power-structure" etc.

warning against:

> The dangerous craft of culling term and phrase
> From languages that want the living voice
> To carry meaning to the natural heart;
> To tell us what is passion, what is truth
> What reason, what simplicity and sense.

Every branch of humanistic study, philosophy, economics, history and literature, can profit by a searching examination of its pathological symptoms, so Sorokin's courageous initiative deserves to be studied as a possibly valuable model in other faculties also. Sorokin had looked hopefully for aid for sociology from psychology and statistics, but he was forced to write off as failures the exaggerated claims to competence in explaining the human condition that were currently made by many social physicists, econometrists and psychometrists, sociometrists, ethicometrists and others. The root of the trouble may readily be discovered from Sorokin's own principles and theories and the remedy is suggested by them as well.

The Failure of Positivism

Sociological study has been based upon facts revealed in the main as sensory phenomena, so knowledge about it has accordingly been sought in a systematic body of factual operations and perceptions aided by logico-mathematical reasoning. "Naturally" may well be the immediate reaction, and Sorokin would be the first to agree that, in a predominantly sensate culture, such a methodology is indeed "natural", Pronouncements such as "there is no meaning to a concept unless it represents an operation which can be performed in a laboratory" may be wisdom in physics or chemistry, but it cannot be adopted to sociology. Hume had shown long ago that the empiricism of "pure sense-perception does not provide the data for its own interpretation". Nevertheless the attempt to explain the universe "as merely interpretative of sense-impressions" had survived. One of the most eminent scientists of the day, Professor A. N. Whitehead, recalled Hume's discovery saying that "interest and importance are the primary reasons for the effort after exact discrimination of sense-data.*" If a "scientific sociology" is regarded as one devoted to the accumulation of sociological empirical facts free from all taint of "subjective" value

*A. N. Whitehead, *Modes of Thought* (Cambridge University Press, 1938), pp. 182,44.

sociological empirical facts free from all taint of "subjective" value judgments, it will end in a blind alley. Such a result is at once the confirmation of Sorokin's diagnosis and a vindication of his wider viewpoint. His book clearly showed up the inadequacy of tremendous efforts by thousands of sociological workers who put all their faith in sensory, empirical methods. Reference has already been made above to the expenditure of time, research grants, publications and devoted human effort by hundreds of writers and researchers in the U.S.A., made in the name of sociology, yet the product in uniformities, factors, causes, or correlations was so meager that it amounted to little or nothing. How little, was probably not recognized. During Sorokin's early years as a professor, many American sociologists had small knowledge of earlier work and little or none of work in other countries. Two years before *Fads and Foibles* appeared, the American Sociology Society had devoted its annual meeting to illustrate the development of sociological thought since the First World War. The relatively very recent short period was chosen because "most instructors, particularly those of the younger generation, have little antiquarian interest and their students vitally important earlier work has become distressingly frequent."* Such a remark recalls a retort to a brash art student, which Justice Holmes used to repeat with relish, "Oh, I see, you want to do something damned smart, straight off."** Appropriately, Sorokin's first chapter in *Fads and Foibles in Modern Sociology* dealt with "Amnesia and the New Columbuses." In it he gave astonishing examples of ignorance of past work and conceit about present virtues. The result has been that "almost all the new discoveries are either mere pompously worded platitudes, painful elaborations of the obvious, purely terminological innovations, or rediscoveries initially discovered long ago.† It is as though some American sociologists deemed a twentieth century birth certificate to be automatically able to confer a degree of wisdom which makes it unnecessary for its holder to exhibit any concern about remarks by such men as Aristotle, St. Augustine, St. Thomas Aquinas, Montesquieu, Hobbes, Bentham, or Burke.

Modern Sociological Theory, H. Becker & A. Boskoff, eds. (New York, Dryden Press, 1958), p. ix, p.v.
**Holmes-Laski Letters*, Howe M. de Wolfe, ed. (Oxford University Press, 1953), p. 1228.
†P. A. Sorokin, *Fads and Foibles in Modern Sociology* (Chicago, Henry Regnery Co., 1956), p. 16.

Sorokin with his long experience, his broad humanistic culture, and his familiarity with the inheritance of the works of genius, felt impelled to make a stand on behalf of the integrity of the life of the mind and for the continuity of thought. *Fads and Foibles in Modern Sociology* might well be prescribed reading for all students of sociology just as pathology must be studied by all who seek to minister to the life and health of mankind. The long discussions at the American Sociological Society mentioned above on "major strands in theory and methodology" reported the "persistence of underlying controversies" which it was hoped have "enriched sociological methodology." Sorokin was referred to as "unquestionably the leading American representative" of the users of the historical method, but nothing was said of his integralist theory linking individual thought and action with social life and cultural patterns — not even in a long and learned paper on "The Changing Prominence of Values," which endeavored with singularly slight success, to derive light and guidance from other recent writers on the subject. When "some specializations in Modern Sociology" were presented in Part III of the collection, this unresolved methodological uncertainty underlay the discussion and inevitably prolonged the confusion. A valiant effort to discover some "basic continuities in the study of small groups" ended with the lame admission that its contribution to general sociology was difficult to estimate, accompanied by the usual blank cheque upon the future when "more research may be expected to have implications" although whether interest in the small group concept would last, was a far from encouraging final doubt. A review of studies of social disorganization revealed "the peculiar adolesence of this particular field, its tendency to blow hot and cold by turns, its sudden embarrassments and hollow pretensions." An attempt to put social stratification in perspective furnished many illustrations of the delusion that the abstract concepts of class and structure can yield fruitful results in sociology before value theory first suffuses them with meaning. On page after page there were admissions of failure and inadequacy, naive observations, verbosity masquerading as profoundity, unnecessary and over-elaborate jargon, all of which obscured the good work and valuable ideas reported in the volume. Nevertheless the distinguished editors thought that it should be "quite acceptable and useful in courses at the undergraduate level," so begging the question whether sociology, as it then stood, could be regarded as a fit subject at that level. The degree of knowledge and of experience of the world which are almost essential prerequisites to its successful study would seem to make it unsuitable for boys and girls fresh from school. That this question should have been raised follows from the admission of two contributors to the volume that "a corpus of tested generalizations is something that cannot now be given to students." Apart from Sorokin's work, sociology seems in no better shape in this respect today.

In 1954 Sorokin's integralist theory of personality and of cultural values might have been thought worthy of consideration as just such a basic generalization in sociology. He can be said to have tested it, insofar as far-reaching sociological generalizations can be tested, by his exhaustive historical enquiry. Students may be expected to be able to understand the elements of their own psychological nature and being, from their unconscious reflex actions, their instinctive drives and urges, their mental awareness and powers of reasoning up to a realization that the world in which they live and the way people think and behave are what they are, mainly because of the creative intuitions and thought of geniuses such as Plato, Aristotle, St. Thomas Aquinas, Descartes, Leibniz, Newton, Darwin, Pasteur, and others. What Sorokin said in this way is not new; what was new, and what has still to be made better known, was that Sorokin built a new, value-oriented sociology upon it with very far-reaching explanatory, predicting, and reformatory power. Sorokin had put this integralist theory of sociological motivation and methodology before the world since 1937 when it was explained in his *Social and Cultural Dynamics* (vol. 2. Chapters 1-12 and Vol. 4. 1941, Chapter 16). He had reiterated it in 1943 in his *Sociocultural Causality, Space, Time.* Nobody who had made even a superficial acquaintance with *Society, Culture and Personality* in 1947 and after could be in any doubt about the nature of Sorokin's sociological analysis or of the need to strive for integrated value-patterns. The Harvard Research Center in Creative Altruism was virtually built upon the concept of an integration of cultural values; the need for it being stressed especially in *The Ways and Power of Love, 1954* (Chapters 5-8). Yet virtually nothing to such effect appeared in the proceedings of the American Sociological Society in 1954 despite mounting evidence in several of the contributions that value theory offered the best hope of progress. "It would be quite proper always to speak of human activity as essentially 'knowing-desiring-norming'," said Professor Howard Becker, paraphrasing Sorokin.* The second editor of the proceedings asserted that "a mass of evidence strongly confirms social and cultural explanations of change and virtually extinguishes, for all but the most recalcitrant minds, the theoretical validity of physical, biological or geographical factors."

* *Modern Sociological Theory,* H. Becker & A. Boskoff, eds. (New York, Dryden Press, 1958) pp. 140.

Sorokin was not the sternest critic of the sociology of his day. "Incalculable losses" have been imputed to "fashions in sociological investigation"; to its "dead ends, errors and false starts . . . hypotheses still dangling for want of verification . . . planless and pointless empiricism, . . . theorizing apart from . . . empirical exploration . . . many series of disconnected investigations with which the science is strewn." This comprehensive denunciation, which is not Sorokin's, was made in the hope that by overcoming such lamentable failures, sociology might one day become "a science rather than a series of facts."*

A soul-searching among sociologists was overdue, so Sorokin's initiative should have been salutary. Sociology had a poor repute. It was something of a laughing-stock in literary and historical circles.** After Sorokin had intervened so powerfully, others took up his theme, including the late Professor C. Wright Mills. His writings upon such popular public themes as *White Collar,* on the American middle classes, (1951) *Character and Social Structure,* (1953, with H. H. Gerth), *The Power Elite* (1956) won him a considerable audience.

When he published *The Sociological Imagination* in 1959 (New York, Oxford University Press) to continue the attack on the extravagances and deficiencies of contemporary and recent American sociology, Sorokin's earlier work *Fads and Foibles in Modern Sociology* had already been before the world for three years. Wright Mills was a professor at Columbia University in New York, Professor Sorokin had just retired after thirty years service as the doyen of American sociologists at Harvard University. Yet Wright Mills, who repeated less convincingly and less adequately many of Sorokin's ideas, never once referred to him, to his book, to his work, or to his ideas. Sorokin makes no complaint but in his autobiography *A Long Journey* (p. 297) he records that Wright Mills wrote to him soon after the

*R. A. Schermerhorn & A. Boskoff, "Recent Analyses of Sociological Theory," *Modern Sociological Theory,* H. Becker & A. Boskoff, eds. (New York, Dryden Press, 1958), p. 76.
**A sample indication of the views held about sociology by two exceptionally well-read men, trained by the Harvard Law School, may be derived from the letters exchanged between Professor Harold Laski and Mr. Justice Holmes between 1916 and 1935. Typical of Laski's opinions were "the longer I work the more convinced I am that the whole tribe of sociologists are categorizing material in an unearthly and quite meaningless way" (Nov. 11, 1924 after reading Simmel and Giddings); "they won't examine definite institutions in a definite way. They spend their time in vast generalizations which mean precisely nothing as soon as you analyze them in any serious way" (Nov. 4, 1924) *Holmes-Laski Letters* Howe M. de Wolfe, ed., (Oxford University Press, 1953), pp. 556, 589.

publication of *Fads and Foibles* expressing "his high evaluation and essential agreement with most of my conclusions."

Wright Mills' own book, *Sociological Imagination*, was the poorer as a result, for he failed to support the forthright stand assumed by Sorokin on behalf of values, although throughout his stimulating volume he recognized the great importance of human valuations. Wright Mills was no dupe of the crude empiricists with their exaggerated devotion to "sampling", "mass observation", "case-studies" and so forth, who, he said "do not usually seem aware that it is a philosophy upon which they stand." The implication that Wright Mills himself had a philosophy of which he was aware, is difficult to vindicate from his writings or from the volume of collected essays published in his honor, *The New Sociology* (1964 New York, Oxford University Press). The predominant impression which that volume makes upon any observer who relies upon it alone, is of a man wrestling energetically with the task of winning personal distinction in his efforts to attain clarity of vision and expression; one willing to flirt with Marxist, Soviet and Cuban revolutionary ideas, but nevertheless unequal to the task imposed by his ambition.* The strange fact emerges that towards the end of his short life in 1962 he planned a *Comparative Sociology* of six to nine volumes as a great work to confer the status of a science upon social theory. L. L. Horowitz, the editor of the commemorative volume devoted to him, describes Mills' objective and outlines his methods in sufficient detail to give the impression that he was searching for ways of tackling a task which Sorokin had already completed in 1937. Just as Wright Mills published his book *The Sociological Imagination* upon a theme which Sorokin had more powerfully illuminated three years earlier, so the abortive scheme for a world history was conceived essentially upon lines already plain in Sorokin's work. It was to be in terms of macroscopic social systems rather than of "social systems in terms of history" as Marx and Toynbee; it was to be removed from highly abstract "ideal-typologies"; it was to be based upon an exhaustive study of "all relevant statistical and systematic knowledge;" it would be "non-ethnocentric" in the effort to transcend the cultural relativism of the anthropologists. There seems to be no evidence to show

---

*It is an impression which is confirmed by Professor D. H. Wrong in "The Failure of American Sociology" (*Commentary*, 1959, p. 28); "Mills' books are full of exciting vistas, imaginative suggestions pointing to overlooked connections in social life, but he inevitably fails to follow them up in any vigorous fashion." The contrast which Sorokin's work provides by its far greater range, insight and synthetic power is striking.

whether Wright Mills ever discussed his plans with Sorokin. It seems unlikely in view of the extraordinary omission of any reference to Sorokin either by Wright Mills or by Horowitz, who nevertheless mentions other writers such as Kroeber and Linton whose writings had been superseded by Sorokin's greater range, precision and philosophic insight. In the same essay Horowitz could write, "we do not have large range sociology because we lack familiarity with historical sources." Nobody could have opened any of Sorokin's twenty or thirty volumes published during the previous forty years without having seen Sorokin's familiarity with historical sources.*

It is not possible here to try to detect Sorokin's influence, or its absence, upon the whole vast output of sociological writing which expanded enormously during his long academic career. Many samples indicate that his theories made relatively little impact upon his contemporaries, including many younger sociologists who had been numbered among his students at Harvard. Sorokin's own philosophy largely explains why this should be so. Academic subjects that have long been professed in Universities acquire a momentum of their own. Children at school must be educated so that they can find their way about when they arrive at a university. Schoolteachers, moreover, were trained by universities; school and college textbooks and courses are all planned in conformity with academic tradition. Considerable courage would therefore be required for any teacher to tell his students in history to dispense with time-honored divisions of the subject into "ancient," "medieval," and "modern," or to disregard accepted and convenient "schools" in English literature such as "Elizabethan," "metaphysical," "Restoration comedy," "Augustan," "classic," and so forth, even though their inadequacy has been a commonplace among reflective students for a long time. Sorokin could not expect suddenly to demote sociological concepts, or pseudo-concepts such as "class," "role," "structure," if virtually the whole of the two million or more students of the subject were being told to concentrate upon them. One of Sorokin's sympathizers and cooperators, Professor C. C. Zimmerman, pointed out in 1959 that the new empiricism

*I. L. Horowitz, ed., *The New Sociology: Essays in Social Science and Social Theory* in honor of C. Wright Mills (New York, Oxford University Press, 1964), pp. 25, 40-46. See also p. 227 where the contrast of "ideographic" and "nomothetic" is made an "issue" . . . "embodying a sizable component" and is discussed in language which is difficult to parse, analyse or translate and where Mills is given credit for "relating social science to value," a task which Sorokin had already undertaken while Mills was an undergraduate.

which dominated sociology, imposing neo-positivist ideas, had been accepted by those who "controlled disposable research and training funds almost entirely . . . they almost dominate the field." It was, he said, difficult to get a publisher for "almost any books of more profound intellectual significance than elementary texts."* Generally, he summarized the trend in American sociology by saying that "all of these psychological-structural sociologies are primarily classificatory, and describe relative static conditions. They hypothecate understanding only stable societies and not the living reality. Their dealings almost solely are with the nexus between the individual and the social order . . ." which, he might have added, was not a success because the cultural values of the individual were rarely made a determining element in that living reality.**

When, in the United States, new and valuable ideas are neglected, or spread very slowly, it would be expecting much to find a better state of affairs overseas. In 1950 Professor Barbara Wootton, later Lady Wootton, published *Testament for Social Science,* writing, she said, as an amateur. It was evident that she had not encountered Sorokin's work, for it would have rescued her from the relativity of moral values by which she was baffled, after having effectively exposed difficulties to which Sorokin's work suggests a solution. She came near to an adequate analysis of culture and she shared Sorokin's realization of the need for "creative altruism." "It is not science we lack, but love . . . and if indeed it is love rather than wit that is lacking, the question is how to get it . . . surely there could hardly be a more constructive line of research . . ."† When Lady Wootton wrote these words Sorokin was already at work on his Harvard Research Center for Creative Altruism.

In Great Britain, the development of sociology since Herbert Spencer and H. T. Buckle had been on the whole on careful, cautious lines, as though in reaction from the confident, dogmatic tone of the pioneers. It remained an interest for amateurs in the main. With L. T. Hobhouse academic sociological speculation became more philosophically oriented, with special concentration upon ethical considerations. Loyal as he has

---

*C. C. Zimmerman, "Contemporary Trends in Sociology," in J. S. Roucek, ed., *Contemporary Sociology* (London, Peter Owen, 1959) pp. 19-20.
**Zimmerman's criticisms can be illustrated from many of the contributions to other symposia, e.g., G. Gurvich and W. E. Moore, eds., *Twentieth Century Sociology* (New York, Philosophical Library, 1945); and L. D. White., ed., *The State of the Social Sciences* (Chicago, U. of Chicago Press, 1956).
†B. Wootton, *Testament for Social Science* (London, Allen & Unwin Ltd., 1950), pp. 183-7.

always been to the ideas of Hobhouse, Professor Morris Ginsberg, who succeeded him, has built constructively upon them. His detached, objective approach and the ideas which he has elaborated in his own calm, reflective manner, have been deeply pondered and firmly based upon a lifetime devoted to the pursuit of truth. He was the first to review, and for many years, the only British sociologist to commend Sorokin's *Social and Cultural Dynamics.* *

He is, like Sorokin, convinced that "the view that sociology and history differ in the kind of knowledge they seek to attain does not appear to be well substantiated."** He, as Durkheim and Hobhouse realized earlier, also shares with Sorokin the view that "the comparative method is the method *par excellence* of sociology,"† so that "the problem of determining the proper units required for comparative study has become more acute now that there is available a vast amount of data from the history of the civilizations and its solution requires the close co-operation of historians and sociologists." Sorokin could be counted upon to welcome Professor Ginsberg's conclusion that "the important thing is to resist the tendency of the social sciences to become isolated from one another and from general sociology which can only flourish by their systematization."††

Curiously, Durkheim has been blamed for diverting American sociologists from the right road. After 1912, with the appearance of his *Elementary Forms of the Religious Life,* it was said, "henceforth, sociologists, especially in the United States, were to turn their backs on the historic and humanistic approaches and to converge on a scientific sociology that found reality in social interaction and science in the mustering and manipulation of data in mass — impersonal yet mathematically precise."*†

---

*P. J. Allen, *Pitirim A. Sorokin in Review* (N. Carolina, Duke University Press, 1963), pp. 278-80.
**M. Ginsberg, *On the Diversity of Morals* (London, William Heinemann, Ltd., 1962), p. 178.
†M. Ginsberg, *op. cit.,* p. 267.
††M. Ginsberg, *op. cit.,* p. 268. See also the summary of Ginsberg's contribution up to 1945 by D. MacRae in "British Sociology," *Twentieth Century Sociology,* G. Gurvitch & W. E. Moore, ed. (New York Philosophical Library, 1945), pp. 580-5. See also D. MacRae, *Ideology and Society* (London, William Heinemann Ltd., 1961), pp. 16-29.
*†F. W. Voget, "Anthropology and Sociology," in J. S. Roucek, ed., *Contemporary Sociology* (London, Peter Owen, 1959), p. 454. It seems doubtful whether

In view of the dearly bought failure of virtually exclusive reliance upon such a methodology it was high time for Sorokin to point out that, without a deeper psychological and historical awareness of the nature and achievements of men and women, "social interaction" and similar pseudo-scientific concepts are sterile. By his example, he sought to restore sociology to humanism. Some other sociologists were then beginning to take a similar line.*

It would be satisfying to an Englishman to believe that the relatively late development of academic concern with sociology, particularly at Oxford, may be partly explained by the consideration that some knowledge about values in social life, to the illumination of which it is here contended that sociology should be predominantly directed, was traditionally, indirectly, and all the more pervasively therefore, conveyed in courses such as *literae humaniores* at Oxford. That it was desirable to supplement and enlarge such a discipline had been given academic recognition by the provision of courses in such subjects as ethics, philosophy, political theory, and economics. They were not alone.

Sociology and Some Related Disciplines

Even in Great Britain there has been a great expansion in sociology in recent years, as a separate study or discipline. At the same time other "social" subjects also have been expanded to consolidate their interest and to extend and to define their subject-matter. Professor Talcott Parsons did well to observe that Max Weber "would have altered many of his

Durkheim's work was sufficiently well-known in the U.S.A. at that time to exert such influence. See, for example, R. Dahrendorf, "European Sociology and the American Self-Image," in *Archives Europeennes de Sociologie,* Vol. II (1961), p. 347.

*K. W. Kapp, *Towards a Science of Man in Society. A Positive Approach to the Integration of Social Knowledge* (The Hague, Nijhoff, 1961). After recounting some of the bad results of studying humanistic questions in separate compartments, after reviewing various efforts to find some principle of integration of an interdisciplinary, historical, or other type, Kapp advocates what is essentially integration through culture, which, however, is a concept not successfully defined. Although Professor Kapp writes in New York City and talks of "social dynamics" and "integration" through culture, he makes no mention of the priority of Sorokin's ideas in these fields. Yet the attempt went on, with scant success, to discover key-concepts in other than the culture field. See, for example, A. Kuhn, *The Study of Society: A Multidisciplinary Approach* (Tavistock, 1966), in which "transaction" and "organization" are offered as integrating ideas but fail to meet the need. Cf *Nature* (1966), pp. 212, 1006.

opinions" (especially in the theory of religion) "if he had had access to the subsequent fifty years toil and research."*

Since Max Weber died, new subjects such as public administration have come into academic prominence. Little more than an extra-curricular interest of a few civil servants and local government officials in Great Britain at first, it has become an academic discipline with a very considerable literature. Its scope is such that there are some topics which it would seem appropriate to transfer to it from sociology. Much of the discussion about "small groups", for example, might be undertaken in an administrative and legal context; much of the discussion about authority, power and domination in "group" theory as well as the study of class and social structure becomes more practical and realistic when viewed in an administrative setting.** That social life on the vast scale that we know today can develop solely by better organization may seem a truism until its implications are worked out by administrators and business managers. In industry, business, and government, where the division of labor is essential, there are inevitably ascending grades of complexity and difficulty from simple manual operations through increasingly involved processes requiring technical and scientific skill, training and knowledge up to the directing level on which the whole complex nature of the operations of the entire organization must be understood and responsibility must be accepted for their daily coordination and direction. It has been found in practice, as every good manual on business management or organization and methods shows, that it is only possible to achieve efficient operation by a "staff and line" manning policy corresponding to the various levels of directing, organizing, technical, and manual operations and responsibilities.

What is true of industry, business, and public administration must inevitably be reflected in social organization and stratification. That every attempt to ignore organizational realities by trying to create a classless, egalitarian society in which the heaviest responsibilities receive neither recognition nor reward has invariably floundered and been abandoned is one of the plainest lessons of history. Of the many reasons for such failures, that provided by business and administrative organization is one

---

*Max Weber, *The Sociology of Religion,* trans. by E. Fischoff (London, Methuen & Co., 1965), p. xxvi.
**Max Weber, *Wirtschaft und Gesellschaft* (Mohr, Tübingen, 1925), Part I, chaps. 12, 13, 14, 15. Part I trans. by A. R. Henderson and Talcott Parsons as *The Theory of Social and Economic Organization* (London, W. Hudge, 1947) with a long introduction by Prof. Parsons; selections also trans. by H. P. Secher as *Basic Concepts in Sociology* (London, Peter Owen, 1962).

of the clearest, yet it is one commonly neglected by politicians and sociologists alike.

Possibly because Max Weber gave "bureaucracy" his attention in his encyclopaedic survey of the social scene, the topic has tended to remain one to which sociologists feel bound to give attention, not always apparently with a knowledge of the very considerable literature contributed by those more directly involved in problems of public administration. The best reciprocal relationships between sociology, political, and administrative theory still have to be worked out if much confusion, overlapping, and duplication of effort is to be avoided.*

Lack of well-defined relations between academic sociology and administrative, political, and legal theory can be remedied to a considerable extent by Sorokin's work. If sociology is to merge into, emerge from, or depend upon an overriding theory of value in the way suggested in this book, the need for definition of spheres of activity may seem to be greater than ever. To formulate interdisciplinary relationships with the aid of value theory, as restated in the light of a historical sociology such as Sorokin's should, however, as proposed at the end of the previous chapter, lead to a better division of labor in the social sciences by allowing sociologists to hand over a whole mass of topics for treatment by specialists who are more thoroughly well-acquainted with particular fields than any sociological theorist is ever likely to become. Relationships should not of course be renounced and sociologists might, if this view is correct, have the satisfaction of seeing general sociological value theory applied by others, from whose labors they may, in turn learn much of a general nature which would illustrate, confirm, or amend that value theory as well.

International and American Recognition of Sorokin

Sorokin's achievement stands out brilliantly, because he asked the right questions, because he meditated long and wisely, because he was

*R. K. Merton, *Social Theory and Social Structure* (Illinois, Glencoe Free Press, 1957); one of the sanest reviews of sociological problems, points to "studies of religious, educational, military, economic and political bureaucracies dealing with the interdependence of social organization and personality formation as an avenue for fruitful research", so opening up a frightening vista of the accumulation of yet more monographs on vaguely conceived topics nevertheless held to be "theoretically significant and practically important." (p. 206) The work of the Royal Institute of Public Administration during the past half century is but one of the professional Societies in the field that got no mention in this context.

meticulous in the choice of methods, because he made the whole history of human civilization and culture his universe of discourse, because he made no concessions to currently fashionable personalities, cliques, or doctrines, because he refused to trim his words to court academic favor, the benevolence of Foundations, or the patronage of publishers seeking "best-sellers." To this category of the outstanding merits to which he owes his success, must no doubt be added "because his tremendous vitality and energy allowed him to remain vigorous and active well past his seventieth year." For in the fierce, competitive, academic world, such staying power is highly necessary for anyone who seeks, as Sorokin powerfully sought (and succeeded) to swim against the tide of "orthodox" fashion.*

Again it is difficult, if not impossible, for a stranger to the American sociological scene to assess adequately the reception which Sorokin's views encountered there over the years. From what can only be interpreted as a studious neglect in certain quarters to mention him or his theories in any scientific manner, and from the frequent failure to give his work any acknowledgment, it seems clear that Sorokin's eminence was later in gaining general recognition in the United States than it has been in other countries where his ideas have been more widely disseminated in translation than those of any other American sociologist. In 1964, after certain members of the American Sociological Association had "written in" his name in addition to the "official" candidates proposed by the governing committee, Sorokin was triumphantly elected its president.

By that time honors had already come upon Sorokin thick and fast. His presence was insistently sought at sociological conferences; he just as consistently declined. Such was the persistence of some of their organizers however that he had to give in and attend. He attended, among others, the 18th International Congress at Nuremberg in 1958 and the 19th Congress at Mexico City two years later. He records with amusement that the paper he then delivered at the insistent wish of the then President of the American Sociological Association, "Variations on the Spencerian Theme of Militant and Industrial Types of Society" commemorating the

---

*Sociology is not singular in giving tardy recognition to new ideas. The great physicist, Max Planck, nearly 90 when he died, reported that "it is one of the most painful experiences of my entire scientific life that I have seldom — in fact, I might say, never succeeded in gaining recognition for a new result, the truth of which I could demonstrate by a conclusive albeit only theoretical proof". He added "a new scientific truth does not triumph by convincing its opponents and making them see the light, but rather because its opponents eventually die, and a new generation grows up that is familiar with it." (M. Planck, *Scientific Autobiography and other Papers* trans. by F. Gaynor [Williams and Norgate] pp. 30, 33, 34.)

Centenary Celebration of Herbert Spencer, was rejected by the editor of the Association's *Review*. (There had been many other applications for permission to print it, so it was very soon published.)

When the International Society for Comparative Study of Civilizations was formed in 1960, Sorokin was unanimously chosen as its first President, which led to his reluctant journey to Salzburg for its first Conference in 1961. President-elect also of the 20th International Congress of Sociology, he found it necessary to journey halfway around the world to attend it as well as other meetings; this proved too exacting, so he resigned, confining himself to journeys within the United States. At home he also received many more pressing invitations than he could possibly accept. In 1962 he had to decline some thirty such appeals for his appearance. Disappointing as it must have been to forego these opportunities, it was clearly impossible to accept them all, so he wisely concentrated upon writing instead.

It is to be hoped that many of his occasional contributions to learned journals and symposia will be collected and published. They include subjects such as "The Integral Theory of Values," "Theses on the Moral Transformations of Mankind," "How are Sociological Theories Conceived, Developed and Validated?" "Theses on Creativity," "Mutual Convergence of the United States and the U.S.S.R. to the Mixed Sociocultural Type," "A Quest for an Integral System of Sociology," "Theses on the Role of Historical Method in the Social Sciences," "Western Religion and Morality of Today," and many others. In addition, a great deal of work and correspondence devolved upon Sorokin 'as his earlier writings were reprinted and translated. Retirement from Harvard therefore was certainly not synonymous with leisure and repose. Nevertheless Sorokin reports time taken off for "music, gardening and loafing."

Honors continued to be offered to him. In 1963 a Festschrift commemorating his achievements* was contributed by fifteen sociologists to convey "the respect, admiration and gratitude that his friends, colleagues and former students have for him." In the same year Professor Philip J. Allen published a volume which he had organized on different lines, *Pitirim A. Sorokin in Review* (Durham N.C., Duke University Press, 1963). Sorokin led the 500 pages of this work with an account of the "Sociology of My Mental Life." It was followed by critical assessments of: "Sorokin as Philosopher," by Professor J. B. Ford; "Sorokin's Philosophy

---

*E. A. Tiryakian, ed., *Sociological Theory, Values, and Sociocultural Change*, (Illinois, Glencoe Free Press, 1963).

of History," by Dr. A. J. Toynbee; "Sorokin and Cultural Mythology," by Dr. O. F. Anderle; "Sorokin's Theory of Social Mobility," by Professor Gösta Carlsson; "Sorokin's Theories on Sex and Society," by David R. Mace; "Sorokin's Psychological Theories," by Professor Alexandre Vexilard; "Sorokin's Rural-Urban Principles," by Professor T. Lynn Smith; "Sorokin's Use of Sociological Measurement," by Professors Matilda W. Riley and Mary E. Moore; "Russia and the United States," by Professor Alex Inkeles; "Sorokin on Law, Revolution, War, and Social Calamities," by Professor N. S. Timasheff; "Sorokin's Formulations in the Sociology of Science," by Professors R. K. Merton and B. Barber; and four separate comments upon the reception of Sorokin's ideas in England, India, Italy, and Latin America. The purpose of the book was to advance by critical appraisal the cause of sociology, so Sorokin wound up the whole with a long "Reply to my Critics."

Professor Allen's notable service in devising, planning, and producing this wide-ranging, searching, survey merits enduring gratitude. No better source is available for all who, after acquiring some understanding of Sorokin's work, wish to see it appraised by other minds, criticized, and placed in perspective in a dialectic between them and Sorokin himself. Both Professor Tiryakian's and Professor Allen's volumes contained a list of Sorokin's published books up to the year 1963 and a selection of titles from his more than two hundred essays, papers, and addresses.

The Trend Towards Value Theory in Sociology

Most of the critical questions put to Sorokin in Professor Allen's volume have been mentioned above. The final paper, by Professors R. K. Merton and B. Barber, may however be referred to again because it voiced doubts and uncertainties that may remain with some readers and it contained some of the most searching queries which have ever been put to Sorokin. Merton, one of Sorokin's ablest students during the 1930's, had also undertaken the collection of the data upon which Sorokin had based his conclusions about variations in scientific theories throughout the ages. Merton had, moreover, already been critical of Sorokin's views.*

Sorokin's theories, said Merton and Barber, are "primarily suited to characterize cultures in the large, not to analyze the connections between

*R. K. Merton, *Social Theory and Social Structure* (Illinois, Glencoe Free Press, 1957), pp. 466-7, 475, 481.

various positions in the social structure and the styles and content of thought which are distinctive of them." Sorokin admitted that he "did not pay sufficient attention to many micro-sociological problems" and that his was indeed a "macrosociology," relating to long periods of time and major changes in social and cultural life. He contended however that he had put first things first and that the priority given to the dominant cultural trends was justified. It is also true, as Merton and Barber pointed out, that Sorokin's classifications of main cultural systems were not free from admixture, as he himself had said. His empirical findings revealed, for example, the existence of ideational or idealistic tendencies within a sensate culture. There has, moreover, been an accumulation of cultural achievement so that some activities, knowledge, and values are carried forward from one cultural era to another as a permanent addition to the patrimony of humanity. Sorokin had of course already discovered this. He never contended that his supersystems, even during their periods of greatest vigor, were free from traces of other, even contrary tendencies. He had pointed to survivals or reactions nascent within the dialectical development, naturally occurring, within every cultural system. As in individual lives, the problem is one of identifying predominant influences and of following their development and change. The identification, and comprehension of the nature of such cultural elements or inherited strains is in itself a great gain for descriptive sociology and at the same time an aid to better and more tolerant understanding, of apparently alien or "foreign" elements within any given cultural system. It is reasonable to believe that an immense toll of human suffering and misery might have been, and still could be avoided by the acceptance and practical adoption of Sorokin's ideas of integralism and cultural relativity. Merely to realize that cultural belief and practices which give meaning and value to life are something for which all people will fight and die might often have sufficed to prevent those wars to the death in which vast numbers of the human race have been exterminated. Today no problem is more vital and urgent than to secure universal recognition of the folly of seeking to impose alien cultural patterns by force because conflict so arising is now a madness liable to involve the destruction by atomic weapons of human lives all over the earth.

On the plane of logic and methodology, Sorokin was able to defend his conclusions by demonstrating that his cultural supersystems are very much more than mere "pigeonholes," very much more than merely arbitrary notions, dreamed up in order to foist a particular private world view of his own upon his readers. The very nature of those supersystems had been defined, not in advance, but after observing the manner in which they were composed of simpler cultural values or "systems," mutually congruent or coherent, all of which being themselves variables, were yet observed to arise together, to develop together and to change together. The supersystems are no reified paper concepts, they are the products of a combination of an immense number of discrete facts.

If it is admitted that the cultural supersystems have been detected as having existed "in their own right," the critics have further queries. If, they said, each supersystem has its own cultural values, its own truth, what criteria does Sorokin himself employ? The answer, already described, is his integralist criterion in which hints or intuitions spontaneously occuring in the minds of *some* men or women, described as of supraconscious inspiration and distinguished from those automatic drives experienced by *all* men and women from the equally unknown source labelled the "subconscious," are utilized by being brought into harmony with bioconscious and socioconscious influences.

Another response was surely available to Sorokin, when asked for his criterion, which, however, he did not make. It is not necessary, upon the view taken here of his work, that he should have any criteria of his own. Obviously he has, and a very potent force his integralist position deserves to be. But as a scientist, it would suffice for him to have discerned, in the vast web and network of recorded human history, the nature of the cultural systems by which the lives of men have in fact been shaped and guided in the past. He can report that for x centuries mankind has given its loyalty in the main to a series of cultural values $a^1, a^2, a^3, a^4 \ldots a^n$; for y centuries the a series was supplanted, again in the main, but with some a hangovers, by a new series, $b^1, b^2, b^3, b^4 \ldots b^n$; only in turn to give way to a third series, $c^1, c^2, c^3, c^4 \ldots c^n$ again with some a and b hangovers which endured for z centuries. In order to present such a scheme in manageable form, it is summarized as a succession of cultural supersystems A $(\leqslant a^1 \ldots a^n)$; B $(\leqslant b^1 \ldots b^n)$; C $(\leqslant c^1 \ldots c^n)$. As a scientist, Sorokin will report that the A system of cultural values is not free from some admixture of b and c values, but that they are never so numerous or so weighty as to make invalid the summation represented by A. Similarly B and C cultural supersystems represent predominantly b and c series of phenomena, although a and c, a and b elements respectively are also to be found in them. The validity of the scheme as a whole is seen in the fact that changes within any supersystem such as A affect all its components $a^1, a^2, a^3 \ldots a^n$ which change together. Such an interpretation depends of course upon the validity of the description of the a, b and c series as "cultural values," and for this criteria are necessary. For Sorokin such criteria emerge from the series of questions by which the *a, b* and *c* facts were elicited. These in turn have here been reclassified by means of the universals of truth or knowledge, beauty or aesthetic value, and good or moral behavior and worth.

The illuminating exchange of views, which has been partially and inadequately summarized here, and which should be followed in the detail in which it is given in *Pitirim A. Sorokin in Review,* provokes further reflection. Unless Sorokin's critics deemed *any* such attempt to characterize historical development to be a mistake, what classification do they regard as being superior to his? Spengler's "childhood, youth, maturity and old age"? Toynbee's score or more of "civilizations"? the traditional "Ancient, Medieval, Modern," among others? A greater scientific adequacy and applicability can be claimed for Sorokin's empirically grounded, cultural classification than for any of these alternative views. Merton and Barber did not make any such comparison; indeed, by referring to Sorokin's "macrosociological" view of the matter as "a first approximation," they may be taken to concede a sufficient element of validity to Sorokin's approach as to make the search for alternative classifications unnecessary. To narrow the problem down to one of giving greater microsociological precision to an accepted macrosociological presentation of the whole of history and the whole of sociology is indeed a major advance which greatly fortifies the thesis of this book. For it implies a recognition that in giving pre-eminence in sociology to a cultural interpretation of the life of mankind in society, Sorokin was indeed on the right road.

To answer the charge of relativism by invoking an "integralist" solution may, however, not seem to be conclusive in the light of the overriding problem of the relativism of all cultural supersystems, the *A, B,* and *C* of the exposition above. It would seem to be open to Sorokin to invoke the argument advanced by Max Planck in discussing the impact of Einstein's discovery in physical science when he declared that "the often-heard phrase, 'Everything is relative' is both misleading and thoughtless." Such an interpretation of Einstein's results would, he held, be "fundamentally erroneous" on the logical ground that "everything that is relative presupposes the existence of something that is absolute." Anything relative can be "meaningful only when juxtaposed to something absolute." In the scientific world of physics that absolute is "the determination of the matrix of the space-time continuum."

Dangerous as is the current fashion of invoking analogies from natural science to explain sociological phenomena, it is a risk which has been taken by Sorokin and others already, so with due caution, it will again be taken now, in full recognition that it is no more than an analogy. In place of "space-time continuum" as the absolute in natural science, may not sociologists substitute the "socio-cultural continuum" as the realm of all those values and as constituting the matrix from which cultural supersystems emerge?*

In all cultural supersystems there are aspects of qualities classed as examples of the true, the beautiful and the good, as illustrated above by the schematic series $a^1, a^2 \ldots a^n; b^1, b^2, b^3 \ldots b^n; c^1, c^2, c^3 \ldots c^n$, so providing the group of universals which form the supersystems $A.B.C.$ Here a^1, b^1, c^1 may stand for aesthetic satisfactions; a^2, b^2, c^2 refer to behavioral and ethical factors, and so on. These universals, A, B, C, enriched by an understanding of the widely divergent forms in which they appear and are used and realized in the various supersystems revealed by the historical record, are classes of universal values for which an "absolute," the socio-cultural continuum, is the matrix. There should be a readier acceptance of such a notion today when art, behavior, morality, music, and other forms of culture exhibit the most heterogenous elements, few of which lack some adherents and advocates. The warfare between enthusiasts for various modes of art, music, and so forth arises because each mode is intolerantly regarded as being the universally valid art, universally valid music, instead of being one mode or form only.

What Professor Allen's survey did for Sorokin's ideas had something of a counterpart in what Sorokin was to do for the American Sociological Association. His Presidential Address at Chicago in September 1965, "Sociology of Yesterday, Today, and Tomorrow," was a model of what such an oration should be. Long experience, vast reading, and mature reflection enabled him to confront the assembled sociologists of the United States with a critical stock-taking of the progress of the discipline they served. Sorokin pointed to the marked change of emphasis in sociology during the preceding forty or fifty years of his active life as Professor, during which time the generalizing, synthesizing, philosophical, sociological systems of the pioneers such as Spencer, Marx, Durkheim, Tarde, Weber, Scheler, Simmel, Spengler, Tönnies, Ward, Sumner, Pareto, Ross, and others had been succeeded by an immense amount of fact-finding, analytical work. Paying tribute to the zeal and energy thus

---

*M. Planck, *Scientific Autobiography and Other Papers*, trans. by F. Gaynor (Williams and Norgate), pp. 46, 47.

displayed, Sorokin proclaimed that it had not lived up to its promise nor had it justified the aggressive, confident tone of its advocates. In his considered view, ninety per cent of the thousand and more "discoveries" which had recently been claimed for empirical, "scientific" sociological work in the behavioral sciences were not discoveries at all. They were mostly either truisms, platitudes, or pompous presentations of the ideas of earlier writers, or they were disguised methodological, philosophical, speculative propositions. Not more than five to ten per cent brought any glint of novelty, and they were all of minor significance.

In these circumstances Sorokin called for, and forecast, the advent of a new era of synthesis and reconciliation of all that was found among the products of the fact-finding research, and its integration into broader, generalized, multi-dimensional uniformities. How is so very desirable and so long overdue a progress to be achieved?

Sorokin placed the main emphasis in his address upon the principles and propositions whose adoption would be best likely to ensure that enriched and more fertile sociology for which everybody was waiting. Throughout his recommendations ran such words as "meaningful," "normative," "sociocultural," "ideological," and "cultural," accompanied by the specific apposition of "culturology" with "sociology." These value-laden ideas did not exclude other aspects of social systems, but such was their predominance that they emphasized again that at the core of Sorokin's doctrine lay a theory of culture. When the implications of that theory are brough out they amount to a theory of value. It has been stressed already above that this was the conclusion to which all the work embodied in *Social and Cultural Dynamics* inevitably seems to lead. A quarter of a century later Sorokin confirmed it in the light of subsequent thought and experience. It is hardly an exaggeration to claim that his great achievement has been to establish the virtual congruence, if not the identity, of sociology with value theory. Although implicit in much modern work, this direct connection does not yet seem to have been made clear and explicit. On the contrary, it is still often neglected.*

---

*Typical is M. Duverger, *Introduction to the Social Sciences,* trans. by M. Anderson from *Méthodes des Sciences Sociales* (Paris Presses Universitaires, 1961; London, Allen & Unwin Ltd., 1964). This popular introduction has the merit of rejecting Durkheim's description of social facts as "things" and of stating that "it is impossible for the social sciences to ignore values" (p. 35), but it does not follow through all the implications of this remark. Owing to the difficulty of detecting bias, it gives in to positivism as "an essential condition of science" (p. 37). Four bibliographical entries refer to Sorokin but nothing is said about his major achievement of resolving the positivist-idealist dualism through his "integral" theory of personality and his

The consequences of this coincidence, congruence, or conceptual fusion are tremendous in the new simplification and unity they bring to humanist studies in general. For what is humanism if it is not a collocation of values? When the same question is applied to sociology, must not the same affirmative answer be given? If not, what other better answer can be suggested?

Failing any, for none seems in sight, sociology and value theory may for all practical purposes be said to rest upon the same foundations. The guiding concepts which dominate humanistic studies, which have their basis in a theory of value, are necessarily interwoven.

By "interwoven," it is certainly not intended to imply that the study of sociology could replace theories of law, history, anthropology, education, art, ethics and other specialized subjects. What is intended is that a well-founded, empirical, sociological exposition of the evolution of values on Sorokin's lines, as a theory of culture, as an account of changes in fundamental value-systems, does bring new perspectives and new order into the presentation of such subjects. The various "sociologies" of law, education, art and so forth fall short of their objectives unless they are treated historically, and, to use a clumsy expression, macrosociologically. Their history must of course arise from within their own context. There can be no question of "sociology" taking them over or of imposing a value pattern upon them. When, however, sociology itself as the general study of the life and activity of men in society is revealed by searching, long-range empirical investigations on Sorokin's lines as throwing up a pattern of values, changing more or less uniformly over time; when it is seen to be itself the source of a theory of value, the hypothesis that this theory of value will be relevant to specialized aspects of the life and activity of mankind is no hazardous, highly dubious speculation. On the contrary, it is logically, philosophically, and psychologically an obvious conclusion.

The use Sorokin himself makes of his discovery in his own presentation of sociology puts the matter into perspective. Discussing the traditional presentation of sociology as predominantly the study of social institutions, "structures," "roles," "status," and so forth, he was led on to consider the "sociology of knowledge," which was developed out of it all, notably by Karl Mannheim in the 1930's and later.

He specifically states:

---

concept of cultural supersystems as the parameters which resolve the vexed problem of the subjectivity of value-judgments.

of the two independent variables, cultural and social, I chose the cultural factor as the more fruitful or more important one that accounts for a given state of science as well as of philosophy, religion, ethics, law, fine arts, polity, economy and social theories. This means that each of these cultural systems is more decisively determined by the rest of the *cultural* systems and supersystems than by the social *structures* of the respective groups having these cultural systems and supersystems .... I made this choice quite deliberately and for several reasons. First because the Marx - Mannheim - Stark - Gurvitch variable (of the "social position of an individual" or the "structure of the social group") cannot account for a large series of fundamental phenomena in the field of *Wissen-und Kultursoziologie* ... Summing up ... the co-operation of the cultural and the social types of *Wissensoziologie* is necessary for adequate cognition of socio-cultural reality but of these two types the cultural *Wissensoziologie* is more important and more fruitful than the social *Wissensoziologie.*"*

The specific thesis that sociology must be equated with theory of value, it must again be emphasized, is not stated in set terms by Sorokin. It is advanced here both as the clear implication of his main conclusions and in vindication of the claim that by them he has succeeded in achieving that major "break-through" to that grand synthesis for which sociology has so long waited, and wanted. Again, Sorokin himself makes no such claim. It is a view advanced in the realization that if it fails, its presentation here may unnecessarily harm Sorokin's reputation as a sociologist — "unnecessarily" because his lifework, his empirical researches, and the "integralist" theory based upon them remain an enduring contribution whatever deductions from them or additions to them may be suggested by others.

Sorokin's value theory as an idea to reshape sociology may be a special instance of a principle of Kant's which Cassirer repeated: "the history of philosophy shows us very clearly that the full determination of a concept is very rarely the work of that thinker who first introduced the concept."**

A pronounced emphasis upon the significance for sociology of cultural values does not of course imply that all study of structural

---

*P. J. Allen, *op. cit.,* pp. 483, 488.
**Ernst Cassirer, *Essay on Man* (New Haven, Yale University Press, 1944; London University Press) p. 180.

sociology is a waste of time. The whole point of challenging the amount of attention given to "roles," "class," "structure," "social action" and so forth, as central themes in much academic sociology, is to show that they must be redeemed by being recognized as vehicles for the conveyance of sociological value judgments and by being defined so clearly as to leave their relation to values in no doubt. Then, when they are viewed historically, the constant changes in the content of the ideas they purport to convey could become apparent. "Structure," for instance, if it is to be retained, will mean one thing in a society where tradition assigns occupation and status, where large landed estates are entailed upon the descendants of their aristocratic owners, and where sons normally follow their fathers' occupations. It will mean quite another thing in a relatively free market for goods, services and labor, as in nineteenth century America. As the free market becomes more restricted because, for example, of Trade Union activities, a reversion to earlier practices becomes evident, for the economic power of some Trade Unions can now be deployed to make feudal barons look like bungling amateurs at the game of holding the public to ransom. "Structural" sociological terms such as "role" and "class" are like empty boxes receiving different contents according to the contexts in which they are used.* Those contents, as it was suggested above, are best filled from specialist knowledge, whether it be of economic history, constitutional law, political theory, or public administration. To expect sociology to embrace all these specialisms in the effort to present a detailed microsociological account of them all, would be to impose a burden which few sociologists are ever likely to be fully equipped to sustain.

So much of the intricate, learned word-spinning on "roles," "class," and "structural" themes by academic sociologists is apt to provoke memories of Sir Winston Churchill's defiant question posed when the British were faced with dire threats by the Nazis and their Führer, "what sort of people do they think we are?" Whatever may be the difficulties of the view taken by Leibniz of the unique character of every living human being, it at least has the great merit of recognizing character, diversity of interests and marked individuality and consequently of doing justice to the spontaneous and very varied development of every single man, woman and

*Robert K. Merton, *Social Theory and Social Structure* (Illinois, Glencoe Free Press, 1957). This valiant effort of over 600 pages by a learned, talented and thoughtful sociologist is one of the best efforts to make something out of "structural" analysis, but it spreads more confusion and uncertainty than light upon the precise meaning of such terms as "structure," "role," etc.

child. Leibniz put all the emphasis upon the active, creative human mind. The tendency of academic "structural" sociology has been to put the emphasis upon the social environment, yet at the same time giving too little attention to the cultural quality of that environment. When the rate of cultural change in that environment in the last generation in many countries of the world is borne in mind, it is difficult to see how structural sociology can present a coherent doctrine. In fact it has failed to do so. How far anthropology, loyal to Terence's maxim that nothing human can lack interest, is able to come to the rescue seems doubtful. Neither is it evident how the stock request for "more research" into "structure" or "role" and so forth would be able to do much to alleviate what is alleged to be the social discontent of the less well-off in a land such as the United States where the common goal of human endeavor is said to be to get ahead quickly in the race for income, possessions and "conspicuous consumption." To suppose that the cultural values by which societies live are of secondary concern in relation to the distribution of the national income or to the pattern of remunerative occupations is to make the error of the Marxists and to disastrously misdirect social policy. In putting all the emphasis upon cultural life, Sorokin was therefore again striving to put sociology in better shape to deal with such problems as these.

Meanwhile, striking independent confirmation of the soundness of Sorokin's historical analysis and general sociological theories is forthcoming from many sides. It is partly revealed by the similar conclusions at which some other sociologists and philosophers have arrived and partly suggested by the continuing failure of others following predominantly "structural" lines of thought to arrive at any positive, practical conclusions at all. Examples of both are available in a composite compilation of the views of fourteen sociologists, anthropologists, artists and philosophers prepared between 1963 and 1965 by the American Academy of Arts and Sciences on the general theme of "the relations between the humanities, the social scientists, the scientists and the arts in contemporary culture."* Since none of the learned contributors referred to Sorokin or to his theories, their work may be taken as an independent, recent, and serious effort to illuminate a subject which he had made his own.

In the volume resulting from the Academy's initiative there were many displays of great erudition, much citation from all manner of

---

*"Science and Culture," *Daedalus* (Prcdngs. of the American Academy of Arts & Sciences, 1965), Vol. 94, No. 1.

previous writers, often of the learned sociological name-dropping variety, which at best is a modern form of the old Scholastic citation of authorities but which often seemed an inconclusive pattern-weaving of notions from which no clear or coherent doctrine emerged. Sociologists and anthropologists seemed indeed to have had singularly little of a positive, practical nature to contribute. It might of course be concluded that in the present state of sociology nothing but such a predominantly negative result is possible and that anybody, such as Sorokin, who proffers more must be suspect. Pessimism on this score, however, is less plausible because those who write on the subject usually give the impression that they themselves are in no doubt about the answers. Few admit, as Sorokin does, to uncertainty about what he describes as "dark areas." In the American Academy's survey, for example, emphatic statements of current needs were proclaimed as though that alone would suffice to produce the transformation of the world. There was a call for a shared culture to which all the peoples of the world should contribute, which should have the character of a living tradition. It was said that everybody should be given access to the range of the world's art and opportunities to participate in new knowledge, new skills and new styles of life, all of which should be expressed in clear and simple terms through a new set of communication devices, including a universal standard world language, so that all might share in the values so revealed. Such was the open-ended program for the whole forward movement of culture. Admirable as it may sound as a program, it is but hollow pretension until all the question-begging words and all the pious aspirations are translated into practical terms. *What* are the "new" skills, "new" styles of life, and so forth? Too many of such current writings upon the pressing problems of the age, recall the fable of the cockroach, who, after listening to a harrowing account of the precarious and dangerous life of a grasshopper in the fields, painted a glowing picture of his own secure and sheltered existence in a warm kitchen and advised his friend, if he valued his life, to become a cockroach. Converted to the alluring prospect, the grasshopper accepted the advice and said "now tell me how to become a cockroach," to which his friend replied "That's up to you. I only advise on policy." Not all the American Academy's advisors were very clear about policy. What should be the content of the values that were to be broadcast to transform the world? What, in short, was the character of the "culture" which was to be married to "science"? Some long and learned discourses on this theme failed to advance matters very far. No clear definition of "culture" emerged. Nor is this surprising because some of the Academy's contributors to the theme were impeded by a previous encyclopedic survey of some six hundred works purporting to illuminate the subject, which had been made in 1952 by two of the most renowned names in American anthropology, A. L. Kroeber and Clyde Kluckhohn. As the failure of that attempt has been described elsewhere, it is unnecessary to do more than refer to it as an obstacle as much as an aid to anybody seeking a sound definition of culture.*

Lacking a definition or a clear description of culture, the American Academy's enterprise, despite the wealth of knowledge and pertinent points it disclosed, was hardly likely to be a source of specific sociological doctrines upon which a transformation of public policy might be planned. In some respects it succeeded in registering what should be definite and permanent gains. Professor Eric Weil's pronouncement on the impotence of "science" to replace, or to render unnecessary, the quest for values in modern culture, should be decisive. He paid a handsome tribute to the analytical linguistic movement which had sought to turn philosophy into a science. It had helped, he said, to eliminate ambiguous statements and it had exposed meaningless questions and pseudo-problems. Too high a price, however, had been paid for such positive results as it had achieved. Real as the dangers may be of going beyond its cramped and narrow discipline, they must be faced if philosophy and sociology are to say anything intelligent about the kind of people we are who live and work in the world to create the arts, the sciences, the technologies, including analytical and pragmatic philosophy as well.

"Facts will not lead us any further," said Weil. "We are faced with a choice and a decision." The facts themselves and the "value free" science which produces them, originate in a world of values, because life is directed by values. As though he might have had Sorokin's views in mind, he went on to point out that "values form value-systems." Values cannot be without relations between themselves. If there were no such relations, no such systems, all values would issue as mere arbitrary choices and so lack justification. Rational discussion would no longer be possible in a world of facts or of values unrelated in some system. The very idea of proof presupposes a prior recognition of values as the foundation of consistency in discourse. Kant long ago perceived that reality would be meaningless if values did not exist. There is no possibility of dealing with facts without involving values, for there would then be no ground upon

*F. R. Cowell, *Culture in Private and Public Life* (London, Thames & Hudson, 1959), pp. 333-341.

which one fact rather than another should be chosen out of the brash and buzzing confusion of the cosmos. Understanding therefore is impossible except upon a basis of values; and to pretend that it can be reduced to science, as "scientism" pretends, is absurd. "Scientism", the belief that only that which is scientifically established can be knowledge or truth, implies that science is a universal measuring rod for values, which is in itself a patently unscientific ideology. Weil caps this vindication of a theory of value, which will be seen to be fundamentally the same as Croce's, by calling for a historical analysis of man's actions and discourses to reveal to man what his world is and what he is himself. Sorokin had performed just such services fifteen years before, but his name was not mentioned in the American Academy's symposium.

It would be easy to cite, from the contributions to that volume, other opinions similarly unanimous with Sorokin's. Professor Daniel Bell deplored the disjunction of culture and social structure without noticing Sorokin's own resolute stand in the matter. Other writers voiced the need for integration in psychological and social life without supporting that argument with the reasoned philosophy developed by Sorokin. Professors René Dubos and Robert S. Morison came close to doing so, and much of what they said powerfully supports Sorokin's earlier conclusions. "Human cultures, like organisms and societies, depend for survival on their internal integration," was the conclusion of Dubos, who added that it would be "an integration which can be achieved only to the extent that science remains meaningful to the living experience of men."

Against a very different background an Indian scholar, Professor Radhakamal Mukerjee, who is no stranger to Sorokin's theories added to his many writings on sociology and philosophy another volume, cited in a previous chapter, on the value theme at the time when the American Academy's symposium was being prepared. Not inhibited as Anglo-American writers are from mentioning such universals as Truth, Beauty and Goodness, he also declared that "the world of values and value orientations belongs *par excellence* to the social sciences."* Professor Mukerjee was ready to carry the discussion to levels of transcendental and metaphysical speculation not usually reached by contemporary Western thinkers, but, while remaining on their level, his wise and important words have a special message strongly supporting Sorokin's general conclusions.

From the vast current outpouring of writing upon the grand themes to

*Radhakamal Mukerjee, *The Dimensions of Values* (London, Allen & Unwin Ltd., 1964), pp. 50, 68, 71.

which Sorokin has contributed his seminal ideas, much more can be found to vindicate and to support his views. He was ahead of his times. Others of course had stressed the supreme importance of values. John Dewey's words have been quoted to emphasize that "a culture which permits science to destroy traditional values, but which distrusts its power to create new ones, is destroying itself." It was against such abdication that Sorokin sought to array sociology, which in America until then had relatively little philosophical inspiration. He entered the fray, to fashion his own value theory as the basis of a revised sociology.

Other Sociological Theories of Today

One of Sorokin's earliest contributions to the study of sociology had been his *Contemporary Sociological Theories* (1928). Still widely used both in America and the English-speaking world and elsewhere in translation, it has survived as an excellent comprehensive historical introduction to sociological thought. When in 1966 he continued his survey of the development of sociology in *Sociological Theories of Today*, he succeeded in 650 pages, in not merely picking up and rounding off the theme of his earlier volume, but providing an unrivalled guide to the labors of others throughout half a century on the subject to which he had devoted his life work. The two books together, with their objective surveys of many and diverse ideas, complement Sorokin's own creative work by providing a dense background of thought and theory produced by other minds, many of them different from his own. The two books are certain to be read and re-read wherever sociology is seriously pursued. *Sociological Theories of Today* is a *tour de force* of which few, if any other, scholars would be capable. The daunting difficulties of the task might well have been thought sufficient to deter Sorokin himself.

Among the great merits of the book are the resolute pursuit of the argument wherever it led, the vast sweep of Sorokin's mind, and the enormous range of his knowledge and experience sharpened by a critical faculty which had long been applied to the task of dissecting fact and fancy, sound ideas and false. Yet, notably in his efforts to be fair to one or two pretentious muddlers, Sorokin writes in the spirit of Leibniz, who, echoing a charitable remark of the younger Pliny, used to say that no book is so bad that some good cannot be got out of it.

At the outset, Sorokin makes plain the standards and basis of his appraisal of the theories with which he deals. They were naturally given by the framework he had constructed out of his life's work, and it is interesting to see how they fare when applied to the task of assessing the work of others. He did not have much difficulty in disposing of the positivistic school and the nominalistic - singularistic - atomistic trend in contemporary general sociology. Those whom he had criticized earlier in *Fads and Foibles in Modern Sociology and Related Sciences* had, during nearly ten years, ample opportunity to try to rebut the trenchant strictures it contained, but no convincing rejoinders had been forthcoming. More suggestive and promising were those other theories of cultural systems which had preceded Sorokin's *Social and Cultural Dynamics,* notably those of Danilevsky, Spengler, Toynbee, F.S.C. Northrop, A. L. Kroeber, W. Schubart, N. Berdyaev, and Albert Schweitzer. They had been surveyed and subjected to Sorokin's critical review in his *Social Philosophies of an Age of Crisis* (1950 Boston, Beacon Press; London, A. and C. Black). Now he enlarged that survey by including accounts and critical appraisals of the work of such writers as F. Znaniecki, H. Becker, and Ortega y Gasset. He was more pleased by the similarities and convergence with his own views which he found in their writings than with points on which they differed or fell short of the integralist conception which he had worked out on the basis of his own ten years of research and reflection leading to the production of *Social and Cultural Dynamics.* In the field of the fine arts and aesthetic appreciation generally, he reviewed the theories of Flinders Petrie, Deonna, Ligeti, F. Chambers and others. "Practically all the theories expect, in the culture to come, a reunification of the supreme values of Truth, Beauty and Goonesss — hitherto separated from one another — into one *summum bonum.*"*

It was not difficult for Sorokin in the light of these fundamental principles to dispose of the efforts to elevate into complete theories of social systems all such notions as "social action", "functional" theories, dialectic theories, as well as all pseudo-behavioral and empirical sociologies.

Sorokin found them deficient also in their ability to order and classify the multifarious phenomena characterizing any social system. "To develop a truly scientific taxonomy remains the task of future sociologists" was the conclusion of his survey of the classificatory systems which he examined and criticized.

However plausible and convincing some contemporary sociological

*P. A. Sorokin, *Sociological Theories of Today* (New York, Harper & Row, 1966), p. 382.

explanations may seem to be, they rest on the surface and owe their apparent eligibility to the circumstance that readers and authors share a common underlying value-system, which today is that of a sensate society. If Sorokin himself does not seem to hammer home the point that it is fallacious to seek any method of introducing any basic order and coherence into such problems as social stratification otherwise than through value theory, it is a criticism certainly implicit in his cultural interpretation of sociology.

When all attempts to find a fundamental solution to problems of "social structure" on other bases fail, as Sorokin effectively shows them to have failed, the superiority of his own explanation by invoking a conceptual scheme for the explanation of sociological facts in terms of cultural values becomes all the more attractive. A similar verdict is also applicable to such efforts as have been made, apart from those by Sorokin, to account for social and cultural change. None has succeeded in improving noticeably upon the earlier views of Spengler, Toynbee, or Kroeber, which Sorokin had already shown to be defective in many respects.

At the conclusion of this magisterial survey, Sorokin repeats his conviction that "the next period of general sociology is likely to be the period of great sociological syntheses." The only alternative he foresees would be a continuation of the present fragmented studies with limited perspectives and modest aims amounting to little more than "a hackneyed, rubber-stamped, greatly mechanized set of dogmas devoid of creative *élan* and cognitive growth."

In other words, the need in sociology is for a broad explanatory scheme which will not merely list, classify, recite, and summarize facts will not be content merely to detect, group, appraise, and arrange values upon some scale of preference; but will be one able to put facts and values within the framework of a broad conceptual scheme or order which is also able to illuminate all other humanistic studies as well.

If this formulation is rejected, the imperative necessity remains to propose a superior solution. Since the partial, piecemeal, positivistic approach to social problems, without any coherently formulated standards of judgment for their assessment, may now be said to have failed to provide a philosophically viable sociology, it is inevitable that there should be a search for standards in other directions. Rightly, the dangers of such a proceeding must be stressed, as the whole vast controversy in favor of value-free concepts has made clear.

Hopes that sociology should aid in finding remedies for the more pressing problems of the age may savor of that pragmatic ambition which is as mistrusted academically as is the idealist school of thought. Yet the value problems rejected by philosophers and historians remain. Hopes that sociology might take them up may well account for the great and growing interest in the subject which, significantly, has arisen precisely at the time when analytical, linguistic emphases threw value-problems out of philosophy. While some sociologists soon became aware of these problems and realized their responsibilities towards them, it can hardly be claimed that their response has been brilliant. Too often their prevalent reaction has been to point out that "more research" is necessary, which may be true, but would be more plausible if clear indications could be given as to how to set about the task.

Among the problems of the day are for example those thrown up by employment in vast factories where, for eight hours a day, men and women become virtually an adjunct to a machine which requires their unremitting response, at as rapid a regular rate as trained hands can achieve, to some uniform repetitive process such as fitting windshield wipers on cars, coating cookies or chocolates, putting dust wrappers on new books, and all the thousand and one such tasks that are brought before workers as they stand in front of conveyor-belts. That an economic reward is hardly an adequate recompense for such soul-killing boredom has been recognized by many progressive factory managers. No longer, with some notable exceptions, is the virtue of industry or "honest toil" extolled, with nauseating hypocrisy as a reward in itself. Research, physical and psychological, has been undertaken by public bodies of which the Industrial Fatigue Research Laboratory of the Department of Scientific and Industrial Research was a pioneer in Great Britain after the First World War. Welfare workers have become trained professionals. Repetitive industry has been revolutionized since the nineteenth and early twentieth centuries with new automatic machines and "ergonomic" studies harnessed to the task of improving the ease and convenience of workers and of lessening the strains imposed upon them. As automation progressively takes over repetitive processes some soulless occupations will be diminished, but at the cost of the replaced workers' jobs. The right use of leisure then becomes more of a problem for many.

Faced with such eminently practical social requirements, traditional sociology is not remarkable for its ready response. Since the problem is one involving the whole human personality, piecemeal tinkering by welfare work and research into industrial fatigue and industrial health cannot provide more than partial solutions, valuable although they can be.

Nothing but an integral solution, as Sorokin has outlined, will enable men
and women to surmount the challenge to their personalities which the
necessity of earning a living presents. A large part of the difficulty is thus
thrown back upon the workers themselves, which is surely justifiable as
long as society does not deny them the means of coping with it. During
the nineteenth century particularly, such means were effectively denied to
vast numbers of industrial workers cooped up in industrial slums where
they had no holidays, no public transport providing cheap and easy egress
to the country even if they had holidays, no gardens public or private, no
civic amenities such as the poor of Ancient Roman times mostly possessed,
no libraries, museums, galleries, bookshops, theaters or concert halls, all of
which would have probably been beyond their means if they had to pay
for admission. In those days to get drunk on cheap gin was said to be the
quickest way from misery everywhere, and the early deaths to which it
often led may have been regarded generally as "a happy release" for many
to whom religion no longer spoke consolation and who had no chance of
achieving that integration of meaningful values through which more savor
might have been added to their lives. Many, if not most, of the difficulties
and evils now plaguing society can be seen to confirm what Sorokin said
about the fate of mankind during the decay of a sensate culture. In
addition to those already referred to in these pages, such as sexual license,
the mounting toll of robbery, violence, and other crimes, there are some
Sorokin did not include. There is the example evident in Great Britain and
elsewhere of the unprincipled, mean swindle of inflation and debasement
of the monetary standard that gives sharp point to Burckhardt's words to
his students in Basle a century ago: "Alongside all swindlers, the State now
stands as swindler in chief."* Yet in England at that time political
leadership and public morality still acknowledged standards that would
now be regarded as quixotic and utopian. Nobody then would have
believed it possible that the British sovereign or a Bank of England
banknote, which they knew to be universally accepted as honest money
throughout the world, would within twenty years after 1945 lose
four-fifths of their value. By being able to cheat with impunity those who,
for patriotic reasons, invested in Government "securities," and State
pensioners, the Exchequer gained a temporary, inflationary profit. It was
very dearly bought at the expense of honor and of the ancient Rule of
Law. Idealistic principles of that sort become a rapid casualty when

---

*J. Burckhardt, *Judgments on History and Historians,* trans. by J. Zohn (London,
Allen and Unwin, 1958), p. 165.

legislation degenerates into administrative devices serving a political party temporarily in the ascendant. Soon the administration itself is involved in mounting trouble as organized workers revolt to demand compensation which the toughest are able to win at the expense of the unorganized and weaker members of society. In such an atmosphere it is startling to recall nineteenth century idealistic notions about the State was a source of morality. Surprising also, perhaps, to record that the standard of fineness of the English gold monetary unit remained unchanged from 1600 to 1914 in spite of wars, famines, and acute commercial and industrial crises, or that the Nomisma of the Byzantine Empire was a stable standard of value from the third to the eleventh century A.D., during a predominantly ideational period, in striking contrast with the debasement of money in the sensate Roman empire. Again, Sorokin's theories receive striking confirmation from an unexpected quarter. Tempting and appropriate as it may be to invoke idealistic eloquence such as that of Edmund Burke on the decline of humanity and honor — "The age of chivalry is gone. That of sophisters, economists and calculators has succeeded; and the glory of Europe is extinguished for ever" — it is unnecessary because here again sensate excesses defeat sensate purposes. It is soon found that inflation in the long run is a curse on sensate standards, that dishonesty is the worst policy, and that if sensate economic welfare is to be assured, something like honest money must be restored. Again this is no new discovery. Adam Smith, almost two hundred years ago described the evils of inflation in language as true today as when he wrote.* Few ministers of finance can have been ignorant of the principle so long proclaimed. Here, therefore, is one more example of the futility of supposing that anything significant is achieved by the passive acceptance of principles.

Still less is to be hoped for as long as false principles prevail. Hardly a day now passes but that some social evil is exposed which Sorokin, a generation ago, put into proper perspective. Reliance upon scientific and technical processes with their insistence that they cannot prescribe ends was already combated by Sorokin. So he would have applauded condemnation of the divorce between knowledge and values symbolized by the underlying agreement between the techno-scientist and the hippie, the one declaring that values are subjective preferences, the other mumbling, "Man, I'm only doing my thing." The learned authors of this diagnosis said they "simply do not know the form of the highest general

*The best modern study of the economics of inflation is that by G. Hutton, *Inflation and Society* (London, Allen and Unwin, 1960).

culture appropriate to contemporary, largely post-industrial society." They were, however, very conscious that "undergraduate education is a shambles" and that postgraduate products were in no better case: " . . . microspecialization of knowledge, narrowness of outlook, a growing inability to define intellectual significance . . . evidence of destructiveness all around us, both in the realm of nature and in the realm of that 'second nature' which is culture . . ."* It was in vivid awareness of such blemishes that Sorokin advocated his integralist reshaping of education. As for the call, by the same learned authors, for reflection "upon human history in all of its breadth and diversity in order to acquire the fullest comprehension of the range of human possibilities and, perhaps, a heightened awareness of the crisis which has estranged us from our humanity and our world" – once again, this was precisely the task to which Sorokin gave his energy.** Everybody can readily discover additional evidence from daily experience and from reading which confirms the need for Sorokin's integralist reformation of education, personality, and cultural life. Equally, if not more important for the fate of Sorokin's theories, would be the discovery of anything that disproves them or requires their modification in some essential particular.

One final consideration remains. In a subject so torn and tossed by controversy, one in which philosophical terms are endlessly subject to minute analysis, definition, and redefinition, in which every single judgment is apt to be picked up, queried, or denied, in which ideas offered in good faith at their face value are stripped of their original significance by being reduced to some meaning to fit some arbitrary scheme favored by their critics; the valuations reported, analyzed, and classified by Sorokin are well able to remain bouyant, for he deals with ideas culled from history. Whatever truths, errors, follies, and stupidities may be thought to mar them, they are not his own. They are given by the record; they are the *explananda* which have still to be faced by any critics who reject

---

*Some years ago an academic friend suggested to groups of young students returning to the U.S.A. by sea with him that they should tell him what they regarded as the directing values in American life. Although the challenge was accepted with eager interest, no coherent answers were forthcoming. As long as educational systems show no better results, there could be no better proof of the need for cultural integration.
**J. H. Scharr and S. S. Wolin, "Education and Technical Society," in *The New York Review of Books,* October 9, 1969, Vol. XIII, No. 6, pp. 3-6. Much else in this issue of the *Review,* titled "The Education Nightmare," confirms the earlier pronouncements of Sorokin.

Sorokin's explanation. In the history of thought, Sorokin reviewed metaphysical theories which modern philosophers have thrown out as nonsense. Upon the rights and wrongs of such destructive criticism Sorokin does not need to pronounce. He was concerned with the evident fact that, once, such views were firmly held. Historically, and sociologically, he is right to call for their recognition on that basis.

It is therefore as a grand conceptual creation that Sorokin's sociology stands before the world. Sorokin would have been the first to welcome a re-examination of the grounds upon which it mainly rests, its massive factual foundation and the hypotheses advanced upon that foundation. Until they are very materially modified, Sorokin's reformulation of sociology as a theory of value which dominates and informs all humanistic studies deserves to be studied and applied because it seems to be the most promising and potentially most fruitful interpretative conceptual scheme yet advanced in order to bring coherence, order, and the promise of splendid progress into sociology or the proper study of mankind.

Sorokin's Contribution to Sociology

Inadequate as any summary statement of Sorokin's contribution to sociology must necessarily be, an attempt will be made in conclusion to bring together some of his main findings and their implications insofar as they relate to the nature and methodology of general sociological theory. Any such summary is inadequate because it is impossible to dissect, analyze, and account for the myriad thoughts, theories, or published opinions of a life so fully charged and as complete as his. As vicarious experience in this sense is impossible, it is inevitably impertinent for anyone to purport to be able to expound, in a mere literary or academic manner, the nature of the mind and thoughts behind the deeds of those who have won lasting renown through action.

The most that will be attempted here, therefore, is to indicate aspects of Sorokin's work which have deepened logical and methodological insights, increased and systematized knowledge, sharpened awareness of the immensely complex task of general sociology, and pointed to the fundamental basis and assumptions upon which hopes of future progress may be founded.

Above all, it is necessary to stress, as this book has sought to do, that Sorokin was the first sociologist to plan and execute a co-operative endeavor to survey the whole of history in the search for the realities behind the social life of mankind. His main contribution is, therefore, to be derived from the results of his ten years labor given to that task. All his work after the publication of his great *Social and Cultural Dynamics* carries forward and develops its message. That is why it has been called a watershed in sociology. From its fertilizing power, new ideas, new uniformities are derived. Much vague, tentative thought about many of the problems of the life of men in societies can now be replaced by specific formulations, and these moreover may be seen to be far-reaching in their implications and application. Such, for example, is his Basic Law of Fluctuation of Governmental Control. All who have lived through a World War, a severe economic depression, or other grave national crisis will recall "emergency powers" taken by their governments to meet unforeseen new difficulties. Sorokin is able to show from the history of Ancient Egypt, Babylonia, Persia, Greece, Rome, Byzantium, medieval and modern Europe, ancient Peru and Mexico, that "when a given organized group faces a grave emergency menacing its existence or its basic values, the governmental control over it tends to become more rigid and severe and tends to expand to embrace many social relationships of its members hitherto free from such control. As the emergency passes and conditions become more nearly normal, the governmental controls tend to relax." So wide a generalization may appear to those who have never tried to theorize on the subject as a statement of experience they recall. But would they apply it to other countries and other times? Would they see that it has applications beyond State action – that it includes, for example, the practice in associations, companies, trade unions and other organized bodies? Or that it explains the real reason for the autocracy of Russian tsars as well as of the Bolsheviks? Such a law shows the frequent futility of armchair denunciations of economists against regimentation and their eloquent pleas for free enterprise when political conditions forbid it. The whole question of individual liberty and state and organized control take on a new aspect in its light.*

Another set of generalizations puts the main cause and conditions of internal and international peace and war in a new perspective. Yet others illuminate the vexed and long debated question about the possibility and nature of the migration of cultural values, explaining what happens when different cultures meet, as well as other matters arising from the differences of standards within single cultural systems. The relevance of all

---

*P. A. Sorokin, *Society, Culture and Personality* (New York, Harper & Row, 1947), p. 466.

such considerations to racial and other international tensions will be evident. All manner of phenomena from the vogue of "best sellers" in literature, music, and the arts up to the confrontation of widely different cultural systems, between, for example, the developed and "under-developed" countries are more vividly seen in that fresh vision of the total universe of sociocultural reality which it is Sorokin's merit to have provided.

Such are but a few of the myriad facets of sociological reality which bear new and more rewarding aspects as a result of Sorokin's life-work. More specifically and more abstractly, the following basic ideas may be suggested as a schematic quintessence of his principles and their application. The following enumeration also cannot pretend to be exhaustive, but it may serve as a guide to Sorokin's work and as a summary of what has already been stated in the preceding pages.**

1 Individual human beings entering into the social relationships which it is the business of sociology to study, are motivated by a complex field of forces composed of unconscious drives (reflexes etc.), of bioconscious drives (of hunger, thirst, and sex, for warmth and shelter, etc.), and of socioconscious controls (involving meanings-values-norms, or cultural forces). New directions arise mainly through the discovery by exceptionally gifted individuals of acceptable, improved ideas which often arise from sources as yet imperfectly known and described as intuition or supraconscious inspiration.

2 Societies, as distinct from casual, haphazard assemblages or congeries of personages between whom there are no clear, perdurable links, are characterized by their power to implant meanings, values, norms within the socioconscious egos of their individual constituent members. Societies can be described or defined, and can only be understood to the extent that evidence is available to indicate the nature of those meanings, values, norms, which constitute their cultural quality at any one time.

3 The distinguishing cultural qualities detectable in socioconscious personalities and societies can be discovered in the history of human achievement, which also reveals periods in which cultural life is shattered by wars and revolutions.

**With the exception of an addition to 13 h, the following summary was seen and approved by Sorokin.

4   The empirical study of "meanings, values, norms" or cultural quality, makes it possible to detect long periods throughout which certain relatively clearly marked patterns of activity, beliefs, behavior, thought and creativity were in the ascendant.

5   Enduring patterns of cultural life may be identified because they exhibit a coherence and congruence between so many varying activities and achievements over periods so long and so full of incident as to put their occurrence beyond the range of mere chance happenings and their true inner nature beyond doubt as "logico-meaningful" cultural systems.

6   Such "logico-meaningful" value systems derive their quality from the dual aspect of man's nature as both a sentient and a reasoning being. A predominance of either quality is reflected in two distinct, or "polar," value patterns. An emphasis upon sentient existence produces sensate patterns of cultural values.

    Emphasis upon imaginative, reasoning, and rational activities may give other-worldly, non-sensate values sufficient importance to entirely subordinate, if not neutralize, sentient motives. Whenever sentient and rational motivation together exert a balanced, equal influence, creative idealist cultures have emerged.

7   When regrouped, the classes of values, meanings, and norms revealed by historical investigation to have commanded the clearest recognition, loyalty, and service in the past are shown to fall into precisely those classes of values discerned and classified by the Ancient Greek philosophers, confirmed and accepted by later thought, as values arising from activities tending to contribute to human knowledge (as aspects of the True); to human delight and aesthetic satisfaction (aspect of the "Beautiful" or Beauty); and to socially acceptable and worthy moral conduct and behavior (forms of the Good Life or the "Good"). A fourth value, that of utility, subserves the continuance of individual and social life and so makes possible the creation of and participation in, cultural values generally.

    All purposeful, socially significant, human activity can be explained by means of these four concepts which are true universals; any attempt to evade them by ignoring values, or by substituting other explanatory principles, or by analytical reduction involves an unsuccessful endeavor to translate them into other and less adequate terms.

8   Individual life and life in society are found to be more vigorous and more rewarding to the extent that they are able to integrate the value

systems in which they participate into coherent, congruent patterns or supersystems embracing as many distinct value systems as possible.

9   The integralist concept is applicable both in individual character formation and to cultural values. An individual is integrated to the extent that his unconscious drives and bioconscious urges are controlled and organized by his socioconscious ego in the service of some system of cultural values, occasionally also being informed or illuminated by intuition or supraconscious energies or inspiration. A culture is integrated when the personalities belonging to a society succeed in achieving a harmonious balance in the energies they devote to the service of knowledge, of aesthetic satisfaction and of morally worthy conduct. Such harmony or integralism is characterized by the mutual triple dependence of each important element or component of personality or culture upon all other important elements or parts as well as upon the whole system, which must also itself depend equally upon all its important elements or parts.

10   "Integralist" cultural supersystems arising from such systematized, congruent, coherent value-patterns can contribute to the definition of culture more completely, and more adequately than has hitherto been possible in sociology, anthropology, history, and literature.

11   A consequence in sociology is to confer a primacy upon cultural values as determinants in any descriptive analysis of social life and to subordinate to them many of the topics hitherto treated with little or no organized reference to value systems. Such, for example, are the topics of "groups", "classes", "roles", "stratification", "social action" and the like, all of which can only be endowed with significance as operative terms when they are interpreted as variables of a cultural supersystem of integrated, congruous values, meanings, norms.

12   A new interpretation of major changes in history results and, with it, a new philosophy of history based upon the hypothesis that, within limits prescribed by physical forces, such as climate, situation, natural and other catastrophes, the critical factor in major changes is a breakdown of formerly dominant cultural supersystems − ideational, idealistic, or sensate.

13   The virtual equation of sociology with this new philosophy of history then follows, since both can be seen to depend upon the rise, breakdown and collapse of dominant value systems. As a result, it is possible to elucidate, *inter alia:*

a   the "How" of sociocultural change given by as full as possible a tally of the recorded facts of history about the nature and quality of cultural life and activities over time.

b   the "Why" of sociocultural change, based upon Sorokin's "Principle of Immanent Change" according to which human mentalities and dispositions formed by a "logico-meaningful" cultural supersystem of mutually congruous consistent values develop, as does life generally, as far as the premises and the potentialities of the nature of the system allow.

c   the "When" of cultural change, based upon Sorokin's "Principle of Limits," according to which human creativity bursts through a cultural supersystem of congruous values when the potentialities of the system have been fully worked out. It is then superseded by another, often radically different supersystem after an uneasy period of cultural disturbance or chaos. However some of the qualities of the older outworn system are often carried forward in varying degrees of modification and force.

d   the impossibility of presenting history as a succession of clear-cut, well-defined, distinct, and rigidly divided "periods", because of the immense power of survival of once-accepted and once-honored values. Some "ideational" values survive, even if in an attenuated or disguised form in subsequent "sensate" periods. Some of the creations of the "idealistic" period of creative humanism similarly continue to be respected in later predominantly "sensate" periods, when they may inspire development and improvement. Nevertheless, and despite a far greater technical competence and critical acumen, people of a "sensate" culture mostly fail to rival the earlier "idealistic" creative brilliance, particularly in the humanities.

e   the subordination to the cultural interpretation of history and sociology of previous efforts to found sociology or a philosophy of history upon factors external to the creative human spirit, such as geographical, climatic, racial, political and economic forces, population problems and the evolutionary struggle for survival; all of which in historical periods of developing civilized and cultural life are relegated to the status of influences, instead of being regarded as primary motive forces.

f   the elimination of such factitious divisions or explanatory categories in history as "ancient", "medieval", "modern" of the textbooks and the "childhood", "youth", "maturity", and "old age" of human societies of Spengler and others.

g   a sociological philosophy of structural sociology in which groups or institutions, their solidarity, antagonism, and mixed forms of organization, their stratification, the social mobility within them, the influence of family, contractual and compulsory relations, government, peace, war and revolution, are classified and explained in the light of the prevalent sociocultural mentality within which they arise.

h   the resolution of the vexed problem of cultural relativity by relating value-judgments to the cultural supersystems from which they emerge. Although such cultural "supersystems" are themselves variables in the long run, they are yet able to serve in the short run as parameters of which specific value-judgments in aesthetics, ethics and science are seen to be functions or modes. Consequently analytical reasoning about such values within any given cultural supersystem involves a circular argument centered upon and referable back to the major premise of the supersystem in question. While each such cultural supersystem has no more than a relative significance, all are based upon the determination of the matrix of the sociocultural continuum which is the absolute from which their meaningful character derives.

14   A revised sociological interpretation of history of this type affords the possibility of cautiously framing some hypothesis about:

a   the general shape of things to come both in the short range and the long range as Sorokin in the 1930's, despite the derision of contemporary optimists, predicted shattering wars, violence and immensely powerful, annihilating explosives.

b   some tentative extrapolation of cultural values of a past epoch or a "vanished" culture, when nothing remains except some few artifacts or other evidence. Thus a strongly traditional, religiously-oriented society would be inferred when none but "ideational" sculptures, etc., survives. An easier, more tolerant set of laws, social customs etc., would similarly be supposed to accompany evidently "sensate" art-forms, such as the late Minoan, or late Etruscan. Such tentative predictions serve as a hostage to criticism. Sorokin's theories would be confirmed if they were verified but would be liable to rejection or modification if they proved to be wrong.

A telegraphic summary outline such as that presented above cannot do more than indicate the main features of Sorokin's contribution which, as a closely-knit, mutually cohesive sociological system, is based upon a vaster range of empirical data than any ever yet offered by any other sociologist. Not only does Sorokin bring in more facts, but he offers hypotheses for their explanation and comprehension which are economic, viable, coherent, and elucidating. By merging sociology and value-theory, Sorokin provides canons and standards of interpretation by which other sociological theories, including those of Comte, Marx, Simmel, Max Weber as well as those of Sorokin's contemporaries, may be tested. He carries further their fruitful insights, such as Hobhouse's "organic harmony", and he provides a fertile source of "growing points" from which notable advances should be possible.

Sorokin has expounded his views, from which the above considerations have been drawn, in upwards of 30 substantial volumes and in more than 200 contributions, many of which are small treatises, to the scientific journals of the world. After the manner of any positive theory advancing novel views, it is a challenge. No mere personal "hunches" derived almost entirely from the books and articles of other theorists, Sorokin's contribution, like the achievements of tireless researchers such as Macaulay or Maitland, among historical records and archives cannot be dismissed by lazy critics who say, "I don't believe it," and pass on quickly to some other theme. If Sorokin is to be controverted, his evidence as well as his interpretation of it must be re-examined with as much care and thought as he himself devoted to its formulation. So far, no critic seems to have been willing to make so detailed a review.

That the vast range and extent of Sorokin's labors on behalf of sociology merit such interest is the note upon which this summary must end. Much more might be said, but sufficient will have been recorded here to indicate that his massive contribution is an exception to the lack, upon which he comments, of any "grand system of sociology" in our time, for with the modesty of the true scholar, he disclaimed any pretensions to originality or genius.

His forty years of exile from his native land, where he is by no means forgotten but is again being discussed, have certainly not been forty years in the wilderness. If American sociology, when he arrived there to teach it, were regarded not as a wilderness but as a jungle, he has by his efforts cleared away many of the weeds and helped it to blossom as the rose. His splendid achievement will rank after the work of Saint-Simon, Comte, Marx, Hobhouse, Max Weber, Morris Ginsberg and others as a landmark in the effort of mankind the better to comprehend their tragic and stormy past, to understand the nature of the problems which still divide and plague them, and, in the light of that new knowledge, to advance with more confident and more assured a step toward their ultimate solution.